This book is due on the last date stamped below.
Failure to return books on the date due may result
in assessment of overdue fees.

FINES	.50 per day

HANDBOOK
of
LESBIAN AND GAY STUDIES

HANDBOOK
of
Lesbian and Gay Studies

DIANE RICHARDSON AND STEVEN SEIDMAN

SAGE Publications
London • Thousand Oaks • New Delhi

Introduction © Diane Richardson and Steven
  Seidman 2002
Chapter 1 © Barry D. Adam 2002
Chapter 2 © Sasha Roseneil 2002
Chapter 3 © Peter M. Nardi 2002
Chapter 4 © Lynda Burke 2002
Chapter 5 © Chrys Ingrahim 2002
Chapter 6 © Stephen O. Murray 2002
Chapter 7 © Verta Taylor, Elizabeth Kaminski
  and Kimberly Dugan 2002
Chapter 8 © Nina Wakeford 2002
Chapter 9 © Gill Valentine 2002
Chapter 10 © Stephen Pugh 2002
Chapter 11 © Anne-Marie Fortier 2002
Chapter 12 © Melinda S. Miceli 2002
Chapter 13 © Kristin G. Esterberg 2002

Chapter 14 © Davina Cooper 2002
Chapter 15 © Tamsin Wilton 2002
Chapter 16 © Debbie Epstein, Sarah O'Flynnand
  David Telford 2002
Chapter 17 © Leslie J. Moran 2002
Chapter 18 © Dawne Moon 2002
Chapter 19 © Marieka M. Klawitter 2002
Chapter 20 © Joshua Gamson 2002
Chapter 21 © Judith Stacey and Elizabeth
  Davenport 2002
Chapter 22 © Stephen Engel 2002
Chapter 23 © Valerie Jenness and Kimberley D.
  Richman 2002
Chapter 24 © Dennis Altman 2002
Chapter 25 © Jyoti Puri 2002
Chapter 26 © David Bell and Jon Binnie 2002

First published 2002

SAGE Publications Ltd
6 Bonhill Street
London EC2A 4PU

SAGE Publications Inc.
2455 Teller Road
Thousand Oaks, California 91320

SAGE Publications India Pvt Ltd
32, M-Block Market
Greater Kailash - I
New Delhi 110 048

British Library Cataloguing in Publication data

A catalogue record for this book is available from
the British Library

ISBN 0 7619 6511 4

Library of Congress Control Number Available

Typeset by SIVA Math Setters, Chennai, India
Printed in Great Britain by The Cromwell Press Ltd, Trowbridge, Wiltshire

Contents

Notes on Contributors

Barry D. Adam is University Professor of Sociology at the University of Windsor, Canada. He is the author of *The Survival of Domination* (Elsevier, 1978), *The Rise of a Gay and Lesbian Movement* (Twayne, 1995), *Experiencing HIV* (with Alan Sears, Columbia University Press, 1996), and co-editor of *The Global Emergence and Gay and Lesbian Politics* (Temple University Press, 1999).

Dennis Altman is Professor of Politics at La Trobe University, Australia, and author of ten books, including *Homosexual Oppression and Liberation* (Outerbridge and Dienstfrey, 1971), *The Homosexualization of America* (St. Martin's Press, 1982), *Power and Community* (Falmer, 1994) and *Global Sex* (University of Chicago Press, 2001). He was a founding member of the AIDS Society of Asia and The Pacific and the Asia Pacific Council of AIDS Service Organizations, and co-chair in 2001 of the Sixth International Congress on AIDS in Asia and the Pacific. He has also published a novel, *The Comfort of Men*, and a memoir, *Defying Gravity*.

David Bell teaches Cultural Studies at Staffordshire University. He is co-author of *Consuming Geographies* (Routledge, 1997) and *The Sexual Citizen* (Polity, 2000), and co-author of *Mapping Desire* (Routledge, 1995), *City Visions* (Prentice-Hall, 2000) and *The Cybercultures Reader* (Routledge, 2000). His most recent book is *An Introduction to Cybercultures*, published by Routledge in 2001.

Jon Binnie teaches Human Geography at Manchester Metropolitan University. He is co-author of *The Sexual Citizen* (Polity, 2000) and *Pleasure Zones* (Syracuse University Press, 2001). He is currently completing a book on globalization and sexuality, to be published by Sage in 2002.

Lynda Birke is a feminist biologist, who has written extensively about the intersections between biological ideas and gender/sexuality. She did research for many years on animal behaviour, focusing on how behaviour and hormones interact; later, she was Senior Lecturer in the Centre for the Study of Women and Gender at the University of Warwick, where her research focused on feminist science studies. Her books include: *Women, Feminism and Biology* (Wheatsheaf, 1986), *Feminism, Animals and Science* (Open University, 1994), and *Feminism and the Biological Body* (Edinburgh University Press, 1999). She has been out in print ever since she wrote a chapter on science and lesbians in the 1970s, while part of the Brighton Women and Science Group – a defiant act for a scientist, who is not supposed to admit to personal details in their writing at all. She lives in North Wales, with her partner and lots of animals (including a dyke dog called Penny).

Davina Cooper is Professor of Law and Social Science Faculty Research Dean at Keele University. She is the author of *Sexing the City* (Rivers Oram Press, 1994), *Power in Struggle* (Open University Press, 1995), and *Governing out of Order* (Rivers Oram Press, 1998). She is currently completing a book on radical political and normative theory. Her research interests include governance conflicts, feminist political theory and socio-legal studies.

Elizabeth Davenport is Assistant Dean for student affairs at the University of Southern California, addressing issues of gender, sexual identity and sexual violence on campus. She is a doctoral candidate in social ethics at USC, currently researching intersections of religion and postmodern family identity. She is also an Episcopal priest, and has worked in diverse ecclesiastical settings in the United States as well as in France, Israel, and her native England.

Kimberly Dugan is an Assistant Professor at Eastern Connecticut State University. Her research focuses on the dynamics between the Christian right and the gay, lesbian and bisexual movement. Current work involves issues of identity and identity salience on movement success and the packaging and promoting of claims in an anti-gay ballot initiative. She also teaches a course on gay, lesbian, bisexual and transgendered lives.

Stephen Engel completed an interdisciplinary Master of Arts in Humanities and Social Thought at New York University in the spring of 2001. At present he is researching how high cultural notions regarding the performative identity and socially constructed nature of reality are gaining expression in outlets of popular or mass culture. His first book, *The Unfinished Revolution: Social Movement Theory and the Gay and Lesbian Movement*, was published by Cambridge University Press.

Debbie Epstein is Professor of Education and Head of the Department of Educational Studies at Goldsmiths College, University of London. Her recent publications include *Schooling Sexualities* (written with Richard Johnson, Open University Press, 1998), *Border Patrols: Policing the Boundaries of Heterosexuality* (co-edited with Deborah Lynn Steinberg and Richard Johnson, Cassell, 1997), and *A Dangerous Knowing: Sexuality, Pedagogy and Popular Culture* (co-edited with James T. Sears, Cassell, 1999). She is currently working on a book with Sarah O'Flynn and David Telford, entitled *Silenced Sexualities in Schools and Universities*.

Kristin G. Esterberg is Associate Professor of Sociology at the University of Massachusetts at Lowell. She is the author of *Lesbian and Bisexual Identities: Constructing Communities, Constructing Selves* (Temple University Press, 1997) as well as numerous articles and book chapters on lesbian and bisexual identity and community. Her second book, *Qualitative Methods in Social Research*, was recently published by McGraw Hill.

Anne-Marie Fortier is a lecturer in the Sociology Department, Lancaster University. She is the author of *Migrant Belongings: Memory, Space, Identity* (Berg, 2000), as well as a number of articles, including publications in *Theory, Culture & Society, Diaspora,* and *The International Journal of Canadian Studies.* She is currently working on representations of multicultural Britain, with a focus on the sexual politics of multiculturalism.

Joshua Gamson is Associate Professor of Sociology at Yale University, and author of *Claims to Fame: Celebrity in Contemporary America* (University of California Press, 1994) and *Freaks Talk Back: Tabloid Talk Shows and Sexual Nonconformity* (University of Chicago Press, 1998) which won awards from the Society for Cinema Studies and the American Sociological Association, and was selected as one of *The Voice Literary Supplement's* 25 favourite books of 1998. He has published numerous scholarly articles on social movements, media and culture, and sexuality and has written about television, popular culture, and lesbian and gay politics for *The Nation, The American Prospect, Tikkun,* and *The Utne Reader.*

Chrys Ingraham is Associate Professor of Sociology at Russell Sage College for women in Troy, New York. She also directs the Helen M. Upton Center for Women's Studies and the Allies Center for the Study of Difference and Conflict. Dr Ingraham is the author of *White Weddings: Romancing Heterosexuality in Popular Culture* (Routledge, 1999), co-editor of *Materialist Feminism: A Reader in Class, Difference and Women's Lives* (Routledge, 1997), and is editor of two new readers *Heterosexuality: A Critical Historical Reader* and *Straight Talk,* both published by Routledge in 2002.

Valerie Jenness is an Associate Professor in the Department of Criminology, Law and Society and in the Department of Sociology at the University of California, Irvine, as well as the Chair of the Department of Criminology, Law and Society. Her research has focused on the links between deviance and social control (especially law), gender, and social change. She is the author of *Making Hate a Crime: From Social Movement to Law Enforcement* (with Ryken Grattet, 2001), *Hate Crimes: New Social Movements and the Politics of Violence* (with Kendal Broad, 1997), and *Making it Work: The Prostitutes' Rights Movement in Perspective* (1993) – as well as numerous articles on the politics of prostitution, AIDS and civil liberties, hate crimes and hate crime law, and the gay/ lesbian movement and the women's movement in the USA.

Elizabeth Kaminski is a graduate student in the Department of Sociology at Ohio State University. Her research interests include gender, sexuality, social movements and women's health. She recently published an article on lesbian health in *The Journal of Lesbian Studies* (2000).

Marieka M. Klawitter is Associate Professor of Public Affairs at the Daniel J. Evans School of Public Affairs at the University of Washington. Her research focuses on public policies that affect work and income. Her work includes studies of the effects of child support policies, welfare policies and anti-discrimination policies for sexual orientation. Professor Klawitter teaches courses on public policy analysis, quantitative methods, women and work and sexual orientation and public policy.

Melinda S. Miceli is an assistant Professor of Sociology at the University of Wisconsin-Eau Claire. She received her doctoral degree in sociology from the University at Albany in 1998. Her dissertation, entitled 'Recognizing all the Differences: Gay Youth and Public Education in America Today', was the culmination of three years of interview, field and document research into the school experiences of gay, lesbian and bisexual youth and the social debate that surrounds them. She continues to conduct research on this topic specifically focusing on examinations of school gay straight alliances as a social movement and the political framing processes used by social movement organizations that support, and those that oppose, the rights of gay, lesbian and bisexual students.

Dawne Moon is an Assistant Professor of Sociology at the University of California, Berkeley. She received her PhD from the University of Chicago in 2000. Her forthcoming book is an ethnographic study of debates about homosexuality within two United Methodist congregations.

Leslie Moran is Reader in the School of Law at Birkbeck College, University of London. He has written extensively on matters relating to gay issues in the law. His monograph, *The Homosexual(ity) of Law* was published in 1996 (Routledge). He has edited special edition's of *Social and Legal Studies* entitled 'Legal Perversions' (1997) and co-edited *Legal Queeries* with colleagues in 1998 (Cassell). His current research is on homophobic violence. He is one of a multi-disciplinary team undertaking the largest study of lesbians, gay men, violence and safety in the UK. The project is funded by the Economic and Social Research Council as part of a 20-project initiative on violence research. The project website is http://les1.man.ac.uk/sociology/vsrp. The team are completing a book provisionally entitled *Violence and the Politics of Sexuality.* He is a member of the Metropolitan Police Lesbian Gay Bisexual Transgender Advisory Group and a member of the management committee of GALOP, the gay and lesbian police monitoring organization.

Stephen O. Murray earned a PhD in sociology from the University of Toronto and was a postdoctoral fellow in anthropology at the University of California, Berkeley. He has worked as a consultant to California county health departments and done research in Canada, Guatemala, Mexico, Taiwan and Thailand. He wrote a series of books about the social organization of homosexualities in various culture areas, culminating in *Homosexualities*, published by the University of Chicago Press in 2000.

Peter M. Nardi is Professor of Sociology at Pitzer College of the Claremont Colleges in California. His is the author of *Gay Men's Friendships* (Chicago, 1999), editor of *Gay Masculinities* (Sage, 2000) and co-editor of *Social Perspectives in Lesbian and Gay Studies: A Reader* (Routledge, 1998), among other books. He is also the editor of *Sociological Perspectives* the journal of the Pacific Sociological Association.

Sarah O'Flynn is a doctoral candidate at Goldsmiths College, University of London Institute of Education. Her interests are in sexuality and education, particularly in relation to inequality. She is currently writing her thesis exploring the links between young women's sexualities and educational achievement. She has worked for the past ten years in secondary schools in London teaching English. She is currently working with young traveller pupils in London, supporting their access to education.

Stephen Pugh qualified as a social worker in 1987, with a particular interest in working with older people. In 1992, he moved into social service management concentrating on field and home care services. Throughout his social work career, Stephen developed interests in carer support, abuse of older people and assessment issues with an underlying emphasis on quality. Since 1995, he has been a Lecturer in Social Work with older people at the University of Salford. With colleagues, Stephen developed a Master's programme in Social Gerontology and is currently Director of Social Work and Social Care at the university. He is currently undertaking doctoral study, exploring service provision for older lesbian and gay men.

Jyoti Puri is Assistant Professor in the Departments of Sociology and Women's Studies in Simmons College, Boston. She is also the Director of the master's program in Gender/Cultural Studies. She has published in the areas of gender and sexuality. Her recent book is entitled *Woman, Body, Desire in Post-colonial India: Narratives of Gender and Sexuality* (Routledge, 1999). An article on a feminist critique of the Kamasutra is forthcoming in the journal of *SIGNS*. She has also authored an article entitled, 'Reading Romances in Postcolonial India', which was published in *Gender and Society*. She is currently working on a book on nationalism for Blackwell Publishers.

Diane Richardson is Professor and Head of the Department of Sociology and Social Policy and Director of the Center far Sender and Women's Studies at the University of Newcastle. She has written extensively about feminism and sexuality and her publications include *Women and the AIDS Crisis* (Pandora Press, 1989), *Women, Motherhood and Childrearing* (Macmillan, 1993), *Theorising Heterosexuality* (Open University Press, 1996) and, as co-editor, *Introducing Women's Studies* (Macmillan/New York University Press, 1997). Her latest book is *Rethinking Sexuality* (Sage, 2000).

Kimberly D. Richman is a doctoral candidate in the Department of Criminology, Law and Society at the University of California, Irvine. Her interests include gender, sexuality, law, the construction and social control of vice and morality, and court processes. She is the author of two articles on the topic of domestic violence, appearing in *Sociological Inquiry* and *Studies in Law, Politics, and Society*. She has also published on victimless crime and homosexuality. Her current research analyses judicial narratives and meaning-making in child custody cases involving gay and lesbian parents.

Sasha Roseneil is Professor of Sociology and Gender Studies and Director of the Centre for Interdisciplinary Gender Studies at the University of Leeds. She is the author of *Disarming Patriarchy* (Open University Press, 1995) and *Common Women, Uncommon Practices: The Queer Feminisms of Greenham* (Cassell, 2000), and co-editor of *Stirring*

It: Challenges for Feminism (Taylor and Francis, 1994), *Practising Identities* (Macmillan, 1999), *Consuming Cultures* (Macmillan, 1999) and *Globalization and Social Movements* (Palgrave, 2001).

Steven Seidman is a Professor of Sociology at the State University of New York at Albany. He is the author or editor of, among other books, *Embattled Eros* (Routledge, 1992), *Queer Theory/Sociology* (Blackwell, 1996), *Difference Troubles* (Cambridge University Press, 1997), and his latest book, *Gay and Lesbian Life after the Closet* will be published next year.

Judith Stacey is the Streisand Professor of Contemporary Gender Studies and Professor of Sociology at the University of Southern California. Her primary research and teaching interests focus on the relationship between social change and the politics of gender, family and sexuality. Currently she is conducting ethnographic research on gay male family and kinship relationships and values in Los Angeles. Her publications include *In the Name of the Family: Rethinking Family Values in the Postmodern Age* (Beacon Press, 1996) and *Brave New Families: Stories of Domestic Upheaval in Late Twentieth Century America* (University of California Press, 1998). She is a founding board member of the Council on Contemporary Families, a group committed to public education about research on family diversity.

Verta Taylor is Professor of Sociology and Member of the Graduate Faculty in Women's Studies at Ohio State University. She is co-author with Leila J. Rupp of *Survival in the Doldrums: The American Women's Rights Movement, 1945 to the 1960s*; co-editor with Laurel Richardson and Nancy Whittier of *Feminist Frontiers*; author of *Rock-a-by Baby: Feminism, Self-Help and Postpartum Depression*; and has published numerous articles on social movement theory, women's movements and the gay and lesbian movement. Her forthcoming book (with Leila Rupp) *What Makes a Man a Man: Drag Queens at the 801 Cobaret*, examines the role of drag performances in the gay and lesbian movement.

David Telford taught economics and social sciences in secondary schools in Melbourne, Australia, before beginning his doctoral studies at London University where he is a research student at Goldsmiths College. His research is on young gay men at university. In addition, he has worked as a researcher at the Institute on a project concerned with the evaluation of Education Action Zones and at the London School of Economics on a project investigating the lives of young lesbian and gay university students and young lesbian and gay homeless people.

Gill Valentine is Professor of Geography at the University of Sheffield where she teaches social and cultural geography, approaches to geography and qualitative methods. She is author of *Social Geographies: Space and Society* (Pearson, 2001), co-author of *Consuming Geographies: You Are Where You Eat* (Routledge, 1997), editor of *Lesbian Geographies: From Nowhere to Everywhere* (Harrington Park Press, 2000) and co-editor of *Children's Geographies: Playing, Living, Learning* (Routledge, 2000), *Cool*

Places: Geographies of Youth Cultures (Routledge, 1998) and *Mapping Desire: Geographies of Sexualities* (Routledge, 1995).

Nina Wakeford is the Director of INCITE – the Incubator for Critical Inquiry on Technology and Ethnography – in the Department of Sociology, University of Surrey (incite.soc.surrey.ac.uk). Her past research include's ethnographic work in the UK and the USA on computing and Internet culture, studies of cybercafés, online discussion groups and new media start-up companies. Currently, she is directing two research projects, one investigating the use of mobile phones in urban spaces, and the other exploring the use of cultural theory and ethnography by product and interface designers. She is the author of *Networks of Desire* (Routledge, 2002), and co-editor with Peter Lyman of *Analyzing Virtual Societies: New Directions in Methodology* (American Behavioral Scientist/Sage, 1999).

Tamsin Wilton is Reader in Sociology at the University of the West of England. She has been a teacher, writer and activist on queer issues since the mid-1980s. Her many publications include *Sexualities in Health and Social Care* (Open University Press, 2000), *Lesbian Studies: Setting an Agenda* (Routledge, 1995) and *EnGendering AIDS: Deconstructing Sex, Texts, Epidemic* (Sage, 1997). She is busy writing her next book, *Who Do Women Want?* which sets out to establish an empirical foundation for social constructionist theories of sexuality.

Introduction

DIANE RICHARDSON AND STEVEN SEIDMAN

The academic study of homosexuality and sexuality in general has 'taken off' in many Western nations. Today, students in many nations across the globe have an opportunity to take courses in sexuality, lesbian and gay studies, or queer theory.

Lesbian and gay studies has produced a body of research and theorizing that is already too extensive and specialized to comprehensively present. In this volume, we aim to provide readers with an overview of the field. We make no claim to have covered all the possible areas of research and theory. Our approach is frankly tilted towards sociology, though feminist, cultural studies, and queer perspectives are in strong evidence. In each chapter, authors have made an effort to present a clear overview of the state of the research in a particular field, the key debates and positions, and to suggest future directions of possible research and theorizing.

HISTORY AND THEORY

Before there developed a sociology of homosexuality, there were medical-scientific theories. These initially appeared over a century ago, but medical models of homosexuality have achieved considerable social influence. They propose various ways of understanding homosexuality, for example, as an inherited or learned identity or as a form of sexual or gender deviance. Still,

almost all of these theories define the homosexual as a separate human or personality type. By the mid-twentieth century in many Anglo-American and European nations, the idea was well established that the homosexual was an abnormal or deviant and dangerous type of person.

There were some dissenters. For example, in England, Edward Carpenter imagined homosexuals as a distinct and superior moral-spiritual human type. Somewhat later, the American sexologist Alfred Kinsey shocked his readers by claiming to demonstrate, on the basis of thousands of interviews, that homosexuality is common among Americans. He argued that homosexuality is less a fixed identity than a general human desire. Nevertheless, in the United States and elsewhere, a psychiatric view of the homosexual as an abnormal human type had gained considerable social influence during the post-World War II period.

The 1950s were a time of heightened discrimination and harassment of homosexuals. In response to increasing gay visibility, the state and other institutions sought to criminalize and repress homosexuality. Homosexuals responded by organizing to advocate tolerance and homosexual rights. For example, in the United States, the Daughters of Bilitis and the Mattachine Society established chapters in major cities across the nation. In Britain also, organizations emerged such as the Homosexual Law Reform Society founded in 1958 and, a few years later, the London-based lesbian organizations Kenric and Minorities Research Group, which had similar goals to the Daughters of Bilitis. Members were divided between essentially two political strategies. On the one hand, some sought to decriminalize homosexuality by arguing that, as a psychiatric disorder, homosexuals deserve treatment not punishment. On the other hand, some aimed to reverse the medical model by claiming that homosexuals were normal people like heterosexuals. At the same time, there also appeared the beginnings of a sociological approach – the homosexual was seen as a victimized social minority.

A big change in Western ideas of homosexuality came in the 1960s and 1970s. The women's and gay liberation movements proposed a view of homosexuality as a social and political identity. For example, some lesbians argued that being a lesbian is a political act that challenges both the norm of heterosexuality and men's dominance. To be a lesbian is to choose to live a life apart from men and to make women the center of one's personal and social life.

Social scientists were also beginning to develop a social approach to sexuality. Some sociologists approached homosexuality as neither normal or abnormal, but considered the way homosexuals created their own identities and subcultures in a hostile society. In the USA and England, the labeling theory of Howard Becker (1963), Edwin Schur (1965), and Kenneth Plummer (1975) and the 'sexual script' approach of John Gagnon and William Simon (1973) emphasized that while individuals may be born with or develop in infancy homosexual feelings, they have to learn to think of these feelings as an identity and to manage this identity in an unfriendly society.

In the mid-1970s, the writings of sociologists, along with the ideas of gays and feminists, contributed to developing a sociological perspective. The meaning and social role of homosexuality was determined by the way people respond to it. This social view became politically important, as it suggested that it was not homosexuality

which was a social problem but a social response to intolerance and prejudice.

There were, however, limits to this developing social understanding of homosexuality. For the most part, sociologists and gay and women's liberationists did not question why it was that society defined people in sexual terms and why sexuality had become an identity. They assumed that there had always been homosexuals and heterosexuals; only the social response varied in different societies.

The 1980s were an important period in gay life. In the USA, the UK, Denmark, Holland, France, Australia, and elsewhere, social movements were creating public lesbian and gay communities. In virtually every major city, gays were creating institutions, organizations, clubs, support groups, and beginning to gain political clout. Despite a great deal of opposition, the gay movement was making great strides towards gaining rights and respect. This period of social and political advancement also witnessed the rise of 'social constructionist' perspectives in lesbian and gay studies.

Although constructionists learned from earlier social approaches made by sociologists, feminists and others, a new wave of thinkers and researchers sought to deepen a social view of homosexuality. Constructionists argued that sex was fundamentally social; the modern categories of sexuality, most importantly, heterosexuality and homosexuality, but also the whole system of modern sexual types and notions of normal and abnormal sexualities, were understood as social and historical facts.

In particular, constructionist perspectives challenged the notion that homosexuals have always existed. This idea was popular in the gay movement. If homosexuals have always existed, then it would seem that homosexuality is natural and homosexuals should be accepted. By contrast, constructionists proposed that while homosexual feelings or desires may have always existed, 'homosexuals', viewed as a distinct identity, have appeared only in some societies. The French social thinker, Michel Foucault

(1980) provided a powerful statement of this perspective.

> As defined by ancient civil or canonical codes, sodomy was a category of forbidden acts; their perpetrator was nothing more than the juridical subject of them. The nineteenth-century homosexual became a personage, a past, a case history, a life form … Nothing that went into total composition was unaffected by his sexuality. It was everywhere present in him: at the root of all his actions … because it was a secret that always gave itself away.

Scholars such as Jeffrey Weeks (1977), Jonathan Katz (1976), Carroll Smith-Rosenberg (1985) and Randolph Trumbach (1977) similarly proposed the thesis of the social construction of 'the homosexual'.

Armed with this new approach to sexuality, constructionists have sought to explain the origin, social meaning, and changing forms of the modern homosexual (e.g., D'Emilio, 1983; Faderman, 1981). Scholars have debated when the notion of 'the homosexual' initially appeared, what social factors account for this development and the different historical emergence of the category 'lesbian', what kinds of subcultures or networks have sustained a homosexual identity, and how societies have responded to these developments.

The 1990s witnessed huge changes in the social and political status of lesbians and gay men in many Western nations. Unprecedented social integration occurred, including the right to marry in Denmark, Norway, Sweden, and most recently Holland. But these changes did not amount to a steady line of progress. There was a powerful anti-gay backlash. In the USA, gay rights laws were overturned, a Christian Right made anti-gay politics the center of its social activism, and anti-gay violence spread. This backlash, along with the AIDS crisis, prompted a renewal of radical activism. In addition, deep internal conflicts within both feminist and gay movements surfaced, proving at once divisive and productive. In particular, women, people of color, bisexuals, and transgendered peoples criticized the movement for promoting an agenda that was too male-oriented, white, middle-class and too narrowly focused on rights and social acceptance.

In a social environment where gays were embroiled in battles within and outside the gay and feminist movements, there appeared a new intellectual and political current: queer theory. Queer theory challenged a key idea of gay thinking and politics: the notion that all homosexuals share a common core of experience, interests, and way of life. By contrast, queer theorists argue that there are many ways of being gay. Specifically, sexual identity cannot be separated from other identities such as race, class, nationality, gender, or age. Any specific definition of homosexual identity is restrictive. For example, to claim that homosexuals are the same as heterosexuals or are promiscuous, gender playful, or campy, applies to some individuals but not to others. Moreover, when a particular idea of being gay becomes dominant or an ideal, it devalues or excludes those who deviate. For example, if we read many Western publications we might think that most gay men aspire to an ideal of beauty that includes being muscular, hairless, slim, short-haired, abled, and white. This ideal devalues and marginalizes gay men who do not exhibit these features.

Approaching identities as multiple and regulatory may suggest to critics the undermining of gay theory and politics, but, for queer thinkers and activists, it presents new and productive possibilities. Queers do not wish to abandon identity but to recognize and value the multiplicity of meanings that are attached to being gay or lesbian. This encourages a culture and movement where many voices and interests are heard and shape gay life and politics. While it might make gay politics messy, it will bring more people into the movement and make possible varied political strategies.

Queer perspectives also aim to shift the focus of analysis and politics away from thinking of gays as a separate group or a minority. Instead, queers focus on a system of sexuality that constructs the self as sexual, that assigns a master sexual identity as heterosexual or homosexual to all citizens, and regulates everyone's sexuality in terms of a norm of sexual normality. Queers aim, then, to broaden sexual theory into a general critical study of sexualities and to expand politics beyond identity politics to a focus on the norms and regulations that control everyone's sexuality. Queer politics is less about legitimating minority sexual identities than widening the sphere of sexual and intimate life freed from state and institutional control.

IDENTITY AND COMMUNITY

For much of this century, homosexuality was seen as a natural, biologically based condition. People were said to be born heterosexual or homosexual. Homosexuals were assumed to have existed throughout history, although societies responded differently, some mildly tolerating, others aggressively hostile.

This perspective was first challenged by the British sociologist, Mary McIntosh (1968). She approached homosexuality as a social role. She asked, why have some societies developed the idea that homosexuality is an identity? McIntosh suggested that some societies establish a homosexual role in order to create boundaries between acceptable and nonacceptable behaviors. By defining the homosexual as an unnatural or stigmatized identity, heterosexuality is made into the norm and ideal. Good, respectable citizens are then expected to be heterosexual.

McIntosh held that while many societies are intolerant of homosexuality, only some societies create a homosexual identity. She did not, however, research where, when, and how such homosexual identities were created. It was her colleague, among others, Jeffrey Weeks (1977) who proposed that it was in late nineteenth-century Europe that the idea of a distinct homosexual identity first developed. Weeks emphasized the role of medical and scientific ideas in creating the notion of a homosexual type of person. The

medical view of the homosexual as an abnormal psychological type gained wide popularity through public scandals or court trials such as that of Oscar Wilde in England.

While the two British sociologists offered broad social and historical approaches to homosexual identity, other sociologists were researching the microsocial dynamics of identity formation. In particular, the labeling approach understood sexual identity as learned through processes of social interaction. For example, Plummer (1975) argued that individuals are not born homosexual, but become homosexual. They have to learn to define their desires as signs of a homosexual identity and they often rely on the support of other homosexuals to accept this identity and to come out. Moreover, while some homosexuals stay isolated, others respond to stereotypes by coming out. Some individuals become part of subcultures and social movements that provide a positive sense of identity, a sense of social belonging, and a social basis to mobilize for rights and respect.

The sociology of sexual identity has developed in two directions from the 1980s to the present. On the one hand, there has been an emphasis on the multiple types of homosexual identities. Sociologists and others point out that individuals are not just heterosexual or homosexual, but these sexual identities are shaped by factors such as gender, class, race, and nationality. Individuals never experience being gay in a general way, but only in specific and varied ways, for example, as a white, middle-class lesbian or a disabled, Korean gay man. Thus, feminists have argued that men and women experience being gay differently because, while men are socially dominant, women are, in most societies, socially subordinate. Accordingly, being a lesbian means not only desiring women but also (usually) living independently of men. Being a lesbian, then, challenges a male dominant social order in a way that is not true for gay men. This perspective suggests a sociology of homosexual identities that views gay lives as enmeshed in social dynamics of class, race, gender, nationality, and so on.

On the other hand, queer approaches to identity emphasize the fluid, performative character of identities. Identities are not learned and then fixed. Rather, identities are produced through behaviors that project a particular identity. The key point here is that actions produce the notion of sexual identity, rather than understanding behavior as an expression of a core psychological identity. For example, lesbians may signal that they are gay by the things they say, the way they look at women, by wearing certain clothes, or using certain words that are socially recognized as indicating a lesbian identity. Although many of us might think that these practices express a core identity, queers argue that they project an identity that is then taken as a psychological core.

Homosexual identities are then a product of the social environment. Individuals are not born homosexuals, nor do they naturally grow up becoming aware that this is who they are. Instead, they must learn to think of themselves as homosexual. Whether they do and how they do depends on the social environment.

Initially, the notion of a homosexual identity was created by medical, scientific ideas. As we saw, the homosexual was defined as an inferior, abnormal human type. Gradually, these ideas were accepted by other social institutions such as the criminal justice system and the government. Homosexuals have not, however, simply accepted these stigmatized identities. They have resisted by challenging a medical model, for example, by affirming their identity as normal, natural, or good. Gays have sought to change their legal and social status, and sometimes to change society.

Sociologists make the point that in order for individuals to challenge a stigmatized identity, they need social support. Although lesbian and gay individuals have often been isolated, they have also formed social networks or communities.

In the early part of the twentieth century, lesbians and gay men relied mostly on informal friendship networks. However, even before the movements in the 1970s, there were bars, baths, house parties, clubs, balls, and cruising areas where individuals formed relationships and developed feelings of community. In many cases, these places mixed straight and gay people. For example, Chauncey (1994) documents a gay world in New York City in the early 1900s where straights and gays or in his terms 'normal' men and 'fairies' mixed regularly – in restaurants, speakeasies and bars. In Harlem, rent parties provided occasions for gay people to meet and party. These social networks made it possible for individuals to fashion positive identities and to find partners and social support.

In the post-war period, these loosely formed social networks became solidly institutionalized. Throughout the 1950s and 1960s, in most European and Anglo-American nations, there were social organizations and institutions such as bars or clubs that were frequented by gay people. For example, historians have documented the development of a public working-class lesbian culture in many American cities that was organized around butch–fem roles. Of course, it was precisely this publicness that made lesbians and gay men easy targets of harassment and sometimes arrest.

The major breakthrough in the evolution of gay communities accompanied the take-off of a lesbian and gay movement in the 1970s and 1980s. A national movement for gay rights and liberation stimulated a remarkable period of community building. In small and large towns and cities across nations such as the USA, England, Australia, Holland, Denmark, and France, lesbian and gay community centers, bars, social clubs, and political organizations became commonplace. The institutionalization of gay subcultures made being gay into a profoundly social identity – indicating not only an individual desire but also membership of a complex, dense social world of institutions, organizations, and social and political events.

Gay institutions were initially formed as safe havens from a hostile world. They provided a positive sense of identity and community. They were often found exclusively in major urban centers. Participation in gay subcultures often meant feeling a strong sense of isolation from the social mainstream.

The role of the gay community has changed somewhat. As gays have gained rights and achieved considerable social integration, two developments are noteworthy.

First, more and more individuals today *choose* to participate in these gay subcultures less for reasons of escaping social disapproval or hostility than because they affirm one's identity and provide a desired way of life. In major urban areas such as London, Amsterdam, New York, San Francisco, Sydney, or Copenhagen, all highly tolerant and sexually integrated social spaces, it is possible for individuals to organize a rich individual and social life around being gay.

Second, it is no longer credible to think of the urban gay community as the heart and soul or the model of gay community life. Gay networks and institutions are to be found in virtually every city, small or large, and many suburbs. Furthermore, there are now a multiplicity of types of communities, from politically oriented ones to social clubs organized around a specific interest such as religion, art, sexual preference, or age, to fairly dense social networks that are sustained by friendships and social events.

INSTITUTIONS

In contemporary western societies sexuality is commonly understood as being a personal and private matter, linked to the body, the individual and concepts of nature. Indeed, sex is often talked about as if it had a certain mysterious quality, encompassing desires, feelings and motives that we cannot easily explain, an area of our lives somehow set apart from the public world and the workings of society. There are, of course, many different theoretical approaches to sexuality along the essentialist–constructionist

continuum (Fuss, 1990). A common view, however, and one which developed through the late nineteenth century and was profoundly influential during the twentieth century, is that sex is determined by biology and not by society.

Theories that seek to establish 'natural' or 'biological' explanations for our sexual practices, relationships and identities, generally referred to as essentialist, contain within them the assumption that sexuality is fundamentally pre-social. Sex is understood in terms of a powerful instinct or drive, usually assumed to be stronger in men than women, which is a product of our biological make-up as human beings. Sexuality, in this model, is regarded as separate to society and 'the social'.

In accepting this sex/society split, many theorists have assumed sex to be not only *pre*social, but also *anti*social. Sex is defined as a natural energy or force that is outside of *and* opposed to society, which needs to be held in check in order to maintain social order. This 'repressive hypothesis' assumes that modern societies depend upon a high level of sexual repression. Social institutions are here associated with constraint and control over people's sexual lives and, importantly, are seen to depend upon sexual repression for their continued existence. Indeed, the release of sexual energy from such constraints would, it is hypothesized, threaten or destroy modern 'civilization' and the social institutions upon which it is founded. For this reason some writers believed that sexuality had the power to transform society. Liberationist writers such as Marcuse (1970) and Reich (1962), for example, drawing on Marxism and the work of Freudian psychoanalysis, argued for the need for greater sexual freedom and expression as a prerequisite to radical social reform.

These traditional assumptions about sexuality, which have their roots in sociology, anthropology, psychoanalysis, and past medical investigations of sex, help us to begin to understand how we think about sexuality in relation to social institutions. How and in what ways are sexual lives 'controlled' and 'regulated'? What are the social institutions that are key to shaping sexualities in contemporary societies?

There has been a good deal of work in lesbian and gay studies on the social regulation of sexuality and how this varies with the changing role of the state, the significance of religion and the law, education, health and welfare policies, and so on. Moreover, the idea that society controls sexuality through repression has been superseded by the Foucauldian view that sexuality is regulated not through prohibition, but is socially produced through definition and categorization. One of the key themes to emerge from such work is the changing nature of state and institutional control. As Foucault (1980), Weeks (1990) and others have documented, since the nineteenth century there have been a number of major shifts in the impact that various social institutions have on people's sexual lives. The declining significance of religion as the authoritative voice on sexuality as medicine and scientific views on sexuality became the dominant discourse, coupled with the increasing secularization of society, has been reflected in a move away from moral regulation of sexuality through organized religion to social control being increasingly exercised through medicine, education, and social policy.

In addition to analyses that have focused on the role of social institutions in the social regulation and production of sexualities, some lesbian and gay studies have asked the question in reverse. How do assumptions about sexuality inform and constitute social institutions and our notions of the 'social world'? This represents a significant development. Although lesbian and gay studies continues to develop existing notions of sexuality and gender, and to document lesbian and gay lives and political struggles, there is an increasing focus on the broader implications of such interventions. For example, a shift from simply asking how the state treats lesbians and gays, to asking how concepts of the state are themselves grounded in assumptions about sexuality. The main project, according to writers such as Warner (1993), is the queering of existing theory rather than the production of theory about queers. This is the point Eve Sedgwick makes in proposing that:

> many of the major modes of thought and knowledge in twentieth century western culture as a whole are structured by a chronic now endemic crisis of homo/heterosexual definition ... an understanding of virtually any aspect of modern western culture must be not merely incomplete but damaged in its central substance to the degree that it does not incorporate a critical analysis of modern homo/heterosexual definition. (1990: 1)

This new wave of lesbian and gay studies overlaps with earlier feminist work on the construction of heterosexuality as naturalized and normalized (Richardson, 1996, 2000a). In their ground-breaking work writers like Adrienne Rich (1980) and Monique Wittig (1979) analysed heterosexuality as a social institution, as distinct from identity or practice. Marriage, with its specific understanding of distinct roles for women and men, is the institutionalized model of 'acceptable' sexuality necessary for social cohesion and stability, and for social inclusion as individuals with full citizenship rights.

Although the parallels and interconnections between feminist and queer theory are not always sufficiently acknowledged, in both cases sexuality, specifically the hetero/homosexual binary, is conceptualized as something that is encoded in a wide range of social institutions and practices. The emphasis is on the relationship between sexuality and social theory; on rethinking the social, on asking what happens to conceptual frameworks if heteronormative assumptions are challenged. How might these kinds of lesbian and gay, feminist and queer, studies inform our understanding of, for example, health, education, organized religion, the law, labor market analysis, or political economy? How might they contest the meanings of 'family', 'the state', 'rights', 'public and private', 'citizenship', and 'the social'?

Lesbian and gay studies has, then, contributed to our understanding of the social regulation and subjective meanings of sexuality produced through social institutions and cultural practices such as, for example, the law, religion, media, and education. More recently, they have also ventured into areas not normally thought of as connected with sexuality in an attempt to rethink 'the social'. Part of the problem in doing such work is the tendency to assume that we know what concepts such as 'social' and 'sexual' mean. As we have pointed out, traditionally, these have been theorized as separate if related spheres. This is hardly surprising. After all, laws, social policy, the economy – these are all constituted as belonging to the public arena, whereas sexuality has traditionally been associated with the private. And despite critiques from feminist writers in particular, the public and the private continue to be thought of as if they were dichotomous. It is this articulation of new ways of thinking about sexuality and the interrelationship with social institutions and practices that is one of the exciting areas for the future development of lesbian and gay studies.

POLITICS

Over the last half century lesbians and gay men have formed groups and organizations that either implicitly or explicitly have been a basis for political action and engagement. After World War II in Europe and the USA a number of 'homophile' organizations were formed in urban centres such as Los Angeles, San Francisco, and London. These organizations were, on the whole, conservative in their demands and moderate in their outlook, embracing the political strategies of a minority group seeking tolerance from the heterosexual majority. By the late 1960s, however, all this was to change. Liberal acceptance by mainstream society, and the social and legal reforms sought by most lesbian and gay activists a decade earlier, were replaced by a more militant and radical lesbian and gay voice that was highly critical of society in general and the way it treated

lesbians and gays in particular. And the language it spoke was that of liberation, of revolution, of political organizing, of mobilization.

In the 1990s a new queer perspective on sexuality and sexual politics emerged which echoed many of the concerns of lesbian/ feminists and gay liberationists before it. Queer politics aims to be transgressive of social norms, of heteronormativity. It is not about seeking social inclusion, but nor does it want to remain on the margins. What queers seek to do is contest the ways in which the hetero/homo binary serves to define heterosexuality at 'the center', with homosexuality positioned as the marginalized 'other', by claiming this space. In so doing, the notion of sexual 'difference' is disrupted, for with no center who or what can one be defined as different to?

Interestingly, alongside the development of queer there has been a turn to reformist politics and agendas, and the rise of what some have referred to as 'gay conservatism' in both the USA and the UK. Books like Bruce Bawer's (1993) *A Place at the Table* and Andrew Sullivan's (1996) *Virtually Normal,* for example, articulated a gay (predominantly male) agenda that aims to deradicalize political perspectives on homosexuality, arguing for assimilation into mainstream society with the enduring centrality of marriage and 'family values'. The demands are for acceptance of sexual diversity, rather than a more fundamental questioning of the social conditions that produce gendered and sexual divisions.

The concept of citizenship, along with questions of social exclusion and membership, also (re-)emerged during the 1990s as one of the key areas of debate within both political discourse and the social sciences. This focus on citizenship has been reflected in the political language and goals of social movements concerned with sexuality. This has been most obvious in the USA, where 'equal rights' approaches have come to dominate lesbian and gay politics, and is increasingly the 'main story' in the UK and elsewhere in Europe.

By the 1990s notions of equality had expanded to encompass not just the rights of individuals (identity and conduct-related rights), but those of family units and intimate relationship-based claims such as partnership recognition, marriage, parenting rights including access to adoption, fostering and custody rights. Although, despite this shift, it is important to recognize that demands for individual rights have not disappeared, campaigns for, for example, unequal age of consent, employment rights, gays in the military, and hate crime, continue to reflect a concern with conduct and identity issues (Richardson, 2000b).

These moves towards a politics of citizenship, both in terms of demands for civic rights and rights as consumers, represent a significant shift in the meaning and focus of sexual politics. It reflects a political agenda that is a far cry from both the queer politics of the 1990s, and the women's and gay movements that flourished in the late 1960s and 1970s, with their demands for radical social change. The political goal of such movements was not to assimilate into, or even to seek to reform the existing sexual/social order, but to challenge and transform it.

John D'Emilio (2000), reflecting on these changes in lesbian and gay movements over the past fifty years, characterizes this shift as a move from an outlook captured by the phrase 'here we are', towards activism about family, school, and work which puts forward a different demand: 'we want in'. From this perspective, equality entails 'equalizing up' within a multicultural model of sexual difference. According to D'Emilio, this process:

> will not be best served by primary emphasis on coming out and building community. Access to and equity within the key structures of American life will instead require that winning allies becomes a priority … As for community building, it can in serious ways work counter to achieving success in other areas. Community building easily becomes insular and separatist. It can unwittingly foster an isolation and marginalization that runs counter to the imperative of political engagement, particularly of the sort that involves winning support from outside one's community. (2000: 50)

The AIDS epidemic has been significant in this shift in gay politics, bringing into sharp relief the lack of legal recognition for non-heterosexual relationships, with consequences for access to pensions, housing, inheritance and other rights, as well as the need for health and social care services that are accepting of, and appropriate to, lesbian and gay relationships. Other specific concerns have also fuelled this re-thinking of lesbian and gay struggles such as, for example, Section 28 which Weeks (1991) argues, mobilized and politicized many non-heterosexual communities, especially in its attempts to exclude lesbians and gay men from what is thought to constitute 'a family'.

On the one hand, it is understandable why 'family' and 'marriage rights' are important to lesbians and gay men in their pursuit of full citizenship, in so far as it has a number of material consequences such as access to housing, health care, parenting rights, tax and inheritance rights, etc. However, this raises a much broader question, in terms of the wider implications of such trends, particularly for lesbian/feminist theory and politics which have developed powerful critiques of heterosexuality, marriage and the family. (Though it is the case that feminists have drawn on the language of citizenship, employing rights language in demands for sexual and reproductive self-determination for instance.) In effect, we are witnessing a normalization process; a gentrification process, if you like, of sexual 'others'. What better way to normalize lesbian and gay men than by marriage and family life? The move is towards making lesbian and gay sexualities respectable, rather than making being anti-gay immoral or unrespectable.

In this 'new deal' where demands are centered upon public recognition of lesbian and gay relationships as well as identities, what, we might ask, are the kind of obligations that are concomitant on the recognition of such rights by states or supra-states? What is the 'deal' based upon in modern, liberal, states? Martha Nussbaum, writing on the theme of sex and social justice, provides some illumination:

> The denial of marriage rights to same-sex couples has socially undesirable consequences ... if gays cannot legally get married, their efforts to live in stable committed partnerships are discouraged, and a life of rootless or even promiscuous non-commitment is positively encouraged. Thus a form of discrimination that has its roots in a stereotype may cause the stereotype to become, in some measure, true. But this state of affairs is irrational: Society has strong reasons to encourage the formation of stable domestic units by both heterosexual and homosexual couples. (1999: 202)

One might say that there is a convergence happening between gay politics and state practice in relation to attempts to maintain and stabilize sexuality as an organizing principle of social life. Yet there remains a tension in western liberal societies, which are becoming evermore plural and diverse and place great emphasis on individualism, between accepting 'difference' and the rights of individuals and, at the same time, upholding heterosexuality as the institutionalized model of sexual relations. This is a tension that has been clear in both the Clinton administration in the USA and in Blair's government in the UK. In the latter case, for example, we have witnessed this 'balancing act' played out in the New Labour government's willingness to push forward on the equalizing of the age of consent at the same time as it has backed down on its promise to remove the infamous Section 28 from the statute books.[1]

As part of this process of gaining access to new forms of citizenship status we also need to acknowledge that we are constituting certain types of sexual citizen as 'good' and 'bad' citizens. Who is the good sexual citizen? 'Good relationships' are defined here in terms of an emphasis on monogamy, commitment, and coupledom. Rights continue to be linked to being in such a relationship. What, then, are the implications for those who are critical of the gendered heterosexual norms underpinning citizenship?

These debates over claims of citizenship represent struggles over the meaning of sexuality. It is not simply a case of whether we are able to reach agreement on particular rights claims or not, though such debates can be just as contentious, but whether the models of citizenship operating, and the theoretical arguments put forward for them, are compatible with the kind of frameworks that have been used by lesbians and gays/feminists/and queers in developing a politics of gender and sexuality. To further illustrate this point, we might consider the recent shift towards a focus on relationship-based rights claims by lesbian and gay movements and campaigning groups, both in the USA and Europe. As a number of feminist writers such as, for example, Christine Delphy (1996) have argued, this kind of model of citizenship reinforces both the desirability and necessity of sexual coupledom, privileged over other forms of relationships, as a basis for many kinds of rights entitlements. Moreover, it represents the integration of lesbian and gay men into a couple-based system of rights originally founded on heterosexual and gendered norms.

The process of organizing around identities such as lesbian and gay has also prompted a great deal of debate about identity as a basis for political action. In stressing the importance of 'coming out', for example, lesbian and gay liberation movements in the 1970s ran the risk of seemingly accepting understandings of sexuality as an 'essential' aspect of self and the idea of a shared common identity. In the 1980s similar debates raged within feminism over the possibility of some kind of collective use of the term 'woman' for political purposes. The question in this case is whether the category 'woman' can be used as a unifying, if not unified, concept.

Although both feminist and gay and lesbian politics have critiqued essentialism, some gay interventions into politics use essentialist ideas strategically, with lesbians and gays conceptualized as a legitimate minority group having an ethnic status and identity (Epstein, 1992). This is a strategy that has been deployed in the USA, where the parallels that have been made with race-based political aims and strategies have been extremely controversial, and it is also being used in the UK in a variety of campaigns. Some critics argue that such tactical use of essentialism will only 'undermine the overall aim of achieving social equality for lesbians and gays' (Rahman, 2000: 122). What is required instead, it is claimed, is to deploy political identities as necessary signifiers of political subjects, a location from which to articulate social and material concerns, rather than an expression of essential sexual selves that define lesbians and gays as an 'ethnic' group. More recently, discussion over whether lesbian and gay identities are re-essentialized through political struggles has been given new impetus by postmodern understandings of identity, where the emphasis is on fluidity and performativity (Butler, 1990, 1997).

Rights do not exist in nature; they are products of social relations and of changing historical circumstances. In the present social climate, we are witnessing more and more rights-based arguments concerned with sexual practices, identities, and relationships. As we struggle to keep up with a rapidly evolving and broadening concept of 'sexual rights', we must also respond by extending and developing our frameworks for understanding the sexual rights discourse. We also need to recognize the wider social implications of such changes. Although it is a contested concept with various meanings (Lister, 1997), citizenship is often associated with membership of the nation state. Clearly, the political strategies used and the rights demands made by lesbian and gay movements are shaped by both local and national contexts. However, with the social and political changes which have led to 'globalization', comes the claim that we are experiencing a globalizing of gay identity and politics that has led to the export of western definitions of sexual identities and practices, as well as gay rights agendas, around the world. The implications of this globalized sexual citizenship, which some critics argue is a form of cultural and sexual imperialism, is a key theme for lesbian and gay studies in the future. As writers such as, for example, Dennis Altman (1996 and in this volume) and Carl Stychin (1998) have noted, we must consider how far lesbian and gay/queer politics developed in the West can be deployed successfully elsewhere.

NOTE

1. Section 28 of the Local Government Act (1988), which outlaws the 'promotion' of homosexuality in state-funded schools and defines lesbian and gay families as 'pretended family relationships', was overturned by the Scottish Parliament in 2000, however, at the time of writing it continues to be the law in England.

REFERENCES

Altman, Dennis (1996) 'Rupture or continuity? The internationalization of gay identities', *Social Texts*, 48: 77–94.

Bawer, Bruce (1993) *A Place at the Table: The Gay Individual in American Society*. New York: Touchstone Books.

Becker, Howard (1963) *Outsiders*. New York: Free Press.

Butler, Judith (1990) *Gender Trouble*. London: Routledge.

Butler, Judith (1997) 'Critically queer', in Shane Phelan (ed.), *Playing With Fire: Queer Politics, Queer Theories*. London: Routledge.

Chauncey, George (1994) *Gay New York*. New York: Basic Books.

Delphy, Christine (1996) 'The private as a deprivation of rights for women and children', paper given at the International Conference on Violence, Abuse and Women's Citizenship, Brighton, UK, November 1996.

D'Emilio, John. (1983) *Sexual Politics, Sexual Communities*. Chicago: University of Chicago Press.

D'Emilio, John (2000) 'Cycles of change, questions of strategy: the gay and lesbian movement after fifty years', in Craig A. Rimmerman, Kenneth D. Wald and Clyde Wilcox (eds), *The Politics of Gay Rights*. London: University of Chicago Press.

Epstein, Steven (1992) 'Gay politics, ethnic identity', in Edward Stein (ed.), *Forms of Desire*. New York: Routledge.

Faderman, Lillian (1981) *Surpassing the Love of Men*. London: Junction Books.

Foucault, Michel (1980) *The History of Sexuality*. New York: Pantheon.

Fuss, Diana (1990) *Essentially Speaking: Feminism, Nature and Difference*. London: Routledge.

Gagnon, John and William, Simon. (1973) *Sexual Conduct*. Chicago: Aldine.

Katz, Jonathan (1976) *Gay American History*. New York: T.Y. Crowell.

Lister, Ruth (1997) *Citizenship: Feminist Perspectives*. London: Macmillan.

Marcuse, Herbert (1970) *Eros and Civilisation*. London: Allen Lane.

McIntosh, Mary (1968) 'The homosexual role', *Social Problems*, 16: 182–92.

Nussbaum, Martha (1999) *Sex and Social Justice*. Oxford: Oxford University Press.

Plummer, Kenneth (1975) *Sexual Stigma*. London: Routledge.

Rahman, Momin (2000) *Sexuality and Democracy: Identities and Strategies in Lesbian and Gay Politics*. Edinburgh: Edinburgh University Press.

Reich, Wilhelm (1962) *The Sexual Revolution*. New York: Farrar, Strauss and Giroux.

Rich, Adrienne (1980) 'Compulsory heterosexuality and lesbian existence', *Signs*, 5 (4): 631–60.

Richardson, Diane (ed.) (1996) *Theorising Heterosexuality: Telling it Straight*. Buckingham: Open University Press.

Richardson, Diane (2000a) *Rethinking Sexuality*. London: Sage.

Richardson, Diane (2000b) 'Constructing sexual citizenship: theorising sexual rights', *Critical Social Policy*, 20 (1): 105–35.

Schur, Edwin (1965) *Crimes Without Victims*. Toronto: Prentice-Hall.

Sedgwick, Eve Kosofsky (1990) *Epistemology of the Closet*. Berkeley, CA: University of California Press.

Smith-Rosenberg, Carroll (1985) 'The female world of love and ritual', in *Disorderly Conduct*. New York: Oxford University Press.

Stychin, Carl (1998) *A Nation By Rights: National Cultures, Sexual Identity Politics, and the Discourse of Rights*. Philadelphia, PA: Temple University Press.

Sullivan, Andrew (1996) *Virtually Normal: An Argument about Homosexuality*. London: Picador.

Trumbach, Randolph (1977) 'London's sodomites', *Journal of Social History*, 11: 1–33.

Warner, Michael (1993) 'Introduction', in Michael Warner (ed.), *Fear of a Queer Planet: Queer Politics and Social Theory*. Minneapolis: University of Minnesota Press.

Weeks, Jeffrey (1977) *Coming Out*. London: Quartet.

Weeks, Jeffrey (1990) *Sex, Politics and Society*, 2nd edn. London: Longman.

Weeks, Jeffrey (1991) *Against Nature: Essays on History, Sexuality and Identity*. London: Rivers Oram Press.

Wittig, Monique (1979) 'The straight mind', *Feminist Issues*, 1 (2): 47–54.

Part I

HISTORY AND THEORY

1

From Liberation to Transgression and Beyond

Gay, Lesbian and Queer Studies at the Turn of the Twenty-first Century

BARRY D. ADAM

In its relatively recent but flourishing history, lesbian and gay studies has moved rapidly through a series of major transformations. Even the act of naming such a body of knowledge is a contested undertaking. Gay and lesbian studies, like the communities and movements associated with it, was perhaps least problematic as a term sometime in the 1980s. Since then, 'gay' and 'lesbian', which were certainly disputed names even as they gained widespread currency in the 1960s and 1970s, have been challenged by such terms as 'bisexual', 'transgender', and 'queer'. A leading journal in the field calls itself *GLQ* to try to avoid the charge of exclusivity. Yet all of these words taken together still cannot capture the full range of interests and topics pursued by scholars who write about the many manifestations of sexual and emotional connection, in their social and cultural contexts, that fall outside of the heterosexual realm. Two-spirited aboriginal people, historical romantic friendships, and acolyte-mentor relationships are but a few of the topics that exceed the terminology, but nevertheless draw together a great many researchers and theorists into communication with each other about how gender, sexuality, identity, power, and culture 'work'.

Perhaps what gives some sense of commonality to these many endeavours is their opposition to the study of homosexuality that preceded them. The Cold War era of the 1950s was occupied almost entirely by a set of ideologies intent on annihilating homosexual desire and its social formations. Whether in legislatures, courts, churches, universities, or the mass media, talk of homosexuality, if permitted at all, turned on the question of whether it was sin, sickness, or crime. Scholarly debate, along with public discussion, largely addressed the issue of which tools of repression would prove most effective: psychiatry, law enforcement, or religious indoctrination. Gay and lesbian studies, then, emerged as an effort to decolonize science in that it sought to break the pathology paradigm and wrest the stories of homosexual experience from the monopoly of the social-control professions.

This transition in thinking from the 1950s to the 1970s exists in a yet larger historical context that merits consideration. The desire to document and celebrate the lives of people with homoerotic expression is as lengthy as literacy itself. Ancient recorded epics, such as the Babylonian *Gilgamesh,* the Greek *Symposium,* and the Roman *Satyricon*, contain central narratives of male sexual friendship, as do some of the oldest surviving texts of China, India, Persia, and Japan. Literacy has been much less available to women, but when nuns were first schooled in writing, female passion soon came into view as well (Murray, 1996). From the late nineteenth century until 1933, Germany became a center of scholarship rooted in gay community – most notably Magnus Hirschfeld's Institute for Sexual Science, itself just one element of a larger gay and lesbian culture (Berlin Museum, 1984). The Nazi regime obliterated this first wave of gay and lesbian studies. By the 1950s, only a few lone pioneers in Europe and North America worked against tremendous odds to rediscover what was now 'hidden from history' (Duberman et al., 1989).

The gay and lesbian studies of the 1970s, then, were something of a 'second wave' like second-wave feminism. Also like women's studies, gay and lesbian studies became possible only because of the larger social climate of change characterized by the so-called 'new' social movements of the 1960s. Movement and knowledge-creation were indistinguishable in a period when civil rights, women's, and gay and lesbian movements sought to take back public and scholarly images and stories about themselves. Like the socialist and national liberation struggles that aimed to break the ideologies that legitimated the subordination of workers and of colonized peoples in Asia and Africa, the new social movements worked to re-found science in ways that better expressed their own experiences. All of these new knowledge projects thought of themselves as engaged in consciousness-raising and liberation by challenging social exclusion and creating the tools of self-empowerment.

Debates in gay and lesbian studies were the debates of movement thinkers about who we are and what we want. Key texts written by Jill Johnston, Adrienne Rich, and Mary Daly functioned as manifestos calling lesbians to act on a new vision of a women-centred society free of patriarchal domination. Similarly, Dennis Altman and Guy Hocquenghem postulated new utopias of free-floating desire unhampered by homosexual and heterosexual identities and boundaries. Gay and lesbian writing was struggling out of a long period of censorship and outright suppression. The promise of liberation was allowing people to glimpse the possibility of a new world free of prejudice, and to dream of radically rearranged societies where people could explore new options in loving and living together.

TRANSITIONS IN THE LATE TWENTIETH CENTURY

There are a good many social and cultural factors that shaped the new lesbian and gay studies in the last quarter of the twentieth century. Shifts in the socio-historical environment of the period, reorganization of movement groups and strategies, and new intellectual trends all contributed to thoroughgoing rethinking of studies of sexuality and gender. Over time, gay and lesbian movements, like the other new social movements around them, moved away from confrontation and radicalism (Adam, 1995). Part of this has to do with the colder political climate of the neo-conservative governments of the 1980s, embodied especially in the Thatcher and Reagan administrations, where reform movements and their constituencies were pressed into a more defensive posture in the face of global capitalism. Part of these changes also has to do with a modicum of success won, especially in advanced, industrial nations, through the attainment of basic anti-discrimination laws and the consolidation of social spaces resistant to police repression. The political strategies that proved most viable in liberal, democratic societies were typically civil rights arguments reliant on judicial and legislative reform. Lesbian and gay politics became somewhat more 'domesticated', or perhaps 'mature', through integration into conventional political channels, and homosexuality tended to become constructed as a minority, parallel to ethnic minorities, in contrast to the gay liberation image of homoerotic desire as a potential in everyone.

The emergence of the AIDS epidemic in the early 1980s emboldened anti-gay forces to try to roll back newly acquired citizenship rights, but perhaps ironically, AIDS also led to new alignments between (some) governments and gay and lesbian communities, as AIDS service organizations were brought into health and social service systems and thus into further integration in mainstream state systems (Altman, 1988; Adam, 1997).

Commercialization also blunted liberationist rhetoric. Gay and lesbian worlds flourished in the post-Stonewall United States and in the European Union, Canada, Australia, and New Zealand, anchored often by commercial establishments, such as bars and discos. Over the years, the growing size of Pride celebrations attracted the interest of major corporations who came to view gay and lesbian communities as underexploited sources of consumer buying power. The overtly political gay and lesbian press of the 1970s faded out as slick commercial magazines promoting fashionable and expensive 'gay lifestyles' came to the fore. This more de-politicized and consumerist environment emboldened a new class of conservative commentators both inside the gay press and in the mainstream press as well. All too often, the prominence of the new conservatives resulted in their being able to put their stamp on the meaning of *gay* and *lesbian* in public discourse, and to construct images of gay community that alienated not only many women, people of colour, working-class people, and youth, but many middle-class white men as well.

In this environment, then, the liberationist project lost sustenance and direction. In his 1990 review of the state of gay and lesbian studies in the United States, Jeffrey Escoffier (1998) lamented the growing disconnection between community and movement politics as the field began to migrate into the academy. A great deal of the new gay and lesbian studies of the 1960s and 1970s grew out of the excitement of discovering a lost history, so much so that early conferences subsumed all other research under the 'history' label. A wide range of people from inside and outside the academy turned up at the New York conferences of the Gay Academic Union in the mid-1970s to report on their findings, and many of these findings found their way into gay and lesbian community newspapers. At that time, even professional scholars pursued gay-related research 'on the side' of their regular work for fear that it would be seen as more stigmatizing than valuable inside universities. But the struggle of lesbian and gay caucuses inside disciplinary associations in the 1970s and 1980s succeeded in creating space inside the academy, and more and more work in the area began to emerge from students and researchers in the universities.

THE EMERGENCE OF LESBIAN AND GAY STUDIES

Ken Plummer's (1992) review of lesbian and gay studies in Europe and North America marvelled at the array of conferences, journals, and bookstores that had sprung up over two decades. Psychologists were displacing the homosexuality-as-sickness view with new investigations into *homophobia,* the irrational prejudice directed against homosexual practices and peoples. Sociologists, anthropologists, and historians were unsettling biological models of sexuality by showing how desire is deeply shaped by cultural context, and how pet notions concerning 'the natural', 'the moral', and 'the desirable' are peculiarly ethnocentric.

Literary critics were exposing histories of censorship and distortion that had suppressed homoeroticism in novels, movies, and biographies.

Gay and lesbian studies was also changing as a result of internal dilemmas, and philosophical currents that affected other philosophies of change such as Marxism, feminism, and postcolonialism. As enthusiastic researchers went out to rediscover gay and lesbian history, they first looked for people much like themselves, only to discover that same-sex desire and relationships took often unfamiliar forms in other eras and cultures. This initial belief in a discoverable homosexual throughout history and around the world came to be known as *essentialism* (Boswell, 1989). Out of the dilemmas of essentialism came a scholarship that sought to understand how (homosexual) desire arose and was lived through in very different social and historical environments. This *social constructionist* view was perhaps best expressed in the work of Jeffrey Weeks in gay and lesbian studies and by Peter Berger and Thomas Luckmann (1966) outside. In a groundbreaking trilogy founded in British history, Weeks (1977, 1981, 1985) showed the complex weave of social, historical, and semiotic currents that produced modern conceptions of what homosexuality is. Though same-sex sexual and emotional connections can be documented in many different societies and historical periods, the modern sense of homosexuality as an identity and a people is a relatively recent development.

Despite important differences in philosophical approach and genealogy, social constructionism tended to be identified as well with the work of Michel Foucault (1978) who treated the ways in which sexuality, and knowledge about sexuality, existed within regulatory regimes that give it shape and meaning. For Foucault, modern gay and lesbian identities and movements could scarcely be simply about 'liberation' because they built on the 'homosexual' category, an invention of western societies to police and contain desire. At the same time though, many of Foucault's followers have forgotten his view that the politics of sexual identities is not just about limitation, but also about the generation of new pleasures and ways of living. This dilemma – or perhaps better said – dialectic continues to fuel debates among scholars and activists who want either to build up or tear apart 'gay' and 'lesbian' categories (Gamson, 1998). Perhaps ironically, the *personal is political* credo of the liberationists was a stimulus for the Foucauldian revolution in social theory. It became increasingly difficult through the 1970s and 1980s to postulate that an essential homosexual waited to be liberated, just as Marxian ideologies ran aground with claims of an unsullied, militant, working class about to spring forth ready to effect a socialist revolution, if only 'false consciousness' could be punctured. Just as feminists began interrogating just what the category of 'women' means in the face of critiques by lesbians, women of colour, working-class women, and third world women, just what it is that unifies gay men or lesbians seemed increasingly difficult to discern. This *deconstruction* of core categories became a major academic industry in the 1990s, identified in social theory with *postmodernism* and in lesbian and gay studies with *queer theory*.

THE RISE OF QUEER THEORY

By the 1990s, *liberation* had given way to *transgression* as a leading project, and gay and lesbian studies had grown immensely, fragmented, and changed direction. Queer theory, set in motion by the pioneering work of Judith Butler (1990) and Eve Sedgwick (1990), strongly reinvigorated work in gay and lesbian studies (or perhaps one should now say, queer studies), set a new course for the area, and resulted in a wave of innovative, critical publications. Queer theory stepped back from the study of homosexuality to the question of how people and desires come to be separated into the two camps of homosexuality and heterosexuality in the first place. Sharing with deconstruction an interest in discovering the underpinnings of linguistic binaries like homosexual–heterosexual, male–female, white–black, and so on, queer theory proposed to delineate the regulatory regimes that sort sexualities and subjectivities into valued and devalued categories. The promise of queer theory was to move beyond the minoritizing logic of the study of a gay and lesbian 'ethnicity' toward an understanding of the ways in which heterosexuality and family pull the cloak of virtue around themselves by manufacturing a deviant *other* into which a great many people can be dumped and dismissed. A good deal of insightful work into the ways in which heterosexual masculinity constructs itself by simultaneously exploiting and denying its homoerotic impulse has emerged from this perspective. Though perhaps not an 'official' queer theorist, Mark Simpson's (1994) provocative essays have exposed ways in which the simultaneous reliance on, and denial of, homoeroticism among men informs everything from football to action movies. In a send-up of the British 'new lad', Simpson (1999: 8–9) observes how the quest for masculinity inevitably involves large doses of male bonding and 'an exhausting schedule of boozing, shagging babes and fighting over football scores which is, in part, a hysterical attempt to ward off any suggestion of poovery and keep the homo tag at bay'.

Queer theory encouraged analysis not only of the overtly homosexual, but also a reading between the lines for patterns of absences and silences through which texts deny same-sex desire. It revealed how the manufacture of a reviled 'homosexual' in western societies has often been a method by which 'heterosexuality' and 'family' assured themselves of their superiority, rather like the way racism has loaded repugnant attributes onto people of colour in order to justify the privileges of white people. Queer theory hoped, as well, to jump the traces of gay/lesbian categories by embracing other outlaws from the patriarchal family often by celebrating boundary crossers

such as transgender people and bisexuals. In one sense, queer theory recaptured a radical moment associated with gay liberation in its affirmation of the widespread nature of homoerotic desire and the artificiality of the homosexual–heterosexual division.

So strong has been the vigour of queer theory that Lisa Pottie (1997) discerns a trend toward the 'selling' of queer theory as a fashionable new commodity among academics and students, at least in English departments receptive to cultural studies. On the other hand, reports from other disciplines in the humanities, social sciences, and natural sciences show more scepticism concerning support for scholarship in the area, where gay, lesbian, and queer studies eke out an existence as an avocation of scholars hired to do other things (Taylor and Raeburn, 1995; Duggan, 1995a; Weston, 1996; Leap, 1998).

Still, queer theory is not without its own difficulties, generating a new range of problems in place of those it addresses. There has been a good deal of suspicion about the degree to which queer theory succeeds in being more inclusive of gender (Walters, 1996) and race (Samuels, 1999; Boykin, 2000). Perhaps of greatest concern to critics of queer theory is the politics that flow (or do not flow) from it (Edwards, 1998). Despite ritual references to the queer movement of the early 1990s, Queer Nation proved to be a short-lived phenomenon and queer theory lives on in the academy with a problematic relationship to gay, lesbian, or queer communities. Though deconstruction of heterosexuality is clearly a primary endeavour of queer scholarship, and many theorists have echoed Esther Newton's call to deconstruct heterosexuality 'first', it is gay and lesbian identities that are far more vulnerable to attack. Heterosexuality and its attendant ideological regime of family values, Hollywood romance, and professional reassurance have an immense cultural apparatus to recreate themselves as 'natural', 'biological', and thus unquestionable. 'Gay' and 'lesbian' are historically recent and comparatively fragile accomplishments that secure a social space that otherwise seems never to be available. Ironically, queer theory's fascination with the hidden homoeroticism of ostensibly heterosexual writing – and most often heterosexual men at that – means that attention is turned away once again from the culture, experience, and self-expression of out lesbians, gay men, and queers.

The queer theory myth that 'gay' refers to sexual essentialism may never have been widely believed among gay men in any case (Adam, 2000). Queer theory expresses just one tendency in gay and lesbian communities: simultaneous with the questioning and reworking of gay and lesbian identities are dynamic historical trends toward an even wider embrace and growth of gay and lesbian identities and cultures. Indeed, it is because gay and lesbian spaces and identities have created a secure place that the queer critique can be launched. The deconstruction of 'gay' and 'lesbian' proceeds by ignoring the strategic values of 'necessary fictions' (Weeks, 1993) which still have utility in creating and protecting safe spaces for gay and lesbian expression. Patricia Hill Collins (1997) observes how deconstruction arrived on the scene just in time to undermine a newly achieved sense of self and collective empowerment among people of colour; something similar might be argued for gay and lesbian communities. Queer theory, following social constructionism, has created such a large chasm between homosexual behaviours and identities, that it may now be time to deconstruct the behaviour–identity binary in order to understand why so many people wish to connect the two.[1] Queer politics even show vulnerability to the 'logic' of the Vatican and the US military in its interest in clearing the social field of the gay and lesbian, portraying homosexual desire as a universal potential, and constructing emigrants from the patriarchal family as deviants. As Eric Savoy (1994: 145) remarks, 'postmodern theory effects an ironic, indeed, an uncanny, return of homosexuality to something very like its *premodern* delineation – an inchoate and not-yet-emergent taxonomy of desires or acts that cannot *quite* be termed a "subjectivity"'.

Its construction of the 'queer' as the negation of respectability shows indebtedness to traditional, especially American, understandings of homosexuality as 'deviance' that tend to cover over the commonalities shared by the larger society. At times, denying gay and lesbian social formations by reducing them to 'desire' is a convergent discourse shared by conservative Christian and queer paradigms that can produce odd effects in real struggles in referendum campaigns and the courts (Patton, 1993; Gamson, 1998).

Queer theory's insistence on the uniqueness of every cultural difference cannot explain what Indonesians or post-apartheid South Africans do get out of adapting gay ideas to their own context (Donham, 1998). To find cross-cultural resemblance or note the interest in things gay among peoples outside Europe and North America is to be accused of promoting a 'transcendental gay or lesbian subject' and of sexual essentialism (Boellstorff, 1999: 478), cold comfort for those who look to the International Lesbian and Gay Association and the International Gay and Lesbian Human Rights Commission for defence of a wide variety of sexual and gender expression around the world.[2] Its claim that 'gay' and 'lesbian' are regulatory regimes cannot reconcile itself to the experience of those for whom such identities offer new possibilities, assurances, and self-realization.

BEYOND QUEER

Even this discussion of lesbian, gay, and queer studies presumes implicit boundaries around a definable field. The sense of a shift toward queer theory – and despite its claims to the contrary – its totalizing tendency to displace alternatives with its own canon, iconography, and preferred genealogy (Duggan, 1995a; Duggan, 1995b), comes up most clearly from a series of conferences in Toronto, Rutgers, and Iowa. A glance through a set of multidisciplinary survey books on lesbian, lesbian and gay, and queer studies reveals a much greater diversity of approaches and paradigms. These books

(Cruikshank, 1982; Abelove et al., 1993; Blumenfeld and Raymond, 1993; Garber, 1994; Wilton, 1995; Beemyn and Eliason, 1996; Zimmerman and McNaron, 1996; Foster et al., 1997; Griffin and Andermahr, 1997; Medhurst and Munt, 1997; Nardi and Schneider, 1997; Ristock and Taylor, 1998) typically offer papers on pedagogy, survival in the academy, and individual disciplines, and reflect an eclectic mix of viewpoints. (Perhaps most notable about this set is that half of them address lesbian studies, and half gay and lesbian or queer studies, but none offer an exclusively gay male focus.) Dorothy Painter and Willa Young (1996: 106) distill a core of lesbian studies notables from their review of lesbian studies course outlines: 'Audre Lorde, Barbara Smith, Adrienne Rich, Joan Nestle, Jewelle Gomez, Marilyn Frye, Lillian Faderman, Gloria Anzaldúa, Judy Grahn, and the Radicalesbians'. *Lambda Book Report* struck a jury of fourteen in 1999 to identify the '100 best' gay and lesbian novels of all time. Both of these attempts to identify a canon turn out to be highly US-centred. Still, the scattered and inconsistent nature of gay and/or lesbian studies courses, as well as their different disciplinary hosts, mean that there is often little overlap in texts from one course to another.

While queer theory has its greatest strength in literary studies, a rich research heritage has also been developing in a wide range of disciplines and topics, including studies of (homo)sexuality in societies around the world, in different historical eras, in various cultural media, in psychology and personal development, in sexuality and relationships, in politics and law, and in various communities defined by ethnicity, gender, religion, age, disability, and identity. Community history projects and archives continue to document lives and cultures (Roscoe, 1995). Programmes of study and research centres have come about in several places (http://www.duke.edu/web/jyounger/lgbprogs.html). And despite the inwardness of gay and lesbian studies in the United States – Terry Goldie (1999: 15) remarks, 'It is as if the Americanness of gay and lesbian studies is a given that requires no justification, no explanation and no apology' – gay and lesbian studies have lengthy histories in the Netherlands, Germany, France, United Kingdom, Canada, and Australia, and are showing vitality in Latin America and South Africa.

At the other extreme from queer theory is the study of AIDS. There is a scholarly tradition that draws on gay, lesbian, and queer studies to understand how AIDS has been manufactured as a moral and political entity in contemporary societies (Altman, 1986; Watney, 1987; Patton, 1990; Adam and Sears, 1996; Epstein, 1996; Levine et al., 1997), but this work tends to be side-lined by a biomedical AIDS research establishment where the lives of people living with HIV tend to be contained within a traditional scientific frame that takes them as objects of study while containing their experiences, aspirations, and activities as nothing more than the 'psychosocial' aspect of medicine. Reinforced by major funding agencies, this AIDS research mainstream refuses the significant questions raised by queer theory concerning the politics of science, that is, who observes whom and for what purposes? Safer sex practices can scarcely be understood apart from what people think and feel about sex, how it is a means of communication with others, and the ways in which people make sense of sexual discourses circulating in society, yet 'normal' science remains untroubled in its rationalist presumptions and agenda of trying to measure and impute personality deficits as 'causes' of unsafe sex (Kippax et al., 1993; Díaz and Ayala, 1999; Adam et al., 2000). While AIDS activists have made important inroads in the conduct of clinical trials and in drug distribution, the limitations of psychosocial research have led to distrust among AIDS service organizations and calls for more genuinely community-based research.

NOW WHAT?

Like postmodern feminism, gay, lesbian, and queer theories continue to struggle over issues of difference and equality (Felski, 1997), that is, how to fully recognize and include the multitude of social locations and experiences of homoerotically-inclined people at home and around the world, without sacrificing all sense of commonality out of which solidary networks become possible. 'Gay' and 'lesbian' remain popular forms of self-identification, experienced less as regimes of sexual regulation, than as bulwarks against heterosexism, supports for personal relationships, and modes of celebration of sensibilities and cultures, but 'gay' and 'lesbian' are at the same time infused with the legacy of metropolitan ghettos and colonization by the pervasive market forces of global capitalism.

Certainly the need for critical reflection on contemporary issues facing lesbian, gay, bisexual, transgender, and queer peoples today remains no less than before. Perhaps in Denmark, where so much of the human rights agenda has been achieved, there is some reason for complacency (Bech, 1998). In the United States, where anti-gay forces wage active campaigns against the equality of gay and lesbian citizens, there is urgent need for more engagement of gay, lesbian, and queer studies with politics. Since 1977, local referenda have been used, election after election, to repeal anti-discrimination legislation (Herman, 1997; Witt and McCorkle, 1997), and since 1995, thirty-three of the United States and the national Congress have succumbed to a panic over 'gay marriage', banning the legal recognition of same-sex relationships. Sodomy laws remain on the books in one-third of the states, from time to time proving not to be the 'dead letters' they are often claimed to be. The national uproar occasioned around admitting that gay men and lesbians are part of the military revealed the pervasiveness of national homophobia (Scott and Stanley, 1994) and the federal government determined to reinforce its system of official denial through continued expulsion of gay and lesbian military people. When murderers are discovered preying on gay men, the mass media are quick to impute collective guilt onto a spectral

gay community supposedly threatening innocent heterosexuals, as in the notorious Dahmer case (Schmidt, 1994). People with AIDS remain vulnerable to the same system of spectralization that, from time to time, presents them as a national threat (Patton, 1990), a phantasm reproduced and policed at every border crossing into the United States, where sero-positive people are subject to detention and expulsion. While the map of homophobia has changed shape over time, it has scarcely faded away. Rabidly anti-gay subcultures flourish in most high schools producing the major class of perpetrators of anti-gay violence (Comstock, 1991). The ability of the Christian Right (Diamond, 1998) to construct a sometimes winning ideology around the idea of an effete, moneyed homosexual class demanding special rights in opposition to God-fearing, family-caring, patriotic Americans requires both cultural deconstruction and what the Marxian tradition refers to as *praxis,* that is, an adequate understanding of the social forces that keep such ideologies in operation and strategies for deflating them among the electorate. A cultural politics of deconstruction can be part of a process of opposing these homophobic projects, but is not enough in itself. Social change cannot be 'reduced to the arena of cultural representation' (Hennessy, 1995: 52). The rather too prevalent reliance by the gay and lesbian press on numbers of gay, or maybe-gay, characters on television sitcoms as a measure of progress trivializes these pressing problems that affect gay and lesbian lives.

So there is still a great deal more to be done in lesbian and gay studies, and there are as well a great many innovative and insightful studies coming out that are sure to impact not only ways in which gay, lesbian, bisexual, and transgender people think about themselves, but also 'mainstream' beliefs and dogmas about how to live and love. Rather than rehearse a new list of the 'greats' in the area, and thus contribute to another exercise in canon-building, in these closing pages I would like to draw attention to perhaps under-appreciated work and underdeveloped research areas. (Developments in literary criticism, fiction, drama, poetry, and biography are reviewed elsewhere in this volume.) These include Steven Seidman's (1996, 1997) volumes that attempt to stimulate a cross-fertilization of semiotics and social science to realize the initial promise of cultural studies in a 'social postmodernism' by turning the tools of postmodernism/queer theory to contemporary public debates. Some scholars are following up the other half of the Foucauldian agenda by documenting the new social formations that have arisen in lesbian, gay, bisexual, and transgender worlds. Particularly noteworthy is new work on household, kinship, friendship, and family (Weston, 1991; Lewin, 1993; Arnup, 1995; Dowsett, 1996; Carrington, 1999; Nardi, 1999).

Ethnographies of same-sex relations and network formation in societies around the world continue to emerge, as have encyclopaedic overviews (Greenberg, 1988; Herdt, 1997; Adam et al., 1999; Murray, 2000). Historical research has been especially rich with separate treatment currently being accorded to each historical era and nation. City-level histories are sketching out in some detail the ways that homosexually interested people have found each other and developed networks and communities. Until recently, students were hard pressed to find sources of the experiences of people of Asian, African, Latin American, and aboriginal descent, but a wealth of work has started to emerge (Beam, 1986; Hemphill, 1991; Ramos, 1994; Martinez, 1996; Douglas et al., 1997; Eng and Hom, 1997; Jacobs et al., 1997; Smith, 1998). Writing by and about transgender people is challenging the pathology paradigms (Bornstein, 1995; Feinberg, 1996; Namaste, 2000), much like gay and lesbian studies challenged its predecessors. Several works offer philosophical reflections, social commentary, or personal perceptions (Adam, 1978; Plummer, 1992; Grosz and Probyn, 1995; Bech, 1997; Phelan, 1997; Stein, 1997; Eribon, 1999; Hollibaugh, 2000). And the cultures and histories of people outside the United States are increasingly coming into print in: Canada (Ross, 1995; Kinsman,

1996; Remiggi and Demczuk, 1998; Lahey, 1999), Australia (Aldrich and Wotherspoon, 2000), the United Kingdom (www.sbu.ac.uk/~stafflag/lagstudies.html), the Netherlands (www.homodok.nl), Germany (www.maennerschwarm.de, www.rosawinkel.de, members.aol.com/SchwulesMuseum), France (Martel, 1999; Eribon, 1999), South Africa (Gevisser and Cameron, 1995), Argentina (Kornblut et al., 1998), the Philippines (García, 1996), and in the work of such individuals as Jacobo Schifer Sikora in Costa Rica, Luiz Mott in Brazil, Rudi Bleys in Belgium, and Massimo Consoli in Italy. There is lots more to be done. Dennis Altman (1998: 18) argues that researchers should

> address such questions as, how do we reduce violence against homosexuals, and alcoholism and suicide within our communities?; is there a universal standard of human rights which should be applied to protect homosexuals in countries as diverse and brutal in their persecution as Iran, China and Romania?; what is the political economy which forces large numbers of transgender people across the world into prostitution and provides them virtually no protection or dignity?

The development of two gay and lesbian African-American church networks in major cities across the United States merits a chronicler. Even the world-wide Metropolitan Community Church is under-documented. The internationally popular Gay Games and the rise of organized athletics have not yet had a lot of scholarly attention paid to them. The aspirations and (limited) venues for gay male fatherhood, outside conventional heterosexual arrangements, need research. This is, of course, only a beginning of a list of many possibilities.

The debates and the diversity of LGBT studies are all signs of its vitality and of a wealth of new opportunities for exploration and development.

ACKNOWLEDGEMENT

Presented to the American Sociological Association, Washington, DC, 2000.

Preparation of this paper was facilitated by a sabbatical leave granted by the University of Windsor, and by visiting scholar status provided by the Center for Cultural Studies at the University of California at Santa Cruz.

NOTES

1 The behaviour–identity binary lends perhaps too great a sense of voluntarism, if not arbitrariness, to identity (Samuels, 1999). The queer orthodoxy concerning the performativity of identity categories participates in what Pierre Bourdieu (1984) calls a 'dream of flying' typical of an upwardly mobile middle class that feels little of the structural constraints that weigh upon many other classes. (It is noteworthy that Judith Butler (1993) has expressed concern over this tendency in the use of the idea of performativity.)

2 It insists that Melanesians are so different, that erections and orgasms occurring between New Guinea males are not homosexual or even sexual (Elliston, 1995), and gives warrant to expatriate Filipinos in New York to denounce Filipinos in the Philippines for showing too much interest in gay identity (Manalansan, 1995). It is dismayed by people with bisexual behavior who choose to identify themselves as gay or lesbian, and cannot understand why they prefer distinction instead of rejecting it altogether (Adam, 2000).

REFERENCES

Abelove, Henry, Barale, Michele and Halperin, David (1993) *Lesbian and Gay Studies Reader.* New York: Routledge.

Adam, Barry D. (1978) *The Survival of Domination.* New York: Elsevier/Greenwood.

Adam, Barry D. (1995) *The Rise of a Gay and Lesbian Movement.* New York: Twayne.

Adam, Barry D. (1997) 'Mobilizing around AIDS', in Martin Levine, Peter Nardi and John Gagnon (eds), *In Changing Times.* Chicago: University of Chicago Press.

Adam, Barry D. (2000) 'Love and sex in constructing identity among men who have sex with men', *International Journal of Sexuality and Gender Studies*, 5 (4): 325–39.

Adam, Barry D., Duyvendak, Jan Willem and Krouwel, Andre (1999) *The Global Emergence of Gay and Lesbian Politics.* Philadelphia: Temple University Press.

Adam, Barry D. and Sears, Alan (1996) *Experiencing HIV.* New York: Columbia University Press.

Adam, Barry D., Sears, Alan and E. Schellenberg, Glenn (2000) 'Accounting for unsafe sex', *Journal of Sex Research*, 37 (1): 259–71.

Aldrich, Robert and Wotherspoon, Garry (2000) *Gay and Lesbian Perspectives, v 1–5.* Sydney: Dept of Economic History, University of Sydney.

Altman, Dennis (1986) *AIDS in the Mind of America.* Garden City, New York: Doubleday.

Altman, Dennis (1988) 'Legitimation through disaster', in Elizabeth Fee and Daniel Fox (eds), *AIDS: The Burdens of History.* Berkeley, CA: University of California Press.

Altman, Dennis (1998) 'The uses and abuses of queer studies', in Robert Aldrich and Garry Wotherspoon (eds), *Gay and Lesbian Perspectives IV.* Sydney: Department of Economic History, University of Sydney. pp. 6–19.

Arnup, Katherine (1995) *Lesbian Parenting.* Charlottetown, PEI: Gynergy.

Beam, Joseph (1986) *In the Life.* Boston: Alyson.

Bech, Henning (1997) *When Men Meet.* Chicago: University of Chicago Press.

Bech, Henning (1998) *Real Deconstructions.* Montreal: International Sociological Association.

Beemyn, Brett and Eliason, Mickey (1996) *Queer Studies.* New York: New York University Press.

Berger, Peter and Luckmann, Thomas (1966) *The Social Construction of Reality.* Garden City, New York: Anchor.

Berlin Museum (1984) *Eldorado.* Berlin: Frölich and Kauffmann.

Blumenfeld, Warren and Raymond, Diane (1993) *Looking at Gay and Lesbian Life.* Boston: Beacon.

Boellstorff, Tom (1999) 'The perfect path', *GLQ*, 5 (4): 475–510.

Bornstein, Kate (1995) *Gender Outlaw.* New York: Vintage.

Boswell, John (1989) 'Revolutions, universals, and sexual categories', in Martin Duberman, Martha Vicinus and George Chauncey (eds), *Hidden from History.* New York: New American Library. pp. 17–36.

Bourdieu, Pierre (1984) *Distinction.* Cambridge, MA: Harvard University Press.

Boykin, Keith (2000) *Washington, DC, 2000.* Speech to the 2000 Millennium March.

Butler, Judith (1990) *Gender Trouble.* New York: Routledge.

Butler, Judith (1993) 'Critically queer', *GLQ*, 1 (1): 17–32.

Carrington, Christopher (1999) *No Place Like Home.* Chicago: University of Chicago Press.

Collins, Patricia Hill (1997) 'How much difference is too much?', *Current Perspectives in Social Theory*, 17: 3–27.

Comstock, Gary (1991) *Violence Against Lesbians and Gay Men.* New York: Columbia University Press.

Cruikshank, Margaret (1982) *Lesbian Studies.* Old Westbury, New York: Feminist Press.

Diamond, Sara (1998) *Not by Politics Alone.* New York: Guilford.

Díaz, Rafael and Ayala, George (1999) 'Love, passion and rebellion', *Culture, Health and Sexuality*, 1 (3): 277–93.

Donham, Donald (1998) 'Freeing South Africa', *Cultural Anthropology*, 13: 3–21.

Douglas, Debbie et al. (1997) *Ma-Ka Diasporic Juks.* Toronto: Sister Vision.

Dowsett, Gary (1996) *Practicing Desire.* Stanford, CA: Stanford University Press.

Duberman, Martin, Vicinus, Martha and Chauncey, George (1989) *Hidden from History.* New York: New American Library.

Duggan, Lisa (1995a) 'The discipline problem', *GLQ*, 2: 179–91.

Duggan, Lisa (1995b) 'Scholars and sense', in Lisa Duggan and Nan Hunter (eds), *Sex Wars.* New York: Routledge.

Edwards, T. (1998) 'Queer fears', *Sexualities*, 1 (4): 471–84.

Elliston, Deborah (1995) 'Erotic anthropology', *American Ethnologist*, 22 (4): 848–67.

Eng, David and Hom, Alice (1997) *Q & A.* Philadelphia: Temple University Press.

Epstein, Steven (1996) *Impure Science.* Berkeley, CA: University of California Press.

Eribon, Didier (1999) *Les Etudes gay et lesbiennes.* Paris: Centre Pompidou.

Escoffier, Jeffrey (1998) *American Homo.* Berkeley, CA: University of California Press.

Feinberg, Leslie (1996) *Transgender Warriors.* Boston: Beacon.

Felski, Rita (1997) 'The doxa of difference', *Signs*, 23 (1): 1–21.

Foster, Thomas, Siegel, Carol and Berry, Ellen (1997) *The Gay '90s.* New York: New York University Press.

Foucault, Michel (1978) *The History of Sexuality.* New York: Pantheon.

Gamson, Josh (1998) 'Must identity movements self-destruct?', in Peter Nardi and Beth Schneider (eds), *Social Perspectives in Lesbian and Gay Studies.* London: Routledge.

Garber, Linda (1994) *Tilting the Tower.* New York: Routledge.

García, J. Neil (1996) *Philippine Gay Culture.* Quezon City: University of the Philippines Press.

Gevisser, Mark and Cameron, Edwin (1995) *Defiant Desire.* New York: Routledge.

Goldie, Terry (1999) 'Introduction: queerly postcolonial', *Ariel*, 30 (2): 9–26.

Greenberg, David (1988) *The Construction of Homosexuality.* Chicago: University of Chicago Press.

Griffin, Gabriele, and Andermahr, Sonya (1997) *Straight Studies Modified.* London: Cassell.

Grosz, Elizabeth and Probyn, Elspeth (1995) *Sexy Bodies.* London: Routledge.

Hemphill, Essex (1991) *Brother to Brother.* Boston: Alyson.

Hennessy, Rosemary (1995) 'Queer visibility in commodity culture', *Cultural Critique*, 29: 31–76.

Herdt, Gilbert (1997) *Same Sex, Different Cultures.* Boulder, CO: Westview Press.

Herman, Didi (1997) *The Antigay Agenda.* Chicago: University of Chicago Press.

Hollibaugh, Amber (2000) *My Dangerous Desires.* Durham, NC: Duke University Press.

Jacobs, Sue Ellen, Thomas, Wesley and Lang, Sabine (1997) *Two-Spirit People.* Urbana: University of Illinois Press.

Kinsman, Gary (1996) *The Regulation of Desire.* Montreal: Black Rose.

Kippax, Susan, Connell, R.W., Dowsett, G.W., and Crawford, June (1993) *Sustaining Safe Sex.* London: Falmer.

Kornblut, Ana Lía et al. (1998) *Gays y lesbianas.* Buenos Aires: Editorial la Colmena.

Lahey, Kathleen (1999) *Are We 'Persons' Yet?* Toronto: University of Toronto Press.

Leap, William (1998) 'Staking a claim on history and culture', *Anthropological Quarterly*, 71 (3): 150–4.

Levine, Martin, Nardi, Peter and Gagnon, John (1997) *In Changing Times.* Chicago: University of Chicago Press.

Lewin, Ellen (1993) *Lesbian Mothers.* Ithaca, New York: Cornell University Press.

Manalansan, Martin (1995) 'In the shadows of Stonewall', *GLQ*, 2 (4): 425–38.

Martel, Frédéric (1999) *The Pink and the Black.* Palo Alto, CA: Stanford University Press.

Martinez, Elena (1996) *Lesbian Voices from Latin America.* New York: Garland.

Medhurst, Andy and Munt, Sally (1997) *Lesbian and Gay Studies.* London: Cassell.

Murray, Jacqueline (1996) 'Twice marginal and twice invisible', in Vern Bullough and James Brundage (eds), *Handbook of Medieval Sexuality.* New York: Garland. pp. 191–222.

Murray, Steven (2000) *Homosexualities.* Chicago: University of Chicago Press.

Namaste, Viviane (2000) *Invisible Lives.* Chicago: University of Chicago Press.

Nardi, Peter (1999) *Gay Men's Friendships.* Chicago: University of Chicago Press.

Nardi, Peter and Schneider, Beth (1997) *Social Perspectives on Lesbian and Gay Studies.* New York: Routledge.

Painter, Dorothy and Young, Willa (1996) 'Lesbian studies syllabi, 1982–1994', in Bonnie Zimmerman and Toni McNaron (eds), *The New Lesbian Studies.* New York: Feminist Press.

Patton, Cindy (1990) *Inventing AIDS.* New York: Routledge.

Patton, Cindy (1993) 'Tremble heteroswine', in Michael Warner (ed.), *Fear of a Queer Planet.* Minneapolis: University of Minnesota Press.

Phelan, Shane (1997) *Playing With Fire.* New York: Routledge.

Plummer, Ken (1992) *Modern Homosexualities.* London: Routledge.

Pottie, Lisa (1997) 'Cross-border shopping and niche marketing', *College Literature*, 24 (1): 183–94.

Ramos, Juanita (1994) *Campañeras.* New York: Routledge.

Remiggi, Frank and Demczuk, Irène (1998) *Sorter de l'ombre.* Montreal: VLB.

Ristock, Janice and Taylor, Catherine (1998) *Inside the Academy and Out.* Toronto: University of Toronto Press.

Roscoe, Will (1995) 'Strange craft, strange history, strange folks', *American Anthropologist*, 97 (3): 448–54.

Ross, Becki (1995) *The House That Jill Built*. Toronto: University of Toronto Press.

Samuels, Jacinth (1999) 'Dangerous liaisons', *Cultural Studies*, 13 (1): 91–109.

Savoy, Eric (1994) 'You can't go homo again', *English Studies in Canada*, 20 (2): 129–52.

Schmidt, Martha (1994) 'Dahmer discourse and gay identity', *Critical Sociology*, 20 (3): 81–105.

Scott, Wilbur and Stanley, Sandra (1994) *Gays and Lesbians in the Military*. Hawthorne, New York: Aldine de Gruyter.

Sedgwick, Eve (1990) *Epistemology of the Closet*. Berkeley, CA: University of California.

Seidman, Steven (1996) *Queer Theory/Sociology*. Cambridge, MA: Blackwell.

Seidman, Steven (1997) *Difference Troubles*. Cambridge: Cambridge University Press.

Simpson, Mark (1994) *Male Impersonators*. London: Cassell.

Simpson, Mark (1999) *It's a Queer World*. Binghamton, New York: Harrington Park Press.

Smith, Barbara (1998) *The Truth That Never Hurts*. New Brunswick, NJ: Rutgers University Press.

Stein, Arlene (1997) *Sex and Sensibility*. Berkeley, CA: University of California Press.

Taylor, Verta and Raeburn, Nicole (1995) 'Identity politics as high-risk activism', *Social Problems*, 42 (2): 252–73.

Walters, Suzanna Danuta (1996) 'From here to queer', *Signs*, 21 (4): 830–69.

Watney, Simon (1987) *Policing Desire*. London: Comedia.

Weeks, Jeffrey (1977) *Coming Out*. London: Quartet.

Weeks, Jeffrey (1981) *Sex, Politics, and Society*. London: Longman.

Weeks, Jeffrey (1985) *Sexuality and its Discontents*. London: Routledge and Kegan Paul.

Weeks, Jeffrey (1993) 'Necessary fictions', in Jacqueline Murray (ed.), *Constructing Sexualities*. Windsor: University of Windsor Humanities Research Group.

Weston, Kath (1991) *Families We Choose*. New York: Columbia University Press.

Weston, Kath (1996) 'The virtual anthropologist', in Bonnie Zimmerman and Toni McNaron (eds), *The New Lesbian Studies*. New York: Feminist Press.

Wilton, Tamsin (1995) *Lesbian Studies*. New York: Routledge.

Witt, Stephanie and McCorkle, Suzanne (1997) *Anti-Gay Rights*. Westport, CT: Praeger.

Zimmerman, Bonnie and McNaron, Toni (1996) *The New Lesbian Studies*. New York: Feminist Press.

2

The Heterosexual/ Homosexual Binary

Past, Present and Future[1]

SASHA ROSENEIL

Much of the most important work in lesbian and gay studies over the past thirty years has cast its gaze backwards in time, to document, analyse and theorize the history of sexuality. Indeed, without the groundbreaking historical work of Lillian Faderman (1981), Michel Foucault (1981), Guy Hocquenghem (1978), Jonathan Katz (1976), Carol Smith-Rosenberg (1975), and Jeffrey Weeks (1977, 1981), there would be no lesbian and gay studies. Their contributions, along with many others, have shaped our understanding of the origins of the categories of the 'homosexual' and the 'lesbian', and of the changing ways in which same-sex sex, relationship and affections have been constructed, lived and spoken of within conditions of modernity. More recently, queer theory has developed new ways of thinking which shift our attention from the historically situated homosexual, lesbian or gay subject, towards a consideration of the ways in which the homosexual/ heterosexual binary itself has been constituted.[2] This chapter draws on both of these bodies of literature, bringing the former into dialogue with the latter. I use each of them as a springboard for a discussion of the ways in which the organization of sexuality around a homosexual/heterosexual binary has changed over time, looking back at the past century, and also thinking about transformations which are currently underway, and offering some speculations about the future.

At the turn of the twenty-first century we are living through a period of intense and profound social change, characterized by many social theorists as a shift from modernity to postmodernity.[3] Sociologists theorizing on both modernity and postmodernity have focused largely on change in the areas of work and production, in relations between nation–states, and in the political sphere, and to a lesser extent, in family life and gender relations; the study of the re-organization of erotic relations has, with a few notable exceptions, not been on the mainstream agenda. While, as this volume indicates, lesbian and gay studies is now a well-established field of academic inquiry, it has yet to really impact upon that which is designated as 'social theory'. Lesbians and gay men and their social movements have begun to appear as characters in the social

worlds described by some mainstream
social theorists – Anthony Giddens (1992),
and Manuel Castells (1997), for example –
but the radical implications of lesbian and
gay theory and queer theory have not yet
been embraced by those who do the broad-
brush theorizing of social change.[4] In this
respect, lesbian and gay theory is in a similar position to feminist and gender theory
and critical race and post-colonial theory, all
of which continue to exist on the margins of
social theory.

Writing as a sociologist, one of my aims
in this chapter is to offer a map of the significant changes which, I believe, constitute
a shift from a modern sexual regime *towards*
a postmodern one. My focus is on processes
of postmodernization in the field of sexuality, and I emphasize that these are transformations in train, which co-exist, often in
tension, with more modern formations of
sexuality. While my focus is on the organization of the sexual, this cannot be understood outside wider analyses of social
relations, particularly the organization of
'cathexis', or intimacy – emotionally charged
affective relations which are not necessarily
sexual – and, of course, gender relations.[5] I
will not attempt a definition which circum-
scribes the 'proper domain' of sexuality,
because what is important about relations of
sexuality is that they permeate, sometimes
indeed saturate, the entire social formation.[6]
Some of what I discuss can be considered
under the rubric of change within the sphere,
and in cultural meanings, of 'family', but
my frame of reference fundamentally cross-
cuts the public/private divide, and is concerned also with shifts in non-familial and
public forms of sociality.

The chapter is divided into two main
sections. In the first, I offer a brief outline of
recent developments in queer theory, which I
suggest provide an important theoretical
framework for lesbian and gay studies to
think about the organization of sexuality.
However, I also point to a number of limitations to queer theory, as it has developed
thus far, from a sociological perspective. The
second part of the chapter then traces some

of the most important changes which have
taken place in the realm of sexuality during
the twentieth century. I discuss the emergence of modern sexual identities, and shifts
in the relationship between 'the homosexual'
and 'the heterosexual', as categories, identities and ways of life during this period. I then
go on to explore what I conceptualize as the
'queer tendencies' which characterize the
postmodernization of relations of sexuality
which is underway – somewhat unevenly –
across the western world. These queer tendencies constitute significant destabilizations
of the heterosexual/homosexual binary, and
raise some important questions for and about
the future of lesbian and gay studies.

QUEER THEORY AND THE HETEROSEXUAL/HOMOSEXUAL BINARY

An understanding of virtually any aspect
of modern Western culture must be, not
merely incomplete, but damaged in its
central substance to the degree that it
does not incorporate a critical analysis of
modern homo/heterosexual definition.
(Sedgwick, 1991: 1)

It was against the backdrop of AIDS and the
American New Right's virulently anti-
homosexual politics of the 1980s, and from
within increasingly large, diverse and
reflexive lesbian and gay communities, that
a new strand of thinking about sexuality
emerged within the humanities in the 1990s:
queer theory.[7] Drawing on post-structuralism,
particularly the work of Michel Foucault
and Jacques Derrida, and on Lacanian
psychoanalysis, and emerging out of and in
dialogue with feminist theory,[8] this rather
amorphous body of work shares a critique of
the minoritizing epistemology which has
underpinned both the majority of academic
thinking about homosexuality and the dominant politics within gay men's communities.[9] In the words of Eve Kosofsky
Sedgwick, in her now canonical *Epistemology of the Closet*, this minoritizing view
sees 'homo/ heterosexual definition ... as an

issue of active importance primarily for a small, distinct, relatively fixed homosexual minority', rather than 'seeing it ... as an issue of continuing determining importance in the lives of people across the spectrum of sexualities' (Sedgwick, 1991: 1). Thus, one of queer theory's foundational claims, as expressed by Sedgwick and quoted above – that an understanding of sexuality, and in particular, of the homo/heterosexual binary, must be central to any analysis of modern western culture – stakes a claim for the knowledge produced from the terrain of queer theory way beyond its immediate audience.

Queer theory identifies the heterosexual/ homosexual binary, and its related opposition, 'inside/outside' (Fuss, 1991), as a central organizing principle of modern society and culture, and takes this binary as its key problematic and political target.[10] Right from the outset, in one of its earliest texts, Diana Fuss's edited collection *Inside/ Out: Lesbian Theories, Gay Theories* queer theory 'call[s] into question the stability and ineradicability of the hetero/homosexual hierarchy, suggesting that new (and old) sexual possibilities are no longer thinkable in terms of a simple inside/outside dialectic' (Fuss, 1991: 1). In common with other poststructuralist understandings of the exclusionary and regulatory nature of binary identity categories, queer theory rejects the idea of a unified homosexual identity, and sees the construction of sexual identities around the hierarchically structured binary opposition of hetero/homosexual as inherently unstable. The fracturing and tensions within the category of homosexuality and the fluidities and non-fixity of various homosexualities are thus foregrounded. Differences between the multifarious, and multiple, sexual, gender, ethnic, political and stylistic identifications of those within the 'queer community' – lipstick lesbians, butches, femmes, FTMs, s/m-ers, switch-hitters, muscle marys, opera queens, bisexuals, transsexuals, the transgendered, those who identify as Black, Asian, Irish, Jewish, Latino ... – become theoretically important.

Equally, heterosexuality is also problematized and is rendered as much less monolithic and unassailable than earlier (feminist and sociological) theory has tended to regard it, and the construction and maintenance of heterosexuality through acts of exclusion *vis-à-vis* homosexuality are placed on the agenda to be studied.[11]

Initially queer theory developed within the humanities largely without reference to the thirty years of research and theorizing about sexuality that has taken place within sociology, despite the clear (and unacknowledged) parallels between the social constructionist understandings of sexuality in the two fields.[12] This has led to some unfounded assumptions of novelty, an overly textual orientation, an underdeveloped concept of the social, and a lack of engagement with 'real' material, everyday life and social practices and processes in queer theory, of which social scientists might rightly be critical.[13] However, there is much that is exciting and important in queer theory for those interested in thinking about the social organization of sexuality. Its interrogation of sexual identity categories, and its enactment of a shift in focus from the margins, on the homosexual, to a focus on the constitution of the homo/heterosexual binary represent important developments in the theorization of sexuality. As Arlene Stein and Ken Plummer (1996) argue in their important article advocating 'a more queer sociology', a queer sociology would bring queer theory's interrogation of identity categories into dialogue with a sociological concern to theorize and historicize social change in the field of sexuality. It would, they propose, see relations of sexuality and cathexis as central dynamic forces within society, focusing attention on the homo/heterosexual binary and on heteronormativity – on studying the 'centre', the 'inside', as well as the margins, and the 'outside'. Stein and Plummer also suggest that a queer sociology can learn from the importance queer theory places on culture. In a postmodern world characterized by 'economies of signs' (Lash and Urry, 1994) and by the increasing aestheticization of everyday life,[14] queer theory's attention to the sphere of the cultural needs to be combined with an analysis of social practices, processes and lived experience.

Thus far queer theorists, true to their post-structuralist roots, have tended to favour analyses of structural and discursive regulation over attention to the resistance and creative agency of human actors in the area of sexuality.[15] Drawing on a Foucauldian paradigm in which subjectification – the production of human subjects – is understood as an essentially negative process of subjection, there has been a sociologically weak theorization of agency at the heart of queer theory.[16] Queer theorists have largely been concerned with analysing the cultural texts and processes through which the hetero/ homosexual binary is produced and reproduced, with how heterosexuality is continuously re-naturalized and re-prioritized, and with how heteronormativity operates as a mode of regulation of identities and cultural and social possibilities.[17] It has also tended to direct its gaze backwards in time, failing to remark upon and engage with contemporary social change.[18] It has barely begun to explore how the hetero/homosexual binary and its hierarchical power relations might be undergoing challenge and transformation in the contemporary world. In contrast, a queer sociology, I would suggest, should seek to transcend the limitations of a post-structuralist ontology, reaching for a compromise between post-structuralism and humanism which enables the theorization of human agency within historical, social and cultural contexts.[19] It would have a keen eye for tendencies towards social change, for shifts, movement and destabilization in established relations of sexuality and cathexis.

So, one of the most important implications of queer theory is that much more than 'adding in' the study of lesbians and gay men is necessary. Doing this – making sure that we consider how to research across sexual differences – is just the starting point; we must take seriously non-normative

sexualities, and must allow lesbians, gay men, bisexuals, transgender people and all those whose lives transgress heteronormative assumptions a place in our analyses. There is a tendency among liberal-minded scholars, in the wake of the challenges of the new social movements, to speak of the importance of attention to 'difference', and in recent years sexuality has been added to the list of differences which it is considered necessary to include, alongside gender, race/ethnicity, and, sometimes, disability. The problem with this is that 'differences' are different from each other, and sexual differences have their own specific difficulties of definition and identification. Differences of sexuality are not always visible, indeed, as Sedgwick (1991) points out, there is an 'epistemology of the closet', based on secrecy and outings, in twentieth-century culture, which constitutes a particular form of domination, unlike others. This means that the act of speaking of differences of sexuality is vital, but we must be aware that pinning them down and delineating membership of sexual categories is impossible; sexuality is often ambiguous, identifications are fluctuating, strategically performed, yet sometimes also ascribed.

CHANGING RELATIONS OF SEXUALITY

The Modern Regime

It is now widely accepted by historians of sexuality that the idea of the existence of 'the homosexual' as a category of person distinct from 'the heterosexual' was born in the second half of the nineteenth century.[20] By the start of the twentieth century there was in widespread circulation a proliferation of medical, legal, literary and psychological discourses for which the hetero/ homosexual binary was axiomatic. So it was that there came into existence

a world-mapping by which every person, just as he or she was necessarily assignable to a male or female gender, was now considered necessarily assignable as well to a homo- or a hetero-sexuality, a binarized identity that was full of implications, however confusing, for even the ostensibly least sexual aspects of personal existence. (Sedgwick, 1991: 2)

In this 'world-mapping' marital heterosexuality occupied the centre, constructed as normal, natural and desirable, with homosexuality as the marginal, perverse, unnatural other, subject to a range of different legal, medical and social sanctions and forms of regulation.

From the 1910s onwards sexologists began to develop an ideal of the married heterosexual couple bound together by sexual intimacy rather than just economic and social necessity.[21] This model of hetero-relationality came to replace the nineteenth-century 'separate spheres' ideology which had underpinned the Victorian family and which had allowed, and even encouraged, strong, sometimes passionate, homo-relational ties of love and friendship.[22] Particular emphasis was placed on persuading women of the importance of fulfilling their emotional and sexual desires through their marital relationship.[23] By the 1950s the idea of 'the primarily sexual nature of conjugality' (Weeks, 1985: 27) was firmly entrenched throughout the western world, and the confluence of sexuality and cathexis within the marital heterosexual relationship became established, supported by a panopoly of cultural forms ranging from Hollywood cinema to women's magazines, as well as by social, legal and political institutions and their policies. Not least among these, of course, was the post-war welfare state, which assumed as its subject the married, heterosexual man and his family.

Under the conditions of the post-war sexual and cathectic regime of hegemonic marital heterosexuality, non-normative relations of sexuality and cathexis were lived at the margins. Steven, Barry and Seidman (1996) and Adam (1995) suggest that although the 1950s are widely perceived to have been conservative, the seeds of the sexual rebellions of the 1960s were sown by the

geographical mobility, prosperity and social liberalization which followed the war, and they point to the emergence of homophile organizations, which began, very tentatively, to claim a public voice for homosexuals, and to the cultural interventions of rock music and the beatniks, which offered a challenge to dominant sexual mores. In 1957 Britain saw the publication of the Wolfenden Report advocating homosexual law reform some 10 years before the passing of the Sexual Offences Act, which decriminalized sex between men over 21 in private. While the 'sexual revolution' of the 1960s is easily and often overstated, the emergence of the women's liberation movement, lesbian feminism, and gay liberation politics from the New Left, and the growth of visible subcultures of lesbians and gay men in the metropolises began to expand the public space of the non-heterosexual margins.[24] The Stonewall riot of 1969, when 'drag queens, dykes, street people and bar boys' responded to a police raid on a Greenwich Village gay bar 'first with jeers and high camp, and then with a hail of coins, paving stones, and parking meters' (Adam, 1995: 81) was an epiphanic moment; it marked the beginnings of the gay liberation movement. Gay liberation ideas and activism spread rapidly around the United States, and around the Anglophone world, to Britain and Australia. At its core was the desire 'to free the homosexual in everyone', to overthrow compulsory heterosexuality and thus eventually, the boundaries between the homosexual and the heterosexual (Adam, 1995: 84).[25] The radical demands of gay liberation (which were to be echoed in the queer politics of the 1990s) faded by the mid-1970s, giving way to a more assimilationist politics demanding equal rights and protection for lesbians and gay men as a minority group, and the 1970s and 1980s saw the growth of self-confident lesbian and gay communities with their own institutions and traditions. Developing in parallel to gay liberation were the politics of lesbian feminism, practised in the everyday lives of many thousands of women across the USA, Canada, Britain and Australia. Lesbian feminism offered women a positive lesbian identity within a close-knit community of women with its own newsletters, publishing houses, book stores, self-help and support groups, food co-ops, social groups, theatre troupes, video collectives and writing groups. Then, in the 1980s and 1990s, the AIDS epidemic, which decimated the population of gay men in the global gay cities, called forth new forms of political activism and self-help welfare organization, and ultimately, at a collective level, strengthened the ties of communality and sociality among those who survived.[26]

One of the traditions of lesbian and gay life that took off in the 1970s, post-Stonewall, was the 'coming out story'. Plummer's (1995) discussion of the telling of sexual stories identifies the coming out story as an archetypal modernist tale, featuring a linear progression from a period of suffering to the crucial moment of self-discovery, and ending with a satisfactory resolution in the form of the achievement of a secure identity as lesbian or gay amidst a supportive community. But while the notion of 'coming out' is firmly rooted in the 'epistemology of the closet' and the modern hetero/homosexual binary, the situation in the late twentieth century in which many millions of people around the world have 'come out' (including an ever increasing number of public figures), and have made their sexual and cathectic relationships with members of their own sex highly visible, has actually served to create the context for the postmodernization of the regime of sexuality and cathexis. As Seidman et al. (1999) argue, for many lesbians and gay men today homosexuality has been so normalized that they are effectively 'beyond the closet'. The 'inside/outside' metaphor has started to lose its saliency.

THE POSTMODERNIZATION OF SEXUALITY

In contrast to classic sociological narratives of the development of modernity, there is some attention given to questions of sexuality within the body of literature which seeks to theorize the post (or late) modern social condition. This work suggests that there is underway a shift in relations of cathexis. In the context of a wider argument about the undoing of patriarchalism, Castells (1997) suggests that the patriarchal family is under intense challenge, and that lesbian, gay and feminists movements around the world are the key to understanding this challenge.[27] Giddens's (1992) argument about the 'transformation of intimacy' and Beck and Beck-Gernsheim's (1995) and Beck-Gernsheim's (1999) work on the changing meanings and practices of love and family relationships posit the idea that in the contemporary world processes of individualization and de-traditionalization and increased self-reflexivity are opening up new possibilities and expectations in heterosexual relationships.[28] With a (rather cursory) nod in the direction of feminist scholarship and activism, their work recognizes the significance of the shifts in gender relations consequent particularly on the changed consciousness and identities that women have developed in the wake of the women's liberation movement.

Giddens considers the transformation of intimacy which he sees as currently in train to be of 'great, and generalizable, importance' (1992: 2). He charts the changes in the nature of marriage which are constituted by the emergence of the 'pure relationship', a relationship of sexual and emotional equality between men and women, and links this with the development of 'plastic sexuality', which is freed from 'the needs of reproduction' (1991: 2). He identifies lesbians and gay men as 'pioneers' in the pure relationship and plastic sexuality, and hence at the forefront of processes of individualization and de-traditionalization.[29]

While there are undoubtedly criticisms to be made of this body of work (e.g. Jamieson, 1998), this literature offers important insights into, or at least raises questions about, contemporary social change. But I now wish to extend this analysis to consider the constitution of the sexual more generally.

Giddens's rather throwaway remark that lesbians and gay men are forging new paths for heterosexuals as well as for themselves is developed by Weeks, Donovan and Heaphy who suggest that 'one of the most remarkable features of domestic change over recent years is … the emergence of common patterns in both homosexual and heterosexual ways of life as a result of these long-term shifts in relationship patterns' (1999: 85).[30] In other words, changes in the organization of intimacy are impacting upon the wider organization of sexuality.

It is my argument that we are currently witnessing a significant destabilization of the hetero/homosexual binary. The hierarchical relationship between the two sides of the binary, and its mapping onto an inside/out opposition is undergoing intense challenge, and the normativity and naturalness of both heterosexuality and heterorelationality have come into question.[31] In addition to the yearning for a 'pure relationship' which is increasingly shared by those on either side of the hetero/homosexual binary, there are, I would suggest, a number of 'queer tendencies' at work, and play, in the postmodern world. I choose to speak of 'tendencies' to suggest the still provisional nature of these social changes, and with the existence of countervailing tendencies in mind.[32]

QUEER AUTO-CRITIQUE

Anyone with a brain could see categories breaking down, assumptions rupturing, clear-cut identities going the way of the Berlin Wall. Hence the 'pomosexual', who, like the queer s/he closely resembles, may not be tied to a single sexual identity, may not be content to reside within a category measurable by social scientists or acknowledged by … rainbow-festooned gays … Pomosexuality lives in the space in which all other non-binary forms of sexual and gender identity reside – a boundary-free zone in which fences are crossed for the fun of it, or simply because some of us can't be fenced in. (Queen and Schimel, 1997: 23)

The first of these 'queer tendencies' is that which is underway within lesbian and gay communities themselves: the tendency to engage in auto-critique at both the individual and collective level which is producing a fracturing of modern homosexual/lesbian/gay identities. As the sheer size and scale of the public spaces which are identified as lesbian and/or gay have expanded exponentially in the past three decades,[33] and the number of those living their lives in relation to these spaces has soared, the policing of identity boundaries has become more difficult; there are, literally, more spaces for difference. 'Queer theory' may be an elite academic practice, but queer theorizing and praxis – the thinking through and enactment of the de-essentializing of lesbian and gay identities – are everyday activities for many within and on the margins of contemporary lesbian and gay worlds.[34] Recent years have seen an upsurge of discussion within the public forums and private spaces of lesbian and gay communities about a range of issues which challenge the assumed coherence and constituency of lesbian and gay communities and the fixity of sexual identities and practices. A 'critical community' has developed within the wider lesbian and gay community, in which new ideas about sexuality, gender, embodiment and identity are being created.[35] Many of the members of this critical community are cultural producers and public intellectuals whose ideas and interventions are circulated in journals, newspapers, exhibitions, installations, 'zines, on the Internet, and through performance.[36] Political groups – such as Transexual Menace and Hermaphrodites with Attitude (Wilchins, 1997) – and activists, writers, performance and visual artists, such as Kate Bornstein, Pat Califia, Leslie Feinberg, Del Lagrace, and Joan Nestle have opened up spaces for re-thinking the relationship between gender, embodiment and sexual desire. Bisexuality, butch and femme, transsex, transgender, and cross-dressing are on the agenda; lesbians having sex with men, and gay men having sex with women are openly discussed, as the regulatory power of modern lesbian and gay identities crumbles. It is the era of 'post-gay' (Sinfield, 1996), or 'anti-gay' (Simpson, 1996), of queer, postmodern stories 'in the making, which shun unities and uniformities; reject naturalism and determinacies; seek out immanences and ironies; and ultimately find pastiche, complexities and shifting perspectives' (Plummer, 1995: 133).[37]

THE DECENTRING OF HETERORELATIONS

Much has been written in recent years about the meaning of the dramatic rise in divorce rates over the past thirty years,[38] about the increase in the number of births outside marriage[39] (and to a lesser extent outside any lasting heterosexual relationship – births to mothers who are 'single by choice'), about the rise in the proportion of children being brought up by a lone parent,[40] about the growing proportion of households that are composed of one person,[41] and the rising proportion of women who are not having children. However, this commentary has tended to focus on the meaning of these changes in terms of gender relations and the family; it has not addressed their implications with respect to the established organization of sexuality. This is surprising because it seems to me that these changes speak of a significant decentring of heterorelations, as the heterosexual couple, and particularly the married, co-resident heterosexual couple with children, no longer occupies the centre-ground of western societies, and cannot be taken for granted as the basic unit in society. Processes of individualization and detraditionalization are releasing individuals from traditional heterosexual scripts and from the patterns of heterorelationality which accompany them. During the last four decades of the twentieth century, the proportion of people living in 'traditional' family households comprising a heterosexual couple with children has fallen significantly, so that by 2000, only 23% of households in the UK were 'traditional' families (Social Trends, 2001). Broadly

similar patterns are observable across Europe, North America and Australia.

Postmodern living arrangements are diverse, fluid and unresolved, constantly chosen and re-chosen, and heterorelations are no longer as hegemonic as once they were. It could be said that we are experiencing the 'queering of the family' (Stacey, 1996), as meanings of family undergo radical challenge, and more and more kinship groups have to come to terms with the diverse sexual practices and living arrangements chosen by their own family members. At the start of the twenty-first century there can be few families which do not include at least some members who diverge from traditional, normative heterorelational practice, whether as divorcees, unmarried mothers and fathers, singles, lesbians, gay men or bisexuals.

This social decentring of heterorelations finds its expression and reflection in popular culture. Consider, for example, the television programmes, particularly the dramas and sitcoms, which have achieved particular popularity recently in Britain, the United States and Australia: *Friends, This Life, Absolutely Fabulous, Ellen, Frasier, Grace Under Fire, Seinfeld, Men Behaving Badly, Will and Grace*. All of these television programmes are fundamentally post-heterorelational in their thematic concerns and narrative drive. Unlike the generation of situation comedies that preceded them, which were almost exclusively focused on co-resident, heterosexual families, these programmes are concerned with the embeddedness of friends in daily life. They offer images of the warmth and affection provided by networks of friends in an age of insecure and/or transitory sexual relationships; friends, in the words of the theme song to the show, 'are there for you', in the bustling big city life of the postmodern world, in which individuals have to carve out lives for themselves.[42]

And in popular music, the enormous success of the *Spice Girls* can be read as an example of the cultural decentring of heterorelations among a teen and pre-teenage female audience which, from the 1950s onwards, has directed the emotional and erotic energy of its fandom towards male popstars and boy bands. The *Spice Girls* have not just offered their fans a range of models of contemporary femininity with which to identify, which includes one – Sporty – that clearly draws on lesbian street style, but also, more radically and uniquely they have captured a generation of girls' passion outside the framework of hetero-relationality and heterosexuality. The question 'who is your favourite Spice Girl?', is as much about which Spice Girl is desired, as about which one is identified with. Moreover, the Spice Girls' 'philosophy' of 'girl power' is a reworking of basic feminist principles about the importance of female friendship, seeking to inspire girls to respect and value themselves and their girl-friends, mothers, and sisters, and challenging the cultural prioritization of masculinity and male needs and desires. It is certainly no accident that each concert in the 1998 Spice-World Tour included in it a cover of Annie Lennox's 'Sisters are Doing it For Themselves' and ended with a rendition of the gay anthem first popularized by *Sister Sledge*, 'We are Family'.

and his normal family, as exemplified in Section 28 of the Local Government Act in the UK, and the Defense of Marriage Act in the United States, which has explicitly named marriage as a heterosexual institution, to the ever growing number of personal ads placed in newspapers by heterosexuals forced to name themselves as such, heterosexuality has become de-naturalized and reflexive.[44] Anecdotally, there appears to have been a dramatic growth in the number of students who think of themselves as heterosexual taking lesbian and gay studies courses in US universities, suggesting, perhaps, a growth of self-conscious thinking about non-normative sexualities among those who would previously have practised their heterosexuality unreflexively.[45] Even women's magazines, once the arch-promoters of a naturalized, normative heterosexuality, are now, occasionally, encouraging their readers to engage in the reflexive consideration of their sexual desires by means of the self-administered questionnaire, which at the end, when scores are added up, refuses to locate readers in clearly demarcated sexual identity categories, but rather valorizes self-awareness and sexual openness.[46]

THE EMERGENCE OF HETERO-REFLEXIVITY

THE CULTURAL VALORIZING OF THE QUEER

Another facet of the destabilization of the homo/heterosexual binary is that heterosexuality is increasingly a conscious state which has to be produced, self-monitored, thought about, and, for some, defended, in relation to its other, in a way that was not necessary when heteronormativity was more secure and lesbian and gay alternatives were less visible and self-confident.[43] It used to be that it was homosexuality that had to be produced and thought-out, with heterosexuality the unreflexive inside that did not have to consider its position. But in recent years, from 'backlash' anxieties about political correctness and the 'threatened' position of the white, heterosexual male

If, as exhorted by queer theory, we take seriously the cultural in our attempts to understand shifts in relations of sexuality, contemporary developments in popular culture become significant indicators of the zeitgeist. It would be sociologically naïve to assume that changes in popular culture necessarily give rise to or reflect transformations in people's everyday beliefs and practices, or to assume that people always behave in consistent ways (so that liking Ellen Degeneres, Julian Clary, or Graham Norton also constitutes a rejection of homophobia); but I would like to propose that the ideas and images of the sexual which permeate our everyday world through popular culture are of considerable importance in framing the cultural imaginaries within which people lead their lives and construct their identities and relationships. It is my suggestion that there is underway, particularly in Britain, a queering of popular culture, a valorizing of the sexually ambiguous, and of that which transgresses rigid boundaries of gender. While sexual and gender ambiguity are not new, the contemporary desire to confuse and transgress the hetero/homosexual binary is of a different order from that of the 1970's and early 1980's culturally elite avant-garde that was exemplified by David Bowie, Patti Smith, Marc Bolan, Bay Searge and the 'New Romantics'. Whereas the gender-benders of this earlier period had something of a freak-show about them, and were a safe distance from their fans, whose normality was reconstituted in contrast with the stars' allowable excesses, the contemporary cultural valorizing of the queer is far more participatory and closer to everyday life. This can be seen in three areas of popular culture: dance culture, fashion magazines and television.

Dance culture is one of the most significant cultural movements in Britain of recent years. As it moved from underground raves into the mainstream, clubbing has become a leisure pursuit for millions of young people, and the fashions, imagery and ideals of dance culture have become the fashions, imagery and ideals of a generation (as the category of 'youth' expands both upwards and downwards, this is a large generation).[47] Dance culture has its roots in the house music born in black gay clubs in New York, Chicago and Detroit, in which boundaries of sexuality developed a fluidity, and to which men and women of a range of sexual and gender identifications were welcomed.[48] Travelling across the Atlantic, via Ibiza, in tandem with the drug Ecstasy, house music spawned a new era of nightclubbing in Britain in the 1990s. Pharmacologically energized and 'loved up', what mattered in the early house music clubs was the warmth and intensity of the sociality between those in the club.[47] In Britain, as in the USA, the clubs where new dance music is tested and hits break, the clubs which lead fashion in music, clothing and attitude, have in recent years been queer clubs: not exclusively gay, but emerging from a gay/lesbian community and identity, usually established and run by gay or lesbian promoters, and destabilizing sexual identity categories by welcoming anyone with a queer enough attitude.[49] It is not sexual identity or sexual practice that matters in gaining admission to the coolest clubs, but rather a way of thinking and an attitude of openness and fluidity: those seeking admission to *Vague* in Leeds, for instance, being required by the transsexual 'door whore' to kiss anyone she demanded. The ideals of celebrating diversity and granting respect are often spelt out on club flyers, on posters, banners inside the club, and by bouncers on the door. 'Queer' has become, in British popular culture, an attitude and a stance which rocks the hetero/ homosexual binary, and is one to which a generation aspires.[50]

Further evidence of the aspirational status of the queer is to be found in advertising in a range of media, and in editorial imagery in fashion magazines. Over the past decade there has been an upsurge in the presentation of queer imagery in the mainstream media, in which sexual and gender ambiguity is foregrounded through the use of non-conventionally gendered and non-heterosexually positioned models and through playful cross-dressing, and homo-erotic desire is regularly explicitly represented or more subtly implied.[51] A large number of companies which clearly wish to be perceived as at the cutting edge of fashion have run advertising campaigns in magazines, on television and free postcards, which are decidedly queer – promoting the fashion houses Calvin Klein, Christian Dior, Jean-Paul Gaultier and Versace, alcoholic drinks such as Black Bush Whiskey and Kronenberg 1664, toiletries (Impulse deodorant), electronic goods and services (On Digital, BT Cellnet, Siemens mobile telephones, mail2web email), airlines (Aer Lingus), furniture (Habitat) and cars (Rover 200) through adverts which play with same-sex sexual possibilities and challenge the heteronormative gaze and its expectations. Some of the images and messages in these advertisements are more open to a range of possible readings than others, but in most the attribution of a positive value to non-heterosexually coded bodies, desires and lifestyles is clearly presented to the viewer. In the context of much greater public discussion of lesbian and gay experiences and the appearance of lesbian and gay characters in soap operas and dramas in British television, the present moment is one in which readings which recognize the non-heteronormativity of the images in these campaigns are more available than ever before.

Finally, television has also in recent years brought a queer sensibility into millions of living rooms. In sharp contrast to the tradition of laughing at homosexual men's gender performances in classic British comedies such as *Are You Being Served?*, and *Carry On* films, I would identify *All Rise for Julian Clary* as marking a significant moment in the sexual history of British televisual culture. Broadcast at prime time on Saturday night on BBC1, *All Rise* enacts a queer reversal of traditional anti-gay humour, and directs attention to the humour inherent in the heterosexuality and traditional renditions of masculinity of the audience. Julian Clary, a highly politicized, 'out' gay man, makes constant, extremely sexually explicit, reference to his own homosexuality, but the show revolves equally around laughing at, and pointing out the absurdity of, normal heterosexual masculinity, particularly that of the police and the military. Clary plays the role of judge and adjudicates according to his own set of queer, camp values on a range of matters brought to him by the audience. Thus the privileging of heteronormative behaviour is reversed and the queer valorized.

A pessimistic critique of the tendencies which I identify as the cultural valorizing of the queer would see them as evidence of the extension of commodity culture into previously uncommodified subcultures, and

of the ability of capitalism to colonize and utilize lesbian and gay identities in its relentless search for profit, exploiting their otherness while maintaining mainstream heterosexual positionality.[52] While there is undoubtedly purchase in this analysis, it is my opinion that such an argument neglects the recontextualizations that are possible within commodity culture, and fails to see how capital might be running to catch up with transformations which are already underway in the ways in which sexuality is lived and imagined. It is surely interesting that at this historical moment queer has become trendy, not just in relatively closed metropolitan networks, but in mainstream popular culture, and in the context of a history of the minoritizing of the non-heterosexual, and of the cultural shame associated with homosexuality, this represents a shift of considerable sociological interest and is worthy of further attention.

FUTURES ...

In this chapter I have taken up the challenge posed by lesbian and gay studies to historicize sexuality, and I have traced some of the shifts in the organization of sexuality which have taken place over the past century. In arguing that we are currently experiencing the postmodernization of relations of sexuality, I propose that at the start of the new millennium we are witnessing a number of queer tendencies in social and cultural life, which together constitute a significant cultural challenge to heteronormativity. These queer tendencies question the normativity and naturalness of heterosexuality, re-configure the hierarchical inside/outside relationship between homosexuality and heterosexuality, and destabilize the binary opposition between the two categories. It is undoubtedly the case that these queer tendencies are impacting upon the general population unevenly, and a future agenda for research should therefore include detailed empirical, ethnographic studies which can explore the extent to which new sexualities are in creation both within and beyond the cosmopolitan centres of the western world. It would be worth investigating, for instance, the extent to which the cultural valorizing of the queer has moved beyond the younger generation that has the sub-cultural capital to partake of cool sub-cultures,[53] given that the changes that start in 'cultural trend-setting areas' (Castells, 1997: 237) generally emanate outwards to permeate the wider culture. It is my hypothesis that there is more than a queer avant-garde at work here, and that the queer tendencies that I have identified are of a profound and general societal significance. Reflexive heterosexual identities are becoming increasingly widespread, and all over the western world heterorelations have a significantly less sure hold on the general population, across the generations.

It might be thought that the argument of this chapter grants too great a significance to the transitory, ephemeral world of popular culture, and that its overall tone is overly optimistic. I would readily acknowledge that there are, of course, countervailing tendencies, in the form of various expressions of sexual and gender fundamentalism, which are particularly strong in the United States,[54] but which have also recently been seen in the United Kingdom in public debates about the repeal of Section 28.[55] Homophobia continues to exist, particularly in schools, and violence against lesbians and gay men remains a serious problem.[56] Moreover, lesbians and gay men do not appear ready to collectively cede their hard-won sexual identities, and many are firm believers in their difference (variously conceived as cultural, biological, psychological and/or genetic) from heterosexuals.[57] When boundaries are transgressed and identities unsettled, the impulse to deploy border guards is strong, and lesbian and gay communities continue to expend much time and energy seeking to stabilize and ground themselves in defensible space. But it is not my argument that we have moved into a post-lesbian and gay era, and nor am I positing a straightforward narrative of sexual liberation, revolution or the final demise of homophobia.

So, where does this leave lesbian and gay studies, if the very categories on which the field is founded are being destabilized?[58] Is there a future for a field if the subjects who study and the objects they study no longer quite inhabit the identities that the field invokes? There have been several terminological responses to the challenges posed by queer auto-critique: to extend its remit, reconfiguring it as 'lesbian, gay, bisexual, transgender studies', to relabel it 'queer studies', or simply, and perhaps consciously post-the-homosexual/heterosexual-binary, 'sexuality studies'. Certainly, I would endorse moves such as these which acknowledge that the terrain of the sexual is constantly shifting. I would also hope that a future agenda for research would involve the interrogation of the new borders and divisions, the new normativities, exclusions and marginalizations which are in creation in the ever changing configuration of the realm of the sexual.

NOTES

1 The ideas in this chapter have been gestating over a considerable period of time. Much earlier versions of the chapter were presented at the 'Law, Sexuality and Gender' conference at Keele University in June 1998 and at the 'Sex Outlaw' conference in Helsinki in October 1998, and at seminars at the Universities of Edinburgh, Leeds (*http://www.leeds.ac.uk/gender-studies*), Sheffield and Sussex, Lancaster University, the University of South Australia, Flinders University, and LaTrobe University. The support of the Economic and Social Research Council (UK) is gratefully acknowledged; time for the further development of the chapter was part the programme of the ESRC Research Group for the Study of Care, Values and the Future of Welfare (CAVA) (award M564281001) at the University of Leeds (http://www.leeds.ac.uk/cava). Thanks to all those who have debated these ideas (often disagreeing with me), particularly Barry Adam, Henning Bech, Gary Dowsett, Nicky Edwards, Denis Flannery, Kirk Mann, Antu Sorainen, Fiona Williams, and members of CAVA.

2 'The Future of the Queer Past Conference', which was convened by George Chauncey at the University of

Chicago in September 2000 provided an exciting space in which those working on lesbian and gay histories could reflect upon and engage with recent developments in queer theorizing.

3 I use the designation 'postmodernity' to refer to the contemporary social formation, fully cognisant of the debate between those who prefer to speak of 'late modernity' (e.g. Giddens, 1991, 1992, 1995; Plummer, 1995) and those who prefer the term 'postmodernity' (e.g. Bauman, 1992; Lash and Urry, 1994). More recently Bauman (2000) has coined the term 'liquid modernity', which captures something of the ever-changing fluidity of the contemporary social condition.

4 An important issue here concerns the definition of 'social theory'. My point is that lesbian and gay and sexuality studies is producing 'social theory', some of which is concerned with historical shifts in the realm of sexuality (e.g. Plummer, 1995; Simon, 1996) but that this tends not to get recognized as such.

5 In referring to the wide-range of close personal affective bonds between individuals, I prefer the term 'cathexis' to the more widely used 'intimacy', which I feel is better reserved for speaking of a very particular type of emotional relationship, one of mutual disclosure in which people participate as equals.

6 There is a parallel here with the feminist insight that categories of gender, and gendered oppressions, extend beyond that which appears explicitly gendered. Psychoanalysis, in particular, offers a world view which 'troubles the border between the sexual and the nonsexual' (Dean, 2000: 270).

7 Texts which have come to assume foundational status within queer theory include: Sedgwick (1991), Butler (1991), de Lauretis (1991), Fuss (1991) and Warner (1991).

8 The relationship between feminism and queer theory is both close and contested. See for example Jeffreys (1994), Wilkinson and Kitzinger (1994), Walters (1996), Weed and Schor (1997). It is important to note that lesbian feminism, particularly the work of Rich (1980) offers a theory which places non-heterosexual affect – 'the lesbian continuum' – both firmly at the centre of the social world and at the centre of its project. Queer theory developed in the context of lesbian feminism, both informed by it, and offering an alternative theoretical trajectory.

9 For a clear discussion of the influences of poststructuralism on queer theory see Namaste (1996).

10 Fuss (1991) draws on psychoanalytic understandings of processes of alienation, splitting and identification, which produce a self and an other, an interiority and an exteriority.

11 See particularly Butler (1991).

12 This point is made by Seidman (1996), Stein and Plummer (1996) and Jackson (1999). The traditions of symbolic interactionism (from Goffman, 1971) and ethnomethodology (Garfinkel, 1967; Kessler and McKenna, 1978) provide conceptual resources for theorizing sexuality and gender which have significant parallels with queer theory.

13 These criticisms are made by, *inter alia*, Warner (1993), Seidman (1996) and Stein and Plummer (1996).

14 On processes of 'culturalization' and the aestheticization of everyday life see Lash (1994) and Crook et al. (1990).

15 For instance, in developing an argument for a queer sociology, Namaste wholeheartedly embraces poststructuralism, but fails to consider the problems which sociologists might encounter in the abandonment of all vestiges of a humanist ontology. I have argued elsewhere (Roseneil, 1995) for the importance of transcending the humanist/poststructuralist binary.

16 See McNay (1999) for a critique of Butler's theory of agency, and McNay (2000), in which she draws on Bourdieu to develop a more hermeneutic and praxeological account of agency.

17 See contributions to Seidman (1996).

18 A recent article by Seidman et al. (1999) is an exception to this.

19 Structuration theory still, in my mind, offers the best solution to the agency/structure conundrum (see Giddens, 1984).

20 The terms appear to have been coined by Karl Maria Kertbeny in 1868, though were not used in print until 1869 (homosexuality) and 1880 (heterosexuality), according to Katz (1983, 1996). See also McIntosh (1968), Plummer (1981), Weeks (1977, 1981, 1985), Foucault (1981).

21 For histories of marriage, see Stone (1979, 1993) and Gillis (1985), and on marriage in the immediate postwar period, see Finch and Summerfield (1991) and Morgan (1991).

22 See Smith-Rosenberg (1975), Weeks (1985), Faderman (1981) and Jeffreys (1985).

23 See Jeffreys (1985).

24 On the rise of the lesbian and gay movement see Adam (1995) and d'Emilio (1983).

25 The most important text of gay liberation was Altman (1971), the arguments of which presage many of those of queer theory twenty years later.

26 See for example Levine, Nardi and Gagnon (1997) and Weeks (2000).

27 Castells (1997) also sees the rise of global informational economy and the technological transformation of biology and reproduction as central explanatory forces in the undermining of the patriarchal family.

28 The research by Finch (1989) and Finch and Mason (1993) on family obligations suggests that family ties are now understood less in terms of obligations constituted by fixed ties of blood, and more in terms of negotiated commitments, which are less clearly differentiated from other relationships.

29 In this acknowledgement of non-heterosexual identities and practices Giddens's work differs from that of Beck and Beck-Gernsheim whose discussion fails to acknowledge its exclusive concern with heterosexuality.

30 Bech (1998, 1999) makes a similar argument.

31 Watney (1988) and Fuss (1991) made early suggestions that such a process was underway.

32 For this notion I owe a particular debt to Sedgwick (1994).

33 On lesbian and gay spaces, see Bell and Valentine (1995).

34 It should not be assumed, however, that there were no internal challenges to lesbian and gay identities before the coining of the concept of 'queer'.

35 The concept of a 'critical community' as the originator of new ideas, which may later be taken up by wider social and political movements, is developed by Rochon (1998).

36 Examples of queer auto-critique: Bristow and Wilson (1993), Califia (1994), Eliot and Roen (1998), Hemmings (1993), Stein (1993), Doan (1994), Bi-Academic Intervention (1997), Munt (1998), Prosser (1998), and Halberstam (1998a, b), Garber (2000).

37 Plummer is more sceptical than I am about the existence of such stories.

38 In the UK, divorce rates have increased fram 2 per 1000 of the married population in 1961 to 13 per 1000 of the married population. Among those who married in the late 1980s around one in eight men and one in six women had separated within the first five years, double the proportion for those who were married 20 years earlier (Social Trends, 2001).

39 By 1999 nearly two-fifths of births were outside marriage in the UK, nearly five times greater than in 1971 (Social Trends, 2001).

40 In the UK by 2000, lone parents families were almost 26% of all families with dependent children (Social Trends, 2001).

41 In the UK in 1961 11% of households consisted of one person living alone; by 2000 the figure was 24% (Social Trends, 2001).

42 For a discussion of the importance of friendship in contemporary social relations see Roseneil (2000).

43 I am hereby disagreeing with Smart who argues that 'the immense verbosity around heterosexual acts has not produced the heterosexual' (1996: 228).

44 Section 28 (1) states that: 'a local authority shall not (a) intentionally promote homosexuality or publish material with the intention of promoting homosexuality; (b) promote the teaching in any maintained school of the acceptance of homosexuality as a pretend family relationship. See Stacey (1991) for a discussion of the relationship between Section 28 and feminist/lesbian theories of sexuality, and Wise (2000) and Waites (2000) on recent debates about repeal of the Section.

45 This claim was made by a number of participants at 'The Future of the Field: Lesbian, Gay, Bisexual, Transgender Studies ' Conference, at the Centre for Lesbian and Gay Studies, City University, New York, April 2001.

46 For instance, *Company*, July 1996.

47 An estimated 4 million people go clubbing regularly in the UK (*Guardian*, 8 February 2002:52 pp.)

48 See Bidder (2001). On the role of Ecstasy in breaking down social barriers within contemporary dance culture see Wright (1999) and Collin (1997).

49 In London, the highly fashionable DTPM (more recently ADTPM) and Fiction identify themselves as 'polysexual' as do Miss Moneypenny's in Birmingham and Sundessential in Birmingham and Leeds. Outside London *Flesh* in Manchester and *Vague* in Leeds pioneered queer clubbing in the early to mid-1990s.

50 My argument here parallels Back's (1996) argument about the emergence of a new hybrid ethnicity characterized by high degrees of egalitarianism and anti-racism amongst young people through popular culture's mixing of black and white cultural codes and styles.

51 See Lewis (1997) on lesbian imagery in women's magazines and Simpson (1996) on men's magazines. Also Clark's (1993) discussion of lesbians and advertising.

52 For positions which interpret the cultural valorizing of the queer differently, see Hennessy (1995, 2000), Jackson (1999) and Chasin (2000).

53 The notion of 'sub-cultural capital' is coined by Thornton (1995) in her discussion of club cultures.

54 See Witt and McCorkle (1997) and National Lesbian and Gay Task Force website for further information about recent anti-gay developments in the United States: *http://www.ngltf.org.*

55 On recent debates about Section 28 see Wise (2000) and Waites (2000), and the Stonewall website (*http://www.stonewall.org.uk*). It should be noted that public opinion on Section 28 seems to favour repeal (NOP poll commissioned for Channel 4, December 1999) *http://www.stonewall.org.uk/template.asp*

56 On homophobic bullying in schools, see Douglas et al. (1998) and Duncan (1999), Mason and Palmer (1996) on queer bashing, and Snape et al. (1995) on discrimination against lesbians and gay men in the UK.

57 See for example Rahman and Jackson (1997) on the persistence of essentialism within lesbian and gay claims for rights. For a critique of the queer embrace of hybridity, see Sinfield (1996).

58 But, it should also be acknowledged that, as Tim Dean argues: 'Sexuality is only partly historical; its other dimension has to do not with nature but with the unconscious and with what Lacan calls the traumatic real – unfamiliar aspects of existence that are no more biological than they are historically produced. If the unconscious were purely a historical construct, it would be manipulable in a way that it clearly is not' (2000: 270). Dean reminds us that in attending to the shifting constitution of the homosexual/ heterosexual binary, we must not forget the psychic dimensions of sexuality.

REFERENCES

Adam, B. (1995) *The Rise of a Gay and Lesbian Movement*. New York: Twayne.

Altman, Dennis (1971) *Homosexual Liberation and Oppression*. New York: Avon.

Back, L. (1996) *New Ethnicities and Urban Culture*. London: Routledge.

Bauman, Z. (1992) *Intimations of Postmodernity*. London: Routledge.

Bauman, Z. (2000) *Liquid Modernity*. Cambridge. Polity.

Bech, H. (1998) 'Real deconstructions: the disappearance of the modern homosexual and the queer', paper presented at the 14th World Congress of Sociology, Montreal, 26 July–1 August.

Bech, H. (1999) 'After the closet', *Sexualities*, 2 (3): 343–9.

Beck, U., Giddens, A. and Lash, S. (1994) *Reflexive Modernization: Politics, Tradition and Aesthetics in the Modern Social Order*. Cambridge: Polity.

Beck, U. and Beck-Gernsheim, E. (1995) *The Normal Chaos of Love*. Cambridge: Polity.

Beck-Gernsheim, E. (1999) 'On the way to a post-familial family: from a community of needs to elective affinities', *Theory, Culture and Society*, 15 (3–4): 53–70.

Bell, D. and Valentine, G. (1995) *Mapping Desire*. London: Routledge.

Bi-Academic Intervention (ed.) (1997) *The Bisexual Imaginary*. London: Cassell.

Bidder, Sean (2001) *Pump Up the Volume*. London: Channel 4 Books.

Bristow, J. and Wilson, A.R. (eds) (1993) *Activating Theory: Lesbian, Gay, Bisexual Politics*. London: Lawrence and Wishart.

Butler, J. (1991) *Gender Trouble: Feminism and the Subversion of Identity*. New York: Routledge.

Califia, P. (1994) *Public Sex: The Culture of Radical Sex*. San Francisco: Cleis Press.

Castells, Manuel (1997) *The Power of Identity. Vol. II The Information Age: Economy, Society and Culture*. Oxford, Blackwell.

Chasin, A. (2000) *Selling Out: The Gay and Lesbian Movement Goes to Market*. New York: St Martin's Press.

Clark, D. (1993) 'Commodity lesbianism', in H. Abelove, M.A. Barale and D.M. Halperin (eds), *The Lesbian and Gay Studies Reader*. New York: Routledge.

Collin, M. (1997) *Altered State: The Story of Ecstasy Culture and Acid House*. London: Serpent's Tail.

Connell, R.W. (1987) *Gender and Power: Society, the Person and Sexual Politics*. Cambridge: Polity.

Crook, S., Pakulski, J. and Waters, M. (1990) *Postmodernization: Change in Advanced Society*. London: Sage.

Dean, T. (2000) *Beyond Sexuality*. Chicago: University of Chicago Press.

D'Emilio, J. (1983) *Sexual Politics, Sexual Communities: The Making of a Homosexual Minority in the United States, 1940–70*. Chicago: University of Chicago Press.

De Lauretis, T. (1991) 'Queer theory: lesbian and gay sexualities. An introduction', *Differences*, 3 (2):

Doan, L. (ed.) (1994) *The Lesbian Postmodern*. New York: Columbia University Press.

Douglas, N., Warwick, I., Kemp, S. and Whitty, G. (1998) *Playing It Safe: Response of Secondary School Teachers to Lesbian, Gay and Bisexual Pupils, Bullying, HIV and AIDS Education and Section 28*. London: Health and Education Research Unit, Institute of Education, University of London.

Dowsett, G. (1996) *Practicing Desire: Homosexual Sex in the Era of AIDS*. Stanford, CA: Stanford University Press.

Duggan, L. (1994) 'Queering the state', *Social Text*, 39, Summer.

Duncan, N. (1999) *Sexual Bullying: Gender Conflict in Pupil Culture*. London: Routledge.

Eliot, P. and Roen, K. (1998) 'Transgenderism and the question of embodiment', *GLQ*, 4 (2): 231–61.

Faderman, L. (1981) *Surpassing the Love of Men*. New York: William Morrow.

Feinberg, L. (1996) *Transgender Warriors: Making History from Joan of Arc to Dennis Rodman*. Boston: Beacon Press.

Finch, J. (1989) *Family Obligations and Social Change*. Cambridge: Polity.

Finch, J. and Mason, J. (1993) *Negotiating Family Responsibilities*. London: Routledge.

Finch, J. and Summerfield, P. (1991) 'Social reconstruction and the emergence of the companionate marriage, 1945–59', in D. Clark (ed.), *Marriage, Domestic Life and Social Change*. London: Routledge.

Foucault, M. (1981) *The History of Sexuality Volume 1: An Introduction*. Harmondsworth: Penguin.

Fuss, D. (1991) *Inside/Out: Lesbian Theories, Gay Theories*. New York: Routledge.

Gagnon, J. and Simon, W. (1967) 'Homosexuality: the formulation of a sociological perspective', *Journal of Health and Social Behaviour*, 8: 177–85.

Garber, M. (2000) *Bisexuality and the Eroticism of Everyday Life*. New York: Routledge.

Garfinkel, H. (1967) *Studies in Ethnomethodology*. Englewood Cliffs, NJ: Prentice-Hall.

Giddens, A. (1984) *The Constitution of Society*. Cambridge: Polity.

Giddens, A. (1991) *Modernity and Self-Identity*. Cambridge: Polity.

Giddens, A. (1992) *The Transformation of Intimacy: Sexuality, Love and Eroticism in Modern Societies*. Cambridge: Polity.

Giddens, A. (1995) *Beyond Left and Right*. Cambridge: Polity.

Gillis, J. (1985) *For Better, For Worse: British Marriages, 1600–present*. Oxford: Oxford University Press.

Goffman, E. (1971) *The Presentation of Self in Everyday Life*. Harmondsworth: Penguin Books.

Halberstam, J. (1998a) *Female Masculinity.* Durham, NC: Duke University Press.

Halberstam, J. (1998b) 'Transgender butch – butch/FTM border wars and the masculine continuum', *GLQ,* 4 (2): 287–310.

Hawkes, G. (1995) *A Sociology of Sex and Sexuality.* Buckingham: Open University Press.

Hemmings, C. (1993) 'Resituating the bisexual body', in J. Bristow and A.R.Wilson (eds), *Activating Theory: Lesbian, Gay, Bisexual Politics.* London: Lawrence and Wishart.

Hennessy, R. (1995) 'Queer visibility in commodity culture', in L. Nicholson and S. Seidman (eds), *Social Postmodernism: Beyond Identity Politics.* Cambridge: Cambridge University Press.

Hennessy, R. (2000) *Profit and Pleasure: Sexual Identities in Late Capitalism.* New York: Routledge.

Hocquenghem, G. (1978) *Homosexual Desire.* London: Allison and Busby.

Hughes, G. (1998) *Imagining Welfare Futures.* London: Routledge.

Ingram, G.B., Bouthillette, A. and Retter, Y. (eds) (1997) *Queers in Space: Communities, Public Places, Sites of Resistance.* Seattle: Bay Press.

Irwin, S. (2000) *Conceptualising Social Change: Family, Work and the Changing Pattern of Social Reproduction.* CAVA Working Paper, http://www.leeds.ac.uk/cava/research/strand1/paper7aSarah.htm.

Jackson, S. (1999) *Heterosexuality in Question.* London: Sage.

Jameson, F. (1984) 'Postmodernism: or the cultural logic of late capitalism', *New Left Review,* 146: 53–92.

Jamieson, L. (1998) *Intimacy: Personal Relationships in Modern Societies.* Cambridge: Polity.

Jeffreys, S. (1985) *The Spinster and Her Enemies: Feminism and Sexuality 1880–1930.* London: Pandora.

Jeffreys, S. (1994) *The Lesbian Heresy.* London: The Women's Press.

Katz, J. (1976) *Gay American History.* New York: Thomas Cromwell.

Katz, J. (1983) *Gay/Lesbian Almanac: A New Documentary.* New York: Harper & Row.

Katz, J. (1996) *The Invention of Heterosexuality.* New York: Plume.

Kessler, S. and McKenna, W. (1978) *Gender: An Ethnomethodological Approach.* Chicago: University of Chicago Press.

Lash, S. (1994) 'Reflexivity and its doubles: structure, aesthetics, community', in S. Lash and J. Urry *Economies of Signs and Space.* London: Sage.

Levine, M., Nardi, P. and Gagnon, J. (1997) *In Changing Times: Gay Men and Lesbians Encounter HIV/AIDS.* Chicago: Chicago University Press.

Lewis, R. (1997), 'Looking good: the lesbian gaze and fashion imagery', *Feminist Review,* 55, Spring: 92–109.

Mason, A. and Palmer, A. (1996) *Queer Bashing: A National Survey of Hate Crimes against Lesbians and Gay Men.* London: Stonewall.

McNay, L (1999) 'Gender, Habitus and the Field: Pierre Bourdieu and the limits of reflexivity', *Theory, Culture and Society,* 15 (1): 95–117.

McNay, L (2000) *Gender and Agency: Reconfiguring the Subject in Feminst and Social Theory.*

McIntosh, M. (1968) 'The homosexual role' *Social Problems,* 16: 182–92.

Morgan, D. (1991) 'Ideologies of marriage and family life', in D. Clark (ed.), *Marriage, Domestic Life and Social Change.* London: Routledge.

Munt, S. (1998) (ed.), *Butch/Femme: Inside Lesbian Gender.* London: Cassell Academic.

Namaste, K. (1996) 'The politics of inside/out: queer theory, poststructuralism, and a sociological approach to sexuality', in S. Seidman (ed.), *Queer Theory/Sociology.* Oxford: Blackwell.

OPCS (1991) *Marriage and Divorce Statistics.* London: HMSO.

OPCS (1993) *Population Trends.* London: HMSO.

OPCS (1991) *General Household Survey.* London: HMSO.

Ponse, B. (1978) *Identities in the Lesbian World: The Social Construction of Self.* Westport, CT: Greenwood Press.

Plummer, K. (1981) *The Making of the Modern Homosexual.* London: Hutchinson.

Plummer, K. (1995) *Telling Sexual Stories* Cambridge: Polity.

Plummer, K. (1998) 'The past, present and future of the sociology of same-sex relations', in P. Nardi and B. Schneider (eds), *Social Perspectives in Lesbian and Gay Studies.* London: Routledge.

Prosser, J. (1998) *Second Skins: The Body Narratives of Transsexuality.* New York: Columbia University Press.

Queen, C. and Schimel, L. (1997) 'Introduction', in C. Queen and L. Schimel (eds), *PoMoSexuals: Challenging Assumptions about Gender and Sexuality.* San Francisco: Cleis Press.

Rahman, M. and Jackson, S. (1997) 'Liberty, equality and sexuality: essentialism and the discourse of rights', *Journal of Gender Studies,* 6 (2): 117–29.

Rich, A. (1980) 'Compulsory heterosexuality and lesbian existence', *Signs,* 5 (4): 631–60.

Rochon, T.R. (1998) *Culture Moves: Ideas, Activism and Changing Values.* Princeton, NJ: Princeton University Press.

Roseneil, S. (1995) 'The coming of age of feminist sociology: some issues of theory and practice for the next twenty years', *British Journal of Sociology,* 26 (2): 191–205.

Roseneil, S. (2000) *Why We Should Care about Friends: Some Thoughts (for CAVA) about the Ethics and Practice of Friendship.* http://www.leeds.ac.uk/cava/research/strand1/paper22Sasha.htm.

Saraga, E. (1998) *Embodying the Social: Constructions of Difference.* London: Routledge.

Sedgwick, E. Kosofsky (1991) *Epistemology of the Closet.* Hemel Hempstead: Harvester Wheatsheaf.

Sedgwick, E. Kosofsky (1994) *Tendencies.* New York: Routledge.

Seidman, S. (1996) 'Introduction', in S. Seidman (ed.), *Queer Theory/Sociology*. Oxford: Blackwell.

Seidman, S., Meeks, C. and Traschen, F. (1999) 'Beyond the closet? The changing social meaning of homosexuality in the United States' *Sexualities*, 2 (1): 9–34.

Silva, E.B. and Smart C. (eds) (1999) *The New Family?* London: Sage.

Simon, William (1996) *Postmodern Sexualities*. London: Routledge.

Simpson, M. (1994) *Male Impersonators: Men Performing Masculinity*. London: Cassell.

Simpson, M. (ed.) (1996) *Anti-Gay*. London: Cassell.

Sinfield, A. (1996) 'Diaspora and hybridity: queer identities and the ethnicity model', *Textual Practice*, 10 (2): 271–93.

Smart, C. (1996) 'Desperately seeking post-heterosexual woman', in J. Holland and L. Adkins (eds), *Sex, Sensibility and the Gendered Body*. Basingstoke: Macmillan.

Smart, C. and Neale, B. (1999) *Family Fragments*. Cambridge: Polity.

Smith-Rosenberg, C. (1975) 'The female world of love and ritual: relations between women in nineteenth century America', *Signs*, 1 (1): 1–29.

Snape, D., Thomson, K. and Chetwynd, M. (1995) *Discrimination against Gay Men and Lesbians*. London: SCPR.

Social Trends (1997) London: HMSO.

Stacey, J. (1991) 'Promoting normality: section 28 and the reputation of sexuality', in S. Franklin, C. Lury, J. Stacey (eds), *Off-Centre: Feminism and Cultural Studies*. London: Harper Collins.

Stacey, J. (1996) *In the Name of the Family: Rethinking Family Values in the Postmodern Age*. Boston: Beacon Press.

Stein, A. (1993) *Sisters, Sexperts and Queers: Beyond the Lesbian Nation*. New York: Plume.

Stein, A. and Plummer, K. (1996) '"I can't even think straight": "queer" theory and the missing sexual revolution in sociology', in S. Seidman (ed.), *Queer Theory/Sociology*. Oxford: Blackwell.

Stone, L. (1979) *The Family, Sex and Marriage in England 1500–1800*. Harmondsworth: Penguin.

Stone, L. (1993) *Broken Lives: Separation and Divorce in England 1660–1857*. Oxford: Oxford University Press.

Stychin, C. (1995) *Law's Desire: Sexuality and the Limits of Justice*. London: Routledge.

Thornton, S. (1995) *Club Cultures: Music, Media and Subcultural Capital*. Cambridge: Polity.

Waites, M. (2000) 'Homosexuality and the new right: the legacy of the 1980s for new delineations of homophobia', *Sociological Research Online*, 5 (1), *http://www.socresonline.org.uk/5/1/waites.html*

Walters, S. (1996) 'From here to queer: radical feminism, postmodernism, and the lesbian menace (or why can't a woman be more like a fag?)' *Signs*, 21 (4): 830–69.

Warner, M. (1991) 'Fear of a queer planet', *Social Text*, 9 (14): 3–17.

Warner, M. (ed.) (1993) *Fear of a Queer Planet*. Minneapolis: University of Minnesota Press.

Watney, S. (1988) 'AIDS, "moral panic" theory and homophobia', in P. Aggleton and H. Homans (eds), *Social Aspects of AIDS*. London: Falmer.

Weed, E. and Schor, N. (1997) *Feminism Meets Queer Theory*. Bloomington: Indiana University Press.

Weeks, J. (1977) *Coming Out: Homosexual Politics in Britain from the Nineteenth Century to the Present*. London: Quartet.

Weeks, J. (1981) *Sex, Politics and Society*. London: Longman.

Weeks, J. (1985) *Sexuality and Its Discontents: Meanings, Myths, and Modern Sexualities*. London: Routledge.

Weeks, J. (2000) *Making Sexual History*. Cambridge: Polity.

Weeks, J., Donovan, C. and Heaphy, B. (1999) 'Everyday experiments: narratives of non-heterosexual relationships', in E.B. Silva and C. Smart (eds), *The New Family?* London: Sage.

Weeks, J. and Holland, J. (1996) *Sexual Cultures: Communities, Values and Intimacy*. Basingstoke: Macmillan.

Wilchins, R.A. (1997) *Read My Lips: Sexual Subversion and the End of Gender*. Ithaca, NY: Firebrand book.

Wilkinson, S. and Kitzinger, C. (1994) 'Dire straights? Contemporary rehabilitations of heterosexuality', in G. Griffin, M. Hester, S. Rai and S. Roseneil (eds), *Stirring It: Challenges for Feminism*. London: Taylor and Francis.

Wise, S. (2000) 'New right or "backlash"? Section 28, moral panic and "promoting Homosexuality"', *Sociological Research Online*, 5 (1), http://www.socresonline.org.uk/5/1/wise.html

Witt, S. and McCorkle, S. (eds) (1997) *Anti-Gay Rights*. Westport, CT: Praeger.

Wright, R.M.A. (1999) The symbolic challenge of a new cultural movement: ecstasy use and the British dance scene 1988–1998, unpublished PhD thesis, City University.

3

The Mainstreaming of Lesbian and Gay Studies?

PETER M. NARDI

Lesbian and gay studies, as well as its more recent variations in queer studies with its emphasis on theorizing and textual analyses, presents a relief from the invisibility of gays and lesbians in a variety of academic disciplines. However, this chapter argues that only a small portion of the research is evident in the core sociology textbooks and research literature. And when it is, the topics, issues, and underlying perspectives tend to focus on gays and lesbians in a fairly conventional way, one often absent of any threat that the social, political, sexual, or moral order will become transformed. While it is important to discuss the everyday lives of gay men and lesbians in order to counteract the stereotypes that exist in many societies today, the tendency to do so results in depictions that often normalize and minimize the complexities of living as gay or lesbian in heterosexually-oriented social worlds. This kind of mainstreaming of gay and lesbian issues involves decontextualizing experiences, that is, failing to provide an analysis of the larger cultural contexts that perpetuate the inequalities that gays and lesbian face. It also occurs through a process of desexualization in which topics about sexuality are usually avoided or discussed only in the most general of terms.

Most theory books continue to overlook queer theory, many social movement books

ignore the gay liberation history, the interpersonal relationship literature typically forgets to include gay and lesbian relationships, and discussions of urban growth give scant attention to gay neighborhoods and communities. We are not typically part of the larger sociological landscape; we are off in our own worlds as if we existed on a separate plane, unrelated to the social contexts that affect everyday life. And when gay and lesbian topics do appear in the sociological literature, they rarely include issues related directly to sexuality, unless it is about AIDS. The topics show up here and there, desexualized, and scattered throughout a few chapters of the 'introductory sociology' textbook, making a token appearance, without any sense of how gay and lesbian lives contest and potentially transform the social order.

This is not a recent phenomenon. Some time ago Arlene Stein and Ken Plummer (1994: 178) made the case that gay and lesbian issues 'inhabit the margins of the discipline'; they called on sociologists to rethink social issues (for example, stratification) and to reread the sociological classics in light of what is known from lesbian and gay studies about heterosexism, homophobia, and the construction of sexuality. Several years later, Plummer (1998b: 609) did not see much progress and succinctly observed that the tension between lesbian and gay studies and sociology remains a weak one; there exists 'a sociological community that marginalizes lesbian and gay concerns; a lesbian and gay community that militates against the constructionism of most socio-logical analyses; a generationally based "queer studies" that favors cultural studies over sociological studies', as well as a bias toward a more white male perspective.

However, change has occurred and gay and lesbian topics have been achieving more attention in the field in the past several years since these essays were first written. Yet there is a price for greater incorporation. Like the gay and lesbian characters who get added to today's televi-sion dramas and situation comedies, there is a co-optation. What changes have occurred in the media are little more than assimila-tionist forms of incorporation in which the dominant culture accommodates the radical perspective into its view and robs 'the radi-cal of its voice and thus of its means of expressing its opposition' (Fiske, 1987: 38). As a form of media, sociology text-books, for example, exhibit an assimilation-ist tone when dealing, if they do at all, with gay and lesbian topics. Gays and lesbians become decontextualized and often desexu-alized not only in the entertainment media but also in the sociological literature.

This may sound overly critical of the work that has been done in the field, (and slighting the most recent research, includ-ing what is in this book) but that is not my intention. Like the struggle for civil rights for gay and lesbian people, mainstream strategies are adopted for practical pur-poses and are sometimes necessary in the earliest stages of liberation, but the long-term outcomes are much more limited. Urvashi Vaid, former director of the National Gay and Lesbian Task Force, wrote powerfully about the mainstreaming trend she was witnessing in gay politics. Consider her sociological insights on the pull between political expediency and cultural transformation:

A mainstream civil rights strategy cannot deliver genuine freedom or full equality for one funda-mental reason: the goal of winning mainstream tolerance ... differs from the goal of winning liberation or changing social institutions in lasting, long-term ways ... How the pursuit of fundamental change mutates (and is mutated) into the more limited goal of tolerance or main-stream integration is a story common to many historic movements that have threatened the status quo. In many ways, the triumph of main-stream civil rights over liberation is the victory of pragmatic politics over moral politics ... We must supplement the limited politics of civil rights with a broader and more inclusive com-mitment to cultural transformation ... [C]ivil rights can be won without displacing the moral and sexual hierarchy that enforces antigay stigmatization ... [G]ay mainstreaming will remain partial and provisional until the underly-ing religious, moral, and cultural prejudices ... are transformed ... Our movement must strive beyond ... mainstreaming ourselves into the center to transforming the mainstream. (1995: 3–4, 179, 180)

I argue that this is the challenge of academic research as well. How can gay/lesbian and queer studies transform the mainstream rather than become assimilated by it? While striving to achieve visibility within sociology, for example, we struggle to get our work read, acknowledged, and developed by those who are not already familiar with the work. Yet we need to be attentive to the myriad ways the appropriation of that work can result in its decontextualization and desexualiza-tion, resulting in minimal transformation of the discipline. Trying to become main-streamed into the canons of sociology may be a short-term objective, but in the long term, mainstream sociology continues untouched.

For years, many activists worked to alter the images of gays and lesbians in the enter-tainment media, in books and newspapers, in political and legal arenas (Nardi, 1997). Some of these gay and lesbian leaders fight for respectability in the magazine articles, up-scale talk and news shows, and in the power triangle of Washington, New York, and Los Angeles, by arguing for assimila-tion in the most mainstream of institutions – the three M's of marriage, the military, and the media. In 2000, the court battles for equal treatment in the Boy Scouts, the Emmy Award for best comedy going to *Will and Grace* (a television show about two gay male characters and their two heterosexual female friends), and the fact that the gay sexual orientation of the winner of the television contest *Survivor* was generally ignored, all illustrate how gays and lesbians are 'becoming ordinary', as *Newsweek* columnist Anna Quindlen (2000: 82) wrote. In addition, controversial books by Michelangelo Signorile (1997), Andrew Sullivan (1996), and Gabriel Rotello (1997) push their mainstream, white, middle-class agenda of achieving places at the table through respectable tactics, traditional family values, and monogamous sex in committed relationships.

The battle lines between the so-called 'assimilationists' and the 'activists' are not newly drawn. The debates over strategies have been around since the earliest homophile movements in the 1950s with the Mattachine Society, the Daughters of Bilitis, and other organizations working to achieve equal rights for those who are different (see D'Emilio, 1983). The arguments invariably center on whether we are just like everyone else, except who we sleep with, or if we are indeed on the margins: the center versus the margin, the normative versus the deviant, the straight versus the queer, assimilation versus transformation.

If over forty years of research about homosexuality tell us anything, it is that generalizations about entire categories of people who organize their lives around various sexual orientations cannot be adequately made. Some of us lead mainstream lives; others of us lead transgressive ones, often linked to variations in race and social class. The lesson from the postmodern and queer theorists is that the variations are often the answer, not just the similarities. We are just like everyone else, and we are not like anyone else. We are centering in the mainstream, and we are contesting on the margins. There is not *a* homosexuality, but homosexualities.

Uncovering this diversity without losing the power to transform critical thought and sociological insights becomes the challenge, then, of gay/lesbian studies. Queer studies has provided us with many ideas, language, and conceptualizations needed to take what has traditionally been seen as studies of gay men and lesbians into areas that go beyond the reification of binary categories of sexual orientation, as Steven Seidman (1996) has argued. If we follow this perspective, we may become less likely to simply reinforce the mainstream with problematic empirical surveys of our buying power and tastes. But we cannot always effectively control the discourse or set the agenda.

Take the issue of same-sex marriage. Starting with mainstream questions leads to investigating how same-sex marriage can work in similar ways as for heterosexual couples. As demonstrated below, this approach is exactly what many introductory sociology textbooks do. What is happening, Vaid (1995: 179) said, is that the goal to liberate 'is now phrased as the modest right to live without discrimination based on homosexual orientation. And the feminist critique of family and gender roles, which was at the heart of gay and lesbian liberation, has turned into our wholesale reproduction of family in gay and lesbian drag.'

On the other hand, if we begin with the queer studies questions, we could investigate the ways lesbian, gay, bisexual, and transgendered people already in their quotidian routines contest the very boundaries of such institutions as marriage and recreate differently structured ways of organizing romantic, sexual, and friendship relationships (Nardi, 1999). In so doing, the work could contribute to the mainstream literature on 'marriage and family' and simultaneously challenge and transform its very premises and findings.

When gays and lesbians argue about their right to marry, it ends up reinforcing marriage as an institution and recreating a class system of the marrieds and non-marrieds (see Warner, 1999). If gays and lesbians were to argue instead about the institution itself by providing models of alternative forms of sexual, familial, romantic, and friendship relationships, could not this open up the broader culture to a potentially greater level of acceptability of diversity than trying to fit gay and lesbian relationships into some Procrustean marriage bed?

A SOCIOLOGY OF SEXUALITIES

Not only do some gay and lesbian spokespeople reinforce the mainstream in making the case for equal rights, but sociology research and writing clearly present gay and lesbian issues from a mainstream perspective as well, if they consider it all. Nearly eight years after Stein and Plummer (1994) called on sociology to rethink the field in light of heterosexism and homophobia, and after almost as many years of gay and lesbian activists, like Vaid (1995), exhorting gay and lesbian leaders to transform the mainstream, there is little evidence that gay and lesbian studies challenges the status quo or that sociology has considered the insights of gay and lesbian studies.

Consider the introductory sociology textbook. Struggling for any recognition has been a project, just as gay/lesbian groups fought to get some non-stereotypical and fair acknowledgement in the media. We remain invisible in many textbooks, while, in others, we are made to look just like anyone else in the marriage chapter, in the sexualities chapter, maybe in the gender chapter, at least no longer as an example in the deviance one along with drug addicts, murderers, and rapists. In a convenience sample of seven introductory sociology textbooks currently sitting on my office shelf (and I have no reason to believe these are in any way atypical of what was published by some of the largest publishers in 1998, 1999, and 2000), the minimal impact on sociology of over forty years of social science research about gays and lesbians is evident. And what little is presented only demonstrates the mainstreaming of the topics. Very little of what is published is used to challenge the

hegemonic structures of contemporary societies.

In Rodney Stark's (1998) seventh edition of his introductory book, not a single gay or lesbian topic is included in any chapter. The social movements chapter makes no mention of one of the most sustained and important organized series of attempts to reform public laws and policies to include equal rights for gays and lesbians. The chapters on gender, politics, religion, family, and urbanization totally ignore gay and lesbian concerns. At the other end of the continuum are textbooks by Anthony Giddens and Mitchell Duneier (2000) and Barbara Marliene Scott and Mary Ann Schwartz (2000), both of which include many examples, photos, and extended discussions on gay and lesbian issues. The former especially provides the best coverage with its many cross-cultural examples and definitions of homosexuality, a discussion of gay parenting and romantic relationships, and information about the biological and genetic debates about sexuality. The Scott and Schwartz textbook presents information on hate crimes and homophobia, social activism, gays in the military issues, and lesbian and gay families.

The remaining four texts give only token mentions of gay issues: Thio (2000), Ward and Stone (1998), and Thompson and Hickey (1999) mostly focus on gay parenting, marriage, and family topics (and two of them bringing up the ethical dilemmas of Laud Humphrey's [1975] infamous *Tearoom Trade* study), and Ferrante (2000) barely discuss anything but HIV/AIDS. In almost all of these cases, the coverage is decidedly mainstream, for example, by focusing on how gay men's and lesbians' relationships are really not that much different from heterosexuals' romantic and marriage alliances. Here is Thio (2000: 294) describing gay and lesbian 'marriages': 'Like heterosexuals, most gay men and lesbians want to get married when they are in love. Though denied the legal right to marry, they tie the knot in about the same way as their heterosexual counterparts.' No evidence is provided showing that 'most' gay men and lesbians want to get married in the 'same way' when in love. And almost nothing is given in this or the other textbooks about how domestic partnerships are barely recognized in most states and corporations, resulting in unequal work benefits, lack of visitation rights for the hospitalized, the absence of inheritance rights for partners, and the numerous other forms of discrimination that accrue to what the textbooks benignly call 'gay marriage' and blindly assume to be an almost equivalent alternative to heterosexual relationships.

Furthermore, virtually none of these textbooks focuses on the lack of federal and state protections against job and housing discrimination that continue to exist based on sexual orientation; the rise in hate crimes against gays and lesbians; the development of gay urban communities; the power of gay, lesbian, transgendered politics and social movements; and the diversity of sexual and friendship relationships. Nothing is presented in chapters on religion, work, socialization, culture, media, race/ethnicity, and aging. Queer theory is absent from the theory sections and the only reference in the methodology sections is about the dilemmas faced by Humphreys (1975) in his thirty-year old study on sex in public places. It is as if gay men and lesbians do not exist in any cultural context but rather live in one that is far away on the margins. Gay and lesbian topics, when presented at all, are limited primarily to chapters on gender and sexuality and family.

There continues to be the need to gain entry into the core sociological literature, but to sit back and accept these minimal crumbs of mainstream recognition is too short term a reaction. The question facing gay and lesbian and queer studies is how to *transform* that literature as well. It will not begin to happen until we are willing to risk studying a topic that seems to be avoided at all costs, namely, sexuality. When sex is discussed in these textbooks it seems to be only in terms of Humphreys' research, the debate on the genetic or biological origins of sexual orientation, or on the transmission of HIV. Issues about the everyday sexual lives of gay men and lesbians, including such topics as sexual partners, sexual identity, and sexual practices, remain mostly invisible.

Mainstreaming typically means studying the ways gays and lesbians are like everyone else – that is, studying everything but *sexuality*. This is somewhat ironic given the stereotypes of the highly sexualized gay male or portrayals as pedophiles and molesters. Although the rhetoric of those opposed to equality for gays and lesbians focuses on deviant sexuality, the research, writing, and public images created by both gay leaders and the academic world in their attempts to mainstream our lives tend to avoid any in-depth discussion of sexuality. But it is in the area of sexuality that the battle lines have been drawn. Some argue that if we study or talk mostly about the non-sexual aspects of gays' and lesbians' lives, we might be able to enter the academic and public mainstream. Or so the argument goes. I would instead proffer that the challenges facing gay/lesbian/queer studies in sociology revolve around how we take on the intellectual project of understanding human sexuality and using this knowledge to redirect the sociological imagination. Again Vaid (1995: 192) phrased it succinctly:

> Gay and lesbian sexuality remains the biggest obstacle to our full acceptance as human beings by the dominant heterosexual culture. We are hated because of how, with whom, and how much (mythic or real) we do it. To win against the right wing, we have to fight back on the sexual battleground, not run away from it. And to do this, we have to figure out how to talk in mixed company – heterosexual as well as across gender lines – about what sex means to us, about our sexual ethics and sexual morality, about our views on sexual promiscuity, and about our sexual secrets.

Vaid argues that no legal and legislative arguments have been successful that rely on the assertion of the normality of same-sex sexuality. Behavior-based arguments fail; status-based ones (especially in terms of minority status) tend to succeed. Vaid

(1995: 193) says: 'The heterosexual norm reacts to us as if every act of homosexual sex were an act of terrorism against heterosexuality.' And it is, she claims. Gays, lesbians, bisexuals, and transgendered people threaten the myth of universal heterosexuality, disrupt the sexist order that women exist to give pleasure to men, liberate the powerful force of sexual desire, and expose a limit to the power of the state and church. And what better examples are there of how the sociological imagination can effectively be refocused than with such topics?

SEXUALITY AND GAY/LESBIAN POLITICS

This absence of discussion on sexuality in sociology is not limited to academic writing. A few years ago some activists organized to counteract what they perceived was a growing anti-sexuality movement by some more assimilationist gay men and lesbians who pushed for a new ecology of relationships by seeking acceptance in the mainstream (Warner, 1999). Let's not air our dirty laundry in public; let's not talk about what we actually do in bed, they say. This desexualization of gay lives is not unique to the entertainment media or sociologists.

Evidence suggests an internecine culture war, one in which some gays encourage a moving away from issues of sexuality and exhibit an increasing concern with mainstream values and lifestyles, thereby exacerbating the inequalities that exist within gay and lesbian communities. A few years ago, Paul Horne and Sam Francis, two young white gay men, decided to launch *Hero,* a bimonthly magazine for gay men that does not include sexually explicit stories or advertisements, and one that emphasizes a pro-monogamy and pro-family outlook. In a *New York Blade* news story written by journalist Wayne Hoffman (1998: 21, 27), appearing in the 14 July 1998 edition, Horne is quoted as saying: 'We're not political, and we're not making a statement. We're just

gay men who are constantly bombarded with sex, and we've just reached a saturation point personally.' They want a magazine that is not 'sex-centric' although it will have sexy photographs. Hoffman wrote:

> *Hero* is part of what some observers say is a blossoming trend in gay media, where editors decide to forego sexually explicit content and make their PG-rated content a central selling point. Several new publications have made similar decisions, both to shift the editorial focus and to attract more mainstream advertisers.

Shawn O'Shea, the editor of the San Francisco biweekly *Spectrum*, was also quoted in the same article: 'We all felt a little uncomfortable selling advertisements that we knew to be blatant prostitution, I've got friends who are prostitutes and I don't put them down, but we want to be read by everybody, including children and families.' He is moving toward eliminating the sex ads, but replied that, 'It doesn't mean we're against sex. We just believe there's a proper time and place for everything. People don't put down *Time* or *Newsweek* for not having sexually explicit stories or advertisements.'

Rick Hyman, president of Netsurf Communications similarly wants to eliminate explicit sexual content and 'pornography' from a proposed gay and lesbian website, partly to attract 'mainstream advertisers, many of whom are uptight' and partly for editorial reasons: 'I think there's a silent majority of gays and lesbians who are tired of the sex, or not interested, or just want to have different experiences... For so long, we were just identified as a culture that was sex-obsessed. Gay people are now ready to say, "We want you to know who we really are"' (quoted in Hoffman 1998: 27).

Notice the implied construction of gays and lesbians as 'the other' – people uniquely obsessed about sexuality in comparison to heterosexuals, and the emergence of another marginal or 'other' category – but, this time within the so-called gay/lesbian community, resulting in a stratification of those who talk about sex and those who strive for mainstream respectability. Using words and phrases like 'silent majority', 'mainstream', 'a proper time and place'; invoking 'children and family'; and comparing the gay press to middle-of-the-road news weeklies, a new wave of young editors and web programmers are desexualizing the lives of gays and lesbians and replacing sex with images and stories that don't scare the masses. Imagine the howls of protest if the same rhetoric came from the Republican Christian right. We are, after all, just like everyone else, as if the heterosexuals were somehow asexual creatures who don't fixate on sex in their publications, movies, advertisements, and TV shows.

Certainly a latent (if not manifest) goal is to attract the advertisers who end up dictating what can be published and who sponsor many gay and lesbian organizations and events. What needs to be asked is who is developing the objectives and creating the impetus for our social movements – the advertisers or the activists? When Absolut Vodka sponsors so many gay and lesbian film festivals, organizational benefits, and gay pride marches, one wonders what the costs of mainstreaming really are. Are the goals to effect social change by questioning the hegemonic order or to provide potential gay and lesbian consumers for the products of capitalism? The arguments over the goals of the April 2000 Millennium March in Washington, DC, who was organizing the event, and what the effects of corporate sponsorship are, illustrate the divisions within the gay and lesbian communities about mainstreaming and commercialism (Gamson, 2000).

CREATING A SEXUALITY RESEARCH AGENDA

The mainstreaming of gay, lesbian, bisexual, and transgendered media images, social movements, and sociology textbook topics is a reflection of what is happening in gay and lesbian and queer studies. After all, textbook authors and television drama writers depend on the research and knowledge that come from the studies many social scientists

develop. But are those engaged in gay and lesbian research also desexualizing the field and avoiding questioning the larger structural issues? Are we also asking questions only within the limitations set by our 'sponsors', that is, the journals, textbook publishers, students, funding agencies, and tenure committees? Are we also running away from a focus on sexuality, afraid to tackle questions that might scare away the 'advertisers' and challenge the dominant order?

I see few studies that focus directly on gay and lesbian sexuality that have not been written by activists or journalists; not many of these are by sociologists. Outside of the research devoted to understanding AIDS, the number of published articles and books that delve into how gay men and lesbians think about, talk about, and 'do' sex is rare in sociology. Much of the interesting work on sexuality has been produced by lesbians: Pat Califia, Susie Bright, JoAnn Loulan, Gayle Rubin and Carole Vance some of whom participated in conferences as far back as 1982, such as the 'Towards a Politics of Sexuality' one at Barnard College in New York. Journalist Doug Sadownick and activist/scholar Eric Rofes have written about gay men's sexuality. But many of these writers are doing so outside the umbrella of sociology.

There have, of course, been some very influential sociological studies done on same-sex sexuality. One of the first studies was Laud Humphreys' (1975) *Tearoom Trade*. Focusing on impersonal and anonymous sex in public toilets, the study remains controversial, but more so for its methodology than its findings, as illustrated in the sociology textbooks. We still refuse to talk about sex, even when the study is about sex, and would rather debate how the data were collected. That study was first published thirty years ago, but other than a collection of articles organized by anthropologist William Leap (1999) how much more do we really know today about how people engage in sex, public or private, let alone who is participating in public sex? Yet debates among various gay groups about public sex proceed without the benefit of data and sociological analyses.

Some other research by sociologists over the years had same-sex sex as its central topic, such as Wayne Wooden and Jay Parker's (1982) research on sex between men in prisons and Wendy Chapkis' (1997) study on women who perform erotic labor. John Gagnon and William Simon's (1973) landmark book *Sexual Conduct: The Social Sources of Human Sexuality* has generated important research and concepts about scripting theory and sexuality. And Philip Blumstein and Pepper Schwartz's (1983) work provided one of the few empirical studies of how gay men and lesbians organize their sexual and romantic lives in comparison to heterosexual couples. It sometimes seems as if the biologists, or the literary culture crowd, or journalists have colonized the research and writing on sexuality. As Seidman (1996: 5) wrote in his history of sex studies in sociology, 'Through the mid-century, sociologists had surprisingly little to say about sexuality … [S]ociologists did not deploy their empirical techniques to study human sexuality.' His review of the indexes of the two leading sociology journals up until the early 1960s uncovered only fourteen articles in each journal under the headings of 'sex' or 'sexual behavior' and most of these did not address issues of sexuality. And it's only since 1998 that an academic journal, *Sexualities,* has had the shifting cultural and social nature of human sexuality as its primary mission (Plummer, 1998a).

Sociologists write about 'doing' gender and a lot has been produced about our social and political lives – and much of this work has been extremely important and necessary – but relatively little seems to be about sexuality, and certainly not in the way our sexuality contests heteronormativity and its assumptions about human sexuality. How ironic. Many would say that the only difference between homosexuals and heterosexuals is what people do and with whom in bed. Yet with the exception of the recent sex survey by Laumann et al. (1994) or the survey research from AIDS studies, we do not know much empirically about how gays and lesbians organize their sexual lives today and the subjectivity of diverse people

engaging in same-sex sex. We are a culture that likes to *talk* about sex, usually in sophomoric ways through mass media gossip, but one that doesn't want to *know* about sex, let alone same-sex sex.

Many erroneously conflate gender with sex, and get away from – or do not even include – any data that discuss sexual practices, desires, or constructions. Why are we so afraid to study sex? Has our wish to present gays and lesbians as more than people who are obsessed with sex affected the way we ask questions and conduct our research? This is somewhat understandable, given how frequently we are contained, harassed, and minimized by those trying to defeat us with simplistic and erroneous sexual information. Just look at the media attention to the problematic 'reparative therapy' that claims to change homosexuals into heterosexuals. But these attacks should only push us toward providing the empirical answers necessary to counteract the emotional diatribes and distortions about gay and lesbian lives.

INTEGRATING SEXUALITY AND SOCIOLOGY

I raise these concerns – and overstate them to a degree – in order to call attention to the omission of sexuality from academic and activist writings and to challenge us to think creatively about how we can generate new research in sexuality that can also be brought into the sociology canon without losing its transgressive edge. Those doing work in gay and lesbian and queer studies need to overcome the resistance to studying sex and develop research strategies that contribute in important ways to understanding all forms of sexuality. But how the profession will greet such research is a powerful concern. We need to challenge the profession of sociology to take seriously one of the most basic of human behaviors and social acts, and to embrace the study of sexuality as a core topic and not some marginal specialty, and one that could saliently transform the mainstream canon.

Where, then, is there work to be done? While some research exists here and there on the following topics, few systematic, scholarly, research projects have made these a central concern:

- How do young gay and lesbian people learn about sexual practices?
- What is considered a sexual act in same-sex interactions and who defines it?
- What is a fetish and how do gays and lesbians participate in various fetish subcultures?
- What is a 'type' and how do gays and lesbians become sexually attracted to various kinds of people (blondes, butch/femme, hairy, tall, interracial)?
- How do gays and lesbians of different races, religions, social classes, and ages, conceptualize various sexual acts (such as issues about penetration)?
- How do we tease out the differences among same-sex sexual desire, behavior, identity?
- What is the meaning for different gays and lesbians of various sexual practices, such as masturbation, anal intercourse, oral sex, and kissing?
- How do we understand attractions between large age differences (old for young, young for old)?
- What do we know about same-sex rape and sexual abuse?
- How effective is reparative therapy – what do we know about 'ex-gays'?
- Who chooses sexual celibacy and why?
- What do we know sociologically about gays and lesbians with high sex drives and those with low sex drives?
- How are multiple partners (simultaneously and sequentially) dealt with?
- How do gay and lesbian elders deal with their sexuality as it changes with age?
- What do we know about impotency among gays and lesbians?
- How much do we know about sex among same-sex friends?
- What is the role of 'fuck buddies' in gays' and lesbians' lives?
- How frequent is sex between lesbians and gay men?

- Who is engaging in same-sex sex in public places and doing what?
- What is the role of pornography for gays and lesbians?
- How is the Internet being used for same-sex sex, cybersex in chat rooms as well as making dates, and viewing pornography?
- What do we know about the role of 'escorts' and 'masseurs' and who answers the ads?
- How much is known about street hustlers today and other forms of male prostitution and sex tourism?

Among all the valuable research on how gay men and lesbians organize their social, political, and psychological lives, these questions rarely are addressed in any depth. Although several such studies are underway and some scholars are developing these topics, especially outside of the United States, they generally do not constitute the central focus of today's researchers. Rather, the mainstreaming of gay and lesbian research has led us to seek answers about fitting in to the existing organizational structures and institutions of society. Thus, to study what some argue is the unique aspect of gays and lesbians, namely how we 'do' sex, not only challenges the place at the table, but also raises questions about the table itself.

Researching same-sex sexuality has the potential to provide intriguing ideas about the complex social dimensions of sexuality for all people, not just gay, lesbian, bisexual, and transgendered people, and to raise provocative insights that take us beyond a psychologizing and biologizing of human sexuality. It is a way of making us ask questions about the mainstream without selling our souls to become a part of it.

REFERENCES

Blumstein, Philip and Schwartz, Pepper (1983) *American Couples: Money, Work, Sex.* New York: Morrow.
Chapkis, Wendy (1997) *Live Sex Acts: Women Performing Erotic Labor.* New York: Routledge.
D'Emilio, John (1983) *Sexual Politics, Sexual Communities.* Chicago: University of Chicago Press.

Ferrante, Joan (2000) *Sociology: The United States in a Global Community.* fourth edn. Belmont, CA: Wadsworth.

Fiske, John (1987) *Television Culture.* New York: Routledge.

Gagnon, John and Simon, William (1973) *Sexual Conduct: The Social Sources of Human Sexuality.* Chicago: Aldine.

Gamson, Joshua (2000) 'Whose Millenium March?' *The Nation.* April 17: 16–20.

Giddens, Anthony and Duneier, Mitchell (2000) *Introduction to Sociology.* 3rd edn. New York: Norton.

Hoffman, Wayne (1998) 'Sex and sensibility: gay media turn away from sex in an effort to woo advertisers and attract new readers.' *New York Blade,* July 17: 21–27.

Humphreys, Laud (1975) *Tearoom Trade: Impersonal Sex in Public Places.* Enlarged edn. Hawthorne, New York: Aldine de Gruyter.

Laumann, Edward, Gagnon, John, Michael, Robert, and Michaels, Stuart (1994) *The Social Organization of Sexuality.* Chicago: University of Chicago Press.

Leap, William (ed.) (1999) *Public Sex, Gay Place.* New York: Columbia University Press.

Nardi, Peter M. (1997) 'Changing gay and lesbian images in the media', in James Sears and Walter Williams (eds), *Overcoming Heterosexism and Homophobia: Strategies That Work.* New York: Columbia University Press. pp. 427–42.

Nardi, Peter M. (1999) *Gay Men's Friendships: Invincible Communities.* Chicago: University of Chicago Press.

Plummer, Ken (1998a) 'Introducing *Sexualities*', *Sexualities,* 1 (1): 5–10.

Plummer, Ken (1998b) 'The past, present, and futures of the sociology of same-sex relations', in Peter M. Nardi and Beth E. Schneider (eds), *Social Perspectives in Lesbian and Gay Studies: A Reader.* London: Routledge. pp. 605–14.

Quindlen, Anna (2000) 'The right to be ordinary', *Newsweek,* 11: September 82.

Rotello, Gabriel (1997) *Sexual Ecology: AIDS and the Destiny of Gay Men.* New York: Dutton.

Scott, Barbara Marliene and Schwartz, Mary Ann (2000) *Sociology: Making Sense of the Social World.* Boston: Allyn and Bacon.

Seidman, Steven (ed.) (1996) *Queer Theory/Sociology.* Cambridge, MA: Blackwell.

Signorile, Michelangelo (1997) *Life Outside: The Signorile Report on Gay Men.* New York: HarperCollins.

Stark, Rodney (1998) *Sociology.* 7th edn. Belmont, CA: Wadsworth.

Stein, Arlene and Plummer, Ken (1994) 'I can't even think straight: "queer" theory and the missing sexual revolution in sociology', *Sociological Theory,* 12 (2): 178–87.

Sullivan, Andrew (1996) *Virtually Normal.* New York: Vintage Books.

Thio, Alex (2000) *Sociology: A Brief Introduction.* 4th edn. Boston: Allyn and Bacon.

Thompson, William E. and Hickey, Joseph V. (1999) *Society in Focus: An Introduction to Sociology.* Third edn. New York: Longman.

Vaid, Urvashi (1995) *Virtual Equality: The Mainstreaming of Gay and Lesbian Liberation.* New York: Anchor Doubleday.

Ward, David A. and Stone, Lorene H. (1998) *Sociology for the 21st Century.* 2nd edn. Dubuque, IA: Kendall/Hunt.

Warner, Michael (1999) *The Trouble with Normal: Sex, Politics and the Ethics of Queer Life.* New York: Free Press.

Wooden, Wayne and Parker, Jay (1982) *Men Behind Bars: Sexual Exploitation in Prison.* New York: Plenum.

4

Unusual Fingers

Scientific Studies of Sexual Orientation

LYNDA BIRKE

Animal models have indicated that [hormones] acting before birth might influence the sexual orientation of adult humans ... we examine the ... pattern of finger lengths, and find evidence that homosexual women are exposed to more prenatal androgen than heterosexual women are; also, men with more than one older brother, who are more likely than first-born males to be homosexual in adulthood, are exposed to more prenatal androgen than eldest sons. (Williams et al., 2000: 455)

some scientists have begun to view both heterosexuality and homosexuality as natural variations of the human condition that are at least as deeply rooted in nature as in nurture. (Hamer and Copeland, 1994: 20)

Questions about the origins of homosexuality would be of little interest if it were not a stigmatized behavior. We do not ask comparable questions about 'normal' sexual preferences, such as preferences for certain physical types or for specific sexual acts that are common among heterosexuals. (Hubbard and Wald, 1993: 95)

Gay genes, different length fingers – the biology of homosexuality seems to be rather newsworthy. What science has to say about

who we are may seem quite distant from our everyday lives. But it matters profoundly because not only does science seek to define how we came to be as we are, but it has also offered attempts at cures aimed at eradicating homosexuality.

If homosexuality is indeed just another 'natural' variation of sexuality, then it may be reasonable for scientists to study how it develops – as the quote from Hamer and Copeland suggests. They might then look for a gene which seems to predispose a man to be gay, or ask whether lesbians have been exposed to high levels of the hormones called androgens. But whether or not it is 'natural', homosexuality has also been a stigmatized behaviour; indeed, all non-procreative sexual practices are condemned and vilified by some people. That social/cultural context profoundly influences the choices scientists make to study one phenomenon rather than another: it is 'deviant' sexualities, not heterosexuality, which is called into question.

My aim in this chapter is to sketch out some of the ways in which science has dealt with the idea of homosexuality. 'Science' (by which I mean the natural sciences, notably biology in this context) is a word we usually take to mean the study of the natural world; it includes, among other things, certain methods, devices and narratives which help to give it its authoritativeness. Thus, to say that something is scientific is to give it great significance in our culture; we believe something more easily if there seems to be 'objective proof'.

Yet whatever its claim to objectivity, science is not neutral; its practitioners live in a particular historical period, in a particular culture. That history and culture influence how they generate hypotheses, how they interpret data, and whether and how they obtain funding or publication. Thus, in a climate in which massive international funding goes to 'mapping' genomes and moving bits of DNA around, 'the' gene has become a powerful cultural icon (Nelkin and Lindee, 1995); it is then hardly surprising that geneticists search for all kinds of genes – including those putatively determining our sexuality.

Throughout this chapter, therefore, I try to locate ideas in their social and cultural context. Although I outline various theories about the biological bases of homosexuality, I argue that there is little evidence of any such biology. But that is not to say that our biology is never involved in our sexuality (which, after all, is often expressed through our biological bodies); rather, we have yet to find ways of talking about biology and sexuality that are liberatory and not determining.

Among other things, biomedicine has drawn heavily on cultural stereotypes of homosexuality that collapse sexual orientation and behaviour onto stereotypical notions of gender division. On the whole, the scientific literature is concerned with what makes someone *a* homosexual; and not just a homosexual, but a gender-stereotyped one. So, the personae of the scientific stories are the effeminate gay man and the butch lesbian. Thus, the scientists reporting on finger length started from the assumption that lesbians had been masculinised by hormones in the womb. What these stereotyped characters actually do is not at issue; it is their (our) lesbian/gay identities, their *essences*, that matter.

Michele Ana Barale has written that 'heterosexuality … seeks to create lesbians whose desires are as apprehensible as its own … the lesbian body itself is made the site for such self-depiction' (Barale, 1991: 237). Science lends authority to such re-creation, telling tales of homosexual desire as a reflection of heterosexual desire, but a desire in which something is amiss. Thus, in many scientific narratives, lesbian desire is understood in terms of masculinity, and markers of such masculinity have been sought in lesbians' biological bodies.

Both heterosexuality and masculinity are the dominant narratives in scientific tales (Butler, 1993; Fausto-Sterling, 1997). That is one reason why the question, 'what makes us gay?' can be asked; for we *are* the other to the heterosexual norm. Without that binary opposition between heterosexual and homosexual, the question would have little meaning. Thus, scientific stories seek out that which is amiss with the lesbian/gay body – what is 'other' about it – be that parts of the brain or parts of the chromosomes.

These are the reasons why I write primarily about homosexuality rather than drawing on more recent concepts of queer, which have little or no parallel in biomedical discourse. Here, the division is usually simply hetero/homosexual, male/female. While some areas of science have recognised greater diversity (sexology, for example, has historically tried to map out sexual diversity), the search for biological *causes* of sexual variation has been mired in dichotomies. Nature, it would seem (or at least as it is described by many scientists) has no space for gender as performance, or as multiple (see Butler, 1993).

Despite newer ideas about sexualities and multiplicity in the wider culture, there has been a recent upsurge of interest in biological *bases* of homosexuality: but why now? Addressing these questions raises, I would argue, crucial Zissues for lesbian and gay studies; although our academic inquiry has included discussion of essentialism (Fuss, 1989; Stein, 1992), we have directly addressed science and its claims much less often. Given the hegemony of the 'new genetics', we need to know whether claims about 'gay genes' really help to reduce discrimination against us, as some have argued. Or do such claims merely reinforce the same tired, old, prejudices? And, if we find fault with them, is simply rejecting or ignoring biology the only answer? Could lesbian/gay studies benefit from a less polarised view of the place of biology? These are themes that I want to draw out in this chapter.

SCIENCE ... IN CONTEXT

Before going into details of scientific theories, however, I want to address a few questions about science. Science has enormous authority; within Western culture, we are more likely to believe claims if they are 'scientific' than if they derive from other frameworks. That is why recent claims about putative 'gay brains' or 'gay genes' are so significant: they were claims made by scientists and published in prestigious journals. As a result, they were widely heralded in the media, which further enhances scientific authoritativeness;[1] headlines typically emphasise that 'scientists have found such-and-such', thus reinforcing the notion that what science creates is certainty. When researchers at the National Institutes of Health in the USA located a gene associated with increased male-to-male courtship among *Drosophila* flies, it was reported as a 'gay gene' in fruit flies (e.g. Highfield, 1995). No matter that this has nothing to do with humans, the headline implies a similar genetic mechanism to that claimed for gay men: 'the' gay gene.

Part of the process of doing science is to construct persuasive arguments. It is not enough just to do the experiments. You must also persuade other scientists (perhaps especially those opposed to your views), as well as people outside the labs. Science is, among other things, a form of rhetoric (Gross, 1990). To persuade requires constructing written and verbal forms that, basically, deflect any potential counterclaims (Latour, 1987).

In addition, scientific arguments rely on material produced by apparatus in the labs – what Bruno Latour (1987) calls the output from inscription devices. To be persuasive, a scientist must draw on tables, graphs, and so on, from some device set up to measure something. Merely observing that 'x affects y' is not enough – you have to demonstrate it quantitatively through graphs: indeed, laboratory work is largely organised around ways of '"framing" a phenomenon so that it *can* be measured and mathematically described' (Lynch, 1990: 170, emphasis in original). In other words, what actually happens in laboratories is not only observation of 'nature' (if, indeed, it *is* nature once inside the lab: Knorr-Cetina, 1983) but also practices which set up 'nature' in measurable ways.

Scientists, moreover, must learn not only to produce such inscriptions, but also to read them. Learning to 'read' nature through apparatus is a central part of scientific training. You have to learn how to see down a microscope, for instance, and how to interpret what you see – even if all you actually see at first is a reflection of your own eyeball (Keller, 1996). In learning to read scientific diagrams, you must learn to generalise from the specific (the particular tissue you see under the microscope, say) to the general (a diagram of 'the' ovary, for example). I am stressing these themes from recent sociological studies of science because they are relevant to thinking about biology and homosexuality. How we learn to read scientific images matters when the paper in question shows us photographs of, say, 'gay brains'. What is it that we are seeing? What does it do to label the fuzzy lines on a photograph as representing 'gay brains'? What has gone into the production of this photograph, and to whom is it directed?

Historically, scientific arguments about homosexuality have assumed that it is a problem whose origins need to be understood. Such assumptions have helped both to 'frame the phenomenon', and to define homosexual behaviour as 'unnatural'. That homosexuality has largely meant stigmatised behaviours contributed to the selling power of the arguments; on the whole, the history of science's involvement in lesbian and gay lives has been a sorry one.

A crucial step in scientific involvement was the development of 'the homosexual' as a specific kind of person (by contrast to homosexual behaviour, which anyone could engage in). Ideas about 'the' homosexual developed particularly during the nineteenth century, alongside theories of evolution, thus setting the scene for speculation about what might *cause* a person to become lesbian or gay.

Biological theories about homosexuality waxed and waned during the twentieth century. Once identified in the early decades of the century, the 'sex hormones' for example, became a focus for several decades. These are the hormones produced by the gonads – ovaries and testes – and which bring about the secondary sexual characteristics at puberty: were these, scientists wondered, the cause of deviant sexualities? But whatever the explanatory potential of these theories, they also contributed to various attempts to use hormones to 'cure' homosexuals of their deviant behaviour (alongside other interventions, including surgery).

Such ideas became less prominent in the wake of the women's and gay liberation movements in the 1970s. Now, there was more emphasis on the ways in which sexuality and gender might be socially constructed. But however useful this move was in counteracting earlier medical abuses, it also allowed anti-gay campaigners to argue that, if it were not 'natural', then we could all just stop sinning and become happy heterosexuals.

That reaction helped to usher in a third phase of scientific theories. Over the last decade, various attempts have been made (often by gay scientists) to trace some biological basis. Brains and genes, rather than hormones, are now explicitly the focus. The recent surge of writing about the putative genetics of homosexuality rests, inevitably, upon the dramatic development – and

power – of the new genetics (Terry, 1997: 288). Through genetic manipulation, 'nature' now offers the prospect of manipulating organisms, of changing their genetic potential. In that sense, Terry suggests, nature and science may seem to be more liberating to some scientists than nurture which may be 'imagined as hostile, hopeless and homophobic' (ibid.: 289).

Underlying these recent claims about gay genes or gay brains (and 'gay' here usually means male homosexuality; lesbians, perhaps fortunately, are typically missing from these accounts) is the belief that homosexuality is, indeed, natural. If it occurs as a variant of brain structure, if the gene can be demonstrated within the variations of the human genome, if homosexual behaviour can be demonstrated in other animal societies, then it occurs 'within nature' and should be accepted as such, advocates believe.

Yet what is 'natural'? Much of the literature searching biological correlates of sexuality assumes that demonstrating a biological link means that 'deviant' sexuality becomes 'natural'. I am always suspicious of this word, 'natural', which covers up a great deal. Does natural mean good, as in so many advertisements for different kinds of food? Does natural imply normal, which can convey both statistical and moral overtones? Or does it mean something that is in 'Nature' with connotations of separation of nature from culture?[2]

One problem with invoking nature is that it frequently implies biological determinism – that is, the notion that some aspects of a person's behaviour are somehow rooted in – caused directly by – their biology. This concerns me because biological determinism tends to arise in arguments defending rigid, traditional roles of gender and sexuality – the kind of rigidity that feminists and others have fought for so long. We all know the kind of thing: hormones that predispose the females among us to the ironing board, or males to the company board.[3]

Apart from my being hostile to such claims for political reasons, they also concern me because of the practical consequences that have followed in the past from such beliefs, such as, for example, attempts to 'cure' homosexuality. I see no reason to be complacent now, or to assume that there will be no more such attempts in the future. I will return to the critiques of biologically determinist ideas later in the chapter, after considering the scientific theories in more detail.

SCIENTIFIC STORIES

There are, inevitably, many interconnecting threads within the various stories science tells about sexuality. To follow them, I want to separate them out into two parts. I do so because they draw on slightly different theories and assumptions; there is, however, a great deal of overlap. One thread follows the story of the sex hormones – from their initial discovery and their mapping onto sex/gender to their links with the organisation of the brain. Here, we find stereotypes of gender divisions re-emerging into molecules; no matter that hormones are just molecules, biomedical stories have allocated them gender: androgens are now routinely referred to as 'male' hormones even though we all produce them (Spanier, 1995). We can find assumptions of 'natural' behaviours – allegedly allocated, of course, to one or the other sex. So, mounting behaviour by a rat is portrayed as masculine and heterosexual, even though females often do it too. We also encounter the mapping of what might be termed the 'homosexual body', defined as measurably different from its heterosexual counterpart (Terry, 1999).

The second thread follows stories of genes and evolution. Here, theories usually assume that the highest aim of organisms is reproduction; individuals must spread their genes around by reproducing. So, the question arises: how did homosexuality (assumed not to lead to many offspring) evolve? Why do the putative genes for it persist? And if they exist, can they be found in other kinds of animals? Again, these questions make assumptions about what constitutes 'natural' behaviours, but they also suggest natural types – those who possess certain genes. Here, it is not the body (as we perceive it) that is directly being mapped, but the hidden codes of DNA that helped to create it. These reified bits of DNA acquire characteristics – the gay gene, the gene for learning disabilities – that can be passed on to any offspring we may have.

THE HORMONAL IMPERATIVE

The notion of homosexuals as a 'third sex', intermediate between men and women, was mooted in the late nineteenth century. It is usually attributed to Karl Ulrichs, who sought greater acceptance for homosexuals like himself, through his emphasis on the homosexual person rather than practices, and based his theory on study of hermaphrodites (Kennedy, 1997). To Ulrichs, being attracted to men indicated a female psyche; so, he hypothesised, homosexual men may have a male body, but the mind of a woman. This notion – that *sexuality* must be either female or male – has persisted. It surfaces in the feelings expressed by many people seeking transsexual transformation, because they feel that their psyches are trapped in the wrong (i.e. of the 'other' sex) body. It surfaces, too, in scientific theories about sexuality and gender.

During the early years of the twentieth century, the search for biological markers of homosexuality focused on external anatomy. This was framed within the normative assumption of two sexes; thus, doctors sought indicators of 'mannishness' in lesbians, such as an enlarged clitoris,[4] or evidence that gay men were physically effeminate (Gibson, 1997; Terry, 1999). The equation is a simple and all too familiar one: to be gay/lesbian is to be partly the 'other' sex.[5]

Running parallel to this search for anatomical markers was the discovery of the steroid sex hormones in the early twentieth century (Hall, 1975; Fausto-Sterling, 2000).

The significance of the gonads (ovaries and testes) had been known for some time – animals, after all, were routinely castrated and the consequent behavioural changes known. But once scientists had identified the steroid hormones, it became possible to attach specific molecules to the actions of the gonads. The steroid hormones, produced by ovaries, testes and adrenals, are androgens (hormones such as testosterone), oestrogens (e.g. oestradiol) and progestins (e.g. progesterone). What differentiates men and women is the average amounts of each kind produced; there is no absolute difference.

Despite that, these molecules were quickly labelled as gendered-names that are with us still, as we habitually refer to 'male' or 'female' hormones (Oudshoorn, 1994; Wijngaard, 1997). That these hormones were characterised as strictly dualistic is not, perhaps, surprising; there has been a long history of reading gender (and other) stereotypes onto nature – molecules are no exception (Schiebinger, 1994; Spanier, 1995).[6] Steroid hormones were being named, moreover, at a time of much debate about the status of women, and of feminist challenges to gender stereotypes (Rosenberg, 1982; Fausto-Sterling, 2000). Although scientists were forced, by the 1930s, to recognise that the steroids did not map quite so easily onto two sexes as they had previously thought,[7] the legacy of the binary division remains.

The locus of gendered dualism has shifted, however, from the gonads to the brain. That is, where previously scientists sought direct causes in hormones produced by adult gonads, they now focus attention on indirect effects before birth. From the 1960s on, scientists have focused on the idea that hormones affect the brain long before the foetus is born, bringing about permanent structural change. And once changed, the brain itself can be 'masculine' or 'feminine' in its response during adulthood to circulating hormones, according to this hypothesis of brain organisation. In studies of laboratory animals, scientists might measure this by measuring the kind of behaviour the animal shows when it is adult (assuming that behaviour can reliably be designated as masculine or feminine[8]).

Part of the context in which the shift to organisation theory took place was the rapid post-war development of ideas borrowed from control systems. Bodies became increasingly portrayed as elaborate machines, their internal processes as tightly controlled systems (see Birke, 1999). The endocrine system was no exception; feedback controls the output of ovaries and testes, via the brain and its own hormones. That is, hormones produced by the gonads (ovaries or testes) are carried by the blood to the brain; there, they influence (feedback) the output of the brain's own hormones, from the hypothalamus. These in turn control the amount of hormones produced by the gonads. It is a self-controlling 'system'. This emphasis on feedback systems implies that deviation from a particular point must be corrected (so allowing for possibilities of external control, through drugs).[9] It also shifted the focus of attention onto the brain, as *the* organ controlling the whole system.

So, sex hormones in the rest of the body became less important than prenatal organisation of the brain by sex hormones for theorists of how gender develops. I say gender here, because that was indeed the primary focus – how we become male or female. How we become gay or straight was, as usual, seen as a *product* of that initial dichotomy. Given the way that gender duality is so often confounded with sexual orientation, it was perhaps inevitable that the idea of hormonal differentiation of the brain would be extrapolated to homosexuality. If brains of men and women differ, the reasoning goes, then so might the brains of homo- and heterosexual folk.

One example of such thinking was Simon LeVay's much publicised claim to have identified 'gay brains' (LeVay, 1991). More precisely, he claimed that he had found differences in a small area of the brain between straight and gay men.

Central to LeVay's claims is the organisation hypothesis – the belief that the brain has been permanently reorganised by sex hormones prior to birth, in ways that will later determine the person's sexual orientation. In the case of gay men, the bit of the brain allegedly involved was smaller than its equivalent in straight men; this area is a small nucleus, the INAH3,[10] of the hypothalamus at the base of the brain. LeVay put the claims more graphically in a later book, when he suggested that gay men simply do not have the brains for straight sex (LeVay, 1993).

The assumptions underlying these claims are unsurprising. First, LeVay starts from the premise that the part of the hypothalamus he studied is involved in sexual orientation, on the basis of other experiments in which the mounting behaviour of rats was altered by damage to similar areas, indicating – some scientists believed – that the animals' sexuality was affected. Second, he refers to claims that parts of the INAH are smaller in women than men (although studies looking at the INAH have reported contradictory results). Third, his study supposes that it is logical to move from these claims to homosexuality. The logic runs thus: gay men and heterosexual women have in common that they are attracted to men. So, he reasoned, perhaps there was something similar between them in the way that their brains have developed.

There are many problems with this line of thought. For a start, the relationship between human sexuality, sexual orientation and gender is immensely complex, involving multiple cultural responses to particular situations. That is partly why some feminist authors have insisted on viewing gender as performance (e.g. Butler, 1993). Gender and sexuality are not something given but are constantly being acted out, performed, recreated. So, what is it that LeVay might be measuring when he says that there are differences in the hypothalamus related to sexual orientation?

It is also notoriously difficult to extrapolate from data from laboratory animals.[11] Interfering with the hormone levels of prenatal or infant rats does alter their later behaviour. Blocking androgens ('male' hormones) in male baby rats makes them less likely to mount (defined as male behaviour) when they are adults. According to some authors (e.g. Dorner, 1976), these interventions created a homosexual rat, because these animals were willing to accept the advances of other males – as does a female in oestrus.[12]

Now the problems, in turn, with that are the underlying assumptions. These are (i) that it is quite simple behaviourally to distinguish 'male' and 'female' behaviour. But, with the possible exception of the physical act of putting a penis into a vagina, there are no behaviours which are the preserve of only one sex. (ii) That homosexual behaviours never occur among non-human animals (also a dubious assumption); and (iii) that only the rat accepting the mounting (female-like) was homosexual. Curiously, Dorner never used the word homosexual to describe the other (male) rat who did the mounting. Possibly that was the rat equivalent of the married man who goes cottaging then denies vociferously any homosexual tendencies.

Even if different studies did agree that there was a consistent difference between the brains of gay and straight people (and even if we could be sure that such pure types of people exist[13]), then what does it mean? The brain is a highly complex and malleable organ, responding continually to change. Any possible difference might just as well be the product of rather different lifestyles (in the case of the LeVay study, many critics pointed to the fact that the brains he obtained from gay men were from men who died of AIDS, which may well have influenced the brain). Or it might have something to do with preferred sexual practices, not sexual orientation *per se*. Or, it might have something to do with the type of partner (not his/her sex): facetiously we might ask whether there is a bit of the brain associated with falling for people with blond hair, or large biceps, or a preference for leather.

Just what *are* scientists measuring when they search for biological bases? They may locate differences in the gross structure of the brain. But differences with respect to what? Any difference in size of particular structures between one brain and another is not of interest *unless those differences* can be made to *mean* something. That is, the brains have to be given meaning through being allocated to particular categories – categories which in turn have meaning within a particular culture. Just as, in the nineteenth century, brain size and shape were linked to race and gender (Genova, 1989), now gender and sexuality are mapped onto specific areas of the brain – because these are significant social categories. There is much less invested culturally in whether your preferences are for large biceps than there is in whether you are gay. And it would be meaningless to focus on gay/straight brains if you were a scientist from a (hypothetical) culture in which divisions of gender and sexual orientation did not exist or did not matter.

Size of structures, moreover, must be defined: where do you measure from? Many structures in the brain do not have clearly defined boundaries separating them – at least to the untrained eye. So before measurements are possible, there has to be consensus about what defines the boundaries of (say) nuclei in the hypothalamus; where do clusters of one type of cell stop and the next start? Similarly, much of the criticism levied against studies reporting gender differences in the corpus callosum (the bands of nerve fibres connecting the two hemispheres of the brain) has centred on discrepancies in what was being measured (Gallo and Robinson, 2000). Anne Fausto-Sterling, analysing scientists' attempts to map the corpus callosum (CC), notes that 'the neuroscientist who wants to study the CC must first tame it – turn it into a tractable, observable, discrete laboratory object … But … this process fundamentally alters the object of study' (Fausto-Sterling, 2000: 120–1).

Not only does extracting and fixing brain tissue forever change it, but measuring three-dimensional structures is tricky. One lab may measure a swelling in the bulbs of the corpus callosum in a different place or way than another lab; one scientist may see significance in one axis of measurement and another see none. In other words, how you read the images you produce is crucial to the findings.

These issues are central to analysing LeVay's study. What he produced in the paper were photomicrographs of thin slices of tissue taken from the hypothalamus of the sampled brains. To most people, these seem to be little more than a random pattern of dots (the nerve cells) and a few interconnecting squiggles (the nerve axons). It is then a leap of imagination to see in these squiggles and dots an area that can be defined as larger in one brain than another. What is significant is that the reader of a scientific article is indeed expected to make that 'leap of imagination': that is crucially part of the rhetoric of science.

The photographs help to 'frame' the phenomenon (difference in brain cells), and thus to define it; once described in this way it is no longer a specific photograph of cells from one specific brain, but must be generalised to constitute 'the' homosexual brain. What are, in practice, possible differences in degree (quantitative differences in the volume of this area of brain) become categorised as differences of type (qualitative differences) – simply because they are defined as 'belonging' to one category or another (gay vs. straight).

Whatever we might think about the search for some marker of homosexuality in the brain, that search relies on notions of brain organisation by hormones long before birth. In turn, that depends on concepts of control systems; implicit here is the idea that the control systems have somehow not worked quite right, their balance is awry. And it is that point that concerns me; while the argument that we are a bit different biologically can be – and has been – used to argue for tolerance, it can also imply that any kind of difference equals not-quite-fitting pathology. For what that can mean in turn is both biological justification for discrimination and for seeking medical 'cures' or 'preventions'.

And it is us – the 'deviants' – whose bodies and lives are thus pathologised: there has been no search for the hormonal or genetic bases of queer-bashing.

GENES AND EVOLUTION

Another approach to seeking homosexuality 'in nature' is to look for patterns between individuals. Scientists might, for instance, look at patterns of homosexuality within families – one approach to asking whether homosexuality might be genetic. These questions gain new potency in the context of genetic manipulation and mapping, which might enable scientists precisely to pinpoint 'the' gene for homosexuality.

Another way of seeking patterns is to ask more general questions about what kinds of animals exhibit homosexual behaviour, and thus ask, how did homosexuality evolve in humans? Thinking about where species came from was altered dramatically and for ever in the nineteenth century by the idea of evolution. Rather than positing that a deity created all kinds of creature (including gay ones), evolutionary theory supposed that animals and plants evolved, through change, from earlier forms. Darwin suggested that this occurs through natural selection; that is, some individuals are able to survive better and so reproduce more successfully, passing on their traits to their offspring.

If species change over time, then how have particular forms evolved? In what ways are they adapted to their environments that allow them to survive? Ancestral giraffes, for example, must have included a few individuals with slightly longer necks; these were better able than their short-necked peers to get at nutritious vegetation higher up. So, they did better and left more offspring. Over time, more and more long-necked animals appeared – natural selection in operation. Similar arguments can be made about other types of organism; how have they evolved?

Inevitably, given the notion of 'the' homosexual as a type,[14] evolutionary theorists have asked about homosexuality (see Ruse, 1982). They start from the assumption that homosexuals generally have fewer offspring; if so, how could homosexuality evolve? Any genes that favoured it ought, the theory goes, to disappear over time as they confer no reproductive advantage.[15]

Homosexuality, then, is like altruism: both present problems to the serious Darwinian theorist, because neither apparently immediately enhance the individual's chances of surviving to reproduce.[16] Homosexuality may be explained in various ways within the theory (see Ruse, 1982, 1988) but all confront the same problem, that homosexuality is neither unitary nor unchanging through history. So just what, exactly, is it that theorists are trying to explain? Merely having a tendency towards homosexuality could be completely ineffective in bringing about evolutionary change – you could have that tendency and still be married and reproduce heterosexually (as many women have had to do throughout history).

Whichever explanation might be favoured, modern evolutionary theories require genetics. Although Darwin had pondered how traits might be inherited, the idea of 'the gene' developed later, from the beginning of the twentieth century. Gradually, it came to represent not only an inheritable trait (like having blue eyes) but also a specific bit of the molecule of DNA (Gudding, 1996). Once the molecular structure of chromosomes was established (comprising centrally the double helix structure of DNA), scientists sought to 'map' the chromosomes, that is, to establish links between particular stretches of DNA and particular characteristics of an organism. Their ability to map chromosomes took off, however, after scientists developed new methods for moving bits of DNA around[17] – the basis of what is loosely called genetic engineering.

For much of the last century, however, studies claiming a genetic link to homosexuality were relatively rare (Allen, 1997). Indeed, it was not until the 1990s that genetic causes of homosexuality hit the headlines. First came studies reporting a greater than expected incidence of male homosexuality among identical twins[18] (Bailey and Pillard, 1991; Pillard, 1997). The use of twins to infer inherited traits is controversial, and this was no exception (see Hubbard and Wald, 1993; Terry, 1997). Bailey and Pillard studied families with identical twins, non-identical twins and pairs of adoptive brothers, to see if there was a correlation between degree of relatedness and homosexuality. If one brother of a pair was gay, and if the trait is substantially genetic, then you would expect to find that the other brother of identical twins is frequently also gay. This, Bailey and Pillard reported, was what they found: 52 per cent of their sample of 56 pairs of identical twins were both gay.

The twin study was quickly followed by Dean Hamer's report, widely publicised as identification of a 'gay gene'. What Hamer and his colleagues had done was to search for a genetic marker, that is, a particular stretch of DNA that might occur more often in homosexual men. Locating a genetic marker is not the same as identifying 'the' gene for something; it implies only that the scientists have found a bit of DNA that seems to be inherited along with the possible gene – like having a rainbow flag attached to your front door. So, if they are looking for a specific gene implicated in a particular genetic disease, they might identify a marker – a bit of DNA – that is close to the gene involved in the disease. By tracking the marker,[19] they may learn more about the inheritance of the disease. Hamer's team looked specifically for markers on the X chromosome, which males inherit from their mothers. Again, they compared pairs of gay brothers to a group of unrelated men. For most such possible markers, there was very little similarity between the two brothers; but, for one tiny bit of DNA, called Xq28, DNA from the two brothers was very similar indeed – much more so than would be expected by chance. What this could mean is that Hamer's team had identified a marker which tends to be inherited more often than expected in homosexual

brothers; the team were careful not to say that this was a cause (although Hamer's later book [Hamer and Copeland, 1994] was subtitled 'The Search for the Gay Gene', so implying direct causation).

'Genes' are not, in practice, all that easy to locate on specific stretches of DNA, whatever we might suppose from media reports of 'new breakthroughs' in genetics. A few genes have been identified through their involvement in particular inherited diseases, such as cystic fibrosis. But much DNA is not so readily identified, and a great deal of it has no known function at present.[20] If scientists move a piece of DNA, and the organism then develops a particular trait, they may not necessarily have moved *the* gene *for* that particular trait; many things might influence how a characteristic develops.

Claims that homosexuality is genetic have, however, faced problems from the belief that '"Animals don't do it, so why should we? … If none of the lower orders engage in sex with the same gender, the motivating factor for homosexuality must not be genetic"' (letter to Dean Hamer, quoted in Hamer and Copeland, 1994: 213). In other words, the writer of the letter believed that homosexuality is purely a human behaviour, not seen in any other species; if so, the writer implied, it could not be biological. Hamer's response to that accusation was to argue that animals are not good role models, even for heterosexuality (they don't date or frequent strip bars, for example).

Another response, of course, is to point to the large number of examples of non-heterosexual behaviour among non-human animals. Bruce Bagemihl's recent book, *Biological Exuberance* (1999) reviews evidence for homosexual behaviour in a wide array of species – mammals and birds, particularly. Its significance, the cover blurb tells us, is that it is a book 'that definitively crushes the argument that homosexuality is not natural'.

Bagemihl draws upon a wide array of scientific studies which have noted (usually in passing or in a footnote) examples of animal behaviour that do not fit the standard model of reproductive heterosexuality. Needless to say, scientists who observed such behaviour, or the pairing of two animals of the same sex to hatch eggs ('lesbian gulls', for instance), have had a tough time; most commonly, they have tried to explain it all away (perhaps one of the animals is not really that sex? Perhaps there were no males around, so the gulls paired up to make the best of a bad job?). Or – of course! – perhaps one of the gulls is a bit too masculine.

A predominant narrative of modern biology is reproduction and the need to pass on the genes. Here, 'nature' is not so much red in tooth and claw (as the saying has it), as forever pregnant. Given that, it is hardly surprising that *any* non-procreative behaviour is simply not seen, or is classified as something else. So, if a female mammal licks the genitals of another female, or if one male sucks the penis of another, biologists are likely to interpret the behaviour as 'social'. 'Sex' is what happens when penises enter vaginas.

Bagemihl suggests otherwise. There are a plethora of examples of overt sexual practices (involving genital manipulation, say) between animals of the same sex, and many more examples of same-sex pairs engaging in rearing offspring, or maintaining lifelong affectional bonds (for a recent example, see Vasey et al., 1998).

Bagemihl compiled data for thousands of species, from a wide range of scientific sources. In that sense, his work has authority simply from the sheer volume of studies on which he draws, even if most of these do not overtly focus on homosexuality in their texts. I commented earlier on the need for students of science to learn 'how to see'. Like learning to see the photograph of hypothalamic cells, the observer of animal behaviour must learn to see or understand what animals do through the dominant set of ideas – in this case, the notion that reproductive success ensures the lineage of one's genes. Because of that, *any* form of non-reproductive behaviour may not be 'seen' as sexual by observing scientists.

Bagemihl's book, however, is aimed at a more popular audience. And it gains persuasive power for readers particularly through the use of photographs and line drawings, illustrating different kinds of animals engaging in various forms of non-procreative behaviour.[21] So, we 'learn to see' homosexuality in nature, to interpret pictures as evidence of its existence. I emphasise this not because I necessarily doubt the pictures, but to stress that we, the readers, are collaborating in producing a story. In the case of this book, that story is about the prevalence of homosexuality in nature, but what does that mean for us?

BIOLOGY AND HOMOSEXUALITY

The last decade of the twentieth century was dubbed the Decade of the Brain; however, one might as well call it the decade of the Search for Homosexual Biology.[22] The long quest continues, for instance, for hormonal causes; two recent instances concern lesbian ears (a study which claimed a difference between lesbian and heterosexual women in specific hearing tasks, McFadden et al., 1998), and our hands, shaped before birth by exposure to testosterone.

If the idea of a lesbian ear lends itself to jokes, then even more so the idea of lesbian finger length (specifically, the ratio of length of first and third fingers; lesbians allegedly often have similar ratios to heterosexual men; Williams et al., 2000). In both cases, the researchers point out that the lesbian traits are similar to those of heterosexual men; hence, the argument goes, lesbians must have been masculinised before birth (the part of the brain involved in hearing, or our hands). Of course, the culprit has to be 'too much' testosterone – lesbians again becoming quasi-men.

So, yet again in the scientific literature, we who are lesbian or gay are cast as an 'intermediate' sex, we are mannish women or effeminate men. Sexuality is once again collapsed onto gender (or, rather, an assumed gender dichotomy), and the diversity of sexual and personal expression among our communities ignored. On the contrary, the biological theories, by basing themselves in binary assumptions, act to *reinforce* those assumptions of rigid gender divisions. And isn't that what we have been trying to move away from in recent years?

Nor does invoking biology get rid of that other prevalent notion that homosexuals are contagious. On the contrary, the genetic story reinvents contagion, through the reproductive narrative of 'spreading genes around'. And it is just that sense of contagion which shadows the new genetics and the notion of a 'gay gene'. For the stated remit of the Human Genome Project is the eradication of genetic diseases, by techniques of genetic engineering to remove problem genes (Bodmer and McKie, 1994). Locating a gene raises the spectre of prenatal diagnoses of 'homosexuality' in a foetus, and subsequent abortion. To be sure, some people may choose the other way, and try to have a foetus bearing the 'gay gene'. But in a largely homophobic society, there is a powerful danger of coercion to abort foetuses with the putative gene – not only because the parent does not want to raise a homosexual child (see Murphy, 1997), but also as a result of societal pressure to reduce the incidence of the gene (genetic contagion). In that sense, the rise of modern genetics has helped to reinforce the possibility of medical intervention.

The recent renaissance of biological theories about homosexuality has many sources. The AIDS epidemic (which facilitated the idea of contagion), the power of Christian fundamentalists in the USA (who believe we are all sinners), as well as the growing economic power of gay men – all these have contributed to this biological backlash against the social constructionism of the 1970s (Terry, 1997).

At the same time, there have been changes within biomedicine. One of these is that medicine no longer accepts degrees of intersexuality at birth; instead, newborns must be allocated to one or the other sex, and surgically altered to fit (see Fausto-Sterling, 2000). Not only does this reinforce binary assumptions about the sexed body, but it also reinforces assumptions that sex and sexuality reside *in* the body.

Alongside that, there has been intense effort to map and to manipulate genes, creating a climate in which 'the gene' is increasingly powerful, as well as fear-provoking (Turney, 1998). One consequence is that 'the gene' has become equivalent to identity, defining who we are (Nelkin and Lindee, 1995: 198). It is hardly surprising, in these changing contexts, that this powerful icon answers a need among some in our communities to find ways of explaining ourselves, to be able to say, 'it's not my fault'.

Jennifer Terry sees this surge of research, however, as a 'swan song of economically comfortable white men ... Maybe biology is a more comforting way to narrate their desires than to make sense of them in terms of cultural and historical contradictions, conflicts, and contingencies' (1997: 288). But, she points out, that claim has proved to be no help at all to troubled, young, working-class men for whom the suggestion of an inbuilt biological trait can sometimes be 'one more reason to commit suicide rather than live in a world so hostile to their desires' (ibid.: 289, citing Acqueno, 1993). So, biology may indeed provide comfortable explanations for some; for others, it poses profound threats, with its implications that everything is fixed. Indeed, there is precious little evidence that alleged biological bases help stop bigotry; all kinds of people have been, and continue to be, persecuted because of their 'biology' (Hubbard and Wald, 1993; Stein, 1998).

Why do some among us so want to find scientific explanations? What is it about 'being homosexual' that requires explaining biologically in a way that 'being heterosexual' does not? We are, suggests historian of science Donna Haraway (1991), obsessed in Western culture with origin stories – tales of creation, of our roots. Seeking biological causes is but one version of that obsession, fuelled by the growing power of genetics.[23] But the trouble with these stories is precisely that they suggest fixity. What worries critics of biological arguments is that, in such tales, we become little more than puppets on a string, acting out the dictates of DNA or hormones. Think about media representation of Hamer's experiments, for example. These very quickly became the discovery of 'the gay gene', reported as something which 'made us gay'. It is 'the' gene which has, uniquely, determined who we are.

But what seems to happen when critics reject biological determinism is that the pendulum swings over to emphasis on social constructionism (see Stein, 1992) – that we become gay through the way that society constructs notions of gender/sexuality. In this account, biology is largely irrelevant to our human development. Social constructionism has, moreover, been seized on by the religious right and interpreted as 'choice' (rather like consumer choice), and used as a justification for homophobia: if it is not biological, they argue, then it is a choice for sinning which we can, should we wish, correct. So, we can swing from theories of genetics to choice and back again – either/or, take your pick.

It's a dilemma for any sociological reflection on who we are, not only for lesbian/gay/transgendered people. Lesbian and gay studies, however, has generally had little to say specifically about biology. To be sure, it has addressed essentialism in general; some writers, such as Diana Fuss (1989), have argued, for example, for less polarity between essentialism and social constructionism. But the search for biological bases continues to maintain the binary, and continues to be insufficiently addressed in our academic inquiry. What is more, the stories of biological bases further perpetuate medical assumptions that gender and sexuality are themselves simple binaries, to be reinforced through surgical 'corrections' of newborns' genitals. Where do these assumptions leave those people who are born intersex?

Certainly, one way out of the dilemma of either biology *or* social constructionism is to look for ways of acknowledging biological factors without assuming them to be

determining (eg. Benton, 1991; Rose, 1997; Birke, 1999). After all, biology must be involved in some ways: *something* affected the length of my fingers before I was born, whether or not that was lesbian hormones. It is precisely this that, I would argue, lesbian and gay studies needs to address in more detail, to ask the question: how might biology be relevant to our inquiries *without* invoking determinism and fixity?

What is happening in the stories of genetic imperative, is that *agency* disappears. By that I mean not only conscious choices and decisions, but also the agency of our bodies; for example, as we grow from a fertilised egg, we change and engage with our own environment in bodily, biological ways. That process is partly biological, partly everything else, all interacting. It thus may be that biological processes are, in some ways, part of the events on the path leading to particular forms of expression of sexuality: but they do not determine. That is important to emphasise, partly because I think it is just a more accurate way to think about biology – as potentially participatory and liberatory but not determining (see also Allen, 1997; Rose, 1997).

Yet could this help overcome the impasse between biological determinism and social constructionism? A number of biologists now seek to attack biological determinism by pointing to the complexity and subtlety of nature's processes. Evolution, for example, can act not only at the level of individuals and their genes, but also at the level of the group; organisms moreover can co-evolve, changing each other in the process.[24] The task now for lesbian and gay theorists, then, is to find ways of bringing these ideas into our theory, to challenge determinist concepts of biology.

Among those who have emphasised complexity in nature and thus begun this task, is Bruce Bagemihl, in his narration of homosexual diversity among animals. He argues that the various expressions of sexuality and gender among other animals illustrates the extragavance, the exuberance, of biological systems (1999: 215). Like several other scientists, he draws on recent ideas about complexity and how order can arise out of (apparent) chaos (see Kaufman, 1995). While most of this scientific work remains far removed from lesbian and gay studies, its relevance here is that it makes room for understanding the world not as simple events (A causes B) but as multiple, complex and pluralistic. So, developing as a gendered individual is a product of many layered and interacting processes.[25]

It seems to me that this vision of multiplicity fits our world of disparate sexualities and genders far, far, better than the predominant ideas drawn from science. Assuming that some people do want to ask questions about where sexualities come from, perhaps we do not have to choose between extremes of biological determinism and social constructionism, bouncing from one to the other like a pendulum. But we will not be able to find a middle ground if we cannot find ways of integrating a more liberatory understanding of biology. If we follow Bagemihl's lead, we can insist on different ways of understanding nature, ways that illustrate extravagance and pluralism. In that world, multiple sexualities are commonplace and there is no pressure (perhaps no need) to agonise over 'how we got to be that way'. But if ideas are going to be borrowed from biology, how much better that it is not the notion that we are all puppets on (genetic) strings. I would much rather be exuberant.

NOTES

1 Nelkin (1987) discusses media coverage of science and technology, asking not only how and why journalists cover particular stories but also how scientists themselves market their stories through press releases.

2 Nature/culture dualism has a long history, and has been much debated. See Soper (1995) and Horigan (1990) for discussion.

3 As I usually avoid ironing, I do find it irritating to come across the claim that females-liking-ironing is all down to biology. See Birke (1999). Am I a lesbian because I lack the crucial ironing genes?

4 There is some irony in this, given the way in which the clitoris was usually missing from anatomy textbooks: such omissions continue. See Moore and Clarke (1995).

5 Throughout the medical literature, sexual orientation is collapsed onto binaries of gender (feminine vs. masculine) and biological sex (male vs. female). No matter that none of these categories *is* absolutely dichotomous (not even biological sex); scientific accounts assume a simple binarism. Not only that, but they also assume that there is a simple relationship between each binary category. Femme lesbians, masculine gay men, or any kind of transgender person, have no place here.

6 Reading existing social divisions onto nature reflects who gets to do science. Early in the Scientific Revolution, relations of gender and race became deeply embedded in the practices of science: its practitioners had to belong to certain categories of class, gender, sexuality. As Donna Haraway cogently observes, 'God forbid the experimental way of life have queer foundations' (Haraway, 1997: 30).

7 The discovery of oestrogens in the urine of that symbol of virile potency, the stallion, shook up previous simple assumptions, as did the discovery that androgens must often be converted into oestrogens in the body for them to have their 'masculine' effects: see Oudshoorn (1994).

8 This is doubtful; again, few behaviours in animals are the sole preserve of only one sex. It is also doubtful that hormones alone are responsible – the behaviour of other animals can affect how an animal grows up (see Birke, 1989).

9 Usually, this is beneficial; giving insulin injections to diabetic people helps to correct their internal feedback of blood sugar levels, for example. But it does open up possibilities of less ethical interventions, such as giving a child a drug to inhibit growth hormones if s/he is growing 'too much'. Here, too, the drug is one which affects feedback controls.

10 The Interstitial Nucleus of the Anterior Hypothalamus. The hypothalamus is organised into various areas, or nuclei, which seem to have slightly different functions within the brain.

11 Speculations about the biological roots of human behaviour always trap themselves in the quagmire of animal examples. But we cannot ever study animal societies without bringing to bear our own cultural expectations; as Donna Haraway (1989) notes, the history of our closest relatives, the other primates, is also a history of how gender, race and colonialism have been read onto nature. The example of 'homosexual rats' is just another instance of ways in which the production of ideas in science emerges *from* a particular culture and historical moment. 'Homosexual rats' are deviant rats; and they are deviant because they have been defined as such through a process of labelling hormones, bodies and brains as dualistically gendered.

12 Female rats only usually accept male mounting when they are in heat (oestrus), but not at other times. And contrary to assumptions that this is purely passive, female rats tend to control much of the encounter.

13 One of the many criticisms of LeVay's study has been that he could never know whether any of the bodies had been of exclusively gay or straight people. His samples came from bodies of people who had died of AIDS;

his classification of 'gay' relied on personal disclosure in medical records, that HIV had been transmitted through homosexual sex. But what if that had been a relatively rare gay encounter, in an otherwise 'heterosexual' life?

14 Interestingly, Morris (1993), in his examination of the work of Oscar Wilde, suggests that it was not ideas of natural selection so much as concepts of Victorian degeneracy which led to anti-gay legislation, directed against a specific type of person. This was, he argues, part of a late nineteenth-century reaction against the implications (for the nuclear family) of Darwinian natural selection.

15 Note that this argument is meant to apply to change over evolutionary time – many millennia. It is only very recently that humans have been able to separate sex and reproduction fairly effectively, and to develop specific forms of reproductive technologies. There has not been enough time for that to exert any impact on evolution.

16 Altruism is usually explained by supposing that it has evolved as a form of helping your relatives (with whom you share genes). But that theory does not explain the recent observation that chimpanzee males tend to form co-operative groups of unrelated males: Mitani et al. (2000).

17 This required new methods, developed in the 1970s and 1980s, of amplifying tiny fragments of DNA, as well as new techniques for 'snipping' the molecule in specific places.

18 Identical (monozygotic) twins have more-or-less identical DNA. Non-identical twins (dizygotic) have 50 per cent of their DNA in common, as do other siblings or parent and child.

19 That is, scientists can track the patterns of DNA in tissue samples taken from members of different generations of a family.

20 Such pieces are called 'junk DNA', because they have no purpose (yet) known to scientists.

21 Greg Myers (1990) notes how the persuasive power of drawings and photographs is enhanced through the interpretive work readers of popular scientific texts must do – reconstructing the story that the pictures of animals, and accompanying text, set up.

22 It is the specific focus on *homo*sexuality in the research that concerns me. Perhaps we do need more research on sex, as Dean Hamer and Peter Copeland urge (1994: 220–1), especially as so many lives have been lost to AIDS. But there remains a dearth of research on *sexuality*: it is we, the deviants, who are always the focus.

23 Significantly, modern narratives of genetics embody many themes of creation drawn from our Judaeo-Christian heritage: see Newman (1995) for discussion.

24 For many years, the notion of group selection was discredited; many evolutionary theorists, however, now believe that evolution operates through many different mechanisms simultaneously, including selection at the level of the whole population. See Rose (1997).

25 Anne Fausto-Sterling (2000) argues for an understanding of multiple sexes, based on her analysis of the complex processes involved in creating sexed bodies. It is

a cultural conceit that we demand only two, she points out, and that generates much suffering as people are forced into binary straitjackets.

REFERENCES

Acqueno, F. (1993) Remarks at Out/Write Conference on Lesbian and Gay Writing and Publishing, Boston, MA (cited by Terry, 1997).

Allen, G.E. (1997) 'The double-edged sword of genetic determinism: social and political agendas in genetic studies of homosexuality, 1940–1994', in V.A. Rosario (ed.), *Science and Homosexualities*. London: Routledge.

Bagemihl, B. (1999) *Biological Exuberance: Animal Homosexuality and Natural Diversity*. London: Profile Books.

Bailey, J.M. and Pillard, R.C. (1991) 'A genetic study of male sexual orientation', *Archives of General Psychiatry*, 48: 1089–96.

Barale, M.A. (1991) 'Below the belt: (un)covering the *Well of Loneliness*', in D. Fuss (ed.), *Inside/Out: Lesbian Theories, Gay Theories*. London: Routledge.

Benton, T. (1991) 'Biology and social science: why the return of the repressed should be given a (cautious) welcome', *Sociology*, 25: 1–29.

Birke, L. (1989) 'How do gender differences in behavior develop? A reanalysis of the role of early experience', in P. Bateson and P. Klopfer (eds), *Perspectives in Ethology, Vol 8: Whither Ethology?* New York: Plenum Press.

Birke, L. (1999) *Feminism and the Biological Body*. Edinburgh: Edinburgh University Press.

Bodmer, W. and McKie, R. (1994) *The Book of Man: The Quest to Discover our Genetic Heritage*. London: Little Brown.

Butler, J. (1993) *Bodies that Matter: On the Discursive Limits of 'Sex'*. London: Routledge.

Byne, W. and Parsons, B. (1993) 'Human sexual orientation: the biologic theories reappraised', *Archives of General Psychiatry*, 50: 228–39.

Dorner, G. (1976) *Hormones and Brain Differentiation*. Amsterdam: Elsevier.

Fausto-Sterling, A. (1997) 'How to build a man' in V.A. Rosario (ed.), *Science and Homosexualities*. London: Routledge.

Fausto-Sterling, A. (2000) *Sexing the Body: Gender Politics and the Construction of Sexuality*. New York: Basic Books.

Fuss, D. (1989) *Essentially Speaking: Feminism, Nature and Difference*. London: Routledge.

Gallo, V. and Robinson, P. (2000) 'Is there a "homosexual brain"?' *Gay and Lesbian Review*, Winter: 12–15.

Genova, J. (1989) 'Women and the mismeasure of thought', in N. Tuana (ed.), *Feminism and Science*. Bloomington, IN: University of Indiana Press.

Gibson, M. (1997) 'Clitoral corruption: body metaphors and American doctors' constructions of female homosexuality, 1870–1900' in V.A. Rosario (ed.), *Science and Homosexualities*. London: Routledge.

Gross, A.G. (1990) *The Rhetoric of Science*. Cambridge, MA: Harvard University Press.

Gudding, G. (1996) 'The phenotype/genotype distinction', *Journal of the History of Ideas*, 57: 525–45.

Hall, D.L. (1975) 'The critic and the advocate: contrasting British views on the state of endocrinology in the early 1920s', *Journal of the History of Biology*, 9: 269–85.

Hamer, D. and Copeland, P. (1994) *The Science of Desire: The Search for the Gay Gene and the Biology of Behavior*. New York: Simon and Schuster.

Hamer, D.H., Hu, S., Magnuson, V.L., Hu, N. and Pattatuchhi, A.M.L. (1993) 'A linkage between DNA markers on the X chromosome and male sexual orientation', *Science*, 261: 321–7.

Haraway, D. (1989) *Primate Visions: Gender, Race and Nature in the World of Modern Science*. London: Routledge.

Haraway, D. (1991) 'The contest for primate nature: daughters of Man-the-Hunter in the field, in D. Haraway, *Simians, Cyborgs and Women: the Reinvention of Nature*. London: Routledge. pp. 81–108.

Haraway, D. (1997) *Modest_Witness@Second_Millennium: FemaleMan meets OncoMouse*. London: Routledge.

Highfield, R. (1995) '"Gay Gene" found in fruit flies', *Electronic Telegraph*, 6 June.

Horigan, S. (1990) *Nature and Culture in Western Discourses*. London: Routledge.

Hubbard, R. and Wald, E. (1993) *Exploding the Gene Myth*, Boston, MA: Beacon Books.

Kauffman, S. (1995) *At Home in the Universe: The Search for the Laws of Complexity*. Harmondsworth: Penguin.

Keller, E.F. (1996) 'The biological gaze' in G. Robertson, M. Mash, L. Tickner, J. Bird, B. Curtis and T. Putnam (eds), *FutureNatural: Nature/Science/Culture*. London: Routledge.

Kennedy, H. (1997) 'Karl Heinrich Ulrichs, first theorist of homosexuality', in V.A. Rosario (ed.), *Science and Homosexualities*. London: Routledge.

Knorr-Cetina, K. (1983) 'The ethnographic study of scientific work: towards a constructionist interpretation of science' in K Knorr-Cetina and M. Mulkay (eds), *Science Observed: Perspectives on the Social Study of Science*. London: Sage.

Latour, B. (1987) *Science in Action*. Buckingham: Open University Press.

LeVay, S. (1991) 'A difference in hypothalamic structure between heterosexual and homosexual men', *Science*, 253: 1034–7.

LeVay, S. (1993) *The Sexual Brain*. Cambridge, MA: MIT Press.

Lynch, M. (1990) 'The externalized retina: selection and mathematicization in the visual documentation of objects in the life sciences', in M. Lynch and S. Woolgar (eds), *Representation in Scientific Practice*. Cambridge, MA: MIT Press.

McFadden, D. and Pasanen, E. (1998) 'Comparisons of the auditory systems of heterosexuals and homosexuals: click-evoked otoacoustic emissions', *Proceedings of the National Academy of Sciences*, 95: 2709–13.

Mitani, J.C., Merriweather, D.A. and Zhang, C. (2000) 'Male affiliation, cooperation and kinship in wild chimpanzees', *Animal Behaviour*, 59: 885–93.

Moore, L.J. and Clarke, A.E. (1995) 'Clitoral conventions and transgressions: graphic representations in anatomy texts, c1900–1991', *Feminist Studies*, 21: 255–301.

Morris, A.R. (1993) 'Oscar Wilde and the eclipse of Darwinism: aestheticism, degeneration, and moral reaction in late-Victorian ideology', *Studies in History and Philosophy of Science*, 24: 513–40.

Murphy, T.F. (1997) *Gay Science: The Ethics of Sexual Orientation Research*. New York: Columbia University Press.

Myers, G. (1990) 'Every picture tells a story: illustrations in E.O. Wilson's *Sociobiology*', in M. Lynch and S. Woolgar (eds), *Representation in Scientific Practice*. Cambridge, MA: MIT Press.

Nelkin, D. (1987) *Selling Science: How the Press Covers Science and Technology*. New York: W.H. Freeman and Company.

Nelkin, D. and Lindee, M.S. (1995) *The DNA Mystique: The Gene as a Cultural Icon*. New York: W.H. Freeman and Company.

Newman, S. (1995) 'Carnal boundaries: the commingling of flesh in theory and practice', in L. Birke and R. Hubbard (eds), *Reinventing Biology*. Bloomington: University of Indiana Press.

Oudshoorn, N. (1994) *Beyond the Natural Body: An Archeology of Sex Hormones*. London: Routledge.

Pillard, R.C. (1997) 'The search for a genetic influence on sexual orientation', in V.A. Rosario (ed.), *Science and Homosexualities*. London: Routledge.

Rosario, V.A. (ed.) (1997) *Science and Homosexualities*. London: Routledge.

Rose, S. (1997) *Lifelines: Biology, Freedom, Determinism*. Harmondsworth: Penguin.

Rosenberg, R. (1982) *Beyond Separate Spheres: Intellectual Roots of Modern Feminism*. New Haven, CT: Yale University Press.

Ruse, M. (1982) 'Are there gay genes? Sociobiology and homosexuality', in N. Koertge (ed.), *Philosophy and Homosexuality*. New York: Harrington Park Press.

Ruse, M. (1988) *Homosexuality*. Oxford: Basil Blackwell.

Schiebinger, L. (1994) *Nature's Body: Sexual Politics and the Making of Modern Science*. Boston: Beacon Books.

Soper, K. (1995) *What is Nature?* Oxford: Blackwell.

Spanier, B. (1995) *Im/Partial Science: Gender Ideology in Molecular Biology*. Bloomington, IN: Indiana University Press.

Stein, E. (ed.) (1992) *Forms of Desire: Sexual Orientation and the Social Constructionist Controversy*. London: Routledge.

Stein, E. (1998) 'Choosing the sexual orientation of children', *Bioethics*, 12: 3–24.

Terry, J. (1997) 'The seductive power of science in the making of deviant subjectivity', in V.A. Rosario (ed.), *Science and Homosexualities*. London: Routledge.

Terry, J. (1999) *An American Obsession: Science, Medicine and Homosexuality in Modern Society*. Chicago: University of Chicago Press.

Turney, J. (1998) *Frankenstein's Footsteps: Science, Genetics and Popular Culture*. New Haven, CT: Yale University Press.

Vasey, P.L., Chapais, B. and Gauthier, C. (1998) 'Mounting interactions between female Japanese Macaques: testing the influence of dominance and aggression', *Ethology*, 104: 387–98.

Wijngaard, M.v.d. (1997) *Reinventing the Sexes: The Bio-Medical Construction of Femininity and Masculinity*. Bloomington, IN: Indiana University Press.

Williams, T.J., Pepitone, M.E., Christensen, S.E., Cooke, B.M., Huberman, A.D., Breedlove, N.J., Breedlove, T.J., Jordan, C.L. and Breedlove, S.M. (2000) 'Fingerlength ratios and sexual orientation', *Nature*, 404: 455–6.

5

Heterosexuality: It's Just Not Natural!

CHRYS INGRAHAM

Since I began teaching courses on gender and sexuality in the early 1980s, I've struggled with debates that claim that heterosexuality is both 'natural and normal'. As a sociologist, I frequently find such positions lacking in that they fail to attend to the social conditions upon which most things depend. In other words, the question is not whether (hetero)sexuality is natural. *All* aspects of our social world – natural or otherwise – are given meaning. The real issue is, how we give meaning to heterosexuality and what interests are served by these meanings?

Consider for example, the case of the child born with the genitalia of both sexes. In some societies to be born a hermaphrodite is revered – the Dine – while in other societies – the United States, for example – this condition is viewed as a deformity in need of correction. Our society signals to the child (and to their family) that they are not natural, born wrong, a mistake of nature, in need of correction. Correction, according to the medical science establishment, includes surgically changing the child's genitalia to either male or female, prescribing hormone medication, and providing socialization counseling to assist the child to become 'appropriately' gendered. For little girls this means learning how to act feminine and for little boys it means learning how to act masculine.

What is it about this condition that elicits the need for intervention? The behaviors the child must learn are integral to the gendered division of labor – what girls and boys learn is their place in relation to the institution of heterosexuality. Without a systematic analysis of this institution various questions go unanswered. For instance, is it possible that there are really more than two sexes? What is really 'natural' here? Why is it that in this instance we allow society to intrude on 'the natural'? What is it about sexual identity that our society is so invested in that it sees this procedure as necessary? But more importantly for the broader question at hand, who decides what counts as appropriate and necessary and under what conditions is their authority legitimate? It is cultural meaning systems that determine (with our agreement, of course) what counts as natural or unnatural. And it is cultural meaning systems that regulate what should be the 'proper' treatment or response to anything 'inappropriate' or 'unnatural'.

Historically, we have witnessed the scientific establishment determine which phenomena can be considered normal and natural only to turn around years later and say they were wrong or that their judgement was premature. Consider the instance of women's entry into higher education. At a time when white middle-class women entering higher education was frowned upon, nineteenth-century scientists discovered that women's reproductive organs would be harmed if they were exposed to a college education. And, in an historical moment when the notion of former slaves being equal to whites was not a popular notion, it was scientists who claimed that people of African descent had smaller brains than those of European lineage. In each case, scientists succumbed to the political interests of their time in formulating and interpreting research on such topics. As social conditions shifted, so too did scientific discovery. In each instance, scientists eventually overturned their previous findings in the face of overwhelming evidence to the contrary.

To argue then for a biological or 'natural' explanation seems to me to be a dead end. It is much more important and useful to ask: Regardless of whether sexuality (or anything for that matter) is naturally occurring, how does our culture give it meaning? In other words, how do we give meaning to (hetero)sexuality? How have we organized it? The question then becomes *not* whether heterosexuality is natural, and therefore 'normal', but, rather how do cultural meaning systems work to normalize and institutionalize heterosexuality? And, more importantly, what interests are served by these processes? In other words, who benefits from the ways we've named, defined, and organized sexuality?

Typically studied as a form of sexuality, heterosexuality is, in reality, a highly regulated, ritualized, and organized set of practices, e.g. weddings or proms. Sociologically, then, heterosexuality as an established order made up of rule-bound and standardized behavior patterns qualifies as an institution. Moreover, heterosexuality as an arrangement involving large numbers of people whose behavior is guided by norms and rules is also a *social* institution.

Heterosexuality is much more than a biological given or whether or not someone is attracted to someone of another sex. Rules on everything from who pays for the date or the wedding rehearsal dinner to who leads

while dancing, drives the car, cooks dinner or initiates sex, all serve to regulate heterosexual practice. What circulates as a given in western societies is, in fact, a highly structured arrangement. As is the case with most institutions, people who participate in these practices must be *socialized* to do so. In other words, women were not born with a wedding gown gene or neo-natal craving for a diamond engagement ring! They were taught to want these things. Women didn't enter the world with a desire to practice something called dating or a desire to play with a 'My Size Bride Barbie', they were rewarded for desiring these things. Likewise, men did not exit the womb knowing they would one day buy a date a corsage or spend two months' income to buy an engagement ring. These are all products that have been sold to consumers interested in taking part in a culturally established ritual that works to organize and institutionalize heterosexuality and reward those who participate.

HETERONORMATIVITY

In the 1970s as second wave feminists attempted to theorize and understand the source of women's oppression, the notion of heterosexuality as normative emerged. In one of the earliest examples of this effort, The Purple September Staff, a Dutch group, published an article entitled 'The normative status of heterosexuality' (1975). They maintain that heterosexuality is really a normalized power arrangement that limits options and privileges men over women and reinforces and naturalizes male dominance.

Ti-Grace Atkinson (1974), The Furies Collective, Redstockings (1975), Rita Mae Brown (1976), and Charlotte Bunch (1975) all contributed to these debates by challenging dominant notions of heterosexuality as naturally occurring and by arguing that heterosexuality is instead a highly organized, social institution rife with multiple forms of domination and ideological control:

Heterosexuality – as an ideology and as an institution – upholds all those aspects of female oppression ... For example, heterosexuality is basic to our oppression in the workplace. When we look at how women are defined and exploited as secondary, marginal workers, we recognize that this definition assumes that all women are tied to men ... It is obvious that heterosexuality upholds the home, housework, the family as both a personal and economic unit. (Bunch, 1975: 34)

In this excerpt from Charlotte Bunch, the link between heterosexuality and systems of oppression is elaborated.

While many of these arguments were made by heterosexually-identified feminists, some of the more famous works were produced by lesbian feminists, making a link to the interests of both feminism and lesbian and gay rights. Adrienne Rich's essay 'compulsory heterosexuality and lesbian existence' (1980), a frequently reprinted classic, confronts the institution of heterosexuality head on, asserting that heterosexuality is neither natural nor inevitable but is instead a compulsory, contrived, constructed and taken-for-granted institution which serves the interests of male dominance.

Historians need to ask at every point how heterosexuality as institution has been organized and maintained through the female wage scale, the enforcement of middle-class women's leisure, the glamorization of so-called sexual liberation, the withholding of education from women, the imagery of high art and popular culture, the mystification of the personal sphere, and much else. We need an economics which comprehends the institution of heterosexuality, with its doubled workload for women and its sexual divisions of labor, as the most idealized of economic relations. (ibid.: 27)

Understanding heterosexuality as compulsory and as a standardized institution with processes and effects is what makes Rich's contribution to these debates pivotal.

Monique Wittig's 'The category of sex' (1976), takes the argument to a different level, declaring heterosexuality a political regime. The category of sex, she argues, is the political category that founds society as heterosexual:

As such it does not concern being but relationships ... The category of sex is the one that rules as natural the relation that is at the base of (heterosexual) society and through which half of the population, women, are heterosexualized ... and submitted to a heterosexual economy ... The category of sex is the product of a heterosexual society in which men appropriate for themselves the reproduction and production of women and also their physical persons by means of a contract called the marriage contract. (Wittig, 1992: 7)

This regime depends upon the belief that women are sexual beings, unable to escape or live outside of male rule.

These positions signal a paradigm shift in how heterosexuality is understood, challenging the very centrality of institutionalized heterosexuality and beginning the work of offering a systematic analysis of heterosexuality. When queer theory emerged in the 1990s, these critical analyses of heterosexuality were revisited and reinvigorated (e.g. Butler, 1990; de Lauretis, 1987; Fuss, 1991; Hennessy, 1995; Ingraham, 1994; Jackson, 1996; Sedgwick, 1990; Seidman, 1991, 1992, 1995; Warner, 1993; Wittig, 1992). In his anthology *Fear of a Queer Planet*, Michael Warner rearticulated these debates through his creation of the concept of 'heteronormativity'. According to Warner:

So much privilege lies in heterosexual culture's exclusive ability to interpret itself as society. Het culture thinks of itself as the elemental form of human association, as the very model of inter-gender relations, as the indivisible basis of all community, and as the means of reproduction without which society wouldn't exist ... Western political thought has taken the heterosexual couple to represent the principle of social union itself. (1993: xxi)

In this same passage Warner relates his notion of heteronormativity to Wittig's idea of the social contract. For Wittig the social contract is heterosexuality. 'To live in society is to live in heterosexuality ... Heterosexuality is always there within all mental categories' (1992: 40). Like whiteness in a white supremacist society, heterosexuality is not only socially produced as dominant but is also taken-for-granted and universalizing.

Steven Seidman in his introduction to the ground-breaking work *Queer Theory/ Sociology* (1996) assesses the role of queer theorists in developing a new critical view of normative heterosexuality. Given the history of sociology as a 'de-naturalizing force', he argues that it is time for queer sociologists to de-naturalize heterosexuality as a 'social and political organizing principle'. Seidman asserts that the contribution of queer sociology is to analyse normative heterosexuality for the ways it conceals from view particular social processes and inequalities.

Drawing on these early arguments heteronormativity can be defined as the view that institutionalized heterosexuality constitutes the standard for legitimate and expected social and sexual relations. Heteronormativity insures that the organization of heterosexuality in everything from gender to weddings to marital status is held up as both a model and as 'normal'. Consider, for instance, the ways many surveys or intake questionnaires ask respondents to check off their marital status as either married, divorced, separated, widowed, single, or, in some cases, never married. Not only are these categories presented as significant indices of social identity, they are offered as the only options, implying that the organization of identity in relation to marriage is universal and not in need of explanation. Questions concerning marital status appear on most surveys *regardless of relevance.* The heteronormative assumption of this practice is rarely, if ever, called into question and when it is, the response is generally dismissive. (Try putting down 'not applicable' the next time you fill out one of these forms in a doctor's office!)

Or try to imagine entering a committed relationship without benefit of legalized marriage. We find it difficult to think that we can share commitment with someone without a state-sponsored license. People will frequently comment that someone is afraid to 'make a commitment' if they choose not to get married even when they have been in a relationship with someone for years! Our ability to imagine possibilities or

to understand what counts as commitment is itself impaired by heteronormative assumptions. We even find ourselves challenged to consider how to marry without an elaborate white wedding. Gays and lesbians have participated in long-term committed relationships for years yet find themselves desiring state sanctioning of their union in order to feel legitimate. Heteronormativity works in all of these instances to naturalize the institution of heterosexuality while rendering real people's relationships and commitments irrelevant and illegitimate.

For those who view questions concerning marital status as benign, one need only consider the social and economic consequences for those who do not participate in these arrangements or the cross-cultural variations which are at odds with some of the anglocentric or eurocentric assumptions regarding marriage. All people are required to situate themselves in relation to marriage or heterosexuality, including those who *regardless of sexual (or asexual) affiliation* do not consider themselves 'single', heterosexual, or who do not participate in normative heterosexuality and its structures.

To expand the analytical reach of the concept of heteronormativity, it is important to examine how heterosexuality is constructed as normative. A concept that is useful for examining the naturalization of heterosexual relations is 'the heterosexual imaginary'.[1] The 'imaginary' is that illusory relationship we can have to our real conditions of existence. It is that moment when we romanticize things or refuse to see something that makes us uncomfortable. Applied to the study of heterosexuality it is that way of thinking that conceals the operation of heterosexuality in structuring gender (across race, class, and sexuality) and closes off any critical analysis of heterosexuality as an organizing institution. It is a belief system that relies on romantic and sacred notions in order to create and maintain the illusion of well-being. At the same time this romantic view prevents us from seeing how institutionalized heterosexuality actually works to organize gender while preserving racial, class, and sexual hierarchies as well. The effect of this illusory depiction of reality is that heterosexuality is taken for granted and unquestioned while gender is understood as something people are socialized into or learn. By leaving heterosexuality unexamined as an institution we do not explore how it is learned, what it keeps in place, and the interests it serves in the way it is practiced. Through the use of the heterosexual imaginary, we hold up the institution of heterosexuality as timeless, devoid of historical variation, and as 'just the way it is' while creating social practices that reinforce the illusion that as long as this is 'the way it is' all will be right in the world. Romancing heterosexuality – creating an illusory heterosexuality – is central to the heterosexual imaginary.

Frequently, discussions about the legalization of gay marriage depend on this illusion. Gays and lesbians are seeking equal access to economic resources such as benefits and see marriage as the site for gaining equity with heterosexuals. The central problem with this position is that it constructs the debates in terms of coupling. All those who do not couple for whatever reason are left out of the discussion. Consider some of the other consequences of participating in the heterosexual imaginary, of perpetuating the notion that heterosexuality is naturally a site for tranquility and safety. This standpoint keeps us from seeing and dealing with issues of marital rape, domestic violence, pay inequities, racism, gay bashing, and sexual harassment. Instead, institutionalized heterosexuality organizes those behaviors we ascribe to men and women – gender – while keeping in place or producing a history of contradictory and unequal social relations. The production of a division of labor that results in unpaid domestic work, inequalities of pay and opportunity, or the privileging of married couples in the dissemination of insurance benefits are examples of this. The heterosexual imaginary naturalizes the regulation of sexuality through the institution of marriage and state domestic relations laws.

These laws, among others, set the terms for taxation, health care, and housing benefits on the basis of marital status. Laws and public- and private-sector policies use marriage as the primary requirement for social and economic benefits and access rather than distributing resources on some other basis such as citizenship or ability to breathe, for example. The distribution of economic resources on the basis of marital status remains an exclusionary arrangement even if the law permits gays and lesbians to participate. The heterosexual imaginary works here as well by allowing the illusion of well-being to reside in the privilege heterosexual couples enjoy while keeping others from equal access – quite a contradiction in a democratic social order.

WEDDINGS

To demonstrate how useful these concepts are in analysing the institution of heterosexuality, consider a practice as pervasive as heterosexual weddings. To study weddings using this theory of heterosexuality is to investigate the ways various practices, arrangements, relations, and rituals work to standardize and conceal the operation of this institution. It means to ask how practices such as weddings become naturalized and prevent us from seeing what is at stake, what is kept in place, and what consequences are produced. To employ this approach is to seek out those instances when the illusion of tranquility is created and at what cost. Weddings, like many other rituals of heterosexual celebration such as anniversaries, showers, and Valentine's Day become synonymous with heterosexuality and provide illusions of reality which conceal the operation of heterosexuality both historically and materially. When used in professional settings, for example, weddings work as a form of ideological control to signal membership in relations of ruling as well as to signify that the couple is normal, moral, productive, family-centered, upstanding citizens and, most importantly, appropriately gendered. Consider the ways weddings are used by co-workers in line for promotions or to marginalize and exceptionalize single or non-married employees. For example, two employees are competing for a promotion. One is single, the other engaged to marry. The engaged worker invites all members of the office, including the hiring committee, to the wedding. Because of the heterosexual imaginary, weddings are viewed as innocuous fun-loving, and as signaling membership in dominant culture. As such, they give people significant advantage in the workplace and are anything but benign.

To study weddings means to interrupt the ways the heterosexual imaginary naturalizes heterosexuality and prevents us from seeing how its organization depends on the production of the belief or ideology that heterosexuality is normative and the same for everyone – that the fairy tale romance is universal. It is this assumption that allows for the development and growth of a $32 billion per year wedding industry. This multibillion dollar industry includes the sale of a diverse range of products, many of which are produced outside of the USA – wedding gowns, diamonds, honeymoon travel and apparel, and household equipment. Also included in the market are invitations, flowers, receptions, photos, gifts, home furnishings, wedding cakes, catering, alcohol, paper products, calligraphy, jewelry, party supplies, hair styling, make-up, manicures, music, books, and wedding accessories, e.g., ring pillows, silver, chauffeurs and limousines. In the name of normative heterosexuality and its ideology of romance the presence and size of the sometimes corrupt wedding industry escape us.

While newlyweds make up only 2.6 per cent of all American households, they account for 75 per cent of all the fine china, 29 per cent of the tableware, and 21 per cent of the jewelry and watches sold in the USA every year. Even insurers have entered the primary wedding market by offering coverage 'if wedding bells don't ring' to cover the cost of any monies already spent on the

wedding preparation. Fireman's Fund Insurance Company offers 'Weddingsurance' for wedding catastrophes such as flood or fire but not for 'change of heart' (Haggerty, 1993). In fact, attach the words wedding or bridal to nearly any item and its price goes up. With June as the leading wedding month followed by August and July, summer becomes a wedding marketer's dream. According to industry estimates, the average wedding in the USA costs $19,104. Considered in relation to what Americans earn, the cost of the average wedding represents 51 per cent of the mean earning of a white family of four and 89 per cent of the median earnings for black families. The fact that 63.7 per cent of Americans earn less than $25,000 per year (US Bureau of the Census, 1997) means the average cost of a wedding approximates a year's earnings for many Americans.

The primary wedding market – marketing directed toward prospective newlyweds – depends on numerous production and labor relations issues that underlie the consumption and accumulation involved in weddings. Veiled in the guise of romance and the sacred, the heterosexual imaginary conceals from view the various troublesome conditions underlying the production of the white wedding.

Probably the most significant wedding purchase is the wedding gown. Industry analysts have noted that most brides would do without many things to plan a wedding and stay within budget, but they would not scrimp when it comes to the purchase of the wedding gown. With the US national average expenditure at $823 for the gown and $199 for the veil, the bride's apparel becomes the centerpiece of the white wedding. Most of us have heard the various phrases associated with the bride and her gown, the symbolic significance attached to how she looks and how beautiful her gown is. The marketing of everything from weddings to gowns to children's toys to popular wedding films to Disney is laced with messages about fairy tales and princesses, the fantasy rewards that work to naturalize weddings and heterosexuality. Even couture fashion shows of world-class designers traditionally feature wedding gowns as their grand finale.

One particularly troubling practice widely engaged in by gown sellers is the removal of designer labels and prices from dresses. In many surveys, from *Modern Bride* to Dawn Currie's interview study (1993), brides indicate that they rely upon bridal magazines to give them ideas about what type of gown to choose. They take the ad for the gown they like best to area stores and attempt to try on and purchase that particular dress. What they encounter is a system of deception widely practiced by many bridal shops. First, sellers remove the labels. Brides ask for a Vera Wang or an Alfred Angelo or a Jessica McClintock and are told to get the number off the gown and the clerk will check their book and see which designer it is. The bride has no way of knowing if she actually has the brand she seeks. As I toured various shops and saw how widespread this practice was, I asked store owners why they removed the labels from the dresses. Without exception they told me that it was to maintain the integrity of their business and to prevent women from comparison shopping. The truth is, this practice is *illegal* and provides shop owners with a great deal of flexibility in preserving their customer base and profit margin. In addition to this federal consumer protection law there are many states which provide similar protections. All in all, bridal gown stores have little to fear: This law is not enforced. And, perhaps more importantly, the romance with the white wedding gown distracts the soon-to-be brides from becoming suspicious of store practices.

If you look at the portion of tags gown-sellers leave in the dresses you will see that most are sewn outside the USA in countries such as Guatemala, Mexico, Taiwan, and China. Nearly 80 per cent of all wedding gowns are produced outside the USA in subcontracted factories where labor standards are nowhere near US standards and no independent unions or regulators keep watch.

The recruitment by US companies to contract offshore labor benefits manufacturers on many levels: cheap labor, low overhead, fewer regulations, and higher profits. And with the proliferation of free trade agreements such as the North Atlantic Free Trade Agreement (NAFTA) and the General Agreement on Tariffs and Trade (GATT), labor and environmental abuses abound. In a survey conducted by UNITE in April 1997 of three factories in Guatemala, it was discovered that one American manufacturer's gowns were being made by 13 year olds in factories with widespread violations of their country's child labor laws, wage and hour laws, and under life-threatening safety conditions. At two of the firms, 14 and 15 year olds worked as long as 10 hours a day earning $20.80 a week.

Another area of the wedding industry dominated by messages about romance is the marketing of diamonds. As part of the fantasy of the ever-romantic marriage proposal, the diamond ring takes center stage. In fact, for 70 per cent of all US brides and 75 per cent of first-time brides, the first purchase for the impending wedding is the diamond engagement ring. The central marketing strategy of the world's largest diamond mining organization, DeBeers, is to convince consumers that 'diamonds are forever'. Once you accept this slogan, you also believe that you are making a life-long investment, not just purchasing a bauble for your bride! In fact, DeBeers spends about $57 million each year in this advertising campaign and has 'committed to spending a large part of [their] budget – some $200 million this year – on the promotion of diamond jewelry around the world' (Oppenheimer, 1998: 8). DeBeers and its advertisers have developed a new 'shadow' campaign to sell to consumers the advice that the 'appropriate' diamond engagement ring should cost at least 'two months' salary' for the groom (*Jewelers*, 1996). This advertising strategy signals to newlyweds, grooms in particular, that anything less is not acceptable. In effect, the diamond industry has made use of heteronormativity and the heterosexual imaginary and has convinced us that purchasing a diamond engagement ring is no longer a want but is 'natural', and therefore, a must. Not surprisingly, according to wedding industry estimates, this message is reaching its target. The average annual expenditure for engagement rings is $3000 (*Modern Bride*, 1996). If that constitutes the equivalent of two months', salary, the groom is expected to earn an annual salary of approximately $26,000 per year, the income bracket many of these ads target. What gets naturalized here is not just heterosexuality and romance but also weddings and commodity consumption.

Hidden behind the romance with diamond rings and wedding jewelry is an industry with a history steeped in intrigue, treachery, and vast wealth. Everyone from global capitalists to governments to political operatives to advertising agencies to jewelry stores are included. The mining, manufacturing, and marketing of diamonds have involved colonial wars, apartheid, racist violence, massive labor abuses, struggles between superpowers, the stability of nations, and the hiring of mercenary armies. Hardly the picture of romance each young woman was taught to want but when things such as diamond engagement rings and weddings are 'only natural', conditions such as these remain unimaginable and invisible to the average consumer.

This process of naturalization begins with children. By targeting girls and young women, toy manufacturers have seized on the current wedding market and the opportunity to develop future consumers by producing a whole variety of wedding toys featuring the 'classic' white wedding and sold during Saturday morning children's television shows. Toy companies, generally part of large conglomerates that also own related commodities such as travel or cosmetics, work to secure future markers for all their products through the selling of wedding toys. Mattel, the world's largest toymaker and major multinational corporation has offices and facilities in thirty six countries and sells products in 150 nations. Their

major toy brand, accounting for 40 per cent of their sales, is the Barbie doll – all 120 different versions of her. Mattel's primary manufacturing facilities are located in China, Indonesia, Italy, Malaysia, and Mexico, employing mostly women of color and at substandard wages. Annually, Mattel makes about 100 million Barbie dolls and earns revenues of $1.9 billion for their El Segundo, California company. The average young Chinese female worker whose job it is to assemble Barbie dolls lives in a dormitory, sometimes works with dangerous chemicals, works long hours and earns $1.81 a day (Holstein et al., 1996).

The staging of weddings in television shows, weekly reporting on weddings in the press, magazine reports on celebrity weddings, advertising, and popular adult and children's movies with wedding themes or weddings inserted, all work together to teach us how to think about weddings, marriage, heterosexuality, race, gender, and labor. Through the application of the heterosexual imaginary, the media cloak most representations of weddings in signifiers of romance, purity, morality, promise, affluence or accumulation, and whiteness. Many newlyweds today experience their weddings as stars of a fairy-tale movie where they are scripted, videotaped, and photographed by paparazzi wedding-goers.

The contemporary white wedding under transnational capitalism is, in effect, a mass-marketed, homogeneous, assembly-line production with little resemblance to the utopian vision many participants hold. The engine driving the wedding market has mostly to do with the romancing of heterosexuality in the interests of capitalism. The social relations at stake – love, community, commitment, and family – become alienated from the production of the wedding spectacle while practices reinforcing heteronormativity prevail.

The heterosexual imaginary circulating throughout the wedding industry masks the ways it secures racial, class, and sexual hierarchies. For instance, in nearly all of the examples offered above, the wedding industry depends upon the availability of cheap labor from developing nations with majority populations made up of people of color. The wealth garnered by white transnational corporations both relies on racial hierarchies, exploiting people and resources of communities of color (Africa, China, Haiti, Mexico, South Asia), and perpetuates them in the marketing of the wedding industry.

Women are taught from early childhood to plan for the 'happiest day of their lives'. Men are taught, by the absence of these socializing mechanisms, that their work is 'other' than that. The arguments that second wave feminists made about institutionalized heterosexuality as the source of male dominance and women's oppression are reinforced by these practices. The possibilities children learn to imagine are only as broad as their culture allows. They are socialized to understand the importance of coupling, appropriate coupling, what counts as beauty, what counts as women's work and men's work, and how to become good consumers by participating in those heterosexual practices which stimulate their interests and emotions and reap the most rewards.

CONCLUSION

Heterosexuality is just not natural! It is socially organized and controlled. To understand how we give meaning to one of our major institutions is to participate as a critical consumer and citizen actively engaged in the production of culture and the social order. Heteronormativity – those practices that construct heterosexuality as the standard for legitimate and expected social and sexual relations – has enormous consequences for all members of a democratic social order, particularly in relation to the distribution of human and economic resources that affect the daily lives of millions of people. When the expectation is that all are equal under the law and that all citizens in a democracy can participate fully

in the ruling of that society, rendering one form of socio-sexual relations as dominant by constructing it as 'natural' is both contradictory and violent. In other words, the heterosexuality we learn to think of as 'natural' is anything but.

NOTE

1 See 'The heterosexual imaginary: feminist sociology and theories of gender', *Sociological Theory*, 12: 203-19, 2 July 1994 for further elaboration of this concept.

REFERENCES

Adams, Mary Louise (1997) *The Trouble with Normal: Postwar Youth and the Making of Heterosexuality*. Toronto: University of Toronto Press.

Atkinson, Ti-Grace (1974) *Amazon Odyssey*. New York: Links Books.

Best, Amy (2000) *Prom Night: Youth, Schools, and Popular Culture*. New York: Routledge.

Brown, Rita Mae (1976) *Plain Brown Rapper*. Baltimore: Diana Press.

Bunch, Charlotte (1975) 'Not for lesbians only', *Quest: A Feminist Quarterly*, (Fall).

Butler, Judith (1990) *Gender Trouble*. New York: Routledge.

Currie, D. (1993) 'Here comes the bride': The making of a 'modern traditional' wedding in western culture', *Journal of Comparative Family Studies*, 24 (3): 403–21.

de Lauretis, Teresa (1987) 'Queer theory: lesbian and gay sexualities'. *Differences*, 3: iii–xviii.

Field, Nicola (1995) *Over the Rainbow: Money, Class and Homophobia*. London: Pluto Press.

Fuss, Diana (1991) *Inside/Out*. New York Routledge.

Graff, E.J. (1999) *What is Marriage for?: The Strange Social History of our Most Intimate Institution*. Boston: Beacon Press.

Harman, Moses (1901) *Institutional Marriage*. Chicago: Lucifer.

Helms, Jesse (1996) 'The defense of marriage act'. *Senate Congressional Quarterly* September 9.C. 1996 Senate proceedings. *Congressional Record*, September 9.

Hennessy, Rosemary (1995) 'Incorporating queer theory on the left', Antonio Callari, Stephen Cullenberg, and Carole Beweiner (eds) *Marxism in the Postmodern Age*. New York: Guilford.

Heywood, Ezra (1876) *Cupid's Yokes*. Princeton, NJ: Co-operative Publishing Company.

Holstein, William J., Palmer, Brian, Ur-Rehman, Shahid, and M. Ito Timothy (1996) 'Santa's sweatshop', *U.S. News & World Report* 16 December.

Ingraham, Chrys (1994) 'The heterosexual imaginary: feminist sociology and theories of gender', *Sociological Theory*, 12, 2 (July): 203–19.

Ingraham, Chrys (1999) *White Weddings: Romancing Heterosexuality in Popular Culture.* New York: Routledge.

Jackson, Stevi (1996) 'Heterosexuality and feminist theory', in Diane Richardson (ed.), *Theorising Heterosexuality.* Buckingham: Open University Press.

Jackson, Stevi (1999) *Heterosexuality in Question.* London: Sage Publications.

Jewelers Circular-Keystone (1996) 'Diamond sales hit record', New York: Chilton.

Katz, Jonathan Ned (1995) *The Invention of Heterosexuality.* New York: Plume.

Maynard, Mary and Purvis, June (eds) (1995) *(Hetero) sexual Politics.* London: Taylor & Francis.

Modern Bride (1996) 'The bridal market retail spending study: $35 billion market for the 90's', New York: Primedia.

Oppenheimer, Nicholas (1998) 'Chairman's statement', *Annual Report.* De Beers.

Redstockings Collective (1975) *Feminist Revolution.* New York: Random House.

Rich, Adrienne (1980) 'Compulsory heterosexuality and lesbian existence', *Signs*, 5 (Summer): 631–60.

Richardson, Diane (ed.) (1996) *Theorising Heterosexuality.* Buckingham: Open University Press.

Sears, Hal D. (1977) *The Sex Radicals: Free Love in High Victorian America.* Lawrence: Regents Press of Kansas.

Sedgwick, Eve (1990) *Epistemology of the Closet.* Berkeley, CA: University of California Press.

Seidman, Steven (1991) *Romantic Longings.* New York: Routledge.

Seidman, Steven (1992) *Embattled Eros.* New York: Routledge.

Seidman, Steven (1993) 'Identity and politics in a postmodern gay culture: some conceptual and historical notes', in M. Warner (ed.), *Fear of a Queer Planet.* Minneapolis: University of Minnesota Press.

Seidman, Steven (1996) *Queer Theory/Sociology.* Cambridge, MA: Blackwell.

US Bureau of the Census (1997) *Statistical Abstracts of the U.S.* Washington DC: Government Printing Office.

Wilkinson, Sue and Kitzinger, Celia (eds) (1993) *Heterosexuality: A Feminism and Psychology Reader.* London: Sage Publications.

Wittig, Monique (1992) *The Straight Mind and Other Essays.* Boston: Beacon Press.

6

The Comparative Sociology
of Homosexualities

STEPHEN O. MURRAY

Comparison requires at least a tentative sense of a phenomenon with sufficiently recurrent instances to make categorization heuristic. Sociologists often abstract entities (such as capitalism, a scientific paradigm, or the Protestant ethic), processes (such as revolution, migration, or urbanization), and attributes (such as class and class-consciousness) that are not directly observable. We routinely compare concentrations and exercises of 'power' despite considerable disagreement about what exactly 'power' is and about whether its exercise increases or reduces it. 'Resources', and, even more so, instances of 'resource mobilization' are open to debate in the discourse about 'social movements'. No less than 'revolution', 'homosexuality' is an abstraction. In both cases, some of the persons regarded by observers as participating in this category define what they are doing as 'revolution' or 'homosexuality', while some others deny that what they are doing is 'revolution' or 'homosexuality'. Many others do not think about distinguishing what they are doing as fitting the category, or contest the label if they encounter it being applied to them.

Many terms in human languages have more than one precise referent (this is called polysemy). One of the sillier of Michel Foucault's pronouncements was that 'sodomy' in western Christendom was an 'utterly confused category'. In fact, its prototypical reference was to placing a human penis in a human anus; putting a human penis into a non-human vagina or anus followed the logic of (in)appropriateness, as did the far-from-universal extension to oral–genital contact. Whether particular behavior was an instance of the category 'sodomy' was often argued in court, but the core meaning and the prototypical behavior that established instances of the category were anal penetration with emission.

Contrary to Foucault's surmise (it certainly was not based on comparative research!), 'sodomite' preceded 'sodomy' in European discourse (i.e., the realm in which he was primarily interested) (see Jordan, 1997).[1] A person with a penchant for committing the act of sodomy was widely conceived by confessors. If someone confessed to the Inquisition (or to Florence's Ufficiali di Notte), the focus was not on a particular act ('that anyone might commit'). The focus was on a pattern and on the network of partners and procurers.

BEHAVIOR, CONDUCT, ORIENTATION

'Sexual orientation' is a modern locution, although 'unmodern' and 'premodern' people also have noticed patterns of desire as well as patterns of behavior. 'Homosexual orientation' is analytically distinct from 'homosexual behavior', the latter being in principle observable, the former is almost always an inference. It seems fairly obvious that there can be orientations without physical consummation. 'Gay virgin' is a conception that makes sense in contemporary gay North America, and most gay men include those who identify as gay, but who have never had same-sex sex, as part of 'gay community' (Murray, 1981, 1996: 204–5).

'Homosexuality' sometimes refers to a sexual orientation, sometimes to behavior, i.e., to a sexual act between persons of the same sex. One cannot infer sexual desire from sexual behavior. As Simon (1996: 72) put it, 'The complexity of motivations to engage in sexual behavior remind us that the desire for sex is rarely, if ever, in the exclusive control of "sexual desire"'.

In that coercion may be subtle, one cannot be sure that sexual contact is chosen and, therefore, is an indication of desire. Economic gain is a common motivation distinct from desire, and not only for those directly exchanging sex for money (prostitutes). Although I have expressed skepticism for what I call 'the blind phallus reverie' ('it doesn't matter where we put it, as long as we get off') of men who do not identify as gay/homosexual (Murray, 1987: 196), it is very clear that many sexual acts between persons of the same biological sex occur without one (or more) being regarded as 'homosexual'.

In general, sociologists are uncomfortable with the psychologistic inference of an 'orientation'. Moreover, there is extremely little evidence for scholars to compare subjective orientations to their sexual desires (or behavior) of those engaged in even recurrent same-sex sexual relations in other societies than post-World War II North America and

Northwestern Europe. Although American sociologists may sometimes study behavior, the category intermediate between acts and orientations that we favor is 'conduct'. Gagnon and Simon (1967) influentially deployed the classic Chicago school distinction between 'behavior' and a recurrent pattern of behavior, 'conduct'. It is recurrence, not approximation of any ideal essence, some 'right way' of enacting 'homosexuality', that is used to distinguish 'conduct' from 'behavior'. The patterning may not be consciously recognized. Unfortunately, no clear threshold number exists for deciding how much behavior constitutes a pattern of 'conduct'. Moreover, analysts are not altogether free of the common-sense view that patterns are recognized by those engaging in recurrent behavior (e.g., that a man who goes to a bar or park every week and has sex with one or more men whom he meets there realizes he is looking for sex at least to an extent sufficient to go there). Still, the conception of 'homosexual conduct' excludes those who tried same-sex sex once or for a brief span of time, then ceased. What they did once or for a while can still be considered 'homosexuality', but the conception of 'conduct' allows us to leave aside questions about whether this or that person is or was 'a homosexual', has become an 'ex-homosexual', etc. We (comparativist sociologists – in contrast to some psychologists and others, such as the geneticist oncologist Dean Hamer) do not claim to know what the 'sexual orientations' are – even of those we directly observe, let alone those of individuals mentioned in forensic, historical, travel, or ethnographic literatures from other times and places.

Along with 'conduct' as a concept not making assumptions about inner 'orientations', another concept from the standard sociological armory is that of 'role'. Its usefulness was beclouded by the Parsonian synthesis during the 1950s of Durkheimian and notably ethnocentric neo-Freudian theories of 'deviance',[2] and the very Parsonian positing of a singular 'homosexual role' in McIntosh's eventually famous 1961 article. In many societies – including the USA of the late 1950s – there are/were 'homosexual roles'. These include occupational roles with concentrations of those who openly pursue or are presumed to pursue same-sex sex, roles played within couples at home and in lesbigay settings (e.g., butch-femme), sexual roles ('top'/'bottom', *activo/pasivo*), and, in many times and places, roles that involve presenting a gender other than the one conventional for the person's (natal/genital/chromosomal) sex.[3]

Even from these examples, one might wonder how useful the notion 'role' could be. Among the reasons I think it is useful are (1) everyone plays multiple roles every day, so that 'homosexual roles' and even a role as a 'homosexual' are not the totality of person-hood,[4] and (2) over time the actor (the indi-vidual) may be cast or cast herself/himself in new roles and drop old roles from his/her repertoire. The second of these is par-ticularly crucial for the insertee role of younger partner in age-stratified homosexual relations (pages, acolytes, boy-actors, boy-wives, initiates of either sex). Some of those playing such roles desire penetration, and some prefer (are 'oriented toward') same-sex sex sexual partners (see Herdt, 1981: 252), but (in role theorizing) saying that someone played such a role does not imply that s/he *is* a 'homosexual' or has a 'homosexual orien-tation'. Similarly, in regard to the first, we need not presuppose that someone who plays homosexual sexual roles does not also play heterosexual ones. A vocabulary of roles removes any need to try to establish if some-one is 'really' a 'homosexual', or is a 'hetero-sexual' dallying with same-sex partners, or is a 'bisexual', or whether a person has primary bisexual or heterosexual or homosexual 'orientation'. Put another way, comparing roles avoids claiming either that 'homosex-ual' ('homosexuality') has an ontological status, or that it has no ontological status, universally or in a particular society – or even within a particular psyche. This allows us to get on with the task of comparing what the roles are in different societies, how rare or common performances of particular roles are in this and that society, etc.

Most of the comparisons of homosexuali-ties across time and space rely on documen-tation recorded by nonparticipants (see Bleys, 1995; Murray, 1999a). Most of them have been censorious, and even much of what was recorded by participants was intended to camouflage the authors as pro-perly censorious, shocked, and appalled recorders of such socially stigmatized conduct. Comparisons of subjectivities about same-sex sexualities are tenuous even across races in the contemporary United States.[5] Even with the seemingly large amount of writing about homosexuality, there is very little at-all-systematic sampling of the population about the meanings of same-sex sex.

Systematic comparison across space and time of homosexual inwardnesses is almost entirely conjectural. What we know some-thing about are sociocultural forms, so we compare roles and conduct, usually includ-ing whatever information about desire and orientation is available – which usually is not much. Even if individuals' motivations are knowable in principle (a proposition many sociologists find dubious), they are not knowable from the kind of records available for comparativists to use.

Given the paucity of funding for research on the meanings of same-sex sex (i.e., on the subjectivities of those who engage to vary-ing extents in same-sex sexual conduct), I cannot foresee the accumulation of the body of data necessary for serious comparative work of homosexual inwardnesses. Although I can fantasize about working with such data, I am interested in sociocultural forms. For me, comparing forms (both of homo-sexualities and of other social patterns) is not just making a virtue of necessity, but a project of consuming interest.

GEOGRAPHICAL PATTERNING

Recognizing that all human categories are at least somewhat fuzzy does not mean that any particular category is heuristic. It seems to me that there are several matters in which 'homosexuality' is heuristic. One might be interested in contrasting rates of homosexual behavior from locality to locality (whether the unit is neighborhood, state, or even cultural area). The pioneering comparative work, the 'Terminal essay' to Richard Burton's multi-volume translation of *The Arabian Nights* (1886) postulated a geographic swath, what he called the 'sotadic zone', in which male–male sexuality was more common than in more temperate regions.[6] There was no reliable data on rates of behavior on which Burton could draw for such comparisons, and there still are not.

After Burton, there have been comparisons of different homosexual patterns within regions, e.g., Herdt (1984) on Melanesia, Murray (1987, 1995a) on Latin America; Roscoe (1998) on Native North America; Murray and Roscoe (1997) on the Abode of Islam, Murray and Roscoe (1998) on Sub-Saharan Africa, though only the first and last of these have any focus on geographical patterning within the region discussed. None of these focus on differing rates of same-sex sexual behavior or different percentages of participants on particular sociocultural roles.

Two pioneering works of considerable erudition, psychoanalyst Wainwright Churchill's (1967) *Homosexual Behavior Among Males* and historian Vern Bullough's (1976) *Sexual Variance in Society and History* focus on what seems to me a dependent variable without much variance: sex-negativity of societies. Bullough reviews material on masturbation and what would now be labeled transgendered roles, in addition to homosexuality in ancient (Jewish, Greek, Roman), Islamic, Chinese, and Hindu civilizations. Churchill relied heavily on Kinsey, while also discussing ancient Greece and Rome and (then-)contemporary Americans and southern Europeans. Their considerable accomplishments have been forgotten, as decidedly less erudite works, notably Foucault (1980), have become foundational to historical gay and lesbian studies.

FORMS OF HOMOSEXUAL RELATIONSHIPS

Instead of geographical patterning, one might be interested, instead, in what is the dominant cultural conception and social organization of same-sex sex in different societies, and what correlates between social organization of same-sex sex and other sociocultural patterns that exist.

The first thing to note is that same-sex sexuality in many times and places has not involved one person visibly differing from the appearance and demeanor expected of a person of that sex in that society. Although gender variants are particularly visible and, therefore, likely to be reported by ethnographers and other kinds of travelers, there is a great deal of homosexual conduct not involving a gender-variant person.

A distinction between same-sex sexual relationships in which the partners differed in age from each other or differed in gender presentation is implicit in Burton (1886). Whether there are status differences between same-sex sexual partners and what the salient (within a society) status that differs is has been my own particular interest, and I shall discuss it further below.

In a number of societies, people have felt that sexual desire for persons of the same sex is an important shared feature and/or that such persons deserve contempt and should be proscribed from acting on same-sex desire and should be punished if they do it. Such beliefs provide not just a basis, but a need to band together and fight against cultural stigmatization and institutionalized persecution what the state (and/or others able to limit life chances) treat as a kind of person ('homosexuals' and various local labels for those with recurrent same-sex sexual desire). Whether 'the homosexual' has any ontological status, laws against sodomy etc. continue to exist, and to provide an umbrella to justify employment discrimination against those thought to be 'homosexual', to take away custody of children from 'homosexuals', etc.

The construction in particular societies of a pathological 'homosexual' criminal is the primary focus of a vast constructionist literature, most notably David Greenberg's magisterial (1988) book *The Construction of Homosexuality*.[7] The focus in this line of work is not (primarily) on how those who engage in same-sex sex conceive themselves and organize their lives, but on how legislators (using the term broadly to include councils of tribal elders) conceive nonconformity to gender norms and to 'sexual object choice' of persons of the same sex. There are marked variations not only in the existence of sanctions against each of these kinds of anomalies but in whether being born with the genitalia of one sex or the other is more important than gender. That is, what from the outside appears to be heterogender homosexuality may be regarded and treated by a particular people as 'heterosexual' insofar as a masculine human is penetrating a feminine human, disregarding their genitalia. Transformed shamans in Siberia are the prototype of this (see Murray, 1992: 293–352, 2000: 314–26).

Relatively few of the imaginable structurings by the relative status of partners in same-sex sex occur in the vast panorama of known societies. This is surprising, given the tradition of anthropologists and other travelers of stressing 'exotic' differences and the tendency not to bother mentioning what is familiar. There are not hundreds or even dozens of different social organizations of same-sex sexual relations in human societies (Murray, 1984: 19–21). As for other cultural domains, only a few categorization systems recur across space and time.

Barry Adam (1979, 1986) proposed a fourfold typology of social structurings of homosexuality: (1) age-structured; (2) gender-defined; (3) profession-defined; and (4) egalitarian/'gay' relations.[8] Two years earlier, historian Randolph Trumbach (1977) demarcated the age/gender distinction, and in subsequent publications has stressed a revolution from age-structured to gender role-structured homosexuality, but Adam told me that he was unaware of Trumbach's (1977) paper in 1979. Similarly, Trumbach told me that he was unaware of Geoffrey Gorer's earlier age/gender dichotomy, which, in turn, seems to me to derive from the implicit distinction in Richard Burton's 'Terminal essay' (first printed privately in 1886). Herdt (1987) labeled the second type 'gender reversed' and the third 'role specialized' (religious or social role). Greenberg (1988) and Murray (1992) dropped a distinct occupationally-defined type, Greenberg adding class-structured. Roscoe (1997: 55) suggested 'status-defined' to include differences between partners in age or in class. It seems to me that one could include gender as a 'status' and counterpoise 'status-differentiated' with the 'modern gay' kind of homosexuality in which sexual and domestic roles are not stratified by status differences (although Carrington [1999] shows less than perfect fit between egalitarian ideology and everyday divisions of labor in gay and lesbian households).

While relationships structured by differences in age, gender, class, or occupation, and by more-or-less egalitarian comradeship may coexist in a single society, one of them tends to be more visible 'on the ground', both among those who are native to the society and in explanation to aliens who ask about same-sex sexual relations. For instance, age-graded male homosexuality was the most-valued and only respected form across ancient Greece. Gender-defined and comradely homosexuality also occurred, and at least the former was labeled – with a term for such a kind of person, *kinaidos* (Winkler, 1990: 45–54). Similarly, many indigenous North American peoples had terms for a gender-variant role labeled by alien observers 'berdache'.[9] They had no labels for males who were masculine by their culture's standards, did male work, and had sexual relationships with other males, or for females who were feminine by their culture's standards and had sexual relationships with other females.

Always and everywhere, there is intracultural (and intrapsychic) diversity. There is a range of homosexualities in a single society, and the dominant discourse of the predominant sexual ideology ('sexual culture') may occlude but does not preclude different kinds of relationships. Even one person may understand the same behavior differently on different occasions with different partners, or even with the same partner. As Adam explained:

> Any single set of cultural institutions never completely contains the full range of human experience and innovation. Social coding practices may be uneven, incomplete, or in transition. Even if sexuality has a culturally specific and internally coherent complex of meanings, and even if culture (in the singular) could be shown to channel desires, there remains a larger universe of experience, maladjustment, and emigrations from prescribed interpretive frameworks. Moreover, the dominant sexual codes of one place take on subterranean aspects elsewhere as a 'little tradition'. (1986: 20)

A role category may be variously interpreted and lived by individuals within a society. Over time, shared new meanings may move even the cultural categories. Also traditions that are overshadowed (by dominant discourses) may nonetheless persist, as, for instance, age-stratified and gender-stratified homosexualities do in current-day Amsterdam and San Francisco.

Beyond his explication of the age-structured type (Adam, 1986), Adam has not elaborated on his typology. Greenberg (1988) and Trumbach (1985 et seq.) have stressed a unilinear evolution from age-structured to gender-structured (and from gender-structured to modern/gay in Greenberg) while mostly disregarding intra-cultural variability and the simultaneity of different structurings of same-sex sexual relations in particular places and times. The rapidly proliferating genre of detailed local histories (of which Chauncey [1994] is the most distinguished exemplar) has documented some variability within a more modulated but hardly more multilinear evolution from gendered to gay homosexuality.

My own work has examined homosexual roles around the world and across time (insofar as data are available). After books on Latin America, an extended Oceania, and

the Abode of Islam (Murray, 1987 and 1995a; 1992; Murray and Roscoe, 1997), I more systematically correlated the presence of types of male and of female homosexuality in records of 'tribal' African societies with other sociocultural patterns, using Human Relations Area Files (HRAF) codings of these latter (Murray, 1998). I then extended this correlational (very explicitly not causal!) analysis to a world sample (Murray, 2000: 420–40). The geographically organized surveys had showed that there were 'premodern' instances of female and male homosexuality not involving status differences, so that egalitarian homosexuality was not impossible before industrial capitalism, the lynchpin of 'modernity'.[10] The organization of cases in *Homosexualities* (Murray, 2000) emphasized that each of the main types (age-stratified, gender role-stratified, not stratified by status differences) occurred in societies varying considerably in scale and technological development.

Some of the patternings that emerged are:

1   Societies with gender-stratified male homosexuality were twice as likely to have matrilineal inheritance than the world average.
2   Inheritance in societies with age-stratified male or female homosexuality were markedly more patrilineal than in regional and global rates of patrilinearity.
3   There is no apparent difference in primary means of subsistence correlating with the different types of homosexuality, male or female.
4   Greater female participation in making a living does not co-occur with gendered male or female homosexuality more often than with age-stratified or non-status-stratified homosexualities.
5   In societies in which boys are freest to engage in sex with girls, they also more freely – or, at least, more visibly – have sex with each other (contrary to claims about 'deprivation' or heterosexual

'outlets' explaining homosexual sexual activity).

6 Societies with egalitarian male homosexuality have longer post-partum sex taboos than do societies with age- or gender-stratified male homosexuality.

7 Relatively egalitarian societies are more likely to have male homosexual relations not structured by differences in age or gender status.

Comparing male and female patternings, the correlates of gender-stratified female and gender-stratified male homosexualities turned out to be quite similar, and the correlates for age-stratified homosexuality are fairly similar. However, such (premodern) egalitarian female-homosexuality as has been attested occurs in quite different kinds of societies than those in which egalitarian male homosexuality has been attested, specifically in those that are in other ways less egalitarian.

The differences in this correlational exercise were attenuated by the occurrence of more than one type in the records about particular societies. Moreover, the extent to which 'traditional' social patterns have survived 'globalization' is certainly open to question, although it seems to me that the 'modern gay' conception and organization of homosexuality have not swept away heterogendered homosexuality in the places I have studied directly (Mesoamerica, Thailand, Indonesia). I have argued that in most contemporary societies, *gay* is known and used by some as a label for 'modern', egalitarian homosexuality, challenging traditional stigmatization of a gender-variant partner in homosexual relations. Nevertheless, outside Anglophone North America, the new container *gay* recurrently has been filled with old negative connotations of sexual receptivity and effeminacy. That is, what has occurred is relexification, substituting a new label for a traditional schemata rather than challenge to and transformation of the stigma of homosexuality (Murray, 1995c, 2000; 393–414).

COMPARING NATIONAL LESBIGAY MOVEMENTS, INDUCING PREREQUISITES

Challenges to traditional stigmas have, nonetheless, occurred. Barry Adam has also pioneered the comparison of lesbigay movements. *The Rise of a Gay and Lesbian Movement* (Adam, 1987, 1995) provides an overview of organized lesbigay resistance and politicking focused on the USA and Canada, but also discussing European and Latin American groups.[11] In 1999 he co-edited a collection of accounts of movements in Brazil, Argentina, Romania, Hungary, the Czech Republic, Japan, and South Africa, as well as in 'first world' countries.

Adam et al. (1999: 344) concluded that a prerequisite of any lesbigay political organizing is the existence of some social space (beyond private-party networks and cruising sites) in which people can develop gay and lesbian identities. Both protecting and enlarging the range of these spaces are recurrent goals of lesbigay politics.[12]

In the United States, and to a considerable extent elsewhere, shifts from agriculture to manufacturing and service occupations allowed men and women who were relatively detached from (or seeking to become autonomous from) their families to make a living outside family control and, often, even beyond family capacity to help secure employment. At least in the eastern United States, the service sector began to grow in the 1830s with the railroad system. Banks and corporate headquarters provided occupational slots, e.g., for 'ribbon clerks'. In the twentieth century, the growing welfare state required new kinds of white-collar and pink-collar employees at the same time that blue-collar jobs (handling ocean freight and manufacturing) became increasingly scarce. The growth and florescence of San Francisco gay culture, in particular, occurred simultaneously with the rapid growth of San Francisco's downtown office space and the virtual end of manufacturing and of handling ocean freight in San Francisco. The shift of jobs to the service sector is a long-term trend, which gained momentum in the 1950s, and still continues in cities around the world.

Dependence upon and residence with families preclude the development of lesbigay neighborhoods and is a considerable obstacle to the formation of lesbigay consciousness, culture and community as these have developed in Anglo North America. The welfare state's takeover of insurance against disaster – the 'safety net' function of the family – has facilitated (however inadvertently!) the development of more extensive and more intensive relationships outside family circles. Among these are the possibilities of same-sex couples living together and clustering of persons with shared or similar sexual orientations into gay communities in North America.[13]

However, in much of the world, the family retains economic functions. The family as a production unit exists to a considerable extent in African, Asian, Latin American and Pacific societies, especially in rural areas. Even urban families that are not production units provide social security in countries far from being welfare states. In societies experienced by most of their inhabitants as capricious and heartless, the family provides more than merely psychological shelter. Someone who is struck down by illness or injury with no family to support him or her, will be reduced to begging in the streets. Examples of this horrific danger are readily visible, so individuals cannot, and had better not, take for granted minimum security being supplied against disability, as citizens of welfare states have. Total dependence on families (both of birth and of marriage) makes political, sexual, and social relationships with non-family members relatively unimportant (Khan, 1997).

In many places, revelation of homosexuality is a basis for expulsion from the home and the economic as well as psychological security provided by the family. Many males involved in homosexual liaisons in many places cultivate family relations to a greater extent than do those who can take them for granted. In some cases, they exercise the right of males who have reached sexual maturity to come and go from home at will (literally 'without question') less than do their brothers.

Moreover, taking prospective sexual partners to where one lives is rarely possible for people who live in extended-family households, especially when the whole family sleeps in one room. In such commercial institutions as do exist for lesbian or gay male sociation, admission prices are prohibitive to many. Most men who would like to go regularly to these places must save money for the special occasion of a visit (see Whitam, 1987: 29; Green, 1999a).

The seeming 'tolerance' for homosexual behavior in some places in which such behavior is not illegal, so long as it does not become too consuming an interest or passion, and so long as it does not involve public gender deviance is far from acceptance of homosexual relations as being equal to or as important as procreative/familial relationships. In regards to the tolerance for discreet homosexuality (or other forms of sexual pleasure) as long as family obligations (of which reproduction is the paramount one) are fulfilled, Khan (1997) wrote of the impossibility of gay life in Pakistan:

> Families are like organisms that extend themselves by absorbing their young, and grow stronger or weaker based on the contributions of the new entrants. This is not just one model of life in Pakistan; it is not a choice; it is the *only* way of life ... If a husband takes care of his family's security needs and produces many children, what he does for personal sexual satisfaction is quite irrelevant – and so long as it is kept a private matter – tolerated ... The most successful gay relationships in Karachi are quiet and heavily compromised. They are almost never the most important relationship for either partner; the family occupies that position.

With only a sketchy identity as a person distinct from the identity as a member of a family, having a 'sexual identity' and/or building an 'alternative lifestyle' are literally inconceivable to many, even in urban centres.[14]

Against a background of increasing wage labor outside family and/or feudal enterprises (particularly agricultural ones), association outside work is more a matter of individual choice. Lesbian and gay networks can increase in density and importance more easily when the family is not the only way of life. Dense, multiplex networks make identity more plausible.

Still, gay consciousness is no more automatic a product of homosexual behavior than class-consciousness is of 'objective class position' or ethnic consciousness of genealogy. Not all the persons with a characteristic consider themselves defined in any way by it, and some deny it altogether. The existence and importance of a characteristic must be realized if there is to be a consciousness of kind: characteristics are only potential bases, and if they are not publicly affirmed, they are tenuous bases. The public conflation of homosexuality with gender deviance, often the only kind of public discourse about homosexuality, makes it difficult and unpleasant to develop any conscious identification with 'that kind' even for those fully aware of sexually desired partners of their own sex. As was said in reference to the United States of the early 1960s, 'In a world in which one is rewarded for concealment and submission, it would be difficult to expect the reverse' (Cory and LeRoy, 1963: 213).

It is clear that same-sex sexual conduct does not automatically produce a sense of commonality or peoplehood. Cruising areas and social networks of homosexually-inclined men partying together exist and have existed with varying degrees of visibility in cities everywhere, while a sense of belonging to a community of those whose identity is based on shared sexual preferences has not. Something more than sexual acts in 'the city of night' is needed to provide a conception of a shared fate. Being harassed, beaten, or robbed by the police or by others is an experience had by many males and more than a few females seeking or engaging in same-sex sexual relationships (enduring or transient ones). Some men in Los Angeles in the late 1940s organized against police incursions, but similar depredations were (and are) conceived as 'normal' risks or even as deserved punishment by many people in many places today. For political mobilization to occur requires a combination of some sense of a kind of person and a sense that such persons should be treated better than they currently are.

The modern 'gay' identity is conducive to such mobilization, but the early European and American movements began with conceptions that in retrospect acquiesced to dominant cultural conceptions of inferiority and deviance. In present-day societies with similar equation and derogation of recurrent homosexuality as a reflex of gender deviance, knowledge of the existence of western 'gay' self-presentation and self-acceptance is available. It is less difficult to believe that 'things have to be this way' even if the 'gay' way is not readily visible in one's immediate vicinity. There is certainly emulation, particularly of American ways. One indicator is the choice of American place-names for gay bars and clubs in other countries. There is also a flow of persons with some experience of American lesbigay lifeways (both American visitors to other countries and returning natives who have gone to school or visited America for other reasons). In 2002, commonality of conventionally gendered persons who love and have sex with other persons of the same sex is easier to think in say, Timbuktu, than it was in 1945 in California or France.

Explicit challenges to the legitimacy of social arrangements (of which targeting for extortion and violence those who are involved in same-sex sexual relationships is frequently one) cannot be made where political censorship is vigilant and generally accepted as being legitimate. However, the diffusion of Internet communication has allowed reports of negative action to be reported quickly and internationally and for texts and images of modern 'gay' homosexuality to reach even remote locations.

Copies of videotapes of sex between masculine males has shown people in many places with stereotypically heterogender homosexuality another way of acting, one that has the prestige of coming from affluent northern Europe and the USA.[15] Globalization of 'safe sex' campaigns (often pushing condoms manufactured in the USA) also has disseminated conceptions of 'modern' homosexuality (in particular by preaching responsibility that is shared by insertors and insertee for reducing possibilities of HIV-transmission).

Conceiving that the existing reality is (1) intolerable and (2) changeable is necessary for the formation of a social movement of any sort. Undoubtedly the Kinsey data[16] and the example of the civil rights movement encouraged the early homophile movement in the United States to begin to think about the number of potential recruits and about the possibility of challenging discrimination. Similarly, black nationalist and feminist movements later inspired American and other lesbigay movements making more self-affirming, less cringingly defensive demands to end discrimination in a widening range of domains (first law enforcement, then employment and housing, more recently, marriage and military service). Similarly, in South Africa the anti-apartheid movement's rhetoric of human rights for all provided a rationale for including sexual orientation among the categories protected by its new legal system. In South Africa, as in the USA, some of the persons who were active in fighting for black rights were gay and moved directly on to advocating for gay rights. The new (1996) South African constitution's bill of rights banned discrimination on the basis of sexual orientation, and South African courts have been following this logic to ensure legal equality for same-sex committed relationships.

The formation of a critical mass of people who viewed themselves as defined to some extent by homosexual desires was the central precondition for mobilization everywhere there has been some mobilization. The feasibility of better treatment and less abject status

was itself disproportionately facilitated by even tiny organizations making even equivocal challenges to the legitimacy of the dominant society's picture of homosexuals.

As the famous experiments of Solomon Asch (1958) show, one person perceiving himself or herself to be the only one opposed to the view of others is unlikely to express dissent. Realizing that even one other person also opposes the consensus greatly increases the likelihood of enunciating contrary views. Two is perhaps the most critical number, enabling the first alliance, but two people cannot create a full range of alternative institutions. Although we are not sure of exactly what number constitutes the threshold,

> arrival at certain critical levels of size enables a social subsystem to create and support institutions which structure, envelop, protect, and foster its subculture. These institutions (e.g., dress styles, newspapers, associations) establish sources of authority and points of congregation and delimit social boundaries. In addition to the simple fact of the numbers themselves, they make possible and encourage keeping social ties within the group. (Fischer, 1975: 1325–26, 1329)

Fischer (1975) argued for the importance of absolute numbers in arguing that the greater the concentration of people, the higher the rate of unconventionality, the greater the subcultural variety, the more intense the subcultures in conflict and competition with others, and, therefore, the greater the likelihood of collective action on behalf of the subculture.[17] He marshaled evidence from a variety of countries showing that city size 'increases or at least maintains the cohesion and identity of ethnic subcultures – in spite of all the disorganizing aspects of urbanization, such as migration, economic change, and [the ready availability of] alternative subcultures' (ibid.: 133). New subcultural institutions are possible with increases and concentrations of persons identifying with some particular oppositional characteristic.

Two of the conditions Weber (1978: 305) identified as increasing the likely success of class-conscious organization are the existence of a large number of persons in the same situation and their geographic concentration. In Anglo North America the congregation into 'gay ghettoes' facilitated homophile and gay mobilizations after World War II (Murray, 1984: 17). Such residential concentration of homosexually-inclined men is precluded where the unmarried males continue to live at home.

The specific pattern of historical development of gay communities in Anglo North America need not be assumed to constitute the only possible route to gay solidarity. Residential concentration may be neither a necessary nor a sufficient condition for lesbigay identify formation or political mobilization. Residential concentration seems less in the 'gay Meccas' of Europe and Asia, Amsterdam and Bangkok, than in North American gay ghettoes. Even if dispersed, number is important, however. Especially for groups that receive no media attention, social networks are a vital basis for social movement mobilization (Snow et al., 1980). D'Emilio (1983) shows that at a time during which favorable publicity was unthinkable, the early Mattachine Society and Daughters of Bilitis drew their members from pre-existing social networks. This pattern has been repeated in West Pacific South-East and South Asian, and Latin American instances (e.g., see Green, 1999a, b, Lunsing, 1999).

The formation of a critical mass of people viewing themselves as defined to some extent by homosexual desires was the central precondition for change in the USA and other western societies. It was facilitated quite out of proportion to the size of the organizations that challenged the legitimacy of the dominant society's policing of homosexual sociation.

Other cultural factors important to what the critical mass did after coming together in the instance of the American gay/lesbian movement include the American tradition of printing dissident views and (some, at least nominal) valuing of freedom of expression. This is a value missing everywhere else in the western hemisphere; not that the value

was sufficient in itself for extension to the homophile press without fight in the courts before the US Supreme Court ordered the US Post Office to cease blocking as 'obscence' anything about homosexuality.[18] Also important to the development of American gay movement(s) is the tradition of voluntary associations deriving from the religious pluralism of the United States.

Some repression against which to mobilize is a prerequisite to politicalization (Adam et al., 1999). In a sense, some repression is good for organizing, though this is a good of which it is easy to get too much, making activism excessively high risk and even lethal (as in most Mesoamerican countries). Moreover, what is good for crystallizing a movement is generally not good for those living in a society, whatever one may think of the value of forging oppositional identities.

CONCLUSION

Although, the lengthy preceding section is based on comparative studies of gay/lesbian movements in different countries, it focuses on cultural particularities that seem to be importantly related to the emergence of the largest and most vociferous (though seemingly not the most successful) movement for gay/lesbian equality. Much more detailed comparison of tactics and of the resources that have been mobilized in different organizations in different places remains to be done. In this chapter, I stressed the intra-cultural variation in regard to types of homosexual relationships. Intranational variation in types, degree, success, etc. of gay/lesbian movements also needs to be addressed – or at least remembered.

Although comparison of national/social patterns is central to the Marx/Weber/Durkheim 'grand tradition' of sociology, comparative sociology of homosexualities is in an infancy of trying to establish enough reliable data to compare patterns, whether patterns of behaviors, of roles, of structural

differentiations, or of sociopolitical mobilization. More and better data are needed to
advance beyond the kinds of generalizations
reviewed here, especially to begin to account
for intrasocietal differences and for the lived
experiences even of those following the
most common script for same-sex sexuality
in a particular time and place.

NOTES

1 The claim that there was no notion of homosexual
personages before late nineteenth-century forensic medical
discourse has stimulated a great deal of disconfirmatory
research, e.g., Richlin (1993); Sweet and Zwilling (1993);
Leupp (1995); Murray (1980, 1995b, 2000).

2 The conflation of statistical and prescriptive norms in
discourse about 'deviance' and 'normal' renders them
unuseful concepts (unless statistical or prescriptive sense
is specified).

3 Against the recent tendency to obliterate it and speak
only of 'gender' I have retained the classical feminist
distinction of 'sex' (male/female by birth and chromosomal
configuration) from 'gender' (enacting masculine or
feminine roles in particular societies). Much 'same-gender'
means masculine–masculine or feminine–feminine (butch–
butch or femme–femme). Much same-sex sex is heterogender (butch/femme role-demarcated) and euphemizing 'sex'
in favor of distending the analytical category 'gender'
makes it impossible to distinguish homogender from
heterogender homosexuality. Also, the ultimate arbiter of
'sex' is chromosomal not genital (genitalia may be altered or
may be unclear; true hermaphrodites are exceedingly rare).

4 Even though there is pressure from others to incorporate a role into a defining part of the self, role-self merger
is not automatic (Turner, 1978), and even after such a
merger, one can still distinguish 'part of the self' from
being (all of) the self.

5 See Murray (1995a: 49–64, 150–69; 1996: 146–68;
1999b).

6 If climate accounts for the differences he postulated,
it is difficult to understand the expansion northward to
encompass Japan and the inclusion of the whole of the
Americas in his sotadic zone, and not including Sub-
Saharan African regions with Mediterranean-like climates.
The part of the 'Terminal essay' on homosexualities across
space was separately printed as Burton (1930).

7 Looking at the anthropological records in the Human
Relations Area Files, developed at Yale University, Ford
and Beach (1951) showed that fewer human societies
negatively sanctioned than accepted some male homosexuality. Data were missing for many societies, and many
of the codings of intolerance (negative sanctions) were
dubious (see Greenberg, 1988: 177–88).

8 The distinctive features of 'gay homosexuality' are
(1) a group consciousness of comprising a distinct kind
and; (2) a separate subculture based on the *possibility* of
same-sex relations that (a) are egalitarian (not gender-
role-bound or involving the submission of the young) and
(b) have the chance to be exclusive (not bisexual) for both
partners (Adam 1979; elaborated in Adam 1987: 6). Like
gender-structured and age-structured relations of same-
sex sexuality, this is an ideal type – 'ideal' in the normative sense of 'aspiration' as well as in the sense of
abstraction from empirical cases that do not fully match it.
It seems impossible sufficiently to stress 'possibility' in it.

9 Based on spurious etymology, the current politically
correct term is 'two-spirit[ed].'

10 There has been a great deal of discourse about the
relationship of 'modernity' to 'modern gay homosexuality' with some *ad hoc* use of comparative material and/or
inclusion of discussions of homosexualities in non-Anglo-
phone societies with little more than the proclamation of
changes accompanying a unilinear traditional-modern-
postmodern evolution (some of the richer examples
include Bech, 1997, Plummer, 1992, Simon, 1996; Simon
and Gagnon, 1986; Sullivan and Leong, 1995).

11 In addition to comparing forms of homosexual
relations and conditions of lesbigay movements, Adam's
earliest (1978) work compared the social psychological
responses to stigmatization by European and American
Jews, gays, and persons of African descent.

12 Note should be taken of lesbigay moral entrepreneurs,
usually operating alone, who seek state aid in repressing
what they regard as unsavory activities of less respectable
others, s&m activities, leather, drag, 'promiscuous' and/ or
'public' sex being recurrent examples. Examples include a
gay man who complained to Boston authorities that sex was
occurring at the Safari Club, a small band of gay New Yorkers
who reported and decried sex in Manhattan sex clubs, the
two San Franciscans who pushed for closing bathhouses
(see Murray, 1996: 111–13), and lesbian feminists attacking
lesbian s&m and 'pornography'.

13 Even though provision of health care remains a
chaos of private and public responsibilities in the USA.

14 Religion reinforces familial values, although to
some degree providing socially-acceptable alternative
same-sex grouping. Buddhist monks are a visible and
important force in South-East Asia. In Northern Mediter-
ranean and Latin American countries, less-than-robustly-
masculine boys are channeled towards the priesthood.

15 Although I am not aware of any studies of the diffusion and reception of representations of butch–butch sex,
I have heard very similar (and independent) assertions of
this importance from men living in at least ten Third
World countries.

16 From the histories that Alfred Kinsey and his associates elicited from white American males during the
1930s and 1940s, it became clear that many men, not just
those who were labeled by themselves or others as 'queer'
had some sexual experience with other males. Although
Freudians continued to propose various causes for being

'homosexual', the 1948 Kinsey report was important in undercutting the plausibility that there was a unitary 'homosexuality' or that same-sex sex was extremely rare.

17 In comparing social movements Oliver and Marwell (1988) showed that the positive effect on collective action of the size of a population with grievances increases with group heterogeneity and with overlapping social circles, even though a lower proportion (and even when fewer individuals) may be mobilized than within smaller populations: 'Paradoxically, when groups are heterogeneous, fewer contributors may be needed to provide a good to larger groups' (p. 1; also see Taylor, 1989: 766–8 and McAdam, 1982, on exclusiveness and high commitment in small movements).

18 The landmark case was *ONE, Inc. v. The U.S. Postal Service* in 1958. On the interlocking of postal censors with local police and local newspapers in suppressing the first gay rights organization in the United States (Chicago's Society for Human Rights in 1925), see Kepner and Murray (2001).

REFERENCES

Adam, Barry D. (1978) *The Survival of Domination.* New York: Elsevier.

Adam, Barry D. (1979) 'Reply', *Sociologists Gay Caucus Newsletter*, 18: 8.

Adam, Barry D. (1995) 'Structural foundations of the gay world', *Comparative Studies in Society and History*, 27: 658–70.

Adam, Barry D. (1986) 'Age, structure and sexuality', *Journal of Homosexuality*, 11: 19–33.

Adam, Barry D. (1987) *The Rise of a Gay and Lesbian Movement.* Boston: Twayne.

Adam, Barry D., Duyvendak, Jan W. and Krouwel, André (1999) *The Global Emergence of Gay and Lesbian Politics: National Imprints of a Worldwide Movement.* Philadelphia, PA: Temple University Press.

Asch, Solomon (1958) 'Group pressure upon the modification and distortion of judgments', in E. Macoby et al. (eds), *Readings in Social Psychology.* New York: Holt. pp. 174–83.

Bech, Henning (1997) *When Men Meet: Homosexuality and Modernity.* Chicago: University of Chicago Press.

Bleys, Rudi C. (1995) *The Geography of Perversion: Male-to-Male Sexual Behavior Outside the West and the Ethnographic Imagination, 1750–1918.* New York: New York University Press.

Bullough, Vern (1976) *Sexual Variance in Society and History.* New York: Wiley.

Burton, Richard Francis (1885–1886) *A Plain and Literal Translation of the Arabian Nights.* Printed by the Kama Shastra Society for private subscribers of the Burton Club, 10 volumes. (Facsimile edition, Denver: Press of the Carson-Harper Co., 1899–1901;

reprinted in 7 volumes, New York: Limited Editions Club, 1934.)

Burton, Richard Francis (1930 [1886]) *The Sotadic Zone.* New York: Panurge Press. (Reprinted, Boston: Longwood Press, 1977.)

Carrington, Christopher (1999) *No Place Like Home: Relationships and Family Life Among Lesbians and Gay Men.* Chicago: University of Chicago Press.

Chauncey, George W., Jr (1994) *Gay New York: Gender, Urban Culture and the Making of the Gay Male World, 1890–1940.* New York: Basic Books.

Churchill, Wainwright (1967) *Homosexual Behavior Among Males.* New York: Hawthorn.

Cory, Donald Webster and LeRoy, John P. (1963) *The Homosexual and His Society: A View from Within.* New York: Citadel Press.

D'Emilio, John (1983) *Sexual Politics, Sexual Communities* Chicago: University of Chicago Press.

Fischer, Claude S. (1975) 'Toward a subcultural theory of urbanism', *American Journal of Sociology*, 80: 1319–41.

Ford, Clellan S. and Beach, Frank A. (1951) *Patterns of Sexual Behavior.* New York: Harper & Row.

Foucault, Michel (1980) *The History of Sexuality.* New York: Vintage.

Gagnon, John H. and Simon, William (1967) *Sexual Conduct.* Chicago: Aldine.

Green, James N. (1999a) *Beyond Carnival.* Chicago: University of Chicago Press.

Green, James N. (1999b) '"More love and more desire": the building of a Brazilian movement', in Barry D. Adam et al. (eds), *The Global Emergence of Gay and Lesbian Politics.* Philadelphia: Temple Press. pp. 91–109.

Greenberg, David F. (1988) *The Construction of Homosexuality.* Chicago: University of Chicago Press.

Herdt, Gilbert H. (1981) *Guardians of the Flute.* New York: Macmillan.

Herdt, Gilbert H. (1984) *Ritualized Homosexuality in Melanesia.* Berkeley, CA: University of California Press.

Herdt, Gilbert H. (1987) 'Homosexuality', *Encyclopedia of Religion*, vol. 6. New York: Macmillan. 445–52.

Jordan, Mark D. (1997) *The Invention of Sodomy in Christian Theology.* Chicago: University of Chicago Press.

Kepner, Jim and Murray, Stephen (2001) 'Henry Gerber: grandfather of America's gay movement', to appear in *Before Stonewall: The Fight for Homosexual Rights.* (ed). by Vern Bullough. Binghamton, New York: Haworth.

Khan, Badruddin (1997) 'Not-so-gay life on Karachi,' in S.O. Murray and W. Roscoe (eds), *Islamic Homosexualities.* New York: New York University Press. pp. 275–96.

Kinsey, Alfred C., Pomeroy, Wardell B. and Martin, Clyde E. (1948) *Sexual Behavior in the Human Male.* Philadelphia: Saunders.

Leupp, Gary P. (1995) *Male Colors: The Construction of Homosexuality in Tokugawa Japan.* Berkeley, CA: University of California Press.

Leupp, Gary P. (1998) "The floating world is wide ...":
some suggested approaches to researching female
homosexuality in Tokugawa Japan (1603–1868)',
Thamyris, 5: 1–40.

Lunsing, Wim (1999) 'Japan', in Barry D. Adam et al.
(eds), *The Global Emergence of Gay and Lesbian Politics*. Philadelphia. Temple University Press. pp. 293–325.

McAdam, Doug (1982) *Political Process and the
Development of Black Insurgency, 1930–1970*. Chicago:
University of Chicago Press.

Murray, Stephen O. (1980) 'Lexical and institutional elaboration: the "species homosexual" in Guatemale',
Anthropological Linguistics, 22: 177–85.

Murray, Stephen O. (1981) 'Socially structuring prototype
semantics', *Forum Linguisticum*, 8: 95–102.

Murray, Stephen O. (1984) *Social Theories, Homosexual
Realities*. New York: Gay Academic Union.

Murray, Stephen O. (1987) *Male Homosexuality in Central
and South America*. New York: Gay Academic Union.

Murray, Stephen O. (1992) *Oceanic Homosexualities*.
New York: Garland.

Murray, Stephen O. (1995a) *Latin American Male Homosexualities*. Albuquerque: University of New Mexico
Press.

Murray, Stephen O. (1995b) 'Some Southwest Asian and
North African terms for homosexual roles', *Archives of
Sexual Behavior*, 24: 623–9.

Murray, Stephen O. (1995c) 'Stigma transformation and
relexification in the international diffusion of *gay*', in
William Leap (ed.), *Beyond the Lavender Lexicon*.
New York: Gordon & Breach. pp. 215–40.

Murray, Stephen O. (1996) *American Gay*. Chicago:
University of Chicago Press.

Murray, Stephen O. (1998) 'Organizations of homosexuality and other social structures in sub-Saharan Africa', in
S.O. Murray and W. Roscoe (eds), *Islamic Homosexualities*. New York: New York University Press.
pp. 283–97.

Murray, Stephen O. (1999a) 'The development of lesbigay
studies in the United States of America', in Raymond
Donovan and Leong K. Chan (eds), *Guide to Lesbian,
Gay and Queer Studies*. Sydney: University of Sydney
Centre for Lesbian and Gay Research. pp. 47–60.

Murray, Stephen O. (1999b) 'Representations of desires in
some recent Gay Asian-American Writings', paper
presented at Society for the Scientific Study of Sex,
Western Region annual meetings in San Francisco,
23 April.

Murray, Stephen O. (2000) *Homosexualities*. Chicago:
University of Chicago Press.

Murray, Stephen O. and Roscoe, Will (1997) *Islamic
Homosexualities*. New York: New York University
Press.

Murray, Stephen O. and Roscoe, Will (1998) *Boy-Wives
and Female Husbands: Studies of African Homosexualities*. New York: St Martin's Press.

Oliver, Pamela E. and Marwell, Gerald (1988) 'The
paradox of group size in collective action: a theory of
critical mass II', *American Sociological Review*, 53: 1–8.

Plummer, Ken (1992) *Modern Homosexualities*. London:
Routledge.

Richlin, Amy (1993) 'Not before homosexuality: the
materiality of the *Cinædus* and the Roman law against
love between men', *Journal of the History of Sexuality*,
3: 523–73.

Roscoe, Will (1977) 'Precursors of Islamic male homosexualities', in S.O. Murray and W. Roscoe (eds),
Islamic Homosexualities. New York: New York University Press. pp. 55–86.

Roscoe, Will (1988) 'Making history: the challenge of
gay and lesbian studies', *Journal of Homosexuality*,
15: 1–40.

Roscoe, Will (1998) *Changing Ones: Third and Fourth
Genders in Native North America*. New York:
St. Martin's Press.

Simon, William (1996) *Sexual Postmodernity*. New York:
Routledge.

Simon, William and Gagnon, John (1986) 'Sexual scripts'
Archives of Sexual Behavior, 15: 97–120.

Snow, David A., Zurcher, Louis A. and Ekland-Olson,
Sheldon (1980) 'Social networks and social movements: a microstructural approach to differential recruitment.' *American Sociological Review*, 45: 787–801.

Sullivan, Gerard and Leong, Laurence (1995) *Gays and
Lesbians in Asia and the Pacific* New York: Haworth.

Sweet, Michael J. and Zwilling, Leonard (1993) 'The first
medicalization: the taxonomy and etiology of queerness
in classical Indian medicine', *Journal of the History of
Sexuality*, 3: 590–607.

Taylor, Verta (1989) 'Social movement continuity',
American Sociological Review, 54: 761–75.

Trumbach, Randolph (1977) 'London's sodomites', *Journal
of Social History*, 11: 1–33.

Trumbach, Randolph (1985) 'Sodomitical subcultures,
sodomitical roles, and the gender revolution of the 18th
century', *Eighteenth Century Studies*, 9: 109–21.

Turner, Ralph H. (1978) 'The role and the person',
American Journal of Sociology, 84: 1–23.

Weber, Max (1978) *Economy and Society*. Berkeley:
University of California Press.

Whitam, Frederick L. (1987) 'Os entendidos: gay life in
Saõ Paulo', in Stephen O. Murray (ed.), *Male Homo-
sexuality in Central and South America* New York: Gay
Academic Union, pp. 24–39.

Whitam, Frederick L. (1995) 'Bayot and callboy:
homosexual-heterosexual relations in the Philippines',
in S.O. Murray *Oceanic Homosexualities*. New York:
Garland. pp. 231–48.

Winkler, John J. (1990) *The Constraints of Desire: The
Anthropology of Sex and Gender in Ancient Greece*.
New York: Routledge.

Part II

IDENTITY AND COMMUNITY

7

From the Bowery to the Castro

Communities, Identities and Movements

VERTA TAYLOR, ELIZABETH KAMINSKI
AND KIMBERLY DUGAN

Communities of people with same-sex desires – whether fairy communities in the early twentieth century, butch-fem communities mid-century, or contemporary lesbian, gay, bisexual, transgender, or queer communities – have been and are essential to both the affirmation of same-sex sexuality and love and to collective resistance to cultural norms of gender and sexuality. The earliest communities made it possible for men interested in sex with other men to find each other. Over time, women, too, gained access to the public places that served as a center of same-sex community life. The first lesbian and gay social movements grew from these existing communities. Without the solidarity and shared identity that is constructed in communities, there would be no gay and lesbian movement. Yet the relationship between movements and communities is complex and sometimes adversarial. Indeed, by the last quarter of the twentieth century, the burgeoning gay and lesbian movement had given birth to new institutions and communities that sometimes came into conflict with the old ones.

In this chapter, we provide an overview of research on gay and lesbian[1] communities concentrating on the United States. We begin by examining the way scholars have applied the term community to identify the networks, identities, territories, and shared culture organized around same-sex desire. Our discussion focuses on the historical rise and development of distinct gay neighborhoods, emphasizing their growth and elaboration in urban areas especially since the 1970s. In addition to demonstrating the role that these communities play in providing companionship and solidarity, we argue that communities are significant not only as social outlets but as political entities as well because they lay claim to public space and foster collective identities that challenge and redefine societal expectations and cultural norms of gender and sexuality. We concentrate our discussion on the relationship between gay and lesbian communities and the gay, lesbian, bisexual, and transgender movement. Social movements emerge among pre-existing social networks where people communicate daily, develop close affective ties, and share cultural values and practices (McAdam, 1986; Morris, 1984; Taylor, 2000). Scholarship within gay and lesbian studies has established that communities are important antecedents of social movements. Here we extend the argument by suggesting that not only are the collective identities formed within gay and lesbian communities necessary to mobilize people into political activism, but, at the same time, gay and lesbian political activism both sustains and fragments gay community.

DEFINING COMMUNITY

Scholars (see, for example, Beemyn, 1997; Chauncey, 1994; D'Emilio, 1983; Esterberg, 1997; Johnson, 1997; Kennedy and Davis, 1993; Levine, 1979; Murray, 1998; Rupp, 1999; Rupp and Taylor, 2002; Stein, 1997) have documented various distinct communities of gay and lesbian people in the United States, particularly attending to those that have developed since the Second World War. Despite such convincing accounts of gay communities, identifying specific criteria for defining community has proven problematic (Murray, 1998: 207). Scholars have competing ways of conceptualizing community. Some define community as a distinct physical territory bounded by time and space. For example, Carol Warren (1998) focuses on the concrete physical settings, including bars and private homes, that constitute the gay community and provide a separate space apart from the larger heterosexist and homophobic society in which individuals can express and celebrate gay identity. Martin Levine (1979) similarly emphasizes the spatial and territorial boundaries that set apart gay residential enclaves in large American cities.

By contrast, others who have researched lesbian and gay communities direct attention to social ties and networks rather than local identifiers such as neighborhood or public spaces. For example, Peter Nardi (1999) uses gay male friendships to draw the parameters of community, and for Susan Krieger (1983) the critical features of lesbian community are social and sexual ties and a commitment to feminist principles. Verta Taylor and Nicole Raeburn (1995) also focus on social ties and

suggest that gay communities are composed of submerged networks of people who affirm same-sex sexuality and love; such networks frequently take root in mainstream institutions such as the workplace.

Verta Taylor and Nancy Whittier (1992) extend the argument that networks are critical to building community. They view the existence of distinctive institutions, cultural activities, and political organizations as essential to the identification of community. Lesbians and gay men accomplish this through the creation of independent institutions and events, such as the annual Michigan Womyn's Music Festival and gay pride marches across the country. Likewise, Esther Newton's (1998: 38) research on what she describes as the 'gay world' focuses on formal political or social movement organizations such as the Mattachine Society and Daughters of Bilitis in the 1950s, as well as social institutions including bars, cafés, and bathhouses and informal social groups or networks. However, she argues that not all gay people – especially people living outside cities and suburbs – are part of the community and suggests that the word 'community' implies a degree of coherence that belies the multiplicity of different lesbian and gay communities over time.

Looking at studies that have examined a range of communities over the course of the twentieth century, nevertheless we can see some common elements. First, communities are characterized by shared identities based on same-sex love and desire, although the names for and understandings of those identities change over time and from place to place. Second, communities are defined by distinct physical space – such as parks, neighborhoods, bars, bookstores, or coffeehouses – in which people gather. Third, communities are built around social networks, institutions, or events. And, fourth, communities are marked by common cultural ideas and practices, including behavior, attire, and language that stand as markers of identity (Rupp, 1999: 103–4).

Although the gay communities we discuss here share these same basic elements, the content of communal identity and culture varies significantly throughout time and in different parts of the country. Within communities, people develop and cultivate networks of friends, meet partners, and define for themselves and for society what it means to be a person who desires and loves someone of the same sex. Sometimes these self-definitions are hotly contested, as, for example, when transgendered people reject the terms 'gay and lesbian' to describe themselves, or people who define themselves as 'gay' or 'lesbian' refuse to ally with the contemporary 'queer' identity (Gamson, 1995). Internal conflicts over identity often take the form of disagreements over the boundaries of communities, which is the case, for example, when women debate whether or not bisexuals are part of the lesbian community (Esterberg, 1997; Rust, 1995). Gay communities change over time in response to these internal identity disputes. In addition, the political and cultural environment profoundly shapes the growth of communities and the possibilities for the emergence of social movements from them (Dugan, 1999; Kaminski and Taylor, 2001).

CONSTRUCTING COMMUNITIES AND IDENTITIES

In the decades prior to the emergence of an identifiable gay and lesbian movement in the 1960s and 1970s, men who desired men and women who desired women were actively forming their own subcultures and communities. Although some scholars argue that gay male communities existed in European cities as early as the sixteenth and seventeenth centuries (e.g. Saslow, 1989; Trumbach, 1989), the communities that emerged at the turn of the twentieth century and flourished in the 1920s and 1930s are the earliest documented gay communities in the United States. In major urban areas, men and women with same-sex desires knew where to find one another, used particular labels to identify themselves, and developed codes of dress and behavior that marked them as particular kinds of people (Rupp, 1999: 102). Barry Adam (1987: 39) points to 'a well-developed gay underground in all the major cities' – including Washington, DC, Philadelphia, New York, Chicago, and Los Angeles – composed of various clubs, bars, restaurants, bookstores, residential neighborhoods, parks, and other meeting places. These early communities, which nurtured a rich public culture, were organized around shared characteristics regarding sexual object choice and gender performance (Chauncey, 1994; Garber, 1989; Johnson, 1997).

A number of social factors facilitated the appearance of these early lesbian and gay communities. Most importantly, urbanization brought large numbers of men and women into close proximity in singles' rooming houses. The lack of privacy combined with the anonymity of city life led to the creation of a sexualized working-class culture in bars and saloons, and, in this context, men and later women began to identify around the basis of same-sex erotic desires and practices. Yet in addition to such large, urban areas as New York City, where we might expect the existence of community at such an early time period, communities organized around same-sex desire also appeared in such places as Salt Lake City, Utah (Rupp, 1999).

Although historians have recorded the existence of pre-Stonewall gay communities and their importance as social outlets for people seeking the companionship of others who desired same-sex relationships, our discussion of these early communities highlights the political impact of community-building. The gay communities that emerged at the beginning of the twentieth century consisted of submerged networks of individuals who constructed a positive collective identity – sometimes in a complex relationship with the emerging medical discourse on 'homosexuality' – and created boundaries between themselves and the larger mainstream heterosexist society. The construction of a collective identity based on sexual-object choice was essential to the later development of a gay and lesbian social movement. Moreover, these communities claimed public space for gays and lesbians and created their own cultural norms that challenged aspects of the dominant gender and sexual system.

George Chauncey's *Gay New York* (1994) presents an extensive study of a gay male community at the beginning of the twentieth century. Chauncey convincingly argues for the political nature of gay communities of the 1910s and 1920s by highlighting the 'strategies of everyday resistance that men devised in order to claim space for themselves in the midst of a hostile society' (ibid.: 5). The strategies men used to create their identities and network with other men with same-sex desires varied by class. Working-class men typically adopted a 'fairy' identity that was characterized by effeminacy as well as same-sex object choice. For example, most fairies took on women's names and called each other by feminine terms of endearment such as 'princess' or 'sister'. While fairies did not typically dress completely in women's clothes, they did often wear one feminine article or piece of clothing that was considered flashy, such as a red tie or suede shoes. They often colored their hair, plucked their eyebrows, or wore cosmetics such as lipstick or face powder. In addition, fairies could be identified by their gestures and demeanor that imitated feminine mannerisms. For example, fairies' style of swiveling their hips while walking was known as 'swishing'.

New York was not the only city in which a fairy culture emerged. Chauncey's description of fairies in New York is consistent with Johnson's (1997) research on a gay community in Chicago. Johnson notes that many gay men in the 1930s adopted the effeminate characteristics of the fairy role. Chauncey (1989) also describes the existence of a fairy role in Newport, Rhode Island, in his research on Navy men who engaged in same-sex sexual relations. Sailors who were accused of homosexuality in a Navy investigation in 1919–20 were typically described as wearing make-up and acting effeminate. As all of these examples illustrate, gender transgression was a salient aspect of many emerging gay male communities.

In addition to the self-defined label of 'fairies', men in gay communities in the 1920s and 1930s came up with other terms for themselves such as 'pogues', and 'two-way artists' based on the type of sexual acts they preferred (Chauncey, 1989). Unlike the terms created by sexologists, the classification system used by gay men did not suggest a dichotomy between homosexual and heterosexual based on sexual object choice. The research by Chauncey (1989, 1994) and Johnson (1997) provides clear evidence that the labels of the medical and scientific community were largely irrelevant to how gay men defined themselves, undermining the view that gay identity and communities arose as a result of sexologists' definition of homosexuality as a separate and deviant category (Faderman, 1978).

Middle-class gay men typically took on a different identity. Objecting to the image of the effeminate fairy, middle-class 'queers' maintained a more masculine style of self-presentation to maintain their respectability (Chauncey, 1994). Chauncey describes how these men utilized a strategy of leading a double life: they participated in the gay subculture on weekends or in the evenings, but passed as straight at work. Although these men were unwilling to identify themselves as queer in the workplace because they did not want to risk losing their jobs, they did make use of gay expressions that had double meanings so that they could identify and network with each other at work but still pass as heterosexual. Similarly, Chauncey's (1989) study of sailors in Newport reports the existence of more masculine men, termed 'husbands', in that community. It was only the fairies, and not the 'straight' men who sought them out for sexual encounters, who took on an identity around their sexual practices and who faced repression as a result.

Although gay men had been visible in the streets of New York and in particular social establishments since the end of the nineteenth century, Chauncey (1994: 301) argues that in the Prohibition years of the 1920s, the working-class fairy culture acquired unprecedented prominence in the mainstream culture of New York City. Drag balls, which had been a part of the fairy culture, became popular attractions and led to what Chauncey terms a 'pansy craze'. By the 1920s, gay social communities had not only developed a subculture and identity for themselves, but their cultural events became well known to the larger public as well. Stories about drag balls appeared in tabloid newspapers, such as *Broadway Brevities* and by the 1930s drag balls were even being staged in Madison Square Garden and the Astor Hotel in midtown (Chauncey, 1994).

The growing public visibility of gay culture is also evident in Eric Garber's (1989) description of the Harlem Renaissance. As Garber notes, same-sex sexuality was often the topic of literature and lyrics written by black artists and intellectuals in Harlem. In addition, gender transgression, same-sex relationships, and other markers of gay culture were visible in Harlem's rent parties, clubs, and speakeasies. The gay culture that emerged in the Harlem Renaissance has some similarities with the culture of the fairies. Like fairies, gay entertainers in Harlem often adopted cross-gender behaviors. Gladys Bentley, for example, was a well-known lesbian musician who performed in a tuxedo and top hat. Drag balls were popular in Harlem as they were in fairy communities elsewhere in New York. Importantly, the terms – such as 'sissies', 'faggots', and 'bulldaggers' – that were used in Harlem to describe those who desired same-sex relationships carried connotations of gender transgression. Although Garber labels the participants in Harlem's gay culture 'homosexuals', 'gays', or 'lesbians', the evidence that he presents suggests that these individuals may have actually used the terms 'faggot' and

'bulldagger' to describe themselves. Thus, like the 'pogues' and 'fairies' described by Chauncey (1989), members of gay communities in Harlem had their own system of classification and labeling that was not equivalent to the sexologists' schemes.

Along with greater racial and class integration than other communities, Harlem in the 1920s made more of a place for lesbians. Like Gladys Bentley, many of the prominent entertainers and artists in Harlem were lesbian or bisexual. The greater involvement of women in the gay community may be a result of African American women's tradition of involvement in the public sphere. In contrast to white women, African American women had a longer history of participation in the workforce. Lesbian subcultures are less well documented because women had less financial independence and access to both work and leisure institutions than men. Despite these constraints, some research suggests that lesbian communities did emerge during the 1920s among working-class women who, by virtue of their economic circumstances, were forced into the public sphere to earn a living. Lillian Faderman (1991) suggests that separate white and African American lesbian communities existed in Chicago in the 1920s, and Vern and Bonnie Bullough (1977) note the evidence of a lesbian community in Salt Lake City, Utah.

Along with describing the cultural characteristics of fairies and queers, Chauncey (1989, 1994) and Johnson (1997) also emphasize the importance of networks in the lives of gay men in urban America. They both describe how gay men's ties with one another not only served as important sources of social and sexual fulfillment but also provided economic assistance and help in finding work and housing. These forms of aid were particularly important to men who had recently moved to the city in order to be closer to gay culture. Chauncey (1994) uses the term 'chain migration' to describe how gay men assisted newcomers to the city, thus facilitating the construction of community. Johnson (1997) notes that many gay men relied on each other for economic support during the Depression. While these networks did not constitute formal organizations, they were extremely important as survival strategies.

As networks of gay men grew and fairy culture became more visible, gay communities also claimed public, physical space. The territories that gays claimed included residential neighborhoods, such as the near north side of Chicago, bars, restaurants, parks, baths, and YMCA centers (Chauncey, 1989; Chauncey, 1994; Johnson, 1997). Although these gay spaces were sometimes confined to specific neighborhoods on the periphery of cities, Chauncey (1994) argues that, in the 1920s, gay culture was prominent in public spaces throughout New York City. Gay men, at the height of the pansy craze, were not just confined to gay neighborhoods such as Harlem, the Bowery, and Greenwich Village, but became prominent in Times Square too. Similarly, Johnson points out that gay men's meeting places were located in the center of downtown Chicago, not on the outskirts.

During the 1930s, however, the public space available to gays began to shrink (Chauncey, 1994). With the onset of the Depression, people began to frown on the consumerism and excess of the 1920s. As a result, social interactions that had been tolerated in the 1920s were becoming more stigmatized in the 1930s. Police began to raid and shut down bars with gay patrons, particularly those located in Times Square. Effeminate-looking men were specifically targeted, as their fairy persona was a marker for their sexual identity. Fairies were therefore pushed back into exclusively gay bars on the outskirts of the city, while less overt and more masculine queers could remain in the public spaces in the urban center. Although gay culture may have become less visible in New York in the 1930s as gays retreated into more private spaces such as house parties and baths, it did not entirely disappear from the public sphere. Gay men continued to have a presence in the city, partly by drawing on the cultural strategies

that they had developed in the preceding decades (Chauncey, 1994; Johnson, 1997).

Some scholars question whether or not these subcultures constitute a gay community because of the 'lack of institutions, collective action, and a willingness to fight back' (Murray, 1998: 212). In our view, community is evident in the appropriation of physical spaces, such as bars or parks or neighborhoods, in the creation of interpersonal networks and strong personal ties, and in the elaboration of gay culture, including language, dress, and mannerisms. Through these cultural enactments, men and women forged a collective self-definition of what it meant to be gay – or, more accurately, what it meant to be a fairy, a bulldagger, a sissy, or a queer. Although a formal social movement is lacking during this period, the identities and networks built in gay communities in the early twentieth century would prove to be essential resources for a later movement. Moreover, the distinctive gay cultures that emerged in this period provided men and women with everyday ways to resist heteronormative gender and sexual codes. Although these turn of the century communities may appear different from current gay communities or movements, it is evident that they constructed positive self-identities, created cultures of resistance, claimed public space, and protected individual men and women who identified with the community.

FROM COMMUNITIES TO MOVEMENTS

Early same-sex communities of men and women facilitated everyday acts of resistance, what Elizabeth Lapovsky Kennedy and Madeline Davis (1993) call 'prepolitical' activism. Such resistance eventually led to formal organization. Significantly, the first short-lived social movement organization in the United States grew out of community institutions. The Society for Human Rights, officially established in Chicago late in 1924, was inspired by the vibrant gay German cultural and political scene. Its founder, who had served in Germany as a member of the American armed forces, sought 'to promote and protect the interests of people who by reasons of mental and physical abnormalities are abused and hindered in the legal pursuit of happiness … guaranteed by the Declaration of Independence' (cited in Katz, 1976: 385). Compared to gay communities in American cities, gays and lesbians in Berlin in the 1920s were more formally organized. One of the main organizations in Berlin was the Scientific-Humanitarian committee founded by Magnus Hirschfeld. Unlike American communities, which often challenged the labels and classification systems of the sexologists, Hirschfeld's committee closely allied itself with the medical establishment with the aim of promoting scientific research on sexuality that would educate the public and promote greater social tolerance. The Nazi regime attacked and eventually destroyed the gay reform movement in Berlin. Similarly, the first gay organization in the United States suffered a swift demise after the arrest of its officers.

The first successful gay social movement, the homophile movement of the 1950s, grew out of the gay and lesbian communities that flowered during the Second World War. Allan Bérubé (1989) suggests that for Americans, the war facilitated same-sex interaction and provided a context in which many men and women could adopt a gay or lesbian identity. Although the official policy stated that homosexuals were not permitted in the military, gays and lesbians were tolerated during the war. The war provided men and women from rural backgrounds with their first opportunity to have contact with gay networks that had previously been confined largely to urban areas. Yet despite the tolerance of homosexuality and the fluidity of gender roles during the war, the cold war political climate of the post-war period brought repression that also facilitated the rise of organized resistance (D'Emilio, 1989b). Veterans who had served honorably found themselves dishonorably discharged for their sexuality, but a few found the voice

to speak out and protest their treatment (Bérubé, 1990). In addition, the attacks on homosexuality in military and civilian life actually spread word of the gay community, making it easier for both interested men and women and hostile observers to find it. Further, the role of San Francisco as the port of debarkation for the Pacific theater increased the city's reputation as a gay mecca (D'Emilio, 1989b: 459). As in Greenwich Village and Harlem, the bohemian culture of San Francisco's North Beach area gave rise to both sexual experimentation and political activism. The police harassment that was so prevalent in gay communities in the post-war period provoked the owners and employees of a number of gay bars to organize the Tavern Guild to fight for the right to serve gay patrons (D'Emilio, 1983).

In such an environment, gay and lesbian communities made individual survival possible and facilitated the construction of a collective identity that challenged cultural norms of gender and sexuality. The research by Elizabeth Lapovsky Kennedy and Madeline Davis (1993) documents a working-class lesbian community in Buffalo, New York, from 1940 to 1960. This community, like others of the time period, was organized primarily around bars and structured by butch and fem roles. Butches enacted their sexual and gender identities by adopting a particular style of dress. Typically, they wore short, greased-back hairstyles, pants, and starched men's dress shirts. Fems, by contrast, did not follow a dress code unique to the lesbian community but instead conformed to the dominant fashion trends for women. Yet fems as well as butches exhibited what Joan Nestle calls 'sexual courage' by making public their same-sex relationships through the simple act of being together on the streets (Nestle, 1981). Kennedy and Davis (1993) convincingly argue that the social networks and solidarity forged by working-class butches and fems were instrumental in mobilizing a gay and lesbian political movement in later decades. Yet during the 1950s, the bar culture remained separate from the emerging political organizations of the homophile movement.

The first lasting gay social movement organization was the Mattachine Society, founded in 1951 by an active member of the Communist Party, Harry Hay. Hay turned to the lively gay community of Los Angeles to recruit his first members, taking copies of a petition opposing the Korean War to the gay male beaches, assuming that any men willing to sign might be likely candidates for a homosexual rights organization (D'Emilio, 1983). Hay turned to the gay community again when a founder of the organization was arrested in a public park, using the case to recruit in gay neighborhoods. Even after Hay and his radical compatriots were forced out of the organization they had founded (Epstein, 1999), the male homophile movement had more success in mobilizing the existing gay community than did the women's organization, the Daughters of Bilitis, which was explicitly founded as an alternative to the bar culture. Despite the gender segregation of most lesbian and gay communities, however, some women and men worked together. A member of the Ell Club in blue-collar Bridgeport, Pennsylvania, just outside Philadelphia, in 1957 described the club as 'bringing closer unity between the boys and girls', since they were all 'working for one goal, to be accepted' (Stein, 1994: 210).

The two major homophile organizations worked to form communities around the goal of winning basic human rights for gay and lesbian people, and they fostered a culture of 'middle-class respectability' (D'Emilio, 1989a: 469). They encouraged gender conformity, especially in dress, and the Mattachine Society worked to repress the 'stereotypical promiscuous image of male homosexuality' (ibid.: 460). As a result of this assimilationist stance, however, women in the bar culture and men who were part of the traditional gay world had little use for these organizations.

Yet what is generally marked as the origins of the contemporary gay and lesbian movement – the Stonewall riot – was not an entirely unique act of resistance to a police raid by bar patrons (Adam, 1987; Cruikshank, 1992; D'Emilio, 1983; Duberman, 1993). Gay men and women – and especially butch dykes and

men in drag – were often the target of police harassment in the 1950s and throughout the 1960s (Adam, 1987: 76; D'Emilio, 1983; see also Duberman, 1993; Epstein, 1999; Rupp, 1999). In 1969, police raided a Greenwich Village gay bar, the Stonewall Inn. On that night, the police action provoked substantial physical resistance from 'drag queens, dykes, street people, and bar boys' (Adam, 1987: 75). The resistance at Stonewall gave birth to 'a large, grassroots movement for liberation' (D'Emilio, 1983: 239).

Gay liberation did not, of course, simply emerge out of nowhere. The movements of the 1960s – the civil rights, New Left, and women's movements – set the stage for the transformation of the gay movement. In contrast to the homophile movement, gay liberationists rejected an assimilationist stance and instead touted gay culture and community as a source of 'pride and strength'. Perhaps most significantly, the movement spun off not only a host of new organizations, but also a wide variety of more explicitly political community institutions to add to the bars and bath houses that had been around for decades, as well as restaurants and coffee houses, bookstores, business guilds, community centers, sports leagues, and support groups of all kinds (Rupp, 1999). The movement originally grew out of the social networks and identities fostered by existing communities, but now the movement was helping to create new community institutions and collective identities. This trend toward agenda setting by local and community-based networks in addition to national level organizations that characterizes the modern lesbian and gay movement is typical of the pattern of development of most of the major social movements spawned in the 1960s and 1970s (Castells, 1997).

THE MOVEMENT AS A SOURCE OF DIVERSE COMMUNITIES AND CONTESTED IDENTITIES

In the wake of the liberation movement, gay communities spread across the country.

Martin Levine's (1979) research suggests that in several American cities, gays and lesbians formed distinct neighborhoods or 'gay ghettos'. Similar to ethnic enclaves, gay ghettos are characterized by separate institutions (such as gay bars, bookstores, coffee houses and other businesses, religious organizations, periodicals, banks, and social welfare organizations), a visible gay culture, and a concentration of gay residents who work and socialize primarily within the boundaries of the neighborhood. One of the first ghettos to fit that description is the well-known Castro district of San Francisco. Called the 'first gay neighborhood', Castro residents created both an active gay business area as well as a distinct culture. The Castro culture in the 1970s was considered a 'carnival where social conventions were turned upside down just for the pleasure of [it]' (Fitzgerald, 1986: 12). The festival spirit of the Castro manifested on Halloween, in street fairs, and on gay holidays, with men dressing as bikers, nuns, Betty Grable look-a-likes, or professionals (Fitzgerald, 1986: 12).

Levine's book *Gay Macho* describes a unique gay identity that emerged out of the communities of the 1970s. In the context of the gay pride movement, many men rejected the stereotype of gay men as effeminate, instead projecting a hypermasculine image. They cultivated the macho look through body building and showed off their muscles in tight Levi jeans and white tank tops. They also adopted other articles of clothing, such as work boots and flannel shirts, that projected a masculine working-class image. Yet their meticulous grooming – clean fingernails, short haircuts, and well-trimmed mustaches or beards – signified that they were not really blue-collar workers. The macho look was so prominent that Levine calls the men who adopted it 'homosexual clones'. Members of this subculture embraced and exaggerated other masculine characteristics, in addition to their styles of dress. By engaging in a sexually promiscuous lifestyle, gay men enacted and magnified an image of sexual prowess that was associated with masculinity in the broader American culture.

As in earlier periods, lesbians in the 1970s typically formed their own subcultures and communities, separate from those of gay men (Taylor and Rupp, 1993). Deborah Wolf's *Lesbian Community* (1979) provides a rich description of a mainly white and middle-class lesbian-feminist community in the San Francisco Bay Area. Unlike members of earlier lesbian communities, the women in this 1970s' community viewed their identity primarily as a political rejection of male domination rather than a manifestation of sexual desire. In the 1970s, the identity that emerged among lesbian communities was greatly influenced by the second wave of the feminist movement. Community members viewed lesbianism as a lifestyle based on the values of cultural feminism, including co-operation, egalitarianism, and an ethic of caring (Taylor and Rupp, 1993). These values were put into practice through the creation of alternative women-centered institutions, including feminist bookstores and coffee houses and a women's music industry. Also, lesbian feminists defied dominant standards of femininity by embracing androgynous styles of clothing, such as blue jeans and t-shirts, and refusing to shave their legs. Thus feminism provided the standards of behavior and dress through which women presented themselves as lesbians.

But these new communities of 'clones' and lesbian feminists did not replace the traditional worlds that gay and lesbian people had built (Buring, 1997; Franzen, 1993). Effeminacy remained as a gay male style, and bar dykes and softball players who embraced more conventionally masculine styles continued to flourish in communities all over the country. At the same time, over the years new identities emerged within increasingly more diverse communities. Arlene Stein's book *Sex and Sensibility* (1997) shows how lesbian identity is defined, negotiated, and revised within lesbian communities. Stein shows that lesbian communities of the 1970s were centered on a feminist discourse that defined lesbianism through political affiliation. By the 1990s, however, lesbian communities had become more fragmented, and lesbian-feminism was no longer the dominant lesbian identity. This 'decentering' of the lesbian community resulted from critiques made by women marginalized by the narrow definition of 'lesbian' that emerged from the 1970s communities. Women of color felt excluded by the largely white and middle-class feminist communities that ignored the issue of racism and celebrated styles alien to their cultures. And 'pro-sex' lesbians – those who emphasized the pleasure over the danger of sexuality – felt that the feminist emphasis on politics over desire was stifling. As a result, lesbian communities of the 1990s diversified and embraced multiple and competing ways of defining and presenting oneself as a lesbian. Lillian Faderman's (1991) account of lesbian life at the end of the twentieth-century notes the multiple subcultures and identities – including 'lipstick lesbians', punk lesbians, and s&m lesbians – that emerged in the 1980s and 1990s, and we would expand this list to include lesbian mothers and lesbians who embrace female masculinity (Halberstam, 1998).

Gay male communities, too, diversified in the late twentieth century. Often perceived as white, male, and middle-class by those outside of these privileged classifications, people of color pointed to the gay community as an inhospitable place for the racial-ethnic diversity (see for instance, Almaguer, 1998; Cochran and Mays, 1998; Hanawa, 1997; Peterson, 1992; Romo-Carmona, 1997; Shah, 1998). The communities that developed post-Stonewall, according to Almaguer (1998: 544), 'were largely populated by white men who had the resources and talents needed to create "gilded" gay ghettos'. Yet men from all racial and ethnic groups identify as gay.

A common dilemma for members of racial-ethnic minority communities stems from the fact that they often feel like outsiders in the gay and lesbian community and invisible in their ethnic communities (Shah, 1998). In writing about Latina lesbians, Mariana Romo-Carmona's describes 'straddling a fence' or trying to fit into two cultures, one Latino and stripped of sexual orientation and the other sexuality-based and without Latino culture (1997: 36; see also Anzaldúa, 1987). Likewise, since South Asian immigrant communities and families provide a safe haven against 'racial hostility and cultural misunderstanding', coming out sparks fear among many South Asian gays (Shah, 1998). Despite the fact that homosexuality has been documented in all parts of the world, there is a lingering perception that homosexual behavior and gay, lesbian, and bisexual identities are a white, western, and middle-class phenomenon. South Asians living in the USA tend to see homosexuality as a 'white disease' (ibid.: 484), despite the fact that in South-East Asia, gay and lesbian organizations have established a significant public presence in the twentieth century. As a result of the invisibility experienced at both ends, South Asian gay and lesbian people have had to create 'their own support groups, organizations, events, and newsletters in the US and Canada, in India and Great Britain (ibid.).

African American gay men, too, have developed 'informal social networks' with other gay men from within black communities in the United States (Peterson, 1992: 154). Although in major urban areas, gay bars are sometimes located in black neighborhoods and some black gay political organizations might exist, for the most part, African American gays generally do not have access to black gay institutions, such as newspapers, businesses, and political organizations. As a result, gay black men often identify and develop friendships and socialize with each other at private events, such as entertainment in people's homes and other privately sponsored parties and dances (Cochran and Mays, 1998; Peterson, 1992).

For gays and lesbians, developing community depends above all on adopting an identity based on sexuality. But in some minority communities, participating in a same-sex sexual act may carry no consequences for one's identity. In Mexican and other Latino sexual systems, as in the world of the early twentieth-century fairies, effeminacy and the nature of the sexual acts one performs determine identity. Unlike the less differentiated exchange common among Euro-American gay men, some Mexican men are either strictly passive or active participants in sexual encounters (Almaguer, 1998: 542; see also Carrier, 1976, 1985). Men who maintain a strict active or insertor role may avoid stigma for such behavior because it is seen as conforming to a masculine role, while those who take a passive role are considered in more feminine terms (Almaguer, 1998: 541–2). As Almaguer (ibid.: 543) writes, the Mexican sexual system actually militates against the construction of discernible, discrete bisexual or gay sexual identities because these identities are shaped by and draw upon a different sexual system.

Bisexuals and transgendered people also blur the boundaries of gay and lesbian identity and community (see Esterberg, 1997; Feinberg, 1996, 1999; Rust, 1996, 1993). Bisexuality is often perceived by those in gay communities as either confusion or a temporary condition (Ochs, 1996). Likewise, transgender persons are often misunderstood and marginalized. Rather than building an identity around sexual object choice, persons who consider themselves transgendered see as central the lack of congruity between their own perception of their gender and the perceptions of others (McCloskey, 1999).

By pointing out the existence of diverse subcultures within the gay and lesbian community, recent studies raise questions concerning the boundaries of the community and the assumption that a unified community exists at the start of the twenty-first century. These concerns are at the heart of Kristin Esterberg's (1997) research on two groups of women, those who identify as lesbian and those who claim the label 'bisexual'. Esterberg suggests that the boundaries between lesbians, bisexuals, and heterosexuals are permeable and constantly renegotiated. Moreover, she calls attention to the multiple and diverse identities of

lesbian and bisexual women based on race and class identification. She concludes that scholars should not describe the lesbian community as if it were monolithic but, instead, should conceptualize it as existing of 'overlapping friendship networks' with blurred boundaries. The gay and lesbian community is a collage of these small and diverse subcultures.

As a result, identity disputes flourish in the movement, often grounded in the difference between an assimilationist versus a liberationist politic (Adam, 1987; Dugan, 1999; Duggan, 1995; Gamson, 1995; Reger and Dugan, 2000; Rupp, 1999). As in the homophile movement, the assimilationist tendency, leading to goals such as civil rights in the military and the workplace and the right to marry, emphasizes the similarity between gay men and lesbians, on the one hand, and straight people, on the other hand. By contrast, gay liberation insists on a 'revolutionary struggle to free the homosexual in everyone, challenging the conventional arrangements that confined sexuality to heterosexual monogamous families' (Adam, 1987: 78). The larger political and cultural environment plays a role in highlighting one tendency or the other: a hostile climate not only inhibits movement growth and activism but may favor assimilationist strategies, whereas a hospitable environment allows for movements to thrive in the pursuit of more fundamental social and political change.

If the growing diversity of gay and lesbian communities has made what is now generally referred to as the gay, lesbian, bisexual, and transgender movement more contentious, the rise of direct political attacks on the movement and the appearance of AIDS in the gay community ironically tended to bring people together and to strengthen gay communities both in urban and rural areas of the United States. In the late 1970s, the ultraconservative New Right led anti-gay crusades in different parts of the country (Adam, 1987; Diamond, 1995). Most notorious was the 1977 landmark case in Florida, where Christian fundamentalist

Anita Bryant and her organization, Save Our Children, successfully moved voters to repeal a newly passed pro-gay anti-discrimination law (Adam, 1987; Button et al., 1997; Epstein, 1999). That next year gay rights laws in St. Paul, Minnesota; Eugene, Oregon; and Wichita, Kansas met with a similar fate at the hands of conservative forces (Button et al., 1997). Save Our Children then took its energy and resources to California in 1978 to support the anti-gay Proposition 6 or Briggs Initiative. This failed initiative, had it passed, would have banned openly gay or lesbian people from teaching in California's public schools (Adam, 1987; Diamond, 1995).

Gay men and lesbians have also come together in the face of the AIDS epidemic. When AIDS first made the news, it was constructed as a 'gay disease'. And, of course, gay male communities were in fact hit hard. Although the incidence of HIV is much lower among lesbians than gay men, the anti-gay rhetoric that emerged during the AIDS crisis targeted both men and women and caused gays and lesbians to work together for protection and survival (Levine, 1998; Weston, 1991). As writer and activist Sarah Schulman put it, 'the coming together of feminist political perspectives and organizing experience with gay men's high sense of entitlement and huge resources proved to be a historically transforming event' (1994: 11). In every region of the country and in both rural and urban areas, the battle against AIDS spawned new institutions, as well as alliances between lesbians and gays and between gays and heterosexuals that added to the institutional completeness of lesbian and gay communities (Murray, 1998).

Further diversification and fragmentation of gay communities occurred, beginning in the early 1980s when groups that took on the identity of 'queer' such as ACT-UP (AIDS Coalition to Unleash Power), Queer Nation, and the Lesbian Avengers, moved liberation philosophy to new heights. Rejecting assimilationist tactics in favor of in-your-face direct action, queer activists held kiss-ins, distributed condoms in public, and engaged in disruptive protests (Duggan, 1995: 173).

If such groups sometimes led to struggles over the meaning of who should or should not be included in lesbian and gay communities (Gamson, 1997), they also spawned new networks of solidarity that secured recognition for participants' identities and interests. Another example of the important role that political movements play in some gay people's lives is illustrated by the new and interrelated community networks that formed among the vast number of gay, lesbian and bisexual employee groups that have spearheaded campaigns to win domestic partnership benefits and other forms of equal treatment for gays in the workplace (Raeburn, 2000). Participation in these types of local activism affirm same-sex sexuality and love and provide a source of identity and support for lesbians and gays working for mainstream corporations.

Sociologists interested in understanding the changes taking place in modern complex societies argue that contemporary social and political movements, such as the gay and lesbian, feminist, environmental, fundamentalist, and other racial and ethnic movements, are major sources of community, meaning, and identity that are replacing earlier more traditional sources such as nationality and class (Castells, 1997; Melucci, 1996; Taylor, 2000). If the networks and positive identities nurtured in pre-Stonewall gay communities supplied the solidarity necessary for lesbians and gay men to organize for social change in the first place, the social movements that emerged out of gay communities have, in turn, affected lesbian and gay communities by expanding the number of supportive social networks available and by securing recognition for a wider range of identities of people with same-sex desires.

CONCLUSION

There is considerable published research demonstrating that since at least the end of the nineteenth century, people with same-sex desires identified others like them, gathered in particular locations, and expressed their sexuality through mannerisms and physical attire. From the fairies of New York to the butches and fems of Buffalo, communities of gay men and lesbians formed identities, built social worlds apart from mainstream heteronormative society, and nurtured a rich and elaborate oppositional culture. These gay and lesbian communities served as sites of resistance by making space where individuals collectively built and negotiated identities that challenged dominant gender and sexual codes. These collective identities, in turn, made possible the emergence of a political movement.

We have focused our discussion on the relationship between gay community and the larger lesbian, gay, bisexual, and transgender movement because recent scholarship has emphasized the key role of interpersonal networks and collective identity in movement mobilization. As we have seen, with the emergence of the lesbian and gay liberation movements in the 1970s, social movement communities began to attract lesbians and gay men in numbers that rivaled the bars and other traditional institutions of gay life. As a result, at the dawn of the twenty-first century, a lesbian or gay man would find that in many areas of the country – not just in San Francisco, New York City, Chicago, and Los Angeles, but in Key West, Florida; Atlanta, Georgia; Columbus, Ohio; and Eugene, Oregon – she or he would find a full range of institutions making it possible to concentrate social relations almost entirely within the lesbian and gay community. Yet disputes over identity and struggles between assimilationist and confrontational tendencies in the movement are common, and some individuals continue to keep their distance from explicitly political gay organizations, making it more accurate to think in terms of multiple communities rather than a unified lesbian and gay community. As a new century and new millennium dawn, communities and movements undoubtedly will continue their complex relationship.

Despite the rich scholarship on diverse gay and lesbian communities, it is important to take stock of the questions that we still need to address. First, while there is beginning to be a literature on gay and lesbian communities in places such as Brazil (Green, 1999; Kulick, 1998), Japan (Leupp, 1995; Robertson, 1998), and South Africa (Murray and Roscoe, 1998), we know much less about gay communities outside the United States and Western Europe. Second, while there is considerable historical research on lesbian and gay communities in the major urban areas of the United States, there is less sociological analysis of the demographic and social charactersitics of diverse contemporary communities. Most notably, we know little about contemporary lesbian and gay communities in the South and much less about gay rural life in America. Finally, the important question arises as to what impact lesbian and gay communities and the social movements they have spawned have had on mainstream culture and politics. In past decades, visible lesbian and gay communities have changed the face of social and political life in the United States, and an important research agenda remains for future scholars to trace these effects.

NOTE

1 When possible we label communities organized around same-sex desire with the specific terms – such as fairy, butch-fem, or lesbian feminist – used by members of those communities to identify themselves. However, when making generalized statements about these communities, we use the terms gay or gay and lesbian for the sake of linguistic simplicity. Our purpose is not to portray all communities organized around same-sex desire as monolithic. To the contrary, our analysis highlights the historical variability and the contested boundaries of such communities.

REFERENCES

Adam, Barry D. (1987) *The Rise of a Gay and Lesbian Movement*. Boston: Twayne Publishers.
Almaguer, Tomás (1998) 'Chicano men: a cartography of homosexual identity and behavior', in *Social Perspectives in Lesbian and Gay Studies: A Reader*.

Peter M. Nardi and Beth E. Schneider (eds), New York: Routledge. pp. 537–52.

Anzaldúa, Gloria (1987) *Borderlands/La Frontera: The New Mestiza*. San Francisco: Spinsters/Aunt Lute Book Company.

Beemyn, Brett (1997) 'Introduction', in Brett Beemyn (ed.), *Creating a Place for Ourselves: Lesbian, Gay, and Bisexual Community Histories*, New York: Routledge. pp. 1–8.

Bérubé, Allan (1989) 'Marching to a different drummer: lesbian and gay GIs in World War II', in Martin Duberman, Martha Vicinus and George Chauncey (eds), *Hidden from History: Reclaiming the Gay and Lesbian Past,* New York: New American Library. pp. 383–94.

Bérubé, Allan (1990) *Coming Out Under Fire: The History of Gay Men and Women in World War Two*. New York: Free Press.

Buechler, Steven M. (1990) *Women's Movements in the United States: Women's Suffrage, Equal Rights, and Beyond*, New Brunswick, NJ: Rutgers University Press.

Bullough, Vern and Bullough, Bonnie (1977) 'Lesbianism in the 1920s and 1930s: a newfound study', *Signs: Journal of Women in Culture and Society*, 2: 895–904.

Burning, Daneel (1997) 'Softball and alcohol: the limits of lesbian community in Memphis from the 1940s through the 1960s', in John Howard (ed.), *Carryin' on in the Lesbian and Gay South*. New York: New York University Press. pp. 203–23.

Button, James W., Rienzo, Barbara A. and Wald, Kenneth D. (1997) *Private Lives, Public Conflicts: Battles Over Gay Rights in American Communities*. Washington, DC: Congressional Quarterly Press.

Carrier, Joseph M. (1976) 'Cultural factors affecting Mexican male homosexual behavior', *The Archives of Sexual Behavior: An Interdisciplinary Research Journal*, 5: 103–24.

Carrier, Joseph M. (1985) 'Mexican male bisexuality', in Fritz Klein and Timothy Wolf. (eds), *Bisexualities: Theory and Research*. New York: Haworth Press. pp. 75–85.

Castells, Manuel (1997) *The Power of Identity*. Malden, MA: Blackwell Publishers.

Chauncey, George (1989) 'Christian brotherhood or sexual perversion? Homosexual identities and the construction of sexual boundaries in the World War One era', in Martin Duberman, Martha Vicinus and George Chauncey (eds), *Hidden from History: Reclaiming the Gay and Lesbian Past*. New York: New American Library. pp. 294–317.

Chauncey, George (1994) *Gay New York: Gender, Urban Culture, and the Makings of the Gay Male World*, (1890–1940). New York: Basic Books.

Cochran, Susan D. and Mays, Vickie M. (1998) 'Sociocultural facets of the black gay male experience', in Michael S. Kimmel and Michael A. Messner. *Men's Lives*. 4th edn. Needham Heights, MA: Allyn & Bacon. pp. 487–504.

Cruikshank, Margaret (1992) *The Gay and Lesbian Liberation Movement*. New York: Routledge.

D'Emilio, John (1983) *Sexual Politics, Sexual Communities: The Making of a Homosexual Minority in the United States, 1940–1970*. Chicago: The University of Chicago Press.

D'Emilio, John (1989a) 'Gay politics and community in San Francisco since World War II', in Martin Duberman, Martha Vicinus and George Chauncey (eds), *Hidden From History: Reclaiming the Gay and Lesbian Past*. New York: New American Library. pp. 456–76.

D'Emilio, John (1989b) 'The homosexual menace: the politics of sexuality in Cold War America', in Kathy Peiss and Christina Simmons (eds), *Passion and Power: Sexuality in History*. Philadelphia: Temple University Press. pp. 226–40.

Diamond, Sara (1995) *Roads to Dominion: Right-Wing Movements and Political Power in the United States*. New York: The Guilford Press.

Duberman, Martin (1993) *Stonewall*. New York: Dutton.

Duberman, Martin (1999) *Left Out: The Politics of Exclusion/Essays/1964–1999*. New York: Basic Books.

Dugan, Kimberly B. (1999) 'Culture and movement-countermovement dynamics: the struggle over gay, lesbian, and bisexual rights', PhD dissertation, Ohio State University.

Duggan, Lisa (1995) 'Introduction', in Lisa Duggan and Nan D. Hunter (eds), *Sex Wars: Sexual Dissent and Political Culture*. New York: Routledge. pp. 1–14.

Epstein, Steven (1987) 'Gay politics, ethnic identity: the limits of social constructionism', *Socialist Review*, 93/94: 9–54.

Epstein, Steven (1999) 'Gay and lesbian movements in the United States: dilemmas of identity, diversity, and political strategy'. in Barry D. Adam, Jan Willem Duyvendak, and André Krouwel (eds), *The Global Emergence of Gay and Lesbian Politics: National Imprints of a Worldwide Movement*. Philadelphia, PA: Temple University Press. pp. 30–90.

Esterberg, Kristin (1997) *Lesbian and Bisexual Identities: Constructing Communities, Constructing Selves*. Philadelphia, PA: Temple University Press.

Faderman, Lillian (1978) 'The morbidification of love between women by nineteenth-century sexologists', *Journal of Homosexuality*, 4: 73–90.

Faderman, Lillian (1991) *Odd Girls and Twilight Lovers: A History of Lesbian Life in Twentieth-Century America*, New York: Penguin Books.

Feinberg, Leslie (1996) *Transgender Warriors: Making History from Joan of Arc to Dennis Rodman*. Boston: Beacon Press.

Feinberg, Leslie (1999) *Trans Liberation: Beyond Pink or Blue*. Boston: Beacon Press.

Fitzgerald, Francis (1986) *Cities on a Hill: A Journey Through Contemporary American Cultures*. Riverside, NJ: Simon & Schuster.

Franzen, Trisha (1993) 'Differences and identities: feminism and the Albuquerque lesbian community', *Signs*, 18 (4): 891–906.

Freeman, Susan K. (2000) 'Community', in Bonnie Zimmerman (ed.), *Lesbian Histories and Cultures: An Encyclopedia*, New York: Garland Publishing Inc. pp. 190–2.

Gamson, Joshua (1995) 'Must identity movements self-destruct? A queer dilemma', *Social Problems*, 42: 390–407.

Gamson, Joshua (1997) 'Messages of exclusion: gender, movements, and symbolic boundaries', *Gender and Society*, 11: 178–99.

Garber, Eric (1989) 'A spectacle in color: the lesbian and gay subculture of jazz age Harlem', in Martin Duberman, Martha Vicinus and George Chauncey (eds), *Hidden From History: Reclaiming the Gay and Lesbian Past*. New York: New American Library. pp. 318–31.

Green, James N. (1999) *Beyond Carnival: Male Homosexuality in Twentieth-Century Brazil*. Chicago: University of Chicago Press.

Halberstam, Judith (1998) *Female Masculinity*. Durham, NC: Duke University Press.

Hanawa, Yukiko (1997) 'Inciting sites of political interventions: queer 'n Asian', in Martin Duberman (ed.), *A Queer World: The Center for Lesbian and Gay Studies Reader*. New York: New York University Press. pp. 39–62.

Herek, Gregory (1997) 'Heterosexuals' attitudes toward lesbians and gay men: does coming out make a difference?' in Martin Duberman (ed.), *A Queer World: The Center for Lesbian and Gay Studies Reader*. New York: New York University Press. pp. 331–44.

Herman, Didi (1997) *The Antigay Agenda: Orthodox Vision and the Christian Right*. Chicago: University of Chicago Press.

Jenkins, J. Craig (1983) 'Resource mobilization theory and the study of social movements'. *Annual Review of Sociology*, 9: 527–53.

Johnson, David K. (1997) 'The kids of Fairytown: gay male culture on Chicago's Near North Side in the 1930s', in Brett Beemyn (ed.), *Creating a Place for Ourselves: Lesbian, Gay, and Bisexual Community Histories*. New York: Routledge. pp. 97–118.

Kaminski, Elizabeth and Taylor, Verta (2001) 'Constructing identities in gay and lesbian communities', in Dana Vannoy (ed.), *Gender Mosaics: Social Perspectives*, Los Angeles: Roxbury Publishing. pp. 75–84.

Katz, Jonathon Ned (1976) *Gay American History: Lesbians and Gay Men in the U.S.A.* New York: Meridian.

Kennedy, Elizabeth Lapovsky and Davis, Madeline D. (1993) *Boots of Leather, Slippers of Gold: The History of a Lesbian Community*. New York: Routledge.

Krieger, Susan (1983) *The Mirror Dance: Identity in a Women's Community*. Philadelphia: Temple University Press.

Kulick, Don (1998) *Travesti: Sex, Gender, and Culture among Brazilian Transgendered Prostitutes*. Chicago: University of Chicago Press.

Leupp, Gary (1995) *Male Colors: The Construction of Homosexuality in Tokugawa Japan (1603–1868)*. Berkeley, CA: University of California Press.

Levine, Martin P. (1979) 'Gay ghetto', *Journal of Homosexuality*, 4 (4): 363–77.

Levine, Martin P. (1998) *Gay Macho: The Life and Death of the Homosexual Clone*. New York: New York University Press.

McAdam, Doug (1986) 'Recruitment to high-risk activism: the case of freedom summer', *American Journal of Sociology*, 92: 64–90.

McCarthy, John D. and Zald, Mayer N. (1977) 'Resource mobilization and social movements: a partial theory', *American Journal of Sociology*, 82: 1212–41.

McCloskey, Deirdre (1999) *Crossing: A Memoir*. Chicago: University of Chicago Press.

Melucci, Alberto (1996) *Challenging Codes: Collective Action in the Communication Age*. Cambridge: Cambridge University Press.

Morris, Aldon (1984) *The Origins of the Civil Rights Movement: Black Communities Organizing for Change*. New York: The Free Press.

Murray, Stephen O. (1998) 'The institutional elaboration of a quasi-ethnic community', in Peter M. Nardi and Beth E. Schneider (eds), *Social Perspectives in Lesbian and Gay Studies: A Reader*. New York: Routledge. pp. 207–14.

Murray, Stephen O. and Roscoe, Will (eds) (1998) *Boy-Wives and Female Husbands: Studies of African Homosexualities*. New York: St. Martin's Press.

Nardi, Peter (1999) *Gay Men's Friendships: Invincible Communities*. Chicago: University of Chicago Press.

Nestle, Joan (1981) 'Butch-fem relationships: sexual courage in the 1950s', *Heresies*, 3: 21–4.

Newton, Esther (1998) 'The queens', in Peter M. Nardi and Beth E. Schneider (eds), *Social Perspectives in Lesbian and Gay Studies: A Reader*. New York: Routledge. pp. 38–50.

Ochs, Robyn (1996) 'Biphobia: it goes more than two ways', in Beth A. Firestein (ed.), *Bisexuality: The Psychology and Politics of an Invisible Minority*. Thousand Oaks, CA: Sage. pp. 217–39.

Peterson, John (1992) 'Black men and their same-sex desires and behaviors', in Gilbert Herdt (ed.), *Gay Culture in America: Essays from the Field*. Boston: Beacon Press. pp. 147–64.

Queen, Carol (1992) 'Strangers at home: bisexuals in the queer movement', in Larry Gross and James D. Woods (eds), *The Columbia Reader on Lesbians and Gay Men in Media, Society, and Politics*. New York: Columbia University Press. pp. 105–8.

Raeburn, Nicole C. (2000) 'The rise of lesbian, gay, and bisexual rights in the workplace', PhD. dissertation, Ohio State University.

Reger, Jo and Dugan, Kimberly (2000) 'Constructing a salient identity: outcomes and continuity in two social movement contexts', paper presented at the American Sociological Association annual meetings, Hilton Washington and Towers and the Marriott Wardman Park, Washington, DC, 12–16 August.

Robertson, Jennifer (1998) *Takarazuka: Sexual Politics and Popular Culture in Modern Japan.* Berkeley, CA: University of California Press.

Romo-Carmona, Mariana (1997) 'Latina lesbians', in Martin Duberman (ed.), *A Queer World: The Center for Lesbian and Gay Studies Reader.* New York: New York University Press. pp. 35–8.

Rupp, Leila J. (1999) *A Desired Past: A Short History of Same-Sex Love in America.* Chicago: University of Chicago Press.

Rupp, Leila J. and Taylor, Verta (2002) *What Makes a Man a Man: Drag Queens at the 801 Cabaret.* Chicago: University of Chicago Press.

Rust, Paula (1993) ' "Coming Out" in the age of social constructionism: sexual identity formation among lesbian and bisexual women', *Gender and Society,* 7: 50–77.

Rust, Paula (1995) *Bisexuality and the Challenge to Lesbian Politics: Sex, Loyalty, and Revolution.* New York: New York University Press.

Rust, Paula (1996) 'Managing multiple identities: diversity among bisexual women and men'. in Beth A. Firestein (ed.), *Bisexuality: The Psychology and Politics of an Invisible Minority.* Thousand Oaks, CA: Sage. pp. 53–83.

Saslow, James (1989) 'Homosexuality in the renaissance: behavior, identity, and artistic expression'. in Martin Duberman, Martha Vicinus and George Chauncey, (eds), *Hidden from History: Reclaiming the Gay and Lesbian Past.* New York: New American Library. pp. 90–105.

Shah, Nayan (1998) 'Sexuality, identity, and the uses of history', in Peter M. Nardi and Beth E. Schneider (eds), *Social Perspectives in Lesbian and Gay Studies: A Reader.* New York: Routledge. pp. 481–90.

Shilts, Randy (1987) *And the Band Played On: Politics, People, and the AIDS Epidemic.* New York: St Martin's Press.

Schulman, Sarah (1994) *My American History: Lesbian and Gay Life During the Reagan/Bush Years.* New York: Routledge.

Stein, Arlene (1997) *Sex and Sensibility: Stories of a Lesbian Generation.* Berkeley, CA: University of California Press.

Stein, Marc (1994) 'The city of sisterly and brotherly loves: the making of lesbian and gay movements in Greater Philadelphia, 1948–72', PhD dissertation, University of Pennsylvania.

Taylor, Verta (2000) 'Mobilizing for change in a social movement society', *Contemporary Sociology,* 29: 219–30.

Taylor, Verta and Raeburn, Nicole (1995) 'Identity politics as high-risk activism: career consequences for lesbian, gay, and bisexual sociologists', *Social Problems,* 42: 252–73.

Taylor, Verta and Rupp, Leila J. (1993) 'Women's culture and lesbian feminist activism: a reconsideration of cultural feminism', *Signs: Journal of Women in Culture and Society,* 19: 32–61.

Taylor, Verta and Whittier, Nancy (1992) 'Collective identity in social movement communities: lesbian feminist mobilization', in Aldon D. Morris and Carol McClurg Mueller (eds), *Frontiers in Social Movement Theory.* New Haven, CT: Yale University Press. pp. 104–29

Trumbach, Randolph (1989) 'The birth of the queen: sodomy and the emergence of gender equality in modern culture, 1660–1750', in Martin Duberman, Martha Vicinus and George Chauncey (eds), *Hidden from History: Reclaiming the Gay and Lesbian Past.* New York: New American Library. pp. 129–40.

Valocchi, Steve (1999) 'The class-infected nature of gay identity', *Social Problems,* 46: 207–24.

Warren, Carol (1998) 'Space and time', in Peter M. Nardi and Beth E. Schneider (eds), *Social Perspectives in Lesbian and Gay Studies: A Reader.* New York: Routledge. pp. 183–93.

Wellman, Barry, Carrington, Peter J. and Hall, Alan (1998) 'Networks as personal communities', in Barry Wellman and S.D. Berkowitz (eds), *Social Structures: A Network Approach, Contemporary Studies in Sociology,* Volume 15, New York: Cambridge University Press.

Weston, Kath (1991) *Families We Choose: Lesbians, Gays, and Kinship.* New York: Columbia University Press.

Wolf, Deborah Goleman (1979) *The Lesbian Community.* Berkeley, CA: University of California Press.

8

New Technologies and 'Cyber-queer' Research

NINA WAKEFORD

Last June, I watched a group of marchers in the New York Gay Pride parade who carried signs saying, 'We're here, We're Queer, and We Have E-mail'. An off-line friend laughed, remarking 'We have FiestaWare too – so what?' (Senft, 1996)

Now, if the computer screen is soon to become *the* screen to the world as well as for our own so-called private production, its space will be *the* contested arena of the symbolic organisation of cultural and economic power. (Case, 1995: 334)

Lesbian and gay studies of electronic communication address the impact of new technologies on the everyday worlds of lesbians and gay men, and those identifying as bisexual or transgendered.[1] Four themes run through existing research: (a) identity and presentation of the online persona; (b) the creation of queer virtual 'space'; (c) the electronic facilitation of social networks and 'virtual community'; and (d) the potential of new technology to transform erotic practice. Studies of new technologies are methodologically diverse, although many rely on first-hand experience of using electronic forums such as newsgroups, web pages and chat lines. As the uptake of electronic communication continues to rise, and the effects of what has been called the Network Society (Castells, 1996) become more apparent, it is likely that this field within lesbian and gay

studies will be of increasing importance, not only because of the number of queer users who access the Internet on a daily basis, but also due to the changes in the way that academic knowledge is being produced and disseminated. Email and the World Wide Web are changing the *ways* in which lesbian and gay studies is developing as well as the *topics* which it encompasses.

In broad terms, new technologies of information and communication consist of all emerging electronic and digital devices and environments – including the computer, the mobile phone and the pager. However, most research concentrates on computer-mediated online services, and activities that are accessible via the Internet. As well as 'online', other terms which are used in this field of study are 'virtual', 'digital' and the popular 'cyber-' prefix.[2] Many of the technologies and skills which are required to access online spaces began to be developed in the late 1980s, and as a result this area of study has a short history, with published works beginning in the mid-1990s and concentrating on the United States.

Whereas film, television and printed mass media have been the focus of substantial research by lesbian and gay scholars (Horne and Lewis, 1996; Berlant, 1997; Gamson, 1998; Gross and Woods, 1999a), studies of the Internet and other analogous forms of mediated communication are understandably much thinner on the ground. Nevertheless despite the field's relatively small size, the variety of approaches – drawing on literary studies, anthropology, sociology, psychology and media studies – contributing to the emerging literature is notable. The label 'Cyberqueer Studies', which I have used to discuss this body of writing (Wakeford, 1997a), encompasses a diverse set of topics, methods, and forms of output. Although many investigations of online communication have developed in an *ad hoc* way at the edges of traditional disciplines, there is an emerging discipline of Internet Studies, into which would fit much of the writing discussed in this chapter.[3]

One notable feature, both of the field of Cyberqueer Studies and Internet Studies more widely, is a focus on the end user of technology and the 'consumption' of new media, rather than a concern with the design of technologies or the economic and political processes which frame consumption.[4] Many studies have been inspired by theoretical frameworks from the cultural studies of science and technology.[5] In this field the term 'cyborg' has been proposed as a metaphor to describe the inevitability of human association with technology and the contradictory possibilities of this relationship for marginalized groups (Haraway, 1985).[6] This framing of the co-construction of humans and technology is cited by many authors writing about sexuality and new technology, although there is little sustained engagement with Haraway's original formulation. Rather, the idea of the cyborg has become a stimulus for researchers to search out the ways queerly identified individuals and groups are using new technologies (e.g. Bromley, 1995; Hall, 1996; Kaloski, 1997).[7]

Given that both studies of the Internet and Queer Theory emerged in the 1990s, it is hardly surprising that cyberqueer research has also been heavily influenced by frameworks derived from Queer Theory. Indeed, writers have engaged with lesbian and gay studies as a whole through the narrower

prism of queer theory, rather than from any other part of the discipline. Therefore certain topics of investigation – such as those related to ideas of identity or performativity – have been prioritised at the expense of focusing on how everyday activities fit into institutional practices.[8] Although theories of prominent writers in lesbian and gay studies have had a substantial impact on the development of cyberqueer research, the reverse is not yet the case. Cyberqueer studies have not made substantial inroads into the discipline of lesbian and gay studies, in contrast with other areas, such as research on HIV and AIDS (Watney, 1997; Patton, 1988; Epstein, 1996). This is probably a matter of disciplinary time lag, as the concerns which are foregrounded in queer studies of the Internet or other new technologies, and the questions which they potentially raise about contemporary lesbian and gay practice, the politics of representation, the operation of social movements and systems of social support/ intervention, are at the core of lesbian and gay research.

THE GROWING IMPORTANCE OF NEW TECHNOLOGIES IN QUEER LIFE

In the UK television series *Queer As Folk*, one of the central characters is shown using an online service to meet possible sex partners. From this portrayal of gay life in late 1990s' Manchester, it appears that such activity, incorporating the swapping of digital photos, has become a common alternative to cruising bars or using telephone chat lines. The growing prevalence of images relating to new technologies and everyday experiences indicates a new media form which is becoming part of many queer lives.

Drama on stage also reflects this trend: Kate Bornstein's play, *Virtually Yours: beta 1.0*, which was performed in San Francisco during 1994, reflected a curiosity about new technologies in the local queer community. Bornstein acts out the experience of being a transgendered activist faced with her girlfriend's decision to begin her own gender transition. Her confusion about the flexibility of sexual orientation, the persistence of desire and the presentation of the body are explored through a juxtaposition of Bornstein's autobiographical reflections and the experiences of playing an interactive computer game. How similar, Bornstein asks, are the paradoxes of contemporary sexual orientation and the experience of new technologies? What use are new virtual worlds for understanding our queer practices? *Virtually Yours* provides one answer, albeit highly ideosyncratic, to the question 'We have FiestaWare too – so what?'. As Bornstein shows, new media can be used as a way to understand the complexities and contradictions of living a contemporary queer life saturated with technology.

Bornstein has produced subsequent work that draws on images of computer processes to describe and interpret transgender experience, and has used ambiguities about sexual identity as a way to characterise online exchanges (Sullivan and Bornstein, 1996). In doing so she has contributed to a growing strand of queer popular culture which reflects the use of computer-mediated communication among queer communities, particularly in North America. In the novel *Prozac Highway* a lesbian comes to terms with her mental illness through virtual intimacy as well as increasing immersion in computer games (Blackridge, 1996). Jeannette Winterson set her novel *The Powerbook* in 'London, Paris, Capri and Cyberspace' (Winterson, 2000). Film-makers have also highlighted how new technologies can be integrated into the everyday. Pratibha Parmar's film *Wavelengths* indicates the possibilities for connection between women through the Internet (Parmar, 1997). The potential anonymity of electronic encounters has proved popular for gay male fiction.

As well as sparking this new theme among producers of queer popular culture, researchers have also noted a shift in modes of meeting others, given the facilities which are offered through electronic communication.

In Tsang's work on gay Asian males online, he claims that for the users of one online service in California in the mid-1990s 'electronic cruising has replaced bar hopping' (Tsang, 1994: 119). Yet statistical estimates of use are extremely difficult to obtain. In February 2000 an audit of Planet Out's website counted 1.6 million unique hits per month.[9] This indicates the popularity of one online service, but does not tell us anything about the identity of the users or the nature of that use. There are no publicly available surveys of Internet use that collect information about sexual orientation. Some of the newer web content providers, such as Rainbow Network Plc, have commissioned their own surveys. Their nationwide survey of 608 'gay people' in 2000 showed that 57 per cent of lesbian respondents and 51 per cent of gay male respondents in the UK were Internet users (Rainbow Network, 2000).[10] One-third of the total sample were using the Internet on a daily basis. Relating these results to other activities, the research results show that 'non-scene gays' tend to be more frequent users than those participating in local gay scenes, and that all users were spending a third of their time online at sites identified as primarily lesbian or gay. These results offer us an overview of how gays and lesbians are integrating the Internet into their daily lives, but there is not yet any longitudinal data which could indicate how uptake is developing among the heterogeneous groups which make up queer communities. The research described here indicates some of the distinctive ways in which this may be happening in the pockets of activity which have already been studied.

THE HISTORY OF QUEER ONLINE SERVICES

A rough chronology of lesbian and gay spaces on the Internet can be pieced together from the accounts of early users and research studies that focus on specific online sites.

In general terms the evolution of queer online forums have kept pace with mainstream Internet services, beginning with gay newsgroups and bulletin boards and now characterised by elaborate queer web content and services. As commercial services for chatting to other users became commonplace, revenue-orientated gay chat spaces increased in parallel (Shaw, 1997). When graphical '3D' worlds became available *Pride!Universe* was created for queer users (Wakeford, 1997a; Taylor, 1999). However, regardless of the specific features of the online forum, many services are short-lived. Some commercially run services, including *Pride!Universe*, have ceased to operate. The situation of local services, run as hobbies or as non-profit-making ventures, is even more precarious. This makes historical research difficult. Unless it is archived, much fieldwork in online spaces is characterised by a 'disappearance of data' (Kotamraju, 1999). Whereas old banners and leaflets may be retained, digital materials are often deleted or lost as new software and hardware systems are upgraded.

The first gay and lesbian online services were based on plain text posted in electronic arenas such as newsgroups and bulletin boards. Newsgroups were one of the earliest forms of globally accessible computer mediated communication.[11] Gay newsgroups emerged in the early 1980s, more than a decade before the growth of commercial cyberqueer spaces (Goodloe, 1997). In 1983 gay users of USENET set up one of the first globally accessible queer online spaces: a newsgroup called *net.motss*. 'motss' is the acronym for Members Of The Same Sex. As is frequently the case, there is little documentation about the first users of this online service. Nevertheless, fragments of the group's history are contained in an archived posting written by one of *net.motss* original users. This account shows how the group gained visibility in a public Internet forum despite pervasive homophobia within newsgroup space.

It [*net.motss*] arose out of some comment in net.singles about having a newsgroup for gay issues, passed on to some folks saying 'yeah, good idea, I'll support it', and then gathering the requisite 'yea' votes. We then presented the results to 'net.groups' or whatever it was called, where it encountered violent opposition. People were sure it would not only scare the horses but that it would scare upper management as well, and lead to Netterdammerung: death-of-the-net-as-we-know-it. I mean, if upper management knew they were spending money so that gay folks could chat clandestinely to find sex partners, what would be next? The whole house of cards would be in danger of falling: first net. singles, then net.lang.c.

Some folks thought that 'net.gay' was too hot a name, and some rather frivolously suggested alternatives. Someone lost to antiquity peeped up with *net.motss*, a pun on MOTOS/MOTSS, and it stuck. It took a lot of calm but relentless and impassioned arguing with people to achieve consensus and to convince folks that this would be wonderful and not a disaster, but I believe that we did. The newsgroup was formed, and the rest is history. About a year later, I got a note from M[name], one of the backbone folks (and at the time spiritual leader of all of USENET), saying that we could consider, if we wanted to, changing the name to net.gay, since there had been no problems and the quality of the group was self-evident. It didn't seem worth pursuing; motss was fairly well-ingrained. (Dyer, 1988)[12]

The 'violent opposition' of early USENET authorities is just one example of how prejudice has shaped queer spaces on the Internet. Early gay forums from the online service provider Prodigy were included in a ban of unsuitable groups by a court in Germany in 1988, although after much outcry they were reinstated. Later the confidence that queer Internet users could maintain a boundary between online activity and their lives elsewhere was severely shaken when America Online (AOL) was found to have passed on private information revealing the homosexuality of a member of the United States military. Such events are equally as significant in the development of cyberqueer online communication as the technical programming advances that appear to be the driving force behind more sophisticated services. Furthermore, they undermine the utopian rhetoric. How far is the Internet global if services can be blocked by one country? To what extent is the impression of anonymity undermined if service providers reveal private information to employers or other authorities? Apparently benign actions can also have consequences on the provision of lesbian and gay content. The website *lesbian.org* was temporarily overloaded and shut down during its initial months online by the volume of users being directed to it via a link set up by a heterosexual pornographic site (Goodloe, 1996).

The process of vote-collecting for USENET groups deemed necessary for the formation of *net.motss* stemmed from Internet culture which championed a democratic space of inclusion (Ludlow, 1996). However, other arenas existed that did not need such collective permission, and could therefore operate outside the surveillance of those who controlled the formally organised spaces. Bulletin Board Services (BBSs) were small regionally focussed services, often with direct local telephone dial-ins to electronic chat spaces.[13] In an ethnographic study Shelly Correll describes the *Lesbian Café* BBS used by women in the Midwest of the United States in the early 1990s (Correll, 1995). Woodland describes a similar gay male service, *Modem Boy High School*, which was populated by users in the Los Angeles area of California (Woodland, 1995). Tsang reports on a BBS in Orange County, California which began in 1991 and attracted many Asian American gay male users (Tsang, 1994). Other relatively unregulated electronic services offering 'live chat', such as IRC, have also been popular. In 1994 three of the *Wired* 'Top 10' list of most populated chat rooms were men4men (#3), MenWhoWant2MeetMen (#6) and YoungMen4Men (#8), names which suggest gay male users or homosexual content (Shaw, 1997). Most of these chat services, on IRC and in BBSs developed a loyal following via personal recommendations rather than widespread publicity. BBSs flourished among early adopters of

computer mediated communication, and until the mid-1990s they operated as social networks which were largely unnoticed by wider queer media.

Internet services based on the use of electronic mail and the World Wide Web grew rapidly with the development of Internet Service Providers and the increasing use of email in educational institutions, particularly among students. As a consequence, email 'discussion lists' developed. The inventory of lists collected at the online *Queer Resources Directory* shows the wide variety of interests and groups with such forums.[14]

Email discussion lists have enjoyed a far higher profile than newsgroups or BBSs among lesbians online, although there are several personal accounts of substantial lesbian activity on the *Backdoor BBS* in San Francisco.[15] Probably the most well-known lesbian list, SAPPHO, was started in May 1987. Early lists such as SAPPHO tended to be facilitated by women working in the computer industry who could use the computers at their organisation to run the mailing list distribution software.[16] These women could spend up to four hours per day administering requests for subscription, dealing with messages being returned by non-functioning email accounts, or simply moderating the discussion which was happening in the forum. Even though in theory its membership is not limited exclusively to lesbians, the majority of participants on SAPPHO identified as lesbians, dykes or bisexual women, and SAPPHO has been represented in several accounts as a lesbian online space (Case, 1995; Wakeford, 1995; Hall, 1996; Isaksson, 1997). By the early 1990s what had begun as a small list of women who mostly worked with computers or in education developed into an important point of entry for any lesbian starting out on an exploration of Internet services. Postings originated not only from university sites, but also from addresses in NASA and the Jet Propulsion Lab (Case, 1995). By 1994 there were nearly 700 subscribers to SAPPHO, and up to 300 postings per day and the main list soon generated regional sublists (Isaksson, 1997). One of these regional lists was in the San Francisco Bay Area of California, established by a new arrival to the city in order to meet other lesbians (Wakeford, 1998a).

In the early 1990s, discussion lists were dominated by subscribers from the United States, in particularly those logging on from educational institutions. Ron Buckmire, who founded the web-based *Queer Resources Directory*, undertook an analysis of the geographical distribution of the mailing list *QueerPlanet* in 1995. Of 319 subscribers worldwide, 42 per cent were from .edu domains, indicating educational institutions in the United States. A further 28 per cent were from .com, .org, or .net domains, usually implying a user in the United States.[17] Although there was such over-representation of Americans on 'global' lists, pockets of queer Internet activity elsewhere began to emerge including several European lists set up by Eva Isaksson. From her base in Finland she established the first Finnish *sapfo* list in 1993, the year that also marked the beginning of dedicated lesbian 'Chat' spaces.[18]

The mid-1990s marked the beginning of a period of intense growth for all lesbian and gay discussion lists. Isaksson documents the surge of lesbian lists in 1994, including the *OWLS* (Older and Wiser Lesbians) list in late Spring, a list for European lesbians *Euro-Sappho* in July, and a US-based alternative to SAPPHO, *DykeNet*, in November. Lesbian lists began to serve increasingly specific groups: *kinky-girls*, *boychicks*, *politidykes* and *lesbian-studies scholars*, for example (Goodloe, 1997). Also in 1994, California-based *www.lesbian.org* was set up by Amy Goodloe, and *soc.support.youth. gay-lesbian-bi* was approved.[19] Other newsgroups with explicit lesbian and gay labels were also approved on USENET, such as *soc.women.lesbian-and-bi* in 1995.

Although most discussion lists continue to be based in the United States, in the late 1990s, European lists began to be facilitated, sometimes operating in languages other than English. By 1997 Isaksson had counted thirty-nine general or topical lesbian email discussion lists which were running on computers in North America with English as their 'default' language, eight additional lists which had local emphasis such as *BA-Sappho* for the Bay Area area around San Francisco, five lists which were run on European computers using the language of the server's host country rather than English and three which were run from European servers in English for Europeans (Isaksson, 1997).

The timeline of lesbian lists constructed by Isaksson has not been replicated for other queer spaces. There is no systematic documentation about the development of gay male newsgroups, email discussion lists or web resources, and also lack of information about the development of online services by or for the transgender population. It is difficult to assess the importance that websites such as *FTM International* have had for the queer population, although they have undoubtedly played an important part in providing access to information and stories which were not previously in wide circulation.[20]

There is also a gap in research on how particular kinds of online services – newsgroup, discussion list, chat, and/or web – are chosen above others on the same theme. This may be a significant factor in determining the future shape of queer Internet services. Early research on gendered use of spaces online, although not taking into account sexual orientation, suggested that for a topic which had both newsgroups and discussion lists, women were more likely to participate in the latter (Clerc, 1996). As the most visible queer Internet services are now based on the Web, researchers would do well to keep track of the consequences for other arenas.[21]

BBSs were usually run on home computers whereas mailing lists were almost always run on Unix servers. Moderators could be likened to the computer hobbyists described in a study of early computers users (Turkle, 1984). Even BBSs which charged for online access were rarely set up with the sole

Figure 8.1 Planet Out Home Page, 1997; Planet Out Home Page, 2001

purpose of making money. Most of the services in Finland described by Isaksson were developed by Kari Koivumaki, a nurse who worked on the *seta.fi* web space on a voluntary basis.[22] Commercially orientated services began to flourish as content providers realised the value of the gay and lesbian online market. In 1996 an Associated Press report noted 'It's the unspoken secret of the online world that gay men and lesbians are among the most avid, loyal and plentiful commercial users of the Internet' (quoted in Gross and Woods, 1999b). More recently *Planet Out* proclaimed that >>> 'The gay and lesbian market is finally accessible en masse through Planet Out Partners, Inc'. Commercial services such as *Planet Out*, Rainbownetwork.com and *Queer Company*, have established themselves – often with expensive advertising campaigns – alongside those run by the pioneers, many of whom subsidised the running of the free services from their own pockets, or from fund-raising drives.[23]

AOL has been at the forefront of providing commercial unmetered access to the Internet, and since the early 1990s it has been the largest domestic Internet Service Provider in the United States. It was host to one of the earliest commercially facilitated lesbian and gay spaces. In 1991 the Gay and Lesbian Community Forum (GLCF) was established with official support of AOL, although one researcher noted that this forum had a distinctly 'corporate air' compared to unofficial AOL areas (Woodland, 1995). As well as lesbian and gay spaces on otherwise mainstream sites, dedicated queer commercial services began in the mid-1990s. *Planet Out* began on the Microsoft network in 1995, quickly also establishing a space on AOL (see Figure 8.1) (Lewis, 1995). *Rainbow Network* began in the UK in 1999 and by February 2001 boasted 47,000 individual subscriptions.

In the late 1990s as the capacities of bandwidth, hardware and software increased, graphic virtual worlds began to appear (McDonough, 1998). For a brief time *Planet Out* joined forces with Microsoft in providing access to a lesbian and gay graphic

world in which the avatars were designed by the lesbian cartoonist Alison Bechdel. Such a development drew upon the more traditional forms of queer popular culture, in this case the 'Dykes to Watch Out For' comic books. Although this 'virtual world' with characters such as the 'Lesbian Avenger' did not survive more than a matter of months, other spaces had a longer lifespan. In October 1996 an alliance of Pride Media, a private company based in San Francisco, Compuserve and Fujitsu Software Corporation announced the launch of *Pride!Universe*. The service relied on the interface of an exisiting mainstream service called *WorldsAway* on the Compuserve network (Taylor, 1999).

As the Internet becomes more widely used, and the content continues to evolve via more sophisticated graphics and animation, the most visible Internet services for the queer user are provided by large commercial organisations, such as *Planet Out* or *Queer-Company*. However, a large number of more informally organised chat spaces and discussion lists continue to exist, as the listings on the *Queer Resources Directory* make clear. Small, more specialised websites continue to be developed, attracting participants on the basis of shared interests in the same way that newsgroups and discussion lists connected earlier users.

Queer digital content is also being created by artists, representing the expression of queer experience through technology. Significant moments in queer history have been explored by creating interactive multimedia content for the web, such as Shu Lea Cheang's web project related to the story of the murdered Brandon Teena (Harrup, 1997). Two such art projects which have been discussed by researchers in terms of theories of queer performance are Linda Dement's CD-ROM 'Cyberflesh Girl Monster' produced from scanned body parts of the clientele of an Australian dyke bar, and Barbara Hammer's *Community Cyberspace Biography* located on the ECHO system in New York (Willis and Halpin, 1996). Independent film-makers such as Hammer have made extensive use of the new media as a way to express contemporary queer experience, and for those within dance and performance studies interactive work online provides a rich new source of material for pursuing lesbian and gay themes.

Most research in cyberqueer studies has focused on the services which were developed around the mid-1990s. At this time many services were free to Internet subscribers and not commercially organised. In the studies described here most researchers managed to avoid the potential logistical and legal wrangles of recruiting subjects via large commercial organisations. Newer online content providers, which are owned and run by well-financed new media companies, have not yet been the subject of sustained analysis. Yet the form and substance of their output pose significant dilemmas about online representation, in particular the strategic development of quasi-brands which cross-cut different types of media. Increasingly this will either encourage or force researchers to address the methodological issues of access to corporate environments.

DOMINANT THEMES WITHIN CYBERQUEER STUDIES

Identity and Self-Presentation

Recent debates within lesbian and gay studies have addressed the nature and viability of identity-based social movements, reflecting a long-standing concern with what constitutes identity claims and processes of recognition (Butler, 1997). Yet since the mid-1990s the meaning of lesbian, gay, bisexual, transgender or queer identity has been challenged by the ways in which new technologies have become part of many people's experiences of being a member of a sexual minority. This shift has not yet been incorporated into the wider debates about social identity within the discipline.

As the *Rainbow Network* survey showed, roughly half of all lesbians and gay men used online services, reflecting the impact of the Internet in the UK by the late 1990s. This new queer sphere of activity presents a challenge to those researchers studying the formation of social identity amongst contemporary queer populations. They must now take on board the potential significance of online experiences in the processes of coming out, meeting others, being politically active, contributing to a 'community', participating in non-normative sexual activities, and other aspects of identification.

New information and communication technologies do not have a straightforward impact on pre-existing queer identities, and certainly not one which can be predicted in advance with any degree of certainty. Indeed, certain marginal sexual identities have been implicated as figures through which cyberspace is understood. This is particularly the case with transgender identity, which has been used as a metaphor through which the impacts of the Internet on identity can be described (Bromley, 1995; O'Brien, 1996). Transgender has been invoked as a metaphor for boundary crossing, fragmentation, and hybrid/cyborgs, as it was in the work of Kate Bornstein (1995), although the potential political risks of so doing have not been explored.

Existing studies of queer sexuality and the Internet have assumed that issues of identity can for the most part be reduced to issues of self-presentation. The creation of an electronic persona online – whether through text or graphics – may permit misrepresentation as well as the opportunity for sustained fantasy or deception. Early Internet studies developed an emphasis on the nature of self-presentation online, and a central motif of this first wave of research was a male user who presented himself as a woman in online interactions (Stone, 1991; Dibbell, 1996). This act was offered as evidence of a 'freeing' of users from the 'constraints' of the gendered body. The emergence of the interest in identity and self-presentation in cyberqueer research is probably a consequence of this framing. Some writers locate their investigations of cyberqueer directly in terms of the flexibility of self-presentation which is supposed to be a feature of interaction in online spaces (Hall, 1996). Equally influential in casting the issue of identity in terms of self-presentation were the writings in the early 1990s of queer theorists Butler (1990) and Sedgwick (1991), who were read as if they were proposing a theory of voluntaristic performance of the queer self. The ideas of performance and performativity were aligned with the concern with identity mutability in Internet Studies. For example, as well as being used to frame Hall's investigation into the discursive practices on SAP-PHO, references to the work of Judith Butler and/or Eve Sedgwick appear in a study of queering discussion lists about female pop stars (Fraiberg, 1995), in an article on the significance of gay male chat spaces (Woodland, 1995) and in an exploration of the relationship between online and transgender identities (Bromley, 1995).

The consequence of equating the presentation of self online with the formation of self-identity is that the relationship between activities involved in creating an electronic character and the ways in which that electronic character is implicated in everyday life and social institutions may be left unclear. Since much of the writing has focused on highly specific questions – the credibility of user nicknames in a particular forum or which forms of talk are censored – it is difficult to tell whether or not we are seeing new forms of queer social identity in any more general sense. Nevertheless, creating a successful online nickname or working out the discursive norms of an online environment are not trivial matters to users, and are significant in terms of the internal functioning of a forum.

Changing the online description of your ethnic identity seems to have a significant impact on the chances of being selected as a conversational partner. Tsang reports the story of 'one BBSer from Taiwan [who] picked 'Caucasian' and found out lots more people wanted to chat with him than when he was "Chinese"' (Tsang, 1994). Such differential treatment can become an informal means of

gatekeeping for a 'virtual community', as is described in the section below.

Studies of online worlds can provide researchers with a rich set of data on how codes are evolving to describe aspects of self and behaviour. Subcultural codes, akin to the hanky code (Miller, 1995), form an important part of the functioning of some online forums (Hall, 1996; Wakeford, 1995; Livia, 1999). A study of the French Minitel, an early form of computer-mediated communication which in many ways is analogous to a text-only chat space on the Internet, illustrates the complexity of abbreviations in gay male electronic chat spaces (Livia, 1999). On the Minitel a gay man may identify himself as VRP BFT/62 80: DISPSOIRS, which is equally opaque as an unknown hanky colour. This highly concentrated Mintel code contains a great deal of information about the user, including occupation, physical attributes, geographical location and availability.

> VRP BFT/62 80:DISPSOIRS appeared on a gay male sex line based in Lille, in northern France. The mysterious letters 'VRP' refer to a vendeur representant placeur (seller, representative, order placer, or sales rep), 'BFT' describes this sales rep as bien foutu (well hung), '62 80' refer not to his height, weight, or other dimension but to the two regions in which he plies his trade: Pas de Calais and Somme. 'DISPSOIRS' is not a misspelling of desespoir (despair) but the important message that this individual is available in the evenings (Livia, 1999: 432).

Due to the pay per minute structure of the Minitel all interactions must be as brief as possible, and significant insider knowledge is assumed in order to decipher the resulting codes. Other online codes reflect the ancestry of lesbian and gay forums in wider computer cultures. The Muff Diva Index ('MDI'), which allowed early lesbian mailing list participants to categorise themselves on scales such as hair length, shoe style, and relative size of their women's music collection (Wakeford, 1995), was an adaptation of the Hacker Index through which early Internet users created a light-hearted way to categorise themselves using the significant attributes and stereotypes of computer hackers. Codes such as the MDI were regularly included in 'signature files' at the bottom of email postings on discussion lists such as SAPPHO in the early 1990s (Hall, 1996). Additionally, by including mottos and quotations in these signature files, users could affiliate themselves with authors or ideas which were already associated with queer culture.

Given the extent of the light-hearted banter reported in chat space and email discussion lists, it would be tempting to dismiss many online exchanges as trivial in terms of a wider lesbian and gay identity politics. However, other researchers, and in particular those who have combined online observations with face-to-face contact, suggest that certain social and political identities are only made possible through Internet exchanges (Yue, 1999; Barry and Martin, 2000). In Taiwan and South Korea queer communities have only existed openly from the mid-1990s. The authors of a study of the effect of the Internet in these countries conclude 'queer communities and subjects use computer-mediated communication to construct their identities and communities on and off the net in a dialectical and mutually informing manner' (Barry and Martin, 2000). They suggest that the possibility of an openly gay identity in Taiwan and South Korea emerged alongside the popularisation of the Internet. Usage of online services in general was much more widespread in Taiwan than in Korea, including thriving BBSs and around eighty MOTSS sites in mid-1999. In Korea it has been more difficult for users to establish such electronic spaces, and most users access content via the web pages of commerical Internet Service Providers. In both countries Internet sites were used both for meeting other lesbians or gay men, and as a primary resource for queer activist information.

Much has been made of the fragmentation of self-identity in contemporary societies. Some writers on sexuality have attempted to describe autobiographically how the Internet has changed their sense of self-identity,

although their accounts show how difficult it is to make such claims without slipping into technological determinism (Haskel, 1996; Case, 1997; Yue, 1999). Yue suggests that constructing a hypertextual narrative which includes records of her online experiences is a way to bring together, however partially and temporarily, the fragments of diasporic identity which she feels cannot be consolidated elsewhere. She presents the act of writing about the desires and possibilities of cyberspace as a way to reconcile potentially conflicting elements of herself; arriving as an immigrant to Australia, being excluded from some gay venues, and working as a political activist. '<interface: reflections of an ethnic toygirl>' (Yue, 1999) was written as a result of this process:

> Scrolling along very much like the tentative pixels of an interactive computer screen, this text performs as a circuit, inviting readers to interline the webs of their configurations into this fabric, which can only be in the beginning of an ongoing platform for further points of critically queer departures. Articulating the oral, the vernacular and the subaltern, 'interface' injects as a kind of postmodern self-writing which presents an emerging visuality and functions as a postcolonial entry into the metropolitan Australian queer culture. (ibid.: 114)

The way in which Yue constructs her 'postmodern self-writing' narrative can be understood as an attempt at expressing the mutual constitution of sexuality and the technology. Her 'postcolonial entry into the metropolitan Australian queer culture' is constructed through the availability and capabilities of Internet technologies.

The Creation of Queer Space

> They're meeting places so free and open and wild and fun they make the Castro Street look Victorian. (quoted in O'Brien, 1999)

Another key topic within cyberqueer writing is the exploration of the kinds of spaces which are created for queerly identified users online. Queer 'spaces' online exist in so far as 'places' are created by the exchange of electronic text as chat contributions or emails, or via a website (Woodland, 1995). Focussing on the interactions alone misses an important component of the spatial contextualisation of those interactions, and the ways in which these spaces are often presented as locations rather than conduits for communication, and described as 'towns', 'rooms' or 'bars'. Yet queer online services have also been described using metaphors of the body. Case suggests that the SAPPHO is the lesbian body on the Internet (Case, 1995).[24]

The quotation which begins this section appeared in an advertisement in *The Advocate* in 1996, and illustrates the way in which many guides and mass media articles about gay and lesbian online services have drawn parallels with well known physical places which are already marked as queer. Such places – San Francisco's Castro district or Manchester's Gay Village around Canal Street – have received substantial attention in lesbian and gay studies, particularly among cultural geographers (Bell and Valentine, 1995, 2000; Ingram et al., 1997). However, tracking down spaces online can be far more difficult. For the most part queer online spaces have been publicised by word of mouth, until the late 1990s' advertising campaigns.[25] Although early Internet Service Providers such as Prodigy, AOL and Apple's *eworld* offered some gay content, this provision is not a good indication of the extent and content of queer online spaces. Hundreds of 'gay-related' message folders outside the Gay and Lesbian Community Forum were frequently better populated than the official queer area on America Online (Woodland, 1995).

Several writers have provided descriptions of the textual means by which queer spaces are created. It is notable that there is more work on the text-based services such as BBSs than the new graphic-based worlds. On a BBS the textual description of a space can be offered to users as they enter the system. The *Lesbian Café* BBS was organised around the image of a bar and associated

features such as a fireplace. 'TJ described the bar using features everyone would recognise as a bar. There was the bar itself, highly polished so she could slide drinks down to her patrons. The pool table was to be a gathering place, but "no-one is to knock the balls off the table". She added a fireplace and a hot tub,' (Correll, 1995: 279). In common with many descriptions, this BBS encouraged the user to imagine an interior with features which encourage interaction. The creator of *Lesbian Café* sought to portray 'a place more grand than any lesbian bar that actually exists', while retaining elements of a scene which would be familiar to many participants (Correll, 1995).

Woodland paints a similar portrait of the *Stonewall Café* (Woodland, 1995). His description illustrates the ways in which online places may be modified in response to participant activity – in this case the addition of the 'bisexual futon'. 'Depending on the imagination of those writing entries, the room's amenities may contain a hot tub (or two, if separatists are online), a fully stocked bar with attractive co-gender bartenders and a range of comfortable furniture: a love seat, some dark booths in the corner, the "dyke couch" and the most recent addition, the "bisexual futon"'. (ibid.). The visions of those who create these spaces range from the everyday – the café and the bar – to more utopic scenes incorporating iconography of paganism or anarchy.

Woodland also describes *Weaveworld*, which draws upon a quite different set of references to either the *Lesbian Café* or the *Stonewall Cafe*.[26] Rather than encouraging the impression of an enclosed location, the user arrives in an outdoor landscape surrounded by statues and within sight of Michel Foucault.

You are standing on the top of a hill covered with fragrant and unfamiliar flowers and grasses. From this vantage you see a large part of Weaveworld, a riotous patchwork of geographies hastily rescued from some ancient peril...

On a large marble pedestal is a statue of two Greek warriors clad in bronze and silver armour...

You see Jorgé Borges, saying 'Oh time, thy pyramids!'

Quentin talks with what appears to be a box containing Schroedinger's cat.
You see the two boys from the statue, wrestling.
You see Michel Foucault in white pants and a leather jacket. (Woodland, 1995)

The layers of gay imagery incorporated into *Weaveworld* encourage the participants to see themselves as participating in a complex environment in which considerable knowledge of queer cultural references is expected. By contrast the graphic environment of Fujitsu's *Pride!Universe* relied heavily on the imagery of science fiction. 'The visual setting for the Universe in the gleaming interior of a space station, including public thoroughfares with sliding doors, meeting places, private spaces, a landscaped garden and other objects of interest' (Pride Media Press Release, October 2, 1996).

The kinds of representations which are created in the virtual architecture of these spaces are significant because they suggest the kinds of participants who are anticipated, and the types of interactions which are expected to happen (Crang, 1994; Wakeford, 1998b). *Modem Boy High School* BBS has developed an elaborate set of spatial metaphors including public spaces (classrooms, a cafeteria, a library) and private spaces (locker rooms) for the 'STUDents' who log on to the system (Woodland, 1995). Although Woodland points out that this sets a 'tone of playful camaraderie amongst users', he also comments that it simultaneously constructs gay men as 'horny, sexually compulsive, adolescent boys'. He concludes, 'ModemBoy gains the comfortable uniformity of a consistent spatial metaphor, but potentially disenfranchises more diverse expressions of queer identity'.

An alternative way of creating queer space is through the exchange of electronic text on a discussion list (Fraiberg, 1995). Although via a discussion list there is no sense of entering a space with defined parameters such as a bar or a landscape, Fraiberg suggests that queer space emerges via the exchange of emails which are sent to the main list address and then distributed to all members. Her study considered the types of interactions which occurred on the discussion lists formed by the fans of Melissa Etheridge and the Indigo Girls, particularly before these musicians had spoken publicly about their lesbianism.[27] Queer consumption of popular culture has frequently involved the appropriation of mainstream stars and fictional characters. Fraiberg suggests 'queering' takes in the course of discussions in which list members speculate about the stars' sexuality and appropriate them as lesbian icons. Lesbian participants, not without resistance from others, create their own narratives about the stars, and then dominate the discussion amongst those who might dissent. The same kind of queering might be said to take place on SAPPHO, although this list is clearly more dominated by overt lesbian-related content than are other interest-based lists.

Although this means of creating queer space has been tremendously successful on the Internet, discussion lists remain largely underground in terms of the official representations of appropriated cultural icons. For example, the television series *Xena Warrior Princess* has attracted a huge lesbian following, which is reflected in discussion list participation and a substantial number of fan organised websites. Lesbian fans have more webpages than any other subgroup of Xena fans. Yet on the official Xena site they are virtually invisible and MCA/Universal never mentions Xena subtext. Pullen comments 'Even the [online] database that promises unlimited information does not recognize the terms "subtext" or "lesbian"' (Pullen, 2000). Unlike discussion lists, many websites which allow discussion are highly regulated by commercial sponsors, and the potential for queering a mainstream site seems restricted.

Social Networks and 'Virtual Community'

Based largely on his own experiences as a participant in a BBS, Howard Rheingold's book *The Virtual Community: Homesteading on the Electronic Frontier* (1993) proposed that electronic communication that allowed people to share information and emotional support encouraged the formation of 'virtual communities'. The book was one of the first widely read statements advocating this new means of sociality, and it was widely referenced in early Internet studies (Shields, 1996; Jones, 1999). The forms of social support to which Rheingold refers includes the rapid sharing of information in everyday crises, for example between parents, as well as sustained emotional bonds which were developed over time in relation to those with long-term illnesses. Rheingold's ideas contributed to an existing concern circulating in the United States about the need to revive 'third spaces' in which people could gather, away from the first and second places of home and work. Cafés, coffee shops, bookstores, bars and hair salons were characterised as being such third spaces. They provided places where community-making could happen, and also were at the heart of democratic society (Oldenberg, 1988). Rheingold suggests that the virtual community is another third space, providing a supplement to traditional meanings of finding information and offering support. The virtual community reflected a specific kind of nostalgia, and offered a potential replacement for the loss of such third spaces in the 'real' world. Whether or not third spaces actually functioned as beneficially as is implied in these debates remains largely unexamined in relation to the notion of virtual community.

Internet researchers have tended to accept Rheingold's position, including many within cyberqueer studies. Woodland cites Oldenberg's work in his study of the *Stonewall Café* and *Weaveworld* (Woodland, 1995). Although other writers do not make such explicit references, cyberqueer studies tend to replicate two assumptions which characterise the virtual community perspective; first, that communication in online spaces is a replacement for 'community' elsewhere; second, that groups of users interacting electronically on a BBS, newsgroup or mailing list, are assumed to have already achieved some kind of community simply through having this communication.

A frequent assertion is that online interactions are a substitute for participation in gay bars, clubs and other organisations of 'the scene'. Correll suggests the primary function of the *Lesbian Café* was to provide a 'sense of community' for women who were isolated from bars, bookstores or community centres (1995). The role of online spaces in providing social venues in the lives of those who identify as queer but are isolated or marginalised – geographically, economically or socially – has been noted by several writers (McKenna and Baugh, 1998; Wincapaw, 2000). Overcoming such isolation seems to be particularly crucial for queer youth seeking advice and support (Gray, 1999; Silberman, 1999). Having access to online services serves as a proxy for face-to-face involvement, and often respondents talk about online participation as the only way to keep in contact with similarly identified others. A respondent to Wincapaw's survey commented: '(I) needed to communicate with other African American L/B/T (Lesbian, Bisexual, Transsexual) women. Hey, I'm the only out black dyke in this white city of 44,000' (Wincapaw, 2000: 55).

Although providing access to an alternative queer sphere of activity, it is unclear how these online services compare with their geographically situated counterparts. Users may participate in a queer forum online, whilst not necessarily identifying in this way elsewhere (Correll, 1995; Wincapaw, 2000). Correll demonstrated that the *Lesbian Café* provided a sense of being with other lesbians, and that this was particularly important for users who described leading otherwise 'straight' lives. Researchers of internet spaces tend to be sensitised to the ways online behaviors may be separated from other activities, and this raises the question of the ways in which participants in other (offline) queer spaces – such as bars and cafés – may be experimenting in analogous ways.

The other assumption involves the nature of 'community' itself. Rheingold's original example, *The WELL* BBS, was an established electronic forum with a large number of regular and long-standing participants, many of whom were based in Northern California. However, it is questionable that we should presume any group of electronic participants thinks of itself as a virtual community. This tends to have been an assumption in Internet Studies, without a clear indication about what might differentiate a social group, a social network and a community. Rather than assuming that any gathering of electronic participants equals a community, looking at the specific kinds of activities in that group – including communication, rules and responsibilities – uncovers a range of ways in which groups of users create configurations of social relationships. Contrasting the Minitel exchanges (Livia, 1999), which may be extremely brief, pseudonymous and cryptic rather than discursive, with the extended ongoing narratives between those with established personas on a discussion group such as SAPPHO (Hall, 1996; Wakeford, 1998a; Case, 1997), illustrates the possibility that electronic communication can facilitate both weak and strong social ties.[28] If Minitel and SAPPHO are both to be characterised as queer virtual communities, researchers will need to develop more subtle ways of describing the very different types of social relationships which predominate in each space.

Even though research on weaker ties largely focuses on seemingly more ephemeral chat spaces, and research on strong ties has highlighted the role of apparently more robust discussion lists, the nature of the group interactions cannot be read off the technical features of the forum. A BBS, for example, may be used for contrasting purposes. Whereas in some BBSs such as those discussed by Tsang, users might change their self-description to attract different interactional partners on different occasions, other BBSs such as the *Lesbian Café* have regulars who maintain a consistent persona which is expected to be free from any deliberate deception.

Research on the activities happening in online forums shows how far users are taking on roles and constructing reponsibilities in ways which might indicate distinctive types of sociality, such as those associated with being a community. Although these activities are understandably varied, many of the cyberqueer studies have concentrated on networks which are used as a way to pass leisure time, such as swapping news or gossip, rather than more overtly political ends. Informal 'chatting' of this kind seems to occur in all computer-mediated forums, although the actual form varies. In graphic worlds, user actions involve both typing in text, the manipulation of a graphical representation of a character, as well as movement through the virtual architecture of rooms (Taylor, 1999), whereas in chat spaces or IRC, most chatting is done with out the conscious and continuous reworking of the participant's persona during the session. Flirting is a frequent feature of these casual interactions (Wakeford, 1995; Wincapaw, 2000). Yet even apparently trivial chat may involve those taking part in understanding complex sets of rules and vocabulary which are distinctive to that cyberqueer arena, such as the Muff Diva Index (Wakeford, 1995). Although individually many of the electronic messages sent and received appear to be mundane and of little importance, the cumulative effect of participation can sometimes have an intense psychological impact on the interlocutors (Haskel, 1996). In the gay media several stories have highlighted the potential of these social networks to enable 'online romances', although when these involve younger queers, they are often framed in terms of the potential vulnerabilities of these users (Silberman, 1999).

Elsewhere in Internet studies, some research has suggested that prolonged use of the Internet may lead to a decline in psychological well-being. However, a study undertaken by psychologists on the impact of newsgroup use for those with 'concealable marginalised identities' – in which were included users of *alt.homosexual* – concluded that participation of a virtual group was 'a crucial part of the demarginalisation process' (McKenna and Bargh, 1998).

The researchers found that 37 per cent of the users 'came out' as a direct result of newsgroup participation. This would widely be regarded as a positive outcome, and highlights the heteronormative assumptions of the previous study. McKenna and Bargh's results concur with first person accounts which suggest that involvement in a gay forum online may lead some users to question their own sexuality, and then come out to themselves and friends (Walsh, 1999).

Although not yet extensively documented by researchers, computer-mediated electronic networks have had a significant impact on political activism. Soon after the first discussion lists were launched, the *Queer Planet* list was established to keep subscribers informed of the latest activist news and events. *Queer Planet* existed purely as an online mailing list, but electronic resources were also built for existing campaigning groups. The *Queer Resources Directory* was started in 1991 as an electronic archive for Queer Nation, and later turned into a more comprehensive resource available on the Web (QRD FAQ document). Digital Queers (DQ), a fund-raising group, also sprung up around the need for queer organisations to have Internet access. DQ began in San Francisco as a social group which held events at large computer fairs and used funds to provide hardware and training for other groups such as PFLAG.[29] More recently the electronic transmission of information between activists in Seoul impacted on the local Film Festival (Berry and Martin, 2000).

Much of the research on lesbian and gay communities has stressed the importance and the nature of boundaries which are established between group members and outsiders. This has also been a feature of writing about the construction of identities within social movements, particularly separatist movements (Green, 1997; Roseneil, 2000). Similarly, the means by which participants are allowed to join or are refused entry to electronic arenas has provoked interest in cyberqueer studies. Such gatekeeping can occur both through the requirement of formal applications to join a service, and more informally through the operation of discursive norms (Hall, 1996).

Although many online services do not require registration for access, a substantial number of spaces such as discussion lists operate a screening policy administered by the list moderator. The 'intro message' sent out by the moderator may be accompanied by the request for email confirmation that the intended user is indeed lesbian or gay. Some lists also require or expect residency in a particular area, and thereby erect another boundary around the group. Often the rationale for this regulation is that offline meetings will be possible (Wakeford, 1998a).

The use of the intro message alongside the requirement of an affirmation about sexuality is intended to prevent lists being taken over by outsiders, usually heterosexuals. However, an extract from one such intro message, from a list in California, shows how debates about 'who is a lesbian' become part of the way in which the screening policy operates. The first section of the intro message reads: 'This list is for lesbians and dyke-identified women ONLY*(* for the purposes of this list, dyke-identified means any woman (born or TS[transsexual]) who identifies as lesbian or bisexual)' (Wakeford, 1998a). This wording reflects an inclusiveness in the San Francisco area about the transgendered population which was not true for other locations. The rule requires only that a user 'identifies as' lesbian or bisexual, and explicitly includes transsexuals under the category woman. In fact when the list was first formed, the intro message was more restrictive, suggesting only 'post-op[eration]' transgendered users were welcome. After several months the moderator changed the message so that it was in tune with the local queer culture, rather than reflecting the policy on other women-centred lists (Wakeford, 1998a). However, intro messages, through an insistence on defining certain qualifications for participation, may construct boundaries which are just as impermeable, or perhaps more impermeable, than those which occur in bars, clubs or other public places where socialising takes place.

Users of discussion lists and other forums which screen participants often describe the resulting forums as 'safe spaces' (Hall, 1996; Wincapaw, 2000). Participants contrast the high number of homophobic insults which are included in the content of unmoderated groups, particularly newsgroups and chat rooms. In addition to attempts to exclude outsiders via the intro message, or the naming of the forum, particular skills have been developed to combat homophobic speech online, and these are passed on informally. These skills include technical knowledge about gaining 'op' status and how to disconnect other users, or means by which posts can be ignored by the system. Hall describes how 'kill files' were encouraged to exclude a user with a particularly aggressive posting style, as she was thought by the majority of the users to be a man. Inventive naming of chat rooms counter the expectations of unwelcome guests. Thus an AOL forum called 'lesbian chat' may be supplemented with 'sensible shoes', the new name acting as a code which will be understood by the intended participants.[30]

Monitoring of participants also may occur in the course of ongoing conversations. In her study of SAPPHO, Hall was particularly interested in investigating the workings of the discursive practices through which users determine the credibility of the participant. This 'online screening process' begins with an assessment of the subscriber's name. Traditionally masculine names are subject to intense scrutiny and require explicit public justification. Participants are also expected to conform to SAPPHO's norm of what Hall calls 'discursive femininity'. This discursive style is characterised by the avoidance of any verbal utterances which might be seen as adversarial – such as 'flaming' – and encouragement of a 'politeness-based communicative ethic' (Herring, 1996). Hall indicates that the list's desire for discursive conformity is

so strong that jokes have been written about the political correctness of the forum. Users are instructed not to raise discussions of men, straight or gay, including past experiences with male lovers, boyfriends or husbands. In maintaining this policy, SAPPHO subscribers were often required to justify their separatism to other lists to which gay men also subscribed, such as GAYNET (Hall, 1996: 164).

Whereas in some forums of the Internet, such as newsgroups, cross-posting is actively encouraged, on discussion lists such as SAPPHO, which are seen as private spaces, cross-posting is against list policy. There is thus a tension on many lists of wanting to encourage new members, and to maintain a strong screening process. Issues of the permeability of boundaries of the forum are therefore frequently at the forefront of the discussion.

Some subscribers feel that the social and cultural diversity of the group is rarely reflected in the conversations that take place within the postings to the list. White, well-educated repondents considered 'race' to be a 'non-issue' in discussion list communication, whereas a woman of colour stressed the intensification of invisibility which occurred in these spaces. 'Race itself doesn't come up until one of "us" walks in the room' this survey respondent replied. She continued 'people – especially articulate folks – are presumed white until proven otherwise' (Wincapaw, 2000: 55).

Existing cyberqueer studies have not yet developed firm indicators of what would constitute 'community' participation in online spaces. 'Regulars' are defined as those who post regularly to the discussion list, or who frequently log on to the BBS (Correll, 1995), but there are few indications of the effects of regular use. McKenna and Bargh's study suggested that the effects that they noticed on demarginalisation were stronger for self-identified posters than 'lurkers' (McKenna and Bargh, 1998). However, other studies suggest that users may think of themselves as participating in a forum even when it is used as a background noise to other activities. When used in this way online participation would be close to the creation of a queer soundscape, a concept which has been described elsewhere in lesbian and gay studies in relation to the use of music in domestic spaces (Valentine, 1995).

New Technology and Erotic Practices

> Synthetic cyberdyke wants non-blonde (fakes OK), non-herbal types for sexual interfacing. (Yue, 1999: 115)

Online environments are a new arena for queer sexual and erotic practices. As portrayed in *Queer As Folk*, text and graphics can be exchanged via a computer as a precursor to face-to-face meetings, in this way fulfilling a similar role to telephone or postal small-ads. Early services from Prodigy and AOL included online 'personals' databases, and these continue to be a popular feature of large web-based environments. However, the possibility of rapid exchange of information electronically has also promoted a new kind of sexual practice – sometimes called 'cybersex' (virtual sex) – in which the experience of computer-mediated communication is constructed *as* sexual experience, rather than being an addition to other activities. Early mainstream writers speculated about the possibilities of elaborate 'teledildonics' (Rheingold, 1993). However, cybersex usually consists of a jointly authored narrative of a sexual encounter, often in spaces which encourage speedy exchange of electronic text, such as chat rooms.[31]

Eroticism online may occur in less explicitly sexual spaces. Replies to Haskel's request for commentaries about lesbian online experiences produced an example of the powerful effects of rapid communication.

> There's often an intense excitement involved. Your screen becomes electric in a very real way. Her name becomes magic, your days are spent in fingering her [tracking online status], talking with her, writing/reading email to/from her. And the intensity builds until the words on the screen become flesh and sound when she reaches over

the distance to touch you. (Deva, quoted in Haskel, 1996: 57)

A variety of new erotic repertoires are being created in the course of such intense exchanges. The material culture of the computer itself has sometimes acquired an aura of queer desire (Haskel, 1996; Tsang, 1994). Haskel writes of her own feelings about the technologies of computing, and the associated cultures of mastery and control.

> Women like my machine. It's not phallic like a flashy mobile phone, but had all its cybernetic thrill. Is the fantasy to master machines and be mastered by them? Or is it simply childhood memories of visits to my mother's office: clicking keyboards, dextrous ladies at their typewriters, smelling good, looking smooth and soft and so in control? I've always found typing sexy. (Haskel 1996: 53–54)

Often, as in the novels *Nearly Roadkill* (Sullivan and Bornstein, 1996) and *Prozac Highway* (Blackridge, 1997) desire appears to cross-cut use of the computer, the forums which are accessed, and the others with whom connections are made. It is difficult to know what or whom are being desired. Both Haskel and Yue use expressions of their own erotic practices as a way to explore the potential implications of new technologies for queer life. This is a theoretical and methodological strategy which has been advocated elsewhere in queer theory (Probyn, 1995, 1996; Halperin). Drawing on her own memories Elspeth Probyn suggests 'ways in which desire may be put to work as method in queer theory' (1995: 4). Rather than locating desire as having an object to which it must be attached, Probyn uses the conception of desire as a productive force with which to make queer connections (1995). Yue's (1999) article 'Interface' seems to employ a similar strategy, including an account of a sexual encounter which is described in terms of an interactive computer game in an arrangement that is similar to Bornstein's *Virtually Yours*. Yue's queer connections bring together not only women and machine, but narratives of cyberfiction, the fetish scene, and urban drug cultures.

<Interface> is an experimental text, at the boundary of artistic intervention and academic commentary, and suggests how Probyn's method might work with an individual biography, resulting in a highly personal view of the erotic potentials of cyberqueer activities.

It is difficult to understand the type of sexual practice which Yue is describing outside the context of the technology and new media through which it is expressed. Her writing illustrates one way in which changing erotic practice throughout the 1990s has begun to incorporate online activities, and the part that new technologies might play in the construction of sexual activities. The fact that in the early 1990s advice about sex toys was offered on SAPPHO (Case, 1995), and this reflects the growing acceptability of public discussion of lesbian use of sex toys during this period, and at the same time demonstrates the importance of SAPPHO as a means by which these discussions and practices could evolve.[32]

Many discussion lists have been set up for the discussion of non-normative sexual practices, such as *kinky-girls* which was formed for the discussion of lesbian S/M. By establishing such discussion lists, their creators were also consolidating or formalising what were sometimes disparate groups of interest. Whereas access to groups of those with marginalised sexual practices has largely been concentrated in urban centres, more remote users might have their first contact with the existence of such queer sexual practices through the Internet. Online spaces may provide the opportunity not only for having cybersex, but also be part of the way sexual practices themselves are defined. The recent research on the sexual practice of 'bare-backing' has demonstrated the extent to which the practices and debates about this behaviour cross-cut any division between 'virtual' and 'real'.

There has been at least one attempt to deploy the technical features of the online service to create a sex-positive queer environment which would subvert the usual practices in online spaces. In *DhalgrenMOO*

a programmer experimented with computer commands which automatically replaced every user's identity with the word 'someone' in an attempt to explore the possibility of creating a 'backroom' (Woodland, 1995). The participant would become part of a narrative that might include the following statements:

Someone enters
Someone brushes up against your leg.
You touch someone's arm. (Woodland, 1995)

However, Woodland points out that both *DhalgrenMOO* and *Weaveworld* are unusual in their unconventional imagery. More common are the descriptions within *Modem Boy High School* BBS that reproduce images which are already in wide circulation. Rather than using new technologies to invent new forms of queer desire, BBSs such as *Modem Boy High School* encourage users to engage in sexual fantasies which have a more easily accessible set of spatial metaphors.

Lesbian and gay studies has recognised the importance of narratives about sex and sexuality (Plummer, 1995). Cyberqueer researchers have documented several kinds of queer sexual practices, but there are no studies of how online narratives about erotic practices might be integrated in the everyday experiences. At this stage most of the innovative erotic practice that draws on the culture or use of new technologies is being developed by lone writers such as Yue, or in fleeting experiments such as the one in *DhalgrenMOO*.

ONLINE DATA COLLECTION

The methods used in cyberqueer studies range from electronically administered surveys and research based on traditional psychological measures to email interviews and participant observation. In conducting studies of online services, cyberqueer researchers have struggled with several distinctive challenges that relate to the technological and social infrastructure of the fieldwork environment. This has led to several new modes of data collection and some experimental data presentation.[33]

Participant observation has long been used in lesbian and gay studies, both in older 'classics' of research (Humphreys, 1970) and in more contemporary work (Green, 1997). However, in conventional studies participation involved covert or overt face-to-face contact with research subjects. Many studies have collected logs of data online through some form of observation, often combining this with electronic participation in, or even administration of, the space (Isaksson, 1996; Goodloe, 1997). Several researchers have gained access to participants for online interviews after having been involved in virtual world or discussion list exchanges, but many have had no face-to-face contact with their research subjects (Hall, 1996; Wincapaw, 2000; Woodland, 1995). Where researchers have participated in offline meetings or conducted more traditional face-to-face interviews, it has tended to be as a supplement to data collected online (Wakeford, 1998; Berry and Martin). The implication of online data collection versus material gathered through face-to-face exchanges has not been raised.

Some cyberqueer researchers have been physically located in the same geographical area as the service or population that they are researching (Tsang, 1994; Wakeford, 1998a; Correll, 1995), but most are not, and it is surprising that most existing work has not questioned the potential effect of researcher location on the kind of data that is collected.[34] One exception is Anna Livia's study of the Minitel, in which she pays close attention to the possible effects of joining *messageries* based in France from the United States (Livia, 1999). Even though in terms of her on-screen interactions she was just as 'close' to a participant in Paris as any French user, she faced two peculiar challenges: the difference in time zones and the financial infrastructure of Minitel. Given

that she was logging on from the United States and respondents were in France, the data was necessarily constructed around different temporal and bodily experience. The other infrastructural restriction was the fact that users paid per minute for their use. Livia had to develop strategies for understanding the linguistic structure of the Minitel acronyms without engaging in long interactions which were expensive for, and resisted by, her participants.

Despite such problems the global range of computer networks does allow research that would have only been previously possible at disproportionate cost. In considering the implications of new technologies for methodology in lesbian and gay studies, it is worth noting that even those with no interest in studying online worlds *per se* have successfully employed the Internet in order to reach a queer sample (Nieto, 1996; Wood, 1997). Other researchers indicate that their participants could only have been reached via online contact, considering the long-standing difficulty of reaching marginal or stigmatised populations, and this is particularly the case for queer youth (Nieto, 1995; Gray, 1999).

The proliferation of queer spaces on the web, in chat spaces, discussion lists and beyond is often not being archived. Although researchers can log discussions as they happen, as can any subscribed user, there is no organisation that is storing queer Internet history. Data which has been generated on older software versions may be particularly at risk in the long term. The problem of disappearing data is not evenly distributed across all services, particularly where content has been created by a corporation. Any archive of the now defunct *Pride!Universe*, if indeed it has been stored, is now part of the digital assets of the corporate alliance that set it up. It is difficult to imagine that researchers in the future will have easy access to such data, and the most likely outcome is most such digital assets will be deleted before they can be archived.

REFLEXIVE WRITING

Studies of queer culture have frequently included the researcher's personal responses to undertaking fieldwork in spaces such as clubs (Wilton, 1995; Amory, 1996). Cyberqueer studies are no exception. Some writers have also experimented with new narrative forms in the presentation of their results. In his review of the state of contemporary ethnography Norman Denzin suggests that qualitative research faces a crisis of representation in which the traditional forms of academic writing are being challenged by such new narrative forms (Denzin, 1998). In the cyberqueer literature research carried out via auto-ethnography includes attempts at reproducing hypertext narratives within the traditional format of an article or book (Haskel, 1996; Case, 1997; Yue, 1999). Texts may combine different typographical fonts and narrative styles to indicate interactions between the researcher and their subjects, or changing perspectives of the author. Sue-Ellen Case's book presents a traditional academic text which is interrupted by an italicised reflexive narrative on the writing and computing experience (1997), whereas Haskel includes the email texts of her exchanges in her article, switching between responses and personal reflections (Haskel, 1996). As well as including email texts, Yue's writing draws on Teresa De Lauretis 'migratory consciousness' and is a deliberate attempt at intervention in the written form of feminist and queer theory in which passages from personal advertisements and computer game narrative are interwoven with commentary. Although other ethnographies, such as the study of the *Lesbian Café* BBS, have been written up in a more traditional style, the experimental work has opened up the possibility of integrating the experience of the online medium into the form of the presentation, and in so doing has increased the repertoire of queer writing styles.

Part of the explanation for the popularity of the auto-ethnographic componant in many cyberqueer studies is the newness of the medium to the researchers themselves. Descriptions of the online space become accounts of the author's own entry into the queer spaces on the Internet. Most are positive about the possibilities about online services without subscribing to the hyperbole of earlier commentaries. Many authors situate their own stories of getting online as part of their introductory remarks and their motivations mirror those of the populations that they describe; a desire to find a safe space online (Case, 1995), or a place to have sex encounters (Tsang, 1994). Explicit commentary on the sexual practices of the authors is occasionally included (Tsang, 1994; O'Brien, 1997). The pioneer writer-moderators, such as Eva Isaksson and Amy Goodloe, have written about their participation as a form of activism, and as a way to realise their lesbian identities.

In some areas cyberqueer studies have reflected methodological trends in mainstream lesbian and gay studies, and a surprising lack of reflexivity. Although the possibilities for researching groups of which you are not a member is feasible via some online services, researchers have stayed close to the environments in which they might normally participate. Lesbians tend to study lesbian-orientated online services, gay men to study gay male-orientated online services. Perhaps an assumption that this raises fewer ethical dilemmas explains the absence of any extended discussion about issues such as the desirability of asking permission before reproducing exchanges verbatim, the level of privacy that should be given to information shared in electronic spaces, and the effect of any research intervention on the group structure. None of these issues have yet been well covered in such studies.

QUEER THEORY ONLINE: QSTUDY-L

The pervasiveness of Internet facilities amongst scholarly researchers has produced new fields for data collection, such as newsgroups or web pages. Simultaneously it has had an impact on the production of academic knowledge in lesbian and gay studies. The production of queer theory itself has been modified by the popularity of online discussion lists, web archives of unpublished papers, and, far from trivial in the popularisation of queer theory, the rapid dissemination by email of gossip. Archives of discussion lists provide snapshots of intellectual history in lesbian and gay studies, including the ways in which online lists become battlegrounds for different intellectual positions. A set of events on QSTUDY-L – a list dedicated to the discussion of queer theory – highlights the symbiotic relationship between queer theory and new communication technologies.

QSTUDY-L is an online discussion list based at SUNY-Buffalo. Created in 1994 out of a previous forum housed at UC Santa Barbara, the archived postings from QSTUDY-L show how intellectual disputes emerged, captivated the list, and then were integrated into subsequent discussions or disappeared entirely. By mid-1995, from a relatively modest beginning, more than a hundred topic threads each month were being posted to the list. The early logs show that contributors were just as likely to be well known authors in lesbian and gay studies as graduate students or independent scholars and activists;[35] Eve Sedgwick participated in a debate of which the subject header was 'Social constructionism and the sodomite'; Gayle Rubin became involved in an exchange on Camille Paglia. QSTUDY-L seemed to epitomise the early hopes for the Internet as a means through which scholars at all levels could share intellectual interests.

The use of QSTUDY-L grew steadily through the late 1990s, but the numbers of widely known published writers who posted to the list decreased. Then, in June 1998, the posters of QSTUDY-L found themselves unexpectedly in the spotlight, targeted in an article by Daniel Harris in the *Harvard Gay and Lesbian Review* as examples of queer theory's academic insularity. Harris' article was based on a spoof posting which he had

written to QSTUDY-L, much like a similar hoax that had been published in the journal *Social Text* mocking the cultural studies of science.[36] Harris's post concerned a translation drawn from 'a mythical French "subjectivist" named Marie Françoise de Ricci' (Harris, 1998). The fictional De Ricci had been inspired by Judith Butler's article 'The lesbian phallus and the morphological imaginary'. De Ricci's invented response was entitled 'Towards a Theory of the Absent Orifice: Labial Engenderings and Oral Antecedents' from which Harris posted a summary of her 'orifice theory'. He admitted that he composed this 'more or less as a Rorschach blot of postmodern cliches, a suggestive but utterly opaque quilt of theoretical slogans culled from the email of other QSTUDY-L subscribers'. Asked by Harris to comment on the utility of de Ricci's work in queer theory, some participants had taken the bait.[37] One spotted it as a parody of the previous debates. When the text of the article in the *Harvard Gay and Lesbian Review* was posted electronically to all subscribers, the aftermath of Harris' hoax reverberated through the electronic community, as it had in the fallout after the spoof article in *Social Text*. Some participants were furious that Harris had used QSTUDY-L not only as a vehicle for a specific critique about what he saw as the over-zealous policing of queer intellectual terrain, but also as a way to engage with queer theorists by deception. Harris accused the most vocal posters on QSTUDY-L of excluding the very minorities whose experiences the list supposedly sought to analyse. His article is highly critical of the alleged worship of the writers of 'the minute anti-canon of sacred texts'.

> Far from protecting the rights of the silenced few it [QSTUDY-L] stamps out dissent, censors minority positions, and legislates conformity to the minute anti-canon of sacred texts written by queer theorists' real oppressors, not Dead White European Males, but the unchallengeable politburo of postmodernist Big Brothers who dictate every word and every email they write (Harris, 1998).

Harris' choice to target QSTUDY-L, and to use it as a foil for his argument, indicates the partial integration of online spaces into the production of queer theory. He presents the list as a 'virtual community' of queer theorists, and his reporting slides from a specific set of debates on this discussion list ('dildo scholarship', 'trucker porno theory', 'gender liminality') to a more general critique of the state of queer theory *in toto* and allegations of abuses of newly acquired 'power and bourgeois respectability' of its key figures.

As an isolated event on a list primarily of scholars, the action hardly caused a ripple in the wider world of lesbian and gay newsgroups and discussion lists. Yet it indicates a significant moment in the integration of online and offline debates in lesbian and gay studies. It is sometimes tempting to treat discourses generated via the Internet less seriously than discussions that occur elsewhere, and undertake a kind of policing of the boundaries of the sites that are considered appropriate for theoretical production.[38] Feminist theorists have recently questioned the utility of such restrictions (Ahmed, 2000). As increasing numbers of students use the Internet as a primary source of information, the archives of QSTUDY-L, which are freely available on the web, are an easily accessible source of data. Several journals have published guides to online resources for lesbian and gay scholars, and the Queer Resources Directory lists several discussion lists for scholars with interests in a specific subfield. Given the proliferation of lists such as QSTUDY-L, lesbian and gay studies needs to understand the impact that online services are having on the development of the discipline, and more consideration will need to be given to the effect of circulation of online material, pedagogically and in terms of research dissemination.

CONCLUSION

Cyberqueer studies have demonstrated the range of ways in which new information and communication technologies impact upon queer lives, and also how queer experience comes to be understood in terms of these technologies. However, studies are often small scale or exploratory studies and not widely read amongst lesbian and gay scholars. More extensive research in this area should be supported, and the emphasis put on the integration of cyberqueer research into a wide range of perspectives as the discipline of lesbian and gay studies continues to develop. In the spirit of encouraging further studies in this area, and in the light of some of the omissions in existing material, this conclusion will point to some possible issues that might be tackled by future research.

The history of queer online spaces reveals not only the piecemeal development of these services, but the lack of virtually any documentation – electronic or otherwise – on the evolution of cyberqueer services. It points to the need for some kind of routine archiving of the spaces which do exist. In the current climate commercially orientated content providers are attempting to demonstrate in their publicity that their users constitute a queer market, rather than a group of individuals with shared interests. The rapid expansion of lesbian and gay services in the 1990s was due largely to the increasing amount of free content and the facilitation of social networks by companies for whom getting loyal users who would use their website was the primary goal. This shift in ownership and control of the dominant content, from hobbyists to commercial content providers, is the most significant structural change in relation to the development of future cyberqueer research. Who is financing and producing cyberqueer content? The call within Internet studies for an 'ethnography of infrastructure' (Star, 1999) is of crucial importance in cyberqueer research, which has tended to ignore the technological and economic infrastructures that frame online exchanges.

The four themes highlighted in this chapter, addressing the issues of identity, space, community and the erotic, reflect the overlap between existing concerns of

Internet studies and contemporary debates in lesbian and gay studies. Overall, the influence of a particular reading of queer theory, for example understandings that centred around self-presentation, provided the theoretical justification for stimulating research questions and has fostered some sense of similarity between studies, but may have hampered the development of alternative frameworks that might have drawn on other developments in queer theory and elsewhere in the discipline. The impact of Internet studies has perhaps led to an overemphasis on traditional views of community, rather than an examination of what assumptions underlie these views, and the potential distinctiveness of queer modes of affiliation that may or may not be exemplified online.

The most significant contribution of cyberqueer studies has been to highlight a new domain of lesbian and gay practice, and new spaces which may be queered. The Internet can be characterised, at least in part, as a new media form, and similar questions may be asked of the Internet as have been asked of television, film or radio. This would add a new set of questions and engage a different set of queer scholars. Issues of representation of queer lives could be brought to the foreground, along with the risks of standardisation and the reproduction of marginality as the large corporate websites overshadow the smaller offerings.

Although cyberqueer studies have been concerned to examine how one creates and maintains a queer persona in online spaces, the focus on the on-screen textual manifestation of such activities tends to have obscured the diverse ways in which this new media may be integrated into everyday lives. Future studies might start to develop models of these practices, and compare them to the inclusion of other media in public and private queer spaces. Issues such as the way in which the Internet fits into queer household structures have not been tackled, although other researchers of new technologies have focused on such questions (Silverstone and Hirsch, 1992). We need to know more about both the mundane

use of email, the reasons why users would participate in exotic utopian spaces such as *Weaveworld*, and how each kind of use fits into their wider social relationships. Methodologies that have been developed in queer media studies have as yet not been influential in writings about the Internet. The analysis of the construction of images that has been carried out in lesbian and gay film studies could be a model for examining web based content. New questions would surely arise such as 'Are ideas such as 'camp' relevant in terms of the images found online?'. These discussions could play a part in bringing cyberqueer studies back into a dialogue with other scholars working on queer cultural studies.

As well as generating new forms of representation, cyberqueer writers have illustrated the ways in which online services have provided spatial metaphors that have encouraged users to think of themselves as participating in activities based in places – online cafés, bars or locker rooms. As well as generating more descriptions of how images are constructed and understood in these arenas, future cyberqueer research could produce more complex models of how activities in such places are constructed, and engage in debates about the usefulness of concepts such as 'interactivity' for queer users. Is there a distinctive kind of queer interactivity, for example? How would interactivity relate to other notions, such as intimacy, which have already been exposed in terms of their normative framing? (Berlant, 1997).

In contrast to other media, the Internet has emerged in parallel with specific cultures of computing and computer mediated communication. As well as being analysed as a new media form, the Internet can also be studied through the ways in which it interacts with the social shaping of artefacts. Cyberqueer writers have touched upon the erotic potentials of artefacts such as the computer, both as things through which erotic contact can be made, and as fetishised objects in their own right. There are fruitful connections here to be made with the ways in which material cultures become associated with queer identities.[39]

Some cyberqueer writers treat the online interaction itself as an object that can be queered (Fraiberg, 1995). Yet as a whole researchers have not paid attention to the ways in which Internet interactions are changing the politics of social movements, or even the ways in which social movements themselves are constituted. Even though there has been an interest in how intra-group discussions frame the constituency and norms of the participants, there has been little work looking at the implications of on-line activist resources for local actions, or the effects of groups such as Digital Queers on voluntary organisations or the policy process. It is important to note that such lack of research attention does not reflect an absence of activism on the Internet.

Finally, cyberqueer research will undoubtedly evolve in the context of further technological change. As new technological goods enabling mediated communication continue to be offered to consumers, some will attract groups of users and new cultures of practice. The most recent example in Europe of a related technology becoming involved in everyday life is the integration of mobile phones use into public spaces. This development has had particular impact on gay areas such as Soho in London. Although the mobile phones have been promoted as portals to Internet services, currently they appear to have different, although overlapping, patterns of use (Brown, Green and Harper, 2001). Whether cyberqueer writers will pay sustained attention to technological object that are related to the Internet other than the computer remains to be seen.

This review has shown that much work still needs to be undertaken to develop the research directions that are underway in cyberqueer studies, as well as to find means to consolidate the field. Meanwhile researchers elsewhere in lesbian and gay studies should be encouraged to engage with the topics that have already been raised, whether it is to challenge the use of theory, debate the importance of the findings, or to draw upon the data about emerging queer practices. Certainly having email has a greater impact on many queer lives than owning FiestaWare, and by shouting about their Internet access the marchers in the quotation that began this chapter expressed both their recognition that the idea of a Network Society was on the horizon, and their desire that others should know that queers were already part of it.

NOTES

1 I would like to thank Aylish Wood, Mary Gray and CW Lipman for their comments on previous drafts of this article; Anna Livia and Karenza Moore for assistance with locating references.

2 For an introduction to Internet studies more widely see Jones (1999), Bell and Kennedy, (2000), Trend (2001).

3 A cross-section of Internet research can be found via the Association of Internet Researchers Web pages *http://www.aoir.org*

4 Research on the domestic consumption of technology emerged in the UK as part of the Economic and Social Research Council's Programme on Information and Communication Technologies (PICT). Articles on such 'domestication' of computers appear in Silverstone and Hirsh (1995). Recent work attempts to locate new technologies in terms of a 'circuit of culture' which takes into account cultures of production and regulation, as well as consumption. This can be seen in du Gay et al.'s analysis of the Sony Walkman (1997).

5 For a history of Science and Technology Studies, see Hess (1997). A useful indicator of current themes preoccupying those undertaking cultural studies of science and technology can be found in Downey and Dumit (1997).

6 The substantial literature which has emerged on the 'cyborg' includes *The Cyborg Handbook*. Further context about Haraway's original formulation can be found in Ross, interview with Donna Haraway; How Like a Leaf Book.

7 Hall's study of SAPPHO begins by citing Haraway's (1985) article 'A Manifesto for Cyborgs' in order to define a new kind of feminism, which some have called 'cyberfeminism'. Haraway's metaphor has also been used to contextualise Bromley's discussion of transgender identity (Bromley, 1995).

8 This has been noted as a wider trend in queer theory itself. It is also a critique which could be levelled

at Internet Studies, particularly the parts which draw heavily on communication studies and studies of discourse.

9 Statistics about Planet Out can be found in their 'Press Kit' on *www.planetout.com*. The February 2000 audit was undertaken by Media Metrix.

10 Caron Lipman offered invaluable help in uncovering this survey.

11 For a full description of the working of newsgroups, see Baym (2000).

12 In 1983 most online users were working within the computer industry, and the account of *net.motss* describes the perceived threat in terms of the values of the computing subculture. Poking fun at the norms of this culture, the writer suggests that *net.motss* was not just a threat to a subsection of the newsgroup hierarchy ('net.singles') but also to the symbolic heart of the whole system: the forum for discussing the computer programming language 'C++'.

13 In 1993 Osborne reported that there were 45,000 BBSs in the United States (Osborne, 1993). Adverts for gay BBSs occasionally occurred in the gay press personal columns around this time, one example being the Eye-Contact BBS in San Francisco's *Bay Times* (January 1993).

14 A full list of current gay related discussion lists can be accessed via the *Queer Resources Directory* at *www.qrd.org*. Previous versions of this list are not archived making it difficult to track the nature of the growth.

15 Anna Livia and Kira Hall, personal communication.

16 Unusually, SAPPHO was started by a heterosexual woman, Jean Marie Diaz ('Ambar') to provide a meeting place for lesbians online. Ambar ran SAPPHO for four years, until in 1991 the list maintenance duties were passed on to 'Zonker' a lesbian subscriber from Boston (Isaksson, 1997).

17 These can be distinguished from domains which clearly denote a country e.g. .uk (UK), or .fr (France).

18 Chat spaces allow the simultaneous exchange of text in the same way as does a BBS. However sevices such as Internet Relay Chat (IRC) did not require users to dial in to a local chat line. Rather IRC could be accessed through the distributed network of the Internet.

19 I would like to thank Mary Gray for supplying me with this information from her ongoing research with this newsgroup.

20 Informal discussions with transgendered persons during fieldwork in 1996–8 in the Bay Area suggested that such websites have played a significant role in the dissemination of information about medical advances and in the facilitation of support networks.

21 Isaksson has suggested that women are attracted to services which require the least user sophistication and the least connectivity time, which explains the popularity of mailing lists amongst lesbians online (Personal Communication, 2001).

22 SETA is the Finnish national organisation for lesbian and gay rights. It was the first organisation of its

kind to purchase its own internet domain in the early 1990s and to start on web server in 1993.

23 *Queernet.org* organised a regular fund-raising drive, in which appeals for funds were distributed by queernet via list moderators to all members of lists which were housed on the queernet server.

24 Case draws on Nicole Brossard's poetic work *Picture Theory*, which imagines the lesbian body as a 'Screen Skin', a 'Screen Skin Utopia' or a 'Hologram' (Brossard, 1990). Case states 'On the computer screen, one lesbian body takes space as Sappho, reconstructed as scrim, interpenetrated by communal messages, traveling through the inter-net, "bundles" and "branches" creating a "Screen Skin Utopia" out into global dimensions' (1995: 340).

25 Q Company organised a national media campaign in the UK in 2001, both with glossy images in mainstream print media, and using large billboard advertisements.

26 *Weaveworld* was created on the LambdaMOO system, developed by Pavel Curtis of Xerox Research. The Lambda software program forms the core of most other MOO spaces. Discussion of bisexuality on LambdaMOO can be found in Kaloski (1997).

27 Fraiberg monitored discussions between November 1993 and July 1994. At this time there were around 700 subscribers to the Indigo Girls list and 400 subscribers to the Melissa Etheridge.

28 Social network approaches to the analysis of Internet communication have proposed that the social ties between users should be a key interest (Garton et al., 1997).

29 Parents and Friends of Lesbians and Gays has a site at www.pflag.org.

30 I have not used real names of current rooms on AOL. However, I would like to thank Kate Bornstein for giving me examples of such renamings (Interview with author 1995).

31 Kaloski discusses the difficulty of defining 'computer sex'. She offers one definition: 'computer sex is typing with one part of the body (usually the fingers of one hand) and allowing the words on the screen, and other parts of your fleshy body, to give you sexual pleasure' (1997: 49).

32 Case says of a subscriber 'She "meets" other lesbians, thus able to keep "abreast" of activist projects, subcultural fashions, and sex radical pleasure practices on the "privacy" of her own screen' (1995: 340).

33 For a discussion of the 'tricks of the trade' developed by Internet Studies researchers in their data collection and analysis see Lyman and Wakeford (1999).

34 Although researchers can verify the area code for the BBS's local call-up number, this does not guarantee that all participants would be logging on from that area. Therefore it is problematic to suggest that a 'local' online service is primarily drawing from local populations unless there is a formal screening process for locally based users.

35 Sedgwick and Rubin have been cited elsewhere as key in the field, including in Roseneil 2000.

36 Cooper (1999) describes the outcome of this hoax.

37 The full text of postings sent after Harris' intervention can be viewed in the archive of the QSTUDY-L list.

38 This is analogous to Joshua Gamson's comments about day time talk shows in *Freaks Talk Back.*

39 Elizabeth Wilson writes of the queering of the poodle (Wilson, 2001: Ch 13).

REFERENCES

Ahmed, Sara (2000) 'Whose counting?' *Feminist Theory*, 1 (1): 96–103.

Albright, Julie (1995) 'Invisible wimmin: the emergence of bisexual identity in text-based virtual reality', paper presented to American Sociological Association Conference, August.

Amory, Deborah P. (1996) *Club Q: Dancing with (a) Differences in Inventing Lesbian Cultures in America.* Levin, Ellen (ed). Boston, Beacon Press, p. 145–160.

Barry and Martin (2000) – on Korea and Taiwan.

Baym, Nancy (1994) 'The emergence of community in computer mediated communication', in S.G. Jones (ed.), *Cybersociety: Computer Mediated Communication and Community.* London: Sage. pp. 138–163.

Baym, Nancy (2000) *Tune In, Log On: Soaps, Fandom and Online Community.* Thousand Oaks, CA: Sage Publications.

Bell, David and Kennedy, Barbara M. (2000) *The Cybercultures Reader.* London: Routledge.

Bell, David and Valentine, Gill (1995) *Mapping Desire: Geographies of Sexualities.* London: Routledge.

Berlant, Lauren (1997) *The Queen of America goes to Washington City: Essays on Sex and Citizenship.* Chicago: University of Chicago Press.

Berlant, Lauren (ed.) (2000) *Intimacy.* Chicago: University of Chicago Press.

Berry, C. and Fran, D. (2000) 'Queer "n" Asian on – and off – the Net: The Role of Cyberspace in Queer Taiwan and Korea', *Web.studies: Rewiring Media Studies for the Digital Age.* David Gauntlet (ed.), London: Arnold, p. 74–81.

Blackridge, Persimmon (1997) *Prozac Highway.* Vancouver: Press Gang Publishers.

Bornstein, Kate (1995) *Gender Outlaw: On Men, Women and the Rest of Us.* Vintage Books USA.

Broidy, Ellen (1996) 'Cyberdykes, or lesbian studies in the Information Age', in *The New Lesbian Studies.* Bonnie Zimmerman and Toni A.H. McNaron, New York: Feminist Press 203–7.

Bromley, Hank (1995) 'Border skirmishes: a mediation on gender, new technologies, and the persistence of structure', paper presented at 'Subjects of Technology: Feminism Constructivism and Identity', Brune/ University, Jone.

Brossard, Nicole (1990) *Picture Theory* (trans) Barbara Godard. New York: Roof Books.

Butler, Judith (1990) *Gender Trouble: Feminism and the Subversion of Identity.* London: Routledge.

Butler, Judith (1997) 'Merely Cultural', *Social Text* (Fall/Winter), 52–3: 265–77.

Case, Sue-Ellen (1995) 'Performing lesbian in the space of technology: Part II', *Theatre Journal*, 47 (3): 329–44.

Case, Sue-Ellen (1997) *The Domain Matrix: Performing Lesbian at the End of Print Culture.* Bloomington, IN: Indiana University Press.

Castells, Manuel (1996) *The Rise of the Network Society.* Oxford: Blackwell.

Clerc, S. (1996) 'Estrogen brigades and "big tits" Threads: media fandom online and off', in L. Cherny, and E.R. Weise, (eds), *Wired Women: Gender and New Realities in Cyberspace.* Seattle, Washington: MIT Press.

Cooper, Geoff (1999) 'The fear of unreason: science wars and sociology' *Sociological Research Online.*

Compuserve/Pride Media Limited (1996) Pride! Universe on Compuserve offers Virtual World for the Gay and Lesbian Communites, Press Release, Columbus, Ohio (2 October).

Correll, Shelly (1995) 'The ethnography of a lesbian bar: the Lesbian Café', *Journal of Contemporary Ethnography*, 24 (3): 270–98.

Crang, P. (1994) 'It's showtime: on the workplace geographies of display in a restaurant in southeast England', *Environment and Planning D: Society and Space*, 12: 675–704.

Davis-Floyd, Robbie and Dunit, Joseph (eds) (1998) *Cyborg Babies: From Techno-sec to Techno-tots.* London: Routledge.

Dawson, Jeff (1996) *Gay and Lesbian On-Line: The Travel Guide to Digital Queerdom on the Internet, the World Wide Web, America Online, Compuserve, plus BBSs coast to coast.* Berkeley, CA: Peachpit Press.

Denzin, Norman (1997) *Interpretive Ethnography: Ethnographic Practices for the 21st Century.* London: Sage.

Dery, Mark (1993) 'Flame wars', *South Atlantic Quarterly*, Fall. Special Issue: Flame Wars: The Discourse of Cyberculture: 559–68.

Dibbell, J. (1993) 'A Rape in Cyberspace' *Village Voice*, December 21, p. 36–42.

Dishman, Jesse Dallas (1995) 'Digital divas: defining queer space on the information superhighway', paper given at Queer Frontiers: The Fifth Annual National Lesbian, Gay and Bisexual Graduate Student Conference, 23–26 March. (1995) Published online: http:// www.usc.edu/Library/QF/queer/papers/dishman. html

Dishman, Jesse Dallas (1997) 'Digital dissidents: the formation of gay communities on the Internet,' MA thesis, University of Southern California.

Downey, Gary Lee and Dumit, Joseph (1997) *Cyborgs and Citadels: Anthropological Interventions in Emerging Sciences and Technologies*, Santa Fe: School of American Research Press.

Duyves, Mattias (1993) 'The Minitel: the glittering future of a new invention', *Journal of Homosexuality*, 25 (1–2) (March–April): 193–205.

du Gay, Paul et al. (1997) *Doing Cultural Studies: The Story of the Sony Walkman*. London: Sage/Open University.

Dyer, Steven (1998) 'Re: origins of soc.motss,' message posted to soc.motss newsgroup 27 May 88, 20:31:15 GMT. Archived at http://www.qrd.org/qrd/electronic/usenet/soc.motss.beginnings

Epstein, Steven (1996) *Impure Science: AIDS, Activism and the Politics of Knowledge*. Berkeley, CA: University of California Press.

Freberg, Allison (1995) 'Electronic fans, interpretive flames: performing queer sexualities in cyberspace,' *Works and Days 25/26*, 13 (1–2). Published online: http://acorn.grove.iup/edu/en/workdays/Frailberg. HTML

Gamson, Joshua (1998) *Freaks Talk Back: Tabloid Talk Shows and Sexual Nonconformity*. Chicago: University of Chicago Press.

Garton, Laura, Haythornethwaite, Caroline, and Wellman, Barry (1999) 'Studying on-line social networks' in Jones, Steve (ed.) (1999) *Doing Internet Research: Critical Issues and Methods for Examining the Net*. London: Sage. p. 75–105.

Goodloe, Amy (1996) *Personal communication with the author*.

Goodloe, Amy T. (1997) 'Lesbian computer networks and services,' *Encyclopedia of Homosexuality*, 2nd ed. Volume I: *Lesbian Histories and Cultures*. Bonnie Zimmerman ed. New York: Garland.

Gray, Chris Hables (ed.) (1995) *The Cyborg Handbook*. London: Routledge.

Gray, Mary (1999) *In Your Face: Stories from the Lives of Queer Youth (Haworth Gay and Lesbian Studies)* Harrington Park Press.

Green, Sarah (1997) *Urban Amazons: Lesbian Feminism and Beyond in the Gender, Sexuality, and Identity Battles of London*. New York: St. Martin's Press.

Gross, Larry and Woods, James D. (eds) (1999a) *The Columbia Reader on Lesbians and Gay Men in Media, Society and Politics*. New York: Columbia University Press.

Gross, Larry and Woods, James D. (1999b) 'Queers in cyberspace, in Larry Gross and James D. Woods (eds) *The Columbia Reader on Lesbians and Gay men in Media, Society and Politics*. New York: Columbia University Press, pp. 527–30.

Hall, Kira (1996) 'Cyberfeminism', in Susan Herring (ed.), *Computer-Mediated Communication: Linguistic, Social and Cross-Cultural Perspectives*. Amsterdam: John Benjamins. pp. 147–70.

Halperin, David (1995) *Queer Foucault: Towards a Gay Hagiography*. Oxford: Oxford University Press.

Haraway, Donna (1985) 'A manifesto for cyborgs: science, technology, and socialist feminism in the 1980s', *Socialist Review*, 80, March-April.

Haraway, Donna (2000) *How like a Leaf: An Interview with Thyrza Goodeve*, London: Routledge.

Harris, Daniel (1998) 'Qstudy-l', Harvard Gay and Lesbian Review, June.

Haskel, Lisa (1996) 'Cyberdykes: tales from the internet', in Nicola Godwin et al. (eds), *Assaults on Convention: Essays on Lesbian Transgressors*. London: Cassell. pp. 50–61.

Herring, S. (1995) 'Posting in a different voice: gender and ethics in computer-mediated communication', in C. Ess (ed.), *Philosophic Perspectives in Computer-Mediated Communication*. Albany, New York: State University of New York Press.

Herrup, Mocha Jean (1996) Metro on Ice Meets Ball and Cheang in *Women and Performance: A journal of Feminist Theory*. Vol. 9, No. 1, Issue 17 p. 151–60.

Hersher, Elaine (1998) 'Navy Barred From Booting Sailor it Says is Gay'. *San Francisco Chronicle* (27 January) A3.

Hess, David (1997) *Science Studies: An Advanced Introduction*. New York: New York University Press.

Horne, Peter and Lewis, Reina, (1996) *Outlooks: Lesbian and Gay Sexualities and Visual Culture*. London: Routledge.

Humphreys, Laud (1970) *Tearoom Trade: Impersonal Sex in Public Places*. Chicago: Aldine Publishing Co.

Ingram, Gordon Brent, Bouthillette, Anne-Marie and Retter, Yolanda (eds) (1997) *Queers in Space: Communities, Public Places, Sites of Resistance*. Seattle: Bay Press.

Isaksson, Eva (1997) Living with Lesbian Lists. Essay published at http://www.lesbian.org/esbian-lists/111.htm

Jones, Steven (ed.) (1995) *Cybersociety: Computer-Mediated Communication and Community*. Thousand Oaks, CA: Sage Publications.

Jones, Steven (ed.) (1998) *Cybersociety 2.0: Revisiting Computer-Mediated Communication and Community*. Thousand Oaks, CA: Sage Publications.

Jones, Steve (ed.) (1999) *Doing Internet Research: Critical Issues and Methods for Examining the Net*. London: Sage.

Kaloski, Ann (1997) 'Bisexuals making out with cyborgs: politics, pleasure, con/fusion', *Journal of Gay, Lesbian and Bisexual Identity*, 2 (1): 47–64.

Knopp, Lawrence (1992) 'Sexuality and the spacial dynamics of late capitalism', *Environment and Planning D: Society and Space*, 10 (6): 651–69.

Kotamrajn, Nalini (1999) 'The birth of web site design skills', *American Behavioral Scientist*, 43 (2): 464–474.

Lewis, Peter (1995) 'Planet Out's Gay Services on Virtual Horizon'. *New York Times*, August 21, P.D3.

Ludlow, Peter and Godwin, Mike (1996) *High Noon on the Electronic Frontier*. Boston: MIT Press.

Martin, Biddy (1994) 'Sexuality without gender and other queer utopias', *Diacritics*, 24 (2–3): 104–21.

McDonough, Jerome (1999) Designer Selves: Construction of Technologically Mediated Identity within

Graphical Multiuser Virtual Environments, *JASIS* 50 (10), p. 855–69.

McKenna, Katelyn and Bargh, John (1998) Coming Out in the Age of the Internet: Indentity "Demarginalization" through Virtual Group Participation. *Journal of Personality and Social Psychology*, September, Vol. 75, No. 3, p. 681–94.

Miller, Neil (1995) *Out of the Past: Gay and Lesbian History from 1869 to the Present.* London: Vintage.

Nieto, Daniel S. (1995) 'Who is the male homosexual? A computer-mediated exploratory study of gay male bulletin board system (BBS) users in New York City', *Journal of Homosexuality*, 30 (4): 97–124.

O'Brien, Jodi (1996) 'Changing the subject', *Women and Performance*: A Journal of Feminist Theory. Vol. 9, No. 1, Issue 17, p. 151–60.

O'Brien, Jodi (1999) 'Writing in the Body: Gender (re) production in online interaction.' In Smith, Marc A. and Kollock, Peter (eds) *Communities in Cyberspace.* London: Routledge, p. 76–106.

Oldenburg, Ray (1989) *The Great Good Place: Cafés, Coffee Shops, Community Centers, Beauty Parlors, General Stores, Bars, Hangouts, and how they get you through the day,* New York: Paragon House.

Osborne, Duncan (1993) On-line with the FBI. *The Advocate,* 6 April, p. 44–6.

Patten, Cindy (1988) *Sex and Germs: The Politics of AIDS.* Black Rose Books.

Probyn, Elspeth (1995) 'Queer belongings: The politics of departaure' in *Sexy Bodies: The Strange Carnalities of Feminism* (eds) Grosz, Elizabeth and Probyn, Elspeth. London: Routledge, p. 1–18.

Probyn, Elspeth (1996) *Outside Belongings.* London: Routledge.

Pullen, Kirsten (2000) 'I-Love-Xena.com: creating on-line fan communities', in David Gauntlett (ed.), *Web Studies.*

Rainbow Network (2000) Analysis of Media Metrix Survey, London.

Rheingold, H. (1993) *The Virtual Community: Homesteading on the Electronic Frontier.* Menlo Park, CA: Addison-Wesley.

Roseneil, Sasha (2000) *Common Women, Uncommon Practices: The Queer Feminisms of Greenham.* London: Cassell.

Sedgwick, Eve Kosofsky (1991) Epistemology of the Closet. London: Harvester Wheatsheaf.

Senft, Theresa M. (1996) 'Performing the digital body – a ghost story', *Women and Peformance*: A Journal of Feminist Theory. Vol. 9, No. 1, Issue 17, p. 9–34.

Seidman, Steven (1993) 'Identity and politics in 'postmodern' gay culture: some historical and conceptual notes', M. Warner (ed.), *Fear of a Queer Planet: Queer Politics and Social Theory.* Minneapolis: University of Minnesota Press. pp. 105–42.

Shaw, D.F. (1997) 'Gay men and computer communication: A discourse of sex and identity of cyberspace. In

Jones, Steve (ed.) *Cybersociety: Computer-mediated communication and community.* London: Sage.

Sheilds, Rob (1996) (ed.) *Cultures of Internet: Virtual Spaces, Real Histories, Living Bodies.* London: Sage.

Sheldon, Glenn (1996) 'Cruising the tearooms in cyberspace,' *Gerbil* 6 http://www.multicom.org/gerbil/cyb.htm

Silberman, Steve (1999) 'We're teen, we're queer, and we've got e-mail', in Larry Gross and James D. Woods (eds), *The Columbia Reader on Lesbians and Gay Men in Media, Society and Politics,* New York: Columbia University Press. pp. 537–9.

Silverstone, Rogar and Hirsch, Eric (1992) *Consuming Technologies: Media and Information in Domestic Spaces.* London: Routledge.

Star, Susan Leigh (1999) 'The ethnography of infrastructure', *American Behavioral Scientist*, 43 (3): 377–391.

Stone, Alluquere Rosanne (1991) Will the real body please stand by? In *Cyberspace: First step,* ed. Michael Benedikt Cambridge: MIT Press: 81–118.

Sullivan, Caitlin and Bornstein, Kate (1996) *Nearly Roadkill: An Infobahn Erotic Adventure.* Consortium Books.

Taylor, T.L. (1999) 'Life in virtual worlds', *American Behavioral Scientist*, 43 (3): 436–449.

Taylor, T.L. (2002) Living digitally: Embodiment in virtual worlds, in R. Schroeder (ed.) *The Social Life of Avatars: Presence and Interaction in Shared Virtual Environments.* London: Springer-Verlag.

Tomas, David (1991) 'Old rituals for new space: rites de passage and William Gibson's cultural model of cyberspace,' in Michael Benedikt (ed.), *Cyberspace: First Steps.* Cambridge, MA: MIT Press, p. 35.

Trend, David (ed.) (2000) *Reading Digital Culture.* Oxford: Blackwell.

Tsang, Daniel (1994) 'Notes on queer 'n Asian virtual sex', *Amerasia Journal,* 20 (1): (Winter): 117–28.

Turkle, S. (1984) *The Second Self: Computers and the Human Spirit.* New York: Simon & Schuster.

Turkle, S. (1995) *Life on the Screen: Identity in the Age of the Internet.* New York: Simon & Schuster.

Valentine, Gill (1995) 'Creating transgressive space: the music of kd lang' *Transactions of the Institute of British Geographers NS,* 20, 474–85.

Wakeford, Nina (1995) 'Sexualised bodies in cyberspace', in Warren Chernaik and Marilyn Deegan, (eds), *Beyond the Book: Theory, Text and the Politics of Cyberspace.* London: London University Press. pp. 93–104.

Wakeford, N. (1997a) 'Cyberqueer', in A. Medhurst and S.R. Munt (eds), *Lesbian and Gay Studies: A Critical Introduction.* London: Cassell.

Wakeford, N. (1997b) 'Networking women and girls with information/communication technology: surfing tales of the World Wide Web', in J. Terry and M. Calvert (eds), *Processed Lives: Gender and Technology in Everyday Life.* London: Routledge.

Wakeford, N. (1998a) 'Urban culture for virtual bodies: comments on lesbian 'identity' and 'community' in San Francisco Bay Area cyberspace', in R. Ainley (ed.), *New Frontiers of Space, Bodies and Gender*. London: Routledge.

Wakeford, Nina (1998b) 'Gender and the Landscapes of Computing at an Internet Cafe' in Mike Crang, Phillip Crang and Jon Dey (eds). *Virtual Geographies: Bodies, Spaces, Relations*. London: Routledge, 1999, 178–201.

Walsh, Jeff (1999) 'Logging on, coming out, in Larry Gross and James D. Woods (eds), *The Columbia Reader on Lesbians and Gay Men in Media, Society and Politics*. New York: Columbia University Press. pp. 540–1.

Walters, Suzanna Danuta (1996) 'From here to queer: radical feminism, postmodernism, and the lesbian menace (or, why can't a woman be more like a fag?)', *Signs*, 21 (4): 830–49.

Warner, Michael (ed.) (1993) *Fear of a Queer Planet: Queer Politic and Social Theory*. Minneapolis, University of Minnesota Press.

Watney, Simon (1997) *Policing Desire: Pornography, AIDS and the Media*. 3rd edn. Minneapolis: University of Minnesota Press.

Willis, Holly and Halpin, Mikki (1996) 'When the personal becomes digital: Linda Dement and Barbara Hammer move towards a lesbian cyberspace', *Women and Peformance*: A Journal of Feminist Theory. Vol. 9, No. 1, Issue 17, p. 233–38.

Wilton, Tamsin (1995) *Lesbian Studies: Setting an Agenda*. London: Routledge.

Wilson, Elizabeth (2001) *The Contradictions of Culture: Cities, Culture, Women*. London: Sage.

Wincapaw, Celeste (2000) 'Lesbian and bisexual women's electronic mailing lists as sexualised spaces', *Journal of Lesbian Studies*, 4 (1): 45–60.

Winterson, Jeanette (2000) *The Powerbook*. London: Jonathan Cape.

Wood, Kathleen M. (1997) 'Narrative iconicity in electronic-mail lesbian coming-out stories', in Anna Livia and Kira Hall (eds), *Queerly Phrased: Language, Gender, and Sexuality*. New York: Oxford University Press.

Woodland, J. Randall (1995) 'Queer spaces, modem boys, and pagan statues: gay/lesbian identity and the construction of cyberspace', *Works and Days 25/26*, 13 (1–2) Published online: http://acorn.grove.iup/edu/en/workdays/WOODLAND.HTML

Yue, Shirley (1999) <interface: reflections of an ethnic toygirl>, *Journal of Homosexuality*, 36 (3/4): 113–34.

9

Queer Bodies and the Production of Space

GILL VALENTINE

Space has been conceptualised in increasingly sophisticated ways by geographers. In the late nineteenth and early twentieth centuries geography was concerned with the identification and description of the earth's surface. Space was conceived by explorers, cartographers and geographers as something to be investigated, mapped and classified (a process enhanced by the development of instrumental, mathematical and graphical techniques). Indeed, this understanding of space underpinned the subjugation and exploitation of territories and populations through the process of colonialism.

After the Second World War a recognition of the deficiencies of regional geography and the need for more systematic approaches to research, combined with geographers' increasing engagement with quantitative methods, led to a shift in the focus of the discipline. The emphasis on the description of uniqueness was replaced by a concern with similarity. Specifically, positivist approaches to geography were concerned with uncovering universal spatial laws to understand the way the world worked. The focus was on spatial order and the use of quantitative methods to explain and predict human patterns of behaviour. Within this explanatory framework space was conceptualised as an objective physical surface with specific fixed characteristics upon which social identities

and categories were mapped out. Space was, in effect, understood as the container of social relations and events. Likewise, social identities and categories were also taken for granted as 'fixed' and mutually exclusive.

In the 1970s this positivist approach to human geography was subject to critique. Radical approaches, most notably those inspired by Marxism, sought to understand space as the product of social forces, observing that different societies use and organise space in different ways; and to explain the processes through which social differences become spatial patterns of inequalities (Smith, 1990). In turn, geography's subsequent engagement with poststructuralism has produced a new sensitivity to social difference and 'the very different inputs and experiences these diverse populations have into, and of, "socio-spatial" processes' (Cloke et al., 1991: 171). Social categories (such as class, gender, sexuality and race) are no longer taken for granted as given or fixed but rather are understood as socially produced through processes of negotiation and contestation and as such are recognised to be multiple and fluid. In the same way, space is also no longer understood as having particular fixed characteristics. Nor is it regarded as being merely a backdrop for social relations, a pre-existing terrain which exists outside of, or frames, everyday life. Rather, space is understood to play an active role in the constitution and reproduction of social identities and, vice versa, social identities, meanings and relations are recognised as producing material and symbolic or metaphorical spaces. As such, Massey (1999: 283) explains that

[space] is the product of the intricacies and the complexities, the interlockings and the non-interlockings, of relations from the unimaginably cosmic to the intimately tiny. And precisely because it is the product of relations, relations which are active practices, material and embedded, practices which have to be carried out, space is always in a process of becoming. It is always being made.

This chapter focuses on queer bodies and the production of space. In doing so it traces the emergence and development of a diverse range of geographical work on sexuality, and thereby necessarily touches on the different ways of understanding and talking about space outlined above. It begins by outlining how material spaces – 'gay ghettos' and lesbian lands – have emerged in urban and rural landscapes respectively. The second section focuses on questions of sexual citizenship, demonstrating how regulatory landscapes vary between nation–states. In doing so this section addresses questions of lesbian and gay politics, anti-lesbian and gay discrimination and homophobia across a range of spatial scales (from the local to the global) and through a focus on specific geographical sites (namely, the workplace and the home). In the third section, the chapter looks at how Butler's notion of performance and performativity are being used as important conceptual tools to think about the production of sexualised space. Finally, the chapter explores the use of spatial metaphors in the theorisation of sexuality.

MATERIAL SPACES: 'GAY GHETTOS' AND LESBIAN LANDS

In the late 1970s and 1980s geographers began to observe that lesbian and gay

lifestyles were creating distinct social, political and cultural landscapes in major cities often dubbed 'gay ghettos' (Weightman, 1981; Knopp, 1990). Initial explanations for this emerging spatial phenomena focused on 'push–pull' migration factors. Writers argued that individual lesbians and gay men who were isolated in small towns and rural areas were both attracted by the sexual lifestyles on offer in the city (Harry, 1974) and pushed out of their home towns by local prejudice and bigotry (Lyod and Rowntree, 1978). Kramer's (1995) account of gay men's lives in North Dakota, USA, paints a bleak picture of what it means to be gay in rural America. The title of Weston's (1995) paper 'Get thee to a big city' sums up her argument that the anonymity offered by urban environments makes them a better place to live a lesbian or gay lifestyle than within claustrophobic rural society. Indeed, she argues that the symbolic contrast offered by the urban/rural dichotomy is crucial to making sense of lesbian and gay identities, being central to the organisation of many 'coming out' stories in which sexual dissidents migrate from the country to the city to escape intolerance and to forge their own identities.

Perhaps the most famous example of a gay urban neighbourhood is the Castro District in San Francisco. The Second World War and the period immediately afterwards are credited with playing an important role in its emergence. It was in the port of San Francisco that service men both departed and returned from overseas duties and it was also here where dishonourable discharges were carried out. Many of those leaving or being dismissed from the services remained in the City. As such, San Francisco developed a reputation for tolerance and for supporting bohemian ways of life. This, combined with California's liberal state laws on homosexuality led to it emerging as a lesbian and gay friendly city. In turn, its reputation attracted queer migrants fleeing from more conservative towns, cities and rural areas.

Initially, a handful of bars and clubs acted as spaces for gay social networks to develop but police raids meant that these were very transient and unstable environments. However, by the 1970s the Castro District had begun to emerge as a distinct gay neighbourhood. Harvey Milk, a dynamic political activist, was influential in its development. He opened a camera shop in the Castro in 1972 and set about organising neighbourhood campaigns and harnessing a gay political vote. Milk was the city supervisor when he was assassinated in 1978 (his story is told in the film *The Life and Times of Harvey Milk*).

The subsequent development of the Castro District, and the emergence of similar gay neighbourhoods in other major cities, have been theorised in terms of the role gay men have played in reconfiguring class relations and the urban land market through a process of gentrification. For example, in the 1970s the Castro District developed a reputation as an area of relatively cheap housing which had the potential for renovation, and as a neighbourhood where it was possible to live a gay lifestyle. As more gay men moved into the neighbourhood bars, clubs, bookstores and other commercial services opened to cater for their needs (Castells, 1983; Lauria and Knopp, 1985). As a result, gay gentrifiers (mainly men) gradually displaced the long-term poor, minority residents, as well as squeezing out low-income lesbians and gay men (Castells, 1983). This also had a knock-on effect on the neighbouring Latino Mission district on one side of the Castro and an African American neighbourhood in the Hayes Valley on the other side (Castells, 1983).

As such, this process of gentrification demonstrates how one oppressed group – in this case gay men (although there is now more of a lesbian presence in the Castro than in the 1970s) – can be complicit in the perpetuation, through strategies of capital accumulation, of social injustices against other minority groups (Knopp, 1992). As Knopp (1998: 159) observes: 'The forging of identities through the economic and political colonisation of territorial spaces (and the related creation of gay-identified places) is much facilitated by class, racial and gender privilege.'

The strength of pink pounds, dollars and Euros have also created gay enclaves in many other North American, European and Australasian cities including, for example, the Marigny neighbourhood in New Orleans (Knopp, 1998); the gay village along Canal Street in Manchester, UK (Quilley, 1995); Soho/Old Compton Street in London (Binnie, 1995); Oxford Street, and the surrounding inner city neighbourhoods of Darlinghurst, Surrey Hills and Paddington in Sydney, Australia (Knopp, 1998). However, Knopp (1995) warns that while this visibility in the urban landscape might be regarded by some lesbians and gay men as liberating, by 'ghettoising' and bounding dissident sexualities these neighbourhoods might paradoxically limit the challenge to heterosexual hegemony in other everyday spaces.

Indeed, gay lifestyles have been commodified as chic cosmopolitanism to such an extent that they have become attractive to the heterosexual market causing new problems of what Knopp (1998) describes as 'managing success'. Lesbian and gay neighbourhoods such as the Castro and Manchester's gay village are increasingly attracting heterosexual visitors eager to consume a bit of the exotic 'other'. Likewise, spectacles celebrating lesbian and gay sexuality such as the Sydney Mardi Gras (which is broadcast on state television and advertised in prime tourist spots around the Opera House and Circular Quay) and the HERO parade in Auckland, New Zealand, are now being marketed for non-gay-identified consumption (Johnston, 1998). Such examples have provoked some anxiety among lesbians and gay men that spaces that were previously considered to be the 'property' of sexual dissidents – effectively collective 'private spaces' as opposed to the heteronormativity of public space – are being invaded and colonised by heterosexuals. This process is feared to be undermining the 'gay identity' of these spaces, so eroding what lesbians and gay men have often taken for granted as safe environments (Whittle, 1994).

A further note of caution is also offered by Myslik (1996) who suggests that the spatial concentration of lesbian and gay men in particular districts of cities makes it easier for heterosexuals to both control and target them. He notes for example, that gay men are more likely to be victimised in gay identified neighbourhoods or cruising areas than on predominantly heterosexual streets. An argument further supported by the bombing in 1999 of a lesbian and gay pub, the Admiral Duncan, in Soho, a gay gentrified area of London, as part of a wider series of hate crimes aimed at a number of different minority groups.

Of course, not all gay venues have a visible presence within the city. Brown (2000) describes many of the gay saunas, bathhouses and cruise clubs, in Christchurch, New Zealand as closeted because they are inconspicuous (especially compared to their heterosexual equivalents) in the urban landscape. This he suggests partially reflects the legal sanctions to which lesbians and gay men have until recently been subjected to and the homophobic nature of the city. While New Zealand now outlaws discrimination on the basis of sexual orientation, homosexuality was actually only legalised in the country in 1985. The invisibility of these venues also reflects the importantce of secrecy to their clientele, many of whom are men-who-have-sex-with-men but who do not identify as gay. They rely on discreet signage and spatial codes to locate these closeted spaces.

Like gay men, lesbians also create their own spaces within cities, although these environments are often less visible to heterosexuals (e.g. Adler and Brenner, 1992; Rothenberg, 1995; Valentine, 1995a). Adler and Brenner (1992) suggest that this is because like heterosexual women, lesbians have less access to capital than men, and because a fear of male violence deters their willingness to have an obvious presence in the landscape. The influence of feminism has also meant that lesbian 'communities' have tended to be more radical, politicised, and less materially oriented than gay men which has stymied the development of businesses and bars run for, and by, women.

Rothenberg's (1995) study of the Park Slope area of Brooklyn in New York shows how women tend to create 'alternative' rather than commercial spaces. Indeed, the institutional bases of lesbian communities are often made up of non-commercial venues such as support groups, self-defence classes, alternative cafés and co-operative bookstores which are promoted by word-of-mouth or flyers and are reliant on the energy and enthusiasm of volunteers rather than paid staff. Many of these spaces are shared with other non-commercial users, only being appropriated and transformed into lesbian spaces on specific days at specific times. In this sense, these institutional bases represent a series of spatially concentrated venues that are reasonably fixed in location and regular but not permanent (Valentine, 1995a). Despite their ephemeral nature, however, they are important locations where lesbian 'communities' are imagined and contested.

Perhaps the most visible lesbian spaces have been those produced in the rural rather than the urban landscape. In the 1970s radical feminists identified heterosexuality as the root of all women's (lesbian, bisexual and heterosexual) oppression. As such, they argued that women needed to establish their own communities that were separated or spatially distanced from heterosexual society in order to avoid (re)producing patriarchy and to enable women to construct a new society beyond men's influence. The countryside was seen to provide more opportunities for women to be self-sufficient and therefore purer in their practices than the city. Essentialist understandings of women as close to nature because of their menstrual cycles and reproductive role meant that some separatists also defined the rural environment as a 'woman's space' whereas the man-made city was blamed for draining women's energy (Bell and Valentine, 1995; Valentine, 1997).

In the USA a circuit of women's farms known as lesbian lands were established.

These communities were based on non-hierarchical lines and effort was put into building new forms of living space. The women did not want to have to go back to, or rely in any way, on patriarchal society so they re-learned old skills such as firemaking, herbal medicine and survival skills, while also developing a women's culture in terms of language, music and books. This belief in women's closeness to nature meant there was also a strong spiritual dimension to these rural communities. The women celebrated the full moon, equinox, solstice and candlemass, and practised goddess worship, witchcraft and other women-centred traditions that symbolised their resistance to patriarchy. Their intention was not only to build self-contained communities but that these 'communities would eventually be built into a strong state of mind and that might even be powerful enough, through its example, to divert the country and the world from their dangerous course' (Faderman, 1991: 217).

However, tensions also arose within and between lesbian lands, particularly over issues such as boy children and even male animals. While some settlements took a non-essentialist view of identity and so allowed male children and animals to remain in lesbian lands, others excluded them in an attempt to create a pure women-only space. The emphasis on escaping patriarchy meant that many lesbian lands promoted the residents' shared identities as women over their differences. Class and issues over ownership of land and dwellings were common sources of dispute, as were sexual jealousies and relationship breakdowns which caused divisions and exclusions. Claims of racism and a lack of tolerance of disabled women were other fissures of difference that split the fragile unity of some utopian communities. Black women and Jewish women felt marginalised by the inherent whiteness of most of the lesbian lands, while the emphasis on the body and shared physical commitment to the land through physical labour meant that many disabled women felt unable to participate

and that the communities did not respond to their needs (although some lesbian lands did attempt to make independent space for disabled lesbians or to create non-racist environments specifically for women of colour) (Valentine, 1997). As well as these internal divisions, these utopian communities often faced hostility and even violence from wider rural society (Greene 1997). As such, it is not surprising that most did not survive very long.

The studies outlined in this section are valuable because they have challenged the invisibility of lesbians and gay men by mapping out the most obvious material spaces that sexual dissidents have created in both urban and rural landscapes. However, they have also been critiqued because in doing so they have implicitly set up lesbian and gay space as an 'exotic' other, leaving everyday spaces outside these ghettos and lesbian lands unquestioned as heterosexual. In addition some, though not all, of these studies, are guilty of talking about sexuality and space as if they were singular and static concepts rather than recognising them to be multiple, fluid and contested.

REGULATORY LANDSCAPES: SEXUAL CITIZENSHIP, THE LOCAL AND THE GLOBAL

Michel Foucault's (1981) work has been particularly influential in shaping understandings of sexuality. He 'explores sexuality as discourse, located within historically and geographically specific contexts of power/knowledge' (Blunt and Wills, 2000). Through his writing he has charted the ways in which sexuality has been made the object of scientific knowledge (e.g. through medicine, psychiatry, sexology, etc.), the ways in which controls are exercised over it (e.g. through censorship) and the ways that certain bodies are rendered 'normal' and others as 'deviant'.

Heteronormativity is particularly evident in the discourses, and practices, of citizenship.

It is institutionalised through the legal, taxation, welfare system, while through the apparatus of the law the state can deny or erase same sex relationships (e.g. Bell, 1995a). As such, lesbian and gay claims to citizenship rights and political legitimacy are not fully established in most modern states (Corviono, 1997). However, there are geographical differences in the degree to which this is so and consequently in terms of what it means to live a lesbian and gay lifestyle in different nation–states (Binnie, 1997).

In some states homosexuality is illegal. For example, under Italian law same sex acts which are defined as against the common sense of decency in the Criminal Code may be punished with a prison sentence of between three months to three years. In many states of the US sodomy, oral sex and 'unnatural sex acts' are criminalised (Isin and Wood, 1999), while in the UK the prosecution of men on assault charges for engaging in consensual same-sex SM activities in the privacy of their homes demonstrated the limits of British sexual citizenship (Bell, 1995a). Even where same-sex relationships are not explicitly outlawed, lesbians and gay men lack basic civil rights in many countries including anti-discrimination protection in relation to employment, housing, education and so on (Andermahr, 1992; Betten, 1993; Valentine, 1996a).

Some Western countries such as Australia, the Netherlands, Denmark, Norway, Sweden and Iceland do recognise lesbian and gay relationships as families or *de facto* marriages. For example, anyone can obtain Dutch nationality if they have been living in a permanent non-marital relationship with a Dutch national for at least three years and have been resident in the country for at least three years. Lesbians and gay men also have the right to 'marry', and can also gain refugee status in the Netherlands on the grounds of persecution because of their sexuality (Binnie, 1997). However, most countries are not so tolerant. As a consequence, '[i]nsofar as marriage between persons of the same sex is not allowed by most legislation, acquisition of citizenship by way of

marriage is impossible for lesbian and gay couples of different nationalities' (Tanca, 1993: 280). As a result, campaigns have been held across Europe to draw attention to the predicament faced by lesbian and gay couples of different nationalities because of discriminatory partnership legislation (Valentine, 1996a). Activists have also sought to highlight the material consequences and rights that follow from the institution of marriage (such as tax benefits, custody rights, adoption, succession to tenancies, inheritance, etc.) from which lesbians and gay men are excluded.

The position is even more complex for those who define themselves outside the heterosexual/homosexual and male/female binaries. For transsexuals and transgendered people citizenship hangs on the question of their right to self-determination in the face of state definitions of their identity as male or female as classified at birth.

A recognition of the uneven contours of citizenship rights between countries (Evans, 1993) has led to the formalisation of transnational networks such as the International Lesbian and Gay Association into a co-ordinated Federation of Lesbian and Gay Organisations. For gay activists such as Peter Tatchell (1992: 75, cited in Binnie, 1997) 'it is through collective solidarity, overriding national boundaries and sectional interests, that we [lesbians and gay men in the European Union] have our surest hope of eventually winning equality'. In July 1992 London staged the first ever Europride festival in which over 100,000 lesbians and gay men from across Europe marched in the largest ever exhibition of European lesbian and gay consciousness. Since then similar festivals have also been held in a number of other major European cities (Binnie, 1997).

Indeed, some writers have claimed that such forms of social identification might threaten the emotional attachment and sense of loyalty people feel to the state and its authority, potentially 'disuniting the nation' (Morley and Robins, 1995). Hobsbawn (1990: 11) observes, 'We cannot assume that for most people national identification – when it exists – excludes, or is always or ever superior to, the remainder of the set of identifications which constitute the social being.' In a 1970s' publication entitled *The Lesbian Nation: The Feminist Solution* Jill Johnston (1973) argued that all women shared a sense of displacement from masculinist US culture and the state. She aimed to inaugurate an autonomous utopian community (see the description of lesbian lands above) that would effectively declare secession from the USA and would form a radical state based on the shared identity of the 'majesty of women' (Munt, 1999). Like other nationalist movements Johnston's vision of a Lesbian Nation also involved a nostalgia for an imagined past and for heroic mythical figures such as the Amazons' warrior women, who were feted for their strength and agency. More recently Queer Nation, which was founded by AIDS activists in New York in 1990, has provided a new political challenge to heteronormative hegemony. Based on a principle of inclusiveness, Queer Nation rejected the old separatisms which have split gay and lesbian communities embracing transvestites, bisexual people, sadomasochists and transsexuals and celebrated subversion, ambiguity and sexual freedom (Bell, 1995b). Through acts of cultural terrorism (see the next section) the intent of queer activists was 'to make the nation a space safe for queers, not just in the sense of being tolerated, but safe *for* demonstration, in the mode of patriotic ritual' (Berlant and Freeman, 1993: 198; Munt, 1998: 14).

While, in different ways, Lesbian Nation and Queer Nation have sought to create radical understandings of citizenship, the economic muscle of the pink pound and the pink dollar have also enabled spaces of sexual citizenship to be constituted through consumption (Binnie, 1993; Bell, 1995b). The rise of consumer power has meant that companies whose products have a large lesbian and gay market must pay more attention to their customers. Bell (1995b) cites the example of Levi, the clothing company, which faced a boycott by lesbian and gay consumers angry over the company's financial contribution to the homophobic scout movement in the USA. Gay tourism has also brought together consumerism and citizenship since 'being able to go on holiday … is presumed to be a characteristic of modern citizenship which has become embedded into people's thinking about health and well-being' (Urry, 1990: 24, cited in Bell, 1995b: 142). As such, gay tourism guides highlight those places where it is safe to be 'out' and identify the different citizenship rights afforded to sexual dissidents around the world.

As these examples of consumption and tourism illustrate battles are not only being fought over queer rights and responsibilities at the spatial scale of the nation but also simultaneously across other scales, from the space of the body to that of the globe. This is perhaps best illustrated through the example of Brown's work (1995) on AIDS activism.

AIDS is a global crisis, within the nation–state of Canada the city of Vancouver is at the heart of its epidemic, and within this city the problem is focused around the neighbourhood of Yaletown, a gay area which is also important for sex trade workers. Here the Vancouver AIDS team, Man-to-Man, is targeting HIV prevention among gay men through outreach work that provides advice and distributes safer sex information and materials. The team draw on their knowledge of the local microgeographies of public sex to instigate safe bodily practices among gay men. They do this by focusing their prevention work in the very locations (such as bathhouses and gay bars) where public sex takes place. In other words Man-to-Man's initiatives are aimed at high risk behaviour: at the very microgeography of the body. However, this outline of the scalar politics of AIDS is not to suggest that each of these spaces: the global, the nation, the city, the neighbourhood, the body, are in any way fixed, bounded, unrelated or opposed to each other (Smith, 1993). Rather, each of these spatial scales are porous, inter-related and provisional spaces which are constituted in and through their relations and linkages with 'elsewhere', with the spaces which stretch beyond them (Massey, 1991). As such, the global and the local are not dichotomous categories. Rather, global processes are both global and local, in that they operate in particular local places but in doing so are themselves reworked by local cultures, while the local is a product of inter-actions between local social relations and global influences (Massey, 1998).

Returning to Brown's (1995) example of AIDS politics, it is evident that, despite Man-to-Man's focus on safe sex practices, its politics are not fixed at the scale of the body. Brown demonstrates this in three ways. First, Man-to-Man's brochures and materials are shared with AIDS groups in other North American cities. Through the process of preventing the spread of HIV locally, it is also implicitly helping to stop the national and global diffusion of HIV. In this way, Man-to-Man's AIDS prevention work is simultaneously local, national and global. Second, Brown draws on the exam-ple of the World AIDS day programmes. These are aimed at furthering understanding of AIDS issues locally and globally and take place in cities around the world. Brown explains how at a World AIDS Day in Vancouver an exchange took place between local HIV prevention workers and those from Mexico and Nicaragua which enabled local responses to AIDS to be compared and contrasted to those in these other countries. As Brown explains (1995: 257), '[I]n this way, the local politics of AIDS in the city are simultaneously – and self consciously – global politics as well.' Finally, Brown docu-ments the success of disembodied forms of information and communication such as telephone help-lines and the Internet in the fight against the spread of the HIV virus. These support services are situated in local offices (in this case in Vancouver) yet are simultaneously global in that they can be accessed anonymously by anyone, anywhere in the world.

Another way of thinking about the spatiality of lesbian and gay citizenship is to consider the everyday sites – such as the workplace and the home – in which rights are constructed, refused and contested.

In the late 1990s Stonewall, the UK lesbian and gay equality campaign group, carried out a survey of lesbian and gay men's experiences of the workplace. Of the 1,873 people who responded, one sixth claimed to have experienced discrimination, one fifth suspected that they had been dis-criminated against, 8 per cent had been sacked because of their sexuality, and one quarter said that because of their sexuality they were too afraid to apply for certain jobs or to specific employers. Most European legislatures do not provide any protection against discrimination on the grounds of sexual orientation (Betten, 1993). Indeed, lesbians and gay men are systematically excluded from some forms of employment, for example, military service.

Discrimination against sexual dissidents at work also extends to workplace culture and the provision of work-related benefits avail-able to employees' 'families' (Betten, 1993; Waaldijk, 1993). While the heterosexual 'family' is seen to complement working organisations by 'providing continuity and the rest and recreations workers need to be pro-ductive, the gay lifestyle is not perceived to be stable or to offer the same restoratives' (Hall, 1989: 126). Many employers adopt a pater-nalistic approach to their heterosexual work-ers, for example, by providing health insurance, sports and leisure facilities and other benefits for their families. However, same sex partners and their children are rarely eligible for the same perks. In such ways employers therefore contribute to defining the rights – or rather lack of rights – of lesbians and gay men and to reproducing heterosexual hegemony in the workplace and beyond.

Heterosexual desire, and constructions of heterosexual attractiveness also shape work-places (McDowell, 1995). Gutek argues that women at work are perceived to be inher-ently sexual in appearance, dress and behav-iour. She says, 'Because it is expected, people notice female sexuality, and believe it is normal, natural, an outgrowth of being female' (1989: 60). Correspondingly, although men are usually perceived to be asexual in appearance, they use 'sex' at work to tease, flirt with, and manipulate women. Indeed, such expressions of hetero-sexuality – which are informed by wider social attitudes and ideologies, are consid-ered so intrinsic to many worker–customer interactions that some employers even train their staff to use scripted heterosexual exchanges when conducting business (Leidner, 1991). As such, having control over workers' corporeal capacities, and interven-ing in their lives to develop aspects of their identities as an occupational resource have become part and parcel of many organisa-tions' strategies. In this culture it is not surprising that some lesbians and gay men go to great lengths to manage their bodies at work (e.g. in terms of dress, adornments, etc.) in order to pass as heterosexual.

In her study of merchant banks in the City of London, McDowell (1995) shows how an informal culture predicated on the use of highly sexualised language, practical jokes, and even actual sexual harassment, which draws on wider societal ideas about gender and sexuality, contributes to producing these institutions as heterosexual environ-ments. Whereas most heterosexuals take for granted their freedom to express their sexu-ality publicly, using their relationships and sexual experiences as common currency in workplace conversations (Pringle, 1988), many lesbians and gay men, conscious of their vulnerability to discrimination from employers and workmates, conceal their sexuality or fabricate heterosexual experi-ences. This often involves maintaining a rigid separation of home and work, for example, by not inviting colleagues back home and by avoiding work social events. However, by creating this artificial public–private split, lesbians and gay men can feel 'out of place' in workplace culture and find it difficult to network with colleagues or to establish authentic friend-ships with workmates. Indeed, missing out on work 'gossip' and being perceived as 'not a good team player' can in themselves become significant barriers to promotion. In this way, sexual dissidents' experiences of discrimination within the workplace are shaped by wider sets of ideas about homosexuality embedded in society, while behaviour such as 'passing' as heterosexual is rendered intelligible through an under-standing of the interconnections between sites such as the workplace and the home. Similarly, the ability of lesbians and gay men to challenge heterosexism and to 'come out' at work is mediated by the amount of support available to them at home and from the wider lesbian and gay 'community'.

Like the workplace, the home is also a complex site where lesbian and gay lives are played out, and which can shape, and yet is also shaped by, wider sets of ideas about homosexuality and the rights of sexual citizens.

On the one hand, the home is often valor-ised by lesbians and gay men as a 'private' place, a place of refuge, affirmation and belonging where they are free to express their sexuality (e.g. through the design and decoration of the space, the symbols and objects on display in it and the relationships and activities which take place there) away from the hostile and discriminatory social relationships that they encounter in wider 'public' spaces such as the workplace. Indeed, for some sexual dissidents the home is constructed as sites of resistance, where lesbian and gay identities and politics can be nurtured and actively asserted. For example, homes are often used as spaces where 'com-munity' social events and political meetings can be held and networks developed. As such, they can become important sites for contesting heterosexual norms and promot-ing lesbian and gay rights (Johnston and Valentine, 1995; Elwood, 2000).

On the other hand, however, the home is not necessarily experienced as a private space. Rather, for lesbians and gay men living in insecure accommodation (e.g. in institutions and rented or public housing) who have little or no legal protection from housing discrimination, the home can still be a constraining or oppressive space shaped by homophobia and a lack of rights. For these sexual dissidents the home therefore is often a place where their sexuality must be concealed for fear of eviction. Though even home ownership does not guarantee that the domestic environment is a 'safe' space. Homes can also be subject to the surveillant gaze and regulation (which can take the form of everything from critical comments to harassment and violence) of others such as heterosexual family members, neighbours and visiting colleagues or 'friends' (Egerton, 1990; Johnston and Valentine, 1995). Again, these responses can be shaped by interconnections with the wider neighbourhood and social climate. Tolerant or liberal local environments can make the home feel a safer place, whereas bigoted, homophobic neighbourhoods are obviously more confining (Munt, 1995; Valentine, 1995a; Elwood, 2000).

In writing about space, geographers have often drawn on a number of dualisms significant in Western thought such as work/home, public/private. These dualisms are invested with power in that they are not two sides of unrelated terms 'A' and 'B'. Rather, '[w]ithin this structure, one term A has a positive status and an existence independent of the other; the other term B is purely negatively defined, and has no contours of its own; its limiting boundaries are those which define the positive term' (Grosz, 1989: xvi). This dualistic way of thinking has structured the way geographers have come to analyse and understand some spaces. For example, the study of the workplace has often been privileged over the space of the home and clear boundaries have been assumed to be drawn between dualisms such as public and private spaces. However, these dualistic ways of thinking about, and analysing, space are increasingly being challenged and resisted. The discussion here of lesbian and gay men's experiences of the two sites, of the workplace and the home, questions the boundaries that are often drawn between the two locations. At the same time it also highlights the fact that 'private' and 'public'

spaces are not fixed and stable categories but rather that the boundaries between them are blurred and fluid.

PERFORMATIVE SPACE: REPETITION AND SLIPPAGE

The first section of this chapter focused on studies of gay ghettos and lesbian lands, in other words, on spaces on the margins, while the second considered some of the sites where sexuality is regulated and contested. The implicit presumption in some of this work was that everyday spaces from the street to the workplace are heterosexual. And that these spaces are stages or pre-existing places where sexualities are played out. However, recently geographers have begun to draw on Judith Butler's notion of performance/performativity as an important conceptual tool to think differently about space (e.g. Bell et al., 1994; Valentine, 1996b). Butler famously argued in her book *Gender Trouble: Feminism and the Subversion of Identity* that 'gender is the repeated stylization of the body, a set of repeated acts within a highly rigid regulatory framework that congeal over time to produce the appearance of substance, of a natural sort of being' (1990: 33). In the same way, space too can be thought of as 'brought into being through performances and as a performative articulation of power' (Gregson and Rose, 2000: 434). This understanding of space is important because it denaturalises the presumed heterosexuality of everyday spaces. The straight street or office environment do not pre-exist their performance, rather, specific performances bring these places into being and these spaces are themselves performative of particular power relations (ibid.).

The repetitive performances which produce everyday heterosexual space take the form of many acts: from heterosexual couples kissing and holding hands as they walk down the street, to advertisements and shop window displays that present images of contented 'nuclear' families; and from heterosexualised conversations that permeate queues at bus stops and banks to the piped music articulating heterosexual desires that fill shops, bars and restaurants (Valentine, 1993, 1995b, 1996b). These acts produce a 'host of assumptions embedded in the practices of public life about what constitutes proper behaviour' (Weeks, 1992: 5) and which congeal over time to give the appearance of a 'proper' or 'normal' production of space. These acts are produced within regulatory regimes which serve to discipline and constrain the performances that are possible. Laws which criminalise public displays of same sex desire and homophobic assaults on lesbians and gay men are just two examples of disciplinary acts that contribute to maintaining the 'naturalness' of heterosexual productions of space.

The power of heterosexuality therefore depends on being able to repeatedly define people and space in particular ways. However, because spaces do not pre-exist their performance but rather are iterative, there are always possibilities that disruptions or slippages may occur in their production, or that the disciplinary regimes which regulate them might fail, with the consequence that powerful discourses are not replicated but are changed or done differently (Gregson and Rose, 2000). In other words, the heterosexuality of everyday space is always partial, in the process of becoming and unstable.

'Lesbian desires and manners of being' (Probyn, 1995: 81) including: subtle signifiers of lesbian identity such as pinkie rings, labris earrings, dress codes, 'gayspeak', music, body language and knowing glances can all (re)produce space in different ways. For example, kd lang is a mainstream musician but also a lesbian icon. A lang track playing in a public space like a shop or a bar can facilitate the materialisation of lesbian space by causing two women to catch each other's eye and establish fleeting contact or even long-term friendships (Valentine, 1995b). In other words, space may be 'sexed through the relational movements of one lesbian body to another' (Probyn, 1995: 81).

Likewise, cruising glances exchanged by two gay men enabling pick-ups to happen, and the consummation of private sexual acts in so-called public spaces such as the beach and the park (Leap, 1999) are further examples of inter-relational performances which produce 'gay(ze) space' (Walker, 1995: 75). These are productions of space that unsettle the presumed hegemony of heterosexuality and disrupt public/private dualisms (Chauncey, 1995).

The possibilities of building on these everyday productions of space to challenge heterosexuality more explicitly by doing public space differently were implicit in queer activist strategies of the late 1990s. As Berlant and Freeman (1993: 198) point out, 'being queer is not about the right to privacy: it is about the freedom to be public'. Under the slogan 'We're here! We're Queer! Get used to it' these activists set out to blatantly queer hegemonic productions of the city streets as heterosexual. '[T]heir exhibitionist agenda was self-consciously to shove the homosexual into America's face' (cited in Munt, 1998: 14). Through disruptive events that parodied heterosexuality, such as holding mock same-sex weddings and kiss-ins in everyday public spaces, they radically reproduced 'public' space as queer space, and in doing so exposed the normative coding of 'public' space as heterosexual (Bell and Valentine, 1995).

These understandings of sexual spaces, which regard them as being brought into being through specific performances, while themselves also being performative of particular power relations (and therefore forever relational, provisional and shifting) mean that we need to employ more intricate cartographic skills if we are to map them (Rose, 1993).

SPATIAL METAPHORS: CLOSETS AND MARGINS

In the 1990s Smith and Katz (1993) highlighted the proliferation of spatial metaphors in the lexicon of social and cultural theory. Mapping, positionality, location, displacement, grounding, centre, margins, borderlands, inside, and outside have all become popular terms. They work for a number of different reasons: they ground abstract meanings, they reflect our bodily positions in space (dimensionality), and they capture the complexity of self/other relations.

Brown (2000: 1) argues that 'the closet' which is used to describe the concealment of lesbians and gay men is an example of a spatialised metaphor that 'alludes to certain kinds of location, space, distance, accessibility and interaction'. The closet as a noun is a small, secluded private place where things are hidden, as a verb it means to isolate, or conceal and as an adjective it implies secrecy. It is difficult to trace its origins (for example, its use might derive from the expression 'skeletons in the cupboard' or from the British term 'water closet' and hence cottaging), but the use of this metaphor to describe lesbian and gay invisibility appears to have come into common parlance in the mid to late 1960s at the time when its material signifier became popular within the home (Brown, 2000). In the 1970s the emerging gay liberation movement turned the notion of 'coming out' into a clarion call.

Unpacking the spatiality of the closet metaphor Brown suggests that it works in a number of different ways. First, it works as a simple comparison. He explains:

> Its *location* and *distance* suggest proximity to some wider (more important, more immediate, more central) room, but it's a certain kind of proximity: one that limits *accessibility* and *interaction*. The ubiquity of gays and lesbians 'everywhere' means that on the one hand they are indeed close at hand, but enclosure of the closet means that they are separate, hived off, invisible and unheard ... by definition a closet has a certain kind of spatial interaction with its room. It is separate and distinct too. It segregates, it hides, it confines. (Brown, 2000: 7)

In this sense, it is possible to understand the oppression of lesbians and gay men through this direct comparison with the everyday material space of the closet.

Second, Brown (2000) draws on interaction theory to show how metaphors such as the closet might be used not as direct comparisons or literal truths but rather to refer to a more limited truth or allusional space in which there is recognition, for example, that gay oppression is both like, and not like, the physical closet. Here he cites Signorile's (1993: xv) map of lesbian and gay United States that marks out a 'Trinity of the Closet' in terms of three powerful geographic locations: Los Angeles, New York and Washington. Los Angeles represents the closet produced by the entertainment industry through its failure to generate positive images of lesbian and gay lives in TV and film. The New York closet is produced by the media industry through its demonisation and negative representation of lesbians and gay men, while the Washington closet is produced through the political system which fails to legislate in gay friendly ways. As Brown (2000: 1) explains:

> Not everyone in these three cities is closeted by these specific power relations, obviously; nor is every oppression in each city symptomatic of the closet for which it stands ... But as an interactive metaphor, the closet's architectural allusions are grounded in places that are conveniently made to hold certain types of oppression over others.

Some geographers, however, have sounded a note of caution about such uses of spatial metaphors, arguing that space is often employed in them in an uncritical, or simplistic ways (Massey, 1993; Smith and Katz, 1993). In particular, the careless adoption of spatial metaphors can imply a fixity or singularity of space, in which space is implicitly conceptualised in 'absolute' (as a container, or set of distinct, mutually exclusive locations) rather than in relational terms. Smith and Katz (1993: 79–80), for example, point out that: 'the uncritical appropriation of absolute space as a source domain for metaphors forecloses recognition of the multiple qualities, types, properties and attributes of social space, its constructed absolutism and its relationality'. Brown (2000: 19) makes a different point when he warns against the danger of unwittingly assuming a divide between so called 'real' or material space and spatial metaphors in which 'real space' is prioritised as the 'more accurate description of causal processes, and [as] therefore more important ... to study'.

The over-simplifications of space, which are evident in the way comparison and interaction theories understand spatial metaphors, are challenged in post-structuralist theory. In examining the spatiality of the closet metaphor in these terms, the 'real' material space of the closet is not understood to provide the authentic meaning of the closet against which comparisons can be made (Brown, 2000). Rather, the emphasis is on the closet's unstable, contested and often paradoxical meanings. For example, Fuss (1991) notes the ironic geography of the closet in that to come out is to simultaneously call into being a closet. Likewise, Sedgwick (1990) observes that the presumption of heterosexuality in everyday life is so strong that it is difficult, if not impossible, for a lesbian and gay man to come out, because new closets are continually springing up around them every time they meet a new person and must once again make the decision about whether to disclose or conceal their sexuality. Others (e.g. LaBruce and Belverio, 1998) have questioned whether the closet is actually a bad thing, arguing that it is not necessarily confining but rather can be a place of safety/privacy, a place of excitement, and even a place of secret influence.

Indeed, a similar argument has been made in relation to what have been termed the spaces of the margins. These are real material locations but also symbolic spaces of oppression that have been reclaimed by writers such as bell hooks as spaces from which to speak. Hooks (1991: 149) describes marginality as: 'a site one stays in, clings to even, because it nourishes one's capacity to resist. It offers the possibility of radical perspectives from which to see and create, to imagine alternatives, new worlds.'

Spatial metaphors such as 'centre' and 'margins' are frequently employed to think about social relations. Yet such positions do not represent marked or differentiated positions. Rather, Gillian Rose (1993: 140) argues that paradoxically we can simultaneously occupy 'spaces that would be mutually exclusive if charted on a two-dimensional map – centre and margin, inside and outside spaces'. For example, lesbians and gay men employed in professional occupations such as the law and banking might occupy just such a contradictory position. On the one hand, being familiar with and close to the centre of power and part of the 'establishment'; on the other hand, being made to feel that they do not belong. They are present but also absent within the workplace. For writers such as Rose (1993: 155) these paradoxical spaces 'threaten the polarities which structure the dominant geographical imagination'. At the same time '[t]hey provide a means to talk about social position and identity in a way that remains contingent, unfixed but still "there"' (Brown, 2000: 17).

In challenging dichotomies, geographers are increasingly 'imagining a somewhere else' (Johnston et al., 2000: 771). While Rose (1993) describes this as a 'paradoxical space', other writers have talked in terms of hybrid space (Bhabha, 1994) or Thirdspace (Soja, 1996). These different conceptualisations of space represent ways of thinking about the world which focus on 'the production of heterogeneous spaces of 'radical openness' (Johnston et al., 2000: 771). Susan Smith (1999: 21) argues that the concept of Thirdspace:

> turns our attention away from the givens of social categories and towards the strategic process of identification. It forces us to accept the complexity, ambiguity and multi-dimensionality of identity and captures the way that class, gender and 'race', cross-cut and intersect in different ways at different times and places.

Further, she goes on to argue that 'Thirdspace may provide an opportunity to move beyond our historic preoccupation with social divisions – with what holds people apart – and think about what is gained from a discourse of belonging'.

ACKNOWLEDGEMENTS

I am very grateful for a Philip Leverhulme Prize which has enabled me to write this chapter and to Diane Richardson and Steve Seidman for waiting patiently for me to deliver it. Some of the material included here has previously been published in Valentine, G. (2001) *Social Geographies: Space and Society* (Harlow: Pearson) and in Valentine, G. (1996) '(Re)negotiating the heterosexual street'. In Duncan, N. (ed.), *Bodyspace: Destablizing Geographies of Gender and Sexuality*. London: Routledge.

REFERENCES

Adler, S. and Brenner, J. (1992) 'Gender and space: lesbians and gay men in the city'. *International Journal of Urban and Regional Research*, 16: 24–34.

Andermahr, S. (1992) 'Subjects or citizens? Lesbians in the new Europe,' in A. Ward, J. Gregory and N. Yuval-Davis (eds), *Women and Citizenship in Europe: Borders, Rights and Duties: Women's Differing Identities in a Europe of Contested Boundaries*. London: Trentham Books.

Bell, D. (1995a) 'Perverse dynamics, sexual citizenship and the transformation of intimacy,' in D. Bell and G. Valentine (eds), *Mapping Desire: Geographies of Sexualities*. London: Routledge.

Bell, D. (1995b) 'Pleasure and danger: the paradoxical spaces of sexual citizenship', *Political Geography*, 14: 139–53.

Bell, D., Binnie, J., Cream, J. and Valentine, G. (1994) 'All hyped up and no place to go', *Gender, Place and Culture*, 1: 31–47.

Bell, D. and Valentine, G. (1995) 'Queer country: rural lesbian and gay lives', *Journal of Rural Studies*, 11: 113–22.

Berlant, L. and Freeman, E. (1993) 'Queer nationality', in M. Warner, (ed.), *Fear of a Queer Planet: Queer Politics and Social Theory*. Minneapolis: University of Minnesota Press.

Betten, L. (1993) 'Rights in the workplaces', in K. Waaldijk and A. Clapham (eds), *Homosexuality: A European Community Issue: Essays on Lesbian and Gay Rights in European Law and Policy*. Dordrecht: Martinus Nijhoff.

Bhabha, H. (1994) *The Location of Culture*. London: Routledge.

Binnie, J. (1993) 'Invisible cities/hidden geographies: sexuality and the city' paper presented at the Social Policy and the City Conference, Liverpool, July.

Binnie, J. (1995) 'Trading places: consumption, sexuality and the production of Queer space', in D. Bell and G. Valentine (eds), *Mapping Desire: Geographies of Sexualities*. London: Routledge.

Binnie, J. (1997) 'Invisible Europeans: sexual citizenship in the new Europe', *Environment and Planning A*, 29: 237–48.

Blunt, A. and Wills, J. (2000) *Dissident Geographies*. Harlow: Pearson.

Brown, M. (1995) 'Sex, scale and the "new urban politics": HIV-prevention strategies from Yaletown, Vancouver', in D. Bell and G. Valentine (eds), *Mapping Desire: Geographies of Sexualities*. London: Routledge.

Brown, M. (2000) *Closet Space: Geographies of Metaphor from the Body to the Globe*. London: Routledge.

Butler, J. (1990) *Gender Trouble: Feminism and the Subversion of Identity*. London: Routledge.

Castells, M. (1983) *The City and the Grassroots*. Berkeley, CA: University of California Press.

Chauncey, G. (1995) *Gay New York: The Making of the Gay World 1890–1940*. London: Flamingo.

Cloke, P., Philo, C. and Sadler, D. (1991) *Approaching Human Geography*. London: Paul Chapman.

Egerton (1990) 'Out but not down: lesbians' experiences of housing', *Feminist Review*, 36: 75–88.

Elwood, S. (2000) 'Lesbian living spaces: multiple meanings of home', *Journal of Lesbian Studies*, 4: 11–28.

Evans, D. (1993) *Sexual Citizenship: The Material Construction of Sexualities*. London: Routledge.

Faderman, L. (1991) *Odd Girls and Twilight Lovers: A History of Lesbian Life in Twentieth Century America*. Harmondsworth: Penguin.

Foucault, M. (1981) *The History of Sexuality, Volume 1*. Harmondsworth: Penguin.

Fuss, D. (1991) *Inside/Out: Lesbian Theories, Gay Theories*. London: Routledge.

Greene, K. (1997) 'Fear and loathing in Mississippi: the attack on Camp Sister Spirit', *Women and Politics*, 17.

Gregson, N. and Rose, G. (2000) 'Taking Butler elsewhere: performativities, spatialities and subjectivities,' *Environment and Planning D: Society and Space*, 18: 433–52.

Grosz, E. (1989) *Sexual Subversions: Three French Feminists*. Sydney: Allen & Unwin.

Gutek, B. (1989) 'Sexuality in the workplace: key issues in social research and organisational practice', in J. Hearn, P. Sheppard, P. Tancred-Sherriff, and G. Burrell, (eds), *The Sexuality of Organisation*. London: Sage.

Hall, M. (1989) 'Private experiences in the public domain: lesbians in organisations,' in J. Hearn, P. Sheppard, P. Tancred-Sherriff and G. Burrell, (eds), *The Sexuality of Organisation*. London: Sage.

Hobsbawm, E.J. (1990) *Nations and Nationalism since 1780*. Cambridge: Cambridge University Press.

hooks, b. (1991) *Yearning: Race, Gender and Cultural Politics*. London: Turnaround.

Hubbard, P. (1999) *Sex and the City: Geographies of Prostitution in the Urban West*. Aldershot: Ashgate.

Isin, E.F. and Wood, P.K. (1999) *Citizenship and Identity*. London: Sage.

Johnson, J. (1973) *The Lesbian Nation: The Feminist Solution*. New York: Touchstone Books/Simon and Schuster.

Johnston. L. and Valentine, G. (1995) 'Wherever I lay my girlfriend that's my home: the performance and surveillance of lesbian identities in domestic environments', in D. Bell and G. Valentine (eds), *Mapping Desire: Geographies of Sexualities*. London: Routledge.

Johnston, R.J., Gregory, D., Pratt, G. and Watts, M. (eds.) (2000) *The Dictionary of Human Geography*. Oxford: Blackwell.

Knopp, L. (1990) 'Some theoretical implications of gay involvement in an urban land market', *Political Geography Quarterly*, 9: 337–52.

Knopp, L. (1992) 'Sexuality and the spatial dynamics of capitalism', *Environment and Planning D: Society and Space*, 10: 651–69.

Knopp, L. (1998) 'Sexuality and urban space: gay male identity politics in the United States, the United Kingdom and Australia', in R. Fincher and J. Jacobs (eds), *Cities of Difference*. London: Guildford Press.

Kramer, J.L. (1995) 'Bachelor farmers and spinsters: lesbian and gay identity and community in rural North Dakota', in D. Bell and G. Valentine (eds), *Mapping Desire: Geographies of Sexualities*. London: Routledge.

LaBruce, B. and Belverio, G. (1998) 'A case for the closet', in M. Simpson (ed.), *Anti-Gay*. London: Freedom Editions.

Lauria, M. and Knopp, L. (1985) 'Towards an analysis of the role of gay communities in the urban renaissance', *Urban Geography*, 6: 152–69.

Leap, W.L. (ed.) (1999) *Gay Space/Public Sex*. New York: Columbia.

Leidner, R. (1993) *Fast Food, Fast Talk: The Routinization of Everyday Life*. Berkeley, CA: University of California Press.

Lyod, B. and Rowntree, L. (1978) 'Radical feminists and gay men in San Francisco: social space in dispersed communities', in D. Lanegran and R. Palm (eds), *An Invitation to Geography*. New York: McGraw-Hill.

Massey, D. (1991) 'A global sense of place', *Marxism Today*, June, 24–9.

Massey, D. (1993) *Space, Place and Gender*. Minneapolis: University of Minnesota Press.

Massey, D. (1998) 'The spatial constructions of youth cultures', in T. Skelton and G. Valentine (eds), *Cool Places: Geographies of Youth Cultures*. London: Routledge.

Massey, D. (1999) 'Spaces of politics', in D. Massey, J. Allen and P. Sarre (eds), *Human Geography Today*. Cambridge: Polity.

McDowell, L. (1995) 'Body work: heterosexual gender performances in City workplaces', in D. Bell and G. Valentine (eds), *Mapping Desire: Geographies of Sexualities*. London: Routledge.

Morley, D. and Robins, K. (1995) *Spaces of Identity: Global Media, Electronic Landscapes and Cultural Boundaries*. London: Routledge.

Munt, S. (1995) 'The lesbian flaneur', in Bell D. and Valentine G. (eds), *Mapping Desire: Geographies of Sexualities*. London: Routledge.

Munt, S. (1998) 'Sisters in exile: the lesbian nation', in R. Ainley (ed.), *New Frontiers of Space, Bodies and Gender*. London: Routledge.

Myslik, W. (1996) 'Renegotiating the social/sexual identities of place: gay communities as safe havens or sites of resistance', in N. Duncan (ed.), *BodySpace: Destablising Geographies of Gender and Sexuality*. London: Routledge.

Pringle, R. (1988) *Secretaries Talk: Sexuality, Power and Work*. London: Verso.

Probyn, E. (1995) 'Lesbians in space: gender, sex and the structure of missing,' *Gender, Place and Culture*, 2: 77–84.

Quilley, S. (1995) 'Manchester's "village in the city": the gay vernacular in a post-industrial landscape of power', *Transgressions: A Journal of Urban Exploration*, 1: 36–50.

Rose, G. (1993) *Feminism and Geography: The Limits of Geographical Knowledge*. Minneapolis: University of Minnesota Press.

Rothenberg, T. (1995) 'And she told two friends: lesbians creating urban social space', in D. Bell and G. Valentine (eds), *Mapping Desire: Geographies of Sexualities*. London: Routledge.

Sedgwick, E. (1990) *Epistemology of the Closet*. Berkeley, CA: University of California Press.

Signorile, M. (1993) *Queer in America: Sex, the Media and the Closets of Power*. New York: Random House.

Smith, N. (1990) *Uneven Development: Nature, Capital and the Production of Space*. Oxford: Basil Blackwell.

Smith, N. (1993) 'Homeless/global: scaling places', in J. Bird B. Curtis T. Putnam G. Robertson and L. Tickner (eds), *Mapping the Futures: Local Cultures, Global Change*. London: Routledge.

Smith, N. and Katz, C. (1993) 'Grounding metaphor: towards a spatialised politics', in M. Keith and S. Pile (eds), *Place and the Politics of Identity*. London: Routledge.

Smith, S.J. (1999) 'Society–space', in P. Cloke, P. Crang and M. Goodwin (eds), *Introducing Human Geography*. London: Arnold.

Soja, E. (1996) *Thirdspace*. Oxford: Blackwell.

Tanca, A. (1993) 'European citizenship and the rights of lesbians and gay men', in K. Waaldijk and A. Clapham (eds), *Homosexuality: A European Community Issue: Essays on Lesbian and Gay Rights in European Law and Policy*. Dordrecht: Martinus Nijhoff.

Urry, J. (1990) 'The consumption of tourism', *Sociology*, 24: 23–35.

Valentine, G. (1993) '(Hetero)sexing space: lesbian perceptions and experiences of everyday spaces', *Environment and Planning D: Society and Space*, 11: 395–413.

Valentine, G. (1995a) 'Out and about: a geography of lesbian communities', *International Journal of Urban and Regional Research*, 19: 96–111.

Valentine, G. (1995b) 'Creating transgressive space: the music of kd lang'. *Transactions of the Institute of British Geographers*, 20: 474–85.

Valentine, G. (1996a) 'An equal place to work? Anti-lesbian discrimination and sexual citizenship in the European Union', in M.D. Garcia-Ramon and J. Monk (eds), *Women of the European Union: The Politics of Work and Daily Life*. London: Routledge.

Valentine, G. (1996b) '(Re)negotiating the heterosexual street', in N. Duncan (ed.), *Bodyspace: Destabilizing Geographies of Gender and Sexuality*. London: Routledge.

Valentine, G. (1997) 'Making space: separatism and difference', in J.P. Jones III, H.J. Nastand, and S. Roberts (eds), *Thresholds in Feminist Geography: Difference, Methodology and Representation*. Rowman and Oxford: Littlefield Publishers.

Waaldijk, K. (1993) 'The legal situation in member states', in K. Waaldijk and A. Clapham (eds), *Homosexuality: A European Community Issue. Essays on Lesbian and Gay Rights in European Law and Policy*. Dordrecht: Martinus Nijhoff.

Weeks, J. (1992) 'Changing sexual and personal values in the age of AIDS', paper presented at the Forum on Sexuality Conference, Sexual Cultures in Europe, Amsterdam, June.

Weightman, B. (1981) 'Commentary: towards a geography of the gay community', *Journal of Cultural Geography*, 1: 106–12.

Weston, K. (1995) 'Get thee to a big city: sexual imaginary and the great gay migration', *GLQ: A Journal of Lesbian and Gay Studies*, 2: 253–77.

Whittle, S. (ed.) (1994) *The Margins of the City: Gay Men's Urban Lives*. Aldershot: Ashgate.

10

The Forgotten

A Community Without a Generation – Older Lesbians and Gay Men

STEPHEN PUGH

A considerable amount of literature is available that is related to older lesbians and gay men, however, it is not, on the whole, gathered within standard texts on gerontology but is dispersed. The nature of the available material is itself diverse, being in the form of explicit research, commentary or narrative/life history. The majority of the texts refer to older gay men, some address issues for older lesbians and gay men alike, while a much smaller percentage is concerned solely with older lesbians.

While this reflection is not based on an empirical analysis, it is also interesting to note that the studies on older gay men maintain a duality of approach, containing both quantitative and qualitative material. The material related to older lesbians, however, is, on the whole, much more narrative in the exploration of issues and relies on a life history approach to tell individual stories.

The difference in approach is interesting both from a research perspective and in the reportage of the material. The quantitative material lends itself to easy gathering and reporting, unlike the narrative style, which requires a much more careful and detailed review. It is important to note that both styles are valid in research terms and much more narrative/biographical research needs to be undertaken related to older gay men. However, the absence of easily reportable material has the consequence that issues related to older lesbians may be overlooked as commentators have difficulty in reviewing the available material.

On the whole, researchers and commentators in exactly the fields of study in which we would expect older lesbians and gay men to be recognized – social gerontology and sexuality – have largely ignored their existence. As such, asking the question – what about older lesbians and gay men? – requires a leap of thought or an inquiry that takes the individual beyond the accepted knowledge base of these disciplines.

This chapter will explore the available literature and identify a number of key themes, such as ageism and homophobia; accelerated ageing; images of older lesbians and gay men; their social support systems and coming out as an older person. Of equal importance are such issues as researching older lesbians and gay men; the theoretical underpinnings of much of the current research and the assumptions that are made in the literature.

One of the difficulties in writing and commentating on issues related to older lesbians and gay men is one of generalization. The temptation is to assume that the experience of being a lesbian or gay man at a time when criminal and social sanctions were severe and real was awful and affected everybody in discernibly negative ways. However, for some people this was not the case, or at least not the reality for all of the time. The problem of generalization is the subsuming of individual experiences within the context of an assumed overall experience. Patently, this acts in a manner which is as oppressive as denying the existence of an entire group and while this chapter will reflect on issues that have affected older lesbians and gay men as a whole, regard must be given to individual experiences which may be very different.

DISCOVERING THAT SOMETHING WAS MISSING

The disappearance of older lesbians and gay men may seem somewhat analogous to a science fiction tale in which everybody over a given age suddenly vanishes as if to avoid tarnishing younger people. Evidence of this disappearance can be illustrated by the *Christopher Street* periodical that asked in November 1977 'where do old gays go? (Kimmel, 1977a).

In 1982 the *New York Daily News,* quoting a gay man stated 'You never see them [older lesbians and gay men] around; after a certain age they seem to disappear. Where do they go? (LaRosa, 1982). A poster for a Toronto gay forum asked 'what happens to homosexuals over 50? (GLHC, 1985). While these comments may seem to have no other relevance than historical – given the

dates – the sentiments expressed are still as valid in the twenty-first century as they were in the 1970s and 1980s.

While gay ageing was 'discovered' by gerontologists in 1969 (Weinberg, 1969), Jacobs et al. (1999) comment that the existence of older lesbians and gay men is not recognized within the broad range of gerontology texts and that this literature either: 'fails to mention elderly gay men and lesbians or provide little discussion of the concerns about aging. This omission reflects the systematic ignoring of and subsequent exclusion of older gay, lesbian and bisexual populations in mainstream gerontology' (1999: 4). There is no simple explanation for this absence of recognition. We could attribute such a state to the function and operation of major systems of oppression – ageism and homophobia. Equally, we could assert that older lesbians and gay men are the victims of their own, extremely successful anonymity. This anonymity was based on the need to avoid detection at times when same sex relationships were either criminalized or subject to severe social restriction and sanction. For older lesbians and gay men, this was a reality through most of their adult lives and will have informed how same sex relationships were established, how they were conducted and even how the imagery of self was formulated. Jacobs et al. comment that '[the] secrecy related to sexual orientation was a common coping response to discrimination, but often resulted in individuals feeling guilty and ashamed of their gayness or lesbianism' (1999: 3). The consequences of the need to maintain this secret, which some have continued into later life, is identified in the literature as being problematic for the individual older lesbian or gay man giving rise primarily to issues of adjustment, imagery and self-identification.

The Sexual Offences Act 1967 decriminalized consensual gay male relationships over 21 years of age in 'private' in England and Wales (the situation in Scotland and Northern Ireland did not change for many years) and began a liberalizing process that has changed the environment in which many younger lesbians and gay men now conduct their lives. The 1967 Act passed into law when the current 80 year olds were aged in their late forties and early fifties. The liberalization, which is a consequence of this change in legislation, did not occur overnight, but in fact has been a gradual process which has developed and quickened in pace over the past thirty or so years.

The implications for older lesbian and gay men – for this group of people who were in their forties and fifties at the time of the change in the law – was little immediate change. It was not until this group were well into their sixties before most could identify any appreciable change in attitude. Such changes in attitude or liberalization that we currently enjoy, still has, in many countries, a backdrop of discrimination. Thus, such areas as the age of consent, rights to recognized relationships, the notorious Section 28 (section 2a of the Local Government Act 1988)[1] and archaic attitudes towards lesbians and gay men in respect of childcare, reflect legitimated discrimination based on sexuality. In Britain, the recent debates in the House of Lords in respect of Section 28 and the age of consent clearly demonstrate that homophobia is alive and well within the English legislature.

Given the existence of official, state-sponsored homophobia, what hope is there for older lesbians and gay men who wish to maintain their respect and dignity at times when they may be dependent on the care of others. Such care may be provided in environments such as residential or nursing homes or even in their own homes.

I am a woman paralysed after a stroke from the neck down. How can I ask my home carer, employed to facilitate my 'independent living' to switch on *Dyke TV* (Channel 4, 1995) when I do not wish to reveal my sexual orientation because the carer has already let me know that their opinion that Beth Jordace's death on *Brookside*[2] (Channel 4, 1995) was better than she deserved because she was a lesbian? (Brown, 1998: 113)

AGEISM

The common experience of all older people is one, in which age-related assumptions impact significantly on every day lives. The acknowledgement of ageism as a system of oppression is relatively recent. Butler defined ageism as: 'a process of systematic stereotyping of, and discrimination against, people because they are old, just as racism and sexism accomplish this for skin colour and gender' (1987: 22). The product of stereotyping is to assume that *all* older people are the same and are thereby treated as a homogenous group. Older people are therefore ascribed identifiable characteristics, which are exhibited by all in the group and recognized by everybody else. Thus, all older people smell, are forgetful, are slow, they live in the past, they are a burden on the rest of society and importantly, being old is a condition that should be avoided (not that one can) at all cost.

The realities of these assumptions are found in such things as television adverts for cosmetics where the imperative is to avoid the signs of ageing. Older people are urged to avoid shopping and travelling at times when younger people are demanding these services. The 'burden' imagery has been very powerful in social policy terms when politicians argue that we cannot afford the demands that older people make on the economically active. Pension arrangements in the UK have been changed in line with this imagery as SERPS (State Earnings Replacement Scheme)[3] has been cancelled and the 'pension link'[4] has been abandoned.

These stereotypes continue into the areas of sex and sexuality where imagery frequently portrays older people as being asexual. The dominant stereotype is based on the assumption that the young body and only the young body is attractive. Thus, those of us who deviate from this image are unattractive, and who could possibly want to have sex with somebody who is unattractive? Exceptions are identified to this general rule, primarily these are male media stars but the recognition of their attractiveness is set in the context of their exceptional appearance given their age.

The media presentation of Viagra has begun to challenge these assumptions as the major user group is identified as older men. Older people's, or in particular, older men's desire for sex has therefore entered our living rooms in discussion with the use of this drug. Unfortunately, this association, while positive in part, has linked older people's desire for sex with the need for chemical enhancement.

When older people's sexuality is acknowledged, it tends to be in the context of pathology and the imagery of the 'dirty old man' comes rushing to the fore. However, the automatic assumption is of heterosexuality. The possibility of same sex relationships in late life is very rarely considered.

Ageism cannot, on its own, provide a satisfactory explanation for the lack of acknowledgement or understanding of the situation in which older lesbians and gay men are placed. The concept of 'jeopardy' and in particular 'multiple jeopardy' may help us to understand more easily the day-to-day reality of the lives of older lesbians and gay men. Norman employs the term 'triple jeopardy' to describe the situation of older black people living in a second homeland. She comments: 'They are not merely in double jeopardy by reason of age and discrimination … but in triple jeopardy. At risk because they are old, because of the physical conditions and hostility under which they have to live, and because services are not accessible to them' (1985: 1). This definition in many ways reflects the position of older lesbian and gay men in terms of the experience of discrimination, ageing, hostility and the lack of suitable services. In essence, this approach identifies the existence of multiple systems of oppression, which intersect and have differing emphases as individual lives are being lived.

As an example, an older lesbian may experience oppression related to her age while out shopping and in doing so she may overhear a pejorative conversation about same sex relationships and feel uncomfortable about the tone of the conversation, given her own sexuality. If this woman was black or experienced a disability, she may equally encounter direct hostility related to her skin colour or her disability. In this respect, this particular older woman's life has been affected negatively by ageism, homophobia, racism and disability oppression at different times as she conducted her day.

Reflecting on individual *vis-à-vis* group experiences, which were identified above, a common misconception related to lesbians and gay men irrespective of age, relates to the belief in the existence of a unitary 'gay community' in which both lesbians and gay men have equal presence and sense of belonging. The implication is that lesbians and gay men have common interests, aspirations and live similar lives. The reality for most lesbians and gay men is far from this. Jacobs et al. identify that 'the "lesbian and gay community" is dispersed throughout mainstream society, as well as centered in particular geographic hubs' (1999: 3).

The hubs that are being referred to are 'gay' urban spaces and in particular evening spaces, which are somewhat euphemistically referred to as villages or quarters. These gay hubs are, on the whole, gay male spaces and are based primarily on conspicuous consumption and sex. Thus class, money and time become important features for those who wish to occupy these urban spaces. The presence of lesbians in these spaces may be, at worst, actively discouraged and, at best, tolerated. Where women-only venues are available, they are likely to be very limited in number.

The emphasis in these spaces may also be very different with a concentration on youth and loud 'boom boom' music in gay male venues. The assumption of 'community' equally ignores the differences in how individual gay men and lesbians network and establish relationships. The commonality rests with a shared experience of oppression resulting from homophobia.

While homophobia is alive and well, a more subtle form of oppression has dominated the lives of lesbians and gay men – that of heterosexism. This form of oppression asserts that heterosexual relations are the norm and that each of us is unquestioningly assumed to be heterosexual. Associated with this ascription of sexuality are assumptions about behaviour, role and the location in which types of activities take place. Thus, the presumption is that *all* men are heterosexual. They go to work, which is invariably in the public sphere, to provide for their family, they participate in or watch team sports, it is their responsibility to do the garden and maintain the fabric of the house. In the same mode, *all* women are heterosexual. Women look after the children and while increasingly they undertake paid employment, this represents a second income for the family. The primary sphere in which women operate is the privacy of the home. It is their responsibility to construct and maintain this home for their husband and family.

While these gender roles are somewhat generalized, they feature prominently in the literature related to older lesbians and gay men, and in particular the research undertaken on older gay men. As we will see, assumed gay male gender role flexibility is viewed very positively in assisting older gay men to adjust to the ageing process. Specifically, the references relate to retirement and exclusion from employment.

These gender assumptions have other and more worrying implications, in particular, for lesbians and gay men, who have levels of dependence on others. In such a scenario, the care giving would be undertaken in an atmosphere of assumed heterosexuality unless otherwise asserted. Thus references in conversation may be made to intimate relationships with the opposite sex – girl friends and boy friends. Potentially, care staff, in spite of the wishes and desires of the people concerned, may contrive such relationships without a thought that the person they are caring for may in fact be a lesbian or gay man.

The experience of oppression is not always and at all times negative. A consequence of homophobia is an experience shared by many hundreds of thousands of lesbians and gay men. The movement into another system of oppression – ageism – as we all age, has for Lukes positive benefits as he asserts that 'gay men cope better with age because deprivation has been their daily fare' (1973: 26). The broad assumption is that coping with oppressions facilitates the development of skills which in turn informs the individual's ability to cope with other forms of oppression.

COHORT EFFECTS

The shared experience of cohorts is particularly important when exploring issues pertinent to older lesbians and gay men. On a broader scale, national and international events which have occurred historically and that have impacted on groups of people in essence can be referred to as cohort effects. As an example, the First World War (1914 to 1918) and the subsequent flu epidemic had a devastating effect on the population in Europe. Both events gave rise to a reduction in the numbers of young men and as a result a reduction in the numbers of men available for marriage, with the result that large numbers of women were not able to marry and thus remained single. This effect is currently working its way through the population as many of these single women are reaching later life.

In attempting to understand this effect in more detail, Ryder notes that 'each cohort has a distinctive composition and character reflecting the circumstances of its unique origination and history' (1965: 845). Jacobs (1990) provides us with the following definition of a cohort effect as 'distinct political and economic experiences (which) separate generations and have lasting impact' (1990: 350). The terms cohort and generation are used interchangeably. However, in demographic terms a generation refers to kinship links while a cohort is a group born at a particular time in history.

A further complication to this debate arises from the concept of period effects which 'emerge from the major events that shape the lives of persons who experience them' (Morgan and Kunkel, 1998: 39). The emergence of AIDS is used as an example of a period effect because it has impacted on the whole population, irrespective of age. While this analysis is somewhat limited, it is possible to conclude that a period effect may produce a groups cohort effect. Thus, AIDS becomes the backdrop for young gay men who are currently exploring their sexuality while for those who are older, it is a disease which emerged after the development of their sexuality and one that should inform a change in sexual behaviour.

Cohort effects also have implications for attitudes towards sex and sexuality. The criminalization of sex between men had the result that many gay men maintained aspects of their lives hidden from the rest of society or entered heterosexual relationships in the belief that this was *normal* and through which they could avoid public scrutiny. During this period, while the threat of criminal sanction was not a threat for lesbians, the reality of severe social reaction gave rise to similar sorts of coping behaviours.

Cohort effects in reviewing issues related to older lesbians and gay men are very influential as they inform such issues as identification of self, association with other lesbians and gay men, how and in what circumstances relationships were formed and in what circumstances they were conducted. Many gay men and lesbians were both individually and by association, labelled as 'sick by doctors, immoral by clergy, unfit by the military, and a menace by the police' (Kochman, 1997: 2).

As a result of this widespread attitude, individual older lesbians and gay men will have conducted their lives to reflect their own circumstances. Thus, some people will have lived openly as a lesbian or gay man and others may well have identified themselves as gay while living with the veneer of heterosexuality. Lee (1989) identifies two solutions for gay men prior to the changes in legislation. The first was to marry and possibly to conduct same sex relationships in secret with an expectation of never living with a lover. The other solution was to remain single with the air of asexuality or disinterest in sex, which by its nature was less of a threat and thereby facilitated the acceptance of the individual gay man. In family histories, how many uncles and great uncles remained bachelors, thereby hiding their gay sexuality?

Inevitably, the covert nature in which many older lesbians and gay men conducted their lives, with the threat of real sanctions if discovered, gave rise to absolute imperative for secrecy. Perhaps a secret gay world consisting of intimate knowledge, of furtive glances and covert introductions. Older gay men undertook the initiation or introduction of younger men into this world. This world of extreme secrecy involved carefully arranged meetings, explicit trust between the individuals, fear of discovery and sometimes financial extortion. In Britain, this world also had a language of its own – Polari – employed to enable gay men to talk in public to each other without discovery, for who would risk telling the police that two men were conversing in Polari without disclosing their own secret?

IMAGES OF OLDER LESBIANS AND GAY MEN

The received wisdom related to older gay men creates an image of: 'loneliness, isolation, sexlessness, poor psychological adjustment and functioning, fearful anxiousness, sadness and depression and sexual predation on the gay young who reject their company and exclude them from a "youthist" gay culture' (Wahler and Gabbay, 1997: 9). Both ageist and homophobic attitudes undoubtedly influence this stereotype. To be a gay older person pours on the misery, not least because it is bad enough to be one or the other, but to be both is to double the misery. The stereotype also involves a necessary referent to younger people – without which older people have no existence. Interestingly, Kimmel (1977b, 1978, 1980) identified that older gay men have little contact with younger men – thereby undermining the assumption of older gay men's predatory behaviour. The basis of this assumption is quite offensive because it potentially facilitates links between older gay men, promiscuity and paedophilia that are unfounded and feed homophobic attitudes.

Older lesbians are frequently portrayed as highly educated, politically liberal, middle-class, professionally employed and unmarried or divorced (Jacobs et al. 1999). In contrast, older heterosexual women are often stereotyped as poorly educated, politically conservative, poor, religiously active, asexual, professionally unemployed and married or widowed.

The literature identifies differing images of older gay men most of which portray positive adjustments to ageing and social networks. Most researchers predicate health in later life with involvement with the wider gay community on the assumption that such involvement equates to a 'healthy' acceptance of sexuality. Little or no contact with the wider community presupposes 'unhealthy' acceptance of sexuality or denial, which inevitably suggests depression and mental illness.

Kimmel's (1977, 1978, 1980) work actually found considerable differences between older gay men, thereby recognizing diversity among older gay men rather than the generalizations upon which the stereotypes have been constructed. Weinberg (1969, 1970) identified that older gay men had reduced their involvement with the gay community with increasing age, but that they were not any more lonely than younger gay men. Francher and Henkin (1973) while equally reporting a reduction in involvement in the wider gay community, also noted an increase in the contact that older gay men had with their social networks, both gay and heterosexual. Some researchers observed that older gay men have many gay

friends but less heterosexual friends and that in general, gay men had significantly more close friends than heterosexual men (Kelly, 1977; Friend, 1980). Older gay men were also reported as being less worried about their sexuality being disclosed and that they had higher levels of self-acceptance and had an improved and stable concept of self (Weinberg, 1969, 1970; Kelly, 1977).

Many older lesbians appear to view their sexuality in terms of emotional intimacy and personal identification with other women (Jacobs et al., 1999). The literature identifies a contradiction relating to living arrangements as older lesbians are reported to be living with a partner or living alone. Most studies identify continued interest and valuing of sex although celibacy was a feature of many older lesbians' lives that, for many, was not a choice. The research identifies that the relationship arrangements involved a belief in monogamy (Minnigerode and Adelman, 1978; Raphael and Robinson, 1980; Tully, 1983; Kehoe, 1986).

Kimmel's (1977, 1978, 1980) and Kelly's (1977) work acknowledged that sex remained important for older gay men and that they remained sexually active. There was also a recording of a decrease in the amount of sex that older gay men experienced and that they engaged in sex with men of their own age group.

Minnigerode and Adelman's (1978) small research study explored differences between lesbian and gay and heterosexual older people in areas such as physical changes, work and retirement, social behaviour, psychological functioning, loneliness, sexual behaviour and reflections on the life course. Their research identified indicators of similarities and generational differences. These findings in part reflect the nature of the research undertaken and are repeated time and time again by numerous researchers (Bennett and Thompson, 1980; Goleman Wolf, 1982; Berger, 1984; Gray and Dressel, 1985; Pope and Schulz, 1990; Adelman, 1991).

Bennett and Thompson (1980) in a study of older Australian gay men found that they were not disengaged from the broader community either by choice or by exclusion. However, they did establish that older Australian gay men were more secretive about their sexuality than younger gay men in Australia and that this may be related to cohort effects or of other perceived risks, such as loss of their job. This is in part supported by Gray and Dressel (1985) who indicate that older gay men were more likely to wish to maintain secrecy about their sexuality than younger gay men, but that this did not suggest any significant alienation from the broader community. Goleman Wolf (1982), in fact, on a very positive note, suggests that heterosexuals could learn and benefit from a gay model of ageing. Berger (1984) notes that the issues for older gay and non-gay people were similar with a major feature being self-acceptance.

ADJUSTING TO THE AGEING PROCESS

In contradiction to the many stereotypes of older lesbians and gay men, a number of commentators have identified that the atmosphere of repression encountered while older lesbians and gay men were growing up and conducting their early adult lives, had in fact assisted them to adjust to ageing. Frencher and Henkin (1973) were the first to propose the idea that 'coming out' as a life crisis assisted older gay men to cope with ageing. Kimmel (1978) also reflects this view. The assumption that is being made is that 'coming out' must be a difficult and painful process and having 'competently' responded to this crisis, older lesbians and gay men have the skills to cope with other life crises, in particular, the move into retirement.

Berger (1980) refers to the term 'mastery of crisis', which was later endorsed by Jeffrey Weeks (1983). Berger comments that:

> There are aspects of the homosexual experience that facilitate adjustment to aging. Social workers who work with the elderly would do well to consider these aspects for what they reveal about adjustment to aging for homosexuals and

heterosexual alike … the coming-out period is a major life crisis, which, when resolved, provides the individual with a stamina unavailable to many others. Today's older homosexual had to resolve a crisis of independence at a young age and at a time less tolerant of sexual nonconformity. He knew that he could not rely on the traditional family supports that heterosexuals take for granted. Whereas older homosexuals are as likely as heterosexual to be alone in old age, they are better prepared for it, both emotionally and in terms of support networks of friends. (Berger, 1982: 238)

Lee (1987) asks whether Berger's assumption is true or whether some puritanical idea that suffering is good for the soul is present in these comments. Lee goes on to identify comments from a number of researchers who, while reporting on differing problems that older gay men experience, all note that these older men have high levels of self-acceptance and self-esteem (Weinberg and Williams, 1974; Minnigerode, 1976; Kelly, 1977).

A competence model, or more accurately – crisis competence – has been used by Berger (1982), Francher and Henkin (1973), D'Augelli (1994) and others to maintain that older gay men are more able to cope with life crises. In reflecting upon the model, Pope and Schulz (1990) and Kooden (1997) identify that older gay men are able to cope in a positive sense with loss and less rigid role expectations. Friend (1980) identified that the changes in social status and role that occur with ageing are less of a problem for older lesbians and gay men because of more flexible gender roles experienced throughout their lives.

This is an interesting reflection on how lesbians and gay men are assumed to conduct their lives and their relationships. Such comments further reinforce the power of heterosexism as a system of oppression, in structuring how relationships should be and are conducted. Thus in same sex relationships there must be a 'man' and there must be a 'woman' to undertake the ascribed roles.

Wahler and Gabbay (1997) in their review of the literature, identify a number of themes related to the adjustment to ageing:

- The similarity between gay and non-gay older people in some of the predictors of successful ageing.
- That self-acceptance can be a critical variable.
- That gay men are better prepared for the process of ageing than non-gay men.
- There are some unique challenges to the gay experience of ageing.

In fact, they go on to identify positive benefits of being a lesbian or gay man in late life as they assert:

> the literature suggests that older gay men may adjust to aging more easily than their non-gay male counterparts. Further, studies indicate that gay men who have grown to a point of acceptance and celebration of themselves experience the highest degree of life satisfaction and positive adjustment to the challenges of aging, both as gay men and as older individuals. (Wahler and Gabbay, 1997: 13)

However, they do identify a note of caution involving older lesbians and gay men who 'lack self-acceptance'. In most of the literature, lack of self-acceptance is inevitably equated to not being 'out' and involved with the wider gay community.

Kimmel (1977) identifies a number of other benefits of being an older lesbian and gay man. Such benefits, he argues, are a consequence of many gay male lives not being disrupted by 'life cycle' changes such as the death of a spouse; role changes of retirement and the movement of adult children away from the home. He goes on to state that older gay men have a more self-reliant attitude in respect of their own needs based in part on higher levels of earned income and more disposable income in later life.

Older lesbians are reported to have adapted well to the ageing process and to have a positive self-image, equally, they do not experience the acceleration of ageing as fast as heterosexual women (Laner, 1979). Patently, older lesbians and gay men do not lead lives separated from family and friends and many of the life-cycle changes identified by Kimmel (1977) do have an impact on people's everyday lives. Older lesbians

and gay men are touched by the death of partners, parents and friends and retirement or exclusion from work has different meanings for different people.

Also, we cannot assume that all older lesbians and gay men's lives have been constructed in the same manner and are therefore formatted to look the same. Many older lesbians and gay men will be mothers and fathers (grandmothers and grandfathers) themselves and any event that affects a child can have very profound change potential. Whitford, commenting on his own research, states that 'a high proportion of all men had children, indicative of the fact that most of these men had been married at some point in their lives' (1997: 92).

The other comment that should be made at this point relates to the underlying assumption that lies behind much of the research. Ageing is viewed as a negative event, which requires adjustment. The researchers are inevitably reflecting broader social constructs in a society, which is fundamentally ageist. These assumptions do not reflect individual experiences or aspirations. For many older people, retirement is a release that enables them to engage in the activities of their choosing, while for others the move away from the labour market is not wanted and ageing is something to be dreaded.

THE CONDITIONS FOR SUCCESSFUL AGEING

The primary condition for gay men in successful ageing is income and access to financial resources. Lee (1987) comments that this is a powerful indicator in the general population regardless of sexual orientation. Education is also a strong indicator and is related to income. This is again related to the whole population of older people and is not specific to sexual orientation. The presence of a life partner is the third in the correlation with happiness in old age (Berger, 1980; Lee, 1987) with loneliness representing one of the major threats to happiness. Ageing itself is the final aspect in the correlation with satisfaction in old age rather than being gay. This in part reflects on attitudes to dependence and the attainment of goals such as a comfortable home and a sex life. These are again related to the whole population and not specifically related to gay male older people.

The message is quite clear, that happiness or satisfaction in later life is dependent on other factors rather than sexual orientation *per se*. However, unlike heterosexual older people, the literature identifies an additional factor for lesbian and gay older people. Whilst this factor is identified differently (Wahler and Gabbay [1997] refer to it as 'self-acceptance'), it relates to publicly disclosing the nature of their sexuality – of being 'out'. The literature asserts that being 'out' is likened to happiness and the test is participation in the gay community by belonging to gay or lesbian organizations. This is a substantial test that heterosexual older people do not have to pass. Whitford (1997) identifies two aspects to participation in the community. The first is a formal measure which relates to participation with gay organizations, while the second is informal and addresses the characteristics of the social networks or friendships that the older person maintains. This measure identifies the number of gay friends and is specific to the majority of friends being gay. The importance of this latter measure rests with the prediction of positive outcomes in terms of adjustment to ageing.

There are a number of assumptions that lie behind such ideas. The first, as identified above, is that being old is a state that has to be adjusted to and is thereby unpleasant or to be avoided. The avoidance of ageing has become a moral imperative. To be young and active is the state we should strive to achieve. For commentators from a political economy perspective, the world of economic activity – work – is the condition that provides meaning to our lives and thereby to be excluded from this on the basis of age is an inequity. The second assumption is

related to being 'out'. The process of coming out can be devastating for some people, for others it can be liberating. To assume that happiness is being out denies individual experiences and again establishes a moral imperative – lesbians and gay men must be out to be happy. Lee's (1989) work cited above identifies that many people maintain wholly satisfying lives while being very private about their sexuality.

Equally, being 'out' is not a fixed and complete state, different levels of knowledge exist in various groupings. Perhaps, in order to ensure widespread knowledge of the person's sexuality, older lesbians and gay men should be made to wear vests at all times with some form of outing statement of self-declaration thus complying with the moral imperative and maximizing the opportunity for happiness. The third point rests with membership of lesbian and gay organizations as a test of the degree of 'outedness'. This again may deny the individual's experience and wishes. In equity, we should assert that heterosexual older people have to join groups in order to satisfy a test of happiness. The theoretical underpinning with this test is *activity theory* (Havighurst, 1963).

THEORETICAL UNDERSTANDINGS APPLIED TO OLDER LESBIANS AND GAY MEN

Much of the research, as identified above, maintains, either explicitly or implicitly, a number of theoretical constructs, which guide assumptions made within the work or its conclusions. The most obvious of these is the link between successful adaptation/adjustment to the ageing process and participation in organized lesbian and gay activities.

Lee (1987) comments that activity theory is not an explanation for ageing but rather a recipe for health in later life. In its simplistic form, activity theory asserts a need to 'keep busy in old age' with an emphasis on formal activity in social organizations as a means for compensating for the loss of roles through retirement or declining physical strength. Furthermore, Lee (1987) identifies a development of this approach with the emphasis on activity with significant others. This is identified as a move towards a symbolic interactionist adaptation of the theory.

The application of activity theory to lesbian and gay male ageing places an emphasis on the need to maintain sexual activity and to build non-sexual support networks. Researchers see this later imperative as compensation for the absence of families, which are so important in heterosexual adaptation to ageing (Friend, 1980; Raphael and Robinson, 1980).

There are a number of assumptions located within much of this work that inform the conclusions drawn, either directly or indirectly. The first is related to the need to continue to be active in later life *per se*. Wholesale adoption of this approach does not facilitate individual expression of ageing or reflect how many people have lived their lives. For the older lesbian and gay man there is a double bind here in that they not only have to maintain activity but they must do so in specific ways – participation with lesbian and gay organizations. Failure to do this would seem to indicate that they have not adjusted to ageing and to their sexuality.

The researchers seem to assume that older lesbians and gay men have either been rejected by their families and thereby live in familial isolation, or are estranged from their children, having come out after years of maintaining their sexuality as a secret. This again simply denies the reality for some individual older lesbians and gay men who are welcomed into their families and maintain good relationships with their children and siblings. Of course, for some older lesbians and gay men coming out did result in rejection, but it is too gross an over-simplification to apply this to all older lesbians and gay men.

The final assumption rests with role adoption and the apparent absence of the 'other' gender in the lives of lesbians and gay men. Once again there are very big generalizations reiterated in the research which imply that gay men undertake homemaking roles while lesbians adopt more masculine roles in domestic settings. Such assumptions appear to rest with heterosexist ideas of male and female roles in partnerships, thereby when two men live together one of them will become the 'woman'. This is equally played out in heterosexual assumptions about sexual activity between couples of the same sex. These ideas are not applied to other same sex groupings such as the armed forces or student accommodation, why, then, should a heterosexual model be implanted in discussions about same sex couples? Here again, individual expression is lost in over-generalized assumptions.

Activity theory is presented in mainstream gerontological texts as a discrete theory that provides a balance for another theoretical construct, that of disengagement theory (Cumming and Henry, 1961). Disengagement theory provides a structural-functionalist explanation of ageing by asserting that we are all socialized to expect to disengage from activities and roles as we age. The 'emphasis in disengagement theory is on the social actor playing out normatively defined role withdrawal in a universal and inevitable process that fills the functional needs of society' (Lee, 1987: 44).

As a result, successful ageing, according to disengagement theory, is dependent on older people accepting the process of disengaging as both inevitable and natural. The failure to disengage places the individual older person as a deviant. The theory recognizes gender differences in individual disengagement based on gender roles and that 'homemaking' is a role from which women do not retire.

The application of disengagement theory to older gay men is located in the assumption that gay men, necessarily in the absence of women, have to undertake 'homemaking' roles. Therefore the shedding of employment roles at retirement is assumed to be less painful and difficult because of the continuation of these other roles (Kutner et al., 1956; Friend, 1980). Hochschild (1975) similarly claims that older gay men are less affected by the disengagement process because they have often lived secret lives which were disengaged from society, thereby disengaging in later life is a return to a state that is already familiar.

Patently, the research which identifies that older lesbians and gay men can achieve high levels of life satisfaction, while not being out, would indicate higher levels of adjustment to ageing by disengagement. Obviously, the counter-argument here is that they were never engaged in the first place and these individuals may experience more difficult adjustment as their heterosexual roles diminish.

Activity and disengagement theory establish moral imperatives related to ageing. Older people must either be involved and active or must reduce their activities to conserve their strength. Both theories deny older people's individual wishes, experiences and life course.

Continuity theory identifies that 'there is a clear tendency for aged people to persist with the same relative levels of activity and attitudes as they grow older' (Palmore, 1968, in Lee, 1987: 45). The approach also identifies that patterns of adjustment to ageing can be identified by the age of 50 years and that a number of personality types are identifiable (Blau, 1957; Clark and Anderson, 1967; Fontana, 1977). Lee (1987) maintains that this approach is very value-laden and implies 'hierarchical ordering of adjustment patterns'. Rather than viewing these as personality traits, Lee urges us to regard them as indicators of coping strategies.

In application, Lee (1987) identifies that in a homophobic society, older lesbians and gay men (he refers specifically to older gay men) have developed strategies for coping with discontinuity. Such an approach is particularly relevant to the current cohort of older lesbians and gay men who grew up in a very hostile society. Kimmel (1977) refers to greater levels of continuity for older gay men because they have not experienced their children growing up and leaving home. However, coming out represents significant discontinuity as a result of the reactions of others and may lead to loss of friends and relatives.

'COMING OUT' OR STAYING IN

The decision to disclose or 'come out' about one's sexuality as a lesbian or gay man can be very difficult and such decisions are made individually. The repercussions can involve rejection by family and friends, loss of employment and for older lesbians and gay men, when they were younger, could have resulted in attempted extortion, imprisonment and exclusion from their children, which still exists in some countries. Disclosure is not a one-off event, but each new relationship or social event may involve a 'coming out' process.

The accepted view within a great deal of the literature denies that 'coming out' can be very positive. An event that brings to an end having to 'pass' as heterosexual and needing to construct pretend families or social life – never daring to admit going to local gay venues. The tension between those out activists and lesbians and gay men who are not as public about their sexuality is often palpable. This tension has a tendency to deny people's very real fears and significant cohort effects, all of which indicates some very different attitudes, particularly between some younger lesbians and gay men and their older counterparts.

Lee (1989) identifies the distinction in attitude and how people conduct their lives based on the current use of language and public displays as one of political confrontation, which he identifies as the exact opposite of 'passing' as heterosexual. This analysis relates to Goffman's (1963) work on stigma, which arises in part as a result of attributes but also the language of relationships. This distinction between public acknowledgement and private acceptance has prompted quite sharp comments, in fact, Berger (1982) considers the relationship between older and younger gay men to be one of mutual aversion:

> to a great extent, older homosexual men do not associate with younger homosexuals, and they believe that younger homosexuals will react negatively to them ... A vicious circle perpetuates

each generation's preconceived attitudes towards the other. Negative attitudes on the part of both generations lead to mutual avoidance ... the results of this process are all too evident in the gay community ... Homosexual rights groups and other civic organizations fail to attract many older gays, and those who do participate rarely occupy leadership positions. (Berger, 1982: 160)

Minnigerode and Adelman (1978) identified that many older lesbians felt that their working lives had been constrained by their sexuality and this was a theme in Chafetz et al.'s (1974) work, where most older lesbians felt that they would have lost their jobs if their lesbianism had been known. A respondent in Tully's (1983) work, selectively disclosed her sexuality, with her family being less likely to be aware of her sexuality than her female friends.

Lieberman and Tobin observe that older gay men view the 'closet' as the 'only anchor left' (1983: 348), MacLean (1982) further comments that militant gay men are 'making a spectacle of themselves' (1982: 16). Vining (1981) provides some insight into this concern by noting that older gay men feel that current attitudes of tolerance and acceptance could change. Lee's (1989) longitudinal research identified that the majority of older gay men did not want to have their sexuality dominate or prefix their identity: 'They have no desire to be known at work or at home as a "gay doctor, gay banker, gay father or whatever"' (1989: 87).

This attitude influences participation in gay-related organizations, 70 per cent of Lee's (1989) sample did not participate in any gay organizations. The decision to participate in such organizations involves recognizing that an issue or theme is relevant or pertinent to their life and that such joining would add to a measure of life satisfaction. For the older lesbian or gay man a further decision is required; that disclosing a closely held secret about their sexuality and the associated risk that this knowledge would become uncontrollably public as other members talk to other people. Of equal importance in this decision is the impact of ageism and sexism in limiting

participation with groups whose membership may be comprised predominantly of younger men and who may not welcome an older woman.

By contrast, gay activists may urge older lesbians and gay men to share their public persona. This attitude is captured by the editor of *The Advocate* who, writing in the mid-1980s, comments:

And what are you hiding from? Aren't you a little tired of the work all this subterfuge requires? ... If your experience of coming out is at all like mine and that of millions of others who have come out, you will find that your friends and acquaintances already know that you are gay. And maybe they will feel a deeper respect for you ... maybe they will reject you ... What then? Read *The Advocate* and other gay media, and you will find gay people creating new realities, like immigrants, in communities of our own construction throughout the country. There is a place for you, too, in all of this, a place where you can be honest and perhaps find love and almost certainly find friendship. (*The Advocate*, 20 August 1985: 5).

This issue of public openness, but more importantly participation and contact with the broader lesbian and gay community, has led researchers and commentators to assert that individual happiness for older lesbians and gay men can only be achieved by such involvement. A number of researchers have drawn a correlation between being openly gay or lesbian and life satisfaction. Friend (1980) maintains that the greater the number of interactive roles in which the person is open about their sexuality, the greater is their self-esteem and necessarily satisfaction with their life. Other researchers (Lee, 1989; Berger, 1982), however, do not draw the same conclusion. Lee in fact comments that his longitudinal respondents 'clearly demonstrated the capacity of gay men to lead personally and professionally rewarding lives, while remaining highly secretive about their sexuality and bearing the burdens of "passing" in a heterosexist society' (1989: 84). Lee's (1989) findings are supported by Adelman (1991), who identified a correlation between high life satisfaction and low involvement with other gay men, low levels of disclosure of the nature of their sexuality and a decrease in the importance of being gay. In a similar vein, Wahler and Gabbay (1997) identified the importance of self-acceptance rather than public acknowledgement.

Participation, as we have seen, involves public acknowledgement of one's own sexuality with all the associated fears and anxieties and possibly acting in a manner that contradicts life-long beliefs and patterns of behaviour. Lee asserts that 'the self-rated happier (gay) elders were much more likely to participate in the gay community than the unhappy' (1989: 89). Given that 70 per cent of his longitudinal sample do not participate with the community, the conclusion to be reached is that this group are unhappy. This directly contradicts his earlier comment identified above.

SOCIAL SUPPORT

The practicalities of social support assume greater significance for the researchers of issues related to older lesbians and gay men, particularly given the image portrayed by Kehoe of 'disapproval and distancing by their relatives, [with older lesbians and gay men] left with no meaningful human contacts' (1991: 137). Francher and Henkin (1973) also noted that while family support may have been withdrawn as a result of the person's sexuality this support had been replaced by friendship networks.

Kehoe's image has added to that of Berger (1980) who states:

> older [homosexual] men are depicted as isolated from other homosexual males, both young and old, who place great importance on the good looks of youth. Older homosexual men are believed to have unhappy sex lives, if any, and to resort to 'tearooms', hustlers and young children for sexual gratification. They become effeminate, are socially unacceptable to other adults and are labeled as 'old queens'. (1980: 163)

Berger's description of the ageing process that gay men undertake involves desperation, a change in personality and eventually a change in sexual expression. Hardly surprising that older lesbians and gay men become socially isolated.

In respect to older people generally, an association is identified between support network and mental health, in particular depression (Phifer and Murrell, 1989; Russell and Cutrona, 1991). If the primary sources of social support for older people are their relatives, the implications for older lesbians and gay men who stereotypically are thought to live much more isolated lives, are higher incidences of depression. However, in their research, Dorfman et al. have identified: 'no significant differences between older homosexuals and heterosexuals with regard to depression and over all social support, despite significantly less family support in the homosexual group … Apparently a homosexual orientation among the elderly does not impede development of a socially supportive network' (1995: 39).

The health-related consequences of this research for 'friends-based social networks' are identified by Dorfman et al. (1995) as:

- Friends are more likely to give freely and without obligations whereas families have increased expectations and demands.
- Friends are more empathic listeners than families who have vested interests in avoiding and denying difficult areas.
- Friends provide fun.

They go on to comment that the shared experience of being gay in a heterosexual world has strengthened the relationships that exist between older lesbians and gay men.

Older lesbians' social support is drawn from within the gay and lesbian community. In times of crisis support is frequently obtained from lesbian friendship networks rather than heterosexual friends, siblings or other family members. Indeed, at such times, there is often a reporting of isolation from the general heterosexual culture. (Albro et al., 1977; Chafez et al., 1974; Minnigerode and Adelman, 1978; Raphael and Robinson, 1980; Tully, 1983). Jacobs et al. (1999) identifies that older lesbians prefer to relate to their own age group for their social and sexual needs, however, 66 per cent of Kehoe's (1986) survey had been involved in a cross-generational relationship where the age difference varied from 20–53 years. The vast majority of older lesbians in Raphael and Robinson's (1980) research had lost a partner at some point, with 53 per cent reporting little support after the loss.

The implications are clear. Older lesbians and gay men, on the whole, have vibrant social lives, which involve mutual support. As individuals, they gain a great deal from these support networks, which may include increased enjoyment and happiness with their lives. Such conclusions would make Berger's (1980) profile of older lesbians and gay men seem irrelevant and not reflective of the reality of older lesbians and gay men's lives.

In terms of more formal support, Jacobs et al. (1999) identify that older lesbians and gay men may be hesitant in approaching and using social services, even if specific services are available. The rationale that they identified for such hesitance in service up-take is located within older lesbians and gay men's own internalized homophobia and historical social stigma. The consequence of this internalized homophobia, defined by Kominars as 'the fear of, and hatred of one's homosexuality' (1995: 29–30) can be low self-esteem, greater isolation and poor social interaction. Jacobs et al. (1999) go on to comment that many older lesbians viewed professionals associated with the support services, as not accepting their sexuality and wanting to 'cure' them.

While support may be drawn from friends, Berger (1982) notes that other institutional arrangements can impact negatively on the wishes of older lesbians and gay men and deny the existence or access of friends at critical times. Berger (1982) cites institutional policies, legal discrimination, medical oversight and social service agencies' neglect for much of

this negative impact. Thus, hospitals and nursing homes may deny access to a gay partner based on a failure to recognize the relationship and families can and do contest wills that leave property to a surviving partner.

ACCELERATED AGEING

Much of the research on issues related to older lesbians and gay men has been conducted in the United States and Australia, and has interestingly identified the issue of self-identification *vis-à-vis* age. The reference to accelerated ageing is purely an issue of self-identification and does not imply that lesbians and gay men experience premature ageing directly as a result of their sexuality. The emphasis on the body young being the body beautiful, within the lesbian and gay community (in particular, the gay male community), reflects the extent of ageist attitudes. The result is that people who are in mid-life are, or feel they are, disregarded and no longer attractive or sought after. This belief is reflected in a colloquialism, which asserts that 'nobody loves a fairy over forty'.

The consequence of this is that some older lesbians and gay men – more notably gay men, identify themselves as old, decades before their heterosexual counterparts. Bennett and Thompson comment that:

> because of the gay community's emphasis on youth, homosexual men are considered middle-aged and elderly by other homosexual men at an earlier age than heterosexual men in the general community. Since these age-status norms occur earlier in the gay subculture, the homosexual man thinks of himself as middle-aged and old before his heterosexual counterpart does. (1991: 66)

The evidence of accelerated ageing is contradictory. Friend (1980) undertaking research in Philadelphia advertised for older gay men with the result that over 90 per cent of the respondents were aged under 64 years – the youngest was aged 32 years. However, Laner (1978) in her analysis of gay and heterosexual contact

adverts in newspapers concluded that there
was no evidence of accelerated ageing.

In terms of age-related norms, Minnigerode
(1976) undertook research to identify how
gay men aged between 25 and 68 years old
defined themselves using chronological
stages in life (young, middle-aged and old)
and placed themselves within these stages.
All the men in their twenties, 80 per cent of
the men in their thirties and 28 per cent of the
men in their forties considered themselves
as young. The rest regarded themselves as
middle-aged. The mean ages for middle-
aged was 41.29 years and 64.78 years for
old age.

Neugarten et al. (1965) established similar figures among heterosexuals, and Minnigerode (1976) concluded that accelerated
ageing did not exist. Kelly (1977, 1980)
asked gay men who were aged between 16
and 79 when these stages in life began and
ended. The conclusion was that the majority
regarded youth as starting before 18 years
and ending at 30, middle-age started and
finished between the ages of 30 and
50 years and old age started at 50 years. The
conclusion reached was that accelerated
ageing did exist.

Bennett and Thompson (1991) employed
a symbolic interactionist approach in their
research on accelerated ageing. Their con-
tention was that gay men live in two worlds –
that of the gay community and that of the
wider society – thus, an examination of the
duality of gay men's experience was essential in understanding attitudes to ageing.
They established that there was no claim for
the existence of accelerated ageing based on
the gay men's self-identification. However,
they did establish that gay men believe that
other gay men view the stages of life as
occurring earlier than with the rest of
society.

This self-identification has affected some
of the research undertaken on issues related
to older lesbians and gay men. However,
interestingly when asked, the people who
self-identify as old recognize a distinction
between the significance of age in the gay
community and the rest of society.

RESEARCH ISSUES

The emerging research related to older
lesbians and gay men does not lead to a
unified theory about gay and lesbian ageing
and, in fact, as Jacobs et al. (1999) have
identified in relation to research associated
with social service needs, there are several
different and often contradictory theoretical
approaches. Equally, some of the literature
and research maintain theoretical stances
drawn from mainstream sociology, which is
not explicitly identified within the material.
Hence, the assertion of both activity and
disengagement theory as themes within the
literature.

Jacobs et al. (1999) in their review of the
literature also maintain that other methodological problems exist in the research,
related to:

- The use of non-probability sampling
  because conceptual and logistical problems make a truly representative sample
  difficult to achieve.
- The nature of the samples employed
  reflect white, middle-class, educated,
  urban dwellers.
- Most studies are descriptive.
- Use of non-standardized measures
  undermines the validity and reliability of
  the studies.
- Single source data collection (usually
  interviews).
- Maintaining a sexist bias by not identifying single sex or unbalanced sex ratios.
- A lack of consistency in defining age
  cohorts.

Harry has identified a number of issues that
are related to the sampling of gay men and
in recognition of changing attitudes
acknowledges that 'considerable progress in
sampling gay men [has been made] since the
days when they were routinely gathered
from the prison and the psychiatric couch'
(1986: 210). These changes reflect the
growing confidence of both the lesbian and
gay male population, and also their availability in easily recognizable places. There

are also a large number of organizations involving and offering services to lesbians and gay men.

Harry (1986) identifies these later points as particularly problematic in trying to establish representative samples for research purposes. The explanation is related to the dominance of young people in gay areas and venues such that: 'the oldest and the youngest groups are less likely to go to gay bars, less likely to belong to gay organizations, to have mostly gay friends, to have many sexual partners and to be coupled. Therefore these groups have fewer opportunities to be sampled due to their lesser involvement in the gay community' (1986: 23). In some respects these comments do not reflect the evidence outlined above about some aspects of older lesbians and gay men's lives – networks and partners, while other elements do reflect patterns of living. The key appears to be involvement with the gay community, which may mean regular attendance at bars and membership of organizations.

Patently, there are not enough bars in the world to accommodate us if we all choose to go out and organizations would be awash with volunteers if we all had to be a member of such a grouping. Lesbians and gay men, irrespective of age, make individual decisions about their involvement with the gay community. For some people, their decision not to disclose the nature of their sexuality would make such participation very difficult, for others the decision not to participate with the community may be based on class, gender or race. Age may be an additional factor in such decision-making.

Sampling lesbians differs by sample source, as noted by Harry (1986). Bell and Weinberg (1978) noted that two to three times more of their lesbian respondents came from personal contacts, and no respondents came from places of overtly sexual activity such as saunas. The implication that is drawn is that lesbian respondents may disproportionately live in couples who have highly domestic lives, and whose main contact with women is through the women's movement rather than lesbian organizations.

Researchers who restrict themselves to those who are in contact with the gay community will inevitably be involved with the over-sampling of the same population and miss large sections of lesbians and gay people who may simply not have access to a local community. In doing so, the researchers open themselves to criticism of skewing their samples and thereby leave open to question the outcomes of their work.

Researchers also need to be aware of the underpinning assumptions that they make about what it is to be a lesbian or gay man. Some of the research that we have seen maintains some very questionable assumptions, which seem to be located within heterosexual models of relationships. A powerful theoretical construct that has been exercised through most of the research related to life satisfaction among older lesbians and gay men is that of activity theory and the link between happiness and community participation. As identified above, this is a test that older heterosexuals do not have to pass, it is contradicted by other research and is based on the premise that coming out leads to happiness.

Harry (1986) offers some advice about advertising for respondents in the media. He notes that press adverts are more likely to be attractive to the educated and thereby produce an over-representation of this group. With a degree of optimism in respect of the budgets available to researchers, he goes on to identify that television reaches the broadest audience.

In all advertizing for respondents, motivation to participate is essential, because it involves the respondent contacting the researcher. This issue applies to all ethically sound research, be it ethnography or market research.

TOWARDS A HAPPIER OLD AGE

Wahler and Gabbay (1997) identify a number of what they refer to as 'unique challenges', for older lesbians and gay men, which includes the dominance of the youth culture in gay communities that gives rise to an early self-definition of age (accelerated ageing). They also identify discrimination as a challenge. Discrimination does exist, both directed towards older people *per se* and also towards lesbians and gay men. Rather than highlight the negative, we should perhaps seek to reinforce the positive with an assertion of the claim for equity. Equity on the part of age as well as equal treatment for all lesbians and gay men irrespective of age.

To assist the process of equal treatment we need to claim our history – to recognize our past. The current cohort of older lesbians and gay men has lived through a number of unique experiences which includes severe oppression. How many younger lesbians and gay men would recognize and understand the significance of the pink and black triangles (the sign of identification that gay men and lesbians were forced to wear in Nazi-occupied Europe)? We are aware of some of the names and lives of some of the more famous lesbians and gay men – Radcliffe Hall, Oscar Wilde and Alan Turin (the person who broke the Enigma code and invented the computer) but what of ordinary lives? What was it like to be a lesbian or gay man growing up in Manchester or New York in the early part of the last century? What skills did they need in order to survive?

Most of the current cohort of older lesbian and gay men will die in the next twenty years or so. Upon their death, we will lose a great deal of our oral history. As a result we will have to rely on the recorded experiences of a few famous lesbians and gay men that will not reflect the day-to-day life experiences of the hundreds and thousands of lesbians and gay men. The other source of material will be that located in the heterosexual world with the consequence that our history will be written through the eyes of heterosexuals. If our claims to 'community' are to mean anything, we must write our own history and therefore we must act now to record this history.

OLDER PEOPLE: MORE SIMILARITIES THAN DIFFERENCES?

The research that has been outlined in this work, while contradictory in places, does identify that there are a number of similarities between older lesbians and gay men and older heterosexuals. Possibly, the experience of ageing in a youth-orientated society is felt more generally than the issues of diversity that are increasingly being recognized as characteristics of older people.

Lee (1987) concludes that older heterosexuals do not have as much to learn from older lesbians and gay men about coping with ageing as Berger (1982) would suggest and that the major variables associated with life satisfaction in later life were health, wealth and loneliness. Of these, health is viewed as the most significant variable (Larson, 1978) with increasing dependence affecting self-esteem and morale (Clark and Anderson, 1967; Atchley, 1977). Lowenthal and Haven (1968) note that even with the moral support of loved ones and a good income, these do not impact significantly in the assessment of life satisfaction when health is poor.

Income levels were a significant variable in assessing life satisfaction for both lesbian and gay older people as well as for older heterosexuals. Lee (1987) comments that age is no leveller and that in fact the rich fare better in later life as they do earlier in life than the poor. An association with social class is drawn, which identifies that the higher the social class, the greater reporting of happiness in late life and that education was linked to class status.

The other major area of diversity in later life is that of cultural identity and black older people. If similar findings are identified in research related to black older people, then the issue is one of age and the social response to ageing. In terms of the response, the most significant point would be related to resources available for older people post-retirement, whether this is income replacement, access to continuing education or health promotion.

'QUEERING' GERONTOLOGY

The preceding decades have generated a lot of research and reflection on issues related to black older people and this in turn has prompted gerontologists to have more regard for the existence of diversity within the group of people generally referred to as 'the elderly'. It stands to reason that a group of people who have passed a socially constructed age barrier and who may have 40-plus years difference in their ages, will have many differences in life experience.

Feminist commentators such as Arber and Ginn (1995) have encouraged us to acknowledge that the experience of late life is in fact the experience of women reflecting differential mortality rates which have the result that women live longer. The current understanding of late life is very different to the days when disengagement theory and political economy were in their own ways thought to be radical reflections on issues related to age and ageing.

The existence and experience of older lesbians and gay men will add to the debate about diversity in late life and encourage further reflections on the experience of ageing. Necessarily this should impact on service delivery with challenges to current practice and the automatic ascription of heterosexuality, in the same way that services have to consider racial and ethnic differences and the needs of, for example, black older people. As such, models of care will need to be developed or refined to encapsulate such diversity.

The contribution to existing debates on age and ageing is important, but it is not the only impact that older lesbians and gay men will make to gerontology. Existing research already challenges our theoretical understandings of ageing in spite of the incorporation of relatively orthodox gerontological theory. 'Queering' the accepted theoretical constructs will in time give rise to better understanding of not only the position of older lesbians and gay men but also older people generally. In contributing to this process an important question that needs to be answered is: can lesbians and gay men make a claim for cultural identity?

The answer to this question will be based on the nature of our differences in relation to heterosexuals. This is not to assert the existence of a 'gay gene' that makes us different, but rather the precepts upon which we conduct our lives, interact with each other and the rest of society and reflect on what is important to us as individuals and as a collectivity. It may mean that the shared experience of oppression and discrimination is the only thing that brings us together in some expression of culture, but it may also mean that there are differences and the recognition of these are vitally important.

How much queering gerontology as a field of study we will experience has yet to be fully explored. However, we can anticipate a significant questioning of theoretical assumptions and the potential of new theoretical constructs. We can also expect the development of new knowledge that is specific to older lesbians and gay men as well as that informed by such studies but related to heterosexual older people. We have waited a long time for the 'discovery' of older lesbians and gay men, we now wait with anticipation for its effect.

NOTES

1 Section 2a of the Local Government Act 1988 forbids local authorities in England and Wales (the section has recently been repealed in Scotland) from devoting resources that promote homosexuality and prevented 'the teaching in any maintained school of homosexuality as a pretend family relationship' (Brown, 1998: 26).

2 Beth Jordace was a lesbian character in a long-running television series who was involved with her mother in the death and subsequent disposal of the body of her violent father.

3 The State Earnings Related Pension Scheme (SERPS) was a British Government initiative, which aimed to increase the value of state pensions.

4 The pension link refers to the annual increase in pensions being tied to rises in average earnings, this link was abandoned to be replaced by a link with inflation with the result that state pensions rise year on year at a much lower level than earnings.

REFERENCES

Adelman, M. (1991) 'Stigma, gay lifestyles and adjustment to aging: a study of later-life gay men and lesbians', *Journal of Homosexuality*, 20 (3/4): 7–32.

Albro, J.C., Kessler, B. and Tully, C.T. (1997) 'A study of lesbian lifestyles', Masters thesis, Virginia Commonwealth University.

Arber, S. and Ginn, J. (1995) *Connecting Gender and Ageing*, Buckingham: Open University Press.

Atchley, R. (1977) *The Social Forces in Later Life.* 2nd edition. Belmont, CA: Wadsworth.

Bell, A. and Weinberg, M. (1978) *Homosexualities.* New York: Simon and Schuster.

Bennett, K.C. and Thompson, N.L. (1980) 'Social and psychological functioning of the ageing male homosexual', *British Journal of Psychiatry*, 138: 361–70.

Bennett, K.C. and Thompson, N.L. (1991) *Accelerated Aging and Male Homosexuality: Australian Evidence in a Continuing Debate.* New York: Harrington Park Press.

Berger, R.M. (1980) 'Psychological adaptation of the older homosexual male', *Journal of Homosexuality*, 5 (3): 161–75.

Berger, R.M. (1982) 'The unseen minority – older gays and lesbians', *Social Work*, 27 (3): 236–42.

Berger, R.M. (1984) 'Realities of gay and lesbian aging', *Social Work*, 299: 57–62.

Blau, Z.S. (1957) *Old Age: A Study of Change in Status.* Ann Arbor, MI: University Microfilms.

Bracher, E.M. (1984) *Love, Sex and Aging*, Boston: Little Brown.

Brown, C. (1998) *Social Work and Sexuality: Working with Lesbians and Gay Men.* London: Macmillan.

Butler, R.N. (1987) 'Ageism', in *The Encyclopedia of Ageing.* New York: Springer. pp. 22–3.

Chafetz, J.S., Sampson, P., Beck, P. and West, J. (1974) 'A study of homosexual women', *Social Work*, 19 (60): 714–23.

Clark, M. and Anderson, B. (1967) *Culture and Aging.* Springfield, IL: Thomas.

Cumming, E. and Henry, W. (1961) *Growing Old.* New York: Basic Books.

D'Augelli, A. (1994) 'Lesbian and gay development: steps toward an analysis of lesbians and gay men's lives', in A.R. D'Augelli and C.J. Patterson (eds), *Lesbian, Gay and Bisexual Identities over the Life Span.* New York: Oxford University Press.

Dawson, K. (1982) *Serving the Older Community.* SIECUS Report (5–6). New York: Sex Education and Information Council of the United States.

Dorfman, R., Walters, K., Burke, P., Hardin, L., Karanik, J. and Silverstein, E. (1995) 'Old, sad and alone: the myth of the ageing homosexual', *Journal of Gerontological Social Work*, 24 (1/2): 29–45.

Francher, J.S. and Henkin, J. (1973) 'The menopausal queen: adjustment to aging and the male homosexual', *American Journal of Orthopsychiatry*, 43: 670–4.

Friend, R. (1980) 'Gayging: adjustment and the older gay male', *Alternative Lifestyles*, 3 (2): 231–48.

Fontana, J.S. (1977) *The Last Frontier.* Beverly Hills: Sage Publications.

GLHC (1985) *Gays and Lesbians in Health Care.* Toronto, Gay Archives.

Goffman, E. (1963) *Stigma: Notes on the Management of Spoiled Identity.* New York: Prentice-Hall.

Goleman Wolf, D. (1982) *Growing Older: Lesbians and Gay Men.* Berkeley, CA: University of California Press.

Gray, H. and Dressel, P. (1985) 'Alternative interpretations of aging among gay males', *Gerontologist*, 25 (1): 83–7.

Harry, J. (1986) 'Sampling gay men', *The Journal of Sex Research*, 22 (1): 21–34.

Havighurst, R.J. (1963) 'Successful ageing', in R.H. Williams, C. Tibbitts and W. Donahue (eds), *Process of Ageing*, Vol. 1. New York: Atherton. pp. 299–320.

Hochschild, A.R. (1975) 'Disengagement theory: a critique and a proposal', *American Sociological Review*, 40: 553–69.

Jacobs, B. (1990) 'Aging and politics', in R.H. Binstock and L.K. George (eds), *Handbook of Aging and the Social Sciences.* San Diego: Academic Press.

Jacobs, R.J., Rasmussen, L.A. and Hohan, M.M. (1999) 'The social support needs of older lesbians, gay men and bisexuals', *Journal of Gay and Lesbian Social Services*, 9 (1): 1–30.

Kehoe, M. (1986) 'Lesbians over 65: a triple invisible minority', in *Historic, Literary and Erotic Aspects of Lesbianism.* London: The Howarth Press.

Kehoe, M. (1991) 'Loneliness and the ageing homosexual: is pet therapy the answer?', *Journal of Homosexuality*, 20 (3/4): 137–41.

Kelly, J.J. (1977) 'The ageing male homosexual', *The Gerontologist*, 17 (4): 328–30.

Kelly, J.J. (1980) 'Homosexuality and ageing', in J. Marmor (ed.), *Homosexual Behavior; A Modern Reappraisal.* New York: Basic Books.

Kimmel, D.C. (1977a) 'Patterns of aging among gay men', *Christopher Street*, November: 28–31.

Kimmel, D.C. (1977b) 'Psychotherapy and the older gay man', *Psychotherapy: Theory, Research and Practice*, 14 (4): 386–93.

Kimmel, D.C. (1978) 'Adult development and aging: a gay perspective', *Journal of Social Issues*, 34 (3): 113–30.

Kimmel, D.C. (1980) 'Life history interviews of aging gay men', *International Journal of Aging and Human Development*, 10 (3): 239–48.

Kochman, A. (1997) 'Gay and lesbian elderly: historical overview and implications for social work practice', *Journal of Gay and Lesbian Social Services*, 6 (1): 1–10.

Kominars, S.B. (1995) 'Homophobia: heart of darkness', *Journal of Gay and Lesbian Social Services*, 2 (1): 29–39.

Kooden, H. (1997) 'Successful aging in the middle aged gay man: a contribution to developmental theory', *Journal of Gay and Lesbian Social Services*, 6 (3): 21–43.

Kurdeck, L.A. (1988) 'Perceived social support in gays and lesbians in cohabitating relationships', *Journal of Personality and Social Psychology*, 54 (3): 504–9.

Kurdeck, L.A. and Schmitt, J.P. (1987) 'Perceived emotional support from family and friends in members of the homosexual, married and heterosexual cohabiting couples', *Journal of Homosexuality*, 14 (3/4): 57–68.

Kutner, B., Fanshel, D., Toga, A. and Langer, T. (1956) *Five Hundred Over Sixty*. New York: Russell Sage Foundation.

Laner, M.R. (1978) 'Growing older male: heterosexual and homosexual', *The Gerontologist*, 18: 496–501.

Laner, M.R. (1979) 'Growing older female: heterosexual and homosexual', *Journal of Homosexuality*, 4 (3): 267–75.

LaRosa, P. (1982) 'Within a minority, another minority', *New York Daily News*, 16 April.

Larson, R. (1978) 'Thirty years of research on the subjective well-being of older Americans', *Journal of Gerontology*, 33: 109–25.

Lee, J.A. (1987) 'What can homosexual aging studies contribute to theories of aging?', *Journal of Homosexuality*, 13 (4): 43–71.

Lee, J.A. (1989) 'Invisible men: Canada's aging homosexuals. Can they be assimilated into Canada's "liberated" gay communities?', *Canadian Journal on Aging*, 8 (1): 79–97.

Lieberman, M. and Tobin, S. (1983) *The Experience of Old Age*. New York: Basic Books.

Lowenthal, M.F. and Haven, C. (1968) 'Interaction and adaptation: intimacy as a critical variable', *American Sociological Review*, 33, 20–30.

Lukes, S. (1973) *Individualism*. New York: Harper.

MacLean, J. (1982) '"Old and growing" report on the first national conference on lesbian and gay ageing', *The Advocate*, 7 January: 15.

Minnigerode, F.A. (1976) 'Age-status labeling in homosexual men', *Journal of Homosexuality*, 13: 43–71.

Minnigerode, F.A. and Adelman, M.R. (1978) 'Elderly homosexual women and men: report on a pilot study', *Family Coordinator*, October, 451–6.

Morgan, L. and Kunkel, S. (1998) *Aging: The Social Context*. California, Pine Forge.

Neugarten, B.L., Moore, J.W. and Lowe, J.C. (1965) 'Age norms, age constraints and adult socialization', *American Journal of Sociology*, 70: 710–17.

Norman, A. (1985) *Triple Jeopardy: Growing Old in a Second Homeland*. London: Centre for Policy on Ageing.

Palmore, E. (1968) 'The effects of aging on activities and attitudes', *The Gerontologist*, 8: 259–63.

Phifer, J.F. and Murrell, S.A. (1989) 'Etiology factors in the onset of depressive symptoms in older adults', *Journal of Abnormal Psychology*, 95 (30): 282–91.

Pope, M. and Schulz, R. (1990) 'Sexual attitudes and behaviour in midlife and aging homosexual males', *Journal of Homosexuality*, 20 (3–4): 169–77.

Raphael, S.M. and Robinson, M.K. (1980) 'Adaptation and age-related expectations of older gay and lesbian adults', *The Gerontologist*, 32 (3): 367–74.

Roadburg, A. (1985) *Aging: Retirement, Leisure and Work in Canada*. Toronto: Methuen.

Russell, D.W. and Cutrona, C.E. (1991) 'Social support, stress and depressive symptoms among the elderly: test of a process model', *Psychology and Ageing*, 6 (2): 190–201.

Ryder, N.B. (1965) 'The cohort as a concept in the study of social change', *American Sociological Review*, 30: 843–61.

Tully, C.T. (1983) 'Social support systems of a selected sample of older women', doctoral dissertation, Virginia Commonwealth University.

Vining, D. (1981) 'The advantages of age', *The Advocate*, 19 March: 22–4.

Wahler, J. and Gabbay, S.G. (1997) 'Gay male aging: a review of the literature', *Journal of Gay and Lesbian Social Services*, 6 (3): 1–20.

Weeks, J. (1983) 'The problem of older homosexuals', in J. Hart and D. Richardson (eds), *The Theory and Practice of Homosexuality*. London: Routledge and Kegan Paul. pp. 177–85.

Weinberg, M.S. (1969) 'The ageing male homosexual', *Medical Aspects of Sexuality*, 3 (12): 66–72.

Weinberg, M.S. (1970) 'The male homosexual: age-related variations in social and psychological characteristics', *Social Problems*, 17: 527–38.

Weinberg, M.S. and Williams, C. (1974) *Male Homosexuals*. New York: Oxford University Press.

Whitford, G.S. (1997) 'Realities and hopes for older gay males', in Jean K. Quam (ed.), *Social Services for Senior Gay Men and Lesbians*. London: The Howarth Press, pp. 79–95.

11

Queer Diaspora

ANNE-MARIE FORTIER

Recent developments in 'queer' and 'diaspora' theories have attended to the complexities of 'postmodern' and postcolonial forms of belonging through their interventions on issues of time, space, identity, and embodiment. More specifically, queer and diaspora are used to host a decisive change of orientation away from primordial identities established alternatively by either nature or culture. By embracing queer and/or diaspora, theories of identity turn instead toward contingency, indeterminacy, power, and conflict.

This chapter examines the intersections of theoretical discourses of diaspora with those of queer, in what has been termed 'queer diasporas' (see also Mort, 1994; Watney, 1995; Gopinath, 1996; Cant, 1997; Eng, 1997; Patton and Sánchez-Eppler, 2000; Sinfield, 2000). A central aim is to examine the implications of presuming a diasporic queer subject. What does it mean to project queer sexualities within a diasporic framework?

Diaspora has been taken up by gay, lesbian and queer theorists in two ways. The first usage refers to the creation of queer spaces within ethnically defined diasporas[1] (Mason-John and Khambatta, 1993; Ratti, 1994; Gopinath, 1996; Leong, 1996; Takagi, 1996; Tamburri, 1996; Eng, 1997; Eng and Hom, 1998). In the narrowest sense, 'queering the diaspora' (Puar, 1998), in this collection of

work, forces a reconsideration of the heterosexist norms supporting definitions of ethnic diasporas. In the broadest sense, it argues for a critical methodology for evaluating ethnic-diasporic formations across multiple axes of difference and in their numerous local and global manifestation (Eng, 1997: 39). The term queer is expanded, in this latter case, to define itself 'against the normal rather than [merely] the heterosexual' (Warner, in Eng, 1997: 50, n35).

Although I will briefly discuss, below, the implications of defining queer against normality, or *as* strange, the main focus of this chapter is on the second usage of 'queer diaspora' that has surfaced in the context of the transnationalization of gay and lesbian identity politics: 'diasporizing the queer' (Puar, 1998). In this context, 'queer diaspora' refers to the transnational and multicultural network of connections of queer cultures and 'communities'. What interests me here is the way in which diaspora is put to work, the way it is mobilized in the definition of a transnational queer culture and 'community'. What is it about 'diaspora' that appeals to queer theorists? What kinds of imaginings does 'queer diaspora' foster? What kinds of spatiotemporal horizons does diaspora sustain when conjugated with 'queer'?[2]

I begin with a short definition of 'diaspora' in critical cultural theory, followed by a close reading of selected texts that suggest a 'diasporic turn' in queer theory. A central aim of this chapter is to examine the sort of claims being made in support of the conjugation of queerness and diaspora. In other words, I critically assess how 'diaspora' has been taken up and put to work together with 'queer' in the formation of an imagined diasporic queer community and culture.[3] In sum, this chapter is an inquisitive rather than a summative piece: I invite readers to reflect upon the claims made in the name of a 'queer diaspora', and to identify issues and questions that are raised by these claims.

THE RENEWED CURRENCY OF DIASPORA

Theoretical discourses about diaspora have noticeably proliferated in recent years, namely, within anti-absolutist critiques of identity formation that attempt to account for the complexities of culture in a transnational, postmodern, postcolonial world (Hall, 1988, 1990; Gilroy, 1993a, 2000; Clifford, 1994; Dhaliwal, 1994; Brah, 1996; Radhakrishnan, 1996; Fortier, 2000). Once used to describe exiled and forced dispersal of Jews or Armenians, 'diaspora' is now widely used to describe transnational networks of immigrants, refugees, guest-workers, and so on. Deployed from a transnational and intercultural perspective in opposition to ethnically absolute approaches to migration, the term converses with other terms such as border, transculturation, travel, creolization, *mestizaje,* hybridity (Clifford, 1994; Gilroy, 1994).

When thinking of diaspora, we must bear in mind that the present circulation of the term in cultural theory derives from the historically specific experience of the 'black Atlantic' (Gilroy, 1993a) and of anti-Zionist critiques of the return to Israel (Marienstras, 1975, 1989; Boyarin and Boyarin, 1993). In the work of Paul Gilroy on black responses to modernity, the themes of suffering, tradition, spatiality, temporality and the social

organization of memory have a special significance resulting from their association with ideas of dispersal, exile and slavery (Gilroy, 1993a: 205; Gilroy, 2000).

Diaspora is not about travel or nomadism. Central to its definition are 'push factors', that is, forced migration or displacement (Clifford, 1994; Gilroy, 1994: 207). Slavery, pogroms, genocide, famine, political persecutions and wars may be sources of the dispersal of populations.[4] Paired with the emphasis on push factors is the stress on conditions of settlement within countries of immigration, which involve the rearticulation of multiple locations, temporalities and identifications in the effort to create new terrains of belonging within the place of migration. As James Clifford writes: 'the term *diaspora* is a signifier, not simply of transnationality and movement, but of political struggles to define the local, as distinctive of community, in historical contexts of displacement' (1994: 306; italics in original).

Diaspora constitutes a rich heuristic device to think about questions of belonging, continuity, and solidarity in the context of dispersal and transnational networks of connection. Defined as decidedly anti-nationalist within critical cultural theory, it has been widely argued that the presence and experiences of diasporic subjects puts any normative notion of culture, identity, and citizenship in question by their very location *outside* of the time–space of the nation. As Paul Gilroy writes, diaspora is a distinctly 'outer-national term which contributes to the analysis of intercultural and transcultural processes and forms. It identifies a relational network characteristically produced through forced dispersal and reluctant scattering' (2000: 123).

More broadly, diaspora has become an emblem of multi-locality, 'post-nationality', and non-linearity of both movement and time. Questions of what it means to speak of home, community, identity, tradition and belonging have been reassessed in the context of the 'age of migration',[5] that is, the global circulation of culture, capital, and people. Notions of diaspora, transnationalism, bordercultures, migrancy, nomadism and homelessness push against the limits of established definitions of nation, community, and tradition. In this context, the renewed currency of theoretical discourses of 'diaspora', with their focus on displacement and transnational networks of connections, inserts itself within a wider shift of focus within contemporary Euro-American social sciences, where the spatial takes precedence over the temporal in understanding social change.[6] In sum, diaspora now signifies a site where 'new geographies of identity' (Lavie and Swedenburg, 1996) are negotiated across multiple terrains of belonging, producing what Avtar Brah (1996: 209) calls a 'diaspora space', located *between* 'the global' and 'the local'.

In the pages that follow, I examine the terms in which a common ground is established between queer and diaspora. Two themes emerge and are discussed in the first two sections, respectively: scattering and diversity, on the one hand, and exile and home, on the other. Running through this thematic structure is a concern about the tendency to ontologize diasporic subjects as emblems of dispersal and fragmentation. In other words, I am primarily interested in the way diaspora is construed as the basis of new cultural forms and identity formation that are conceived as inevitable outcomes of dispersal. Reading Frank Mort's words about a 'well-established homosexual diaspora' (1994: 202), and Alan Sinfield's response 'we know what he means' (2000: 103), I am intrigued by the kind of imaginary mapping conjured up by 'diaspora'. Without denying that there exists a 'productive exchange of information and enthusiasms' between British, American and Canadian activists and intellectuals (Mort, 1994: 202), I am interested in the shift away from viewing this as a transnational network of 'a *specific* group of actors' (ibid.; emphasis added) to seeing this as a symptom of a 'well-established diaspora'. As I state earlier, what interests me here is the emergence of a diasporic imagination in queer studies.

DIASPORIZING THE QUEER I: SCATTERING AND DIVERSITY

Scattering, diversity and relational networks of multi-local connections are largely what inspired some queer theorists and activists to find in diaspora a useful alternative to earlier considerations of gay/lesbian community and identity politics based on the ethnicity model.[7] Inviting their readers to consider the diasporic character of gay and lesbian communities dispersed world-wide, they seek to reveal the limits of cultural nationalisms, while finding, in diaspora, a useful heuristic device to think about the transnational character of gay/lesbian politics and culture (Walker, 1995; Watney, 1995; Gopinath, 1996), illuminate the 'complex nature of queerness in the postmodern world' (Patton and Sánchez-Eppler, 2000), or (re)think the problematic of home (Eng, 1997: 31). Overall, texts on queer diasporas move into a new spatialization of queer belongings, one which claims to recognize and problematize difference within unity (Gopinath, 1996; Puar, 1998).

In an article on the international implications of gay and lesbian politics in Europe and the USA, UK activist and writer Simon Watney finds the metaphor of diaspora:

> seductively convenient to contemporary queer politics. Unlike the tendency of seventies and eighties lesbian and gay theory to develop overly monolithic notions of identity and cultural politics, the concept of diaspora is suggestive of diversification, of scattering, fracturing, separate developments, and also, perhaps, of a certain glamor. It also suggests something of a sense of collective interest, however difficult this may be to pin down. It implies a complex divided constituency, with varying degrees of power and powerlessness. (1995: 59)

A recurring tension surfaces in reflections on queer diaspora, between the political imperative for transnational solidarity in the face of the violences experienced by queers world-wide, and the need to recognize that 'same-sex eroticism exists and signifies very differently in different … contexts'

(Gopinath, 1996: 123). Local struggles are also determined by locally specific forms of legal, political, religious and moral discursive formations. Moreover, 'queer' subjects themselves are multiple and diverse in all contexts, by virtue of their gender, class, ethnic, generational positions.

For example, Watney's main concern is for the political imperative to recognize the specificity of national struggles and issues in gay and lesbian politics, while identifying the transnational relational network that connects the dispersed queer political 'communities' within an 'imaginary unification' (1995: 60). Likewise, Frank Mort speaks of a 'well-established homosexual diaspora, crossing nation states and linking individuals and social constituencies, especially in the Western metropolitan centres', while he insists on recognizing the influence and significance of locally specific struggles and identity practices within the transnational network (1994: 202–3).

Encoding transnational queer culture and politics as diasporic may be read as a gesture that further emphasizes the new spatiotemporal horizon of queer consciousness in the postmodern 'global' world. One which is located between the constraining 'local'/ national, and the immodest pretensions of the 'global', but where both are reconfigured within an entangled web of connections. The question that arises is, how are 'the global' and 'the local' reconfigured? How are differences (local, cultural, national specificity) marked and recirculated into a new collectivity, a new 'we' cast within a diasporic unity?

Gayatri Gopinath alerts us to the 'dangers involved in framing queer sexuality diasporically' (1996: 123). Dangers that result from neo-colonial relations between 'the West' and 'the Rest' *within* the 'queer diaspora'. This may take on different forms, such as assumptions of the relative passivity of the non-Euro-American 'other', whose encounters with queer culture and politics are 'read solely as mimicry' (ibid.: 124). A number of authors have critically assessed the cultural imperialist thesis of globalization

in relation to queer culture and politics. If the influence of Euro-American discourses of gay/lesbian or queer cultures is powerful, they argue, local national responses to the globalization of queer culture are far from passive and are utterly diverse and creative (Altman, 1996, 1997, and in this volume; Morris, 1997; Manalansan, 1993, 1995).

This relates to the question: 'Whose queerness?', which Gopinath asks in view of highlighting the Euro-American centricity in definitions of what queer sexuality and queer culture consist of. One of the two examples of the diasporization of queer culture that Watney identifies, for instance, is the circulation of 'our queer cultural divinities' – including 'Divine, John Waters, Derek Jarman, Pasolini, Virginia Woolf, Elizabeth Bishop, Sylvia Townshend Warner, Morrisey, Frank O'Hare, k.d. lang' (1995: 65) – leading him to proclaim 'We have our own queer canon, and it is nothing if not diasporic' (ibid.). This proclamation immediately confines and defines the queer canon within Euro-American culture, whilst its diasporic character is founded on the multi-local 'origins' of its key protagonists.

A corollary question thus surfaces: whose diaspora? If diaspora signifies dispersal – hence movement and displacement – and diversity – founded on ideas of difference – who, then, are the moving and diverse subjects? A close reading of Watney's text is telling in this respect.

Watney's idea that diaspora evokes a 'certain glamor' is indicative of the tendency to use it merely as a voguish synonym of wandering and travel. The second, and seemingly closest, example he finds to a queer diasporic experience is:

> our direct experience of overseas travel, as well as of queer culture and its constitutive role in our personal lives. Few heterosexuals can imagine the sense of relief and safety which a gay man or lesbian finds in a gay bar or a dyke bar in a strange city in a foreign country. Even if one cannot speak the local language, we feel a sense of identification. Besides, we generally like meeting one another, learning about what is happening to people 'like us' from other parts of the world. (Watney, 1995: 61)

Watney's statement suggests that overseas travel is shared by 'us' universally. Obscuring racial, ethnic, class, and gender-based power relations that exist within the unifying 'us', Watney deploys diaspora as an emblem of undifferentiated mobility, not only presumed accessible to all, but presumed experienced by all. The experience of travel Watney is alluding to is most often than not founded on privilege and, for white Euro-American males, freedom of movement. Watney's traveling subject is disembodied: this body is invisible, unmarked, unquestioned, unchallenged. Yet as Jasbir Puar eloquently argues in her account of her travels, not all bodies move freely through borders. Her traveling body was also a body that was 'traveled upon': marked and read as threatening, inferior, undesirable other, 'some bodies must always negotiate the discursive structures that render [them] Other' (1994: 93).

The notion of bodies being traveled upon also suggests the ways in which the movement of some takes place through the fixing of others (Ahmed, 2002). Watney's travels towards other men 'like him' suggests that they must stay in place if their difference is to be apprehended and recirculated within the new diasporic horizon to create 'further diasporic diversity' (1995: 64). His own notion of diaspora is premised upon a pleasureseeking idea of traveling and crosscultural encounter that hides the power relations constitutive of the very conditions surrounding his movements: the 'exploitative nature of, sexual exchange behind, and economic motivations of interactions between those who travel and those who are traveled upon' (Puar, 1994: 91). His narrative involves 'modes of encounter that suggest the proximity of [gay men and lesbians] in different spaces within a globalized economy of difference. *But being "in it" clearly does not mean we are "in it" in the same way.'* (Ahmed, 2000: 171; emphasis added).

My point here is not to probe the motivations and practices of Watney-the-traveler himself, but it is to question the effects of exemplifying a queer diaspora through

travel. Who travels and who stays put? What is the relationship between them? How are those who stay put included into the folds of diasporic unity? To put it simply, what is the status of these subjects within the wider diasporic picture?

In Watney's text, the cultural complexity of a global gay culture is marked by local specificities located in the 'Orient', and which are then recast in an exercise of diasporic diversification:

> Moreover, local responses to the injustices surrounding most aspects of the [AIDS] epidemic are already bringing into being new, articulate groupings of men in countries such as India and the Philippines, where homosexual acts were not related to notions of identity before the epidemic. This will lead to still further diasporic diversity. For example, it is clear that there is no single answer to such questions as how one thinks of oneself if one is Indian, British, and gay. One man will identify as a black man, another as a gay Asian, and a third may reject the validity of the category gay altogether. There can be no easy resolution to such issues, nor is resolution required. On the contrary, it is the conflict between a gay political imperative to think of its constituency as unified and homogeneous, and the actual constantly changing complexity of gay culture as it is lived, that stimulates most of our greatest challenges today. (1995: 64)

In an interesting connection of global and local spheres, the gay diasporic constituency is signified by marking and locating 'diversity' and 'complexity' in the non-Western world and on non-white bodies. In addition, the use of the figure of the Indian British gay man as an emblem of the potential tensions and impossible resolutions that such diversification may ensue represents the challenges facing 'us' today. In contrast to the disembodied, unmarked *traveling* diasporic queer, diasporic *diversity* is marked on the Asian (British) male body, who becomes at once the origin of difference and a potential threat to unity.

Watney's encounters with 'people "like us" from other parts of the world' involve both differentiation and homogenization in the very production of the signifier 'queer diaspora'. He speaks of a universal diasporic 'we' by translating how 'they' live and struggle within communities, families, nations, and so on, into a 'we' that speaks (Ahmed, 2000: 173). Hence the formation of queers as diasporic agents 'involves a universalism predicated on a prior act of differentiation' (ibid).

The idea of a queer diaspora speaks of the fantasy of getting closer to the Other, but this is a fantasy that also elicits some tensions about the difficulties of imagining a 'unified and homogeneous' constituency without addressing the power structures that invariably operate within the 'community'. 'Queer diaspora' is put to work here as an image that is possible by concealing the relations of inequality and power that are an inherent part of it. Watney's 'our' reinstates the distance between 'us' and 'them' within his diasporic imagination, where differences remain fixed into place and simply add on to each other within the gradual diversification of diaspora. The constituency here is far from homogeneous; and perhaps the problem lies in this very conception of community as being based on commonality wrapped in the veneer of equality. While I support the political project of unifying against sexual oppression of all forms, the conceptual underpinnings of this project need to be interrogated since they impact on the politics of 'community' itself. I shall return to this point in the concluding section.

DIASPORIZING THE QUEER II: EXILE AND HOME

Although traumatic displacement is a distinctive feature of diasporic dispersal, *reducing* diaspora to forced dispersal holds the potential problem of assuming the primacy of an original placement. In other words, by establishing the defining moment of diaspora solely in its inception – the traumatic uprooting from geographically located origins – it is easy to reduce diaspora to its connection with a clearly bounded timespace: the 'homeland'. Indeed, relations with the

homeland are, for many social theorists, crucial in ascertaining diasporas and diasporic subjects (Conner, 1986; Safran, 1991; Tölölyan, 1996; Cohen, 1997). Consequently, such accounts risk engulfing diasporic populations into culturally unified groupings by virtue of their presumed 'common origin' and shared commitment to the homeland. These texts follow 'the familiar unidirectional idea of diaspora as a form of catastrophic but simple dispersal that enjoys an identifiable and reversible originary moment – the site of trauma' (Gilroy, 2000: 128).

Several queer theorists, seemingly aware of the limitations of such a reductionist view, dissociate 'origins' with the idea of a single, unitary cultural–geographical space in their version of 'queer diaspora'. Although some, like Michael Warner, dismiss the idea of a queer diaspora precisely because there is 'no locale from which to wander' (1993: xvii) – thus sustaining the foundational status of the homeland – others establish a connection between queer, diaspora, and exile, secured through the shared experience of forced movement away from an original home that does not occupy the same definitional status. For some, 'queer diaspora' rests on claims about the condition of exile and estrangement experienced by queer subjects, which locates them outside of the confines of 'home': the heterosexual family, the nation, the homeland. In this section, I explore the connection between moving out and coming out within the narrative of migration-as-emancipation that characterizes much of the discourse on queer migrations.

Described as a 'traumatic displacement from the lost heterosexual "origin"' by David Eng (1997: 32), queer migrations are conceived, by others, as a movement towards another site to be called 'home'. Thus Alan Sinfield writes:

> Indeed, while ethnicity is transmitted usually through family and lineage, most of us are born and/or socialized into (presumably) heterosexual families. We have to move away from them, at least to some degree; and *into,* if we are lucky,

the culture of a minority community. 'Home is the place you get to, not the place you came from', it says at the end of Paul Monette's novel, *Half-Way Home*. In fact, for lesbians and gay men the diasporic sense of separation and loss, so far from affording a principle of coherence for our subcultures, may actually attach to aspects of the (heterosexual) culture of our childhood, where we are no longer 'at home'. Instead of dispersing, we assemble. (2000: 103; italics in original)

The heterosexual family is posited as the originary site of trauma. This is evocatively expressed by Sinfield, who draws attention to how the 'diasporic sense of separation and loss' experienced by gay men and lesbians results from being cut off from the heterosexual culture of their childhood, which becomes the site of impossible return, the site of impossible memories. 'Everybody else had a childhood', writes Paul Monette about the imposed silence on young lesbians and gay men's growing-up stories (in Cant, 1997: 6). But the interesting twist to the narrative of the exile is that queers constitute a different diaspora because the originary site of trauma is not the basis of coherence. In a noteworthy reversal, 'home', here, is not an origin, but rather a destination; there is no return, only arrival. And it is an arrival that is always deferred. The queer diasporic journey is one of 'envisioning ourselves beyond the framework of normative heterosexism', but gay men and lesbians are 'stuck at the moment of emergence. For coming out is not once-and-for-all' (Sinfield, 2000: 103). Sinfield's suggestion of home as always in the making, endlessly deferred, hints at a radical discomfiture of the idea of 'home' as a space of coherence and continuity, also found in utopian visions of diaspora as radically anti-nationalist (Gilroy, 2000).

To be sure, both queer and diaspora compel us to re-think the problematic of home. '[S]uspended between an 'in' and an 'out' ... – between origin and destination, and between private and public – queer [and diasporic] entitlements to home and a nation-state remain doubtful' (Eng, 1997: 32). The notion of 'diaspora' opens up 'a

historical and experiential rift between the locations of residence and the locations of belonging' (Gilroy, 2000: 124). This 'in-betweenness' is conceived as a constitutive feature of diaspora identity (Clifford, 1994; Brah, 1996). However, exclusively defined in spatial terms, diasporic in-betweenness comes to a halt when it comes to gender and sexual identities. In this respect, 'queer' expands the idea of in-betweenness to include sexualities located between the polarized heterosexual/homosexual.

Hence the conjugation of queer with diaspora potentially produces a wedge between fixed gender roles and sexualities and brings to the fore the question of the reproductive moment of diaspora. When conjugated with 'queer', the anti-nationalist proclivities of diaspora are amplified through the narrative of migration as homecoming rather than as homeleaving, where 'home' is not (re)produced in the heterosexual family. Indeed, many diasporic cultural forms repeat nationalist biopolitics that posit the heterosexual, patriarchal family as the preferred institution capable of reproducing traditions and an original culture. In such cases, the indeterminacy of a dispersed and fragmented identity is solved by gendered encodings of culture, where definitions of authenticity are defined by ideas about family, fixed gender roles, and generational responsibility: women as reproducers of absolute cultural difference, men as protectors of cultural integrity and allegiance, and generations as bearers of cultural continuity and change (Gilroy, 1993b; Gopinath, 1995; Fortier, 2000; Gilroy, 2000). Queer diasporas, for their part, decidedly 'propagate' outside of the nation-building narrative where the heterosexual family is the essential building-block in the construction and elevation of the nation. In short, the invocation of queer diaspora potentially denaturalizes 'any claims on the nation-state and home as inevitable functions of the heterosexual' (Eng, 1997: 35).[8]

Which is not to say that queer or diaspora could be simply read as emphatic refusals of the home(land). Queer and diasporic narratives of belonging often deploy 'homing desires' (Brah, 1996: 180): the desire to *feel at home* achieved by physically or symbolically (re)constituting spaces which provide some kind of ontological security in the context of migration. As David Eng states, 'despite frequent and trenchant queer dismissals of home and its discontents, it would be a mistake to underestimate enduring queer affiliations to this concept' (1997: 32). For example, the widespread narrative of migration as homecoming, within queer culture, establishes an equation between leaving and becoming, and creates a distinctively queer migrant subject: one who is forced to get out in order to come out. Books such as Paul Monette's *Halfway Home,* where 'home' is a destination, or John Preston's *Hometowns: Gay Men Write about Where they Belong,* where home is 'where we come from' and conjures up stories of 'exile, abandonment, redemption, salvation, reconciliation' (1991: 14), reproduce a model of home as familiarity, where strangeness is cancelled out. In their refusal of home, queer migrant subjects reclaim a space to be called 'home'.

The very pervasiveness of the trope of home in narratives of queer migrations should alert us to the ways in which it is re-inscribed as a desired site of familiarity, comfort and belonging. What remains under-theorized here, however, is the very model of home as familiarity.[9] In this respect, Sinfield's narrative inserts itself within the logic of pathological ideas of diaspora according to which it will only be 'treated' by a movement toward 'home'. By conflating diaspora (or queer) and exile, he transforms 'diaspora yearning and ambivalence … into a simple and unambiguous exile *once the possibility of easy reconciliation with either place of sojourn or the place of origin exists*' (Gilroy, 2000: 124; emphasis added). Sinfield is uncomfortable with the indeterminacy of lesbian's and gay's 'home'; his reversed narrative maintains a linear trajectory that posits homecoming as a desirable destination. For Sinfield, people move away from 'home'

and '*into, if we are lucky*' (second emphasis added), a gay or lesbian subculture. This is highly reminiscent of the prototypical immigration narrative, where immigrants are perceived to move *from* one culture *into* another, thus assuming 'cultures' to be neatly bounded and separately located within distinct territories. Sinfield's 'subculture' constitutes a timespace that is distinct and separate from the '(heterosexual) culture of our childhood', and puts an end to the sense of loss; it brings an end to migration. 'Home' is the antidote to dispersal. Yet not all queer migrants leave home in order to come out[10], nor do they all entertain the desire to move (in)to what Lawrence Schimel labels queer 'cultural homelands' (1997).

Schimel takes a more critical view in his text about 'cultural homelands' within US gay and lesbian culture (such as San Francisco's Castro, New York City's Greenwich Village, Key West, or Northampton). Drawing on the distinctly anti-nationalist inclinations of diaspora as it has been used by anti-Zionists (Marienstras, 1975, 1989) and post-colonial critics (Hall, 1990; Gilroy, 1993a, 2000; Clifford, 1994), Schimel likens queer 'cultural homelands' to 'mini-Zions' by virtue of their quasi-mythical status: 'our visits feel like a return home, even if we've never set foot there before' (1997: 167). His use of the Jewish imagery is meant as a caution against nationalist projects that seek to negate diaspora. A self-identified post-Zionist Jew, Schimel is critical of the Zionist project whereby the nation–state appears as the institutional means to terminate diaspora dispersal (1997: 172): much like Sinfield's subculture, the 'return to the homeland', brings diaspora to a halt. Schimel's political project, in contrast, aims at rehabilitating diaspora by defining it as a fruitful and original mode of existence that thrives through dispersal. He thus views with a glimpse of hope the emergence of a queer diaspora where it has become possible to connect with queer culture without having to live *within* queer 'mini-Zions'.

Gays are beginning to embrace our diaspora as well, choosing to stay home and come out wherever we are rather than moving to our mini-Zions of gay culture. And many of us in these Zions are choosing to leave, to form smaller enclaves outside of these arenas, to live queer lives in suburbia or rural sectors ... now it is possible not to be the only openly-gay man in Small Town USA, and it is more and more possible to interact with gay culture through mass media – magazines, films, the internet – from anywhere in the world. (ibid).

Embracing diaspora, for Schimel, means being able to be out and to stay 'at home', wherever that may be. For him, the project of queer diaspora will be fully achieved when gays and lesbians no longer have to get out in order to be out. His intervention is interesting for it raises important issues with regards to the ways in which queer theory has tended to constitute queer subjects and queer spaces.

Schimel not only questions the assumption that queers live in urban areas, but that they should. 'Sure, it's fun to visit these cities,' he writes, 'but they're no longer as essential to being gay as they once were' (ibid). Schimel hence proposes a redefinition of the sexual geography of queer theory, whose urban–rural binary has only recently been brought to light (Halberstam, 2000). Conceived as a space that nurtures a variety of sexual cultures, the 'urban' is accepted as the location *par excellence* for queer subjects to inhabit. In contrast, small town and rural areas are conceived as sexually homogeneous, where 'dissident sexuality is rarer and more closely monitored' (Rubin, 1993: 23). Consequently, queer subjects are constructed as *urban* subjects, thus making the rural queer an outsider, one whose choice of residence – which is sometimes also the choice to 'stay put' – seems somewhat out of place within queer studies. As Judith Halberstam (2000) suggests, the rural is the closet of the urban.

Within queer studies, the focus on urban centres as queer spaces of inhabitance, and the ensuing neglect of small town and rural areas are brought into question at a time when queer culture is more easily accessible. Schimel suggests that the emergence of

a diasporic consciousness is facilitated by the proliferation of queer *sites of connection* in popular culture: magazines, films and the Internet. In the trails of Benedict Anderson, Schimel asserts the impact of the mass media and new technologies in the construction of a sense of shared belonging between individuals who are geographically dispersed. Yet a number of considerations need to be addressed. First, the political and economic conditions surrounding the production of, and access to, these sites. Just like moving to the city is not accessible to all as it entails considerable costs (Rubin, 1993), the cost of the mass media and, especially, the new technologies required to connect to the 'diaspora', could exclude a number of individuals from participating in such sites. Second, one should be cautious about assuming that sites of connection are homogeneous or conflict-free zones. They may be 'entered' from an array of subject positions and 'read' in a range of ways, thus producing a multiplication of queer identities and subjectivities. As Nina Wakeford (1997) has noted in relation to 'cyberqueer', and Alexander Doty (1993) with respect to the mass media (see also Doty and Gove, 1997), users of these sites of connection have a range of definitions of what being gay or lesbian or queer means. In addition, the scrutiny of 'sites of connection', such as Internet sites, would reveal how various encounters are produced through intersecting relations of dialogue and conflict.[11]

This being said, queer spaces, whether virtual or physical, can also constitute important spaces of refuge, either from the straightworld(s), or even 'from *other* lesbian, gay, transgender, queer worlds' (Wakeford, 1997: 31; italics in original). The 'sense of relief and safety' Watney finds in gay bars when he travels abroad is telling of how vulnerable one might feel, as a 'queer' subject, walking in the streets of an unknown city. Similarly, the gay and lesbian 'subculture', for Sinfield, offers the ontological security of being 'at home' in a cultural, social, or physical space, thus not having to defer 'being out'. For Watney and for Sinfield, these sites of connection are also sites of emergence as they constitute desirable destinations of safety and comfort against the dangers of the streets and the often traumatic separation from hetero-sexual families. In addition, going to the gay bar, or moving within a lesbian subculture solves, even if momentarily, the ontological problem about belonging to the 'lesbian and gay' culture in a heterosexist, homophobic world. Likewise, the proliferation of ethnic-based lesbian and gay groups over the last decades in many Euro-American cities is partly a result of the sense of exclusion and, in some cases, the violence of a racist lesbian and gay 'community'. Hence if the idea of 'home' deployed in notions of 'queer diaspora' remains sentimentalized as a space of comfort where one seamlessly 'fits in' and belongs, it is also embedded in the struggles to create and maintain spaces of belonging and comfort in the face of adver-sity within or without the 'lesbian and gay community'.

The relationship between violence, sexu-ality, and space thus needs to be addressed more extensively than I have suggested here.[12] For a large number of lesbians and gays, space may be used to claim and per-form a recognizable sexual identity that has been marginalized. So if, as I suggest, the theoretical emphasis on diaspora as the new basis of identity formation must attend to the violent processes of fixing some bodies into 'difference' or into place, it must also attend to the relationship between violence, safety, and 'home', whose boundaries may be maintained and enforced as a survival strat-egy and a quest for safety and comfort (Moran, forthcoming).

CONCLUSION

In their respective theoretical formations, both diaspora and queer subjects have been positioned as outside modern narratives of the nation, offering alternative perspectives on the 'historical and cultural mechanics of belonging' (Gilroy, 2000: 123): 'diaspora' by making 'the spatialization of identity problematic and interrupt[ing] the onto-logization of place' (ibid.: 122), and 'queer' by problematizing heteronormative dis-courses and denaturalizing gendered nation-alisms. In this chapter, I examined what happens when diaspora and queer are brought together. More specifically: what does it mean to diasporize queer culture and politics? Extending from the conclusions that can be drawn from the above discus-sion, I would like to point out some of the questions and directions for future research that the above discussion might suggest.

First, 'queer diasporas' are part of the increased currency of what I call *diasporic horizons*, that is, the projection of, in this case, queer belongings and culture, within a spatio-temporal horizon defined in terms of multi-locality, cultural diversity, dispersal, and conflict. More to the point, the explo-ration of the ways in which diaspora is put to work in narratives of collective identity and culture, indicates the significance of consi-dering diaspora not as an accomplished fact, but, rather, as a process, as a concept that is mobilized to produce imagined remains of belonging. I begin to examine this process in this chapter, by asking what kinds of spatio-temporal horizons diaspora fosters in the narratives of queer theorists. As I argue else-where (Fortier, 2001), it is worth consider-ing the extent to which collective identities in the postmodern, postnational, global world, are lived and represented in terms of diaspora, and to illuminate how a diasporic consciousness manifests itself and con-verses with other forms of consciousness (for example, national consciousness; immi-grant consciousness; ethnic consciousness, and so forth). In doing so, definitions of identity, namely, of transnational networks of connections, are understood as the out-come of a number of mediations that weave together multiple locations and histories.

This relates to the relationship between diaspora and globalization. On the one hand, discourses about the diasporization of queer culture and politics emerge in the context of increased connectivity, largely facilitated by the development and availability – albeit still limited – of new information technologies. One the other hand, and more importantly, the very use of diaspora *rather* than that of 'global' to talk about transnational queer culture and politics is telling of the resistance to the cultural imperialist tendencies often associated with globalization. It is also suggestive of a kind of sexual geography that diaspora conjures up: a 'diaspora space', as Avtar Brah puts it (1996: 209). Composed of genealogies of displacement and genealogies of 'staying put', diaspora space inserts itself between localism and globalism and proposes a conception of identity as a positionality that 'is not a process of absolute othering, but rather of entangled tensions' (Clifford, 1994: 307). The space of diaspora weaves new webs of belonging that trouble spatial fields of 'nation', 'home', territory, 'community'.

This leads onto the second point I want to consider: how the shift to diaspora away from ethnicity or nation marks a turning point in relation to thinking about ideas of community that are not defined in terms of commonality, but, rather, configured in terms of difference, dispersal, (dis)connection, diversity, and multilocality. Much recent theorizing on community still assume an equation between community and commonality. Yet there is little discussion about the enduring appeal of 'community', and how the 'we' is produced or performed in a variety of ways. Do communities necessarily entail the suppression of difference? Can communities come together without presumptions of 'being in common'? One of the tensions that surfaces in queer considerations of diaspora is precisely the tension between dispersal and diversity – which calls for a recognition of difference not as foundational, but as historically specific – and the political imperative for solidarity and connectivity or, in Simon Watney's terms, the 'political imperative to think of its constituency as unified and homogeneous' (1995: 64). While he pointedly suggests that such a tension is productive rather

than destructive, he nonetheless returns to a conception of community as homogeneous. The point I am trying to make is that the turn to diaspora signals a shift away from such a conception of community founded on 'being-in-common' or 'having-in-common'. Researching how communities come to be imagined as well as how they come to be inhabited in the everyday world may reveal the complexities of the lived experience of 'community', while providing further insights into its enduring appeal. Are they guarantors of safety? As stated earlier, are they necessarily conflict-free zones (see note 11)? Can communities exist in virtual worlds, where members never 'face' each other? (see Wakeford in this volume).

The enduring appeal of community as 'being in common' needs to be scrutined as well. More specifically, how are communities brought together? What are the social processes involved in imagining and constructing a queer diasporic community? How does diasporizing the queer produce a 'community' that involves the movement of some bodies though the fixing of others (Ahmed, 2000)? How does diasporizing the queer affect the inclusion/exclusion of diasporic subjects who have relationships to multiple nations (Gopinath, 1996; Puar, 1998)? On what terms does the diversification of the transnational queer network operate?

Third, suggesting that diaspora is a project that is put to work might imply that there is an actor, as well as intent, behind the project.[13] One of the aims of this chapter is precisely to inquire into how queerness is projected within a diasporic horizon, and in the name of whom. Yet the question of who are the 'actors' of this diaspora remains open. Frank Mort points to it by specifying that the diasporic network is largely the doing of North American and European activists and intellectuals. Hence a more general investigation of the political movements themselves, with a focus on the actors – their aims, projects, desires, conflicts, but also their actual lived experience of 'diaspora': their movements, access to resources, local struggles, and so on, would provide important insights into the material conditions surrounding the formation of diaspora as an imagined space of belonging (Adam et al., 1999).

Likewise, the relationship between the transnationalization of queer culture, and the commodification of queerness is another area of inquiry that could be further developed. The circulation of 'queer' culture within the transnational network of commodity capitalism is undoubtedly a contributor to the 'diasporization' of queer culture. More research into the conditions of production, circulation and consumption of these 'commodities' and 'sites of connection' would also contribute to further grasp of the material conditions surrounding the formation of a queer diaspora space (Binnie, 1995; Bell and Binnie, 2001).

Fourth, an important area of research that I mentioned at the beginning of this chapter, but did not focus on, is the *queering of diasporas*. Indeed, there is an increasing body of work that seeks to force a reconsideration of the heterosexist norms supporting definitions of diasporas. Such research largely focus on ethnically defined diasporas, but they offer important inroads into broader considerations about the conditions and effects of diasporizing queer sexualities. For instance, the effects of theorizing difference within unity, in terms of the kinds of identities and differences this produces and maintains.

Also, queering diaspora challenges naturalist assumptions about the heterosexist foundations of both the nation and ideas of 'home', which is not to say that queer is a refusal of home and ideas of family that are often associated with it. Closer scrutiny into multiple evocations of home/land within narratives of queer diasporas would offer a more complex, and less uniform view of ideas of home and nation (see note 9).

Finally, a noteworthy contribution of queering the diaspora is to raise important questions about queer activism for full citizenship. For Gayatri Gopinath, there are uninterrogated assumptions that 'queers, for the most part, have unproblematic access to the state and to "queer citizenship"'

(1996: 120). Members of the South Asian diaspora, she argues, cannot take citizenship for granted. Hence diasporic queerness is constructed at the interstices of various strategic negotiations of state regulatory practices and multiple national spaces (ibid.: 121). More research of this type would be called for if we are to continue to interrogate the heterosexist and Western assumptions of identity politics. In addition, this research would provide deeper insights into the sites of diversity and connections between different experiences of queer diasporic subjects in different parts of the world.

More generally, a closer scrutiny of how gays, lesbians, transgender, transsexuals, and other queer subjects inhabit new transnational spaces of belonging, could lead into more detailed considerations of multiple ways in which individuals move between, and within, these spaces. In turn, these could bring to light the ways in which new forms of solidarity, attachment and reterritorialization come about in a world largely defined in terms of flows, scapes and mobilities. For one of the fascinating aspects about diasporic identities and cultures, is how they are shaped through *both* movement and attachment, how they are *at once* deterritorialized and reterritorialized, in what might be aptly called, following Paul Gilroy (1993a: 190), the social dynamics of rootings and routings (Fortier, 2000: 17).

ACKNOWLEDGEMENTS

A draft version of this paper was presented in the 'Queer Theory' seminar series at the Institute for Women's Studies, Lancaster University, October 2000. I am grateful for the useful comments and discussion that followed my presentation. I would also like to thank the following colleagues from the Faculty of Social Sciences Women's Writing Group (Lancaster University) for their comments on an even earlier draft: Sara Ahmed, Anne Cronin, Vicki Singleton, Mimi Sheller, Imogen Tyler. And thanks to

Diane Richardson for her patience and
efficiency in this project.

NOTES

1 For example, the East Asian diaspora, the South Asian
diaspora, the African diaspora, the Irish diaspora, and so on.
2 While I am fully aware of the debates around the term
'queer' itself, I use 'queer', here, in a very pragmatic way.
That is, I adopt the term as it is used in the texts I discuss,
where it refers to a political and cultural platform based on
homosexual identities. With the exception of Alan Sinfield,
who retains the phrase 'gay and lesbian', all the writers I
refer to speak as, or about, 'queers'.
3 Benedict Anderson's notion of 'imagined community'
(1983/1991) has now become a key concept in accounts of
the formation of collective identities. Anderson's work
centred on the formation of the modern nation and the
impact of print capitalism in the construction of a sense of
shared belonging between individuals who are geographically dispersed, and who will thus most probably never
meet. 'Community', here, is used not in the more traditional sense of geographically located microcosms of
daily interaction, but, rather, in the sense of an imaginary
terrain of belonging or identification. For Anderson, the
nation and nationhood are 'cultural artefacts', with their
own 'style in which they are imagined' (1983/1991: 13
and 15). When applied to other contexts, such as the
transnational queer community, the question then is: how
is the community imagined? What are its organizing principles? Who is included and excluded?
4 A wider understanding of 'diaspora' would also
include severe economic or climactic constraints as a
factor that forces a large number of people to emigrate and
disperse to different parts of the world. The emigration of
over 27 million Italians since 1800 is considered, by some,
as the constitutive basis of an Italian diaspora (see Tomasi
et al., 1994; Gabaccia, 2000). Others have contested this
view in an attempt to distinguish diasporas from immigrants and ethnic groups (Tölölyan, 1996; Clifford, 1994)
on the grounds that diaspora, unlike immigrants, are
forced to emigrate, and do not simply move from one
culture into another but rather negotiate multi-local ties.
Finally, some adopt a mediating position, refusing to
establish a typology of migrations and rather seeking 'the
links between the historical experiences of migration and
displacement' (Kaplan, 1996: 137; also Fortier, 1998;
2000) that different migrant subjects may share. The final
viewpoint is the one I adopt here; it implies a shift away
from a conception of diaspora as an accomplished fact,
towards one that examines diaspora as a process.
5 This phrase is borrowed from the title of a book on
the impact and scale of migration at the dawn of the
twenty-first century. See Castles and Miller (1995).

6 As manifested in the shift from debates about
modernity/postmodernity to debates about globalization.
7 The construction of identity is a key theme that has
long since concerned gay and lesbian writers and activists.
Some have suggested an identity politics based on the
ethnicity model, by way of conceiving the gay and lesbian
'community' as a subculture, or a 'cultural community',
with its distinct cultural practices and 'traditions'; a thesis
that has been contested by others. On this topic, see
Cohen, 1991; Sinfield, 2000; Takagi, 1996; Epstein, 1987.
8 Even in 'queer nation' – and in spite of the conflicted
uses of this phrase – such myths of reproduction are challenged by forcing a reconsideration of the naturalized
status of the family as the cornerstone of the nation.
9 For a more detailed analysis of multiple evocations of
'home' in narratives of queer diaspora, see Fortier (2001).
10 The Cuban-American lesbian writer Anchy Obejas
questions this assumption when she asks: 'What if we'd
stayed? What if we'd never left Cuba? ... What if we'd
never left [?] ... I wonder, if we'd stayed then who, if anyone ... would have been my blonde lovers, or any kind of
lovers at all ... I try to imagine who I would have been if
Fidel had never come into Havana sitting triumphantly on
top of that tank, but I can't. I can only think of variations of
who I am, not who I might have been' (in Espin 1996: 83).
11 Consider Shelly Correll's study of 'The Lesbian
Cafe' bulletin board system, where 'newbies' and 'bash-
ers' meet within a same queer cyberspace (Correll, 1995).
12 See the website of the *Violence, Sexuality and
Space Research Project*, Manchester University; *http://
les1.man.ac.uk/sociology/vssrp/home.htm* (accessed
31.01.01)
13 Thanks to Anne Cronin for bringing this point to my
attention.

REFERENCES

Adam, B., Duyvendak, J.W. and Krouwel, A. (1999)
*The Global Emergence of Gay and Lesbian
Politics: National Imprints of a Worldwide Movement.*
Philadelphia, PA: Temple University Press.
Ahmed, S. (2000) *Strange Encounters: Embodied Others
in Post-Coloniality.* London and New York: Routledge.
Altman, D. (1996) 'Rupture or continuity? The internation-
alization of gay identities', *Social Text*, 14 (3): 77–94.
Altman, D. (1997) 'Global gaze/global gays', *GLQ*, 3 (4):
417–36.
Anderson, B. (1983/1991) *Imagined Communities.*
London and New York: Verso.
Bell, D. and Binnie, J. (2001) *The Sexual Citizen.*
Cambridge: Polity.
Binnie, J. (1995) 'Trading places: consumption, sexuality
and the production of queer space', in D. Bell and
G. Valentine (eds), *Mapping Desire: Geographies of
Sexualities.* London: Routledge. pp. 182–99.

Boyarin, D. and Boyarin, J. (1993) 'Diaspora: generation and the ground of Jewish Identity', *Critical Inquiry*, 19 (4): 693–725.

Brah, A. (1996) *Cartographies of Diaspora: Contesting Identities*. London and New York: Routledge.

Cant, Bob (ed.) (1997) *Invented Identities? Lesbians and Gays Talk About Migration*. London: Cassell.

Castles, Stephen and Miller, Mark M. (1995) *The Age of Migration. International Population Movements in the Modern World*. London: Macmillan.

Clifford, James (1994) 'Diasporas', *Cultural Anthropology*, 9 (3): 302–38.

Cohen, E. (1991) 'Who are "we"? Gay "identity" as political (e)motion (a theoretical rumination)', in D. Fuss (ed.), *Inside/Out. Lesbian Theories, Gay Theories*. London and New York: Routledge. pp. 71–92.

Cohen, R. (1997) *Global Diasporas: An Introduction*. Seattle: University of Washington Press.

Conner, W. (1986) 'The impact of homelands upon diasporas', in G. Sheffer (ed.), *Modern Diasporas in International Politics*. New York: St Martin's Press. pp. 16–46.

Correll, S. (1995) 'The ethnography of an electronic bar. The Lesbian Café', *Journal of Contemporary Ethnography*, 24 (3): 270–98.

Dhaliwal, A. (1994) 'The traveling nation. India and its diaspora', special issue of *Socialist Review*, 24 (4).

Doty, A. (1993) *Making Things Perfectly Queer: Interpreting Mass Culture*. Minneapolis: University of Minnesota Press.

Doty, A. and Gove, B. (1997) 'Queer representation in the mass media', in A. Medhurst and S. Munt (eds), *Lesbian and Gay Studies: A Critical Introduction*. London and Washington: Cassell. pp. 84–98.

Eng, D. (1997) 'Out here and over there: queerness and diaspora in Asian American studies', *Social Text*, 15 (3–4): 31–52.

Eng, D. and Hom, A. (eds) (1998) *Q & A: Queer in Asian America*. Philadelphia: Temple University Press.

Epstein, S. (1987) 'Gay politics, ethnic identity: the limits of social constructionism', *Socialist Review*, 17 (3/4): 9–54.

Espin, O. (1996) 'The immigrant experience in lesbian studies', in B. Zimmerman and T. Mcnaron (eds), *The New Lesbian Studies: Into the Twenty-First Century*. New York: The Feminist Press. pp. 79–86.

Fortier, A.-M. (1998) 'Calling on Giovanni: interrogating the nation through diasporic imaginations', *International Journal of Canadian Studies*, 18: 31–49.

Fortier, A.-M. (2000) *Migrant Belongings: Memory, Space, Identity*. Oxford: Berg.

Fortier, A.-M. (2001) '"Coming home": intersections of queer memories and diasporic spaces', *The European Journal of Cultural Studies*.

Gabaccia, D. (2000) *Italy's Many Diasporas*. London: UCL Press.

Gilroy, P. (1993a) *The Black Atlantic. Modernity and Double Consciousness*. London: Verso.

Gilroy, Paul (1993b) 'It's a family affair: black culture and the trope of kinship', in *Small Acts: Thoughts on the Politics of Black Cultures*. London: Serpent's Tail.

Gilroy, Paul (1994) 'Diaspora', *Paragraph*, 17 (3): 207–12.

Gilroy, Paul (2000) *Between Camps: Nations, Cultures and the Allure of Race*. London: Allen Lane, The Penguin Press.

Gopinath, Gayatri (1995) 'Bombay, U.K., Yuba City: Bhangra music and the engendering of diaspora', *Diaspora*, 4 (3): 303–21.

Gopinath, G. (1996) 'Funny boys and girls: notes on a queer South Asian planet', in R. Leong (ed.), *Asian American Sexualities: Dimensions of the Gay and Lesbian Experience*. London and New York: Routledge. pp. 119–27.

Halberstam, Judith (2000) 'Male fraud: counterfeit masculinity and the case of Brandon Teena', paper presented in the Queer Theory Seminar Series, Institute for Women's Studies, University of Lancaster, Autumn 2000.

Hall S. (1988) 'New ethnicities', in K. Mercer (ed.), *Black Film British Cinema*. ICA Documents, 7: 27–31.

Hall, S. (1990) 'Cultural identity and diaspora', in J. Rutherford (ed.), *Identity. Community, Culture, Difference*. London: Lawrence and Wishart. pp. 222–37.

Kaplan, C. (1996) *Questions of Travel: Postmodern Discourses of Displacements*. Durham, NC, and London: Duke University Press.

Lavie, S. and Swedenburg, T. (1996) 'Between and among boundaries of culture: bridging text and lived experience in the third timespace', *Cultural Studies*, 10 (1): 154–79.

Leong, R. (ed.) (1996) *Asian American Sexualities*. London and New York: Routledge.

Manalansan, M. (1993) '(Re)Locating the gay Filipino: resistance, postcolonialism, and identity', *Journal of Homosexuality*, 26 (2–3): 53–72.

Manalansan, M. (1995) 'In the shadows of Stonewall: examining gay transnational politics and the diasporic dilemma', *GLQ*, 2 (4): 425–38.

Marienstras, R. (1975) *Être un peuple en diaspora*. Paris: Maspero.

Marienstras, R. (1989) 'On the notion of diaspora', in G. Chaliand (ed.), *Minority Peoples in the Age of Nation-States*. Trans. T. Berrett. London: Pluto. pp. 119–25.

Mason-John, V. and Khambatta, A. (1993) *Lesbians Talk. Making BlackWaves*. London: Scarlet Press.

Monette, P. (1992) *Halfway Home*. London: SMP.

Moran, L. (forthcoming) 'Poetics of safety: lesbians, gay men and home', in A. Crawford (ed.), *Crime and Insecurity*. William Publishers.

Morris, R. (1997) 'Educating desire: Thailand, transnationalism, and trangression', *Social Text*, 52–3: 53–79.

Mort, F. (1994) 'Essentialism revisited? Identity politics and late twentieth-century discourses of homosexuality', in J. Weeks (ed.), *The Lesser Evil and the Greater Good*. London: Rivers Oram Press. pp. 201–21.

Patton, C. and Sánchez-Eppler, B. (eds) (2000) *Queer Diasporas*. Durham, NC, and London: Duke University Press.

Preston, J. (1991) *Hometowns: Gay Men Write about Where they Belong*. New York: Plume.

Puar, J. (1994) 'Writing my way "home". Traveling South: Asian bodies and diasporic journeys', *Socialist Review*, 24 (4): 75–108.

Puar, J. (1998) 'Transnational sexualities. South Asian (Trans)nation(alism)s and queer diasporas', in D. Eng and A. Hom (eds), *Q & A: Queer in Asian America*. Philadelphia, PA: Temple University Press. pp. 405–22.

Radhakrishnan, R. (1996) *Diasporic Mediations: Between Home and Location*. Minneapolis and London: University of Minnesota Press.

Ratti, R. (ed.) (1994) *Lotus of Another Color: An Unfolding of the Gay and Lesbian South Asian Experience*. Boston: Alyson.

Rubin, G. (1993) 'Thinking sex: notes for a radical theory of the politics of sexuality', in H. Abelove et al. (eds), *The Lesbian and Gay Studies Reader*. London and New York: Routledge. pp. 3–44.

Safran, W. (1991) 'Diasporas in modern societies: myths of homeland and return', *Diaspora*, 1 (1): 83–99.

Schimel, L. (1997) 'Diaspora, sweet diaspora: queer culture to post-Zionist Jewish identity', in C. Queen and L. Schimel (eds), *PoMoSexuals: Challenging Assumptions About Gender and Sexuality*. San Francisco: Cleiss Press. pp. 163–73.

Sinfield, A. (2000) 'Diaspora and hybridity: queer identity and the ethnicity model', in N. Mirzoeff (ed.), *Diaspora and Visual Culture: Representing Africans and Jews*. London: Routledge. pp. 95–114.

Takagi, D. (1996) 'Maiden voyage: excursion into sexuality and identity politics in Asian America', in S. Seidman (ed.), *Queer Theory/Sociology*. Cambridge, MA, and Oxford: Blackwell. pp. 243–58.

Tamburri, A. (ed.) (1996) *Fuori: Essays by Italian/American Lesbians and Gays*. West Lafayette: Bordighera.

Tölölyan, K. (1996) 'Rethinking diaspora(s): stateless power in the transnational moment', *Diaspora*, 5(1): 3–34.

Tomasi, L., Gastaldo, P. and Row, T. (eds) (1994) *The Columbus People: Perspectives in Italian Immigration to the Americas and Australia*. New York: Center for Migration Studies.

Wakeford, N. (1997) 'Cyberqueer', in A. Medhurst and S. Munt (eds), *Lesbian and Gay Studies: A Critical Introduction*. London and Washington: Cassell. pp. 20–38.

Walker, B. (1995) 'Une critique du nationalisme culturaliste: l'idée d'une nation gaie', in F. Blais, G. Laforest, D. Lamoureux (eds), *Libéralismes et nationalismes*. Québec: Les Presses de l'Université Laval. pp. 211–26.

Warner, M. (ed.) (1993) *Fear of a Queer Planet*. Minneapolis: Minnesota.

Watney, S. (1995) 'AIDS and the politics of queer diaspora', in M. Dorenkamp and R. Henke (eds), *Negotiating Lesbian and Gay Subjects*. London and New York: Routledge. pp. 53–70.

12

Gay, Lesbian and Bisexual Youth

MELINDA S. MICELI

As gay and lesbian subcultures and politics have become more mainstreamed in America and Western Europe, more visible gay and lesbian public figures, media images, and narratives have emerged (Vaid, 1995; Harris, 1997). In this more tolerant atmosphere, and with access to information and role models, small, but rapidly enlarging, groups of g/l/b teenagers have also emerged throughout the United States, Canada, Western Europe, and Australia. They are making themselves visible and demanding to be treated equally. Individual acts of 'coming out' by g/l/b youth have solidified, in many ways, into an act of 'coming-out' for this population, which was once thought of as either non-existent or rightfully hidden.

This new visibility of g/l/b youth has caused cultural, social institutional, and political controversy that seems to be perpetuated by the inherent qualities of this population. As a group, g/l/b youth are a sexual minority and, because of age, they have no legal standing. Their sexuality has placed them at the center of controversy in their homes, schools, and communities. At home, g/l/b youth often find themselves submerged in struggles over morality, identity, and acceptance. In their schools, g/l/b students face battles for tolerance, inclusion, and their own safety. In their communities, and often in even larger public arenas,

g/l/b youth frequently become symbols in political debates over the limits of inclusion and tolerance, over the extent of civil rights, over the separation of Church and State, and over their nation's responsibility to protect and nurture all of its children.

In this chapter, I provide a summary of the research on contemporary g/l/b youth, give an account of the local and national political debates that surround them, and offer an analysis of the effect this population and their activities have on the academic fields of gay and lesbian studies and sociology, in general.

RESEARCH ON GAY, LESBIAN, AND BISEXUAL YOUTH

Despite the recent increase in visibility, gay, lesbian, and bisexual youth are still one of the most under-researched groups of children and adolescents. This stems, in part, from the historic 'invisibility' of this population. In reaction to the stigma and prejudice surrounding homosexuality, most of these young people have kept their sexual orientation secret. Therefore, locating a sizable population of gay youth for a large-scale research project is extremely difficult, if not impossible. Smaller-scale qualitative interview and field studies may be more feasible in terms of sampling, but contain their own set of difficulties. The first hurdle often encountered in these types of studies involves the ethics of researching minors. Academic researchers must struggle to get institutional approval to research gay youth because it generally involves interviewing minors without parental consent. The legality surrounding this issue makes many university Human Subjects Review Boards wary. Even when research is approved and funded, sampling remains an issue. The best starting points for a snowball sample of g/l/b youth is often a support group or youth drop-in center. This poses a serious question about how representative the samples used in these studies actually are. They tend to disproportionately consist of 'out', urban, and male youth in need of and receiving support. Significantly missing from the research on g/l/b youth, then, are accounts of rural, 'closeted', and female youth who are not seeking, or not receiving, support.

Because of these methodological difficulties, the statistics describing young gay, lesbian and bisexuals vary. In attempting to estimate the number of g/l/b teens and young adults, some researchers use comparative estimates of the percentage of gays and lesbians in the population as a whole. These estimates range from about 2 per cent to about 10 per cent of the total population. If we use these percentages to estimate the number of gay and lesbian youth between the ages of 14 and 17, we get a range of 267,000 to 1,333,500, based on 1990 census data (Durby, 1994).

Another issue that has complicated the research on gay, lesbian, and bisexual youth concerns the question of the 'origins' of homosexuality. Is it a biologically or genetically determined trait or a socially acquired trait? After over a hundred years of scientific research into this question, no conclusive evidence has been found to fully support either answer. Whatever the determining factors, most researchers do seem to agree that the questioning of, and uncertainty about, sexuality are common in early adolescence.

This includes the emergence of same-sex attractions and affections. Given the social stigma surrounding homosexuality, this period of adolescence can be particularly trying for gay, lesbian, and bisexual youth.

With little support or accurate information available to them, gay, lesbian, bisexual, and 'questioning' adolescents may have great difficulty coping with their emerging feelings. Many g/l/b youth face the anxiety and fear of potentially being rejected by their family and peers, who may consider homosexuality a sin, or a form of deviance. As a result, many adolescents choose to hide, deny, repress, and keep silent about their sexual feelings (Cook and Herdt, 1991). This dynamic makes g/l/b youth a unique minority group in some significant ways. Most other minority groups can at least count on the emotional support of their families to help them learn how to cope with discrimination and oppression. Gay, lesbian, and bisexual youth are often rejected rather than supported by their families. For the most part, even those fortunate enough to have supportive families still do not receive the empathy and coping lessons that other minority youth receive, unless other family members are gay. This type of isolation can have many effects on individuals, including: loneliness; high anxiety and nervousness; substance abuse; depression; and thoughts of, and attempts at, suicide (DeCrescenzo, 1994).

Much of the little research that has been done on gay and lesbian youth has been sparked by reports of exceptionally high suicide rates in this population. In 1989, the US Department of Health and Human Services (USDHHS) published a report on youth suicide that concluded gay and lesbian youth are at a significantly higher risk of suicide than their heterosexual peers. The report states that approximately 30 per cent of youth suicides are committed by gays and lesbians (Gibson, 1989). If we take the high end estimate that 10 per cent of adolescents are gay or lesbian, than we could estimate that gay and lesbian youth are three times more likely to commit suicide than their heterosexual peers.

Many researchers have studied gay and lesbian youth suicide. Some have argued that the figures are really much lower than the USDHHS's report; and some have argued that they are higher (Durby, 1994). Once again, the difficulty in obtaining exact numbers stems largely from the difficulty of obtaining representative samples of the g/l/b youth population. Diane Raymond (1994) has argued that even when using a conservative estimate, approximately 1,500 gay and lesbian teenagers kill themselves every year. This makes suicide the leading cause of death among gay and lesbian youth in the USA.

Another danger that g/l/b youth may face is becoming homeless. The fear, anxiety, ignorance, misinformation, and prejudice that families may have about homosexuality, all too often, result in the child being kicked out of the home, or running away because of a physically or emotionally abusive home environment (Anderson, 1987; Savin-Williams, 1989). Becoming homeless presents many dangers for adolescents, including substance abuse, prostitution, and crime (DeCrescenzo, 1994).

Much of the sociological and psychological research on gay, lesbian and bisexual youth stresses the importance of understanding their experiences in relationship to that of other stigmatized groups. Social theorist Erving Goffman (1963) made the distinction between 'discredited' and 'discreditable' stigmatized groups. 'Discredited' groups are those whose stigma is readily obvious and incapable of being hidden, such as skin color or a physical deformity. Those in 'discreditable' groups have some stigmatizing characteristic that is not readily discernible and can be hidden. This is the category into which homosexuals fall. Members of discreditable groups who choose to hide, or fail to make obvious their stigmatized characteristic, are continually at risk of being found out or of having their otherwise 'normal' identity stigmatized.

According to Martin and Hetrick (1988), this 'discreditable' feature creates specific problems and issues for homosexual adolescents. Gay, lesbian or bisexual adolescents have to cope with a stigma that is not only discreditable to others' perception of their identity, but is also discrediting to their own perception of their identity. This self-discrediting aspect of the stigma occurs because many g/l/b individuals do not become aware of their sexuality until adolescence or later in life. Dennis Anderson (1994) refers to this as a 'crisis of self-concept', because these adolescents feel that they are suddenly, and involuntarily, joining a stigmatized group. As a consequence, g/l/b adolescents may go through a complex stage of negotiating their difference with themselves and with the larger culture. Erik Erickson (1968) described adolescence as a period in which there is a strong desire for sameness with one's peers. The desire for sameness is 'spoiled' (to use Goffman's term) for adolescents who are coming to realize that their affectional and sexual desires mark them as different.

According to Hetrick and Martin, 'The primary task for homosexually oriented adolescents is adjusting to a socially stigmatized role' (1987: 25). The social withdrawal, which can be a coping strategy for any stigmatized individual, can lead to extreme isolation for gay, lesbian or bisexual youth because they may not be able to find any support in their family.

The isolation experienced by gay youth has three compounding components: social, emotional, and cognitive. Martin and Hetrick cite cognitive isolation as being unique to those with a 'discreditable' stigma. They point out that many gay youth have no access to information about homosexuality and no exposure to real life models of gays, lesbians or bisexuals. They describe the effects of this cognitive isolation as follows: 'There is little or no opportunity for the homosexually oriented adolescent to discover what it means to be homosexual. Therefore, they cannot plan or sometimes even conceive of a future for themselves' (1988: 167).

Along with this cognitive isolation from others, Martin and Hetrick (1988) state that there may also be cognitive dissonance within the individual. In attempting to cope, the gay youth may try to deny their sexuality or separate themselves from it. In trying to deny it to themselves, they act out, for others and for themselves, heterosexual norms. This causes a great deal of internal anxiety, because it leads to an almost constant state of self-monitoring – making sure not to give any signs that they may be homosexual. At this crucial time when young people are learning that sexual desire is part of their developing selves, sexuality, for the g/l/b youth, becomes a threat to the social integration that socialization entails.

Although it is still far from easy for gay, lesbian and bisexual youth to find their place in a society that, generally, sees them as abnormal, the situation can be improved. While past research focused on the problems and negative impacts of homosexuality, recent research has begun to investigate programs that can help g/l/b youth develop healthy and positive lives (Herdt and Boxer, 1993; Martin and Hetrick, 1988; Sears, 1992). One key factor in accomplishing this is to provide opportunities for these youth to meet and socialize with one another. Other critical needs revealed by the research include: educating family and peers about homosexual issues; having accurate information about homosexuality available in the schools; and providing positive adult gay and lesbian role models.

The conclusions of this empirical social science research have been reflected in an even larger and more journalistic body of literature on g/l/b youth (e.g. Due, 1995; Owens, 1998; Chandler, 1995). These books promise to offer the reader a window into the 'real-lives' of g/l/b youth. Generally, these books tell the stories of g/l/b youth that have been abstracted through interviews with journalists. They are written in tones that seek to give rise to sympathy from heterosexual audiences, and recognition and hope for g/l/b audiences. In these books, g/l/b youth tend to be portrayed as either victims or young, brave, cultural warriors. Although this body of literature has done a good job of exposing this population and giving them a

human face, none of the books have offered an analysis of the experience and lives of g/l/b youth, and none have offered any concrete suggestions for social change. The combination of academic literature (the little that exists) and these narrative accounts of the experiences of a select few g/l/b youth creates an image and understanding of them as either victims who should be pitied or survivors who should be admired. Little else is added to fill in this image.

CRITIQUE OF THE LITERATURE ON GAY YOUTH

Most of the previous research on g/l/b youth, because it is primarily concerned with developmental issues, concentrates on the developmental problems of g/l/b youth (Hunter, 1987; Hetrick and Martin, 1987; and Schaecher Goggin, 1993; Durby, 1994). This body of literature, which began to emerge in the late 1980s, is heavily informed by the literature on 'the homosexual identity formation process' that began in the 1970s and continued through the 1980s (e.g. Plummer, 1975; Cass, 1979, 1984; Troiden, 1979, 1988, 1989). These models seem somewhat simplistic by today's understandings of social construction of identity and in relation to the contemporary work of postmodern, queer, and gay and lesbian theorists. However, at the time they were written, the research on homosexual identity formation models was a progressive move in the scientific understanding of homosexuality. The important significance of these models is that they offered a scientific perspective on homosexuality that assumed it to be a normal, rather than deviant, sexual identity. This did much to shift the focus of research in many disciplines away from finding the cause of the abnormality of homosexuality and its cure. The literature on developmental models, instead, calls for focusing attention on determining ways to assist the homosexual person successfully through the stages of self-acceptance in a hostile social climate.

The literature on gay youth has made some similarly progressive, if limited, steps. Prior to the late 1980s, gay youth were considered either nonexistent or invisible. One major importance of the early work on gay youth by Herdt (1989a), Herdt and Boxer (1993), Martin and Hetrick (1988), James Sears (1992), and others is that it has authenticated the population by documenting the existence of self-identified gay youth, and it has persuasively asserted that these youth should be assisted in coming to terms with their identity rather than cured. Although this may seem rather minor in terms of gay and lesbian or queer studies, personally and politically it has had an important impact of the lives of g/l/b youth. The body of literature has impacted the way many families, counselors, and teachers come to understand g/l/b youth, and has caught the attention and sympathy of some political figures in positions to improve the experiences of g/l/b youth as a minority group.

A major drawback of this same perspective presented in the majority of the literature is that it largely focuses on the negative aspects of growing up gay, lesbian, or bisexual, giving the impression that homosexuality invariably leads to suffering and unhappiness. Although this might win public sympathy for the population, it is not a full account of g/l/b youth. What is missed by such a perspective is an understanding of g/l/b youth who have successfully avoided such negative experiences and outcomes, and the variables that contributed to such success. Some of the more journalistic accounts (Chandler, 1995; Due, 1995) do present some positive 'success stories' of g/l/b youth. However, these accounts do not provide a social analysis of the factors that contribute to a happy rather than a tragic story.

The increasing prevalence of politically active gay youth suggests that many g/l/b teens, while still coping with a socially stigmatized identity, are adopting proactive strategies for dealing with this identity. These strategies seem to be distinctively and fundamentally different from the intrapsychic defensive coping strategies suggested

in previous research (e.g. Martin, 1982; Hetrick and Martin, 1987; Robertson, 1987; Savin-Williams, 1989; Cook and Herdt, 1991). These young adults are seeking to fight the stigma and the social institutions that enforce it on them rather than accept or adapt to the stigma. In communities across the United States, Canada, Western Europe, and Australia there is evidence that g/l/b youth are organizing local grassroots movement to challenge the social stigma that has been assigned to them, and to change the institutions that affect their lives.

In the United States, g/l/b students have rallied to bring attention to and make gains for their cause across the country. In Massachusetts g/l/b youth fought to get a statewide safe schools act passed. This state law protects g/l/b students from discrimination and harassment, and establishes efforts to educate students about g/l/b issues. In Utah, students fought a long and heated battle for the right to have a g/l/b student group. In Wisconsin, Jamie Nabozny successfully sued his school and was awarded approximately $1 million dollars in compensation for the severe abuse he suffered at school because he is gay. These more visible cases have sparked what could be called a grassroots social movement of g/l/b student groups in schools across America. Seven hundred such groups have been established since 1985.

In the United Kingdom, there has been a national battle over 'Section 28', which is the section of the local government act passed in 1988 that bans local authorities from 'promoting' homosexuality. Here too, g/l/b students have lent their voices and stories to the movement to repeal this ban. Their actions played a part in the repeal of the measure in Scotland. In Canada, g/l/b students have led struggles to lift book bans and to establish support for g/l/b student groups in Canadian schools. In Australia, a lawsuit filed by a single gay male student seeking compensation for the abuse he suffered at school resulted in a windfall of accusations of abuse by other g/l/b students. Fifty g/l/b students and faculty have banded together in a lawsuit against Australia's public schools.

These large and small movements of g/l/b youth offer a social, cultural, and institutional critique that is largely missing from the body of literature seeking to understand their lives. The existing body of literature offers a simplistic analysis of the experiences of g/l/b youth as merely personal struggles to accept their 'spoiled' identity. It does not examine the cultural and institutional forces that impose the normative standard of heterosexuality on developing adolescents. Some of the previous research does acknowledge the heterosexism in the culture and within social institutions, but the discussion is generally limited to the fact that g/l/b youth must struggle to adapt to it. There is little analysis of the purposeful social construction of these heterocentric institutions that have both means and ends. Left unchallenged, these institutionalized structures of sexual hierarchy are assumed to be organizational reflections of natural laws of human sexual behavior. Also left unexamined are the ways that both these institutionalized and naturalized qualities of 'the stigma' affect the experiences and identity development of g/l/b youth. Documenting and publicizing the problems of g/l/b youth are important to developing and instituting programs and policies to assist them. However, if we only view this population as a group struggling with a stigmatized identity, then we are missing crucial aspects of sociological knowledge.

In order to analyse all the factors and issues that are missing from the previous studies of g/l/b youth, we must move beyond a solely social-psychological developmental approach. We need to undertake an analysis of changes in the broader social, cultural, and political climate, as well as the social movements that have emerged around the issue of g/l/b youth rights. These movements are largely centered on changing public schools, because gay youth spend a large amount of time within these social institutions. Considering this, research on g/l/b youth must analyse public education as a social institution that enforces the norm of heterosexuality and the stigma of homosexuality. Such an analysis will also provide insight into the potentially powerful effect that changes in public schools' culture and organization of normative heterosexuality might have on the larger society.

To develop such a social analysis, social scientists need to shift the focus away from individuals' management of stigmatized identities. We need to conduct research that seeks to empirically examine the social function of this stigma, the various ways in which it is institutionalized, and the ways in which youth challenge this socially structured process. Focusing primarily on the obstacles and risks gay youth face will only lead to temporary solutions at an individual level, and leave the obstacles firmly in place. Many contemporary gay youth clearly understand this point. For example, when I asked 16-year-old Vincent what he thought about the impact of efforts made to help gay students like himself, he replied: 'In my opinion they have failed. They have done nothing to help young gay people – other than having a support group. They tried, but they don't know how to. They ignore the big circle of how things work and just make little holes here and there' (Miceli, 1998: 53). To reach this broader understanding, social scientists must work past the limitations of developmental models, and past the simplistic sociological and cultural understandings of g/l/b youth that have been informed by them. We need to work on building strong, empirically grounded, social structural analyses.

Developing such an analysis can begin with a re-examination of the concept of stigma. The terms 'stigma' and 'stigmatization' are so commonly used in social science literature and in popular culture that we often take their actual meaning for granted. Erving Goffman (1963) was the first, and perhaps the only, sociologist to seriously attempt to define stigma. Social scientists have since used the term widely, but largely failed to further explore and document the structural qualities of stigma and stigmatization as a social process. Ainlay et al. (1986) assert, 'In some ways social scientists may have legitimized stigma by suggesting that it is only human, if not "natural", to perceive and rank differences between ourselves and others. Such understanding suggests that people cannot change and may excuse them from feeling they should try.' In other words, the concept of stigma is too often used to rationalize the control and oppression of those defined as socially abnormal.

The term stigma has become one that is often troubling to a sociological analysis. It has been widely misunderstood and misused as being a natural quality or attribute of individuals. This misuse of the term has done much to squash its powerful potential to direct social and institutional analysis of oppressed groups. This phenomenon is reflected in the literature on g/l/b youth. 'Stigma', if the term is to be properly and effectively applied, must be understood as a systematic process of social control through socially constructed and institutionally enforced devaluations of purposely chosen individual characteristics. It is the power, social functions, and institutionalization of this process that should be the primary focus of social scientific investigations of 'stigmatized' populations such as g/l/b youth.

GAY YOUTH AS SOCIAL SUBJECTS AND ACTORS: INSTITUTIONALIZED POWER AND RESISTANCE

As mentioned earlier, the vast majority of attention that has been paid to gay youth since the late 1980s has been prompted by clashes occurring within local public schools across the United States, Canada, Western Europe, and Australia. Examining these localized conflicts, and both the local and national responses to them, provides a critical inroad into the real lives and experiences of g/l/b youth that serves as an excellent basis for a social structural analysis. Gay, lesbian, and bisexual students'

school experiences also, when examined critically, illuminate many of the more abstracted theoretical analyses offered by queer, and gay and lesbian studies across various disciplines. Therefore, researching this population is critically important to the empirical grounding of gay and lesbian studies.

The debates over g/l/b inclusions into public education are situated within the context of the power/knowledge dynamics of sexual identity first documented by Michel Foucault (1976, 1980). Foucault insightfully argued that people in positions to claim authority over knowledge – scientists, religious leaders, educators, etc. – are also in the position to use that knowledge to claim power over individuals by defining them, categorizing them, and placing meaning on them. The positions, opinions, and motivations of all the participants in the debates over g/l/b inclusions in schools – g/l/b youth, teachers, school administrators, parents, community members, politicians, etc. – are shaped by their understanding of the meanings of homosexuality and sexual identity that they derived from scientifically, religiously, and culturally produced knowledges. Gay students develop their sexual identity within these meanings, but also within the environment of hostility, abuse, controversy, and support, or lack of support, that surrounds them. In all of these situations, as well as in many others, they are labeled and defined by others, or forced to define themselves to others, within the limiting normative discourse of sexual identity.

It is particularly challenging for g/l/b youth to try to find and assert a positive identity, of which homosexuality or bisexuality is only one aspect, within social institutions such as public schools. As Warner states, 'the sexual order overlaps with a wide range of institutions and social ideologies. To challenge the sexual order is sooner or later to encounter those institutions as problems' (1991: 5). The institutionalization of norms and knowledges about sexuality and sexual identity is in some ways an interesting paradox. On the one hand, institutions serve to define, enforce, and regulate norms of society (in this case sexuality) in a way that naturalizes them and makes them a routine, transparent, and unquestioned part of everyday life; on the other hand, this seemingly innate uniformity can be quickly exposed as a purposeful social construction when challenged by those who do not conform to its order.

There is a sizable body of literature within the social sciences that theorizes and documents public education as a social institution that functions not only to provide students with cognitive skills but also to instill cultural norms, beliefs, and values in students. Although the role of public education in the socialization of children is well established in the literature, the social purpose and consequence of this role is debatable. Those who take what is often termed a functionalist perspective assert that schools should socialize students into the dominant and accepted cultural norms of the larger society. Doing this is necessary and helps to assure the equal smooth functioning of society (Durkheim, 1956, 1961; Parsons, 1959). Critical theorists acknowledge that the socialization that takes place in schools reflects the dominant norms and values of the larger society; however, they disagree with the assumption that these are 'accepted' norms (Apple, 1995; Arnot and Weiner, 1987; Bourdieu and Passerson, 1990; Giroux, 1988). Critical theorists argue that they are the norms and values of the dominant class, race and gender, but they are not 'accepted' freely. They are imposed. The result of this process, then, is the upholding of social injustice, not the assurance of equality.

Critical theorists have effectively critiqued the claim of education's neutrality. For example, Bourdieu and Passerson (1990) used the concept of 'symbolic violence' to signify the process by which the knowledge and beliefs consistent with the interests of the dominant order are portrayed as both natural and necessary. In Bourdieu's view, schools have considerable power because they appear to be neutral transmitters of the best and most valuable knowledge. This enables schools to promote the unequal aspects of society, while seeming to be objective and fair. Bourdieu and others (e.g. Sears, 1992; Giroux and McLaren, 1989) argue that schools promote a hegemonic curriculum, which is a curriculum that simultaneously legitimizes the dominant culture and marginalizes or rejects other cultures and knowledge forms (Stanley, 1992).

The concepts of hegemonic curriculum, and the related concept of hidden curriculum have been the subject of much theoretical contemplation, and have informed many investigations into educational practices. These previous studies have examined the ways in which upper and middle class, white and male culture, history, morals, behaviors, norms, and values are taught and enforced in schools through the power of a hegemonic process in which they are also naturalized, neutralized, and made invisible. Heterosexuality has largely been ignored as a significant part of this hegemonic process within public schooling (with the exception of Sears, 1992 and Unks, 1995). A critical perspective on the heterosexual norms of the schooling process is significantly missing from the literature on g/l/b youth and on education generally.

The concept of 'hegemonic heterosexuality', or 'heteronormativity', although not investigated in relation to the schooling process, has been established in feminist, gay and lesbian, and queer academic literature. The emphasis of poststructuralist, postmodern, and queer theory is on analysing the production of 'heterosexual hegemony' and the effect that this has on the lives of individuals and on society. Much like feminist theories' application of the concept of 'compulsory heterosexuality' (Rich, 1983; Ingraham, 1996), these theories address heteronormativity as an important and powerful social force used to coerce, oppress, and control the lives of individuals. I argue that it is important to use this theoretical approach to analyse the power and social force of heteronormativity at work in the lives and experiences of g/l/b youth. I have applied this approach to an analysis of institutions of public education and my findings suggest that this force significantly shapes the lives and identities of g/l/b youth (Miceli, 1998).

Normative heterosexuality is enforced rather explicitly in the environment, or 'culture', of public schools. In overt ways, it is enforced by the immense visibility of heterosexuality within the school environment – in the halls, in the cafeteria, at after school activities and functions, etc. The ways in which high school students, as well as administrators and teachers, incorporate heterosexual activities, behaviors, and language into the social aspects of the school establish and enforce a culture and ideology in which heterosexuality is exclusively the norm of acceptable behavior, discussion, and even feeling. In some ways, it seems that the explicitness of heterosexuality within the environment and culture of high schools would be almost immediately obvious to anyone who spends even a few hours in any school. However, as with many things, this observation, to a large degree, depends on one's perspective. In this case, heterosexual behavior and language are integrated and normalized to such a degree within school culture that they have become the 'natural', often translated into 'neutral', high school environment. Because of this, things like male–female displays of affection, discussions about same-sex relationships, school dances, proms, anti-gay jokes and insults, and harassment of g/l/b students are not viewed as 'explicitly heterosexual'. Instead they are generally perceived as part of the normal high school environment and a culture of teenage behavior. This is often how administrators, school board members, teachers, parents, and students interpret the environment of public schools.

Gay youth find themselves, therefore, defined as outside of the norm. Gay, lesbian, and bisexual students speak of public high schools as a 'straight world' with a normative order and culture of heterosexual feelings, meaning, ideologies, and behaviors that they know they are both outside of and surrounded by everyday. In ways that are very real and tangible to them, g/l/b students feel this environment as a social force shaping their lives. These students experience the environment of schools as not only explicitly heterosexual, but also explicitly intolerant of homosexuality. The evidence that there is an actual structure and force of heteronormativity in public schools can be found in g/l/b students' reports of the behaviors, ideas, and emotions they feel they are forced to repress while at school, and the punishment they face when they fail to adhere.

Every g/l/b student I spoke with gave at least one (most reported several) instance of verbal and/or physical harassment they or someone they knew experienced because they were gay, or suspected of being gay. Gay students describe their high school environments in a variety of ways, ranging from isolating and uncomfortable, to openly hostile to anyone who is openly gay, or perceived to be gay. To whatever degree they feel their school enforces heteronormativity, g/l/b students continuously monitor and modify their behavior to adjust to it. The following are examples of g/l/b students' experiences with, and perception of, the institutionalized heteronormativity of their schools. 'I knew that I could never walk down the halls holding my girlfriend's hand, you know, like straight people could, without getting harassed or beat up ... So, like, my girlfriend and I were really careful and restricted our contact at school' (Ani) (Miceli, 1998: 136). This statement illustrates that g/l/b students like Ani learn that heterosexual signs of affection are valued at her school and homosexual signs of affection are punished.

The following statement shows that a specific 'subversive action', like two girls holding hands in the hall, is not required to prompt efforts to ensure heteronormativity.

School sucks, I mean, it just sucks. But you all know that. It seems like it gets worse every day. The more visible I become the more people throw cookies at me ... The worse thing that ever happened was a guy throwing me up against a locker yelling all sorts of things that I can't remember, but they were just the usual things, in my face … It's annoying, it's something every-day. (Rick) (ibid.: 137)

Rick's experience illustrates that just his mere presence as a 'visible' gay male is per-ceived by some students as a threat to the heteronormative school culture and, there-fore, must be punished.

For Mary and her friends, such punish-ment came when they tried to establish a space for g/l/b students at their school.

> I had never been attacked at school until after I started the group [a g/l/b support group at her high school]. And then, I was verbally approached, I was cornered by like four guys, but that was just because of the activism I had been doing at school, and I just walked away from them. But, I mean, they threatened to kick my ass or what-ever … But, things that had happened to other people had just been horrid, I mean absolutely horrid. I mean, this one kid had rocks, these huge rocks, thrown at his head because he dared to speak up and he dared to say that he wanted this group. (Mary) (ibid.: 1998: 137)

Experiences like these are common to gay, lesbian and bisexual youth who attend public schools. The prevalence of harass-ment reported by g/l/b students provides empirical evidence to support the assertion that heteronormativity is a prominent social force in the culture of these public schools. Most students have been taught socially constructed meanings of sexual identity. They understand hetero/homosexuality to be a natural binary that proves heterosexuality to be normal, natural, and desirable, and proves homosexuality to be abnormal, deviant, and punishable. These students also get the message that the stigmatization of homosexuality is a natural and valued part of school culture. This power/knowledge of sexuality serves as a social force in the lives of all students. Most students respond to this force by repressing any thoughts or behav-iors, in themselves or in others, that are out-side of these norms. Those students who fail to do this suffer the consequences.

One of the simplest conclusions to make from any examination of public schools is that homosexuality, and the existence of gay

and lesbian people are rarely, if ever, mentioned in the curriculum. This lack of information on, or complete exclusion of, gay issues from classroom instruction and discussion is readily apparent to g/l/b youth. They express concern that this lack of infor-mation serves to reinforce heteronormativity and stereotypical understandings about g/l/b people. They believe that this lack of infor-mation is causally related to the harassment faced by g/l/b students. Some students also make a causal link between the lack of infor-mation and the struggles some g/l/b youth have dealing with their sexual identity in a positive way. Without access to accurate information about g/l/b people, these students are more likely to internalize the negative messages and 'accept' their 'stigma' and the limitations it places on them.

On the few occasions when students remember a teacher broaching a g/l/b related topic, they generally report that it was not handled well.

> Once in American History class our teacher was talking about how the slaves were treated walk-ing down the street when they first became free and he tried to compare it … to like gays and les-bians. He tried to like make an analogy to show the inequality … and one of these big macho sports guys in the class repeated like 'gay men', and this girl Janine, who I'd always been friends with said, 'Ewe, I don't want to hear about that!' … And [the teacher] goes 'Sorry, I didn't mean to bring it up we'll just change the subject.' You know, he should have been able to handle it better than that. (Becca) (ibid.: 144)

From Becca's account of this incident, we can see that there is opportunity in the general curriculum of public schools to discuss g/l/b issues. It is also evident from this exam-ple that teachers have to be knowledgeable and skilled to effectively teach about these issues within this heteronormative environ-ment. Becca's statement also illustrates that teachers, too, are subject to the power of the school culture of heteronormativity. In this case, the teacher's small step outside the bounds of this collective conscience was announced by a student, and this alone was enough to coerce the teacher back in line.

The absence of information on the issue of homosexuality, which is often stated to be a neutral position, is, in fact, part of the practice of heterosexual hegemony. Speaking only of heterosexuality in schools within cultures and societies where meanings and knowledge about sexual identity are entrenched in a heterosexual/homosexual binary that privileges and naturalizes heterosexuality and oppresses and dehumanizes homosexuality, reinforces the power of this binary. The culture, curriculum, and formal structure of the public schools attended by most g/l/b youth are infused with messages about sexual identity. These social institutions are organized forces of heteronormativity that shape the experiences and identities of g/l/b students in significant ways.

GAY YOUTH AS AGENTS OF SOCIAL CHANGE

Gay youth generally experience their public high schools as isolating, uncomfortable, and unsafe. Many g/l/b students endure the effects of this heteronormative institution alone and in silence; others are fortunate enough to find friends and some support outside of school walls to help them cope with the hours they must spend within them; and a few attempt to change their schools by claiming a voice and a space for g/l/b students. Many g/l/b youth demonstrate a rather sophisticated sociological understanding and analysis of the ways in which schools as a social institution affect their lives. This understanding goes beyond a feeling that they are uncomfortable at school, that they do not like school because they do not fit in there, or that being g/l/b, in-and-of itself, makes them feel uncomfortable. Many gay youth have an acute understanding of the ways in which sexual identity is socially defined and the 'stigma' of homosexuality is socially enforced. They see it in the cultural stereotypes, media images, ignorance, and institutionalized structures and practices such as those that take place at their schools. For some, having such an analysis of the situation is frustrating because they feel powerless against the strength of these institutionalized forces. Others feel a sense of personal contentment in knowing that these meanings were socially constructed. Some even feel empowered by the knowledge of a tangible force that can be resisted and changed.

Although it can be documented that the process of normative heterosexuality is institutionalized and, therefore, produces a systematic negative impact on g/l/b youth's experiences and identities, the political activity of some g/l/b students in the United States, Canada, England, Scotland and Australia provides evidence that this hegemonic process has not been fully successful. The most complete form of hegemony, in theory, works as an invisible exercise of power of the dominant group over the subordinate group – causing those who are oppressed to be blind or passively resigned to the power being exercised against them. Some gay youth are demonstrating that they are both aware of, and actively resistant to, the institutionalized forces of normative heterosexuality and stigmatized homosexuality. These students are transcending the socially and culturally conventional perspective of sexual identity as a solely personal and individual experience, and are testifying to the institutional and social causes of the problems of g/l/b youth. Such testimonies have not gone unnoticed.

At the local level, the efforts of some g/l/b students to change some of the heteronormative elements of their school generally result in considerable school and community debate. Their attempts to establish places for support for, and information about, g/l/b issues in their schools are generally (at least initially) perceived as a threat to the order and function of the school.

Foucault's (1976; 1980) power/knowledge dynamics of sexuality are crucial to both local and national debates over g/l/b student inclusions into public schools. The positions, opinions, and motivation of all of the actors in these debates reveal that they have all been informed, to a large degree, by their understandings of sexual identity, which they derived from scientifically and culturally produced knowledges of homosexuality. To justify and give power to their adamant resistance, individuals and social movement organizations opposing these inclusions generally draw from socially constructed and religious based knowledges of g/l/b sexual identities. They see homosexuality as abnormal, deviant, and immoral, and, therefore, believe it has no place in the public education of children. The following example of this type of opposition comes from the leader of a US organization called Citizens for Excellence in Education.

> Today, the secular world tells us to learn tolerance. Our schools tell our children 'you must learn to be tolerant of all people and all behaviors.' ... The current use of 'tolerance' in our schools was concocted by the homosexual/lesbian lobby to interject into all our children's classrooms, and their tender accepting minds, that homosexuality is just another normal lifestyle ... Christians are to be held responsible to God for not opposing the evils of our time. Parents must protect their children from the homosexual teaching and recruitment going on right now in our classrooms, through homosexual courses like 'Project 10.' Our children's minds are being openly polluted by homosexual 'tolerance' teaching. (Simonds, 1997: 1)

This typical statement of opposition to g/l/b students' efforts to improve their schools illustrates that the rejection largely rests in the person's or group's belief in the knowledge that homosexuality is an immoral behavior. Therefore, they assert that gay youth do not constitute a valid minority group and are unworthy of the rights they are seeking.

According to many who oppose the efforts of g/l/b youth, the real problem that needs to be addressed in schools is not the detrimental effect that heteronormativity has on g/l/b students, but rather, is the cultural climate that prompts even the consideration of granting such rights to a group of social deviants. The above statement points to the validity of this fear by drawing on the belief that homosexuals are 'deviants' and

'recruiters' who don't really want civil rights as much as they want to 'convert' young minds to their 'evil lifestyle'. Without reliance on religiously and socially produced stereotypical meanings of homosexuality, this assertion of the social problem of g/l/b youth has no basis.

Gay, lesbian, and bisexual youth, and the individuals and groups who support them are making attempts to counter the power of these socially constructed and institutionalized knowledges by framing the problem in different terms. Statements of justification and support for the changes g/l/b students seek are defined not in terms of sexual morality or deviance, but rather in terms of fundamental democratic rights. The following is a typical example of this type of argument from a US organization called People for Education Regarding Sexual Orientation Nationally (PERSON).

> Is it not precisely the role of education, and schools, to prevent ignorance? Yet, schools continue, through their own ignorance and fears, to censor all fair and accurate information about LGBT [lesbian, gay, bisexual, transgendered] people. And what is the result? Obviously, LGBT young people grow up isolated, afraid, lacking self-esteem or role models, disliking themselves ... LGBT young people, denied their right to the truth about themselves through appropriate schooling, experience a host of societally-imposed problems: harassment, hate violence, parental abuse, job discrimination, medical mistreatment, etc. Schools are failing in their responsibilities to these young people. (Miceli, 1998: 254)

Statements like these attempt to effectively articulate the negative experiences of g/l/b youth as a social problem with social causes and consequences. In these statements, the causality for the well documented problems of this population is named as the lack of information and environment of intolerance in public schools. They implicate a major social institution as a causal agent for the sufferings of g/l/b youth and they call for a social remedy.

Although the controversies and conflicts that surround their sexual identity often complicate the lives of g/l/b students, many of them are able to clearly articulate the core issues and the rational solutions to this social problem. The problem, according to many outspoken g/l/b youth is the preponderance of falsities, or one dimensional perspectives, about homosexuality that have been institutionalized by schools, religions, the state, and the media to create ignorance and fear about g/l/b people. The problems this causes for g/l/b students, they argue, can be alleviated by giving students the 'other side of the story' and giving them the skills to decide for themselves what they believe to be true.

These seemingly simple and rational answers proposed by g/l/b youth, too often, become buried, or disregarded, in the reality of power struggles and identity politics at the national level. However, increasing numbers of g/l/b youth are speaking up and making their opinions heard on this issue. The addition of this young cohort to the arena of identity politics and public debate offers the potential of significantly impacting these arenas. Gay students' participation in these discussions often simplifies debates by getting past the discursive rhetorics of politically charged and divisive identity politics, and by exposing knowledge claims as socially constructed strategies for power and control over identities, institutions, and culture.

G/l/b students' assertions and redefinitions of sexual identity are forcing institutions of public education to adapt their heteronormative structure and culture, and, therefore, are causing a shift in power. These students are naming their schools as institutions that are causing them harm through a process and structure of hegemonic heterosexuality. Some of them are demanding that schools take steps to rectify this damage.

CONCLUSION

The dynamics of power and knowledge are palpable in the lives of g/l/b students. The defining and oppressive power of institutionalized knowledges of sexual identity that are entrenched in the structural heteronormativity of public schools is evident in gay youth's accounts of the physical and psychological trauma they experience in school. For them school is a place where they are continually reminded they are not accepted and where they are denied access to knowledge that might allow them to fight back. These young adults spend much time and energy struggling against socially constructed and enforced knowledges and sexual identity categories that seek to define and control them, with or without their acquiescence.

However, the empowering and liberating properties of knowledge are also evident in the political activities of some gay youth. As they gain access to alternative information about g/l/b people and sexual identity, many g/l/b youth are able to use this new knowledge to empower themselves to resist the social forces of 'stigmatization'. Some deploy this power in an effort to transform the institutions that produce and enforce this social force. These g/l/b students understand that heteronormativity is an institutionalized aspect of their school, and the larger society in which they live, but they do not accept it as natural or necessary. They believe that, in democratic societies based on the principles of free speech and equality for all, knowledge about g/l/b people who are 'normal', productive, contributing citizens, and other understandings that are contradictory to the negative daily messages they receive at school should, rightfully, be made available to all students.

The emerging debates over g/l/b student groups and inclusions in public schools can push our thinking about the power and knowledge of the social construction of sexual identity, the institutionalization of heteronormativity, the purpose and goals of public education, and the rights of citizenship. On the one hand, because this issue is positioned beyond definitional boundaries, it is easily made invisible and can be summarily dismissed from consideration. On the other hand, when students themselves declare that there is a problem, then schools are forced to at least consider the issue. The topic of 'homosexuality' becomes visibly and immediately embodied in the lives of these students rather than in images, stereotypes, and abstract moral rhetoric.

The actions currently being taken by g/l/b students and their supporters in public schools throughout the world signal an important moment in the 'history of sexuality'. As Foucault (1976), and many others after him, have documented, the meanings, understandings, and socially produced knowledges of sexuality have varied historically and culturally. These transformations in the inscribed meanings of sexuality have varied along with other social, cultural, economic, and political changes. Historically, sexuality – as an identity, as a behavior, as a moral compass – has been a popular and effective weapon, used to define, regulate, and subvert in battles over power and control in all realms of society. Through the discursive strategies utilized by all parties, these struggles, regardless of the victor, generate some degree of new understanding of sexuality and identity. Contemporary g/l/b students may be propelling us towards a significant shift in the knowledge and power of sexual identity. These young people are asserting sexual identities that transcend the current socially defined boundaries. By doing this, they are sparking discussion, debate, and conflict that could potentially play an important part in changing meanings of sexuality and sexual identity, and altering our understanding of how these factors fit in with culture, politics, and the institutions of society.

The exact path and extent of this change, of course, cannot be accurately determined at this point in time. There is a need for much more research in this area from a wide range of academic disciplines if we are to fully understand the lives and potential social impact of this population of contemporary g/l/b youth. Gay, lesbian, and bisexual youth have only begun their fight. There is much left to be done.

REFERENCES

Ainlay, S., Becker, G. and Coleman, L.M. (1986) *The Dilemma of Difference: A Multidisciplinary View of Stigma.* New York: Plenum.

Altman, D. (1982) *The Homosexualization of America.* Boston, MA: Beacon.

Anderson, D.A. (1987) 'Family and peer relations of gay adolescents', *Adolescent Psychiatry*, 14: 162–78.

Anderson, D.A. (1994) 'Lesbian and gay adolescents: social and developmental considerations', *High School Journal,* special edition: 13–19.

Apple, M.W. (1995) *Education and Power.* 2nd edn. New York: Routledge.

Arnot, M. and Weiner, G. (eds) (1987) *Gender and the Politics of Schooling.* London: Hutchinson in association with Open University Press.

Bell, A.P., and Weinberg, M.S. (1978) *Homosexualities: A Study of Diversity Among Men and Women.* New York: Simon and Schuster.

Bell, A. *et al.* (1981) *Sexual Preference: Its Development in Men and Women.* Bloomington, IN: University of Indiana Press.

Bidwell, C. (1965) 'The school as a formal organization', in J.G. March (ed.), *Handbook of Organizations.* Chicago, IL: Rand McNally.

Bourdieu, P. and Passerson, J.C. (1990) *Reproduction in Education, Society and Culture.* Newbury Park, CA: Sage.

Bravmann, S. (1996) 'Postmodern queer identities' in Steven Seidman (ed.) *Queer Theory/Sociology.* Cambridge, MA: Blackwell. pp. 333–6.

Cass, V.C. (1979) 'Homosexual identity formation: a theoretical model', *Journal of Homosexuality*, 10: 77–84.

Cass, V.C. (1984) 'Homosexual identity: a concept in need of definition', *Journal of Homosexuality*, 9: 105–26.

Chandler, K. (1995) *Passages of Pride.* Los Angeles: Alyson Books.

Coles, R. and Stokes, G. (1985) *Sex and the American Teenager.* New York: Harper and Row.

Cook, J. and Herdt, C.H. (1991) 'To tell or not to tell: patterns of self-disclosure to mothers and fathers reported by gay and lesbian youth', in K. Pillemer, and K. McCartney (eds), *Parent and Child Relations Across the Lifespan.* New York: Oxford University Press.

Cusick, P.A. (1983) *The Egalitarian Ideal and the American High School.* New York: Longman.

DeCrescenzo, C. (ed.) (1994) *Helping Gay and Lesbian Youth: New Policies, New Programs, New Practice.* Binghamton, NY: Harrington Park Press.

Dennis, D.I. and Ruth E.H. (1986) 'Gay youth and the right to education', *Yale Law and Policy Review*, 4: 445–55.

Due, L. (1995) *Joining the Tribe: Growing Up Gay and Lesbian in the '90s.* New York: Doubleday.

Durby, D.D. (1994) 'Gay, lesbian, and bisexual youth', in T. DeCrescenso (ed.), *Helping Gay and Lesbian Youth*. Binghamton, New York: The Haworth Press, Inc.

Durkheim, E. (1956) *Education and Sociology*. Translated by P. Fauconnet. Glencoe, IL: The Free Press.

Durkheim, E. ([1925] 1961) *Moral Education: A Study in the Theory and Application of the Sociology of Education*. Glencoe, IL: The Free Press.

Durocher, C. (1990) 'Heterosexuality: sexuality or social system', *Resources for Feminist Research*, 19: 13–19.

Edwards, W.J. (1996) 'A sociological analysis of an invisible minority group: male adolescent homosexuals', *Youth and Society*, 27: 334–55.

Epstein, D. (ed.) (1994) *Challenging Lesbian and Gay Inequalities in Education*. Buckingham: Open University Press.

Erickson, E. (1968) *Identity, Youth, and Crisis*. New York: W.W. Norton.

Foucault, M. ([1976] 1990) *The History of Sexuality Volume 1: An Introduction*. New York: Vintage Books.

Foucault, M. (1980) *Power/Knowledge: Selected Interviews and Other Writings, 1972–1977*. Translated by C. Gordon, L. Marshall, J. Mepham and K. Soper. New York: Pantheon Books.

Gallois, C. and Cox, S. (1996) 'Gay and lesbian identity development: a social identity perspective', *Journal of Homosexuality*, 30: 1–30.

Gamson, J. (1989) 'Silence, death, and the invisible enemy: AIDS activism and social movement "Newness"', *Social Problems*, 36: 351–67.

Gibson, P. (1989) 'Gay male and lesbian youth suicide', *US Department of Health and Human Services Report of the Secretary's Task Force on Youth Suicide*, 3: 110–142.

Giroux, H.A. (1988) *Schooling and the Struggle for Public Life*. Minneapolis, MN: University of Minnesota Press.

Giroux, H.A. and McLaren, P. (eds) (1989) *Critical Pedagogy, the State, and Culture Struggle*. Albany, NY: SUNY Press.

Giroux, H.A. and McLaren, P. (1993) *Between Borders*. New York: Routledge.

Goffman, E. (1963) *Stigma: Notes on the Management of a Spoiled Identity*. New York: Simon & Schuster Inc.

Goggin, M. (1993) 'Gay and lesbian adolescence', *Sexuality in Adolescence*, S. Moore and D. Rosenthal (eds). London: Routledge.

Goodman, J. (1996) 'Lesbian, gay, and bisexual issues in education: a personal view', in D.R. Walling (ed.), *Open Lives, Safe Schools: Addressing Gay and Lesbian/Issues in Education*. Bloomington, IN: Phi Delta Kappa Educational Foundation. pp. 9–16.

Harbeck, K. (1994) 'Invisible no more: addressing the needs of gay, lesbian, and bisexual youth and their advocates', *High School Journal*, special edition: 170–80.

Hayes, W. (1991) 'To be young and gay and living in the '90s', *Utne Reader*, March/April: 94–100.

Harris, Mary, B. (1997) *School Experiences of Gay and Lesbian Youth*. Binghamton, NY: Harrington Park Press.

Herdt, G. (ed.) (1989a) *Gay and Lesbian Youth*. New York: Harrington Park Press.

Herdt, G. (1989b) 'Gay and lesbian youth, emergent identities and cultural scenes at home and abroad', *Journal of Homosexuality*, 17: 1–41.

Herdt, G. and Boxer, A. (1993) *Children of Horizons*. Boston: Beacon Press.

Hetrick and Martin. (1987) 'Developmental issues and their resolution for gay and lesbian adolescents', *Journal of Homosexuality*, 14: 25–43.

Hunter, J. and Schaecher, R. (1987) 'Stresses on lesbian and gay adolescents in schools', *Social Work in Education*, 9 (3): 180–90.

Ingraham, C. ([1994] 1996) 'The heterosexual imaginary: feminist sociology and theories of gender', in Steven Seidman. (ed.), *Queer Theory/Sociology*. Cambridge, MA: Blackwell. pp. 168–93.

Inving, J. ([1994] 1996) 'A place in the rainbow: theorizing gay and lesbian culture', in Steven Seidman (ed.) *Queer Theory/Sociology*. Cambridge, MA: Blackwell. pp. 213–40.

Karp, S. (1995) 'Trouble over the rainbow', D. Levine et al. (eds), in *Rethinking Schools: An Agenda for Change*, New York: The New Press. pp. 23–35.

Katz, F.E. (1964) 'The school as a social organization', *Harvard Educational Review*, 34: 428–55.

Margruder, B. and Wider-Haugrud, L.K. (1996) 'Homosexual identity expression among lesbian and gay adolescents: an analysis of perceived structural associations', *Youth and Society*, 27: 313–33.

Martin, D.A. (1982) 'Learning to hide: The socialization of the gay adolescent', *Adolescent Psychiatry*, 10: 52–65.

Martin, D.A., and Hetrick, E.S., (1988) 'The stigmatization of the gay and lesbian adolescent', *Journal of Homosexuality*, 16: 163–83.

Martin, W. (1996) *With God On Our Side: The Rise of the Religious Right in America*. New York: Broadway Books.

McDonald, G.J. (1982) 'Individual differences in the coming out process for gay men: implications for theoretical models', *Journal of Homosexuality*, 8: 47–60.

McIntosh, M.([1968] 1996) 'The homosexual role' in Steven Seidman (ed.), *Queer Theory/Sociology*. Cambridge, MA: Blackwell. pp. 33–40.

Miceli, M. (1998) 'Recognizing all the differences: gay youth and public education in America today', Dissertation, University of NY at Albany.

Millett, K. (1984) 'Beyond politics? Children and sexuality', in C.S. Vance (ed.), *Pleasure and Danger,* New York: Routledge.

Owens, Robert E. (1998) *Queer Kids*. Binghamton, NY: Harrington Park Press.

Parsons, T. (1959) 'The school class as a social system: some of its functions in American society', *Harvard Educational Review*, 29: 297–319.

Plummer, K. (1975) *Sexual Stigma: An Interactionist Account.* New York: Routledge.

Plummer, K. (1990) 'Understanding childhood sexualities', *Journal of Homosexuality*, 20 (1/2): 231–49.

Raymond, D. (1994) 'Homophobia, identity, and the meaning of desire: reflections on the cultural construction of gay and lesbian adolescent sexuality', in J.M. Irvine (ed.), *Sexual Cultures and the Construction of Adolescent Identities.* Philadelphia, PA: Temple University Press. pp. 115–50.

Remafedi, G. (1987) 'Homosexual youth: a challenge to contemporary society', *JAMA*, 10 July, 258.

Rich, A. (1983) 'Compulsory heterosexuality and lesbian existence', in A. Snitow et al. (eds), *Powers of Desire*, New York: Monthly Review Press.

Robertson, R. (1987) 'Young gays', in J. Hart and D. Richardson, *The Theory and Practice of Homosexuality.* London: Routledge and Kegan Paul.

Rofes, E. (1989) 'Opening up the classroom closet: responding to the educational needs of gay and lesbian youth', *Harvard Educational Review*, 59: 444–53.

Rubin, G. (1984) 'Thinking sex: notes for a radical critique of sexuality', in C.S. Vance (ed.), *Pleasure and Danger.* New York: Routledge.

Savin-Williams, R.C. (1989) 'Coming out to parents and self-esteem of gay and lesbian youth', *Journal of Homosexuality*, 18: 1–35.

Savin-Williams, R.C. (1990) *Gay and Lesbian Youth: Expressions of Identity.* New York: Hemisphere.

Schneider, M. (1989) 'Sappho was a right-on adolescent: growing up lesbian', *Journal of Homosexuality*, 17: 111–30.

Sears, J.T. (1992) *Sexuality and the Curriculum: The Politics and Practices of Sex Education.* New York: Teachers College Press.

Seidman, S. (1995) 'Deconstructing queer theory or the under-theorization of the social and the ethical', in Steven Seidman and Linda Nicholson (eds), *Social Postmodernism: Beyond Identity Politics.* Cambridge: Cambridge University Press. pp. 116–40.

Seidman, S. (1996) 'Introduction', in Steven Seidman (ed.), *Queer Theory/Sociology*, Cambridge, MA: Blackwell. pp. 1–29.

Simonds, R. (1997) *President's Report July 1997.* National Association of Christian Educators/Citizens for Excellence in Education. Box 3200, Costa Mesa, CA 92628.

Stanley, W.B. (1992) *Curriculum for Utopia: Social Reconstruction and Critical Pedagogy in the Post Modern Era.* Albany, NY: SUNY Press.

Sullivan, T. and Schneider, M. (1987) 'Developmental and identity issues in adolescent homosexuals', *Child and Adolescent Social Work*, 4: 13–23.

Troiden, R.R. (1979) 'Becoming homosexual: a model of gay identity acquisition', *Psychiatry*, 42: 362–73.

Troiden, R.R. (1988) *Gay and Lesbian Identity: A Sociological Analysis.* New York: General Hall.

Troiden, R.R. (1989) 'The formation of homosexual identities', *Journal of Homosexuality*, 17: 43–73.

Unks, G. (1993) 'Thinking about the homosexual adolescent', *High School Journal*, special edition: 1–6.

Unks, G. (ed.) (1995) *The Gay Teen: Educational Practice and Theory for Lesbian, Gay, and Bisexual Adolescents.* New York: Routledge.

Uribe, V. (1994) 'Project 10: a school-based outreach to gay and lesbian youth', *High School Journal*, special edition: 109–13.

Vaid, U. (1995) *Virtual Equality: The Mainstreaming of Gay and Lesbian Liberation.* New York: Doubleday.

Walling, D.R. (ed.) (1996) *Open Lives, Safe Schools: Addressing Gay and Lesbian Issues in Education.* Bloomington, IN: Phi Delta Kappa Publications.

Warner, M. (1991) 'Fear of a queer planet', *Social Text*, 9 (14): 1–17.

Wolpe, A.M. (1988) *Within School Walls: The Role of Disciplining Sexuality and the Curriculum.* London: Routledge.

Woog, D. (1995) *School's Out: The Impact of Gay and Lesbian Issues on America's Schools.* Boston: Alyson.

Zera, D. (1992) 'Coming of age in a heterosexist world: The development of gay and lesbian adolescents', *Adolescence*, 27: 848–54.

13

The Bisexual Menace

Or, Will the Real Bisexual Please Stand Up?

KRISTIN G. ESTERBERG

What is bisexuality? Is it an identity that a person holds, something one *is?* Is it a behavior, something one *does?* Is it stable, or does it shift and float and change? Is bisexuality distinct from heterosexuality and homosexuality? Is it a little bit of both, or neither? Does bisexuality disrupt the dichotomous way in which we are used to thinking about sexuality? (One is either straight *or* gay.) Does bisexuality have the potential to end sexual categories altogether? Or does it constitute a new, third category (straight *or* gay *or* bisexual)?

In the early part of the twenty-first century, bisexuality seems to be everywhere and nowhere. Popular magazines like *Newsweek* proclaim that bisexuality is 'coming out' in 'pop culture, in cyberspace, and on campus' (Leland, 1995: 44). *Essence* declares that bisexuality among Black women is 'out of the closet' and 'more common than you think' (Abner, 1992: 61). Even *The Economist* has gotten into the act, with a 'Christmas special' article on gays and bisexuality in Latin America (*The Economist,* 1999). Bisexuality seems highly visible, newly chic, and yet at the same time socially invisible. While to some social commentators the 'bisexual menace' might

seem to be knocking at society's door, bisexual invisibility – or what Kenji Yoshino terms bisexual erasure – is much more common (Yoshino, 2000).

Talk about bisexuality abounds (perhaps especially on daytime television – see Gamson, 1998). Bisexuality is the 'natural' state of sexuality – what everyone 'naturally' would be, before society has its way with you. And bisexuality does not exist. Bisexuals are 'really' straight or gay or something else – or would be, if society hadn't had its way with them. In popular discourse, bisexuals are often seen as a menace. Called 'vectors of disease', bisexuals are blamed for bringing AIDS and sexually transmitted diseases to 'innocent' wives and children and polluting the 'purity' of the lesbian community. Bisexual desire is seen as raging out of control, as bisexuals are portrayed as sexual swingers having multiple, simultaneous erotic relationships with 'anything that moves' (as the title of one bisexual journal ironically puts it). Bisexual sex is sometimes imagined as group sex, a tangle of sweaty, unidentified body parts (Garber, 1995). And bisexuals are seen as hopelessly confused: as fence sitters, unable to make up their minds about what they 'really' are.

At the same time, bisexuals are, at least in some quarters, lauded as postmodern, chic, and truly queer. In an historical moment that celebrates uncertainty and flux and delights in transgression, bisexuality fits the bill. Unlike more vanilla monosexuals – lesbians, gay men, straights – bisexuals alone have the ability to 'mess with' dualistic thinking about sexual identity. Because bisexuality does not fit neatly into the dominant categories – neither homosexual nor heterosexual, but both/and – bisexuality is sometimes seen as the sexual category to smash all sexual categories.

In both academic and popular discourse, bisexuality has been imagined in countless ways. Bisexuality has been variously defined as behavior, as identity, and as anti-identity. It has been seen as essential and, at the same time, as socially constructed. In the face of this slippery category, this chapter will look at some of the ways in which bisexuality has been conceived. The chapter will consider the difficulties involved in attempting to define bisexuality, the political debates raging about bisexuality, and some of the issues relating to bisexual invisibility.

A SERIES OF OPPOSITIONS

In popular discourse, bisexuality has primarily been defined as a series of oppositions. In one formulation, bisexuals and transgenders are seen on one side, the 'queer' side, versus lesbians and gay men on the other (Humphrey, 1999). In this formulation, lesbians and gay men are seen as more conventional – monogamous, more like straights. Gamson (1998) argues, for example, that same-sex desire as practiced by lesbians and gays is portrayed as 'morally acceptable' on daytime TV talk shows. Bisexuality, on the other hand, is portrayed as promiscuous and hence morally suspect. Queers, thus, are counterposed with 'nonqueers' (Ault, 1996). Sometimes this queerness is lauded, as when queer activists seek to deconstruct social

labels, seeing them as oppressive and regulatory. At other times and by other actors, this queerness is seen as perverse and perverted – not only by the right wing, but also among lesbians and gays (Gamson, 1995; Ault, 1996; Humphrey, 1999).

Another scenario, promoted at least at times by the mainstream lesbian and gay movement and by many in the bi movement, sees lesbians, bisexuals, and gay men as having interests in common. In this formulation, bisexuals are presumed to share a common base of oppression with lesbians and gay men. Bisexuals are lumped together with lesbians and gays (lesbigays), who must unite against straight oppression. Because all three desire – at least potentially, in the case of bisexuals – those of the same sex, and because this desire is stigmatized and legislated, lesbians, gays, and bisexuals' common interests in ending heterosexist oppression are emphasized over potential sources of difference.

In yet another formulation, lesbians are counterposed with all of those who 'love men' (Jeffreys, 1999). From the vantage point of lesbian feminism, bisexuals are seen as trading on heterosexual privilege and selling out the lesbian movement (see also Rust, 1995). In a sex-obsessed world, lesbians alone (and primarily feminist lesbians) are seen as standing firm against patriarchy.

Finally, in an opposition that is more often put forward by bisexual people themselves than by others, monosexuals are counterposed to bisexuals (Rust, 1992; Yoshino, 2000; Ault, 1996). Monosexuals – lesbians, gays, and straights – are seen as rigid, overly focused on gender as a basis for relationship. As Paula Rust argued in 1992: 'Heterosexuals and homosexuals treat biological sex as a necessary criterion; another person must be of a particular sex in order to be eligible as a romantic partner' (p. 298). For bisexuals, however, biological sex is only one of a number of different criteria that might be important in selecting partners. Bisexuals are thus seen as more flexible, having a unique ability to cross gender boundaries.

Why are these oppositions important? First, they reflect deeply held assumptions about the dualistic nature of Western thought. As any number of identity theorists have noted, the notion of sexual identity is rooted in modern Western culture and thought. In modern Western thought, the individual, who is presumed to have something called a self, reigns supreme. Prior to the mid to late nineteenth century, individuals simply did not *have* something called a sexual identity. Some time around the latter part of the nineteenth century, the terms *homosexual* and *heterosexual* entered into common parlance in Europe and the United States, and by the end of the twentieth century became the predominant way in which sexual desire was organized. By the late twentieth century, a Western man who experienced desire for men could hardly resist being labeled homosexual. Sexual desire is presumed to translate into a particular identity, a type of being (Foucault, 1980).

We tend to see things in terms of binaries: male/female, hetero/homo, black/white, dominant/subordinate. Because of the binary structure of Western thought, we tend not to recognize intermediate categories like bisexuality or transgenderism. When we do, we tend to interpret them in terms of the dominant categories (Ault, 1996). Thus, bisexuality is often treated in conjunction with homosexuality or lesbianism and much less often considered in its own regard.

These oppositions also reflect people's fears about bisexuality. For lesbians, gays, and straights, whose understandings of themselves are rooted in a clear separation of heterosexual from homosexual, bisexuality can raise powerful fears. Bisexuality – and nonconformist sexuality more generally – question the rigid hetero/homo distinction and, as Steven Seidman argues, 'the coding of sexuality by gender preference' (1993: 121). For straights, bisexuality can raise the specter of the dangerous pleasures of same-sex desire. For lesbians and gays, bisexuality raises the possibility of having to re-think one's own sexuality, acceptance of which is often hard won. Especially for those who are immersed in a lesbian or gay community and politics, the loss of identity can be devastating (Clausen, 1999; Young, 1992).

These oppositions tell us, too, about shifting political alignments. Debates about the nature of bisexuality reflect political questions as much as empirical ones. They force lesbians and gays to re-visit the question of political strategy. Contemporary lesbian and gay organizing reflects an 'ethnic' model of identity (Epstein, 1987). According to this model, lesbians and gays are an identifiable, relatively 'fixed' percentage of the population and, like other 'minority' groups, in need of civil rights protection (Duggan, 1995). The task of the recent lesbian and gay movement has been to develop a lesbian and gay community along an ethnic community model, with relatively firm boundaries, and to press for those civil rights. If sexual identities are not rigid and fixed, then what are the implications for a political strategy based on coming out? By shattering an essentialist notion of sexuality, bisexuality fundamentally shakes up the ethnic model of being gay (Seidman, 1993: 121).

The debates about bisexuality also highlight that sexual categories are social constructions, and especially in the case of bisexuality, fuzzily constructed ones indeed. Defining bisexuality feels a little bit like pinning jello to a wall. The jello oozes down in dribs and drabs, leaving a sticky trail. The material itself fails to hold shape.

TRADITIONAL SOCIAL SCIENTIFIC THINKING ABOUT BISEXUALITY

If popular discourse about bisexuality is steeped in Western dualisms, so is social scientific thinking about it. Bisexuality is often lumped together with lesbianism or homosexuality (see Fox, 2000, for a review), and bisexuality is often mechanistically reduced to behavior. Still, social scientists have thought about bisexuality in a number of different ways, some more productive than others.

One of the first to think about sexuality as a continuum was Alfred Kinsey (1948, 1953). Kinsey suggested in the late 1940s and early 1950s – a time in US history known more for its conformism than its sexual exploration – that bisexual behavior was far more widespread than previously understood. He argued that exclusive heterosexual attraction and behavior stood at one end of a continuum; exclusive homosexual attraction and behavior at the other. The vast majority of people are somewhere in the middle, with greater and lesser amounts of heterosexual and homosexual attraction mixed together. He expressed this continuum as a 7-point scale (with exclusive heterosexuality, ranked 0, at one end of the scale; equal attraction to men and women, 3, in the middle of the scale; and exclusive homosexuality, 6, at the other end of the scale). Using this scale, he argued that same-sex attraction and behavior were much more common than people had previously believed. In fact, something like 46 per cent of the men and 26–28 per cent of the women he studied had reported at least some erotic attraction or experience with a member of the same sex (Rust, 1995: 29).

Criticisms of the Kinsey scale have abounded. Some argue that bisexuality is not one dimension, as the Kinsey scale implies, but two. That is, bisexuality should not be seen as in the middle of heterosexuality and homosexuality. Instead, we should think of attraction toward women and men as consisting of two separate, unrelated dimensions. One might have a lot or a little of either, but one's attraction toward men may be wholly unrelated to one's attraction toward women (Stokes et al., 1998; Storms, 1980).

Others have argued that bisexuality is not two-dimensional but multidimensional. Weinberg, Williams and Pryor (1994) have argued that definitions of bisexuality must incorporate sexual feelings, sexual activities, and romantic feelings. Thus, they adapted Kinsey's scale to incorporate these elements. In the most complex adaptation of the Kinsey scale, Klein developed a complicated 21-point scale measuring past, present,

and ideal ratings of sexual attraction, sexual fantasies, lifestyle, sexual behavior, emotional preference, social preference, and identification of the self (Klein et al., 1985).

These models of bisexuality are useful in that they encourage us to reject dualistic thinking. As Marjorie Garber pessimistically notes, however, 'we have made virtually no progress since [Kinsey's] time in understanding bisexuality's place in sexual and cultural life' (Garber, 1995: 252). At the same time, however, with the exception of the unwieldy Klein grid, these models tend to conflate past and present. If a woman used to desire sexual relations with men, but now desires them with women, is she bisexual or lesbian? A little of each? Did she used to be heterosexual in the moment of experiencing that desire for men? In speaking of her 'journey through sexual identity' as she moved out of a lesbian identity, Jan Clausen asks, 'how many months or years would it take to change me into that alien life form, a heterosexual woman?' (1999: 227). These models also may not reflect how individuals themselves think of their sexuality. Is a self-proclaimed bi-dyke a Kinsey 5?

These alternative models notwithstanding, much traditional social science research uses a behavioral definition of bisexuality. A quick tour through almost any social science database or search service will reveal hundreds of articles about bisexuality and AIDS. This research, which became prominent in the late 1980s and 1990s as the AIDS epidemic spun seemingly out of control, focuses almost exclusively on a behavioral definition of bisexuality. In these articles, bisexuality is by and large nonproblematically seen as having sexual relations with both men and women. Primarily dealing with AIDS prevention, this research focuses predominantly on 'men who have sex with men' (MSMs) who may also have sex with women. This literature does not, by and large, concern itself with whether the men call themselves or think of themselves as bisexual. Rather, these articles are concerned with sexual behaviors that may put men and women at risk of acquiring HIV.

TYPOLOGIES OF BISEXUALITY

In a number of respects, most traditional social science definitions of bisexuality do not particularly clarify the matter. Sexuality, and perhaps especially bisexuality, seems much more complicated than the models allow. Is a lesbian who occasionally sleeps with men 'really' bisexual, even though she continues to think of herself as lesbian? Is a married man who occasionally fucks men bisexual, even if he thinks of himself as straight? What about a gay man and a lesbian who have sex with each other on occasion? Is theirs queer sex? Bisexual sex? Straight sex? And what *is* sex, anyway? What particular combinations of body parts and desires have to come together in order for something to be called sex? What do these folks have in common – anything? And what do they have in common with, say, men or women in prison who engage in same-sex relations inside, but only heterosexual relations outside? Bisexuality is, to say little else, diverse. Some have argued that there are, in fact, wholly different types of bisexuality. So, for example, Garber (1995) finds the following typology of bisexuality mentioned in the literature. (There are other typologies as well; see, for example, Stokes et al., 1998).

- *Latin bisexuality*: a form of bisexuality found in Latin societies in which men may engage in sexual behavior with both men and women (see Murray, 1995). As long as the men play an 'insertive' role, they are not considered homosexual (or, indeed, bisexual). Men who play a 'passive' role are considered homosexual, again, even if they also engage in sexual behavior with women.
- *'Defense' bisexuality*: a form of bisexuality found in societies that stigmatize homosexual behavior. (This form implies that bisexual individuals would 'really' be gay in the absence of negative social attitudes.)

- *Secondary homosexuality* (sometimes called 'situational' bisexuality). This form of bisexuality is said to occur when otherwise heterosexual people lack opportunities for a different-gendered partner (for example, in prisons or the military). Again, note that the implication is that the individuals are 'really' straight.
- *Married bisexuality*: a form of bisexuality that exists when individuals who are (heterosexually) married take same-sex partners as lovers.
- *'True' bisexuality*: equal interest in male and female partners.
- *Experimental bisexuality*: experimenting with bisexuality along the way to a more permanent gay or straight identity. Here, the implication is again that bisexuality is simply a phase – a common assumption still among many gay men and lesbians. Still, the stereotype has some elements of truth. In one longitudinal study of 216 bisexual men, about one third of the sample moved toward homosexuality over the course of a year (Stokes et al., 1997).
- *Technical bisexuality*: relationships with partners who are transgendered or, in some cultures, members of a 'third' sex.
- *Ritual bisexuality*: an example of this form would be that documented by Herdt (1982, 1997) in Papua, New Guinea, in which all adolescent males pass through a ritualized period of sexual relations with older males.

These typologies of bisexuality are interesting in that they encourage us to move, at least in small ways, beyond stereotyped images. Ironically, however, behavior-based conceptions of bisexuality such as these may also contribute to the erasure of bisexuality (Yoshino, 2000). Each of these bisexual 'types' is rooted in a behavioral definition of bisexuality. With the exception of 'true' bisexuality, these ways of typifying bisexuality assume that the individual is 'really' something else (or would be, given the opportunity). In some respects, these ways of thinking about bisexuality are like asking how many angels can dance on the head of a pin. (How many can dance? As many as they like, if one believes in angels; none, if one doesn't.) Traditional social scientific ways of thinking all assume that one could somehow objectively (and, hence, accurately) label someone (a research subject) as bisexual, based on some algorithm of behavior and preferences. These attempts at definition essentialize bisexuality and largely sidestep the issue of self-conception. How do individuals themselves think about their sexuality? If one does not think of oneself as bisexual, is one?

We know that there is a vast gap between behavior (and desire) and identity. As Paula Rust's (1992, 1995) research on lesbian and bisexual women clearly shows, very little separates contemporary Western lesbians and bisexual women in terms of sexual history and behavior. It is the meaning they make of their experiences that leads some women to think of themselves as bisexual and others as lesbian. Like the bisexuals in her sample, most of the lesbians had had erotic or romantic experiences with men – sometimes substantial experience. Yet the lesbians tended to discount their experiences with men in considering their sexual identities. What was most important to them was current behavior. Bisexual women, on the other hand, tended to focus on feelings of attraction. Using a strict behavioral definition of bisexuality, contemporary lesbianism is erased.

Traditional conceptions of bisexuality also see *gender* in dichotomous terms. That is, bisexuality is seen as attraction to or sexual behavior with both genders. There are assumed to be two, and only two genders, which correspond to biological sex: male and female. Yet as Kenji Yoshino (2000) provocatively argues, we leave intersexuality out of the picture in thinking about bisexuality. That is, we would not think of a man as being bisexual if he were attracted to both men and intersexed people, even though this would constitute attraction to two different biological sexes. (Tellingly, we don't have a

social label for such a man.) Nor would we think of a woman as bisexual if she were attracted to both butch and fem women: two genders, but one biological sex. We would think of her as lesbian. Thus, our thinking about bisexuality tends to reify dualistic and biologically based notions of sex and gender.

This is not, then, entirely satisfactory. Much recent thinking about gender has attempted to challenge its presumed biological basis. Research into the intersexed (Kessler and McKenna, 1985; Money, 1988) as well as recent works by transgendered activists shows far greater variability in biological sex, let alone gender expression, than is commonly assumed.

RACE, CULTURE, BISEXUALITY

The emphasis on identity in modern Western culture raises particular questions in thinking about culture, race, and bisexuality. Different societies in different time periods clearly organize sexuality differently. When we look cross-culturally, we find ample evidence of what we might call bisexual behavior. So, for example, anthropologist Gilbert Herdt (1982, 1997) has extensively documented same-sex behaviors among the Sambia of Papua, New Guinea. In this society, all adolescent males experience a period of ritual same-sex expression with an older male. As adults, the males sexually initiate adolescent boys into adulthood, and most adult males also enter into sexual relationships with women. Are all Sambia men bisexual? Not according to the concepts of their culture. What does it mean to use such a term outside of its cultural context?

Similarly, a number of anthropologists and sociologists have documented what some have called a Latin model of homosexuality (or Latin bisexuality) (Carrier, 1992; Murray, 1996). In this model, already mentioned, males who engage in sexual activity with other males are not considered homosexual as long as they otherwise play culturally approved masculine roles. Men who play an active role in anal intercourse do not violate traditional masculine roles, and thus, those who do so are not considered gay. Those who play a passive role, however, are. On behavioral grounds, one might call those who play an active role bisexual, for they are often married or have relationships with women as well. But again, no word for bisexuality exists in this socially structured form of sexuality.

Some have suggested that, for a variety of reasons, African American and Latino men in the United States may be more likely to engage in bisexual behavior while still retaining a heterosexual identity (Peterson, 1992; Stokes et al., 1998). The reasons are various: racism within the predominantly white gay and lesbian community; a desire to retain connections to one's family of origin and racial/ethnic community; and lower socio-economic status, which brings with it increasing opportunities to engage in same-sex behavior. Poor and marginalized men, for example, are more likely to engage in male prostitution or to be imprisoned. But these men may not think of themselves as homosexual or bisexual. Again, what does it mean to think of these men as bisexual when they, themselves would not?

BISEXUAL IDENTITIES

Strikingly, another literature focuses more on the question of bisexual identity than behavior (Dobinson, 1999; Esterberg, 1997; Rust, 1995; Whisman, 1996). That is, how do people come to see themselves as bisexual? What does bisexuality mean to the people who see themselves in that way? Instead of seeing bisexual identity as indelibly rooted in behavior, this work focuses on individuals' understandings of themselves as bisexual.

Much of this literature questions the notion of identity itself – and challenges the notion that sexual identities are fixed, essential, or unchanging. In my earlier research (1997), for example, I examine the identity

accounts, or stories, that bisexual women in a Northeast community use to understand their experiences. Rather than seeing identities as fixed or essential parts of the person, I argue that identity accounts arise within the particular communities and social settings in which women find themselves. As women make sense of their desires, attractions, and relationships, they come to see themselves in culturally available terms. As a bisexual movement developed through the 1980s and 1990s, women who experienced desire for both men and women could increasingly think of themselves as bisexual.

In the particular community I studied, I identified four dominant accounts of bisexual experience. Some of the women I interviewed saw themselves as 'not quite heterosexual'. Their bisexuality consisted of an openness to experiences with women, even though they had primarily had erotic and romantic relationships with men. Others saw themselves as openly, sometimes proudly bisexual. These women tended to be active in creating a politicized bisexual presence within the lesbian/gay community. A third account was expressed by women who came to bisexuality from the vantage point of lesbian feminism. These women had previously thought of themselves as lesbian; in coming to understand their desire for men, they came to think of themselves as bisexual. A final group of women rejected the impulse to label their identity at all, preferring to see their sexuality as fluid, in the moment. Labels – even seemingly expansive ones like bisexuality – felt restrictive.

Others have developed the concept of sexual fluidity (Fox, 2000; Golden, 1987; Esterberg, 1997), a notion that has even gained some social currency as queer politics and queer identities proliferate (see, for example, Gideonse, 1997). More recent studies of lesbian and bisexual women have suggested that sexual identities are far more changeable over the life course than dichotomous conceptions of sexuality suggest. Most previous models of homosexual identity have seen identity development as occurring in one direction only: from straight to lesbian or gay (Cass, 1979, 1983/1984; Troiden, 1988). Yet, as Carla Golden (1987, 1994) and others have argued, women may embrace very different sexual identities at different points in time, depending on their political commitments, their life cycle stage, and the social contexts in which they find themselves. (Tellingly, scholars who focus on sexual fluidity have been far less likely to consider men, leading some scholars to argue that women's sexuality is more fluid than men's. We might ask what this says about the researchers themselves and the social construction of men's sexuality.)

Interestingly, considerably more attention has been paid to those who claim a bisexual identity en route to a lesbian/gay one. Relatively little attention has been paid to those who move from a gay or lesbian identity to a bisexual one – or to those who experience numerous, multiple shifts in identity (from straight to lesbian to bi to lesbian, for example). Yet it is clear that these changes exist for significant numbers of people, at least among bisexual women. In Rust's sample of women who currently identified as bisexual, 84 per cent had seen themselves as lesbian at an earlier point in their lives; 64 per cent had switched between lesbian and bisexual identities two or more times (Rust, 1995).

BECOMING BISEXUAL

How do people become bisexual? Interestingly, relatively little attention has been paid to this question (although see Stokes et al., 1997; Phillips and Over, 1995). Although researchers and social commentators have focused intensively on the question of how people 'become' gay, with frequent recourse to biological explanations, this question is much less frequently raised in the literature on bisexuality. Social researchers, for whatever reason, have been remarkably less driven to find a biological basis for bisexuality than they have for homosexuality. (There are a few, however,

who look for such a link; see Van Wyk and Geist, 1995, who argue for a multi-factored explanation for bisexuality that includes, for women, early exposure to masculinizing hormones.) Why is this so? Perhaps it is because bisexuality brings up the messy notion of choice, raising the question of whether (and how) bisexuals make active choices about their sexuality.

Still, at least some researchers have thought about how people 'become' bisexual. Drawing on the stage models of identity acquisition used to describe homosexual identity development (Cass, 1979, 1983/ 1984; Troiden, 1988), Weinberg et al. (1994) argue that bisexual identity develops in a series of stages. In their study of San Francisco bisexuals involved in what they called the 'sexual underground', Weinberg et al. identified four stages of bisexual identity development. The first stage involves a period of initial confusion, followed by a stage in which the individual both finds and accepts a bisexual identity. Settling into the identity is the third stage, followed by a fourth stage, continued uncertainty about the identity.

BISEXUALITY AND FEMINISM

Some of the sharpest debates about bisexuality have occurred within lesbian communities, as lesbians have argued vigorously and acrimoniously about lesbians who have come to have sexual and romantic relationships with men (Ault, 1994; Rust, 1995). Feminist lesbians have tended to be hypercritical of bisexuality. In my own research, one former lesbian who became involved with a man received hate mail. Others are called by the unfortunate term 'hasbian', a term Stacey Young notes defines a woman *only* in terms of what she once was' and implies that the former lesbian is a 'has-been' (Young, 1992: 77). These kinds of experiences are well documented in personal narratives by bisexuals (see, for example, Hutchins and Kaahumanu, 1991).

Why are the debates about bisexuality so fierce within lesbian communities? The answer lies, at least in part, in the influence that lesbian feminism has had on the development of lesbian community life. As a political theory, lesbian feminism high-lighted the issue of choice and suggested that any woman could be a lesbian. From this followed the lesbian imperative: if one *could* be a lesbian, one *should* be. Interest-ingly, Paula Rust (1995) notes that many early lesbian feminists believed that all women were inherently bisexual. Lesbians were encouraged to choose relationships with women as a political statement. Lesbianism thus becomes a political choice.

Lesbian feminism sees lesbians as work-ing against male domination because, by choosing women, lesbians are denying men services and working to build political, social, and economic relationships among women. They also hold out the possibility to heterosexual women that they, too, can become lesbian and move out from under men's patriarchal domination. In this way, bisexuality is perceived as a threat to lesbian visibility, and bisexual women are seen as traitors, ones who have fallen away from the fold (Ault, 1994; Rust, 1995). Although lesbian feminism has been eclipsed by newer forms of lesbian social organization (Stein, 1993, 1997; Esterberg, 1997), this position on bisexuality is by no means old fashioned or merely a byproduct of the 1980s. See, for example, Jeffrey's recent article (1999), in which she argues that bisexual women – because they *could* choose women but do not – are 'conformists'. In her view, bisexual women pose a threat to lesbian visibility and reinforce compulsory heterosexuality.

MONOGAMY AND CHOICE

Debates around monogamy and choice have been fierce. Bisexuality highlights the notion that people can have a choice in their sexuality. Although heterosexuals, lesbians, and gays also have the capacity to exercise

choice in acting on their desires, the question of choice retains greater significance for bisexuals. Even if individuals do not neces-sarily choose *desire,* a position many for-merly lesbian bisexuals claim, they can certainly choose to act on it or not. The question of choice is, perhaps, especially resonant among the Christian right, who see the choice of sexual identity, which they extend to lesbians and gays as well, as a sin-ful one (Esterberg and Longhofer, 1998). But issues of choice are tricky among the left as well (Ault, 1996), and especially among lesbian feminists, as we have seen. In the face of the mainstream lesbian/gay movement, which maintains that sexual orientation is biologically based, immutable, and fixed, bisexuals raise the possibility that sexual orientation is not so fixed after all, a position that many in the lesbian and gay movement see as undercutting their political position.

Is the issue of choice so contentious and personally threatening among gay men as it is among lesbians? Perhaps not to the same degree. As Vera Whisman (1996) argues, gay men are less likely to rely on narratives of choice to account for their sexuality. In her study of 72 New York gay men and les-bians, she found relatively few men, com-pared with women, who believed that their sexual identity was a choice. Because they are more likely to draw on dominant accounts of sexuality – that they are born 'that way' – gay men are perhaps less likely to feel threatened by bisexual choice. For if one believes that one is born lesbian or gay, the existence of bisexuals (who presumably have a choice) will not unsettle one's own identity in the same way.

By its very nature, bisexuality also raises the issue of monogamy. Can bisexuals be monogamous, Lenore Norrgard (1991) asks? She answers: some are, but not all, and she goes on to defend nonmonogamy as a valid choice for bisexual people. In popu-lar discourse, bisexuals are as a matter of course presumed to be nonmonogamous, in a way of thinking that folds bisexuality into behavior. Monogamous bisexuals (serially or not) are rendered invisible. 'At any given time, one's a lesbian if one's involved with a woman and one's straight if one's in a relationship with a man,' argued one of the interviewees in my study (Esterberg, 1997: 166). Another argued, 'if a woman is bisexual, the inherent assumption is that she is expressing her sexuality with both women and men partners', something she called 'emotionally irresponsible' (ibid.).

Like the question of choice, the issue of monogamy, too, may resonate somewhat differently among gay men and lesbians, nonmonogamy having a much more accepted history among gay men. Numerous accounts of pre-AIDS gay men's social life have emphasized the acceptance of non-monogamous, sometimes anonymous sex (Murray, 1996; Esterberg, 1996). As Martin Levine (1992) argues, the advent of AIDS signaled the end of a hypersexualized gay male culture. A 'relational ethos' began to characterize the organization of gay men's erotic life. At the same time, the mainstream gay movement, with its newfound emphasis on 'gay normalcy' characterized, for example, by freedom to marry campaigns and a renewed emphasis on religion and spirituality, has signaled a move away from non-monogamous sex.

Kenji Yoshino (2000) argues that gays and straights alike have an interest in defining themselves in opposition to bisexuals through the institution of monogamy. First, as Yoshino notes, monogamy is a societal norm. And although straights, with their access to legal marriage, have perhaps greater investment in that norm than gays, still monogamy has, especially in recent years, become a norm among many lesbians and gays. Some gays, as Yoshino notes, distinctly wish to 'retire' societal stereotypes of gay promiscuity (see, for example, Kirk and Madsen, 1989). Bisexuals threaten the norm of monogamy. Although, of course, there need be no necessary relationship between having the *potential* for relationships with both sexes and actually having them, this distinction is not often made. Yoshino further

argues that bisexuality raises the issue of sexual jealousy among straights and gays alike. Even if a bisexual is involved in a monogamous relationship with a nonbisexual, holding a bisexual identity continually brings to the fore the lover's potential inadequacy. Thus, he argues, straights and gays have a vested interest in the erasure of bisexuality.

BI POLITICS, BI MOVEMENTS

The 1980s and 1990s saw a flowering of bisexual organizing in the United States, as bisexuals sought to counter their invisibility. This period saw, as Paula Rust (1995) details, the creation of a number of autonomous organizations, groups, networks, and newsletters. Several path-breaking anthologies were published (Hutchins and Kaahumanu, 1991; Weise, 1992), and bisexuals – many of them movement-affiliated – appeared on numerous day time talk shows (Gamson, 1998). Articles on bisexuality appeared in mainstream magazines and newspapers, leading some to proclaim a new bisexual chic.

One strategy bisexual activists have used extensively entails alignment with the lesbian/gay movement and an attempt to force lesbians and gays to include bisexuals in their organizing. This strategy has been, to a certain extent, successful, as many mainstream lesbian/gay activists have added the word 'bisexual' to their organizations and activities. Yet the inclusion of bisexuals under a lesbigay umbrella is by no means certain. (See, for example, Humphrey's [1999] discussion of 'queering' the lesbian/gay caucus of the UK public-sector trade union.) Paula Rust notes, ironically, that the lesbian/gay movement is, in some respects, responsible for the creation of a bisexual movement in the first place.

In a very real sense, the lesbian/gay movement created bisexuals as an oppressed group by creating a discourse in which lesbians/gays and heterosexuals, but not bisexuals, were defined into political existence. Thus, the lesbian/gay movement not only altered the political arena by creating a new political tradition; it also created the need for a bisexual movement. (Rust, 1995: 257)

Other bisexual activists have sought to organize under a queer umbrella. The rise of queer politics in the 1990s may be a more welcome home for those bisexuals who value the trangressive nature of their sexuality. As Lisa Duggan argues, this new 'queer community', if it can be called that, 'is unified only by a shared dissent from the dominant organization of sex and gender' (1995: 165). If queer activists seek to challenge traditional dichotomies of gay/ straight, male/ female, then bisexual activists fit right in. Queer organizing also represents a more youthful 'in-your-face' style of activism, anathema to some within the more staid lesbian and gay movement. Yet the queer umbrella, while it may shelter a number of diverse groups and practices – lesbians, gay men, bisexuals, transgenders, sadomasochists, and others – also functions, as Ault (1996) argues, as a 'cloaking device'. In that sense, bisexuals may be as invisible within a queer movement as within a lesbian and gay one.

Bisexual organizing holds enormous challenges. Despite recent 'discoveries' of bisexuality, the issue of bisexual invisibility is paramount.[1] In becoming visible, however, bisexuals run the risk of creating a fixed identity. Identities, as queer and postmodern theorists have argued, are inherently limiting and subject individuals to social regulation. Yet identities may also hint at liberation, as Steve Seidman argues, by holding out the promise of political agency (1993: 134). The attempt to organize around bisexual identity thus poses the danger of fixing boundaries and limiting possibilities at the same time as it creates possibilities for women and men to articulate their desires and create a public space for them.

Learning from some of lesbian feminism's mistakes, bisexual organizers have sought to remain open about inclusion and the nature of bisexual identity. As a group

that has been most subject to erasure, bisexual organizers are sensitive to the needs for individuals to define themselves. But can bisexual organizing ultimately avoid an ethnic model of social movement organizing? That remains to be seen.

BYE-BYE BINARY? THE POTENTIAL OF BISEXUALITIES

What's not okay is to lie about the complex attractions that often culminate in simple labels. What's unacceptable is to bully the border-crossers. What's got to stop is the rigging of history to make the either/or look permanent and universal. (Clausen, 1999: xxviii)

What are the chances that sexual identities as we know them today will actually disappear? Will bisexuality usher in an era of unlabeled sexuality? Are we at the brink of just such a queer moment, in which the hetero/homo divide collapses into an unlabeled ambisexuality, in which gender plays no more role in sexual choices than eye color or the way someone walks or cuts their hair? The existence of those who prefer not to take an identity, who prefer to remain unlabeled, might hint at such a possibility.

Marjorie Garber seems relatively optimistic. She argues that 'bisexuality itself, or bisexualities themselves, put into question the viability of a "politics of identity" at all'. Practically speaking, she argues that the animosity between lesbians and gays, on the one hand, and bisexuals, on the other, 'underscores the fact that these secure identities and divisions are already on the way out. To acknowledge this is not to accept defeat but to recognize success' (Garber, 1995: 87). I remain less sanguine about the inevitability of this success. The tenacity with which heterosexuals hold onto heterosexual privilege and the deeply institutionalized nature of heterosexual life, on the one hand, combined with the deep investments that lesbians and gays have made in their sexual identities and movements, on the other, lead me to believe that the collapse of binary thinking is not imminently on the horizon. What may be on the horizon is a recognition that sexuality is far more complex than previously realized. At best, perhaps we can recognize that the categories we've come up with are not universal and, in Jan Clausen's words, stop bullying the border crossers.

NOTE

1 In regards to the repeated 'discovery' of bisexuality, Marjorie Garber asks: 'Is sexuality a fashion – like platform shoes, bell-bottomed trousers, or double-breasted suits – that appears and then disappears, goes underground, only to be 'revived' with a difference? Is it that 'news', by its very nature, must always be 'new' to be noticed? Do we need to keep forgetting bisexuality in order to remember and rediscover it?' (Garber, 1995: 20)

REFERENCES

Abner, Allison (1992) 'Bisexuality out of the closet', *Essence*, 23 (6): 61–6.

Ault, Amber (1994) 'Hegemonic discourse in an oppositional community: lesbian feminists and bisexuality', *Critical Sociology*, 20 (3): 107–22.

Ault, Amber (1996) 'Ambiguous identity in an unambiguous sex/gender structure: the case of bisexual women', *Sociological Quarterly*, 37 (3): 449–63.

Carrier, Joseph (1992) 'Miguel: sexual life history of a gay Mexican American', in Gilbert Herdt (ed.), *Gay Culture in America: Essays from the Field*. Boston: Beacon Press. pp. 202–24.

Cass, Vivienne C. (1979) 'Homosexual identity formation: a theoretical model', *Journal of Homosexuality*, 4: 219–35.

Cass, Vivienne C. (1983/1984) 'Homosexual identity: a concept in need of definition', *Journal of Homosexuality*, 9: 105–26.

Clausen, Jan (1999) *Apples & Oranges: My Journey Through Sexual Identity*. Boston: Houghton Mifflin.

Dobinson, Cheryl (1999) 'Confessions of an identity junkie', *Journal of Gay, Lesbian, and Bisexual Identity*, 4 (3): 265–9.

Duggan, Lisa (1995) 'Making it perfectly queer', in Lisa Duggan and Nan D. Hunter (eds), *Sex Wars: Sexual Dissent and Political Culture*. New York: Routledge.

Epstein, Steven (1987) 'Gay politics, ethnic identity: the limits of social constructionism', *Socialist Review*, 93/94: 9–54.

Esterberg, Kristin (1996) 'Gay cultures, gay communities: the social organization of lesbians, gay men, and bisexuals', in K. Cohen and R.C. Savin-Williams (eds), *The Lives of Lesbians, Gay Men, and Bisexuals: Children to Adults*. Fort Worth, TX: Harcourt.

Esterberg, Kristin (1997) *Lesbian and Bisexual Identities: Constructing Communities, Constructing Selves*. Philadelphia: Temple University Press.

Esterberg, Kristin and Longhofer, Jeffrey (1998) 'Researching the radical right: Responses to anti-lesbian/gay initiatives', in Janice Ristock and Catherine Taylor (eds), *Inside the Academy and Out: Lesbian/ Gay/Queer Studies and Social Action*. Toronto: University of Toronto Press.

Foucault, Michel (1980) *The History of Sexuality Volume 1: An Introduction*. New York: Vintage Books.

Fox, Ronald C. (2000) 'Bisexuality in perspective: a review of theory and research', in Beverly Greene and Gladys Croom (eds), *Education, Research, and Practice in Lesbian, Gay, and Transgendered Psychology: A Resource Manual*. Thousand Oaks, CA: Sage. pp. 161–206.

Gamson, Joshua (1995) 'Must identity movements self-destruct? A queer dilemma', *Social Problems*, 42: 390–407.

Gamson, Joshua (1998) *Freaks Talk Back*. Chicago: University of Chicago Press.

Garber, Marjorie (1995) *Vice Versa: Bisexuality and the Eroticism of Everyday Life*. New York: Simon & Schuster.

Gideonse, Ted (1997) 'The sexual blur', *The Advocate*, 736: 28–34.

Golden, Carla (1987) 'Diversity and variability in women's sexual identities', in Boston Lesbian Psychologies Collective (ed.), *Lesbian Psychologies: Explorations and Challenges*. Urbana and Chicago: University of Illinois Press. pp. 18–34.

Golden, Carla (1994) 'Our politics and choices: the feminist movement and sexual orientation', in Beverly Greene and Gregory M. Herek (eds), *Lesbian and Gay Psychology: Theory, Research, and Clinical Applications*. Thousand Oaks, CA: Sage. pp. 54–70.

Herdt, Gilbert (1982) *Rituals of Manhood: Male Initiation in Papua New Guinea*. Berkeley, CA: University of California Press.

Herdt, Gilbert (1997) *Same Sex, Different Cultures: Exploring Gay and Lesbian Lives*. Boulder, CO: Westview Press.

Humphrey, Jill C. (1999) 'To queer or not to queer a lesbian and gay group? Sexual and gendered politics at the turn of the century', *Sexualities*, 2 (2): 223–46.

Hutchins, Loraine and Kaahumanu, Lani (eds) (1991) *Bi Any Other Name: Bisexual People Speak Out*. Boston: Allyson.

Jeffreys, Sheila (1999) 'Bisexual politics: a superior form of feminism?', *Women's Studies International Forum*, 22 (3): 273–85.

Kessler, Suzanne J. and McKenna, Wendy (1985) *Gender: An Ethnomethodological Approach*. Chicago: University of Chicago Press.

Kinsey, Alfred C., Pomeroy, Wardell B. and Martin, Clyde E. (1948) *Sexual Behavior in the Human Male.* Philadelphia: W.B. Saunders.

Kinsey, Alfred C., Pomeroy, Wardell B., Martin, Clyde E. and Gebhard, Paul H. (1953) *Sexual Behavior in the Human Female.* Philadelphia: W.B. Saunders.

Kirk, Marshall and Madsen, Hunter (1989) *After the Ball: How America Will Conquer its Fear and Hatred of Gays in the 90's.* New York: Plume.

Klein, Fritz, Sepekoff, Barry and Wolf, Timothy J. (1985) 'Sexual orientation: a multi-variable dynamic process', in Fritz Klein and Timothy Wolf (eds), *Two Lives to Lead: Bisexuality in Men and Women.* New York: Harrington Park Press. pp. 35–48.

Leland, John (1995) 'Bisexuality emerges as a new sexual identity', *Newsweek*, 126 (3): 44–50.

Levine, Martin P. (1992) 'The life and death of gay clones', in Gilbert Herdt (ed.), *Gay Culture in America: Essays from the Field.* Boston: Beacon.

Money, John (1988) *Gay, Straight, and In-Between: The Sexology of Erotic Orientation.* New York: Oxford University Press.

Murray, Stephen O. (1995) *Latin American Male Homosexualities.* Albuquerque: University of New Mexico Press.

Murray, Stephen O. (1996) *American Gay.* Chicago: University of Chicago Press.

Norrgard, Lenore (1991) 'Can bisexuals be monogamous?' In Loraine Hutchins and Lani Kaahumanu (eds), *Bi Any Other Name.* Boston: Allyson.

Peterson, John L. (1992) 'Black men and their same-sex desires and behaviors', in Gilbert Herdt (ed.), *Gay Culture in America: Essays from the Field.* Boston: Beacon Press.

Phillips, Gabriel and Over, Ray (1995) 'Differences between heterosexual, bisexual and lesbian women in recalled childhood experiences', *Archives of Sexual Behavior*, 24 (1): 1–20.

Rust, Paula (1992) 'The politics of sexual identity: sexual attraction and behavior among lesbian and bisexual women', *Social Problems*, 39 (4): 367–86.

Rust, Paula (1995) *Bisexuality and the Challenge to Lesbian Politics: Sex, Loyalty, and Revolution.* New York: NYU Press.

Seidman, Steven (1993) 'Identity and politics in a "postmodern" gay culture: Some historical and conceptual notes', in Michael Warner (ed.), *Fear of a Queer Planet: Queer Politics and Social Theory.* Minneapolis: University of Minnesota Press. pp. 105–42.

Stein, Arlene (ed.) (1993) *Sisters, Sexperts, Queers: Beyond the Lesbian Nation.* New York: Plume.

Stein, Arlene (1997) *Sex and Sensibility: Stories of a Lesbian Generation.* Berkeley, CA: University of California Press.

Stokes, Joseph, Damon, Will and McKirnan, David (1997) 'Predictors of movement toward homosexuality: a longitudinal study of bisexual men', *Journal of Sex Research*, 34 (3): 304–12.

Stokes, Joseph, Miller, Robin and Mundhenk, Rhonda (1998) 'Toward an understanding of behaviourally bisexual men: the influence of context and culture', *Canadian Journal of Human Sexuality*, 7 (2): 101–13.

Storms, M.D. (1980) 'Theories of sexual orientation', *Journal of Personality and Social Psychology*, 38 (5): 783–92.

The Economist (1999) 'Living la vida loca', 18 December: 81–83.

Troiden, Richard (1988) *Gay and Lesbian Identity: A Sociological Analysis.* Dix Hills, New York: General Hall.

Van Wyk, Paul H. and Chrisann S. Geist (1995) 'Biology of bisexuality: critique and observation' *Journal of Homosexuality*, 28 (3–4): 357–73.

Weinberg, Martin S., Williams, Colin J. and Pryor, Douglas W. (1994) *Dual Attraction: Understanding Bisexuality.* New York: Oxford University Press.

Weise, Elizabeth Reba (ed.) (1992) *Closer to Home: Bisexuality and Feminism.* Seattle: Seal Press.

Whisman, Vera (1996) *Queer by Choice: Lesbians, Gay Men, and the Politics of Sexuality.* New York: Routledge.

Yoshino, Kenji (2000) 'The epistemic contract of bisexual erasure.' *Stanford Law Review*, 52 (2): 353–461.

Young, Stacey (1992) 'Breaking silence about the "b-word": bisexual identity and lesbian-feminist discourse', in Elizabeth Reba Weise (ed.), *Closer to Home: Bisexuality and Feminism.* Seattle: Seal Press. pp. 75–87.

Part III

INSTITUTIONS

14

Imagining the Place of the State

Where Governance and Social Power Meet[1]

DAVINA COOPER

Analysis of the state within lesbian and gay studies has been limited. This is not to say the state is entirely absent; however, it tends to remain in the background, tangential to the topic discussed. Even lesbian and gay political science has generated little analysis of the state, focusing instead on theoretical issues such as rights and citizenship, or empirical questions of political effectiveness. Consequently, drawing together conceptions, analyses and theories of the state from lesbian and gay studies feels a rather archaeological endeavour: sifting and piecing fragments together from other fields; fragments constructed with other goals in mind. At the same time, the concerns of state theory are not unfamiliar to lesbian and gay studies. How public bodies regulate sexuality and reproduce sexual inequalities, the potential that is present for using the state in more progressive or radical ways: these questions underlie much scholarship in the field. However, unlike theoretical work on gender and class, these questions have not tended to generate an analytical infrastructure regarding the state.

We can explain this, perhaps curious, neglect in several ways. Altman (1982: 110) and others (e.g., Cohan, 1982) have focused on the impact of lesbian and gay studies' disciplinary background, politics departments not forming a significant academic base. From the perspective of my discussion here, two other factors are more relevant. The first concerns the specific relationship between lesbian and gay movements and the state which, until recently, has almost exclusively revolved around exclusion, discrimination and violence: not a context likely to generate accounts of a multifaceted, nuanced state. The second factor is Foucault. Although lesbian feminist writing has demonstrated more ambivalence, Foucault's intellectual impact on critical western gay and queer scholarship since the early 1980s is hard to overstate. While Foucault's main influence in the field has been on the ways sexual identity is understood, his work has also helped to generate a paradigmatic shift in lesbian and gay social science away from a top-down model of power and the state to a concern with discourse, subjectivity, and more recently, governmentality.

I begin this chapter by mapping out the contours of existing research on the state within lesbian and gay studies. Because much of the work approaches the state tangentially, this chapter adopts a broad brush perspective, focusing on some of the many encounters within lesbian and gay studies. As will become clearer later on, my understanding of the state weaves together several themes: national identity, political force, governance, institutionalised policy-making, and territory. The first part of the chapter sketches some of the ways in which these concepts have been used, focusing on liberal, western states: the focal point for much writing in this area. At the same time, I also draw upon a growing literature on non-western states (e.g., Alexander, 1994; Brown, 1999; Green, 1999; Lunsing, 1999; Phillips, 1997; Sweet, 1995). Research on the sexuality–state interface outside the western, liberal tradition is a particularly important area of development: both for the insights generated about particular states as well as for its theory and potential to problematise and particularise assumptions that have come out of western encounters (e.g., see generally Gupta, 1995).

In the second section, I pull together the fragments discussed to offer a way of thinking about the state that is less splintered. This forms the groundwork for the final part of the chapter, which outlines three possible research pathways. The first concerns the convergence of gay politics and state practice in stabilising and entrenching sexual orientation as an organising principle around a hetero/homo binary divide. The second addresses the effects of a radical transgender perspective on lesbian and gay state politics. The third considers the distinct contribution lesbian and gay scholarship can make to understanding the state, by highlighting the role of desire in motivating state practices.

STATE ENCOUNTERS

From discrimination to discipline

While the changing approach of many states towards homosexuality has led writers to explore how states can further lesbian and gay equality, probably the largest body of research concerns the way in which states have constructed and responded to sexual difference in more ostensibly negative ways. Historical accounts alongside analyses of the present have identified the ways in which states subordinate, exclude, harass, prohibit and marginalise bodies, subjectivities, activities and places associated with homosexuality. Much of this writing is based upon liberal paradigms. Centring on the discriminatory treatment meted out to gays and lesbians through family policy, employment and criminal law, in particular, liberal legal scholarship, has generated detailed studies of the problem alongside proposed remedies. While assessing the intricacies of legal frameworks has merit, to the extent liberal scholarship portrays the problem as confined to formal discrimination, ignores the intersection of sexuality with other social relations, and fails to engage with the more complex, uneven and contested ways in which the state regulates and shapes sexual practice, its contribution needs supplementing by more theoretical and critical accounts.

Since the 1970s, such analyses have been forthcoming from several quarters, influenced by feminism, Marxism, and more recently poststructuralist analysis. Here, I want to focus on Foucault's impact on lesbian and gay 'state' scholarship, particularly in relation to ideas of power and governance. The idea of power as 'creating' rather than simply denying particular outcomes is not unique to Foucault (1980); however, Foucault's work usefully drew attention to the idea of power as working through, rather than against, agency. In other words, power is not primarily the process of crushing another's will or of causing them to act against their own identified interests. Rather, power works most effectively when – by mobilising the capillaries of the social – it shapes the knowledge, behaviour, interests, even desires of its subjects. In this way, state power does not simply circumscribe the options available to an already constituted subject, but actively shapes the subjectivity it simultaneously and subsequently confronts (see Pringle and Watson, 1992: 64).

Foucault's analysis of public power generated a wave of lesbian and gay scholarship exploring the production of discourses, disciplinary techniques, and processes of regulation. In analysing state-generated discourse, legal decisions proved a particularly fruitful terrain because court judgments offer socially powerful, oral and written texts (see Moran, this volume). While writing has tended to concentrate on the changing character of particular discourses, such as 'the homosexual', the *effects* of discourse are an equally important site of analysis lest it be assumed that discourses and their effects are identical. The law, for instance, may construct a homosexual subject (or subjects) (e.g., Mort, 1980: 42): 'the unfit lesbian mother' or 'degraded gay sado-masochist', but there is a crucial social space between this discursive production and the way diverse communities understand and constitute themselves. This space is not a vacuum, however; it is a heterogenous place of contestation, partial communication, a refusal or inability to hear, as well as processes of domination.

Analysing the impact of state-generated truths about social subjects and practices requires us to look at the interrelationship between discourses and other governing techniques. For instance, Leslie Moran (1991: 156–8) has explored how the discursive production of homosexuality as 'risk' was linked, by the British state in the mid-1950s, to investigative and other disciplinary techniques in order to promote national security, and improve Britain's relations with the USA (see also D'Emilio, 1989; Sullivan, 1999). At the same time, state power may be more effective when it remains both unannounced and undefended; disciplinary effects are not always anchored in contemporaneous discourses. For instance, CCTV cameras and police officers pacing streets may dampen down expressions of gay intimacy regardless of the reasons for which surveillance was initiated. Similarly, lesbian co-parents may continue to avoid physical affection in front of their children long after periods of state censoriousness have declined or ceased.

While writing on state discourse and discipline has tended to focus on specific techniques, other work has attempted to offer a broader analysis of state practice. Two different directions are evident here: the first centring on regulation, the second on governmentality. Analysis of state regulation focuses on the way governments structure rather than direct practice. Franzway et al. (1989: 18) describe regulation as a strategy that uses rules and order to manage conduct. While rules can forbid, their primary effect is to shape the social landscape upon which action takes place, frequently by carving out a temporal and geographical domain within which certain events are permitted or forbidden.[2] For instance, in Britain, the state has regulated homosexual activity according to rules that identify where and with whom sex is permitted. Thus regulatory policies can combine liberalisation in one domain with a more restrictive approach elsewhere (see Altman, 1982: 121; also Mort, 1980: 40). Gary Kinsman (1996b) explores this strategy in his work on governing people with AIDS. According to Kinsman, the classificatory divide between responsible and irresponsible subjects was deployed not just as a discursive framework, but also as a way of enabling the 'responsible' to be governed through modes of self-regulation, such as advice, while the criminal law, policing and coercive public health measures controlled 'irresponsible' subjects.

State coercion can be seen as identifying the limits of regulation which, as a technique of governance, tends to assume that the majority will act 'rationally', keeping themselves within the parameters of legitimate conduct. However, just as we cannot assume that the discursive construction of subjectivity will generate coterminous subject identities, so the production of rules and norms does not necessarily mean compliance or success (see, generally, Sunstein, 1990). Exploring the gap between governmental practice and actual outcome can be found in foucauldian work on governmentality: the particular mentalities, arts and regimes of government and administration (Dean, 1999: 2; see also Foucault, 1991). While Nikolas Rose (1994) declares that the will to govern is eternally optimistic, failure, he also argues, is inevitable (see also Hunt and Wickham, 1994). Indeed, according to Rose and Miller (1992: 181), it is around the difficulties and failures of governing that programmes of government are elaborated.

The ongoing tension between the will to govern within liberal states and the inability of governing apparatuses to achieve their desired outcomes provides the terrain for studies of governmentality that have built upon Foucault's (1991: 103) conceptual decentring of the state. While analyses of governmentality have tended to focus on more mainstream areas of social and economic policy, lesbian and gay studies is beginning to explore the potential of this approach (e.g., see Goldberg-Hiller, 1998: 525–6; Kinsman, 1996b). Two aspects of governmentality studies are particularly helpful to understanding the state's response to sexuality. The first is the claim that governments rule 'at a distance' geographically and relationally (see Rose, 1999; also Cooper, 1998). Indirect and mediated rule emerges from the tension between the ambitious ruler or government seeking to extend their remit, and the importance to liberalism of sustaining what is perceived as a relatively autonomous civil society (or private sphere) (Rose and Miller, 1992).

The second key element is that of governmental rationality. In relation to liberal western societies, governmental rationality is concerned, according to Burchell (1996), with the art of government. This has several elements: the way in which governing by different agencies becomes constituted as legitimate; how reality and its 'problems' are rendered thinkable and amenable to political programming and strategy; the changing aspirations of liberal governance; and the way in which its subjects are conceptualised (Rose, 1994: 42; see also

Rose and Miller, 1992; Simons, 1995: 36). According to Mitchell Dean (1999: 32)

> One of the features of government is that authorities and agencies must ask questions of themselves, must employ plans, forms of knowledge and know-how, and must adopt visions and objectives of what they seek to achieve. The 'welfare state', for example, can be understood less as a concrete set of institutions and more as a way of viewing institutions, practices and personnel.

The developing field of governmentality has encountered criticism on various grounds (see Curtis, 1995; O'Malley et al., 1997); it does, nevertheless, offer a fruitful field of scholarship for lesbian and gay political studies. For instance, it provides a framework for exploring changes and conflicts in governments' perceptions of their role and capabilities in relation to homosexuality, in the light of new knowledges about sexuality, subjectivity and new framings of the 'problem'. One example of such an approach to analysing anti-gay US policy is provided by Janet Halley (1999), in her examination of the Clinton administration's response to 'gays and lesbians in the military', popularly described as 'Don't ask, don't tell' (see also Herek et al., 1996; Rimmerman, 1996). Although Halley does not explicitly draw on the field of governmentality, her short monograph, *Don't*, focuses on the changing way in which state policy understood lesbian and gay sexuality revolving around the imagined relationship between homosexual status and conduct. Halley refutes the claim that the policy under Clinton was more liberal and sympathetic to lesbians and gay men; that it moved from excluding persons to excluding activities. 'Every moving part of the new policy is designed to *look like* conduct regulation in order to *hide* the fact that it turns decisively on status' (1999: 2). One key theme of *Don't* is the intensified and particular deployment of the notion of homosexual propensity in US military policy post-1993. Exploring the complex ways in which propensity as an actuarial prediction, and as a pathological, personality trait, are combined to generate workable knowledge for military governance, Halley provides a close study of the governmentality of sexuality.[3]

Activism Against the State and the Pursuit of Change

Halley's work is useful in linking the production of knowledge to conflicts and disagreements within the US state over the right approach to homosexuality in the military. For, in the main, studies in governmentality, focusing on the practices, objectives and vision of government, have tended to sideline the pressures placed upon government to reform. A similar, although somewhat less polarised, division is apparent within lesbian and gay studies where research and writing that focus on regulation and governmental power sit at a distance from analyses of social movement attempts to revise state policy and practice. In the following brief overview of writing on lesbian and gay state activism I want to address three interlinked questions: how does work on lesbian and gay campaigning imagine the state? What can we learn about the structure of the state from research into political conflicts over sexual orientation policies? And are there legitimate limits to state intervention to *prohibit* discrimination?

Academic scholarship on lesbian and gay activism has taken several directions. One dominant strand has embraced a liberal perspective leading priority to be placed on removing formal discriminatory provisions such as the criminalisation of sexual activity, alongside arguments for state protection in order to safeguard lesbians and gay men from the hostility and discrimination of others. Liberal ideology shapes not only the character of the claims made, but how the state is also understood. While bias is perceived as encoded within the state's operations, this is seen as a residue of history rather than an inherent aspect of modern, western states. A similar optimism on the part of campaigners structures and motivates pressures for reform. In his

discussion of AIDS campaigning, for instance, Hodge (2000) argues that, in comparison with others who organised politically, white, middle-class male activism was distinguished by its sense of assumed entitlement from the state.

Not all lesbian and gay actors, however, have demonstrated such a confident sense of expectation. Leaving to one side, for the moment, processes of 'structural selectivity' in which the state's form generates a skewed response to different interests (see, generally, Jessop, 1990), critics have explored the gate-keeping, self-interested activities of white, male campaigners that have limited the involvement and influence both of lesbians (Schrodel and Fiber, 2000: 12), and other Black gay activists (Boykin, 2000). Ambivalence about lesbian and gay reform campaigns has also come from two other directions; the first questions the desirability of the state becoming the primary means of pursuing equality intervention; the second questions the goals and techniques of reform movements themselves. Critical voices arguing for restraint in the rush for state-based equality have emphasised the *relational* quality of the state. The liberal scholar, William Eskridge (1997), for instance, has argued that anti-discriminatory state policies should not dominate civil society. In particular, 'private' bodies such as churches and religious universities should be allowed to express and act upon their opposition to lesbian and gay 'lifestyles'. From a different perspective, echoing earlier work by feminists and socialists critical of an overly-optimistic, reliant relationship with the state, Wendy Brown (1995) has criticised identity-based state activism, on the grounds it misrepresents the state as neutral, and fixes identity around the experience of injury and suffering. Eskridge and Brown's positions are interesting because of their explicitly normative stances. However, in the main, critical writing avoids a normative approach; instead many writers, ambivalent about the agenda and techniques of reform based organisations, have focused their energies on studying more oppositional, expressive and grass-roots social movement organisations (Berlant and Freeman, 1993; Brown, 1997; Hodge, 2000).

In contrast to liberal scholarship and activism, radical critics and activists tend to portray the state as neither autonomous, omnipotent nor democratically accountable. Instead, the state is seen as *one* site of concentrated power (others include the church and large corporations), anchored to a sea-bed whose terrain is structured by social inequality. Radical activism asks the state to act, but it does so less politely and less hopefully. It sees the state less as an entity marked by anachronistic prejudices, than as a site of power mobilised against vulnerable, unpopular constituencies. But why does the state act in this way? For all its sophistication in analysing movement struggles, radical lesbian and gay analysis offers a thin interpretation of the forces shaping and structuring state form and practice. Even where the state is described in lesbian and gay scholarship as 'heteropatriarchal', 'racist' or 'capitalist', there is little theorisation or detailed analysis of what this means.

One illustration of this gap is Lisa Duggan's influential article, 'Queering the state' (1994).[4] Duggan's analysis problematises the way in which the politics of the state are generally being left to lesbian and gay civil rights strategies (ibid.: 6). Arguing for a queerer approach in the face of right-wing antigay mobilising, Duggan (1994: 9–11) urges lesbian and gay activists to invert special rights discourse to highlight and counter the state's promotion of heterosexuality. She also proposes the reformulation of sexual difference as a form of *dissent*, understood not simply as speech, but as a constellation of nonconforming practices, expressions, and beliefs (ibid.: 11). Duggan's proposals are useful, but, to the extent one looks for an analysis of the state, her discussion disappoints. Despite the title, the article offers no conceptualisation of the state, queer or otherwise. This is not so much a criticism of Duggan since she does not explicitly suggest her paper would do

otherwise. Nevertheless, it illustrates how far the state has become evacuated as an analytical concept amongst radical gay theorists, that even an article on queering the state does not explore the form and character of the state itself.

One body of social movement writing to provide a more detailed account of the state, particularly of the linkages between different apparatuses, is the research on western struggles between gay and right-wing forces over government policy and legislative reform (Altmore, 1995; Duggan, 1994; Durham, 1991; Herman, 1994, 1997; Smith, 1994). In the US context, writers have examined the 'gay rights' battles waged between lesbian and gay forces and the Christian Right through the constitutional systems and processes of different states. One technique popularised in the last decades of the twentieth century was that of 'direct democracy' as conservative religious forces introduced local ballot initiatives to outlaw current and future gay rights protection (Donovan et al., 2000; Herman, 1997; Magleby, 1998). With state governments forced to give effect to successful local referenda, often in the face of their own contrasting political stance, lesbian and gay activists turned to the courts seeking to have the new ballot-driven legislation declared unconstitutional.

Juridical struggles between gay and right-wing American forces provide a vantage point from which to examine the intricate constitutional and political arrangements between different state bodies. While accounts of the state often treat it as an aggregate of its apparatuses, or focus on one state arena as illustrative of others, writing on 'direct democracy' centres on the differences between state arenas as well as the links, particularly legal and political, that operate between city government, local referenda, state government and courts. At one level, these linkages are strings pulling state and local government to attention, to be held to account, to act. At another level, the linkages are more contested, and contradictory, as I discuss further below.

Entering the State and its
Satellite Dilemmas

Research on mobilising the complex links between different state bodies raises the question of whether there is anything coherent or unified about the state. While the links between apparatuses such as local government, the courts, the national executive, legislature, police force and army identify institutional connections, is this the extent of the state's unity? Or is the state unified by the power relations it condenses, the projects it pursues, and the constraints it shares? While Marxist state scholarship has tended to stress the state's overall coherence *vis-à-vis* capitalism, one interesting source of potential fracturing was posed by Althusser (1971: 140) in his discussion of Ideological State Apparatuses (ISAs). According to Althusser '[T]he resistance of the exploited class is able to find means and occasions to express itself there [in contrast to Repressive State Apparatuses], either by the utilization of their contradictions, or by conquering combat positions in them in struggle'. From a different direction, feminist work in the 1980s and early 1990s moved from an assumption of structural constraints to an emphasis on contingency and the ongoing struggle for hegemony amongst political forces (Pringle and Watson, 1992: 63).

In the main, debates about state coherence and unity have not surfaced within lesbian and gay studies. While the scholarship on institutional gay rights conflicts throws light on these questions, for the most part it does not engage with state theory in any sustained or explicit way. One cluster of scholarship that does focus more directly on the state, and thus can illuminate debates on state unity and coherence addresses the entry of lesbian and gay forces onto the terrain of the state itself. To what extent does such 'entryism' undermine or reinforce the thesis of state unity?

Work on lesbian and gay entry has taken two primary directions. The first, predominantly US focused, concerns the preconditions and criteria for policy effectiveness (e.g., Haeberle, 1996). Encompassing the entry of both gay individuals and gay concerns, its focus is the institutional mechanisms, coalitions and policy orientations that have enabled lesbian and gay demands to make it onto government agenda, either through political clout or by converging successfully with pre-existing state interests (see, generally, Bailey, 1999: Ch. 11; Button et al., 1997; Wald, 2000: 15–18). While useful in exploring some of the conditions for lesbian and gay effectiveness in particular policy arenas, such as city governments, research in this area nevertheless sidelines wider, more theoretical debates about the state, particularly its relationship to economic, racial and gendered forms of power. Thus, it does not use the experience of lesbian and gay policy-making to address questions of state coherence or fragmentation. Instead, it tends to assume two things: first, that variation as a result of different, operative 'political opportunity structures' is possible; and second, that lesbian and gay political agenda are broadly compatible with prevailing state frameworks oriented around liberal equality.

The second direction research on lesbian and gay political entryism has taken focuses on instances where activists have gained apparently unmediated access to the state's terrain in their own right, as politicians and officials (e.g., see Rayside, 1998). One instance that raises, particularly acutely, the issue of convergence between gay and state agenda concerns the lesbian and gay municipal developments in Britain during the 1980s (Carabine, 1995; Cooper, 1994a, 1994b, 1995; Lansley et al., 1989; Tobin, 1990).[5] Although, in many respects, the policies developed here were framed in terms of liberal equal opportunities and non-discrimination, their confident, assertive style, emphasis on symbolism and the needs of young gay men and lesbians, and their 'arithmetic' understanding of intersecting oppression owed much to the feminist and liberation politics out of which many lesbian and gay local government actors emerged (see Cooper, 1994a). Local government lesbian and gay policies provide a good example of the capacity, hinted at by Althusser (1971), of progressive forces capturing a politically 'vulnerable' state apparatus. However, leaving to one side the question of whether local government can be considered an ISA, this reading has to be tempered in two respects. First, lesbian and gay urban policy development underwent complex, internal containment processes as a result of which initiatives and discourses were organised out or modified. Second, when internal processes broke down, external forces intervened: in the 1980s, in Britain, this included the Thatcher central government and right-wing media, as well as more local conservative and religious constituencies.

Both internal and external processes highlight the limited capacity of state bodies to 'step out of line'. When such transgressing of parameters occurs, other bodies will use the institutional links between them to drag the recalcitrant authority back (see also Cooper, 1998: Ch. 5). However, the overall dominance of a particular project, regime or perspective does not just rely on institutional articulations. Non-state bodies, with an interest in the outcome, may also be involved. In the case of British local government, media ridicule and a publicised loss of credibility proved powerful incentives, alongside the deployment of law, personnel hierarchies, and financial support to re-establish the status quo. But despite such a reversion, troublesome state bodies may also have a more pervasive influence on state projects as a whole. Sexual orientation, by the turn of the 21st century, had become far more accepted as an integral element of state equal opportunities policies. At the same time, convergence across different state bodies should not be overstated. Despite the pervasiveness of certain discourses, policies and structures, state apparatuses operate in different ways. Indeed, this might be seen as an integral aspect of a complex, unified state, as well as signifying resistance to political hegemonising impulses.

The question of unity is not restricted to the agenda and processes operating between different state arenas, it also needs considering in relation to other aspects of the state's identity. In the second part of the chapter, I explore the relationship between different aspects of the state in more detail. One issue raised is that of boundaries. If the state is a meaningful concept then identifying its boundaries may be important. And if the state is a multifaceted entity, this complicates the question of boundaries further, since each state facet will have its own 'limits'. Within lesbian and gay studies the question of state boundaries arises, particularly prominently, in relation to the voluntary sector. From writing on AIDS service and policy organisations (Altman, 1994; Brown, 1997; Kinsman, 1992) to bodies such as the Gay and Lesbian Taskforce in Australia (Hart, 1992), analysts have explored the extent to which lesbian and gay voluntary organisations have become part of the state through the state's provision of funds, policies and staffing.

While views on the question of state incorporation remain moot, the important point is not, I think, to answer definitively whether the voluntary sector is or is not 'within', but rather to examine the issues such a question throws up. Voluntary sector studies reveal the fuzzy character of the state/civil society boundary – a fuzziness deployed and exploited when governing takes place 'at a distance' (Rose, 1996; see also Mitchell, 1991: 90). For governments to 'step back' from governing directly, they require a range of organisations to adopt a regulatory function: to promote norms, rules and particular truths, and to monitor, audit, and select. In some sectors, private commercial bodies have fulfilled this role, but within the lesbian and gay community, the voluntary organisation is a more common model. Yet, to say that voluntary organisations are incorporated within state relations of governing does not mean they necessarily exercise state power or reflect the balance of class, gender, and racialised relations that the state condenses. Indeed, one can see such a sector as subject to the conflicting tendencies of state and community, as being both inside and out, at varying, overlapping degrees of intensity. This is not just the case where the state tries to co-opt, in the face of community organisations' attempts to maintain autonomy and distance; the situation is far more complicated. As voluntary organisations try to build strong bridges to some aspects of the state (its legitimacy and resources, perhaps), while disidentifying with others (the state's coercive function and condensation of social power), state forces engage in a parallel endeavour (Cooper, 1995: 66). In the process, both attempt to hegemonise their interpretation of the relationship in order to sustain legitimacy within their wider community.

Sexing State Form and Relations

So far I have mapped accounts of the state that draw upon 'external' as well as 'internal' perspectives. While the former treat the state as an entity that governs and is subject to pressures from the outside; 'internal' analyses open up the 'black box' of the state to explore the struggles that take place within and across. While some writing combines both approaches, much of the literature in the field prioritises one or other perspective. I now want, however, to turn to a third strand of scholarship. This overlaps both 'internal' and 'external' analyses, but tends to be explored separately. It concerns the way in which the state's form and structures are themselves sexualised (Cooper, 1995: 67–74). This extends from the interface between sex and state violence (Enloe, 1993; McClintock, 1992) to the figurative deployment of sexuality to imagine relations between nations (Stychin, 1998: 100–2).

Work on the sexualised state parallels, while also building upon, path-breaking work on the gendered or male state (Brown, 1992; Mosse, 1985; Watson, 1990; Yuval-Davis, 1997). Unlike more conventional scholarship which treats sexual policies as ontologically distinct from the state itself,

writers in this area have portrayed the state's sexual agenda as a reflexive project that attempts to sustain a particular corporate, national identity, at the same time as it shapes and regulates the sexual possibilities of its citizens or subjects.[6] It is the mutually constitutive relationship between nation-state identity and the governance of social practice, both according to a heterosexual logic, that has provided a focus for writers such as Jacqui Alexander (1994) and Oliver Phillips (1997). Jacqui Alexander's (1994) work on the Caribbean, for instance, explores how reproducing the heterosexual character of the nation–state works to delegitimise and often criminalise sexual practices and relations that do not involve 'procreative' sex. Thus, the particular histories of building 'post-colonial' states can cause homosexuality to be figured, in some instances, as an external form of invasion or contagion (Alexander, 1994: 15; see also Phillips, 1997; Stychin, 1998: 61, 63)[7] in contrast to its more insidious status within certain western contexts (Moran, 1991; Mosse, 1985).

Nation-building work may be intent on reproducing and sustaining a heterosexual identity, but from an 'external' vantage point, nation–states may appear sexually otherwise. Schwartzwald (1993), writing about Quebec, explores the way in which national identity has been both juxtaposed against, and articulated to, homosexuality. Carl Stychin (1998: 99) continues this analysis in terms of how discourses constitute nations through the attribution of sexual identities. According to Stychin (ibid.):

> This theme is well established in the context of the Canadian federal system ... that the federation is a marriage between French and English, a heterosexual metaphor in which French Canada ... takes on the female role ... But the construction of national identities is not limited to a heterosexual frame. The relationship between Quebec and the ROC [rest of Canada] has long been constructed in homosexual ... terms.

The figurative sexualities of nations, and the relationships between them, opens up a host of metaphorical possibilities: heterosexual, bisexual, gay, lesbian, queer, while the nuances added by the complex gendering of butch, femme and camp promises new readings and interpretations of international relations.

TOWARDS A POLYCENTRIC ACCOUNT

The State's Identities

Is the state itself best defined by its legal form, its coercive capacities, its institutional composition and boundaries, its internal operations and modes of calculation, its declared aims, its functions ... or its sovereign place in the international system? Is it a thing, a subject, a social relation. (Jessop, 1990: 339)

My discussion so far has mapped the spread of state scholarship within lesbian and gay studies. Together, these literatures draw attention to different aspects of the state. Liberal writing on state discrimination, and Foucauldian work on regulation and governmentality highlight the power, techniques and effects of state policies, provide an account of how the state 'thinks' and acts, and the limits to its interventions, but do not, for the most part, assume intentionality or agency. In other words, state actions and processes, even paradoxically state thought, emerge out of the way political hegemony or rationality is organised, rather than constituting the workings of an inner institutional ego. Work on lesbian and gay mobilising depicts an embodied state open to pressure from the 'outside'. From one perspective, this is a state ready to reform its archaic edges, from another politically forced to accommodate movements against the interests encoded at its core. Writing on lesbian and gay entry, in contrast, shifts from a morphology of embodiment to the invocation of a structured terrain, raising questions about state form, 'selectivity' (Jessop, 1990: 148–9), the relationship between different state arenas, and the boundaries of the

state's territory. Finally, writing on the sexualised state collapses the space between the two. Analyses of the sexual identity of the nation-state bestow upon it both agency and intentionality. At home, the state promotes its preferred sexual logic while its international identity is sexually inflected by the wider forces of the global arena.

Are these different perspectives contradictory and inconsistent? Is our choice to select between them or is there a way of bringing their insights together to construct a fuller, richer account? For many scholars, activists and policy-makers, the state still most closely resembles a leviathan (cf. Hobbes, 1914): a power-infused monster whose reach embraces, coerces, even suffocates civil society. While this image reflects a pervasive, and for this reason, important understanding of the state, my analysis seeks to draw from less reified, as well as less essentialised, accounts (Boyd, 1994; Watson, 1990; see also Cooper, 1995). In contrast to those Foucauldians who have replaced state theory with studies of governmentality, and those feminists who question whether the abstracted character of the term has anything worthwhile to offer (e.g., Allen, 1990), I want to hold on to the state as an analytical concept for two primary reasons. First, it reflects the way in which political and governmental power is understood, both by those who perceive themselves to wield it has well as by those who experience their subjection to it. Second, as I go on to discuss, the state identifies a particular set of connections or configurations that both accentuate the nature of political power as well as giving it a specific form.

Given the slippage and retranslation inherent in the movement of concepts, what counts as part of the state will vary according to time, place and outlook (e.g., see Gupta, 1995; Held, 1989; Jessop, 1990: 347–9). Within liberal western discourse, at the turn of the twenty-first century, the state operates as an organising principle of power and governance that pulls together, in geographically specific configurations, a combination of roles, practices, powers, technologies, institutions and spaces. These include the state's condensation and coordination of social relations (Kinsman, 1992: 222), its governmental functioning, nation–state identity, arenas (Pringle and Watson, 1992: 53), and the relations of authority, accountability, law and resources that connect them. While the state organises these 'identities' into a complex configuration, identities are not always equally in focus. Depending on the context, different identities or dimensions will come to the fore – a plasticity often ignored by state theorists. Thus, the state may seem to function primarily as the nation's representative within international relations or as the source of coercive power over citizens and territory. However, regardless of which identity or dimension appears paramount, and regardless of the extent to which political forces present this or that identity as *defining* the state, such identities or dimensions do not exist in a vacuum. First, they are always articulated to other state identities that, however obscured in a particular context, will continue to shape their meaning and impact – just as gender identities are always shaped and structured by other social relations, such as class and ethnicity. Second, the state's identities take their meaning from, and operate within, specific socio-economic, political and cultural contexts (see also Mitchell, 1991). For instance, just as a gay identity only has meaning within the terms of wider sexual norms and practices, so the state's identity as, for instance, the site and means of exercising public, legitimate violence is carved out of, and operates across, a terrain of contested norms, understandings and practices of violence. Identity is not a façade – a front or garment – behind which reality lurks; rather, it identifies a location within and relationship to wider social processes.

It is the complex, productive relationship between the state's different identities – their particular configuration at any given instance – that is central to the state's functioning as an organising principle. While the state's identities interrelate,

overhang, and separate in various ways, overlap is crucially important. If the bodies identified as state bodies are not the places where governance occurs, if states are no longer primary international actors or the nation no longer identifies a territory across which states have political power (e.g., see Steinberg, 1994), if the primary chains of articulation between state organs – financial, legislative, guidance, control – slide apart or if governance becomes detached from dominant socio-economic interests, the state may not necessarily unravel (although this is possible), but it will come to identify a different, probably far more diffused structure of power and governance.

The Emergence of Sexuality as a Social Organising Principle

In the discussion that follows, I draw upon this framework to explore developments within lesbian and gay scholarship. But first I need to introduce briefly another element: the place of sexuality within social relations of power. In an attempt to avoid privileging particular relations, such as economic class or gender, *a priori,* and in an attempt to move beyond a model of asymmetrical, antagonistic groups, writers have looked for metaphors through which the intersection of different social relations can be understood. One approach some feminist theorists have adopted is to equate social relations with axes of power (de Lauretis 1990: 131; Fraser, 1989: 165; cf. Fraser, 1997: Ch. 1). This metaphor successfully evokes two ideas: first, social relations constitute subject positions at both axis ends (as well as, possibly, along it); second, social location depends on where axes intersect. While an improvement upon binary class models of oppression, axes are also limited in that they reduce social relations to points along a linear continuum, and imply a single meeting point. My preference, therefore, is for the concept of 'organising principles' used by various authors in different ways (e.g., see Seidman, 1997: 227). In contrast to the state which organises the institutionalisation, depersonalisation and governmentalisation of power, *social* organising principles identify, can be read off from, and work to reproduce, the complex configurations of social inequality based on race, gender, class, and age, among others.

I have set out this approach in more detail elsewhere (Cooper, 2000). Here, I just want to draw attention to three aspects of relevance to the following discussion. First, social organising principles go beyond identifying relations between situated subjects (men/women, lesbians/heterosexuals). They span out to include organisational processes, and everyday practices, as well as social norms and values that historically and culturally have been articulated to, affected by, or which have structured particular social locations. Thus, organising principles of gender draw together the public/private divide, norms of intimacy, individualism, and forms of personal agency as well as the specific ways in which men and women live and relate. Second, organising principles are not linear. Power does not move incrementally along an axis of subject positions. While social organising principles are defined by the asymmetry at their core, this may take shape in contradictory ways. Third, organising principles are not simply imposed from 'above'. Although the role of the state or status quo in sustaining particular inequalities is enormous, the constitution of gender, ethnicity or economic class also depends upon community and individual practices that echo, challenge, disrupt and give nuance to more hierarchical processes.

NEW DIRECTIONS

Drawing upon these frameworks, in the remainder of this chapter, I want briefly to identify three research pathways that address the state in different ways. The first asks: to what extent, and in what ways, do lesbian and gay movements work with the state to solidify a binary divide? The second asks:

what impact does destabilising gender have on lesbian and gay state activism? And the third asks: what follows from the encoding of desire within the logic of state practice?

Splitting the Hetero/Homo Binary

The concept, organising principles, provides a useful framework for exploring exchanges between different social relations as they evolve over time. Not only are the internal dynamics and relationships between particular organising principles in constant flux, but new principles evolve, while older ones expire. We can see this process of change in relation to sexuality within liberal western societies. Sexuality has, arguably, shifted from functioning primarily as a terrain or register of practice refracting asymmetrical relations of race, class, gender and geography (see, generally, Foucault, 1981) to posing as a social organising principle constituted around the hetero/homo divide (see also Seidman, 1997: 227–9). While a large part of the responsibility for sexuality's emergence as an unequal binary relationship can be laid at the door of the state, lesbian and gay communities and activists have also participated in consolidating this process.

The rise of the modern lesbian and gay movement involved, among other things, forging sexuality as a distinct organising principle, irreducible to other social relations such as gender (Rust, 1995: 253). Yet, in suggesting that sexuality came to function as a distinct organising principle, I am not denying the intersections between organising principles,[8] including most particularly the relationship between sexual identity and gender (cf. Jeffreys, 1996; and see Wilton, 1996).[9] I also do not want to suggest that lesbian and gay forces alone have the political power to determine the form sexual formations will take, or that all late twentieth-century lesbian and gay activists sought to distance themselves from other political movements. Rather, my point is threefold.

First, the hetero/homo divide emerged as the pivot around which lesbian and gay politics and identity were forged. While the more liberal wing of the movement worked to declare the divide misplaced: that respectable lesbians and gay men had been positioned on the 'wrong' side of the border, more radical gay and queer forces positioned themselves as *the* other – the site from which normative heterosexuality could be effectively challenged. Second, the divide came to stand in for more than the gendered patterning of intimate/sexual relationships, encompassing in its train the sexualised organisation of labour, social histories, cultural qualities (camp, straightness), as well as patterns of everyday life and community formations. Third, and most pertinent to my discussion here, lesbian and gay forces were not responding to a predetermined social regime in which sexuality's binary construction was already immutably determined by state, economy, and church.

The emergence of lesbian and gay social movements and identity has been the subject of considerable historical research that I cannot do justice to here. The point, however, that I want to emphasise is the role played by lesbians and gay men in the production of a sexual divide. Heterosexual forms of social organisation generate a range of stigmatised others, but to the extent that heterosexuality as a social and political patterning remains naturalised, such others are likely to be fragmented and diffused – a series of activities, styles, and exclusions scattered across the hinterland of the social rather than converging across a single frontier of (il)legitimacy. Thus, socially meaningful binary divisions are formed, at least in part, in the process of collective identity formation and social struggle. While neither identity formation nor social struggle can be separated from the wider social, economic and political transitions that have brought them into being (e.g., see Kinsman, 1996b: Ch. 2), this does not detract from the processes through which they help to gel a social location and form of personhood that the state simultaneously both feeds and confronts.

This is not a unified nor a static process. Not only is the character of the divide shifting, but the ways in which state and communities converge is both varied and in transition. Yet, to the extent we are witnessing liberal western states move towards a stance of formal gay equality, we need to consider whether the binary hetero/homo divide is vanishing or remaining as a basis of *non*-asymmetrical distinctiveness. Queer, bisexual and other sexual forces have suggested the divide is reconfiguring: that mainstream lesbian and gay movements in alliance with the state are causing inequalities of resources, entitlements, freedoms, authority and discursive/cultural recognition to be organised along new lines. While bisexual activists and commentators have relocated the dichotomy between mono and bi-sexualities: between those that challenge and those that consolidate dichotomous thinking (e.g., see James, 1996; Rust, 1995, 1996), sexual minority advocates, such as Gayle Rubin (1989: 279), focus on the divide between respectable and illegitimate sexualities.

Whether the sexual dichotomy at the heart of organising principles of sexuality has left sexual orientation behind for new divides, whether it has exploded, bringing forth a multitude of different inequalities in its wake, remains an open question. In relation to thinking about the state however, it opens up the following line of inquiry: (1) how does the convergence between lesbian and gay communities and the state vary across different aspects of the state's identity?; (2) are some state identities reorganising around new sexual divides, while others sustain the current hetero/homo dichotomy?; and (3) to what extent are lesbian and gay forces consolidating, challenging or undermining these shifts?

Transgender and the Destabilising of Orientation

In the destabilising of the hetero/homo dichotomy, one force to gain greater prominence is that of transgender (e.g., see Califia, 1997; Namaste, 1996; Raymond, 1996; Stone, 1991; Whittle, 1996). The discrimination, marginalisation and violence experienced by people who cross, and sometimes straddle, the gender divide are seen as reason to identify transgendered people as a significantly subordinated constituency. Here, however, I want to approach transgender from a different perspective: one less focused on the discrimination, serious as it is that many transgendered people face, than on the gender problematic that radical transgender politics raises for lesbian and gay state activism.

The contrasting, but intertwined, trajectories of transsexuality and transgender have intersected lesbian and gay politics at several junctures: organisationally, in the growing, but highly contested, inclusion of transsexual and transgendered activists within lesbian and gay groups and social movements (e.g., Humphrey, 1999); historically, in the interwoven relationship between gender-ambiguous identity and practices and lesbian/gay communities (Cahn, 1996; Innes and Lloyd, 1996; Meyer, 1996); and, ethically, in the challenge transgendering poses to the viability of lesbian and gay sexual identity being based on a solid knowing and identification of gender.

Traditionally, conventional transsexual politics converged with dominant gender principles. Both worked from the premise that a gender divide existed; the question was whether and how it could be authentically crossed. While cross-gender identification was generally represented by mainstream transsexual and state forces as a psychological or physiological condition beyond the individual's control, crossing – to the extent it was possible – required hard work, commitment and biological transformation. In a sense, we can see this earlier politics as a contractual one in which transsexuals offered to externalise their 'inner' gender to the best of their ability, doing whatever was required to make the performance a convincing one (see, generally, Stone, 1991). In

return the state granted the transfer of gender partial (if not proper) effect. Whittle (1998: 397) argues that this approach placed those MTF (males to females) who could 'pass', in control of the movement's politics, leading to a focus on privacy rights that would allow them more fully to live their gender without the slippage of their prior sex being revealed. From this perspective, little, if any, common ground with gays and lesbians existed. Indeed, homosexuality functioned as the transsexual 'other' – whose claims had to be publicly forsaken if the performed gender was to be officially realised.

In contrast, the alliances transgender activists' forged with gays, and to a lesser extent lesbians, in several countries in the 1990s revolved around a different gender politics. Coalitions were based, first, on the recognition that someone could be both transsexual and gay, and, second, on their shared location as minorities (cf. Whittle, 1998: 391). Transgender also provided, at least rhetorically, a cutting edge for a queer politics that sought to go beyond the hetero/homo binary to embrace all those disadvantaged and marginalised by the dominant sexuality/gender system. At the same time, some activists and scholars moved beyond a 'third sex' position to argue that the transgendered person, as a dissonant, complexly legible body, provided a genre through which imaginings of gender could be productively disrupted (see Stone, 1991: 296; Whittle, 1998).

It is this third foundation that raises particularly interesting questions for the future of sexual orientation as a stable category in interactions with the state. If changing gender no longer requires particular genitals but is simply the performance or expression of masculinity or femininity (see Pratt, 1995: 88) – subjectively chosen identifications or 'registers' – what implications does this hold for gay and lesbian politics?[10] If butch lesbians and FTM (females to males) are both perceived as more masculine than the biological male who expresses 'feminine' behaviours and attitudes, what constitutes a lesbian, gay or even heterosexual relationship? Is it based on the particular gendered nexus of behaviour, identification, and emotional display; and can it therefore remain constantly in flux: for instance, heterosexual on the street, lesbian under the sheets?

While this approach to gender is open to criticism on several grounds (Jeffreys, 1996), most particularly its voluntarist assumptions that gender is mutable and chosen rather than socially constituted and relatively stable. My interest here is in the implications of this approach for the way sexuality and the state intersect. Paisley Currah (1997: 1374–76), for instance, has drawn attention to an interesting puzzle regarding the interface of gender and sexuality in the US regulation of marriage. '"Same-sex" marriage is already legal, or more precisely, ... many states have been unable to successfully regulate marriages between those whose sexual identity, gender identity or even sexual orientation confounds the predictable relationship assumed by state law to exist between sex, gender identity, and sexual orientation' (Currah, 1997: 1374). Transgender politics, like radical lesbian feminism, raises core questions about the ideological thrust of lesbian and gay demands. Namely, do lesbian and gay political campaigns implicitly consolidate as natural conventional conceptions of gender? Does the hetero/homo divide work to reinforce the gender one? While state bodies and technologies deploy a biologically contingent approach to gender, should lesbian and gay campaigns draw more explicitly from a different model (Currah, 1997) in which gender is far less stable? For, if lesbian and gay movements retain a biologically-based or at least social conception of gender, what implications does this have for state-based activism if gay movements work alongside or confront transgender movements working with radically different perspectives? Are state bodies going to be required to mediate or choose between them?

To the extent that the nation–state and public sector mobilise gender as a meaningful

form of classification (e.g., see Pratt, 1995: 162), how gender is defined is important, from the question of fixing identity at birth, migration or death (Namaste, 1996: 196–7), to its impact upon healthcare, employment, and the juridical regulation of sexual relationships (Califia, 1997: 234; Smith, 1997). However, the risk of adopting a more fluid approach is that it may trivialise gender's social significance and consequences. How can these be acknowledged and tackled without being reinforced? One strategy is for lesbian and gay forces to link gay equality to the erasure of gender as an official category of state practice.[11] To the extent that biological differences are significant, such as the capacity to bear children, or the specific health risks associated with male or female reproductive bodies, these can be identified discretely rather than as part of a broader cluster of gender characteristics. However, this strategy may be of limited benefit or even counter-productive if organising principles of gender still operate in other areas of social life. There is also a further difficulty. To advocate social movement pressure on the state as the way of eliminating gender poses a limited understanding of the state's polycentric relationship to social power. While campaigning may sometimes be effective, it is not the primary way in which the state negotiates, enacts and responds to organising principles of gender and sexuality.

The Desiring State

A prostitute tells me that a magistrate who pays her to beat him confessed that he gets an erection every time he sentences a prostitute in court. (McClintock, 1992: 70)

So far, my discussion has focused on the intersection of lesbian and gay forces with the state in relation to the consolidation of sexual binaries and the destabilisation of gender. The final issue I want to address raises a quite different concern: namely, the sexualised character of the state itself. The two issues already discussed, while they intimately concern the state, do not tell us anything special or distinct about it. But can we use work on sexuality to give the state texture in ways not simply analogous to the interface between the state and race, gender or class? Sexuality as a social organising principle may still be centred on heterosexuality, with homosexuality its socially constituted other, but as I suggested earlier, social organising principles are not restricted to asymmetries between socially situated persons. Thus, sexuality both organises and is coupled to the incitement of other domains and practices according to a 'logic' of desire, climax, corporeality and lack. Earlier, I referred to the figurative sexualisation of the nation–state, here I want to focus on the desiring state. Some work in this area already exists: from George Mosse's (1985) scholarship on the ambivalent libidinal politics and practices of the German Nazi Party to the sexualised violence of armies (Enloe, 1993). Other analyses have focused on institutional displacement: for instance, judicial vengeance and the production of sacrificial victims in the prosecution of gay sado-masochism (Moran, 1996: 186), and feminist work on the symbolic assualting of women during the sexualised and humiliating ordeal of rape trials (e.g., Smart, 1995: 84).

To talk about the state as desiring does not assume a reified state actor, although it includes this aspect of the state's identity. It also encompasses the way erotic energy can be found in projects or technologies of governance, often as an unintended effect of state practice. Yet, the liberal state's relationship to desire is an uncomfortable one. Fascist states may exalt in a displaced libidinal energy, but for the most part, desire, other than in its patriotic, competitive expression, is defined as inappropriate for a liberal state, whose processes fetishise rationality, impartiality, objectivity and lack of emotion instead (see also Cooper, 1999), a distancing nicely captured in Butt and Hearn's (1998) discussion of corporal punishment in Britain.

Ambivalence about the state's own desires also affects the state's relationship to

the sexual identities, practices, and agenda of others. It leads to the privatisation, regulation, prohibition, but also, paradoxically, to the *intensification* of those identities and practices perceived as particularly, uncomfortably or contagiously sexual. For instance, despite appearing ostensibly hostile to sexual conduct between prisoners, the state generates, through its institutional structures and policies, its socially specific form, just as, according to Meyer (1996), it produces the particular contained, directed, thwarted organisation of sexual desire and conduct among military personnel.

Exploring how sexuality articulates to state desire is an important and underdeveloped area of state analysis. Yet, in the process of inquiry, attention also needs to be given to the impact of privatisation and the extension of capitalist market relations within modern, liberal states. Nation – states, such as Britain, are allying themselves increasingly with corporate capital – their bodies colonised by the drive, agenda and practices of market actors. At the same time, there is a considerable tension between the two in relation to questions of desire. Various scholars and activists have explored the ways in which capitalism mobilises sexuality and desire in the workplace, as well as *vis-à-vis* consumption (e.g., Hearn et al., 1989; Marcuse 1991); in contrast the state's deployment of desire to generate interest in its services and products seems far less apparent. Indeed, the reverse seems more often the case.

One site with the potential to both trouble and incite the state's ambivalent relationship to desire concerns the growth and growing recognition of sexualised citizenship identities (e.g., Richardson, 1998, 2000; Weeks, 1998). To the extent that citizenship is limited to the demand for equal rights – including equal consumption – for sexually identified communities such as lesbians and gay men, any challenge to the prevailing sexual logic of state practice remains minimal. However, if a sexual citizenship goes further to introduce into the public sphere and polity norms and practices based upon erotic desire, this opens up questions about the sexualised character of the state in ways that cannot be so easily forestalled. Thus, the move towards a sexualised citizenship – taking desire and intimacy out of its private box – poses the possibility of making demands that the state's desires – the emotional/psychological charge that both incites and emanates from its practices, structures, culture and relations – be also made explicit, justified and, perhaps most radically, democratised.

CONCLUSION

In this conclusion, I want briefly to revisit two issues addressed earlier. While these do not exactly constitute new directions, they highlight 'orientations' discounted in recent years. The first concerns lesbian and gay studies' neglect of the factors shaping state action: the question, posed in its most basic form, of why the state regulates sexuality in the way it does. The second issue is somewhat different: it concerns the way political scholarship and activism have been grounded in a politics of experience and identity at the expense of ideology.

The question of why the state acts as it does – the interests or social power that it condenses and organises – proved of far more concern to an earlier generation of Marxist-influenced, gay scholarship (e.g. Mort, 1980: 48), than to lesbian and gay scholars of the 1990s. Yet, despite the Foucauldian insistence that what matters is 'how', understanding the forces or conditions that structure, skew and continuously renegotiate state practice is important to avoid two assumptions: first, that the state is a neutral and open terrain; second, that its reproduction of social inequality is a fully immanent tendency, emanating exclusively from internal state processes. But this in turn begs the question: what is the relationship between state and wider forces? While acknowledging the relationship is not one-way, how do wider forces and the environment shape state practice? To say,

for instance, that the state 'condenses' the prevailing heterosexual balance of power – in line with a similar movement *vis-à-vis* race, gender and class (see Jessop, 1990: 149–50) tells us little. In the case of western, liberal states, it does not mean that the state is governed exclusively by a prevailing heterosexual logic, any more than that the state, scale-like, mirrors the prevailing balance between the two. While it has become almost a post-structuralist cliché to describe the state as uneven, mutable, and contradictory, the impact of these discontinuities on the capacity of different forces to shape state practice has received inadequate attention within lesbian and gay scholarship. Likewise, more work is required on the impact of different social processes and systems. How does the polycentric state's response to explicit social movement pressures intersect the structuring role played by sexual norms, discourses, covert interests, and ongoing social pathways upon state practice (see more generally Cooper, 2001)?

The final issue I want to raise concerns terrain at the heart of lesbian and gay state activism. For some sexual 'minorities' on the economic and normative boundaries of propriety, middle-class lesbians and gay men seem increasingly secure: focally positioned by a sexual binary that leaves others invisible. Not surprisingly, these perceptions have generated demands that lesbian and gay organisations widen the terms of inclusion, affirm their outsider status, or risk being displaced by a new 'vanguard'. In the face of claims by some lesbian feminists that bi and trans issues are not 'theirs', others are convoking a shared ground (Humphrey, 1999). But while such responsiveness is in many ways admirable, it does raise important political questions about the ideological basis for these new alliances. Namely, is sexual outsider status – as experience or identity – a sufficiently meaningful foundation for political mobilising?

Without denying the value of collective identity, I want to suggest that political organising on the basis of social experience or location, whether as gay, or more broadly as sexual outsiders/minorities, carries several risks. Not only does it pose the possibility of cementing identity boundaries against those who cannot be classified as belonging, but it also offers too vague a foundation from which a transformatory politics might spring. Contrary to the implicit assumptions of liberal political science, there is no single gay politics, no unitary gay 'interest' whether expressed discretely or in coalition with other 'oppressed groups'. What we have are a diverse spread of political aspirations from formal equality through radical democracy to the elimination of organising principles of class, race, gender, and sexuality. This pluralism is recognised by many scholars within lesbian and gay studies. However, there is still a tendency to see this diversity as the result of our multiple formed locations. What is missed in this interpretation is the role and importance of perspective or ideology in shaping political agenda.

I want therefore to close with two propositions: first, the need for normative political theorising which, while recognising the power and importance of social location, centres political aspirations that remain irreducible to location. This form of scholarship is already being undertaken by theorists such as Shane Phelan (1995), but without an explicit state focus. In addition, we need to explore the state's facilitation and 'management' of current gay politics. While the excesses of identity politics are often placed at the door of feminism and other new social movements, the state is implicated here too. In the case of liberal, western regimes, for instance, how does the particular configuration of state identities work to promote a sexual politics, based not only on formal rights, but according to a 'welfare' imperative which centres on 'raising' those with less? In addressing this question, we need to ask: what would be the consequences if lesbian and gay forces engaged with state bodies and state technologies in ways that repudiated these leanings, according to political perspectives that explicitly centred norms, ideology and vision? How would our states respond?

NOTES

1 My thanks to Didi Herman, Diane Richardson and Carl Stychin for their help and feedback on this chapter. Thanks also to Nick Cartwright for his research assistance.

2 In the process, rules 'hail' and thus recognise subject identities, even when they restrict the activities certain subjects can engage in.

3 By focusing on the relationship between conduct and status, Halley, and others writing in this field (see also Stychin, 1996), implicitly raise questions about liberal forms of governing. For instance, liberalism tends to believe it is more legitimate to target conduct than identity since the latter is often represented as immutable whereas conduct is perceived as a matter of choice. But does targeting conduct simply provide a disingenuous way of governing identity 'at a distance', given the interrelationship between the two? Halley describes how US military policy did not just target conduct retroactively, it also targeted conduct that had not yet occurred. Its focus on 'propensity' meant status functioned as evidence of the likelihood of acts occurring. From this perspective, we can thus identify other elements of liberal rationality, including the desire for risk minimisation combined with an auditing of danger, that draws on the military's capacity for high levels of surveillance and observation of individual conduct, speech, and possessions. At the same time, the policy also suggests a more conservative, authoritarian form of governance in which the state seeks to control the sexual identity and desires of particular governmental employees; in this way the military marks the boundary line of liberal governmentality.

4 Since the early 1990s, Queer has proven a major theoretical and activist meeting point, with its emphasis on the fluid, unstable nature of sexual identity; the political necessity of transgressing social rules and conventions; and the centrality of those constituencies deemed most unacceptable to the mainstream polity. See, generally, McIntosh (1993); Phelan (1997); Seidman (1997); Smyth (1992).

5 An analytics of government (Dean, 1999: 30–2) might also provide a useful vantage point from which to analyse municipal lesbian and gay politics. This perspective might ask: how did local government practices function to illuminate certain phenomena, e.g., anti-gay prejudice and discrimination, while obscuring others, such as the naturalised status of heterosexual norms? How did councils constitute themselves as legitimate actors within this field, and to what extent were they successful in doing so? What forms of thought were employed: how was sexuality conceptualised within local government and what relationship was it seen as having with socially constituted communities and persons?

6 It can thus be contrasted with the partially homologous, counter-identification of Queer Nation, see Berlant and Freeman (1993).

7 There is also an interesting parallel literature on the genealogies of Ireland's sexualisation (Flynn, 1997; Hanafin, 1998) that suggest its postcolonial identity is less contingent on heterosexuality than is suggested by Phillips' (1997) work on Zimbabwe and Alexander's (1994) work on the Caribbean.

8 As Biddy Martin (1994; see also 1992) argues, erotic relations are intimately tied to social principles of class, gender and race, as is the sexualisation of identity and role (see D'Amico, 1996). See also work on sexuality, race, and class in post-apartheid South Africa (e.g., Gevisser and Cameron, 1995), and wider debates about whether any necessary relationship exists between inequalities of gender, class and sexuality (e.g., Stychin, 2000).

9 The interpretive struggles between radical lesbian feminists, who placed gender or women at the heart of their understanding of sexual regulation (e.g., Jeffreys, 1994), and those lesbians who identified the relationship as far more contingent (e.g., Calhoun, 1996; Califia, 1997: 255) have proved a major struggle within community and academic arenas.

10 Among commentators and scholars it has led to turf wars over historic and more current figures who cross-dressed. Were they first and foremost lesbians who dressed and lived as men for safety, convenience or pleasure, or women who identified as male (see for instance, Califia, 1997: Ch. 4)?

11 Because a politics of gender fluidity is more concerned to free gender than to erase it, the gendered character of other aspects of the state, such as its values and norms might seem less problematic.

REFERENCES

Alexander, J. (1994) 'Not just (any) body can be a citizen: the politics of law, sexuality and postcoloniality in Trinidad and Tobago and the Bahamas', *Feminist Review*, 48: 5–23.

Allen, J. (1990) 'Does feminism need a theory of the state?', in S. Watson (ed.), *Playing the State: Australian Feminist Interventions*. London: Verso. pp. 21–37.

Altmore, C. (1995) 'Drawing the line: issues of boundary and the Homosexual Law Reform Bill campaign in New Zealand (Aotearoa), 1985–86', *Journal of Homosexuality*, 30: 23–52.

Althusser, L. (1971) *Lenin and Philosophy and Other Essays*. London: New Left Books.

Altman, D. (1982) *The Homosexualization of America*. New York: St. Martin's Press.

Altman, D. (1994) *Power and Community: Organizational and Cultural Responses to AIDS*. London: Taylor and Francis Ltd.

Bailey, R. (1999) *Gay Politics, Urban Politics: Identity and Economics in the Urban Setting*. New York: Columbia University Press.

Berlant, L. and Freeman, E. (1993) 'Queer nationality', in M. Warner (ed.), *Fear of a Queer Planet: Queer Politics and Social Theory*. Minneapolis: University of Minnesota Press. pp. 193–229.

Boyd, S. (1994) '(Re)placing the state: family, law and oppression', *Canadian Journal of Law and Society*, 9: 39–73.

Boykin, K. (2000) 'Where rhetoric meets reality: the role of Black lesbians and gays in queer politics', in C. Rimmerman, Wald, D., and Wilcox, C. (eds), *The Politics of Gay Rights*. Chicago: Chicago University Press. pp. 79–96.

Brown, M. (1997) *Replacing Citizenship: AIDS Activism and Radical Democracy*. New York and London: The Guilford Press.

Brown, S. (1999) 'Democracy and sexual difference: the lesbian and gay movement in Argentina', in B. Adam, Duyvendak, J.W., and Krouwel, A. (eds), *The Global Emergence of Gay and Lesbian Politics*. Philadelphia: Temple University Press. pp. 110–132.

Brown, W. (1992) 'Finding the man in the state', *Feminist Studies*, 18: 7–34.

Brown, W. (1995) *States of Injury: Power and Freedom in Late Modernity*. Princeton, NJ: Princeton University Press.

Burchell, G. (1996) 'Liberal government and techniques of the self', in A. Barry, Osborne, T., and Rose, N. (eds), *Foucault and Political Reason*. London: UCL Press. pp. 19–36.

Butt, T. and Hearn, J. (1998) 'The sexualization of corporal punishment: the construction of sexual meaning', *Sexualities*, 1: 203–27.

Button, J., Rienzo, B., and Wald, K. (1997) *Private Lives, Public Conflicts*. Washington, DC: Congressional Quarterly.

Cahn, S. (1996) 'From the muscle moll to the butch ball player: mannishness, lesbianism, and homophobia in US women's sport', in M. Vicinus (ed.), *Lesbian Subjects: A Feminist Studies Reader*. Bloomington and Indianapolis: Indiana University Press. pp. 41–65.

Calhoun, C. (1996) 'The gender closet: lesbian disappearance under the sign women', in M. Vicinus (ed.), *Lesbian Subjects: A Feminist Studies Reader*. Bloomington and Indianapolis: Indiana University Press. pp. 209–32.

Califia, P. (1997) *Sex Changes: The Politics of Transgenderism*. San Francisco: Cleis Press.

Carabine, J. (1995) 'Invisible sexualities: sexuality, politics and influencing policy-making', in A. Wilson (ed.), *A Simple Matter of Justice*. London: Cassell.

Cohan, A.S. (1982) 'Obstacles to equality: government responses to the gay rights movement in the United States', *Political Studies*, 30: 59–76.

Cooper, D. (1994a) *Sexing the City: Lesbian and Gay Politics within the Activist State*. London: Rivers Oram.

Cooper, D. (1994b) 'A retreat from feminism? British municipal lesbian politics and cross-gender initiatives', *Canadian Journal of Women and the Law*, 7: 431–53.

Cooper, D. (1995) *Power in Struggle: Feminism, Sexuality and the State.* London and New York: Open University Press/NYU Press.

Cooper, D. (1998) *Governing out of Order: Space, Law and the Politics of Belonging.* London: Rivers Oram.

Cooper, D. (1999) 'Punishing councils: political power, solidarity and the pursuit of freedom', in S. Millns and N. Whitty (eds), *Feminist Perspectives on Public Law.* London: Cavendish. pp. 245–69.

Cooper, D. (2000) 'And you can't find me nowhere: relocating identity and structure within equality jurisprudence', *Journal of Law and Society,* 27: 249–72.

Cooper, D. (2001) 'Against the current: social pathways and the pursuit of enduring change', *Feminist Legal Studies,* 9: 119–148.

Currah, P. (1997) 'Defending genders: sex and gender non-conformity in the civil rights strategies of sexual minorities', *Hastings Law Journal,* 48: 1363–85.

Curtis, B. (1995) 'Taking the state back out: Rose and Miller on political power', *British Journal of Sociology,* 46: 575–89.

D'Amico, F. (1996) 'Race-ing and gendering the military closet', in C. Rimmerman (ed.), *Gay Rights, Military Wrongs: Political Perspectives on Lesbians and Gays in the Military.* New York: Garland Publishing. pp. 3–46.

Dean, M. (1999) *Governmentality.* London: Sage.

de Lauretis, T. (1990) 'Eccentric subjects: feminist theory and historical consciousness', *Feminist Studies,* 16.

D'Emilio, J. (1989) 'The homosexual menace: the politics of sexuality in Cold War America', in K. Peiss and C. Simmons (eds), *Passion and Power: Sexuality in History.* Philadelphia: Temple University Press. pp. 226–40.

Donovan, T. et al. (2000) 'Direct democracy and gay rights initiatives after *Romer*', in C. Rimmerman (eds), *The Politics of Gay Rights.* Chicago: University of Chicago Press. pp. 161–90.

Duggan, L. (1994) 'Queering the state', *Social Text,* 39: 1–14.

Durham, M. (1991) *Sex and Politics.* Basingstoke: Macmillan.

Eaton, M. (1995) 'Homosexual unmodified: speculations on law's discourse, race, and the construction of sexual identity', in D. Herman and C. Stychin (eds), *Legal Inversions: Lesbians, Gay Men, and the Politics of Law.* Philadelphia: Temple University Press. pp. 46–73.

Enloe, C. (1993) *The Morning After: Sexual Politics at the End of the Cold War.* Berkeley, CA: University of California Press.

Eskridge, W. (1997) 'A jurisprudence of coming out: religion, homosexuality, and collisions of liberty and equality in American public law', *Yale Law Journal,* 106: 2411–74.

Flynn, L. (1997) 'Cherishing all her children equally: the law and politics of Irish lesbian and gay citizenship', *Social and Legal Studies,* 6: 493–512.

Foucault, M. (1980) *Power/Knowledge.* New York: Pantheon.

Foucault, M. (1981) *The History of Sexuality.* London: Penguin.

Foucault, M. (1991) 'Governmentality', in G. Burchell, Gordon, G., and Miller, P. (eds), *The Foucault Effect: Studies in Governmentality.* Hemel Hempstead: Harvester Wheatsheaf.

Franzway, S., Court, D., and Connell, R.W. (1989) *Staking a Claim: Feminism, Bureaucracy and the State.* Cambridge: Polity.

Fraser, N. (1989) *Unruly Discourses: Power, Discourse and Gender in Contemporary Social Theory.* Cambridge: Polity Press.

Fraser, N. (1997) *Justice Interruptus.* New York: Routledge.

Gevisser, M. and Cameron, E. (eds) (1995) *Defiant Desire.* New York. Routledge.

Goldberg-Hiller, J. (1998) 'Entitled to be hostile: narrating the political economy of civil rights', *Social and Legal Studies,* 7: 517–38.

Green, J. (1999) 'More love and more desire: the building of a Brazilian movement', in B. Adam et al. (eds), *The Global Emergence of Gay and Lesbian Politics.* Philadelphia, PA: Temple University Press. pp. 91–109.

Gupta, A. (1995) 'Blurred boundaries: the discourse of corruption, the culture of politics, and the imagined state', *American Ethnologist,* 22: 375–402.

Haeberle, S. (1996) 'Gay men and lesbians at City Hall', *Social Science Quarterly,* 77: 190–7.

Halley, J. (1999) *Don't: A Reader's Guide to the Military's Anti-Gay Policy.* Durham, NC and London: Duke University Press.

Hanafin, P. (1998) 'Rewriting desire: the construction of sexual identity in literary and legal discourse in postcolonial Ireland', *Social and Legal Studies,* 7: 409–29.

Hart, J. (1992) 'A cocktail of alarm: same sex couples and migration to Australia, 1985–90', in K. Plummer (ed.), *Modern Homosexualities.* London: Routledge.

Hearn, J. et al. (1989) *The Sexuality of Organization.* London: Sage.

Held, D. (1989) *Political Theory and the Modern State.* Cambridge: Polity.

Herek, G. et al. (eds) (1996) *Out in Force: Sexual Orientation and the Military.* Chicago: University of Chicago Press.

Herman, D. (1994) *Rights of Passage: Struggles for Lesbian and Gay Legal Equality.* Toronto: Toronto University Press.

Herman, D. (1997) *The Antigay Agenda: Orthodox Vision and the Christian Right.* Chicago: Chicago University Press.

Hobbes, T. (1914) *Leviathan.* London: J.M. Dent and Sons.

Hodge, G.D. (2000) 'Retrenchment from a queer ideal: class privilege and the failure of identity politics in AIDS activism', *Environment and Planning D: Society and Space,* 18: 355–376.

Humphrey, J. (1999) 'To queer or not to queer a lesbian and gay group? Sexual and gendered politics at the turn of the century', *Sexualities,* 2: 223–46.

Hunt, A. and Wickham, G. (1994) *Foucault and Law: Towards a Sociology of Law as Governance*. London: Pluto Press.

Innes, S. and Lloyd, M. (1996) 'G.I. Joes in Barbie land: recontextualizing butch in twentieth-century lesbian culture', in B. Beemyn and M. Eliason (eds), *Queer Studies: A Lesbian, Gay, Bisexual, and Transgender Anthology*. New York: New York University Press. pp. 9–34.

James, C. (1996) 'Denying complexity: the dismissal and appropriation of bisexuality in queer, lesbian, and gay theory', in B. Beemyn and M. Eliason (eds), *Queer Studies: A Lesbian, Gay, Bisexual, and Transgender Anthology*. New York: New York University Press. pp. 217–40.

Jeffreys, S. (1994) *The Lesbian Heresy*. London: the Women's Press.

Jeffreys, S. (1996) 'Heterosexuality and the desire for gender', in D. Richardson (ed.), *Theorising Heterosexuality*. Buckingham: Open University Press. pp. 75–90.

Jessop, B. (1990) *State Theory*. Cambridge: Polity.

Kinsman, G. (1992) 'Managing AIDS organizing: "Consultation", "partnership", and the national AIDS strategy', in W. Carroll (ed.), *Organizing Dissent: Contemporary Social Movements in Theory and Practice*. Toronto: Garamond. pp. 215–31.

Kinsman, G. (1996a) *The Regulation of Desire: Homo and Hetero Sexualities*. Montreal: Black Rose Books.

Kinsman, G. (1996b) 'Responsibility as a strategy of governance: regulating people living with AIDS and lesbians and gay men in Ontario', *Economy and Society*, 25: 393–409.

Lansley, S., Goss, S., and Wolmar, C. (1989) *Councils in Conflict: The Rise and Fall of the Municipal Left*. Basingstoke: Macmillan.

Lunsing, W. (1999) 'Japan: finding its way?', in B. Adam et al. (eds), *The Global Emergence of Gay and Lesbian Politics*. Philadelphia: Temple University Press. pp. 293–325.

Magleby, D. (1998) 'Ballot initiatives and intergovernmental relations in the United States', *Publius: The Journal of Federalism*, 28: 147–163.

Marcuse, H. (1991) *One Dimensional Man*. London: Routledge.

Martin, B. (1992) 'Sexual practice and changing lesbian identities', in M. Barrett and A. Phillips (eds), *Destabilizing Theory*. Cambridge: Polity. pp. 93–119.

Martin, B. (1994) 'Sexualities without genders and other queer utopias', *Diacritics*, 24: 104–21.

McClintock, A. (1992) 'Screwing the system: sex work, race, and the law', *Boundary 2*, 19: 70–95.

McIntosh, M. (1993) 'Queer theory and the war of the sexes', in J. Bristow and A. Wilson (eds), *Activating Theory: Lesbian, Gay, Bisexual Politics*. London: Lawrence and Wishart. pp. 30–52.

Meyer, L. (1996) 'Creating G.I. Jane: the regulation of sexuality and sexual behavior in the women's army corp during World War II', in M. Vicinus (ed.), *Lesbian Subjects*. Bloomington and Indianapolis: Indiana University Press. pp. 66–84.

Mitchell, T. (1991) 'The limits of the state: beyond statist approaches and their critics', *American Political Science Review*, 85: 77–96.

Moran, L. (1991) 'The uses of homosexuality: homosexuality for national security', *International Journal of the Sociology of Law*, 19: 149–70.

Moran, L. (1996) *The Homosexual(ity) of Law*. London and New York: Routledge.

Mort, F. (1980) 'Sexuality: regulation and contestation', in Gay Left Collective (eds), *Homosexuality: Power and Politics*. London: Allison and Busby Ltd. pp. 38–51.

Mosse, G. (1985) *Nationalism and Sexuality*. New York: Howard Fertig.

Namaste, K. (1996) 'Tragic misreadings: queer theory's erasure of transgender subjectivity', in B. Beemyn and M. Eliason (eds), *Queer Studies: A Lesbian, Gay, Bisexual, and Transgender Anthology*. New York: New York University Press. pp. 183–203.

O'Malley, P. et al. (1997) 'Governmentality, criticism, politics', *Economy and Society*, 26: 501–7.

Phelan, S. (1995) 'The space of justice: lesbians and democratic politics', in A. Wilson (ed.), *A Simple Matter of Justice*. London: Cassell. pp. 193–220.

Phelan, S. (1997) 'The shape of queer: assimilation and articulation', *Women and Politics*, 18: 55–73.

Phillips, O. (1997) 'Zimbabwean law and the production of a white man's disease', *Social and Legal Studies*, 6: 471–92.

Pratt, M.B. (1995) *S/he*. Ithaca, New York: Firebrand Books.

Pringle, R. and Watson, S. (1992) 'Women's interests and the post-structuralist state', in M. Barrett and A. Phillips (eds), *Destabilising Theory: Contemporary Feminist Debates*. Cambridge: Polity. pp. 53–73.

Raymond, J. (1996) 'The politics of transgenderism', in R. Ekins and D. King (eds), *Blending Genders*. London: Routledge. pp. 215–23.

Rayside, D. (1998) *On the Fringe: Gays and Lesbians in Politics*. Ithaca, New York, and London: Cornell University Press.

Richardson, D. (1998) 'Sexuality and citizenship', *Sociology*, 32: 83–100.

Richardson, D. (2000) 'Claiming citizenship? Sexuality, citizenship and lesbian/feminist theory', *Sexualities* 3: 255–272.

Rimmerman, C. (ed.) (1996) *Gay Rights, Military Wrongs: Political Perspectives on Lesbians and Gays in the Military*. New York: Garland Publishing.

Rose, N. (1994) 'Expertise and the government of conduct', *Studies in Law, Politics and Society*, 14: 359–67.

Rose, N. (1996) 'Governing advanced liberal democracies', in A. Barry, Osborne, T., and Rose, N. (eds), *Foucault and Political Reason*. London: UCL Press.

Rose, N. (1999) *Powers of Freedom*. Cambridge: Cambridge University Press.

Rose, N. and Miller, P. (1992) 'Political power beyond the state: problematics of government', *British Journal of Sociology*, 43: 172–205.

Rubin, G. (1989) 'Thinking sex: notes for a radical theory of the politics of sexuality', in C. Vance (ed.), *Pleasure and Danger: Exploring Female Sexuality.* London: Pandora. pp. 267–319.

Rust, P. (1995) *Bisexuality and the Challenge to Lesbian Politics: Sex, Loyalty, and Revolution.* New York: New York University Press.

Rust, P. (1996) 'Sexual identity and bisexual identities: the struggle for self-description in a changing sexual landscape', in B. Beemyn and M. Eliason (eds), *Queer Studies: A Lesbian, Gay, Bisexual, and Transgender Anthology.* New York: New York University Press. pp. 64–86.

Schrodel, J.R. and Fiber, P. (2000) 'Lesbian and gay policy priorities: commonality and difference', in C. Rimmerman, Wald, K., and Wilcox, C. (eds), *The Politics of Gay Rights.* Chicago: Chicago University Press, pp. 97–118.

Schwartzwald, R. (1993) 'Symbolic homosexuality, false feminine, and the problematics of identity in Quebec', in M. Warner (ed.), *Fear of a Queer Planet: Queer Politics and Social Theory.* Minneapolis: University of Minnesota Press. pp. 264–99.

Seidman, S. (1997) *Difference Troubles: Queering Social Theory and Sexual Politics.* Cambridge: Cambridge University Press.

Simons, J. (1995) *Foucault and the Political.* London and New York: Routledge.

Smart, C. (1995) *Law, Crime and Sexuality.* London: Sage.

Smith, A.M. (1994) *New Right Discourse on Race and Sexuality.* New York: Cambridge University Press.

Smith, A.M. (1997) 'The regulation of lesbian sexuality through erasure: the case of Jennifer Saunders', in J. Dean (ed.), *Feminism and the New Democracy.* London: Sage. pp. 181–97.

Smyth, C. (1992) *Lesbians Talk Queer Notions.* London: Scarlet.

Steinberg, P.E. (1994) 'Territorial formation on the margin: urban anti-planning in Brooklyn', *Political Geography*, 13: 461–76.

Stone, S. (1991) 'The empire strikes back: Posttranssexual manifesto', in J. Epstein and K. Straub (eds), *Body Guards.* New York: Routledge. pp. 280–304.

Stychin, C. (1996) 'To take him at his word: theorizing law, sexuality and the US military exclusion policy', *Social and Legal Studies*, 5: 179–200.

Stychin, C. (1998) *A Nation by Rights.* Philadelphia: Temple University Press.

Stychin, C. (2000) '*Grant*-ing rights: the politics of rights, sexuality and European Union', *Northern Ireland Legal Quarterly*, 51: 281–302.

Sullivan, G. (1999) 'Political opportunism and the harassment of homosexuals in Florida, 1952–1965', *Journal of Homosexuality*, 37: 57–81.

Sunstein, C. (1990) 'Paradoxes of the regulatory state', *University of Chicago Law Review*, 57: 407–41.

Sweet, D. (1995) 'The church, the Stasi, and socialist integration: three stages of lesbian and gay emancipation in the former German Democratic Republic', *Journal of Homosexuality*, 29: 351–367.

Tobin, A. (1990) 'Lesbianism and the Labour Party: the GLC experience', *Feminist Review*, 34: 56–66.

Wald, K. (2000) 'The context of gay politics', in C. Rimmerman, Wald, K., and Wilcox, C. (eds), *The Politics of Gay Rights.* Chicago: Chicago University Press, pp. 1–28.

Watson, S. (1990) 'The state of play: an introduction', in S. Watson (ed.), *Playing the State: Australian Feminist Interventions.* London: Verso. pp. 3–20.

Weeks, J. (1998) 'The sexual citizen', *Theory, Culture and Society*, 15: 35–52.

Whittle, S. (1996) 'Gender fucking or fucking gender? Current cultural contributions to theories of gender blending', in R. Ekins and D. King (eds), *Blending Genders.* London: Routledge. pp. 196–214.

Whittle, S. (1998) 'The trans-cyberian mail way', *Social and Legal Studies*, 7: 389–408.

Wilton, T. (1996) 'Which one's the man? The heterosexualisation of lesbian sex', in D. Richardson (ed.), *Theorising Heterosexuality.* Buckingham: Open University. pp. 125–42.

Yuval-Davis, N. (1997) *Gender and Nation.* London: Sage.

15

Lesbian and Gay Health

Power, Paradigms and Bodies

TAMSIN WILTON

THE GREAT DIVIDE?

As with so many aspects of lesbian and gay studies and, indeed, women's studies before it, the academic study of health has a dynamic relationship to political activism around health policy issues. Theory and research feed into activism and vice versa; indeed, academics and activists are sometimes the same individuals. However, unlike other subject areas in lesbian and gay studies, research into health issues and problems tends to be located in a professional arena, that of health and social care practice. This unique combination of factors means that scholarship in the field of lesbian and gay health is split into what can seem like two completely separate halves. This split is partly disciplinary and partly to do with the intentions and motivation of two contrasting groups of scholars. It is very marked, to the extent that work done in one arena may remain very unfamiliar to those working in the other.

The first body of work consists of research located in the policy arena or in practice. This is the aspect of lesbian and gay health studies that is probably the most visible from the point of view of lesbians and gay men outside the academy. It is largely produced by researchers (including practitioners) working from within the broad field of health studies. They aim to focus attention on the health care needs of lesbians and gay men, to encourage greater recognition of homophobia as a malign influence on health and life chances, and to improve health care provision to lesbian and gay service users.

The end product of work of this kind includes articles in practice journals, reports directed at policy-makers, papers or poster presentations at conferences and study days for nurses and other health care professionals. Education and information are also targeted at lesbian and gay community members in the form of educational articles in the pink press, or healthcare handbooks (examples include Shernoff and Scott, 1988; Weatherburn, 1992; McClure and Vespry, 1994; Gill, 1996; Wilton, 1997a).

The second body of work is very much theoretical and concerned with abstract questions. Generally produced in universities, by academics who study health as a contested concept and medicine as a discourse, it incorporates work in disciplines such as sociology or cultural studies, or in multi-disciplinary areas such as queer studies/ sexuality studies, or theories of the body. Here, issues to do with sexual orientation are generally integrated into debates about subjectivity and identity, medical power, the social construction of gender and the medicalisation of gender and sexuality (examples include Hausman, 1995; Waldby, 1996; Rosario, 1997; Shildrick, 1997; Wilton, 1997b; Mort, 1997/2000). Although the focus of such work is more likely to be 'purely' intellectual than policy-orientated, many of those carrying out research in this arena are motivated by a more or less implicit concern for social justice and hence for the greater well-being of queer people. Moreover, as I shall argue here, the more pragmatic and policy-driven kinds of research require at least some understanding of theoretical work on sexuality and health in order to underpin future development.

Any overview of health as a topic of concern within lesbian and gay studies needs, therefore, to explore the relationships between activism, policy/practice research and discourse-based scholarship. Here, I have chosen to start by discussing two very different forms of political activism around health; AIDS activism and the involvement of lesbians in the women's health movement. The discussion then continues with an exploration of more formally academic work on lesbian and gay health from the policy/practice perspective. The second section introduces the more theoretical body of work concerned with analysing medical discourses of gender and sexuality, and the chapter concludes with an assessment of the relationship between these strands of activity and their contribution to the embryonic discipline of lesbian and gay health studies.

TWO KINDS OF HEALTH ACTIVISM

The forms taken by health activism reflect and grow out of the political history of activist movements at different points in time and at various geopolitical locations. Thus, AIDS activism differs in many important ways from activism around lesbian health. The reasons for this are complex, and are to do with such factors as political and professional power, socio-economic inequalities, shifting norms in an increasingly media-filtered mainstream culture and (especially) the influence of sexism on these and other issues.

When, in the early 1980s, the HIV epidemic first made itself felt among the urban gay communities of the United States, it sparked the formation of a new activist community, made up largely of privileged, educated, white gay men for whom such a direct experience of social exclusion was new and bitter (Wilton, 1992; Kayal, 1993). The increasingly coalitional nature of AIDS activism in the USA, as more and more marginalised groups became affected, was a new experience for many of the gay men involved. Although some had experience of lesbian and gay politics, health was never high up the gay rights agenda in the US (see, for example, Jay and Young, 1978, 1994). Even in Britain, where a welfare state and a national health service underpin a very different sense of entitlement, the Campaign for Homosexual Equality (CHE) and the Gay Liberation Front (GLF) paid little attention to health care (see Cant and Hemmings, 1988; Power, 1995).

Lesbian health activism, in contrast, grew out of the women's health movement and employed many of the strategies developed in the wider context of feminist healthcare politics. As an integral element of the second wave of the Women's Liberation Movement (WLM), the women's health movement was, by definition, part of a long-lasting social and political struggle for rights. Moreover, with issues such as reproductive rights, free access to abortion and the struggle against rape and domestic violence at the top of the agenda, sexuality was an integral element of the feminist struggle (Smart and Smart, 1978).

Not only did lesbian health activists cut their teeth on such issues, they also had to fight *within* feminism, against the heterosexual majority who thought lesbian issues unimportant or who believed that to include lesbians would bring feminism into disrepute (Abbott and Love, 1985; Nestle, 1987; Cruikshank, 1992). Nor was the infant gay movement much better. Since so many gay men were hostile to feminism (Cruikshank, 1992; Power, 1995) and unwilling to acknowledge either lesbian oppression or their own sexism, lesbian issues dropped down the agenda of the gay liberation movement.

Finding themselves marginalised within feminism and gay liberation, large numbers of lesbians abandoned both mainstream gay politics and the women's movement. This historical moment – from the early 1970s to the mid-1980s – was, at least in Britain and the USA, the heyday of lesbian separatism. As a political strategy, separatism required lesbians to devote their energy and time to other lesbians, an approach that included establishing separate clinics for lesbians. The first, begun in New York City in 1973 (Waitkevics and Stein, 1978), established a model that is still relevant, as demonstrated by the slowly growing number of lesbian clinics and well-woman drop-in centres around Britain today (Wilton, 1998).

SCHOLARSHIP OUT OF ACTIVISM

The contrasting forms of activism over lesbian health and HIV/AIDS[1] have given rise to very different bodies of academic work. Work on HIV/AIDS, which may be assumed under the loose umbrella of lesbian and gay studies, takes many forms. Indeed, there has been a dazzling profusion of AIDS-related scholarship by and about gay men and (to a lesser extent) lesbians. This body of work encompasses social science (Altman, 1986; Waldby, 1996), cultural studies (Boffin and Gupta, 1990; Wilton, 1997b), media studies (Crimp, 1988; Crimp with Rolston, 1990), fine art studies (Gott, 1994), literature (Mars-Jones and White, 1988; White, 1997), film studies (Patton, 1991; Gever,

1993), policy studies (Patton, 1985; Wilton, 1992; King, 1993), social history (Fee and Fox, 1988; Kayal, 1993), philosophy (Sontag, 1988) and many other elements.

As lesbian and gay studies/queer studies consolidates its academic position, a queer scholarship of AIDS seems fully integrated into the discipline (see, for example, Abelove et al., 1993; Creekmur and Doty, 1995; Seidman, 1996; Nardi and Schneider, 1998). So variegated and cross-disciplinary has the study of AIDS become, however, that it exceeds the boundaries of anything which could plausibly be called 'health studies'. Social scientific research methods of the most familiar and mainstream kind - surveys, questionnaires, interviews – stand side by side with elite theoretical musings on popular cultural artefacts seldom admitted into the study of health.

This proliferation across disciplinary boundaries is typically postmodern and very much in tune with the *Zeitgeist* of the academy. However, it remains unfamiliar territory to those who actually work in the field of AIDS care, whose training is still largely innocent of input from the humanities and cultural studies. This element of the scholarship of AIDS might more properly be said to belong in our second category of lesbian and gay health studies, discourse-based theory. Yet those scholars, such as Susan Sontag (1988), Catherine Waldby (1996) or Paula Treichler (1988 a, b), who employ sophisticated discourse analysis to understand the social and cultural impact of the pandemic, clearly intend their work to contribute to the struggle against AIDS. This is the first point at which it starts to become clear that high theory and pragmatic policy-driven research are inseparable elements in lesbian and gay health studies.

DYKES WITHOUT A THEORY: LESBIAN HEALTH RESEARCH

The sheer range of AIDS-related work, from cutting-edge discourse analysis to routine epidemiological data collection, is in sharp contrast to scholarship in the field of lesbian health. Here, relatively few of those working in the field are established academics and almost no theoretical work has been carried out on the complex foundational questions on lesbian health. AIDS acted as a catalyst for plenty of high-theory work on the gay male body, its surfaces, vulnerabilities, representations, health/sickness and its capture by competing discourses (e.g. Bersani, 1988; Hewett, 1990; Meyer, 1998). Of course the contribution made to AIDS theory by lesbian academics and activists has ensured that the lesbian body is a presence – albeit a shadowy one – in AIDS theory (Wilton, 1997b; Richardson, 2000b). However, the paradigmatic body-at-risk, as represented in high theory texts on HIV/AIDS, continues to be a white, gay male body.

The socio-cultural phenomenon that is AIDS (as distinct from the bio-medical emergency that is the HIV pandemic) has engendered a polyvocal and cross-disciplinary body of theoretical work that deconstructs notions of health, pathology, (male) homosexuality, masculinity, medicine and the body. Apart from its footnote status within this body of work, the whole notion of 'lesbian health' is, by comparison, profoundly under-theorised and remains a taken-for-granted concept in most published work on the subject (Wilton, 1997c)[2].

Voices from practice

With the exception of the deconstructive strand of AIDS scholarship, most published work on lesbian and/or gay health is situated within the professional context of health and social care practice. Typically, practitioners who are themselves lesbian or gay carry out pieces of research with the aim of improving one or more aspect of service provision to lesbian or gay service users in their own area of expertise. Since health and social care services are, by their nature, not generally located in academic institutions, opportunities

to engage in research may be limited and, in any case, will have very different parameters from those which apply to university researchers.

Research of this kind has, therefore, often been carried out by student practitioners in post-basic training, who may make use of their time in a higher education environment to carry out studies for undergraduate dissertations or postgraduate theses. Examples include Stewart's (1997) study of the experiences of lesbian mothers, or Das's (1996) account of homophobia in medical training. There is still a real shortage of reliable data on many lesbian and gay health issues, so there is greater than usual potential for even an undergraduate dissertation to make a meaningful impact in the literature, especially if it is reworked as an article in the practice literature or presented at a practice conference. However, this also gives rise to the risk that work of variable quality may be published and, sadly, this is already the case in some areas of the health and social care practitioner literature on lesbian and gay issues[3].

A parallel strand of more formal practitioner-initiated research in this field is carried out by more experienced professionals who have succeeded in getting funding for specific projects. Often this work is supported by professional bodies, such as (in the USA) the Gay and Lesbian Medical Association or (in Britain) the Royal Colleges, who recognise the need for practice improvements in order better to meet the needs of their lesbian and gay clients. The British model for research of this kind is the Royal College of Nursing (RCN)'s working party on lesbian and gay nursing issues.

Set up in response to pressure from lesbian and gay nurses, the working party has carried out a substantial body of work on many aspects of the nursing care of sexual minorities, and has produced several key *Statements* on important issues such as the nursing needs of lesbian and gay patients (RCN, 1994) or the vexed question of next-of-kin status in families with lesbian or gay members (RCN, 1998). These *Statements* are the chief means by which the RCN establishes and maintains good professional practice in nursing, so the existence of these examples represents a significant step forward. The RCN working party has also published widely in the nursing literature, ensuring that research findings and implications for practice are disseminated widely through the profession. More recently, this model has been taken up by the Royal College of Midwives (RCM), who funded a survey of lesbian mothers to identify strengths and weaknesses in service provision (Wilton and Kaufmann, 2001). The RCM also established a working party to devise a formal Policy Statement on the maternity care of lesbian mothers, drawing on the expertise of academics in the field as well as experienced midwives and midwife tutors.

Important interventions in practice, such as the work done in the USA by the Institute of Medicine (Solarz, 1999) or in Britain by the Royal Colleges, are almost invariably instigated by practitioners who are themselves lesbian or gay. For example, the RCM's ground-breaking programme was initiated in response to a lesbian student midwife who contacted the College to express deep concern at the homophobia she experienced during her own professional training. It is therefore important to recognise that work of this kind remains impossible in those areas where homophobia retains a powerful professional, cultural or political sanction (Rosenblum, 1996). It is still the case that, for those working in the health care professions, openly asserting a lesbian or gay identity demands real courage.

The final element in this practice-orientated field is research carried out by trained professional researchers, usually employed by universities, using funding obtained from the larger institutional funding bodies, such as England's Health Development Agency (formerly the Health Education Authority), New Zealand's Health Funding Authority or the US Department of Health and Human Services. It is notoriously difficult to persuade funding bodies that work of this

kind is relevant or important, and homophobic stigma remains an obstacle both in terms of obtaining funding and in carrying out work in practice areas. Farquhar (1999: 81) is fairly typical in meeting stubborn resistance from staff working in genito-urinary medicine (GUM):

> a 'flagship' GUM service, … which had initially agreed to participate in my research, declined at the last moment to do so (after full ethics committee approval had been granted), on the grounds that it was not possible to find a member of clinic staff willing to take named responsibility for liaising with a study on lesbian sexual health.

Nevertheless, it is certainly easier now to obtain funding than has ever been the case in the past, and the body of knowledge generated by this means is growing rapidly. Such studies vary greatly in scale and scope, from small-scale survey work carried out in a local area (examples include Dockery, 1996; Mugglestone, 1999) to major studies with a national focus, of which the most significant recent example is the Institute of Medicine report on lesbian health in the United States (Solarz, 1999).

Characteristics

This important and growing body of work is almost always funded out of the public purse. There seems to be little funding available from commercial sources in the private sector, with the important exception of work on HIV/AIDS which, at least in the USA, is often funded by drugs companies hoping to improve their standing with the gay community. In Britain, local authorities or local healthcare trusts have funded some key studies in their area.

In relation to this body of work it is often difficult to detach 'lesbian and gay health' from *sexual* health or, indeed, from a specific focus on HIV prevention. On one level, this is problematic, since it powerfully reinforces the social construction of lesbian and gay identities as primarily sexual and of lesbians and gay men as sexual deviants interested in little else. In terms of a public health agenda, locating lesbian and gay health under the umbrella of sexual health makes it very difficult to explore either the wider consequences of homophobia for health or the impact of heterosexism within the medical profession.

However, concern to prevent the continuing spread of the HIV/AIDS pandemic may often lead to a recognition of the wider needs of gay men and/or lesbians for health education more generally. AIDS charities may fund research into a broad spectrum of gay health issues, often in collaboration with community groups. In Britain, for example, research into such gay-related issues as homophobic bullying in schools, or into safe sex practices, has been supported by charities such as the AIDS Education Research Trust (AVERT), the lesbian and gay campaigning group Stonewall or the Terrence Higgins Trust. By their very nature, such projects may adopt a more or less critical perspective on existing services, so are more likely to be based in established academic centres of excellence than carried out by practitioners.

Non-governmental organisations (NGOs), such as human rights groups, may also fund research into lesbian and/or gay health, as may service-user groups or single-issue health charities such as, for example, the British mental health charity, MIND. Such groups may be particularly interested in exploring questions of equitable treatment or access to services, and they may or may not collaborate with government agencies, depending on the local political situation.

Increasing global concern for human rights has been an important means of getting fundamental questions of lesbian and gay health and well-being onto political agendas. At the European and Atlantic Governmental Preparatory Conference in Vienna in 1994, the International Lesbian and Gay Association and the International Gay and Lesbian Human Rights Commission both presented formal Statements on the human rights of lesbians and gay men (Rosenblum, 1996). Human rights organisations have been slow to recognise the significance of sexual orientation as a valid human rights issue, but this situation shifted rapidly in the last decade of the twentieth century.

This shift has had a significant impact on lesbian and gay health politics and research. In Canada, for example, the Michigan Organization for Human Rights (1991) funded a major survey of lesbian health. South Africa, although in dire need of investment to underpin its collapsing economy, has enshrined lesbian and gay civil rights in the new, post-apartheid constitution. This offers (at least in theory) powerful political support for groups concerned with the health and well-being of lesbian and gay South Africans.[4] A recent study of the health education and care needs of lesbian, gay and bisexual residents of Cape Town, carried out by local community group the Triangle Project, was funded by the Health Systems Trust and the Department of Health (Griffin, et al., 1998).

Lesbians and gay men who are citizens of countries of the European Union may soon make good use of the Human Rights Act, which came into force across the Union in October 2000, to underpin legal challenges against homophobic and/or heterosexist health care provision. The Act specifically prohibits discrimination against individuals on the grounds of sexual orientation (MacEarlean, 2000) and, since its remit covers all public services, it is likely to have a positive impact on health care. It is not possible at the time of writing to predict the response of health care providers, but it will arguably be much more difficult to justify spending public money on research or services that fail to take account of the needs of lesbian and gay service users.

FUTURE RESEARCH QUESTIONS
FOR POLICY AND PRACTICE

Clearly it is not possible, in the space available here, to detail all the research that remains to be done in the field of lesbian and gay health from a policy/practice perspective. Nor is it possible to predict the directions such research might take in response to shifts in local, national or international policy agendas. In Britain, for example, the policy agenda of Tony Blair's New Labour government is dramatically different from that of the Tories under John Major or Margaret Thatcher. In particular, a determined focus on health inequalities and social exclusion has resulted in a redirection of funds towards primary care and a recognition of the social factors that contribute to ill health. This suggests that the time is ripe for researchers to argue that sexual orientation functions as a mode of social exclusion in homophobic societies, and that homophobic bias is a public health problem. Certainly, new thinking on sexuality and citizenship (e.g. Richardson, 1998; 2000a) would support such a move.

However, research into sexualities and health is far from straightforward. Both sexual orientation and health are contested concepts and are, in any case, contingent on many other social and cultural factors. A cursory glance at two issues, breast cancer and homophobia, will serve to illustrate the breadth and complexity of this research area.

Lesbians and Breast Cancer: A Moot Point

The vexed question of lesbians and breast cancer offers a cautionary tale about the difficulties of establishing links between sexual orientation and vulnerability to disease, and about the importance of accurately representing research findings.

There is an assumption current in many lesbian communities that lesbians are at increased risk of developing breast cancer relative to non-lesbian women. This assumption, importantly, is *not* based on comparative research. Rather, it is a conclusion reached by extrapolating from research findings which indicate that childlessness, failure to breastfeed, obesity and excess consumption of alcohol may result in increased risk of developing malignant breast disease (Kerner, 1995). By assuming that these factors are likely to be characteristic of lesbian populations, you reach a position where you can *hypothesise* a greater relative risk for lesbians.

However, these extrapolations need to be treated with some scepticism. First, we do not know what proportion of lesbians have children, and methodological problems mean that this situation is unlikely to change in the forseeable future. Even if we did have this information, it is still *childlessness,* rather than being a lesbian, which is significant. The protective factor, breastfeeding, remains the same *whatever your sexual orientation.*

Even those research findings which seem to indicate that lesbians are disproportionately likely to be obese or to abuse alcohol need to be treated with caution. They are almost all from the United States, where excess consumption of both food and alcohol is high on the list of health-damaging behaviours for the population in general, and all have real problems with sampling and sample size. There is, for example, a strong possibility that lesbians recruited by researchers are particularly likely to have problems with food and alcohol ab/use, simply because the very nature of recruiting 'hard to reach' groups means that samples are often drawn from a community culture based in bars and clubs (Whisman, 1996). Even if it were the case that lesbians are more likely to experience problems with food and/or alcohol than non-lesbian women, any increase in breast cancer risk is due to obesity and alcohol abuse, *not* lesbianism.

This single example demonstrates just how complex is the relationship between sexual orientation and health. It also suggests that researchers need to take care not to present data in such a way that it risks contributing to homophobia. Those who manipulate existing data on obesity, alcohol ab/use and breastfeeding to suggest that lesbians are a high risk group for breast cancer, may be inadvertently colluding with homophobic claims that lesbians are sick or unnatural.

HOMOPHOBIA AND HEALTH: UNCHARTED TERRITORY

It is important to bear in mind that the extent to which lesbian and gay citizens are discriminated against by political adminstrations, legislatures and social infrastructures varies widely between countries. Such institutional homophobia clearly has consequences for health and access to services, and little comparative research has yet been carried out into the experiences of lesbians and gay men in different health care and policy systems. Someone accustomed to the very high levels of institutional homophobia found in Britain or the USA may be surprised by countries such as Sweden or Denmark where the situation is very different (Tatchell, 1990; Griffin and Mulholland, 1997).

This suggests, among other things, that a researcher trying to understand the consequences of homophobia for health needs to take an international perspective. It does not take a vivid imagination to recognise that the health and well-being of a gay man living in the redneck depths of Alabama is likely to be very different from that of his counterpart in Copenhagen or Gothenburg. The fundamental question, in whatever socio-political context, is *why* is the health care profession failing to meet the needs of its lesbian and gay service users? In order to begin exploring this question, we must turn to the second, theory-based, strand of research in lesbian and gay health studies.

QUEERYING MEDICAL POWER

This deconstructive approach to lesbian and gay 'health' has to do with more abstract questions than those addressed in a policy/practice context. The two central issues here seem to be, first of all, the 'grand question' of sexual identity (or orientation or preference, depending on your model of sexuality) and, secondly, that central theme of the sociology of health and illness, the

power of the medical profession and its role in the cultural construction of difference. The two are, of course, closely entwined. In fact, taking sexual orientation as a 'case study' exposes with particular clarity the role of medical discourse in social control, and the appropriation of the body by the medical profession. This makes it particularly frustrating that sexual orientation is so widely ignored within mainstream health studies, precisely the discipline that concerns itself with such issues (see, for example, Jones, 1994; Moon and Gillespie, 1995; Turner, 1987/1995; Annandale, 1998; Petersen and Waddell, 1998).

The medicalisation of homosexuality is a product of the history of the medical profession in European culture. Since the time of the Enlightenment, Western scientific medicine has been extraordinarily successful in establishing its professional dominance and credibility. In particular, the profession has asserted a privileged claim to scientific objectivity, claiming that its descriptions of, and explanations for, human behaviours are disinterested and transparent accounts of the 'real' world. The hegemony of medicine as a paradigm, world view and social institution enables its practitioners to speak with great authority about what is normal and what is deviant. In particular, medicine has co-opted the authority to distinguish categorically between health and dis/ease, both of bodies and of behaviours, and to act on bodies in order to destroy disease.

Historically, a medical model for homosexuality replaced older notions of sin, as the power of organised religion was superceded by that of organised medicine. This shift in paradigm was enormously significant, since it marked a shift in attention away from behaviours to identities. As Foucault so famously explained:

> As defined by the ancient civil or canonical codes, sodomy was a category of forbidden acts; their perpetrator was nothing more than a juridical subject of them. The nineteenth-century homosexual became a personage, a past, a case history ... a type of life ... with an indiscreet anatomy and possibly a mysterious physiology ...

The sodomite had been a temporary aberration; the homosexual was now a species. (Foucault, 1976: 42–3)[5]

Social historians disagree about the consquences of this for the formation of a homosexual social identity and for the development of homosexual communities (see Weeks, 1985; essays in Duberman et al., 1989; Boswell, 1994). However, there were important consequences for the relationship between people whom we now think of as lesbian or gay, and the medical profession. In particular, biomedical research into the 'cause' of homosexuality could not happen *unless* same-sex erotic desires and activitives were at some point conceptualised as symptoms of an individual disorder (whether physiological or psychological).

LOOKING FOR THE OUTWARD SIGNS OF QUEER DESIRE

Biomedicine has successfully commandeered the body as its professional territory, and has accrued enormous social, cultural and political power by establishing monopoly rights over the business of identifying and 'curing' organic disease processes. Biomedical professionals therefore have an investment in claiming that forms of human difference have their origin in the body. This is particularly so for those differences that are socially significant, such as gender, or socially troublesome, such as criminality or homosexuality. It is therefore hardly surprising that biomedical researchers have constructed a disease model for homosexuality, since this enables them to get funding to explore its symptomatology, identify its aetiology (causes) and, by implication, suggest strategies for prevention and cure.

There is not the space here for a detailed summary of the history of biomedical theories of homosexuality (for summary accounts see Ruse, 1988; Byne, 1994; Rosario, 1997; Wilton, 2000b). It is, however, worth pointing out that such theories have been driven at least as much by developments in medical

technology as by socio-cultural factors. As new technical developments enabled the medical gaze to extend its surveillance from the surface of bodies (with the unaided eye) to its cells, endocrine system, brain structure and chromosomes, theories of the origin of homosexuality have followed. Where early medical researchers spent their time measuring the depth of 'sex variant' women's vaginas with a crude depth indicator bodged out of a piece of wire wound round a finger, their twenty-first-century counterparts rely on magnetic resonance imagery of brain tissue, or strive to isolate individual chromosomes (for a summary see Wilton, 2000b).

With the exception of social Darwinism and its socio-biological explanations for homosexuality as an aid to species survival, the essentialist theories of homosexuality are all located within a primarily clinical paradigm (see Birke, this volume). Moreover, they all rely on what Foucault (1976: 43) called 'a kind of interior androgyny, a hermaphrodism of the soul'. In other words, whether the cause of homosexuality is sought in the brain, the DNA, the endocrine system or early childhood experiences, the underlying assumption is that desiring men is an inherently female characteristic, and desiring women is inherently male.[6]

Researchers are therefore, in essence, trying to track down evidence of a fault in the biological mechanisms which they see as responsible for producing sexual difference in human beings. Studies to date seem also to have assumed that the best way to identify such evidence is to do comparative measurements of the *size* of specific physiological elements within a binary sex framework. In other words, if some part of the human anatomy is generally larger in women than in men, it will be larger in gay men than in heterosexual men, and smaller in lesbians than in heterosexual women.

To this end researchers have expended much time, energy and money in measuring penises, anuses, vaginas, pelvic basins, clitorises, nipples, fingers and even ears (Ruse, 1988; Wilton, 2000a). On a microscopic level, different structures in the brain have been measured (LeVay, 1993), as have chromosomes and the level of so-called 'sex-hormones'. As many critics have pointed out (see essays in Gonsiorek and Weinrich, 1991; Terry and Urla, 1995; Rosario, 1997), such research is unlikely to produce anything of scientific worth. Any social scientist will tell you that establishing a working definition of 'gay' and 'straight' is dauntingly complex, yet biomedical researchers are often extraordinarily cavalier about assigning their research subjects to one category or another. For example, Simon LeVay, the US researcher who claims to have identified physiological differences between gay and straight men's brains, labelled all his female cadavers as heterosexual by default, purely on the basis that there are not many lesbians around (LeVay, 1993).

Nor are the purported physiological distinctions between women and men as clear-cut as they are generally claimed to be. Supposedly generalisable findings about sex differences in brain structure seem to be particularly weak. Neuroanatomist and psychiatrist William Byne (1994: 295) warns that, 'Of the supposed sex differences in the human brain reported over the past century, only one has proved consistently replicable: brain size varies with body size. Thus, men tend to have slightly larger brains than women.'

The history of biomedical research aimed at identifying the cause of homosexuality seems naïve and anachronistic from a social scientific perspective. The complex social and cultural factors which police and produce 'gender', 'sex' and 'sexuality' have been rigorously theorised, and bio-essentialist hypotheses compare badly with social constructionist models of sexuality. As Mary McIntosh pointed out as long ago as 1968:

> The failure of research to answer the question [whether homosexuality is an innate or acquired condition] has not been due to lack of scientific rigour or to any inadequacy of the available evidence; it results rather from the fact that the wrong question has been asked. One might as well try to trace the aetiology of 'committee

chairmanship' or 'Seventh Day Adventism' as of 'homosexuality'. (McIntosh, 1968: 31)

In short, homosexuality is a social role and, as such, is simply not a proper object for biomedical scrutiny. Social constructionist theories, drawing on research in anthropology, social history, cultural studies and sociology, constitute a substantial and impressive body of evidence that undermines the epistemological and ontological foundations of biomedical models of sexual orientation (see Foucault, 1976 and essays in Stein, 1990; Seidman, 1996). The question now becomes, not 'what are the biomedical causes of the homosexual condition?' but 'why and how does biomedical science claim the authority to explain homosexuality?'

MEDICINE AND THE SOCIAL CONTROL OF GENDER AND SEXUALITY

To answer this question we must examine the social control function of biomedical science and, in particular, its role in policing and reproducing a binary regime of gender. As we have seen, 'scientific' hypotheses about the cause of the homosexual condition inevitably depend upon some variation of a gender-inversion model for same-sex desire and eroticism. This unthinking acceptance of what I have called a heteropolar model of gender and sexuality (Wilton, 1996 a, b) tends to produce quite catastrophic collapses in biomedical logic. Take, for example, Dean Hamer and Peter Copeland's discussion of the likely impact of the chromosome block, Xq28, on sexual attraction:

> There is no way to be sure yet, but it's unlikely the same version of Xq28 associated with male homosexuality also is associated with lesbianism … If Xq28 influenced sexual orientation by directing a person's sexual attraction, it would be unlikely to influence both gay men and lesbians, because the objects of their affection are *just the opposite*. (Hamer and Copeland, 1994: 289, my italics)

So this, apparently highly sophisticated, hypothesis concerning a genetic origin of same-sex desire is predicated upon an unproblematised socio-cultural metaphor of 'opposite sexes'. Yet in what sense may male and female humans be said to be 'opposite'? Are we here talking about bodily configuration? If so, the notion of opposites can only refer to a naïve kind of genital functionalism, whereby penis is the 'opposite' of vagina in the way that plug is the 'opposite' of socket or foot is the opposite of sock. The everyday language of sexual oppositeness makes it fairly obvious that the model has been appropriated from physics, where 'opposites attract' and a sexual 'charge', rather like electricity, moves of necessity from one pole (the male) to the other (the female). Here, male sexual potency is constructed as an electromagnetic charge that builds up (from friction, or simply from unstoppable production within the body) and must be discharged onto a body bearing the opposite polarity. It is this socio-cultural story of heteropolarity that provides the unquestioned structuring logic of almost all biomedical models of gender.

Moreover, because heteropolarity produces gender as a function of uni-directional sexual desire and activity (you are a man *because* you want to put your penis in a vagina and a woman *because* you want a penis in your vagina), it is not possible to disengage gender from the erotic or vice versa. So scientists carry on trudging endlessly (and somewhat randomly) through the spaces of the body, seeking physical signs of female matter out of place in the gay male body.[7] As Byne comments (1994/2000: 295), 'the notion that gay men are feminized and lesbians masculinized may tell us more about our culture than about the biology of erotic responsiveness'.

The doctrine of heteropolarity lies at the heart of the medical profession's unhelpful relationship with those of its service users who are not heterosexual men. Moreover, it infests cultural stereotypes of other forms of difference, including 'race' and disability. White supremacist discourse produces,

and depends upon, constructs of race that are sexually marked in specific ways. The sexual voracity of women of colour, the black super-penis, the lascivious Asian or Oriental schooled in the erotic arts, these and other constructs of racialised sexuality serve to demarcate the boundaries of white European sexuality as controlled and civilised. To be white is to be in firm control of the animal within and hence to be destined master of those 'races' whose animal sexuality marks them as child-like, savage, needful of mastery (Fausto-Sterling, 1995; McClintock, 1995; Tolen, 1995). It is not difficult to recognise the heteropolar paradigm of necessary gender hierarchy here. The subordination of racialised 'others' to white dominance mirrors the subordination of women (childlike, closer to nature, needful of mastery) to men in European culture.

Thus a critical examination of the construction of 'homosexuality' in medical discourse offers intellectual support for a coalitional approach to key questions of social justice and human rights. The social exclusion and political marginalization of queers, women and people of colour stand in a particular relationship with a bioreductionist paradigm of difference. Questions of masculinity, femininity and the erotic are closely interwoven within this paradigm to produce bodies that are marked with signs of disorder. One key element of a critical study of lesbian and gay 'health' must be to identify the role of medical science in this complex project of social control.

MEDICINE MAKING GENDER: SEX REASSIGNMENT SURGERY

Any such critical deconstruction of medical discourses of gender introduces contradictions into lesbian and gay health studies. Importantly, this has consequences for political coalitions and health advocacy. At the heart of such contradictions lies an apparently marginal issue: transsexuality.

Increasingly, the umbrella of minority sexuality is seen to encompass individuals whose experience or performance of gender is at odds with their assigned biological sex. The inclusiveness of queer politics means that both activism and service provision within queer communities are more and more likely to be addressed to 'lesbian, gay, bisexual and transgender' individuals.[8] In terms of lesbian and gay health issues the question of transsexuality introduces two, deeply contradictory, issues for consideration.

The first is that, if transgender and transsexing people are indeed part of the 'queer nation', their healthcare issues have a place on the political and research agendas. This is far from insignificant, since there are many key health problems associated with the various forms of gender crossing. The standards of care associated with sex reassignment surgery (SRS) are extremely variable, and remarkably little is known about the long-term implications for physical and emotional well-being of the surgery itself, ancillary cosmetic procedures and the necessary life-long dependence on high doses of artificial hormones (Califia, 1997; Hausman, 1995). We also lack information about the attitudes of health and social care practitioners to service users whose 'manning' or 'womanning' (Ekins, 1997) is non-conformative. Research questions such as these may fit the existing lesbian and gay healthcare needs agenda in a relatively straightforward manner.

Less straightforward are issues to do with the theory and clinical practice of SRS, and what these suggest about the medicalisation of gender and sexuality and about the heteronormalising role of the medical profession. After all, the diagnosis of transsexuality was invented by a clinician who was at a loss to know how to respond to a male patient who insisted that he was female (Califia, 1997). Indeed, as Bernice Hausman (1995) so meticulously argues, the very idea of *gender*, as currently understood, arose out of the need for clinicians to justify surgical interventions on the bodies of babies born with ambivalent genitalia.

Before this time, 'gender' was a term used only in the study of languages.

It is perhaps ironic that what started out as a technical term, coined in response to these developments in genital plastic surgery, subsequently became a keystone of feminist theory and activism. Gatens, who identifies Robert Stoller's work on transsexuality as the originary moment of 'gender', writes that:

> his work was generally hailed as a breakthrough in the area of sexuality and socialization. As such it was quickly taken up by feminist theorists as offering theoretical justification for the right to equality for all independently of sex. His work has been used by Greer, Millett, Oakley … Chodorow, Dinnerstein and Barrett, to name a few. (Gatens, 1991: 142)

It is salutory to remember that this was a major paradigm shift. The ability theoretically to detach something called 'gender' (meaning masculinity or femininity) from biological sex (meaning maleness or femaleness), which is now so taken for granted and which remains so fundamental to both feminists and queer theorists, dates only from the late 1960s. Far from being a marginal issue then, clinical discourses of transsexuality and intersexuality turn out to be the very foundations of contemporary Western constructs of gender as a property of bodies. This has major implications for lesbian and gay health studies, particularly for any critique of the medical model of homosexuality which, as we have seen, insists that same-sex desires are somehow caused by a fault in the body's gender programming.

The ramifications of SRS for our critique of the medical model of gender/sexuality are therefore profound. It would be difficult to argue that sex reassignment surgery represents a radical challenge to the heteropolar model that, I have argued, remains dominant in western scientific medicine. Sociologists Dwight Billings and Thomas Urban firmly locate the socio-medical construction of transsexualism at the heart of biomedicine's professional colonisation of ever increasing areas of social and cultural concern. They write:

There is hardly a more dramatic instance of contemporary professional authority than so-called 'sex-change' surgery. Physicians perform cosmetic surgery yet certify that their patients have undergone a change of sex ... public acceptance of sex-change surgery attests both to the domination of daily life and consciousness by professional authority as well as the extent to which many forms of deviance are increasingly labelled 'illness' rather than 'sin' or 'crime' ... Sex-change surgery privatises and depoliticises individual experiences of gender-role distress. (Billings and Urban, 1996: 99)

The key problem for research and activism in the broad area of sexuality and health seems, then, to be that advocacy and support for the right of transsexual or transgender individuals to high standards of care and treatment in *all* aspects of health and social care delivery must go hand in hand with an informed and rigorous critique of the politics of SRS. For, although the numbers of individuals seeking SRS are relatively small, the theory and clinical practices of sex-reassignment have clear implications for the medical politics of gender and sexuality more generally (Wilton, 2000b).

INCLUDING A SOCIOLOGY OF THE BODY

Lesbian and gay health studies may initially appear to be a relatively simple issue. Yet, as we have seen, even basic research into healthcare policy and practice is fraught with contradiction and difficulty. This is because both sexual orientation and health are, by definition, located in various ways in *bodies*. And the dynamic relationship between our selves or subjectivities, our bodies and the social and cultural worlds we inhabit are extraordinarily complex. It is not difficult to see that those social and cultural worlds discipline and constrain our bodies, our behaviours and our identities in ways that impact on our health and the expression of our sexual desires, and this recognition underpins most practice/policy research into lesbian and/of gay health.

However, our bodies, behaviours and identities are also *produced* by the social and cultural worlds that we inhabit. This dynamic, too, has profound implications for health, and for the activities and power of the medical industry. Therefore the more abstract, discourse-based, theoretical work on sexualities and health, which can seem so far removed from the practical concerns of most healthcare researchers, is in fact an entirely necessary element of lesbian and gay health studies.

DIRECTIONS FOR THE FUTURE

Given the interwoven strands of practice-based, empirical research and more abstract, theoretical work which constitutes lesbian and gay health studies, any attempt to predict the direction of future developments within such a vast and multi-disciplinary field can be little more than informed guess-work. However, there are important gaps in the existing literature, and it is increasingly likely that funds will be available to carry out the work needed to fill in some of the missing pieces in our knowledge.

In practical terms, research is needed to underpin human rights-driven political demands for egalitarian access to good quality health care. Here, there is an urgent need to develop a more sophisticated, empirically grounded understanding of the impact that homophobia has on the health and well-being of individual lesbians and gay men. The complex cultural and psychological parameters of homophobia require that such research is carried out in different localities, cultures and nations, and that it takes into account the intersections of homophobia with racism and sexism, as well as its observable tendency to undergo historical shift (Neild and Pearson, 1992; Kennedy and Davis, 1993).

Related to this is the need to identify and challenge the heterosexism that permeates medicine at every level. This requires interventions in the education and training of health care professionals, and such interventions must be evidence-based. Existing data on the knowledge, attitudes and practices of staff (Stern, 1993; Wilton, 2000b) needs to be supplemented with text-based analyses of medical discourse and with research into health policy at micro and macro levels.

The social, political and medical struggle against HIV, and its disproportionate impact (at least in the industrialised nations of the West) on the gay community, will continue to demand research activity. So, too, will the need to expand our knowledge of lesbian sexual health and of lesbian health more generally through the life-course.

However, there is precious little point in research activity of any kind unless it informs changes in practice. It is notoriously difficult to ensure that research findings – even the most pragmatic ones to do with the effectiveness of clinical therapies – are widely enough disseminated among practitioners. Here, the extraordinary efforts which were made by the AIDS community to ensure that combination therapies were used appropriately and effectively (Gay Men's Health Crisis, 1998) offer a sound model of best possible practice. The unique coalition between activists, user groups, physicians and drugs companies, presents a powerful example of what can be done to navigate the power relations of capitalist medicine – albeit in the wealthiest nation in the world. It offers a template for those working on other lesbian and gay health issues, who want to ensure that their findings lead to improvements in practice.

The more theoretical element of lesbian and gay health studies has its roots in so many disciplinary areas that it is more difficult to predict or suggest future developments. However, it is clear that a heteropolar model of same-sex desire remains stubbornly dominant in biomedicine, and continues to underpin *all* 'scientific' research into sexual orientation. Given that this biomedical model of sexuality seems little short of naive to social scientists and cultural theorists, its continued dominance within medical

science indicates that medicine suffers from a profound intellectual insularity. This suggests a fairly urgent need to develop ways of speaking across the traditional disciplinary and epistemological divide between the social and the physical sciences. Lesbian and gay health studies may yet prove to be the catalyst for the demolition of this stubborn divide.

All research into lesbian and gay health, whether empirical or theoretical, traces the points of intersection of biopower (Gastaldo, 1997) with medical constructs of health and pathology, sexual normalcy and deviance, professionalism and consumerism. As such, lesbian and gay health studies forms a potent element in the wider project of lesbian and gay studies in its focus on the (embodied) power relations that both discipline and engender all of us. Hopefully, therefore, a scholarship of health will become less marginal within lesbian and gay studies.

NOTES

1 I am, of course, aware that lesbian health includes the subject of HIV/AIDS. Indeed, one feature of the early days of AIDS activism was the anger of some lesbians that gay men expected them to get involved and offer support, when gay men had shown remarkably little interest in struggles around lesbian health. Sadly there is not enough space here to trace the complex relationship between lesbians and the AIDS community. Interested readers are referred to Leonard (1990); Schwartz (1993); Patton (1994); Richardson (1994).

2 The untimely death of Tessa Boffin sadly ended her work examining the construction of lesbian sexuality and the lesbian sexual body in discourses of safe sex. Tessa was almost alone in tackling these issues (see Boffin, 1990).

3 This is one instance where it is probably a good idea *not* to give references. Anyone who has done more than dip a toe into the literature will know what I mean ...

4 Visiting the Triangle Project in Cape Town, I found it located in the office block formerly used by the African National Congress (ANC), an unambiguous indicator that lesbian and gay rights are regarded as an integral part of the agenda for a reconstructed South Africa.

5 'La sodomie – celle des anciens droits civil ou canonique – était un type d'actes interdits; leur auteur n'en était que le sujet juridique. L'homosexual du xixe siècle

est devenu un personnage: un passé, une histoire…une forme de vie…avec une anatomie indiscréte et peut-être une physiologie mystérieuse…Le sodomite êtait un relaps, l'homosexuel est maintenant une espece.' (Michel Foucault, 1976: *Histoire de la Sexualité 1: La volonté de savoir Paris*, Editions Gallimard. p. 59

6 Which means that, if two men desire each other they must both be 'feminine' and hence … lesbians? And lesbians must be …

7 Makes you feel sorry for them …

8 For example, *New Internationalist* Magazine's special issue (October 2000) on the global politics of sexuality was promoted thus, '"Out South" – this month's *New Internationalist* – takes a look at life for sexual minorities be they lesbian, gay, bisexual or transgender'.

REFERENCES

Abbott, S. and Love, B. (1985) *Sappho was a Right-On Woman: A Liberated View of Lesbianism.* New York: Stein and Day.

Abelove, H., Barale, M.A. and Halperin, D. (eds) (1993) *The Lesbian and Gay Studies Reader.* London: Routledge.

Altman, D. (1986) *AIDS and the New Puritanism.* London: Pluto.

Annandale, E. (1998) *The Sociology of Health and Medicine: A Critical Introduction.* Cambridge: Polity.

Bersani, L. (1988) 'Is the rectum a grave?', in D. Crimp (ed.), *AIDS: Cultural Analysis, Cultural Activism.* Cambridge, MA: MIT Press.

Billings, D. and Urban, T. (1996) 'The socio-medical construction of transsexualism: an interpretation and critique', in R. Ekins and D. King (eds), *Blending Genders: Social Aspects of Cross-Dressing and Sex-Changing.* London: Routledge.

Boffin, T. (1990) 'Angelic rebels: lesbians and safer sex', in T. Boffin and S. Gupta (eds), *Ecstatic Antibodies: Resisting the AIDS Mythology.* London: Rivers Oram.

Boffin, T. and Gupta, S. (eds) (1990) *Ecstatic Antibodies: Resisting the AIDS Mythology.* London: Rivers Oram.

Boswell, J. (1994) *The Marriage of Likeness: Same-Sex Unions in Pre-Modern Europe.* London: HarperCollins.

Bristow, J. and Wilson, A. (eds) (1993) *Activating Theory: Lesbian, Gay, Bisexual Politics.* London: Lawrence and Wishart.

Byne, W. (1994) 'The biological evidence challenged', reprinted in R. Nye (ed.) (2000) *Sexuality.* Oxford: Oxford University Press.

Califia, P. (1997) *Sex Changes: The Politics of Transgenderism.* San Francisco: Cleis.

Cant, B. and Hemmings, S. (eds) (1988) *Radical Records: Thirty Years of Lesbian and Gay History.* London: Routledge.

Creekmur, C. and Doty, A. (eds) (1995) *Out in Culture: Gay, Lesbian and Queer Essays on Popular Culture.* London: Cassell.

Crimp, D. (ed.) (1988) *AIDS: Cultural Analysis, Cultural Activism.* Cambridge, MA: MIT Press.

Crimp, D. with Rolston, A. (1990) *AIDS Demo/Graphics.* Seattle: Bay Press.

Cruikshank, M. (1992) *The Gay and Lesbian Liberation Movement.* London: Routledge.

Darty, T. and Potter, S. (1984) 'Lesbians and contemporary health care systems: oppression and opportunity' in T. Darty and S. Potter (eds), *Women-Identified Women.* Palo Alto, CA: Mayfield.

Das, R. (1996) *The power of medical knowledge: Systematic misinformation and the perpetuation of lesbophobia in medical education.* Paper presented at the Teaching to Promote Women's Health Conference, Women's College Hosital, University of Toronto, Canada: June.

Dockery, G. (1996) *Final Report on the Sexual Health Needs of Lesbians, Bisexual Women and Women who have Sex with Women in Merseyside/Cheshire.* Liverpool: SHADY.

Dorenkamp, M. and Henke, R. (eds) (1995) *Negotiating Lesbian and Gay Subjects.* London: Routledge.

Duberman, M., Vicinus, M. and Chauncey, G. (eds) (1989) *Hidden from History: Reclaiming the Gay and Lesbian Past.* Harmondsworth: Penguin.

Ekins, R. (1997) *Male Femaling: A Grounded Theory Approach to Cross-Dressing and Sex-Changing.* London: Routledge.

Farquhar, C. (1999) 'Lesbian sexual health: deconstructing research and practice', unpublished PhD. thesis, London: South Bank University.

Fausto-Sterling, A. (1995) 'Gender, race and nation: the comparative anatomy of "Hottentot" women in Europe, 1815–1817', in J. Terry and J. Urla (eds), *Deviant Bodies: Critical Perspectives on Difference in Science and Popular Culture.* Berkeley, CA: University of California Press.

Fee, E. and Fox, D. (eds) (1988) *AIDS: The Burdens of History.* Berkeley, CA: University of California Press.

Foucault, M. (1976) *The History of Sexuality: An Introduction.* Harmondsworth: Penguin.

Gastaldo, D. (1997) 'Is health education good for you? Rethinking health education through the concept of biopower' in A. Petersen and R. Bunton (eds) *Foucault, Health and Medicine.* London: Routledge.

Gatens, M. (1991) 'A critique of the sex/gender distinction', in S. Gunew (ed.), *A Reader in Feminist Knowledge.* London: Routledge.

Gever, M. (1993) 'Pictures of sickness: Stuart Marshall's "Bright Eyes"' in M. Gever, J. Greyson and P. Parmar (eds), *Queer Looks: Perspectives on Lesbian and Gay Film and Video.* London: Routledge.

Gill, E. (1996) 'Three cheers for smears', *Diva*, Oct./Nov. pp. 54–5.

Gonsiorek, J. and Weinrich, J. (eds) (1991) *Homosexu-
ality: Research Implications for Public Policy.* London:
Sage.
Gott, T. (ed.) (1994) *Don't Leave Me This Way: Art in the
Age of AIDS.* Melbourne: National Gallery of
Australia/Thames and Hudson.
Griffin, K. and Mulholland, L. (eds) (1997) *Lesbian
Motherhood Across Europe.* London: Cassell.
Griffin, G., Stein, N. and de Pinho, H. (1998) *Divided in
Ourselves: Cape Town Gay Men, Lesbians and Bisexu-
als Talk about their Health Education and Care Needs.*
Cape Town: Triangle Project.
Gruskin, E.P. (1999) *Treating Lesbians and Bisexual
Women.* London: Sage.
Hamer, D. and Copeland, P. (1994) *The Science of Desire:
The Search for the Gay Gene and the Biology of Behav-
ior.* New York: Simon and Schuster.
Hausman, B. (1995) *Changing Sex: Transsexualism, Tech-
nology and the Idea of Gender.* London: Duke Univer-
sity Press.
Hepburn, C. and Gutierrez, B. (1988) *Alive and Well: A
Lesbian Health Guide.* Freedom, CA: The Crossing Press.
Hewett, L. (1990) 'Projections', in T. Boffin and S. Gupta
(eds), *Ecstatic Antibodies: Resisting the AIDS Mytho-
logy.* London: Rivers Oram.
Jay, K. and Young, A. (eds) (1978, 1994) *Lavender
Culture.* New York: New York University Press.
Jones, L. (1994) *The Social Context of Health and Health
Work.* London: Macmillan.
Kaufmann, T. and Lincoln, P. (eds) (1991) *High Risk
Lives: Lesbian and Gay Politics after THE CLAUSE.*
Bridgport: Prism Press.
Kayal, P. (1993) *Bearing Witness: Gay Men's Health
Crisis and the Politics of AIDS.* Boulder, CO: Westview.
Kennedy. E. and Davis, D. (1993) *Boots of Leather, Slip-
pers of Gold: The History of a Lesbian Community.*
London: Routledge.
Kerner, K. (1995) 'Health Care Issues' in K. Jay (ed.),
*Dyke Life: From Growing Up to Growing Old, a Cele-
bration of the Lesbian Experience.* London: Pandora.
Lauver, D., Karon, S., Egan, J., Jacobson, M., Nugent, J.,
Settersten, L. and Shaw, V. (1999) 'Understanding les-
bians' mammography utilization', *Women's Health
Issues,* 9 (5): 264–74.
Lemelle, A., Harrington, C. and LeBlanc, A. (2000) *Read-
ings in the Sociology of AIDS.* New Jersey: Prentice-Hall.
Leonard, Z. (1990) 'Lesbians in the AIDS crisis', in ACT
UP/New York Women and AIDS Book Group (eds),
Women. AIDS and Activism. Boston: South End Press.
LeVay, S. (1993) *The Sexual Brain.* Cambridge, MA: MIT
Press.
LeVay, S. (1996) *Queer Science: The Use and Abuse of
Research into Homosexuality.* Cambridge, MA: MIT
Press.
MacErlean, N. (2000) 'Justice finally breaks the wedlock
deadlock', *The Observer.* 1st October (*Cash* supple-
ment): 16–17.

Mars-Jones, A. and White, E. (1988) *The Darker Proof:
Stories from a Crisis.* London: Faber and Faber.
Marshall, J. (1983) 'The medical profession', in
B. Galloway (ed.), *Prejudice and Pride: Discrimination
against Gay People in Modern Britain.* London:
Routledge and Kegan Paul.
McClintock, A. (1995) *Imperial Leather: Race, Gender and
Sexuality in the Colonial Contest.* London: Routledge.
McClure, R. and Vespry, A. (eds) (1994) *Lesbian Health
Guide.* Toronto: Queer Press.
McIntosh, M. (1968), 'The homosexual role', reprinted in
K. Plummer (ed.) (1981), *The Making of the Modern
Homosexual.* London: Hutchinson.
Meyer, R. (1998) 'Rock Hudson's body', in D. Bright
(ed.), *The Passionate Camera: Photography and
Bodies of Desire.* London: Routledge.
Michigan Organization for Human Rights (1991) *The
Michigan Lesbian Health Survey.* Michigan: MOHR
(Special Report).
Moon, G. and Gillespie, R. (eds) (1995) *Society and
Health: An Introduction to Social Science for Health
Professionals.* London: Routledge.
Mort, F. (1997/2000) *Dangerous Sexualities: Medico-
Moral Politics in England since 1830.* London:
Routledge.
Mugglestone, J. (1999) *'Are you sure you don't need
contraception?'* Report of the Bolton and Wigan
Lesbian Health Needs Assessment. Bolton: Bolton
NHS Trust.
Muir-Mackenzie, A. and Orme, J. (eds) (1996) *Health of
the Lesbian, Gay and Bisexual Nation Conference
Report.* Plymouth: The Harbour Centre/Plymouth
Eddystone Group.
Nardi, P. and Schneider, B. (eds) (1998) *Social Perspec-
tives in Lesbian and Gay Studies: A Reader.* London:
Routledge.
Neild, S. and Pearson, R. (eds) (1992) *Women Like Us.*
London: The Women's Press.
Nestle, J. (1987) *A Restricted Country: Essays and Short
Stories.* London: Sheba.
Patton, C. (1985) *Sex and Germs: The Politics of AIDS.*
Boston: South End Press.
Patton, C. (1991) 'Safe sex and the pornographic verna-
cular', in Bad Object-Choices (eds), *How Do I Look?
Queer Film and Video.* Seattle: Bay Press.
Patton, C. (1994) *Last Served? Gendering the HIV
Pandemic.* London: Taylor and Francis.
Petersen, A. and Bunton, R. (eds) (1997) *Foucault, Health
and Medicine.* London: Routledge.
Petersen, A. and Waddell, C. (eds) (1998) *Health Matters: A
Sociology of Illness, Prevention and Care.* Buckingham:
Open University Press.
Power, L. (1995) *No Bath but Plenty of Bubbles: An Oral
History of the Gay Liberation Front, 1970–1973.*
London: Cassell.
Richardson, D. (1994) 'Inclusions and exclusions:
lesbians, HIV and AIDS', in L. Doyal, J. Naidoo and

T. Wilton (eds), *AIDS: Setting a Feminist Agenda*. London: Taylor and Francis.

Richardson, D. (1998) 'Sexuality and citizenship', *Sociology*, 32 (1): 83–100.

Richardson, D. (2000a) 'Claiming citizenship? Sexuality, citizenship and lesbian/feminist theory', *Sexualities*, 3 (2): 255–72.

Richardson, D. (2000b) 'The social construction of immunity: HIV risk perception and prevention among lesbians and bisexual women', *Culture, Health and Sexuality*, 2 (1): 33–49.

Rosario, V. (ed.) (1997) *Science and Homosexualities*. London: Routledge.

Rosenblum, R. (ed.) (1996) *Unspoken Rules: Sexual Orientation and Women's Human Rights*. London: Cassell.

Royal College of Nursing (1994) *The Nursing Care of Lesbians and Gay Men: An RCN Statement*. London: RCN.

Royal College of Nursing (1998) *Guide for Nurses on 'Next-of-Kin' for Lesbian and Gay Patients and Children with Lesbian or Gay Parents*, London: RCN.

Ruse, M. (1988) *Homosexuality: A Philosophical Inquiry*. Oxford: Blackwell.

Saraga, E. (ed.) (1998) *Embodying the Social: Constructions of Difference*. London: Routledge and Open University.

Schwartz, R. (1993) 'New alliances, strange bedfellows: lesbians, gay men and AIDS', in A. Stein (ed.), *Sisters, Sexperts, Queers: Beyond the Lesbian Nation*. New York: Plume.

Seidman, S. (ed.) (1996) *Queer Theory/Sociology*. Oxford: Blackwell.

Sheffield Health (1996) *Lesbian Health Needs Assessment*. Sheffield: Sheffield Health.

Shernoff, M. and Scott. W. (eds) (1988) *The Sourcebook on Lesbian/Gay Health Care*. Washington, DC: National Lesbian and Gay Health Foundation.

Shildrick, M. (1997) *Leaky Bodies and Boundaries: Feminism, Postmodernism and (Bio) Ethics*. London: Routledge.

Smart, C. and Smart, B. (eds) (1978) *Women, Sexuality and Social Control*. London: Routledge and Kegan Paul.

Solarz, A. (ed.) (1999) *Lesbian Health: Current Assessment and Directions for the Future*. Washington, DC: Institute of Medicine/National Academy Press.

Sontag, S. (1988) *AIDS and its Metaphors*. Harmondsworth: Penguin.

Stein, E. (ed.) (1990) *Forms of Desire: Sexual Orientation and the Social Constructionist Controversy*. London: Routledge.

Stern, P. (ed.) (1993) *Lesbian Health: What are the Issues?* London: Taylor & Francis.

Stewart, M. (1997) *We just want to be ordinary: Lesbian parents talk about their birth experiences*, unpublished Master's dissertation, University of the West of England, Bristol.

Tatchell, P. (1990) *Out in Europe: A Guide to Lesbian and Gay Rights in 30 European Countries*. London: Rouge/Channel 4.

Terry, J. and Urla, J. (eds) (1995) *Deviant Bodies: Critical Perspectives on Difference in Science and Popular Culture*. Indianapolis: Indiana University Press.

Tolen, R. (1995) 'Colonising and Transforming the Criminal Tribesman: The Salvation Army in British India' in J. Teery & J. Urla (eds) *Deviant Bodies: Critical Perspectives on Difference in Science and Popular Culture* Bloomington: Indiana University Press.

Treichler, P. (1988a) 'AIDS, homophobia and medical discourse: an epidemic of signification', in D. Crimp (ed.), *AIDS: Cultural Analysis, Cultural Activism*. Cambridge, MA: MIT Press.

Treichler, P. (1998b) 'AIDS: gender and biomedical discourse: current contests for meaning', in E. Fee and D. Fox (eds), *AIDS: The Burdens of History*. Berkeley, CA: University of California Press.

Turner, B. (1987/1995) *Medical Power and Social Knowledge*. London: Sage.

Waitkevics, H.J. and Stein, J. (1978) 'Lesbian health issues', in G. Vida (ed.), *Our Right to Love: A Lesbian Resource Book*. Englewood Cliffs, NJ: Prentice-Hall.

Waldby, C. (1996) *AIDS and the Body Politic: Biomedicine and Sexual Difference*. London: Routledge.

Weatherburn, P. (1992) 'Alcohol and unsafe sex', *Rouge*, 11: 12–14.

Weeks, J. (1985) *Sexuality and its Discontents: Meanings, Myths and Modern Sexualities*. London: Routledge and Kegan Paul.

Whisman, V. (1996) *Queer by Choice: Lesbians, Gay Men and the Politics of Identity*. London: Routledge.

White, E. (1997) *The Farewell Symphony*. London: Chatto and Windus.

Wilton, T. (1992) *Antibody Politic: AIDS and Society*. Cheltenham: New Clarion.

Wilton, T. (1996a) 'Which one's the man? The heterosexualisation of lesbian sex', in D. Richardson (ed.), *Theorising Heterosexuality*. Buckingham: Open University Press.

Wilton, T. (1996b) 'Genital identities: an (idiosyncratic) foray into the gendering of sexualities', in L. Adkins and V. Merchant (eds), *Sexualising the Social: Power and the Organization of Sexuality*. London: Macmillan.

Wilton, T. (1997a) *Good For You: A Handbook on Lesbian Health and Wellbeing*. London: Cassell.

Wilton, T. (1997b) *En/Gendering AIDS: Deconstructing Sex, Texts, Epidemic*. London: Sage.

Wilton, T. (1997c) 'Healing the invisible body: lesbian health studies', in G. Griffin and S. Andermahr (eds), *Straight Studies Modified: Lesbian Interventions in the Academy*. London: Cassell.

Wilton, T. (1998) 'Gender, sexuality and healthcare: improving services', in L. Doyal (ed.), *Women and Health Services*. Buckingham: Open University Press.

Wilton, T. (1999) 'Towards an understanding of the cultural roots of homophobia in order to provide a better midwifery service for lesbian clients', *Midwifery*, 15: 154–64.

Wilton, T. (2000a) *Sexualities in Health and Social Care: A Textbook*. Buckingham: Open University Press.

Wilton, T. (2000b) 'Out/performing ourselves: sex, gender and cartesian dualism', *Sexualities*, 3 (2): 237–54.

Wilton, T. and Kauffman, T. (2001) 'Lesbian mothers' experiences of midwifery care: report of the Royal College of Midwives Survey', *Midwifery*.

16

Innocence and Experience

Paradoxes in Sexuality and Education

DEBBIE EPSTEIN, SARAH O'FLYNN
AND DAVID TELFORD

May 26, 2000. Friday

School officials here apologized today to
parents who were outraged by a health
survey, given to some students as young
as 11, that posed specific questions about
sexual orientation and behavior, drug and
alcohol use and other intimate details.
(*New York Times*)

July 30, 2000. Sunday

Sound the trumpet! The moral majority is
on the march again. The Section 28 debate
is just the latest in a long line of controversies about sexual values that have gripped
Britain since the 1950s. Abortion, divorce
and gay rights appeared to change the
moral landscape forever. Now, it seems,
the conservatives are in the ascendant once
more. Is this the end of liberal progress?
(*Independent on Sunday*, London)

October 14, 2000. Saturday

It's a family issue

Families should carry the burden of curb-
ing teen pregnancies, according to
Premier [of Victoria, Australia] Steve
Bracks. Mr Bracks said he didn't believe
condoms, the contraceptive pill or the

morning-after pill should be provided in
schools. (*Herald Sun*, Melbourne)

As the extracts from newspapers in
Australia, the United Kingdom and the
United States quoted above show, the media
across the Anglophone world is preoccupied
with questions on sex education, young
people, and sexuality. In the United States
and Canada, a search of headlines in newspapers across the country reveal repeated
articles about teenage pregnancy, 'premature' sex/uality, and gay sex among young
people. Australian and New Zealand newspapers, too, reveal deep concerns about
these issues. In South Africa the news of
sexual violence against schoolgirls is in the
papers almost daily. In the UK during 2000
several papers took part in a concerted campaign against the repeal of Section 28
of the Local Government Act 1988, which
prohibited the 'promotion of homosexuality' by Local Authorities.[1] This was taken as
an opportunity by some papers to mount a
campaign against any move towards a
greater tolerance of queer[2] sexualities in
schools.

Our focus, in this chapter, will be on the naturalization and policing of heterosexualities,

mainly through homophobia and heterosexism, in educational institutions in late
capitalist Anglophone countries (particularly Australia, Britain, Canada, New Zealand
and the United States). We have drawn on
the literature from all these countries but,
because of our location in the UK, we have
often used British events as exemplars of
tendencies in several countries, while, of
course, also acknowledging the extensive differences between countries.[3] Our concentration on the normalization of heterosexuality
here derives from a wish to, as Richard Johnson puts it, 'render heterosexuality visible to
critical scrutiny and to make it, in some
sense, politically accountable' (1997: 5; see
also Richardson, 1996).

Our thinking, in this respect, can be seen
in a direct line of descent from Adrienne
Rich's influential article 'Compulsory
heterosexuality and lesbian existence'
(1980), in which she proposed the notion of
'compulsory heterosexuality' to explain
how heterosexuality was rewarded, maintained and reproduced, while lesbianism
was punished and stigmatized. In the inter-
vening years, others have built on, adapted
and taken issue with her ideas (for example,
Butler, 1990; Steinberg et al., 1997). Her
work has been criticized for being over-
simplistic and reductive, as well as appearing almost to evacuate lesbianism of sexual
desire (see, for example, Rubin and Butler
1998; Sedgwick, 1990: 36–7) and for ignoring the experiences of women of colour
(Lorde, 1984).[4] Similarly, 'compulsory
heterosexuality' has been subject to the critique of being over-determining, and thus
denying the agency of women. Judith Butler,
for example, suggests that 'compulsory heterosexuality' is simply 'another totalizing
frame' (Butler, 1990: 18; de Lauretis, 1994).
And, of course, her focus on lesbianism does
little to explain the position of gay men
(Sedgwick, 1990: 36–7). However, the idea of
'compulsory heterosexuality' is a powerful
one, which continues to be a key idea for
researchers in sexuality. Indeed, Judith
Butler's queer reworking of compulsory
heterosexuality – in which she draws also on

the writings of Wittig (1981, 1992) – as a
'heterosexual matrix' (Butler, 1990) is one
we have found particularly useful in pointing to the performance of gender and the
ways that it is culturally understood through
a lens that assumes attraction to and desire
for the Other, who is of the opposite sex.

Epstein and Johnson (1998: 6) have
argued that in the sexual, as in other
domains such as 'race' (hooks, 1984), the
relationship between the centre and the
margins is one in which:

> marginalized categories turn out to be crucial in
> the self-production of the 'centred' ones (white,
> heterosexual, middle-class and so on), a process
> most noticeable (in relation to sexuality) in
> public displays of homophobia by politicians and
> in the media, but also important in the daily lives
> of those in schools.

We follow on from this position to explore the
production of (hetero)sexuality in primary/
elementary, secondary/junior high school
and university education. This may seem a
long way from lesbian and gay (or queer)
studies, which have, typically and understandably, focused on the experiences of lesbians, gay men, bisexual and transgendered
people rather than on how 'straight' is produced. However, our examination of the
dominant tradition in sexuality, that is heterosexuality, is built on those studies of lesbian
and gay experiences (see, for example,
Abelove et al., 1993; Nardi and Schneider,
1998; Plummer, 1992; Seidman, 1997)
which, taken together, give rise to questions
about the possibility of stability in sexual
categories. We will, in this context, write
about both straight and queer sexualities,
examining them as relational categories that
structure definitions, understandings and
social dynamics of both dominant and
subordinated categories.

We begin with a discussion of educational
institutions and the political economy of
education to contextualize our argument that
education is a key site for the production of
compulsory heterosexuality. This is followed
by an exploration of the relationship between
'innocence' and 'experience'/'knowing' and
'not knowing' in the context of sexuality,

education and popular common sense ideas about the meaning of childhood and phases of 'growing up'. We then move into an examination of the ways in which both formal and informal curricula are (hetero)sexualized and (hetero)sexualizing. In each section, we will use examples from primary (elementary) and secondary (junior high) schooling and from university education.

HETEROSEXUAL HEGEMONIES AND MORAL MAJORITIES

Schools and universities are places where the education of, for the most part, the young takes place. This happens not only in the official spaces of curriculum and classroom, but also in the micro- and often very unofficial cultures of students, teachers and others connected with particular sites (for example, Local Education Authorities and governing bodies in the UK, School Councils in Australia and School Boards in the United States). All phases of education share certain features: some people (teachers) are meant to be passing knowledge to others (students); they are places where learning is institutionalized; they all have transient populations of students, though staff may stay for longer or shorter periods of time; and they are all places where appropriate knowledges are defined, taught, measured and examined (Foucault, 1977). There are also significant differences between the different phases. These are related to the age of the students and to notions of developmental phases. When considering sexuality in schools 'appropriate knowledge' is especially contested, particularly during the compulsory years of schooling.

The controversy surrounding the UK government's attempt between February and July 2000 to repeal Section 28 of the Local Government Act 1988 provides a clear example of this contestation. Similar politics around sexuality and school (on both sides of the divide) exist in the USA, Canada, Australia and New Zealand and in

some European countries. Of course, the particular negotiations that take place vary from country to country, partly as a result of different formations of 'left' and 'right', of 'moral majority' and 'sexual liberal', of the relative power of religion and of civil/secular society. Here, we take the British context as a case study of such negotiations.

In the UK, the campaign against the repeal of Section 28 by much of the press, by religious leaders and by a well-organized faction in the House of Lords, significantly influenced the new *Sex and Relationship Education Guidance for Schools* (DfEE, 2000). These guidelines arise partly from long-standing concerns about the high rate of teenage pregnancies in the UK.[5] David Blunkett, then the Secretary of State for Education, also hoped that by producing more coherent sex and relationships education guidelines Section 28 would be seen to be redundant. The guidelines seem to borrow from practice in the USA on preventing teenage pregnancy, despite the high rate of teenage pregnancy there, and from the Netherlands in Europe, where the teenage pregnancy rate is low. At one level, they offer a profoundly anti-sex message, borrowed particularly from anti-sex campaigns in the USA. For example, the requirement for teachers to stress the reasons for delaying first sexual intercourse is mentioned explicitly several times (Introduction.5, Introduction.9, 1.7, 1.18, 2.16, 2.22, 3.5) and implied in a number of other parts of the *Guidance*. At the same time there is to be more emphasis on 'relationship education' as in the Netherlands, rather than what James Sears (1992: Introduction) has described as the 'techno-rational' approach that has pervaded sex education up to now in the USA and, we would add, the UK. The *Guidance* treads a tightrope, attempting both to stress the desirability of marriage to please the churches and those on the Right, and simultaneously expounding a more liberal view about individual sexuality in order to keep its election pledge to those lesbian and gay rights campaigners, broadly on the left:

It is up to schools to make sure that the needs of all pupils are met in their programmes. Young people, whatever their developing sexuality, need to feel that sex and relationship education is relevant to them and sensitive to their needs. The Secretary of State for Education and Employment is clear that teachers should be able to deal honestly and sensitively with sexual orientation, answer appropriate questions and offer support. (DfEE, 2000, para. 1.30)

However, in a clear reference to Section 28, the same paragraph ends with the statement that, 'There should be no direct promotion of sexual orientation'. Since the document also requires teachers to stress the preferability of 'marriage and stable family relationships', one can only assume that heterosexuality is not perceived as a sexual orientation.

Of course, the stress on marriage presents the DfEE with another dilemma, since large numbers of children do not live in families where they have two parents of the opposite sex who are married to each other. In order that children's own family relationships should not be devalued, teachers are instructed to preach a message of tolerance of other sexualities and to recognize the value of stable relationships as well as marriage. The *Guidance* deals with this problem in the following terms in its introduction:

As part of sex and relationship education, pupils should be taught about the nature and importance of marriage for family life and bringing up children. But the Government recognises ... that there are strong and mutually supportive relationships outside marriage. Therefore children should learn the significance of marriage and stable relationships as key building blocks of community and society. Care needs to be taken to ensure that there is no stigmatisation of children based on their home circumstances. (ibid. Introduction: 4)

Perhaps the most important part of this *Guidance*, however, is that this is the first time that schools in the UK have been given a systematic national framework (as opposed to piecemeal government circulars) for sex and relationship education. Therefore there will be much greater scrutiny of how sex education is being taught, though

it is difficult to assess what the overall impact of this *Guidance* will be when it is implemented in its final form. It represents the political tensions surrounding sex education (and the limits of tolerance of lesbian, gay and bi-sexualities) in the UK, comparable to those in other industrialized Anglophone countries. It attempts a negotiation, or a settlement between these tensions, within which teachers will have to manoeuvre. For pupils in school, it clearly advocates an ideal and presumed majority subject position of non-sexual heterosexuality, where children and young people 'recognise' heterosexuality and are constituted through its discourses but also are expected not to consolidate sexual identity through sexual performances, which therefore remain subterranean and transgressive in nature. We will be returning to the issue of students' performances of sexuality later.

The past twenty years have seen the imposition of marketization and managerialism on schools (Epstein and Kenway, 1996; Gewirtz et al., 1995; Whitty, 1994) and, more recently, public sector universities. In this context, success in the educational market depends on achievement in publicly recognizable forms, like examination results – although courses in lesbian and gay, queer and/or women's studies may benefit or lose out from market driven education, with fluctuations in fashion and student demand. Competitively driven education has consequences in a number of areas, including the ways that sexualities can be and are learnt and expressed within these institutions. Investments of time and money are more likely to be spent by institutions to ensure greater publicly recognized achievement, which will in turn accrue more investment and funding, than on more controversial programmes of sex education for example. It is not just that such programmes might infringe the law as it stands both in some US states and in the UK, but also that bad publicity would have an impact on future funding. Therefore even when there are, within institutions, individuals with the power ostensibly to effect change, any attempt to do this is a very risky business (Bickmore, 1999; Epstein, 1997c; Kaeser, 1999; Silin, 1995).

Without radically altered sex education programmes in schools, it is unlikely that more widely held heterosexist views will ever be challenged and yet it is necessary to secure that challenge first before such programmes will be allowed. This is not necessarily easy to come by given the politics current in the various countries to which this chapter refers. Nor have the 'middle way' 'social liberals' represented by Clinton/Gore in the USA and Blair in the UK been very brave in relation to sexuality as evidenced by Clinton's responses to the gays in the military affair at the beginning of his presidency and the Blair government's anxious consultation with the churches over sex education (discussed previously). In the meantime, on the Right of the political spectrum, leaders are openly homophobic. The right-wing Liberal government of Australia is not receptive to liberal (small l) ideas about sexuality and this is repeated at state level in a number of states. Western Australia, for example, has regulations similar in effect to Section 28 and in mid-2000 John Howard, the Prime Minister of Australia, moved swiftly to legislation to overturn a court judgement that allowed access by lesbians to *in vitro* fertilization. George W. Bush has expressed his opposition to any measures to improve equality for lesbians and gays in the USA, while the ex-leader of the UK Conservative Party, William Hague, in an article in the influential British tabloid, the *Daily Mail* (23 January 2000), made clear his views in favour of maintaining Section 28 (Hague, 2000). Underpinning these views was a particular definition of 'tolerance'. Mr Hague defined tolerance as 'a minority accepting and understanding the experiences and beliefs of the majority'. It is this principle that governs much policy on sex education in schools and indeed in universities as well. Foucault (1978) has documented the historical processes whereby sexuality has come to occupy the central position of a person's identity in contemporary Western society.

As Ken Plummer observes, 'Sex has become the Big Story' (Plummer, 1995). It is for this reason that sex education has become such a battleground and the need to shore up heterosexuality is perceived to be crucial to the maintenance of other key institutions.

Furthermore, schools and universities in the Anglophone countries since the 1990s have been organized around an obsession for academic achievement. In the UK, Australia, New Zealand and the USA, governments have made this a priority, believing that a more highly knowledge-based society, particularly in new technologies, will generate greater wealth. In the UK, teachers' salaries and promotions (at schools and, increasingly, at universities) are to become ever more closely wedded to the production of student results with the introduction of performance management and performance-related pay in schools. Since the late 1990s this discourse of achievement discourse has become hegemonic and it is one, as we will show, that has particular effects on the ways that sexuality is construed and constructed within secondary schools.

Despite many constraints and silences, schools and universities have spaces where sexualities are not only permitted, but even required in either formal or informal contexts. In the early years of education, the 'home corner' provides a space for children's fantasies of heterosexual family, while elementary school children need a certain 'sexual literacy' about, for example, desirable pop stars and athletes in the pursuit of friendship. In secondary schools, the 'prom' (in the American context) or school disco provide a space where, however uncomfortably, students are expected to interact, producing themselves as feminine and masculine in iconically heterosexual and exaggerated ways. The heterosexualization of this process is often unremarked and young people are seen generally within a developmental discourse of 'normal' gender development. However, the homophobia endemic in schools and directed at those young men in particular, who are alternatively masculine, makes clear that heterosexuality is indeed compulsory.

Heterosexually successful school students often make a successful transition into the heterosexual economies of colleges and universities. The clubs and societies of UK, Australian and New Zealand universities and the fraternities and sororities of the United States and Canada are places where heterosexual credentials must be proved, for popularity depends on this. Without such heterosexual credentials, many young lesbian and gay students are likely to find themselves excluded from 'the university life', from informal networks of learning and sites of informal cultural exchange. This means they often do not know what is going on or have access to the 'in' stories. Such exclusions are painful and for young people who are already disadvantaged by locations of class or race or dis/ability, it may be impossible to sustain a gay identity, when a heterosexual one provides them with a key strategy for inclusion. In this way a rehearsal of normative heterosexual adulthood is coerced from students. Furthermore, there is a growing body of research that explores how even in elementary education heterosexuality is used as a resource by children (Epstein, 1997b; Letts IV and Sears, 1999; Renold, 2000).

It would, however, be a mistake to assume that there is no room for manoeuvre in educational institutions. As Gramsci (1995) pointed out, hegemony is never total or, in more Foucauldian terms, where there is power, there is always resistance (Foucault, 1977, 1980). Schools and colleges are also sites of cultural struggle. Power does not operate simply in one direction. In all of our research, and in the research of others, we have come across pockets of opposition to dominant forms (see, for example, Appleby, 1995; Davis, 1999; Epstein and Johnson, 1998; Griffin and Andermahr, 1997; Kehily and Nayak, 1996; Pinar, 1998; Rhoads, 1994). Often the ways in which discourses of sexuality, learning, age, class and race are configured in the micro-politics of the classroom, school or university allow for

quite powerful resistances to happen. These may in the end be disarmed by the institution but they do show that the institution is being challenged. A key strategy of the institution to retain power seems to be to allow protest but to contain it in particular areas. Speech is zoned (Steinberg, 1997); what can be said in some places, is not possible in others. Thus, in some educational locations and within some discourses it is possible to speak about sex and sexuality in progressive, even radical, terms. However, closets are often built around these locations, which both affords protection on the one hand but limits the challenge to the institution on the other. For example, in *Schooling Sexualities*, Epstein and Johnson (1998) describe how the Year 5 children (aged 9–10) in Mr Stuart's class deliberately refrained from gossiping about their teacher after he had come out to them on the grounds that, as one girl said, 'Most grown-ups are, um, grown-up about it but some aren't really.'

INNOCENT IGNORANCE AND 'APPROPRIATE' KNOWLEDGES

Young children, according to common-sense understandings, are innocent. They neither do, nor should they, know anything about sexuality. The fear is that contemporary children 'grow up too soon' or are 'not yet ready' for sexual knowledges. In the words of John Patten, who was at the time the Conservative Secretary of State for Education in the UK, children 'should not even be thinking about beginning to be understanding, never mind understanding' particular items of sexual knowledge (*Daily Mail*, 24 March 1994). This is a pervasive theme in debates about sexuality and sex education in Anglophone countries. John Patten's views are shared by the so-called 'moral majority' of the United States, by the right-wing tabloid and broadsheet press of the UK,[6] and by some Christian and other moral traditionalist groups in Australia and New Zealand.

In contrast, feminists, sex educators and others have long argued that not only is 'childhood innocence' an excuse for keeping young children ignorant but it is dangerous to the children (cf. Silin, 1995). Stevi Jackson, writing in the early 1980s (1982), pointed out that the notion of childhood innocence was a way of keeping children ignorant and thereby both denying them access to power and justifying their powerlessness. Children, she suggested, are not allowed to deny adults the right to touch or kiss them in situations that are not perceived by other adults as abusive. How many young children have been told to 'kiss x or y goodbye' when they would rather not do so?[7] Similarly, she pointed out, women are more likely to be touched by men without invitation than vice versa, employees are more likely to be touched by employers, and so on. Jenny Kitzinger (1988; 1990) took this argument further, calling for a critique of the way that the concept of 'childhood innocence' is used in the treatment (by the media, for example) of child sexual abuse. She argued that this supposed 'innocence' itself constituted a form of eroticization of children, making it titillating and exciting. On the other hand, she suggested, children who have been sexually abused lose their innocence (since they are no longer ignorant) and become fair game, legitimate victims of abusers. Thus, an eight-year-old girl can be described by a High Court judge as being 'no angel' and men who abuse can get off with extremely light sentences on the grounds that the knowing child tempted them and led them on.

Of course, as Stevi Jackson argues, the ideology of childhood innocence is profoundly gendered. It is little *girls* who are simultaneously (hetero)sexualized and meant to retain their innocence. Writing about a television documentary on little girls who take part in beauty pageants, Jackson says:

> The little girl [in the beauty pageant] is just acting out a more stylized version of the usual little girl performance – and in one sense knows nothing about sexuality while in another knows a great deal. She is probably ignorant about the mechanics of heterosexual sex, yet she knows that being attractive, flirtatious and cute wins a positive response from adults – and little girls know this even if they don't enter beauty contests. (1999: 139)

While we would agree with Jackson that the sexualization of young children is highly gendered, it is important to remember that little boys are also inscribed within discourses of heterosexuality. The extreme femininity of little girls may construct them as hetero/sex objects, but little boys are required to prove that they are 'real boys' in ways that mark them as masculine, even macho, and therefore (by definition) heterosexual. Furthermore, as Valerie Walkerdine has argued, the eroticization of little girls is profoundly classed (and we would added racialized) as well as gendered (Walkerdine, 1997). Corruption, degradation and immorality are not far away from perceptions of the working-class child or child of colour, particularly when they are girls. Such children are perceived as giving in too easily to temptation and become sexualized in femininity or 'violenced' in masculinity. Thus any child not brought up in a white, middle-class, heterosexual family is potentially sullied and defiled by their surroundings, ultimately because of their failure to be normatively middle class.

We would also agree with the claims made by Kitzinger and by Jackson that discourses of childhood innocence are profoundly damaging to children (girls and boys). The moral traditionalist claim that knowing about sexuality constitutes the corruption of children is, moreover, profoundly anti-educational. As Jonathan Silin so powerfully argues:

> Unlike some, I do not want to protect children from pain during a romanticized period of innocence, nor do I see children as a way to purchase immortality. Rather I want to argue that too much of the contemporary curriculum brings a deathly silence to the being of childhood and not enough of it speaks to the things that really matter in children's lives or in the lives of those who care for them. I want to argue that the curriculum has too often become an injunction to desist rather than an invitation to explore our life worlds. The

curriculum remains lifeless as long as it is cut off from the roots and connections that feed it. (1995: 40)

Silin is writing, here, about death and dying, specifically from AIDS. However, much the same could be said about sexuality, and, indeed, Silin supports this view in his important book.

The desire to preserve 'childhood innocence' is one which we would recast as an attempt to enforce 'childhood ignorance' and which seems to represent the triumph of hope over experience. Children in primary/elementary schools in late capitalist countries, at least, are already knowledgeable about and interested in sexuality in a whole host of different ways. Indeed, we would argue that primary schools are suffused with sexuality in ways which are recognizably similar to the sexual cultures of secondary schools and universities, but that also differ from them in significant ways. Even the youngest children constantly use the discourses of heterosexuality which abound in playgrounds and classrooms as a resource that they can draw on in the making and breaking of friendships, in the investments they make in different versions of themselves as girls and boys, and in their relationships with adults. Emma Renold (2000), for example, describes how girls in primary schools talk very explicitly about the heterosexual attractiveness or otherwise of their classmates and how this enters into the social dynamics of the peer group (see also Connolly, 1995a; Epstein, 1995a; Epstein, 1997a; Epstein et al., 2001 a).

Questions of innocence/ignorance and (being) knowing about sexuality are played out somewhat differently in secondary schools. As children move from the primary/elementary phase, into secondary/junior high schools, there is an expectation that they will be beginning to find out, to know more about sex and sexuality. Young people, at this stage, are expected to know about sexuality, but sexual activity is undesirable. There are particular fears, here, about the rates of teenage pregnancy, on the one hand, and of the seduction, even corruption,

of young men by predatory gay men on the other.

While not wanting to downplay the real sexual vulnerability of some young women, it is worth considering how far those who become pregnant do so because it constitutes specifically an oppositional version of success to school-based success, structured around desire (as against a 'different' version of success because of limited options outside school). It also often puts them beyond schooling, or modifies the meaning of schooling by allowing young women to assert their adulthood. This seems especially true of those young women in secondary schools who specifically state a desire to get pregnant. Thus, young women who gain sexual knowledge (as evidenced by the pregnancies) are no longer innocent, are excluded from gaining school-based knowledge and kept ignorant. Indeed, in the UK, the Social Exclusion Unit's report into *Teenage Pregnancy* (SEU, 1999) specifically comments on the fact that pregnancy seems to signify the end of education for many young women. The government's commitment in this document, to keeping young mothers at school, has yet to be tested in practice. However, the document itself draws attention to the fact that UK schools seem to find it particularly difficult to accommodate continued academic achievement with an active student sexuality and/or parenting roles:

> Attention to ensuring a pregnant teenager continues to receive education is often very weak, and the Unit heard innumerable examples of pregnant girls pushed out of school on grounds of pregnancy or 'health and safety'. This is particularly damaging while educational provision for those out of school remains so poor: an example of a 13 year old receiving only 6 hours education a week from 20 weeks was not at all untypical and for many teenagers this is the beginning of permanent detachment from education. (SEU, 1999: para. 8.22)

Yet in some ways this has to be the case. It is no good promising the rewards of adulthood for a developed heterosexuality and then telling those of whom this is overtly true, that they still have to go to school. As Bullen, Kenway and Hey observe:

> There is much about youthful gender identities and relationships and gendered labour and sexual market(s) that eludes New Labour. With regard to teenage mothers, it tackles their so-called social exclusion without recognising how for some young women social exclusion is multi-dimensional. Indeed, for some, to be excluded from the labour market and to be economically dependent on the state are not the worst possible risk scenarios. In contrast, exclusion from hetero-sexist forms of teenage desirability and relationships is understood as a high-risk scenario (Hey 1997) and teenage pregnancy cannot be addressed if such matters are ignored or trivial-ised. (2000: 449)

The ways in which allowable knowledges about sexuality are inflected by class, dis/ability, embodiment and ethnicity are revealed strikingly in the case of Helen, a year 9 (13–14 years) student of Greek Cypriot origin who was admitted to a girls' state comprehensive school in the UK. She had cerebral palsy. The school had admitted other students with cerebral palsy and so this in itself was not new. In fact her dis-ability[8] was at the mild end of the cerebral palsy spectrum. Within about 12 weeks however, towards the middle of the spring term 1999, this student had been perma-nently excluded (that is, expelled). A variety of reasons were given but the main one was that she had been found masturbating[9] in the toilets.

The fact that Helen was constituted as disabled within the school, both physically and in terms of her ability to learn had an important impact on the perception of her sexuality and the status it was accorded. Had Helen's educational attainment been higher, she would probably not have been excluded – to permanently exclude a high achieving student does not make good eco-nomic sense in the educational market place. Conversely, student sexuality is also often seen as constitutive of 'ability' with the 'over-sexed', underachieving working-class girl the one who becomes pregnant and drops out of school. Helen's learning disability meant that she should not be sexual but also paradoxically the presence of her sexual behaviour appeared to consti-tute the 'severity' of her learning disability.

Furthermore, disabled people are meant to be, for the most part, asexual. As Shakespeare et al. point out: 'Just as children are assumed to have no sexuality, so disabled people are similarly denied the capacity for sexual feeling. Where disabled people are seen as sexual, this is in terms of deviant sexuality, for example, inappropri-ate sexual display or masturbation', (1996: 10). However, as Epstein (1996) has shown, this assumption of asexuality is, in practice within the presumption that it will be a heterosexual version of asexuality.

Helen's case also suggests not only that heterosexual hegemony is maintained through the active suppression of female sexual desire (Fine, 1988) but that the man-ifestations of such desire must therefore also have a transgressive potential to be exploited by students in school and against schooling. This is a point emphasized in the work of Mary Kehily and Anoop Nayak (Kehily and Nayak 1996; Kehily and Nayak 1997; Nayak and Kehily 1997). The final consequences of such transgressions are often, though not always, less than empow-ering. However, such events and their ever-present possibility mean that students' sexual knowledges and expression consti-tute a source of considerable anxiety to the institution, which is obliged to look for ways of containing or expelling the trans-gressive meanings that can be attached to student expressions of sexuality – often before it considers the welfare of the student concerned.

For many, possibly most, young people who leave school to go into higher educa-tion, college or university provides a space within which they can deepen and widen their sexual experience. Universities and colleges are the places within the educa-tional system where (hetero)sex stops being taboo and enters the realm of the expected. Young people are no longer expected to be innocent/ignorant about sexuality, but either to have or to gain sexual knowledge and experience during their courses. There is an assumption, among most heterosexual young people and their families, that this is the place and period during which potentially long-term partners, even spouses, will be found. Similarly, the majority of queer young people who have elected to go into higher education want to further the interrogation of their sexual-selves. They presume that their college or university will provide an environment that is *more* supportive of sexual difference than they have previously experienced because of the relaxation of heteronormative attitudes experienced in their previous homes and secondary schools. The 'dynamics of their closets' (Sedgwick, 1990; Smith et al., 1998) and the borders that their environments have placed around their desires are likely to be well known to them. Nevertheless the queer young person frequently anticipates that higher education will provide a social and sexual intersection, enabling them to expand their personal ties and networks within a freer cultural environment. They may view university or college as offering the potential for sexual emancipation, personal liberation, and the opportunity of being treated as an equal in a heterocentric world.

However, when students arrive at university, they are likely to discover that social permission to be sexual is tenuous for those who do not conform to the prescriptions of normative heterosexuality. Heterosexual expectations of straight friends and family, as well as the governances of the hidden or micro curriculum continue to police the boundaries of their lives (Stevens and Walker, 1996). The thread of heteronormativity that has woven its way through their primary and secondary schools is there too in college, feeding the hidden anti-queer discourses of higher education. We have shown, above, how sexuality – especially in non-normative form – is both prohibited and pervasive in primary and secondary schools. In universities, by contrast, there are likely to be discussions of lesbian and gay themes (and maybe even bisexual and transgender

ones) generally, a broader awareness and understanding of sexual differences and even a tacit official approval on the macro level. This is likely to show itself in a number of ways: first, in inclusion of references to lesbian, gay, bisexual and transgendered identities in references to minority or disadvantaged groups, particularly in the social sciences; secondly, in the existence of courses that are specifically about lesbian, gay and/or queer themes, particularly within literary studies; and thirdly, in the intellectual work of openly queer academics (for example, Seidman, 1995; 1997). There are, also within the university sector, a number of out academics, some of them very famous, working specifically in the field of sexuality[10].

Nevertheless, the same heterosexism that pursued queer pupils through primary and secondary school lies just under the surfaces of higher education. Consequently, many non-heterosexual students, particularly those who occupy 'sexual margins', feel that they have little choice other than to distance themselves from mainstream university life and *do* their sexuality elsewhere.

For those attending college or university in or near large urban centres *doing* one's (homo)sexuality elsewhere means, for the most part, in the commercial 'gay scene' near to where their college or university is located. In more isolated university settings, however, queer young people can experience something akin to a 'siege mentality' where they are sequestered and/or rely predominantly on chance contacts they make within the university, via the Internet, or through queer groups often established as part of the Students' Union. However, such recognition is always risky. For example, the University of Georgetown in Washington, DC, has attempted to disallow the existence of a lesbian and gay society, a move that was found to be unlawful in a court challenge (Lorenz, 2000). Similarly, at the same university, a queer studies course taught within English was pilloried in the press (Inglebretson and Edward, 2000). In both urban and rural settings, therefore, the university or college is a site of and for heterosexuality, where an often-narrow heterosexuality is performed and where gender and sexual differences are marginalized. The halls of residence, the student bar or other social spaces are often threateningly straight (McNaron, 1991; Taulke-Johnson and Rivers, 1998). This is when queer students realize that they may have cast off the heterosexism of their secondary school only to rediscover, somewhat ominously, that the same heterocentric agenda exists within the now constricting confines of higher education.

Furthermore, in these economic rationalist times, it is increasingly difficult for young people to leave the family home in order to go to university. This has a particular impact on students identifying as queer, who might previously have found a space on the commercial gay scene away from home. For these young people, continued financial dependence on their parents, and/or living in the parental home, makes coming out problematic. It holds young people in a state of *economic childhood* beyond the years of legal minority, giving economic power to compulsory heterosexuality by making young queers nervous of coming out to their parents in case this leads to the end of their studies as well as to disruption of their familial relationships (which is frequently feared by those thinking of coming out within families).

TEACHING AND LEARNING (HETERO)SEXUALITIES

All educational institutions, at whatever phase, have both formal and informal curricula. The formal comprises what is overtly taught, the content of the curriculum. The informal, or hidden, curriculum is much harder to pin down, since it consists of almost everything else. Although, for the sake of clarity, we are dividing the formal and the informal, in practice they are intertwined and bleed into each other. Formal

and hidden curricula are formed and understood in relation to each other. No formal teaching can take place outside the context of the hidden curriculum and the hidden curriculum draws on aspects of the taught curriculum. Social relations, forms of pedagogy, curriculum content, micro-cultural processes and dynamics, even the life histories of students and staff, all contribute to the learning and teaching that goes on within educational sites. Sometimes the hidden curriculum can be at odds with what is apparently being taught. Thus, teaching from a post-modern or queer perspective in sexualities courses in universities may be in tension with the discursive practices outlined above, which make non-normative versions of sexuality at the very least uncomfortable.

The Formal Curriculum

Overt teaching about sexuality in primary/elementary schools is to be found only in formal sex education classes as part of the Personal, Social and Health Education (PSHE) curriculum. In middle/secondary/high schools, sex education will continue to be part of PSHE but there may also be some work around sexuality in the syllabi of various subject areas, particularly English, Drama and Social Studies (or Sociology). At university, sexuality may be studied overtly in a number of curriculum areas including sociology and cultural studies, psychology, medical sciences, gender or women's studies – and, of course, Lesbian and Gay Studies. In primary and secondary schools, sex education in the UK, the USA, Australia and New Zealand has historically been focused on reproduction with one's heterosexuality assumed – the sexuality of default. The secondary English curriculum may be used to explore all kinds of sexual dilemmas from heterosexual teenage passion in *Romeo and Juliet*, love, lust and adultery in a range of poetry and novels and may even, though unusually, explore same sex attraction and love (Harris, 1990). At universities, particularly in social sciences and literary studies, there may also be courses in lesbian and gay studies, or queer theory, although these may be more prevalent in the United States than elsewhere. Furthermore, as Sheila Jeffreys points out, in her elite Australian university:

> I teach a lesbian and gay politics course with the support of my department of Political Science at the University of Melbourne. My course is called 'The Politics of Sex Reform Movements' because the students pointed out that the title that included the words lesbian and gay might impede their chances of employment. The very fact that my course has to be closeted in this way suggests some of the political difficulties of such teaching. My course and my department are exceptional in Australia. Departments of Political Science often contain no teaching about women or feminism, let alone lesbians. (1997: 142)

The extent of specific teaching about sexuality, however, is limited both in time and content. In UK primary schools, for example, children in Year 5 (aged 9–10) are likely to have four or five lessons in sex education, which is likely to be based on the biological. In Ontario, Canada, animal reproduction is included in the grade three Health and Physical Education curriculum, while puberty and human reproduction are taught in grades 5 and 6 (Bickmore, 1999). In general, teachers in this phase are nervous about sex education. They are in a difficult place, here. Often primary school teachers, who teach across the curriculum, have little or no training in how to do sex education. Furthermore, they are likely to be legitimately anxious about the reactions of some parents and, worse, of the popular press, if they stray into territory considered by moral traditionalists to be too risky (even risqué).

Cahill and Theilheimer (1998) ask why it should be harder to imagine children in kindergarten classes acting out events at Stonewall in June 1969, when a group of gay people fought back against police harassment, than to imagine them playing at being Rosa Parks or Martin Luther King during events in Montgomery, Alabama, at the start of the Civil Rights Movement.

They point out that children are part of multigenerational families 'in which elders, the child her- or himself, and/or the child's future offspring may be gay' (Cahill and Theilheimer, 1998: 40). But, as most readers would recognize, it is almost impossible to imagine the Stonewall scenario being played out (and in a positive way!) in schools, particularly during the early years and elementary phases. While citizenship education may, in theory, have the potential to create a space for such a play, there is no evidence that this has been the case in those places that have adopted it (for example, parts of the USA and Victoria in Australia). Furthermore, if discourses of desire are missing, as Michelie Fine (1988) argues, or forcibly expelled, as Epstein and Johnson (1998) suggest, at the secondary phase, how much further are they from the realms of the sayable in primary classrooms?

The formal sex education curriculum of secondary schools is much more likely to focus on the dangers of sex and desire, especially on the 'evils' of HIV transmission, rather than the social context of sexuality. In most secondary schools, such discussion as there is in the official spaces of schooling will be in terms of conception, contraception and the spread of sexually transmitted diseases, especially HIV, all within an assumed heterosexual norm. At the same time, the advent of the HIV/AIDS pandemic has meant that, in many countries, sex education has assumed a new urgency over the last two decades. Most recently, in South Africa (and notwithstanding President Mbeki's statement, just prior to the July 2000 AIDS conference held in Durban, that HIV does not necessarily lead to AIDS), the government and donor agencies have begun to spend enormous sums in the attempt to develop a sex education curriculum that will reduce the rate of transmission among young people, Nevertheless, the findings reported by Hillier et al. (1999: 71) are typical in this respect: 'In the formal classroom curriculum, an assumption that students were heterosexual meant that safe sex and sexuality issues were dealt with only in the context of heterosexuality.' The curriculum spaces in schools (as opposed to universities) that are most likely to allow possibilities for exploring queer sexualities are English and Drama, and Sociology. English teaching, in the UK, the USA and Australia has a tradition of commitment to exploring social justice issues as well as working in the affective domain through literature and drama and there have been moves by the American National Council for Teachers of English, to take on questions of sexuality (Misson, 1999; Spurlin, 2000). School sociology courses may well include something about sexuality under the heading of gender and/ or deviance – where exploration of queer sexualities are still most likely to be found.

As discussed earlier, many students imagine university/college to be a freer sexual environment, than school. For many heterosexual students, this may well prove to be the case. For those who do not conform heterosexually, higher education may provide a site of possibility for coming out, particularly where high school has seemed to be an impossible location. Indeed, the literature is uni-vocal in suggesting that attitudes within the academy have changed from the days when there was complete silence in the curricula and the administrations actively campaigned against activists (see, for example, D'Emilio, 1992; Tierney, 1993; 1997; Tierney and Rhoads, 1993). The pace and spread of change, however, vary considerably. John D'Emilio concludes that 'for the most part, the 1970s was a decade characterised by organisation and networking. The 1980s have witnessed the production and sharing of knowledge. I expect that the 1990s will be the time when we see significant movement toward the institutionalisation of queer studies in higher education'. (1992: 169) It is interesting to compare D'Emilio's prediction made at the start of the last decade with what we have witnessed within institutions of Western academia. While some of the changes have been significant – and the publication of books like this one is an example of that – they have not been uniform. At best, the development of

queer studies courses, in their various forms, and the inclusion of queer studies within non-specialist courses has been patchy (Tierney, 1997).

There is little doubt that distinct heterosexual biases continue to exist and are embedded in the curricula and pedagogical practices in universities. There appear to be two projects for which writers in the field are calling. First, pleas for the implementation of curricula that are more inclusive of queer issues, one that is supported by more tolerant/aware pedagogical practices (Lopez and Chism, 1993; Piernik, 1992). This requires a redesign of the existing heterocentric curricula and the modification of the pedagogical practices of many university teachers to incorporate the specific learning needs of non-heterosexual students. The second project is a corollary of the first, and produces demands to 'educate' straight students about negative effects of their heterosexist attitudes (Wallick, 1995) and to disrupt heteronormativity (Britzman, 1995). McCord and Herzog (1991) suggest that programmes that help students understand that discrimination and abuse are not justifiable responses can also help to expose latent/blatant heterosexist attitudes amongst straight students. As Linda Eyre points out, however, there are inherent dangers and contradictions in this and similar approaches: 'Pedagogical practices explicitly intended to challenge the heteronormativity and heterosexism ... [and] ... work towards social change risk reproducing the very aspects of injustice that they seek to rectify' (1993: 191, 195). Some of the approaches employed in teaching may *harm* the success of curricula and pedagogical practices that aim to be queer inclusive and/or disruptive of normative heterosexuality. These include what Eyre (1993) describes as the 'add-on' approach, the 'homosexual' guest speaker, and workshops on heterosexism. There are, perhaps, dangers in further isolating straight students from pro-queered perspectives through some mismanaged attempts to incorporate Queer Theory into the mainstream curricula because many heterosexual students have limited reference points from which to engage with queer themes or, as Deborah Britzman argues, because those in dominant, unmarked groups, often feel they have an entitlement to maintain their ignorance (1995: 159). Parallels can be drawn, here, between debates about whether feminism and 'multiculturalism' should be 'mainstreamed', taking their place within, for example, core courses in sociology, or whether they should be taught in separate classes labelled, variously, 'women's studies', 'gender studies', 'African-American studies', and so on (see, for example, Coate, 2000, and Nardi in this volume).

The Hidden Curriculum

There is no possibility of predicting exactly how queer curricula may be read by straight (or even queer) students. The way students make sense of any formal curriculum is dependent on a complex combination of their own personal biographies and social positions and the hidden curricula of the institutions in which they are educated. Therefore, 'to boldly go' where no straight writing course/history class etc. has thought of itself going before, could cause a backlash of heterosexism that can abandon queer students to feel further marginalized, and further entrench straight students' heterocentric attitudes. The fact that 'a few' straight students are offended is not the real concern. Rather, of greater consequence is the missed opportunity to advance the political project of troubling and disrupting heteronormativity. We are not arguing, of course, that curricula should not be queered. Rather, we would suggest that the unpredictability of response, our inability to know who the addressee of any curriculum or pedagogy 'really' is (Ellsworth, 1997), must be taken into account and acknowledged.

Children and young people bring all kinds of different experiences in relation to sexuality to school and college and these, along with the particular local cultures of the institution, form an important part of the hidden curriculum of sexuality.

As we have argued above, and as the work of Emma Renold (1999; 2000) shows, sexuality pervades primary school playgrounds and classrooms and children draw on it as a resource for constructing themselves as boys and as girls. This takes a variety of forms from imaginative games involving heterosexual family life and talk about 'dating', 'dumping' and 'going out' (Epstein, 1997b) to name-calling and abuse of those who, for whatever reason do not 'fit' as properly masculine or feminine (but perhaps particularly masculine) (Boldt, 1996; Connell, 1989; Connolly, 1995b).

Children's play and talk are profoundly heterosexualized and form an important part of any hidden curriculum. As Bronwyn Davies shows:

> Heterosexuality is continually constructed in the children's talk as they separate and heighten the difference between themselves as male and female. So pervasive is this construction that even the most simple initiative on a girl's part, such as asking a boy for a pencil, can be overlaid with compromising (hetero)sexual meanings. The boys, in contrast are not compromised by (hetero)sexuality. (1993: 123)

But it is, of course, not only the children's play that produces heterosexuality within the hidden curriculum of primary schools, but forms of organization, the assumptions and expectations of teachers that children will live in heterosexual families and the heteronormativity of various books and other resources (VanEvery and Wallis, 2000).

Similar processes are at work in secondary schools and universities. In secondary schools, the dominating discourses of 'standards' and 'achievement', discussed above, have a huge impact on the hidden curriculum. In schools 'ability' is measured in relation to age and educational attainment. It is strongly inflected by psychological developmental discourse, which in turn has a preoccupation with sexual development. Walkerdine (1990) has explored the implications for women and girls of a male-centred discourse 'of the rational, independent, autonomous child as a quasi-natural phenomenon who progresses through a universalized developmental sequence towards the possibility of rational argument' (1990: 29). In this context, the functionalist logics of the hidden sexuality curriculum demand there should be a smooth progression, with an emergent heterosexuality appearing in the later years of compulsory school but not fully developed until the end of compulsory schooling. In this logic gay sexuality is often recuperated as a stage, an immature sexuality, on the way to fully-fledged heterosexuality. Its more radical meanings are then contained within the heterosexual hegemony of the school. David Denborough argues: 'If sex is upheld as a symbol of adulthood, and adulthood is seen to represent control over one's own life and an end to constant domination, then it makes sense that young people speak of and participate in sex in order to make claims to adult identity. Sexuality comes to represent freedom' (1996: 3). Denborough's analysis needs refining in fact, as it is only *hetero*sexuality that is invested with meanings of adulthood in schools. The promise of adulthood is a key strategy of heterosexism in schools.

Two key aspects of the hidden curriculum of secondary schools – Cartesian rationality and emphatic masculinities – may make it possible for gay male student identities to exist publicly within these spaces. They must, however, be presented in ways that are recognizable within school contexts, that is, in terms of 'rational argument' and/or as hegemonically masculine 'real boys', for example through being good at team games like rugby or football (Epstein, 1997a). In terms of the Cartesian rational, it is perhaps the case that defences of gay male sexuality become realistically possible in the later years of secondary education when intellect is re-valorised as a form of masculinity (Redman and Mac an Ghaill, 1997) and also significantly when the 'Macho lads' are likely to drop out of school. Furthermore, such rationality may only work for the white, middle-class gay young man (and then only partially) for, as Mac an Ghaill shows, gay young men from ethnic minorities are particularly liable to be subject to a combination of bodily desire (for their 'blackness') and disgust (with their gayness) by their teachers and peers (Mac an Ghaill, 1994).

Universities, perhaps even more than schools, are characterized by appeals to the rational. It is unusual for writers about higher education to consider the hidden curriculum of universities (see, however, Epstein, 1995b). Here, the importance of rational thinking, the economics of higher education (for example, are students forced to live with parents because of cost?) and the politics and relationships of students and staff all play a part in forming the framework for university education.

These relationships include: family, ethnic and cultural background, religion, the importance of primary and secondary school, political ideology, socio-economic status, friends (heterosexual and queer), the wider 'gay scene' and issues of gender non-conformity (Lottes and Kuriloff, 1992; 1994; Nora et al., 1996; Waldner-Haugrud and Magruder, 1996). Another important part of the hidden curriculum for queer students is involvement with LGBT or queer social/political groups and other political activities. Similarly, as Nina Wakeford (this volume) shows, new information technologies may provide opportunities for the expression and support of deviant sexualities. Personal ties and social networks can also lend support to the young person by providing a means of escaping from the heteronormative expectations of family and peers and afford a discursive space in which to build a sexual identity (Rhoads, 1994). But, overwhelmingly, the hidden curriculum is produced by a straight, often threatening, environment in which, according to Evans and D'Augelli (1996: 215), queer students in US universities reported that:

- 75 per cent experienced verbal abuse.
- 25 per cent were threatened with violence at least once.
- 22 per cent were chased or followed and 5 per cent had been spat on.
- 17 per cent have had personal property damaged.

- 64 per cent feared for their personal safety on campus.
- Most hid their sexual identity from their roommates or other students.

Significantly, 'nearly all expected the "average" lesbian or gay man to be harassed on campus' (Evans and D'Augelli, 1996: 215). Most of these incidents were not reported to the university authorities and many queer students made changes to their daily routines to avoid hardships. Many gay or bisexual men in Evans and D'Augelli's study feared for their personal safety and those fears were based on previous experience of personal violence or attacks to property. We would argue that these experiences are not only relevant for non-heterosexual students, but for many who do identify as heterosexual. The often violent policing of queer sexualities also constitute a means through which heterosexual masculinities and femininities are regulated, particularly those that are, in some way, non-normative (for example, gentle boys/young men, assertive girls/young women, celibate students of either gender). Indeed, it is worth asking whether the attacks on apparently queer students by apparently straight ones is a way of dissociating oneself from any aspersions on one's sexuality.

CONCLUSION

We have suggested, in this chapter, that childhood is highly regulated through discourses of innocence and experience and that this shapes education in profound ways. Compulsory heterosexuality for children and young people is, to a large extent, written through assumptions of and demands for innocence (ignorance?). We have traced the ways that these discourses are expressed at different stages in education and in different educational sites. We have suggested, furthermore, that what happens in education is tightly bound up with the organization and regulation of the heterosexual family. Myths

of happy heterosexuality abound at every stage from the play house of the nursery school to the dating games of secondary/junior high schools and universities. The particular ways that this happens are, of course, nuanced by local, institutional micro-cultures but are also shaped by the exigencies of more global political economies of education.

Where Foucault (1980) suggests that power and knowledge are inextricably entwined, what we have argued is that knowledge in educational settings is constructed as heterosexual. The paradox is that educational institutions are charged with the production and passing on of knowledge, but, at the same time, young people and children are only supposed to gain particular knowledges, especially where sexuality is concerned. This means that young people can sometimes use their sexual knowledges as forms of resistance to the demands and discourses of schooling/university and at others, they can use them to access networks of power and popularity, and even academic achievement.

Much research in the field of sexuality and education to date has focused on the dual questions of the victimization of young lesbian, gay and bisexual people, and the development of sexual identities. In this context, it is often difficult to write without setting up binaries and, indeed, our own chapter has divided queer and straight, formal and informal curricula. What is needed, at this point, are ways of interrogating the structures of education that recognize and explore both the fluidities and fixities of educational institutions. Here, careful attention must be paid to the ways that people (young and old) do sexuality through gender, ethnicity, class and the body and vice versa. Rather than assuming that young people bring their sexuality to school with them, and investigating how educational institutions respond to that, we would suggest that explorations of how institutions themselves produce and constrain sexualities are likely to be generative in future research.

NOTES

1 Section 28 infamously prohibits Local Authorities (that is, local government) from 'promoting homosexuality', labelling same-sex relationships as being 'pretended family relationships'. When the Thatcher government in 1988 passed it, there were protests in the UK and nearly all the 'western democracies'. The Blair Government was finally defeated in the House of Lords on the repeal of Section 28 at the end of July 2000. It seems unlikely that a further attempt to repeal the Section will be made before the next general election in Britain.

2 We recognize that terminology is always contested, and not everyone likes the term 'queer', which can be seen as derogatory. However, we will use it in this chapter for two reasons. First, we find the litany of identities, 'lesbian, gay, bisexual, transgendered, transsexual' awkward to use, breaking the flow of writing. Secondly, 'queer' suggests something more of the fluidity of sexual identities, which we would argue exists among both heterosexual and non-heterosexual people. While we are probably more materialist in our analysis than many queer theorists, we are certainly indebted to queer theory for much of it.

3 This chapter is based on (and, in part, quotes from) our significantly longer and fuller review of the literature for the American Educational Research Association's *Review of Research in Education* (Epstein et al. 2001b). For an excellent review of the literature on sexuality and education from the United States see Tierney and Dilley (1998).

4 Elspeth Probyn, however, points out that Rich's project is to 'combine the specificity of individual female bodies with a larger feminist politics' (Probyn, 1990: 177) and, in particular, that she is very specific about her own white, Jewish lesbian body.

5 Between 1977 and 1996 the USA had much the highest rate of live births per thousand women between the ages of fifteen and nineteen in comparable countries. It was followed by (in order) New Zealand, the UK, Canada and Australia. New Zealand is the only one of these countries to show a significant reduction in the rate of teenage pregnancies over this period (SEU, 1999).

6 Unlike geographically larger countries, the UK has a large number of national daily papers. The tabloids tend to be more scandalous and read by much larger numbers than the more 'highbrow' broadsheets. Right wing tabloids include the *Sun* (owned by Rupert Murdoch), with the largest readership of any national daily newspaper, and the *Daily Mail* (which has traditionally been closely associated with the Right of the Conservative Party). Right-wing broadsheets include *The Times* (also a Murdoch paper) and the *Telegraph*.

7 It may be that this is less likely to happen in quite so overt a form now. However, given the power differential between children and adults, it is not easy for children to feel empowered to refuse a kiss proffered by an adult, especially one with whom they have close relationships.

The difficulty is that denying children the physical expression of affection is likely to be damaging in a different way. Thus programmes that purport to teach children how to refuse 'bad touches' and distinguish between 'good' and 'bad' ways of touching and cuddling present significant difficulties. We would like to thank Rebecca Boden for pointing this out to us.

8 The language to use when talking about 'dis/ability' is a minefield and is different in different countries. We agree with the argument that dis/ability is socially constructed and thus use the term 'dis/ability' when talking about the general case, to indicate social construction. In talking about Helen, specifically, however, we talk of her 'disability'. The use of 'disabled person' or 'person with a disability' is also contested. We have followed the use in Shakespeare et al. of 'disabled person'.

9 Of course, as Foucault notes, masturbation is a key perversion in the history of sexuality (Foucault, 1978; see, also Sedgwick, 1994 particularly the article or on 'Jane Austen and the Masturbating Girl').

10 One should not, however, underestimate the difficulties that such high profile outness may bring. See, for example, Valentine (1998).

REFERENCES

Abelove, Henry, Barale, Michèle Aina, and Halperin, David M. (1993) *The Lesbian and Gay Studies Reader.* London: Routledge.

Appleby, Yvon (1995) 'Voices from the heart-land: lesbian women and education', unpublished PhD, University of Sheffield.

Bickmore, Kathy (1999) 'Why discuss sexuality in elementary school?', in William J. Letts IV and James T. Sears (eds), *Queering Elementary Education: Advancing the Dialogue about Sexualities and Schooling.* Lanham, MD: Rowman & Littlefield.

Boldt, Gail M. (1996) 'Sexist and heterosexist responses to gender bending in an elementary classroom', *Curriculum Inquiry*, 26 (2): 113–31.

Britzman, Deborah P. (1995) 'Is there a queer pedagogy? Or, stop reading straight', *Educational Theory*, 45 (2): 151–61.

Bullen, Elizabeth, Kenway, Jane, and Hey, Valerie (2000) 'New Labour, social exclusion and educational risk management: the case of "Gymslip Mums"', *British Educational Research Journal*, 26: 441–56.

Butler, Judith (1990) *Gender Trouble: Feminism and the Subversion of Identity.* New York and London: Routledge.

Cahill, Betsy J. and Theilheimer, Rachel (1998) 'Stonewall in the housekeeping area: gay and lesbian issues in the early childhood classroom', in William J. Letts IV and James T. Sears (eds), *Queering Elementary Education: Advancing the Dialogue about*

Sexualities and Schooling. Lanham, MD: Rowman and Littlefield.

Coate, Kelly (2000) *The History of Women's Studies as an Academic Subject Area in Higher Education in the UK: 1970–1995.* Unpublished PhD, Institute of Education, University of London.

Connell, R.W. (1989) 'Cool guys, swots and wimps: the interplay of masculinity and education', *Oxford Review of Education*, 13 (3): 291–303.

Connolly, Paul (1995a) 'Boys will be boys? Racism, sexuality, and the construction of masculine identities amongst infant boys', in Janet Holland, Maud Blair and Sue Sheldon (eds), *Debates and Issues in Feminist Research and Pedagogy.* Cleveland, Philadelphia and Adelaide: Multilingual Matters Ltd in association with the Open University.

Connolly, Paul (1995b) 'Racism, masculine peer-group relations and the schooling of African/Caribbean infant boys', *British Journal of Sociology of Education*, 16: 72–92.

Davies, Bronwyn (1993) *Shards of Glass: Children Reading and Writing Beyond Gendered Identities.* St. Leonard, NSW: Allen and Unwin.

Davis, James Earl (1999) 'Forbidden fruit: black males' constructions of transgressive sexualities in middle school', in William J. Letts IV and James T. Sears (eds), *Queering Elementary Education: Advancing the Dialogue about Sexualities and Schooling.* Lanham, MD: Rowman and Littlefield. pp. 49–59.

de Lauretis, Theresa (1994) *The Practice of Love: Lesbian Sexuality and Perverse Desire.* Bloomington, IN: Indiana University Press.

D'Emilio, John (1992) *Making Trouble: Essays on Gay History, Politics and the University.* New York: Routledge.

Denborough, David (1996) 'Power and partnership? Challenging the sexual construction of schooling', in Louise Laskey and Catherine Beavis (eds), *Schooling and Sexualities.* Geelong: Deakin Centre for Education and Change, Deakin University.

DfEE (2000) *Sex and Relationship Education Guidance For Schools.* London: Department for Education and Employment.

Ellsworth, Elizabeth (1997) *Teaching Positions: Difference, Pedagogy, and the Power of Address.* New York and London: Teachers College Press.

Epstein, Debbie (1995a) '"Girls don't do bricks." Gender and sexuality in the primary classroom', in John Siraj-Blatchford and Iram Siraj-Blatchford (eds), *Educating the Whole Child: Cross-Curricular Skills, Themes and Dimensions.* Buckingham: Open University Press. pp. 56–69.

Epstein, Debbie (1995b) 'In our (New) Right minds: the hidden curriculum in higher education', in Louise Morley and Val Walsh (eds), *Feminist Academics: Creative Agents for Change.* London: Taylor and Francis.

Epstein, Debbie (1996) 'Keeping them in their place: hetero/sexist harassment, gender and the enforcement of heterosexuality', in Janet Holland and Lisa Adkins (eds), *Sex, Sensibility and the Gendered Body.* Basingstoke: Macmillan. pp. 202–21.

Epstein, Debbie (1997a) 'Boyz' own stories: masculinities and sexualities in schools', *Gender and Education*, 9 (1): 105–115.

Epstein, Debbie (1997b) 'Cultures of schooling/cultures of sexuality', *International Journal of Inclusive Education*, 1: 37–53.

Epstein, Debbie (1997c) 'What's in a ban? Jane Brown, Romeo and Juliet and the popular media', in Deborah Lynn Steinberg, Debbie Epstein and Richard Johnson (eds), *Border Patrols: Policing the Boundaries of Heterosexuality.* London: Cassell. pp. 183–203.

Epstein, Debbie and Johnson, Richard (1998) *Schooling Sexualities.* Buckingham: Open University Press.

Epstein, Debbie and Kenway, Jane (1996) 'Discourse: studies in the cultural politics of education', Special Issue. *Feminist Perspectives on the Marketisation of Education*, 17 (3).

Epstein, Debbie, Kehily, Mary Jane, Mac an Ghaill, Maírtín, and Redman, Peter (2001 a). 'Girls and boys come out to play: making masculinities and femininities in school', *Men and Masculinities: Disciplining and Punishing Masculinities*, 4 (2): 158–72.

Epstein, Debbie, O'Flynn, Sarah and Telford, David (2001 b) '"Othering education 2001": sexualities, silences and schooling', in Walter Secada (ed.), *Review of Research in Education*, Vol. 26. Washington, DC: American Educational Research Association. pp. 127–81.

Evans, N. and D'Augelli, Anthony (1996) 'Lesbians, gay men and bisexual people in college', in R. Savin-Williams and K. Cohen (eds), *The Lives of Lesbians, Gays and Bisexuals.* Orlando, FL: Harcourt Brace College Publishers.

Eyre, L. (1993) 'Compulsory heterosexuality in a university classroom', *Canadian Journal of Education*, 18 (3): 273–84.

Fine, Michelle (1988) 'Sexuality, schooling and adolescent females: the missing discourse of desire', *Harvard Educational Review*, 58 (1): 29–53.

Foucault, Michel (1977) *Discipline and Punish: The Birth of the Prison.* Trans. Alan Sheridan. Harmondsworth: Penguin.

Foucault, Michel (1978) *The History of Sexuality, Volume 1, An Introduction.* Harmondsworth: Penguin.

Foucault, Michel (1980) *Power/Knowledge: Selected Interviews and Other Writings 1972–1977.* Hemel Hempstead: Harvester.

Gewirtz, Sharon, Ball, Stephen and Bowe, Richard (1995) *Markets, Choice and Equity in Education.* Buckingham: Open University Press.

Gramsci, Antonio (1995) *Antonio Gramsci: Further Selections from the Prison Notebooks.* Edited and translated by Derek Boothman. London: Lawrence and Wishart.

Griffin, Gabriele and Andermahr, Sonya (1997) *Straight Studies Modified: Lesbian Interventions in the Academy.* London: Cassell.

Hague, William (2000) 'Mr Blair shows nothing but contempt for parents,' *Daily Mail.* 23 January: 10.

Harris, Simon (1990) *Lesbian and Gay Issues in the English Classroom: The Importance of Being Honest.* Buckingham: Open University Press.

Hey, Valerie (1997) *The Company She Keeps: An Ethnography of Girls' Friendships.* Buckingham: Open University Press.

Hillier, Lynne, Harrison, Lyn, and Dempsey, Deborah (1999) 'Whatever happened to duty of care? Same-sex attracted young people's stories of schooling and violence', *Melbourne Studies in Education,* 40 (2): 59–74.

hooks, bell (1984) *Feminist Theory from Margin to Center.* Boston, MA: South End Press.

Inglebretson S.J., Edward, J. (2000) 'When the cave is a closet: pedagogies of the (re)pressed', in William Spurlin (ed.), *Lesbian and Gay Studies and the Teaching of English: Positions, Pedagogies and Popular Culture.* Urbana, IL: NCTE.

Jackson, Stevi (1982) *Childhood and Sexuality.* Oxford: Basil Blackwell.

Jackson, Stevi (1999) *Heterosexuality in Question.* London, Thousand Oaks, New Delhi: Sage.

Jeffreys, Sheila (1997) 'Revolting lesbians in the politics department', in Gabriele Griffin and Sonya Andermahr (eds), *Straight Studies Modified: Lesbian Interventions in the Academy.* London: Cassell.

Johnson, Richard (1997) 'Contested borders, contingent lives: an introduction', in Deborah Lynn Steinberg, Debbie Epstein and Richard Johnson (eds), *Border Patrols: Policing the Boundaries of Heterosexuality.* London: Cassell.

Kaeser, Gigi (1999) 'Love makes a family: controversy in two Massachusetts towns', in William J. Letts IV and James T. Sears (eds), *Queering Elementary Education: Advancing the Dialogue about Sexualities and Schooling.* Lanham, MD: Rowman & Littlefield.

Kehily, Mary Jane and Nayak, Anoop (1996) '"The Christmas Kiss": sexuality, story-telling and schooling', *Curriculum Studies: The Sexual Politics of Education,* 4 (2): 211–28.

Kehily, Mary Jane and Nayak, Anoop (1997) '"Lads and Laughter": humour and the production of heterosexual hierarchies', *Gender and Education: Special Issue: Masculinities in Education,* Christine Griffin and Sue Lees (eds). 9 (1): 69–88.

Kitzinger, Jenny (1988) 'Defending innocence: ideologies of childhood', *Feminist Review. Special Issue: Family Secrets, Child Sexual Abuse,* 28: 77–87.

Kitzinger, Jenny (1990) ' "Who are you kidding?" Children, power and sexual assault', in Alison James and Alan Prout (eds), *Constructing and Reconstructing Childhood.* London: Falmer Press.

Letts IV, William J. and Sears, James T. (1999) *Queering Elementary Education.* Lanham, MD: Rowman & Littlefield.

Lopez, G. and Chism, N. (1993) 'Classroom concerns of gay and lesbian students: the invisible minority', *College Teaching,* 41 (3): 97–103.

Lorde, Audre (1984) *Sister Outsider.* Freedom, CA: Crossing Press.

Lorenz, Jay Kent (2000) 'Blame it on the weatherman: popular culture and pedagogical praxis in the lesbian and gay studies classroom', in William Spurlin (ed.), *Lesbian and Gay Studies and the Teaching of English: Positions, Pedagogies and Cultural Politics.* Urbana, IL: NCTE.

Lottes, I. and Kuriloff, P. (1992) 'The effects of gender, race, religion, and political orientation on the sex role attitudes of college freshmen', *Adolescence,* 27 (107): 675–88.

Lottes, I. and Kuriloff, P. (1994) 'The impact of college experience on political and social attitudes', *Sex Roles,* 31 (1–2): 31–54.

Mac an Ghaill, Mairtín (1994) *The Making of Men: Masculinities, Sexualities and Schooling.* Buckingham: Open University Press.

McCord, David M. and Herzog, Harold A. (1991) 'What undergraguates want to know about homosexuality', *Teaching of Psychology,* 18 (4): 243–44.

McNaron, T. (1991) 'Making life more liveable for gays and lesbians on campus', *Educational Record,* 72 (1): 19–22.

Misson, Ray (1999) 'The closet and the classroom: strategies of heterosexist discourse', *Melbourne Studies in Education,* 40 (2): 75–88.

Nardi, Peter M. and Schneider, Beth E. (1998) *Social Perspectives in Lesbian and Gay Studies: A Reader.* London and New York: Routledge.

Nayak, Anoop and Kehily, Mary (1997) 'Masculinities and schooling: why are young men so homophobic?', in Deborah Lynn Steinberg, Debbie Epstein and Richard Johnson (eds), *Border Patrols: Policing the Boundaries of Heterosexuality.* London: Cassell.

Nora, A. Cabrera, A. Hagedorn, L. and Pascarella, E. (1996) 'Differential impacts of academic and social experiences on college-related behavioural outcomes across different ethnic and gender groups at four-year institutions', *Research in Higher Education,* 37 (4): 427–51.

Piernik, T. (1992) 'Lesbian, gay, and bisexual students – radically or invisibly at risk', *Campus Activities Programming,* 25 (6): 47–51.

Pinar, William F. (1998) *'Queer Theory in Education.* Mahwah, NJ: Lawrence Erlbaum Associates.

Plummer, Ken (1992) *Modern Homosexualities: Fragments of Lesbian and Gay Experience.* London: Routledge.

Plummer, Ken (1995) *Telling Sexual Stories: Power, Change and Social Worlds.* London: Routledge.

Probyn, Elspeth (1990) 'Travels in the postmodern: making sense of the local', in Linda J. Nicholson (ed.), *Feminism/Postmodernism.* London and New York: Routledge.

Redman, Peter and Mac an Ghaill, Maírtín (1997) 'Educating Peter: the making of a history man', in Deborah Lynn Steinberg, Debbie Epstein and Richard Johnson (eds), *Border Patrols: Policing the Boundaries of Heterosexuality*. London: Cassell. pp. 162–82.

Renold, Emma (1999) 'Presumed innocence: an ethnographic exploration into the construction of sexual and gender identities in the primary school', unpublished PhD, University of Wales, Cardiff.

Renold, Emma (2000) '"Coming Out": gender, (hetero)sexuality and the primary school', *Gender and Education*, 12 (3): 309–26.

Rhoads, Robert A. (1994) *Coming Out in College: The Struggle for a Queer Identity*. Westport, CT: Bergin & Garvey.

Rich, Adrienne (1980) 'Compulsory heterosexuality and lesbian existence', *Signs*, 54 (4): 631–60.

Richardson, Diane (1996) 'Heterosexuality and social theory', in Diane Richardson (ed.), *Theorising Heterosexuality*. Buckingham: Open University Press. pp. 1–20.

Rubin, Gayle and Butler, Judith (1998) 'Sexual traffic', in Mandy Merck, Naomi Segal and Elizabeth Wright (eds), *Coming out of Feminism?*, Oxford: Blackwell.

Sears, James T. (1992) *Sexuality and the Curriculum: The Politics and Practices of Sexuality Education*. New York: Teachers College Press.

Sedgwick, Eve Kosofsky (1990) *Epistemology of the Closet*. Berkeley, CA: University of California Press.

Sedgwick, Eve Kosofsky (1994) *Tendencies*. London: Routledge.

Seidman, Steven (1995) 'Deconstructing queer theory or the under-theorisation of the social and the ethical', in Linda Nicholson and Steven Seidman (eds), *Social Postmodernism: Beyond Identity Politics*. Cambridge: Cambridge University Press.

Seidman, Steven (1997) *Difference Troubles: Queering Social Theory and Sexual Politics*. Cambridge: Cambridge University Press.

SEU (1999) *Teenage Pregnancy*. London: Social Exclusion Unit.

Shakespeare, Tom, Gillespie-Sells, Kathleen and Davies, D. (1996) *The Sexual Politics of Disability*. London: Cassell.

Silin, Jonathan G. (1995) *Sex, Death and the Education of Children: Our Passion for Ignorance in the Age of AIDS*. New York and London: Teachers College Press.

Smith, G., Kippax, S. and Chapple, M. (1998) 'Secrecy, disclosure and closet dynamics', *Journal of Homosexuality*, 35 (2): 53–73.

Spurlin, William J. (2000) *Lesbian and Gay Studies and the Teaching of English: Positions, Pedagogies and Cultural Politics*. Urbana, IL: NCTE.

Steinberg, Deborah Lynn (1997) 'All roads lead to ... problems with discipline', in Joyce E. Canaan and Debbie Epstein (eds), *A Question of Discipline: Pedagogy, Power and the Teaching of Cultural Studies*. Boulder, CO: Westview.

Steinberg, Deborah Lynn, Epstein, Debbie, and Johnson, Richard (1997) *Border Patrols: Policing the Boundaries of Heterosexuality*. London: Cassell.

Stevens, C. and Walker, B. (1996) 'How residential college students adjust socially and emotionally to first year university', *Higher Education Research and Development*, 15 (2): 201–21.

Taulke-Johnson, Richard A and Rivers, Ian (1998) *Providing a Safe Environment for Lesbian, Gay and Bisexual Students Living in University Accommodation*. Department of Psychology, University of Luton.

Tierney, William, G. and Rhoads, Robert (1993) 'Enhancing academic communities for lesbian, gay, and bisexual faculty', *New Directions for Teaching and Learning*, 53: 43–50.

Tierney, William G. (1993) 'Academic freedom and the parameters of knowledge', *Harvard Educational Review*, 63 (2): 143–60.

Tierney, William G. (1997) *Academic Outlaws: Queer Theory and Cultural Studies in the Academy*. London and Thousand Oaks, CA: Sage Publications.

Tierney, William G. and Dilley, Patrick (1998) 'Constructing knowledge: educational research and gay and lesbian studies', in William J. Pinar (ed.), *Queer Theory in Education*. Mahwah, NJ: Lawrence Erlbaum Associates. pp. 49–71.

Valentine, Gill (1998) '"Sticks and stones may break my bones": A personal geography of harassment' *Antipode* 30 (4): 305–32.

Waldner-Haugrud, L. and Magruder, B. (1996) 'Homosexual identity expression among lesbian and gay adolescents: an analysis of perceived structural associations', *Youth & Society*, 27: 312–33.

Walkerdine, Valerie (1990) *Schoolgirl Fictions*. London: Verso.

Walkerdine, Valerie (1997) *Daddy's Girls*. Basingstoke: Macmillan.

Wallis, Amy and VanEvery, Jo (2000) 'Sexuality in the primary school', *Sexualities*, 3 (4): 409–424.

Wallick, M. (1995) 'Influence of a freshman-year panel presentation on medical students' attitudes toward homosexuality', *Academic Medicine*, 70 (9): 839–41.

Whitty, Geoff (1994) 'Consumer rights versus citizens' rights in contemporary society', *Education, Democracy and Reform*. Auckland: University of Auckland.

Wittig, Monique (1981) 'One is not born a woman', *Feminist Issues*, 1 (2): 47–54.

Wittig, Monique (1992) *The Straight Mind and Other Essays*. Hemel Hempstead: Harvester Wheatsheaf.

17

Lesbian and Gay Bodies of Law

LESLIE J. MORAN

Lesbian and gay scholarship has produced a wealth of material about the significance of law in the production and regulation of same sex sexuality. Its early origins are explored in Lauritsen and Thornstad's study, *The Early Homosexual Rights Movement (1864–1935)* (1974). They draw attention to the particular historical, legal, (the criminal law's total prohibition of sexual relations between men), and intellectual (predominantly the 'psy' sciences, psychology, psychiarty, sexology)[1] contexts out of which this scholarship emerged. Early scholars such as Magnus Hirschfeld (1898), writing on German law and John Addington Symmonds (1928) addressing English law, analysed the interface of legal prohibition, gender, desire and emerging notions of identity and argued for decriminalisation. While contemporary lesbian and gay scholarship is no longer limited to the confines of the criminal prohibition, or the explicit project of decriminalisation, law and its relation to sexual identity and sexual practices continues to be a pervasive theme. At the same time legal scholarship on lesbian and gay issues has had a different history. A sign of this is to be found in the absence of essays on legal scholarship from collections that purport to survey the field of lesbian and gay studies. How is this state of affairs to be explained? It might point to the lack of lesbian and gay legal scholarship. It might suggest a different or slower development of lesbian and gay studies in law. It might be explained as a failure to take account of the flowering of lesbian and gay legal scholarship. In various ways this chapter will offer some insights into the factors that have worked to produce this state of affairs. Its main objective is to offer an insight into the wealth of scholarship in law that addresses lesbian and gay issues. First, it will examine the disciplinary and methodological factors that have influenced the emergence of lesbian and gay legal studies. It will then explore the rich diversity of approaches that make up this growing field of legal scholarship and offer an overview of some of the key themes and current controversies that are emerging within the broad church of lesbian and gay legal scholarship. Finally, it will reflect upon the significance and value of a lesbian and gay legal studies. But before turning attention to specifically legal studies of lesbian and gay issues I want to return to the work on law and same sex sexuality that is to be found across the spectrum of lesbian and gay scholarship. This will provide a background and context in which to consider the factors that have influenced the development of lesbian and gay legal studies and through which the distinctive contribution of legal scholarship might be considered.

BEFORE THE LAW

It is impossible to document all instances of lesbian and gay work that address the law question. The following selection draws attention to the diversity and wealth of that body of work and includes some of its key texts. History scholars such as Goodich, *The Unmentionable Vice: Homosexuality in the Later Mediaeval Period* (1979) and Boswell, *Christianity, Social Tolerance and Homosexuality* (1980) have produced material that offers important insights into the history of law, in particular the regulation of same sex relations through the law of the Catholic Church (known as Canon law) in Europe in the mediaeval period. Bray's work, *Homosexuality in Renaissance England* (1982), examines the historical shift from regulation of same sex relations through the law of the Church to regulation through the secular law of the State in early modern Protestant England. It is a study that has particular importance in a wider global context of colonisation. Studies by Katz (1992), Kinsman (1987) and Wotherspoon (1991) provide historical studies that examine the impact of the colonial expansion of the English legal tradition in the USA, Canada and Australia respectively. Mary McIntosh's ground-breaking study, 'The homosexual role' (1968) and Norton's *Mother Clap's Molly House* (1992) document the operation and impact of law and law enforcement campaigns in early eighteenth-century urban England. Jeffrey Weeks' *Coming Out* (1977) is a pioneering study of law reform debates and activism in the UK. George Chauncey's, *Gay New York* (1994) provides a wealth of data on the role of law in the generation and regulation of gay space in twentieth-century urban America. Copley's work on France (1989) focuses on sexuality and law in a continental European context. Lillian Faderman's work is a still rare example of work that makes reference to lesbians and law (1981, 1983).

Within the social sciences, Laud Humphreys' study, *The Tearoom Trade* (1970)

is a ground-breaking sociological study. It explores the impact of criminal prohibitions on the behavioural practices of men who have sex with men. Within the field of political economy, Phelan (1997) and Kaplan (1997) provide examples of innovative work that examine a range of legal themes relating to justice, citizenship and community. Burke's, *Coming out of the Blue* (1993), Leinen's, *Gay Cops* (1993) and *A Matter of Justice* (Bhurke, 1997) are pioneering studies of gay and lesbian sexuality in the context of policing and more generally in the administration of law and order in Anglo-American contexts. Herek and Berrill's (1992) work on hate crime, and Gary Comstock's (1991) study of violence against lesbians and gay men, raise important questions about the operation of criminal law and the process of criminal justice; about the ability of law to recognise systematic violence, to protect individuals from that violence, and to punish those who perpetuate that violence. Work by Lobel (1986), Taylor and Chandler (1995) and Leventhal and Lundy (1999) has begun to explore violence within lesbian and gay domestic relationships and legal responses to it.

Finally, in the realm of literary and cultural studies, Linda Hart's work *Fatal Women* (1994), examines the relationship between lesbian sexuality and violence by women, in texts ranging from popular culture to criminology and law. Sally Munt's study of feminist interventions in the field of detective fiction, *Murder by the Book?* (1994) raises some important questions about lesbian sexuality, law and popular culture.

Together this work has generated much knowledge about the relationship between law and lesbian and gay sexuality. However, in many instances neither the scholars who wrote the work nor those who resort to it would think of it as legal scholarship. In turn, many legal scholars would not consider these works and the wealth of information that they contain about law, to be legal studies. In part, this state of affairs relates to the particular difficulties that identity politics has generated for the method of law and legal scholarship. Law purports to be merely concerned with the legality, or otherwise, of acts and institutions not identities. In part, it can be explained by way of the disciplinary boundaries that prescribe the objects and method of enquiry and separate one topic and mode of inquiry from another. In order to develop the emergence of the study of lesbian and gay issues within legal studies and to understand the reception of lesbian and gay work in that field, account has to be taken of the nature of the object of study of law. Attention also has to be given to the dominant methodological traditions of legal study. It is to these issues that I now want to turn.

THE OBJECT AND METHOD OF LEGAL SCHOLARSHIP

Legal scholarship has its roots in the western legal tradition (Berman, 1983; Goodrich, 1986). The western legal tradition has two branches; the Common Law, associated with the English legal system and the Civil Law, with its roots in the legal systems of continental Europe. Legal scholarship in Common Law and Civil Law have a common heritage. The common origins of the method of legal scholarship lie in mediaeval continental universities. The first object of study in mediaeval times was not the contemporary law of the town, city, region, or State but the study of the law of an empire that had collapsed, the Roman Empire. Thus, legal scholarship began as the study of an already largely dead law; the rediscovered texts of Roman Law. This ancient written law and commentaries upon it were the object of legal scholarship.

The study of these texts drew extensively upon another well-established scholarly practice that focused attention upon the reading of texts: the monastic practices of reading and commenting upon religious texts. As with the study of religious texts, the study of law developed as a search for

the truth (of law) within the text (of law). As a practice of textual analysis, the relationship between the legal scholar and the text is very specific. Legal scholars are servants of the law. Scholarship is understood as a passive practice of revelation rather than creation. Legal scholarship has developed as a set of practices dedicated to the language of law: of reading the written law and revealing its meaning; of making commentaries in the margins of the text of law; forging links between the many rules in the text to create a unity out of diversity; of explaining distinctions between various rules; outlining the meaning of concepts in the rules; expounding principles not apparent on the surface of the text but supposedly located below, behind or above the text and always already present in it. The aim of this scholarship was to celebrate the law's internal perfection and its autonomy. This tradition of legal scholarship celebrates and preserves law as an archaic and esoteric language. It invests the legal text with special significance and polices its meanings. These specific practices of interpretation deploy a particular method of truth to produce the truth of law. The truth of law is always already in the text of law.

The truth of law can only be found by reading the text of law. The decisions of judges merely explain the 'true' meaning of the text, their decisions are not statements of law. The decisions of others who interpret the law, whether they be State officials, business people, or lay persons, are largely ignored as their interpretations do not formally represent the law. Attention must always focus on the primary texts of law. Finally, as the truth of law is only to be discovered in the text of law, legal scholarship is not to be concerned with the social origins, the social significance of law, its political authority, impact, morality or its relationship to the wider economic or cultural context.

What emerges when we apply the logic of this method to the study of same-sex genital relations in law? First, as a general rule, these relations only appear as objects of law and legal study in a very specific context, by way of particular texts; the written law.[2] The primary texts of the law take various forms: Constitutions, Codes of Law, Statutes. Constitutions are the foundational legal text of a State.[3] They set out the legal basis of the State. Usually they provide a basic description of the institutions of the State, its procedures, powers and responsibilities. The nature of citizenship, the basic civil rights, are usually to be found in the Constitution and amendments to it. Beyond the Constitution, Codes of Law are texts of law that purport to be exhaustive expositions of rules on particular aspects of law, such as human rights or the criminal law (which is understood as law concerned with relations between the State as the keeper of public order and the individual) or civil law with its focus on legal relations between persons. In contrast to Codes of Law, statutes tend to be partial, particular and incomplete statements of rules on a topic, enacted on an *ad hoc* basis. While it is undoubtedly true that Constitutions, Codes of Law and Statutes in many and various ways relate to lesbian and gay relations, a search of these primary sources will find almost no reference to 'lesbian' or 'gay', 'sexual identity', 'sexual orientation' or 'sexual identity'. South Africa's new Constitution, for example, is the first Constitution that has a specific reference to sexual orientation.

However, the absence of such terms does not lead to the conclusion that same sex relations are outside the ambit of Constitutions in particular or written sources of law in general. Let us consider the case of the Constitution of the USA. The infamous decision of the US Supreme Court, Bowers v. Hardwick (1986),[4] addressed the question of sexual orientation and the Constitution. In August 1982 police of the State of Georgia entered the bedroom of Michael Hardwick. They found him having consensual anal intercourse with another man. He was arrested and charged with the crime of sodomy under Georgian law. The Attorney General, a law officer of the State of Georgia, took the decision not to take the matter to trial. In response, Hardwick took the opportunity to challenge the legality of the Georgia sodomy statute. He claimed that the Federal Constitution of the USA gave him fundamental rights that had been violated by the prohibition of consensual sodomy in the Georgian Statute. There is no reference to lesbian or gay, sexuality, sexual preference, sexual orientation or sexual identity in the Constitution or its Amendments. Harwick's argument drew upon the existing language of the Constitutional text to argue for rights that might protect his sexual practices (and thereby his sexual identity) from State interference. He explained his 'rights' by reference to 'the due process clause', 'the Fourteenth Amendment', 'privacy' and the 'Ninth Amendment'. Hardwick's action failed. The Supreme Court, which has the final say on all questions relating to the meaning of the US Constitution, concluded that consensual homosexual sodomy, even in the privacy of the home, could not be understood in terms of a fundamental right protected by the Constitution. Common to both the practice of the Supreme Court and Hardwick's claim is the practice of reading sexuality into the text in general and the specific language of the text of the law that on the surface appears to make no reference to it. All parties to the case utilised previous decisions of the Courts where the Courts had reflected on and given specific meaning to the language of the Constitutional text, to support their arguments. The example of Bowers v. Hardwick draws attention to the way in which sexual practices and issues about sexual identity might appear in law by way of archaic terms, such as 'sodomy' and by way of strange and esoteric 'legal language' that seems, on the face of it, to be remote from matters of sexuality.

This state of affairs is not unique to Constitutional codes or practices of reading those particular texts of law. Criminal codes (purporting to set out an exhaustive list of acts that threaten public order) and criminal statutes, such as sexual offences statutes, make almost no reference to 'lesbian' or 'gay'. However, archaic terms such as buggery, sodomy, soliciting, importuning, indecency, to name but a few, might make reference to, and in some instances, make exclusive reference to, same-sex sexual relations and particular sexual identities.[5] Likewise, civil codes and statutes, for example relating to domestic and family relations rarely make a direct reference to lesbian or gay. In turn, terms such as 'parent', 'family', 'child', 'marriage' rarely make reference to the heterosexual imperative that is almost inevitably 'discovered' in by way of the legal method of reading the text of law.

Let us turn to another example to illustrate these points. This time the example is the UK case of Fitzpatrick v. Sterling Houing Association (Fitzpatrick, 1999). This case deals with a statute relating to housing tenancies. The House of Lords (the final court of appeal in the UK) had to decide whether, in the context of the law (the Rent Act 1977) regulating domestic housing tenancies, 'spouse' or 'family' could be defined to include the same sex partner of the recently deceased. The court concluded that 'spouse' did not include a partner in a same-sex domestic relationship, but such a relationship might fall within the legal meaning of the word 'family'. Again, we see that questions of sexual identity and sexual practices are made to appear in law not so much by way of an explicit reference to sexuality but by way of words that make up the pre-existing text of law, even where those words might seem to be remote from sexuality or indifferent to it. But to stop at this point would be premature. We need to examine the impact of legal method on the appearance of same-sex genital relations in law in more detail.

The method of law demands that meaning is produced according to specific rituals, in particular, by way of the citation of earlier examples of the use of key terms in decided cases of particular courts. Citation is a practice of repetition through which the appearance of the consistency of meaning is produced across time and space. Through citation the experience of law's authority is an experience of stability

and duration; of wisdom made ancient (Goodrich, 1990).

However, while repetition might lead one to conclude that the method of legal scholarship limits, restricts and prohibits new meaning, such a conclusion would misunderstand the practice of citation and the process of repetition. Repetition is also an important technique by which change is created in law. Change effected by repetition merely draws attention to the way in which, in law, changes in meaning must be produced by reference to past decisions and past authority.

A good example of repetition to create novelty is to be found in an article on, 'Developments in gay rights' in *The New Law Journal* (Kirby, 2000). In considering the exciting developments in the House of Lords' decision in Fitzpatrick v. Sterling Housing Association, referred to above, where the Court concluded that a long-term gay partner was a member of 'the family' of the deceased, the author, Kirby, examines the Court's decision in the following way. He focuses upon 'the authorities' that one of the judges, Lord Slynn, used to reach his decision; Brock v. Wollans, a case decided in 1949, Hawes v. Evenden from 1953 and Watson v. Lucas of 1980. How does the citation of these older cases work to produce the pre-existing truth of the 'new' meaning of 'family' arising in the Fitzpatrick case? Let us look briefly at each case and the effect of their conjunction.

All are cited on the basis that they 'explain' the meaning of the term 'family'. Brock v. Wollans, which concerned 'informally adopted children', concluded that 'family' might include informal as well as legally binding relationships. In Watson v. Lucas the court concluded that 'family' could include a long-term mistress. Hawes v. Evenden is presented as a case that accepted that an unmarried heterosexual partner in a relationship, where there were children, could be a member of the 'family'. And finally, Watson v. Lucas reached the same conclusion in the absence of children.

A first reaction to these cases might be that they have nothing whatsoever to do with same-sex relationships, as they appear to be exclusively concerned with 'family' in a heterosexual context. As such, they could be said to provide no authority in support of the conclusion reached in the case of Fitzpatrick. Following these cases, as precedent, could lead to a conclusion hostile to lesbian and gay partners as members of the 'family'. While such a conclusion is possible, it is not the outcome in this case. So what is the 'true meaning' of these cases? Kirby explains that these cases 'illustrated how the word [family] had been applied flexibly' (Kirby, 2000: 550). He draws attention to the way the appeal judge, Lord Slynn, searched for the underlying principle demonstrated in these cases, and found 'flexibility'. More specifically, the resort to these cases and the particular reading offered of them enabled Lord Slynn to present his new reading of 'family' as not only inclusive of same sex relations but as a meaning that was already embedded in previous decisions; as something that had already happened in the past.

This example is of interest in various ways. It draws attention to the method of law used to reach a legal conclusion. Neither judge nor legal commentator move beyond the law to explain or justify the dramatic shift in meaning evidenced in the decision of the final court of appeal. It also draws attention to the importance of repetition in legal decisions and in legal scholarship. Saying something new in law has to be done by saying the same old thing; discovering something new in the past, giving novelty the gloss of age.

LEGAL SCHOLARSHIP

These reflections on the object and the method of law provide the context in which contemporary legal scholarship on lesbian and gay issues has emerged. I now want to consider how legal scholars have responded to the rise of lesbian and gay activism and scholarship. There is a fast-growing body of legal literature that addresses lesbian and gay issues. Much of the work is to be found

in the law journals of North American universities and an increasing number of monographs and scholarly articles are coming from other Common Law jurisdictions such as the UK, Australia, Canada and New Zealand. While some of this scholarship has emerged within the context of the dominant tradition of legal scholarship, there is much work that lies beyond. I now want to turn to examine the different approaches to lesbian and gay issues within legal scholarship.

The 'Black Letter' of Law

In contemporary legal scholarship adoption of the methods I have outlined above is known as the 'black letter' or positivist approach to law. This continues to be a dominant approach within legal scholarship. As a mode of scholarship addressing questions of lesbian and gay practices and identity, 'black letter' legal scholars have been concerned with cataloguing and describing those written and unwritten (judge-made) rules and juridical practices that make reference to and produce sexual relations between persons of the same sex in law. This scholarship tends to proceed by way of an examination of established topics of legal scholarship such as the criminal or civil code, through categories such as sexual offences, or family law, civil rights and human rights. It documents the ancient and esoteric language of the law and collects and catalogues the citations through which its meaning is produced, policed and perpetuated. Responses to the conclusion that the law produces and sustains the social exclusion of lesbians and gay men might take various forms. The evidence of social exclusion in law might be presented as a justification for law reform. This takes issues of sexuality out of the frame of legal scholarship and turns them into questions of politics, morality, or sociological enquiry. The law scholar might suggest 'existing' legal concepts and devise forms of legal language for new legislation. On the other hand, a scholar steeped in the positivist tradition might embark upon a search for an 'existing' legal rule, or an obscure interpretation of a key term, or offer a re-reading of a case that reveals an 'underlying' principle that might overcome the limits of the existing meanings of the text of law.

This mode of scholarship seeks to preserve the methodological and disciplinary requirements of traditional legal scholarship that support the idea of law as an autonomous practice. While this approach may respond to the political, social and moral issues raised by lesbian and gay experience, activism and scholarship, it must formally deny that these concerns are the stuff of legal practice in general or of legal scholarship in particular.

By way of this dominant tradition much pioneering work has been done to document the law and to produce guides to the law that address the legal needs of lesbians and gay men (Crane, 1982; Gooding, 1992). Much important work is to be found in the field of domestic and international human rights law (Heinze, 1995; Waaldijk and Clapham, 1993; Wintermute, 1995). This scholarship addresses the formal absence of any reference to lesbian, gay, or sexual orientation in both domestic and international human rights declarations. It particularly works to discover the always already said of principles and rules within the text that will render the inferior legal status of same-sex sexual relations as contrary to human rights (Kaplan, 1997). To date the rule and principle that has proved to be most successful in certain situations is that of privacy.[6] Anti-discrimination rules and principles (Bamforth, 2000; Chapman and Mason, 1999; Majury, 1994; Wintermute, 1995) and liberty and equality (Kaplan, 1997) have become more recent legal objects of consideration.

The virtues of this approach to scholarship are various. Here the existing law is both the problem and the solution for lesbians and gay men. Resort to concepts and principles that are said to be previously unarticulated or unspoken, offer a solution that appears to be already present in the law. This solution appears to avoid the trials and tribulations of reform through the political process. In particular it avoids the dangers of majority rule, a feature of the democratic process that is particularly problematic for reforms associated with a minority interest. Resort to legal principle is also presented as a better option as it is resort to the cool reason of law rather than the passion of politics. It is a resort to the certainty of tradition and continuity that is said to be the law rather than the uncertainty of novelty and change that is politics. But these advantages have a cost. They demand that we forget that the courts have long been implicated in producing, sustaining and perpetuating the social exclusion of lesbians and gay men. They also preserve and perpetuate the myth of the divide between law and sexuality, law and politics, law and society.

Law Beyond the 'Black Letter'

A second approach to lesbian and gay issues within legal scholarship is to be found within an approach to law that is more closely aligned with legal philosophy, which in the Anglo-American world is called Jurisprudence.[7] The contemporary origins of legal philosophy's concern with lesbian and gay sexuality is to be found in the context of debates that emerged out of proposals produced by the Wolfenden Committee (1957), a UK governmental committee, to decriminalise certain sexual relations between men over the age of 21 in private in England and Wales.[8] These proposals for reform gave rise to a debate about the relationship between law and morality. The reform proposals were supported by H.L.A. Hart, a well-known English legal philosopher, in *Law, Liberty and Morality* (1963). Adopting a libertarian perspective associated with the writings of J.S. Mill, Hart argued that there ought to be a limit to the reach of the law. The law should not interfere in the private lives of individuals where the acts in question cause no harm. In contrast to this, Lord Devlin (a retired judge from the House of Lords) resorted to a utilitarian/communitarian argument in *The Enforcement of Morals* (1965). Lord Devlin argued that the law should reflect and enforce prevailing morality (which in this instance, he argued, was hostile to homosexuality). Law should also follow the will of the majority, which he suggested was against decriminalisation. These perspectives still inform much activism, law reform initiatives and scholarship. They have been particularly evident in the context of initiatives that focus on the importance of 'privacy'.

More recently scholars have expanded the range of legal philosophical positions used in support of lesbian and gay initiatives to include natural law and natural rights (Mohr, 1988; Bamforth, 1997). Those who adopt a natural law and natural rights position argue that there is a set of fundamental laws or rights that are basic to any good ordered society. Natural law and natural rights are offered as that foundational morality. Their origin and authority are not the institutions of the State or the practices of democracy but in their divine origin or in the assertion that they are inherent in the very idea of good order in society. In practice, they offer an absolute yardstick by which the worth of man-made (positive) laws might be challenged. They also provide a set of underlying principles through which the existing law might be interpreted. Finally, they offer a goal that law makers ought to strive for when forming and reforming the law.

This resort to natural law and natural rights by gay scholars is somewhat surprising. It is a legal philosophy that has traditionally been used by those hostile to lesbian and gay rights. A good example of this use of natural rights is to be found in the writings of John Finnis (1983, 1993). Finnis argues that the heterosexual couple and family are the basic building blocks of any good ordered society. For Finnis natural law and natural rights are fundamental laws and rights that produce the social order as a heterosexual order. In this scheme of things lesbians and gay men are antithetical to a good and ordered society and their claim to rights within such a society must be denied.

Gay philosophers and legal scholars have challenged this hostile stance and attempted to rewrite natural law/rights for a lesbian and gay politics. Good examples of this work are to be found in Richard D. Mohr's book *Gays/Justice* (1988) and in Nicholas Bamforth's study, *Sexuality, Morals and Justice* (1997). Both argue for a secular metaphysics of morals (natural rights) as a moral basis for the recognition of lesbian and gay rights and the reform of law. The very humanity of lesbians and gay men and the need to recognise and respect that humanity are the basis for the inclusion of lesbians and gay rights within the scheme of those fundamental rights that are the foundation of any well ordered society.

Mohr applies this perspective to develop a critique of US constitutional law. Bamforth pursues his project at a more abstract level, through a critique of various schools of legal philosophy. He offers a legal philosophical position that might have significance in any jurisdiction, be it national or international. Both authors clearly demonstrate the viability of a natural law/natural rights position in support of recognition of lesbian and gay rights.

In general by bringing morality into the frame of legal studies this brand of legal scholarship departs from the dominant 'black letter' or positivist position. Law is not just a set of rules but a moral order intimately concerned with justice. Legal scholarship might legitimately resort to something (morality) outside the law in order to develop a critical analysis of the rules and the concepts deployed in law. Sources of authority might include references to philosophical texts and argument. At the same time, the turn to legal philosophy in general and morality in particular often sustains a focus upon the isolated text of law. The text of law is the source and manifestation of an underlying morality. Thus, an interest in questions of morality and justice is not necessarily inimical to many of the methodological requirements, limits and restraints of the traditional method of legal scholarship. Nor does an engagement with questions of morality necessarily lead to a willingness to think about the law in terms that might draw attention to the cultural, political and historical factors that inform and invest law and legal practice.

LEGAL STUDIES BEYOND 'LAW'

The two approaches to questions of lesbian and gay sexuality in law set out above now need to be set within the context of a much more diverse picture of legal scholarship, particularly found within the Common Law world. The twentieth century has seen the emergence of a wide range of schools of legal thought: American legal realism, the law in context movement, socio-legal studies, sociology of law, critical legal studies and legal studies informed by Marxism, theories of race and feminism.[9] While it is impossible to go into any detail about these schools of legal scholarship, each, in different ways, brings the social, the cultural and the political within the parameters of legal study. They challenge the positivist conceptions of the object of legal study. They also challenge the methodological assumptions and practices of positivist legal scholarship. Each demands that legal scholarship pursues the study of law by way of questions of power, the politics of social order (and disorder), the practices of social inclusion and social exclusion. In various ways they incorporate work undertaken in the social sciences and the humanities into legal studies.

It is in this context that lesbian and gay legal scholarship has been most receptive to the social sciences and, more recently, arts and humanities, in general and material generated by way of lesbian and gay studies in particular. This material has been directly incorporated into legal studies and legal scholarship alongside more traditional legal material such as legislation and judicial decisions. Other intellectual perspectives and developments such as Marxism and post-Marxist, post-structuralism and feminism have also been of particular importance. Evidence of this is to be found in a wide selection of legal scholarship on lesbian and gay issues (Backer, 1998; Bowers, 1997; Boyd, 1999; Davies, 1999; Eaton, 1994, 1995; Halley, 1993, 1994; Herman, 1994, 1995; Loizidou, 1998; Moran, 1996, 1997, 1998; Robson, 1992, 1998; Stychin, 1995, 1998, 2000). More recently, exciting developments within postcolonial scholarship, critical race theory and Latino/latina critical scholarship have begun to influence lesbian and gay legal scholarship (Hutchinson, 1999; Jefferson, 1998; Phillips, 1997, Valdes, 1998, 1999).[10]

While the legal work that falls within these parameters is diverse it has certain common characteristics. Methodologically it stands opposed to the positivist tradition of legal scholarship. It is also in contrast to the legal scholars who take up the moral philosophy of legal theory. While taking law as the object of study these scholars employ not only legal theory but also literary, political and social theory in their work. The critiques that emerge challenge the divide between law and politics. They seek to examine and explore the place of law within the wider social order. Law is both constituted by and constitutive of the wider social order. Another common focus of this body of work is identity. Dominated by perspectives that emphasize the social, cultural and political factors at work in identities, much of the work has focused upon law as a context in which identity is given form and meaning in societies. Lesbian and gay sexualities are not so much outside the law, and as such something the law might respond to, but something always already in the law as a social and political practice, generated through legal categories and legal practices. It is a body of work that explores the strategic significance of identity, its positive effects, its limits, and its problems in and through the law.

KEY THEMES: FRAGMENTS AND CONTEXTS

My focus upon the methodological distinctions that have influenced the emergence of lesbian and gay legal scholarship has produced a picture of the diversity of that scholarship. Any attempt to embark upon 'key themes' of such a diverse body of work raises problems. 'Key themes' tend to prefix and totalise scholarship. They also might suggest some rationalist project that underlies, guides and interconnects lesbian and gay legal scholarship. Lesbian legal scholar, Ruthann Robson cautions against such approaches in the opening pages of her book *Sappho Goes to Law School* (1998). The specific context of her reflection is the enterprise of writing a book about lesbian legal theory. She draws a parallel between such a project and our knowledge and understanding of Sappho. While Sappho is a name that refers to someone who lived in the past, Robson suggests that 'knowledge' of Sappho is a 'largely fantastical' project (1998: xiv). The fantastical quality of our 'knowledge' about Sappho is given graphic form in Monique Wittig and Sande Zeig's book, *Lesbian Peoples: Material for a Dictionary* (1979). Their entry for Sappho is an empty page. The meanings given to the name Sappho tell us more about our hopes, desires and expectations than they do about Sappho herself. Robson explains that to write the book of lesbian legal theory is as, 'problematic as Sappho' (1998: xv). Robson draws a parallel between telling the full story of Sappho's life which is 'largely fantastical' and the problem of reducing the complexities of lesbian identity to a singular 'lesbian legal theory'. Such a project is, in part, problematic as it will fail to tell the totality of lesbian diversity. Its fantastical quality demands that we procede with some caution. However, its 'fantastical' quality is also something to be celebrated as it draws attention to lesbian legal theory as a space through which existing worlds might be reimagined and transformed and new worlds created. Thus, rather than thinking of what follows as a summary of the absolute truth, or totality or uniformity of lesbian and gay legal studies, I would suggest we follow Robson's suggestion that it be thought of as a series of fragments and contexts that are

influencing, informing and generating the rich diversity of lesbian and gay legal studies. I offer five snapshots: the identity debates; criminalisation and its discontents; human rights the new hegemony; violence and the politics of hate; and institutional struggles.

The Identity Debates

The identity debates are a long and pervasive theme within lesbian and gay legal scholarship (and in more general writings on same-sex relations and law) that have their origins in the nineteenth century (Moran, 1996). They take the form of a question, 'what is the nature of identity?' Answers take a binary form. Lesbian and gay identity is nature or nurture; the manifestation of essence or effect of society; biology or culture; born or made; genes or lifestyle; unchangeable or malleable. For a long time activists, reformers and scholars have promoted the idea of homosexual practices and thereby homosexuality as nature, essence and more recently genetic. From this point of departure, it is argued that legal vilification, criminalisation, and other modes of legal exclusion are irrational. Law ought to concern itself with behaviour that is subject to the will, and thereby subject to control and the fit object for punishment when the will, subject to the control imposed by law, fails.

In contrast to this essentialist view of identity is work that takes (homo)sexuality as a social, cultural, political and historical phenomenon. Here the interface between law and homosexual identity is neither necessary nor inevitable, being a site of and an effect of political struggle. Change might be advocated to recognise the legitimacy of lesbian and gay sexuality and to reduce the negative effects of law that produce and perpetuate its inferior and marginal status.

Identity debates informed by post-structuralism have raised a particular challenge to these ways of thinking. In contrast to earlier manifestations of the identity debates that took identity as a natural or social given, the post-structural position questions the significance of identity. Particular attention has focused upon the inability of any identity category to be an exhaustive expression of the individual and the failure of categories of identity to stand for the fullness or totality of that person. Gail Mason's work (1997) addresses these issues in the context of work on violence against lesbians. She examines the way in which the identity category 'women', used in work on violence against women, assumes that all women are heterosexual. Thereby violence against women is given a heterosexual context. That heterosexual context is also a context of intimacy; most violence against women is violence by men who are known to those women who are objects of violence. In part this threatens to exclude and distort lesbian experiences of violence which, for example, is more likely to be violence performed by strangers and may not be reducible to a heterosexual context. At the same time Mason's argument is not merely that lesbian experiences of violence are different from other types of violence against other women. She also raises the question about the inter-relationship between these identity categories; between 'lesbian' and 'woman' in the experience of violence as a lesbian. The experience of anti-lesbian violence is intimately connected with but different from violence against women. In simple terms, lesbian brings together sexuality, that might point to distinctions between women and gender that suggest connections between women who might be separated by sexuality. Phelan, a lesbian political theorist, has addressed questions of identity in the context of the interface between race, ethnicity and lesbian sexuality (Phelan, 1997). She again draws attention to the way identities fail to represent the fullness and diversity of the individual. They put in place a series of assumptions that Phelan characterises as 'ontological separatism'. Identities separate out the racial, the ethnic and the sexual. Thus, Phelan notes, lesbians are always assumed to be white, and women defined by

racial and ethnic characteristics are assumed to be heterosexual (see also Eaton, 1995; Hutchinson, 1999). Francisco Valdes's work has explored these issues in the context of gay male identity and latino identity (Valdes, 1998, 1999). Peter Kwan (1997) considered the inter-relationship between American Chinese identity and sexuality in his study of the police response and police reactions to the gay serial killer Jeffrey Dahmer.

This work points to some of the limits of identity politics, in particular, the failure of our existing concepts of identity not only to name individual experience but to name collective experiences. One of the effects of this is to be found in the context of anti-discrimination law that puts the assumptions of 'ontological separatism' into practice (Eaton, 1995); you must be black or gay, latina or lesbian. Where sexual orientation is absent from the categories named in anti-discrimination provisions, sexuality might be used to trump other forms of discrimination and deny access to a remedy. Even where all categories are reflected in the law, the either/or logic might prevail, leading to the marginalisation or denial of important aspects of the experience of social exclusion and the legal claim. Legal scholars have also drawn attention to the ways in which 'ontological separation' is also political separation between individuals and between communities. This has the potential to produce conflicts between groups who are socially excluded as they fight for access to limited legal resources. It feeds a logic that produces hierarchies of exclusion; of good victims and bad victims, of the deserving and undeserving minority (Hutchinson, 1999; Valdes, 1997, 1998). It infuses disputes about the validity of claims upon the law and informs disputes about lesbian and gay rights as special or exceptional (and thereby unworthy) rights claims.

The challenge is to conceptualise the ontological and political connections. The point of departure for lesbian and gay legal scholarship has been the idea of 'intersectionality', a concept borrowed from feminist critical race scholarship. It emerged as a tool to explain, analyse and critique the marginalisation of black women within both critical race scholarship and feminist work (Krenshaw, 1989, 1991). It points to the either/or logic of these two critical and political perspectives. It draws attention to the way 'ontological separatism' feeds into essentialist notions of identity.

However, various lesbian and gay legal scholars have commented upon the limits of 'intersectionality' and offered critiques (Hutchinson, 1999: Kwan, 1997; Valdes, 1999). For example, Gail Mason (2001) has drawn attention to the way 'intersectionality' is a metaphor that has a limited capacity to adequately capture the simultaneity of the many axes of social distinction. Following Elizabeth Grosz (1994), Mason suggests that there is a gridlike formation implicit in the idea of intersection that:

> conceptualises differences or race, sexuality or gender as autonomous structures external to the individual subject. The dilemma is that before one axis can intersect, cross, cut or passover another, it must already exist, elsewhere, in a state of divergence or separation from the others. Each axis must function independently from, outside of, of prior to, its intersection with other axes. (Mason, 2001: 66)

In contrast to this, Mason argues that we need metaphors that conceptualise the way in which differences are always already implicated in each other.

Other lesbian and gay scholars have offered alternative terms. Kwan has proposed 'cosynthesis' (1997: 1257). Valdes has attempted to develop a complex of analytical categories including 'interconnectivity', 'multiplicity', 'complexities of compoundedness', 'positionality' and 'relationality' (Valdes, 1997: 55). In part, these terms seek to explain and produce the ontological complexity that is the experience of the individual. The multiplicity that makes up the individual experience also has another significance. It purports to draw attention to the way individuals' experiences are interconnected, generating thereby a common or a 'universal experience' (Hutchinson, 1999; Kwan, 1997). Thus, in part, these terms seek to explain and produce the social bonds that connect individuals and make alliances possible (Phelan, 1997).

This is a new and rapidly developing aspect of lesbian and gay legal scholarship. There is as yet no consensus over the most useful or insightful metaphor. Phelan's work rings a note of caution as to the political significance of these developments. The connections, she suggests, are likely to be volatile and unstable, filled with contradictions and ambiguities, due to the diversity that is imminent in any situation. At best these connections ought to be thought of in terms of temporary alliances that may have specific and limited goals and objectives (Phelan, 1995, 1997).

Criminal Preoccupations

Another preoccupation in legal scholarship is the criminal law. In part, this can be explained by the fact that when same-sex relations did appear in and through the law, they tended to appear most frequently by way of archaic terms such as buggery or sodomy or gross indecency, which are legal terms associated with the criminal law. It was in this context that sexual relations between persons (predominantly men) of the same sex came before the law. This focus on criminal law is one important factor that has contributed to the dominance of a concern with gay men in same-sex legal scholarship. It has given rise to a very gender-specific concern with law as a form of social prohibition and gender-specific demands for decriminalisation that is usually understood in terms of liberation and freedom (Majury, 1994: Stanko and Curry, 1997).

In part this also reflects the general absence of references to the sexuality of women in law and the particular silence relating to sexual relations between women in law. However, there is a growing body of work, much of it inspired by feminism that draws attention to the fact that women's experience of law in general is different from that of men and in particular that lesbians' experience of law is very different from that of gay men (Robson, 1992, 1998; Majury, 1994: Mason, 1995, 1997b; Boyd, 1999). These differences might be explained in terms of the different economic position of women, the different social status of women, the different priorities of women, and the different social experiences of women (Majury, 1994; Boyd, 1999). As histories of the sexual relations between women in law emerge it becomes clear that same-sex sexual relations between women rather than being absent from the field of law were policed in different ways by way of different legal categories in different spheres of law, for example, by way of the regulations of the family and patriarchal relations found in private law rather than by way of public law, in particular the criminal law (Crompton, 1980; Faderman, 1981, 1983; Robson, 1992). To read the law's response to genital relations between men as the same as the regulation of genital relations between women would be a mistake. This suggests that established agendas of scholarship may perpetuate silences rather than offer a challenge to them. Different agendas and different approaches might be necessary.

In those places where decriminalisation has been achieved and where a strong feminist and lesbian and gay movement has emerged, the lesbian and gay legal agenda has become more diverse. This reflects and produces a recognition of the close relationship between sexuality and gender and the idea of sexuality as an identity and a lifestyle. Demands for law reform are no longer confined to a focus upon criminal law or the prohibition of specific (homo)sexual practices but expand into aspects of private law: domestic relations, employment, property, housing and succession, taxation, parenthood and children. In the realm of public law the wider ambit of relations between the state and the individual is being addressed: lesbian and gay exclusion from the military, access to state education (especially sex education), freedom of expression, censorship and the media,

prisons, access to welfare, benefits the protection of sexual minorities in the State Constitution.

Human Rights: The New Hegemony

International law, in particular the international law of human rights, has become a site of intervention and critique of growing importance. This might be explained in various ways. In part it reflects the globalisation of liberal democratic political traditions which, with the fall of communism, have taken on global significance. Human rights is the new hegemony. In part it reflects the growth of international and supranational legal orders, such as the European Convention of Human Rights, which have provided remedies against the State. In part it reflects the impact of these developments within individual States. For example, in the UK a minor revolution is taking place by way of the Human Rights Act 1998, which came into effect in October 2000. Based upon the European Convention of Human Rights, it seeks to provide a new human rights foundation for law in domestic law. Lesbian and gay scholarship on human rights is both a reflection of and an important contribution to such developments (Heinze, 1995; Waaldijk, 1993; Wintermute, 1995).

However, this human rights revolution does not offer an instant or pervasive solution for all lesbian and gay legal ills as is sometimes suggested. For example, the UK Parliament refused to include specific reference to sexual orientation in the Human Rights Act. The US experience shows that a strong focus on fundamental civil rights in the US Constitution has provided no guarantee that lesbian and gay rights will necessarily be recognised or protected. Lesbian and gay legal scholars have questioned the popularity and usefulness of legal concepts such as 'privacy' (Kendall, 1992), 'equality' (Majury, 1994) and the use of 'sexual orientation' as the basis for anti-discrimination initiatives in particular and human rights more generally (Bamforth, 2000; Majury, 1994; Wintermute, 1995). All, in different ways, point to the limited success of the human rights agenda. In turn, they point to new limits on the progess of change for the benefit of lesbians and gay men. At best, human rights might open up new landscapes for activism within and in relation to the law.

Violence and the Politics of Hate

A rapidly emerging issue in lesbian and gay activism and legal scholarship is violence (Jenness and Broad, 1997; Mason and Tomsen, 1997; Mason, 2001; Moran, 2001). Out of community activism, often in response to acts of extreme violence come 'victim surveys'. These seek to document violence and calculate the extent of violence that is otherwise hidden from official view. In the USA the National Lesbian and Gay Taskforce has played a key role co-ordinating data from local victim surveys. In the UK, Stonewall, a national lesbian and gay lobby group produced the first national victim survey on homophobic violence (Mason and Palmer, 1996).[11] Demands for changes in the day-to-day practice of policing and institutional change have followed. In the USA, law reforms to promote further data collection, the Hate Crime Statistics Act 1990, have been introduced. Demands for new offences and changes to the scale of punishment have been other initiatives (Jennes and Grattet, 2001).

The resort to the phrase 'hate crime' within this context is of special interest. 'Hate crime' is rapidly solidifying into a new legal term. It is used to separate 'ordinary crime' from crimes of hate. This separation is associated with calls for new offences and more generally with calls for more severe punishment. In the UK the police have produced a definition of 'hate crime': 'Hate crime is taken to mean any crime where the perpetrator's prejudice against any identifiable group of people is a factor in determining who is victimised' (ACPO, 2000, Introduction, 2). As the

police handbook notes, 'this is a broad and inclusive definition' (ibid., Introduction, 2). This inclusive approach is to be contrasted with much North American experience where there have been many stuggles over the categories of 'hate' that are to be accommodated in the phrase 'hate crime'. In particular there have been and continue to be ongoing battles to include homophobic violence under the category of 'hate' (Jennes and Grattet, 2001; Jacobs and Potter, 1998).

These struggles are of interest in various ways. They point to a new dimension to the relationship between law and same-sex genital relations. This relationship can no longer be thought of in terms of law as a means whereby particular sexualities might be prohibited and excluded. While the incorporation of homophobic violence within 'hate crime' is concerned with practices of social exclusion, by way of violence and by way of the failure of the police and criminal justice to take that violence seriously, it is also a demand by lesbian and gay men for the law to produce a new socially inclusive social order. Law has become a positive force to protect and preserve sexual identity rather than a negative force to be limited. Of particular significance is the requirement that this new legal and social order is to be produced by reference to particular identity categories, which are understood as group identities rather than individual or personal identities. This heralds a departure in law, which has traditionally formally avoided any identity category other than the abstract category of 'persons'.

It also heralds the emergence of new contexts that will problematise and challenge lesbian and gay identity politics. While this is not the place to develop a full-blown critique of 'hate crime' in a lesbian and gay context, some of the problems will be briefly outlined. While the generic approach to 'hate crime' found in the new UK police guide might avoid the problem of separating out forms of hatred and types of identity to which the various hatreds relate, we should note that 'domestic violence' is excluded from the UK definition of 'hate crime'. This echoes the US experience in which violence against women has been excluded from the category of the 'hate crime'. The reasons for this exclusion are various. One justification is that laws, policies and procedures that address violence against women are already well established. Here 'hate crime' is an initiative that seeks to develop services otherwise denied. However, much feminist scholarship continues to challenge any assumption that violence against women is adequately dealt with. Other arguments are even more problematic. One is that such is the level of violence against women, that to call it 'hate crime' would be politically unacceptable as it would reveal too much 'hate'. Another is that 'hate crime' is understood as an act of violence motivated not by personal animosity but by hostility to a group identity (Jacobs and Potter, 1998, Ch. 5). Both arguments, in different ways, are profoundly problematic. They suggest that the category of 'hate crime' might perpetuate and generate new silences and reinscribe, rather than challenge, the personal and political divisions. The suggestion that violence performed by someone who is in an intimate relation with the victim is experienced as less traumatic than violence motivated by a more abstract hatred has the potential to be profoundly reactionary. It also has the potential to create new opportunities for blaming the victim. Finally, it assumes that it is possible to separate out violence, gender and sexuality. Mason's work on violence against lesbians clearly problematises such arguments (1997 a, b).

A major challenge for future lesbian and gay scholarship arises when resort to law is advocated by lesbians and gay men, when law is taken as a resource to protect, preserve and institutionalise sexual identity. This relation to law is a demand to have access to the violence of law. It is a demand that is in stark contrast to much of lesbian and gay legal scholarship that has, in so many instances, documented the operation of law as violence and offered critiques of law's violence against lesbians and gay men. Ruthan Robson's reflections on violence as a lesbian resource in her book on

lesbian legal theory, is a rare example of an attempt to address this question (cf. Scalettar, 2000).

In the chapter, 'Incendiary categories: lesbian/violence/law' (Robson, 1998), Robson gives an overview of recent jurisprudential and philosophical scholarship (Cover, 1986; Derrida, 1992) that has drawn attention to the relationship between law and violence. Law's violence is manifest not only through the capacity to punish, which in certain jurisdictions may take the extreme form of taking life itself, but in the capacity to draw and enforce distinctions and to impose meanings (the violence of the word).

Robson draws attention to various problems that might arise by way of our resort to the violence of the law through hate crime legislation. She points to that particular context as a moment not only when lesbians and gays resort to law's violence but, in the context of the US Hate Crimes Statistics Act, are simultaneously subject to it. This occurs by way of qualifications that were added to the Act in response to the inclusion of 'sexual orientation' as a recognised category of hatred. The reference to 'sexual orientation' was not to be interpreted as a positive reference to lesbian or gay sexuality. Robson also suggests that we experience law's violence in that Act through the distinctions between various identities to be found in the Act. More generally she suggests that a desire for law's violence will impose limits on lesbianism by way of distinctions between good lesbians and bad lesbians and through normalisation of lesbian identity. As such, she points to the contradictions that lesbians (and one might add gay men) are likely to face in demanding access to law's violence.

Robson also wants to argue for another relation to violence. She 'want[s] to claim violence as an attribute of lesbianism' (1998, 16). She suggests that this violence be re-named, by way of a different metaphor, fire, that has a gender-specific resonance. This, she explains, is a violence that appears to be ultimately against the violence of law, and is a challenge to law. As such this is 'good violence', that provokes an 'emancipatory change' in contrast with the 'bad violence' of law that conserves and is conservative.

While Robson raises some important questions about the relation between lesbian/violence/law, her analysis seems to hesitate when the relation to law's violence is addressed. The renaming of violence as 'fire' seems in part to be an attempt to distance lesbian from violence at the same time as it seeks to make the connection. Likewise lesbian violence as a violence outside law's violence repeats the separation in another guise. Lesbian violence as good violence is the closest we get to the proximity of lesbian and violence. It would be churlish to demand that such a pioneering piece of scholarship should provide, even if it were possible, all the answers. What it does do is draw attention to a difficult issue that urgently needs to be addressed.

Institutional Politics

Finally, a theme that has pervaded this chapter has been the disciplinary and institutional context and the struggles in and through which lesbian and gay issues might come into being within legal scholarship. In part, the picture painted is one of many different approaches to that scholarly agenda. The linear narrative format of the chapter promotes the idea that these different approaches are to be understood as successive, suggesting a movement towards an ultimate scholarship that in turn generates an ultimate truth. Implicated in this is an idea of 'progress' and, more specifically, an idea of progress as conflict in which each successive approach struggles against the status quo for dominance both within the institutional context of legal scholarship in general and within the specific context of lesbian and gay legal scholarship (cf. Robson, 1998). It is perhaps in this context that the debate about the inability of identity to fully represent an individual and the challenge of diversity within and between individuals has

an immediate significance. Investments in different methodological positions are implicated in identity formation in and through scholarship. Rather than the emergence of an underlying logic, the realisation of an absolute truth, we perhaps need to think of this body of work as evidencing an on-going struggle with many sites, contexts, identities. Its diversity ought not to be thought of in terms of a logic of either/or. Rather than methodologies in conflict, in an either/or stuggle for dominance the challenge is to think in terms of interconnections and alliances.

CONCLUSION

There is much to celebrate in the rise of such a rich and complex body of legal work. Signs of an emerging discipline of lesbian and gay legal studies are to be found in many contexts. However, it would be wrong to conclude that this flowering of activity has been sufficient to create a recognised discipline in legal studies or that this work has found a home within institutions of legal education where scholarship takes place.

In part, this state of affairs is a reflection of the continuing domination of positivist legal studies. Here lesbian and gay matters continue to be thought of as matters more appropriate in disciplines other than law as they raise political, social and cultural issues that are remote from legal scholarship. Nor does it necessarily follow that those institutions that adopt a more catholic approach to legal scholarship are less hostile to lesbian and gay issues (Robson, 1998). Legal studies remains largely heterocentric in its view of the world and there continues to be considerable indirect and sometimes direct hostility within the institutions of legal studies to issues relating to lesbians and gay men.

The question of whether there ought to be a separate category of lesbian and gay legal scholars also raises important issues about both the possibility and strategic significance of a distinct form of scholarship or a discipline of lesbian and gay legal studies. While the activities of all legal scholars engaging with lesbian and gay matters are overtly or covertly informed by a politics of identity, the rich diversity of topics, questions and approaches challenges any attempt to reduce that body of work by reference to problematic identities. Nor can this body of legal scholarship be reduced to work that is only informed by matters of sexual identity. In turn, the issues of sexuality, identity, sex and gender raised within this body of legal scholarship have a wide significance, from discreet questions relating to specific legal problems to questions that address the very nature of law and of legal scholarship. While strategic considerations may support the move towards lesbian and gay legal studies, to counteract the pervasive heterocentric view of the world and the violence of exclusion that it is built upon, at best, such developments should be thought of as stages in a process rather than an end in themselves.

Finally, I want to return to the relationship between this body of legal studies and lesbian and gay studies. This raises an immediate problem. It seems to presuppose and reproduce existing divisions within disciplines (between law and the social sciences, between the social sciences and the arts) that in its most challenging manifestation lesbian and gay studies might problematise and refuse. Perhaps the issue has significance in another way; it draws attention to the previous marginality of legal studies within lesbian and gay studies that has to date been most successful in the context of the arts, cultural studies and the social sciences. The failure to incorporate legal studies within earlier compilations of lesbian and gay scholarship may also point to assumptions within the established social sciences and the arts about the nature of legal studies which has assumed that legal scholarship is confined within the long methodological tradition of 'black letter' (positivist) conceptions of legal scholarship. Ironically, the absence of law from lesbian and gay studies threatens to reproduce the dominant tradition of legal scholarship and

has distanced legal scholarship from the emerging field of lesbian and gay studies, perpetuating the marginalisation of legal studies within the social sciences and arts.

While some types of legal scholarship might confirm some of these assumptions and divisions, in its diversity legal studies offers a dramatic challenge to them. Legal scholarship may offer many challenges to the way matters of law have been raised and addressed in lesbian and gay scholarship outside of legal studies. These challenges may be varied, for example, positivist legal scholars can offer insights into the technical aspects of law absent from other disciplines. A legal scholarship that incorporates work undertaken in the social sciences and the humanities into legal studies can challenge assumptions about law and legal studies found within lesbian and gay scholarship. Different insights into the nature of law and legal practice can be provided. Furthermore new insights into the application of, for example, semiotics, historiography, poststructuralism or queer scholarship are also to be found in lesbian and gay legal scholarship. In many and different ways lesbian and gay legal scholarship offers to transform the way law is thought about.

NOTES

1 Important texts within this corpus of writing include Krafft-Ebing's *Psychopathia Sexualis* ([1876] 1947) and Havelock Ellis's *Studies in the Psychology of Sex,* Vol. 1 *Sexual Inversion* (1897). Cesare Lombroso's classic study, 'The Female Offender' (1895), is a rare example of the use of these developments within the sciences to explain female criminality in the context of the new discipline of criminology. Wayne Dynes's, *Homosexuality: A Research Guide* (1989) provides a rich though now somewhat dated bibliography of material.

2 In that branch of the Western legal tradition that has developed out of English law, a second source of law is recognised, unwritten law, or the law declared by judges. As the legal method described here presupposed the existence of a code its deployment in the context of a living law that was not codified (for example, in England) is particularly interesting. Far from changing the method of

legal scholarship, in the absence of a code, the project of legal scholarship became an attempt to organise the complex of written and unwritten law into a code like text; to synthesise the existing complex body of *ad hoc* legislation and judicial decision into a single coherent logical synthesis of underlying principle, and specific rules.

3 The United Kingdom is a rare example of a State that has an unwritten constitution. As such it is not possible to point to a single legal text setting out the basic legal structure, institutions, powers and responsibilities of the State.

4 While most of my examples are drawn from the Common Law world, it would be wrong to conclude either that the form of legal scholarship, or that the stability of the object of law and legal scholarship, or the persistence of a particular legal method illustrated by way of these examples, is peculiar to legal studies within the Common Law. A similar story could have been told by way of examples drawn from scholarship within the continental Civilian legal tradition.

5 There is much evidence that from early mediaeval times the regulation and prohibition of same-sex genital acts have been referred to in written law. This knowledge might generate an expectation that the relevant legal rules would have been the object of study within the dominant tradition of legal scholarship. Originally found in Canon law (the laws generated and administered by the Catholic Church) and later in Criminal law, neither body of law was the focus of attention within mediaeval or early modern legal scholarship. As contemporary law, both were outside the parameters of academic study based upon the dead corpus of Roman law. Furthermore, neither were fit objects of academic study as they did not relate to the law of property or the law of obligations, which were the predominant concern of legal scholars. At best, they were referred to, albeit briefly, in the scholarly writings of those who practised law in the courtroom.

6 For example, in the European Court of Human Rights, Dudgeon (1981; 1982), Norris (1989), Modinos (1993) and more recently under the International Convention on Civil and Political Rights, the case of Toonen (1994).

7 In the USA most Jurisprudence teaching in to be found in Philosophy Departments rather than in Schools or Faculties of Law. This is not the case in other Common Law jurisdictions such as the UK, Australia or New Zealand.

8 Various scholars have traced the impact of the Wolfenden reforms in other Common Law jurisdictions. For example see Kinsman (1987) on Canada and Wotherspoon (1991) on Australia.

9 There are several useful guides to these different perspectives on law; Freeman (1994) and Hunt (1978). Sexuality and lesbian and gay issues have yet to gain credibility and the status of 'jurisprudential perspectives' and therefore are not to be found in these texts. In the USA the scholarship informed by these perspectives is more likely to be found in the social sciences, political theory or philosophy faculties and departments not law schools, which still have a strong focus upon legal education as a professional training. This is not the case in other Common Law jurisdictions.

10 Another area of new work that challenges some of the assumptions about the nature of sexuality and the relations between sexuality and gender in law is to be found in transgender scholarship; (Sharpe (1998, 1999) and Whittle (1998, 2000)).

11 Two recent victim surveys have been produced in Scotland. Both focus on Edinburgh (Morrison and Mackay, 2000; Plant et al., 1999).

REFERENCES

ACPO (2000) *ACPO Guide to Identifying and Combating Hate Crime.* London: Metropolitan Police Service.

Backer, L.K. (1998) 'Queering theory: an essay on the conceit of revolution in law', in L. Moran, J. Monk and S. Beresford (eds), *Legal Queeries.* London: Cassell. pp. 185–203.

Bamforth, N. (1997) *Sexuality, Morals and Justice.* London: Cassell.

Bamforth, N. (2000) 'Sexual orientation discrimination after Grant v. South West Trains', *Modern Law Review,* 63 (5): 694–720.

Berger, N. (2000) 'Queer readings of Europe: gender, identity, sexual orientation and the (im)potency of rights politics at the European Court of Justice', *Social and Legal Studies,* 9 (2): 249–70.

Berman, H. (1983) *Law and Revolution.* Cambridge, MA: Harvard University Press.

Boswell, J. (1980) *Christianity, Social Tolerance and Homosexuality.* Chicago: University of Chicago Press.

Bowers (1986) Bowers v. Hardwick 92 L Ed 140–65.

Bowers, L. (1997) 'Queer problems/straight solutions: the limits of a politics of "Official recognition"', in S. Phelan (ed.), *Playing with Fire: Queer Politics, Queer Theories.* New York, Routledge. pp. 267–91.

Bowley, M. (2000) 'Gay rights – the second front', *New Law Journal,* 26 May: 803–4.

Boyd, S. (1999) 'Family law and sexuality: feminist engagements', *Social and Legal Studies,* 8 (3): 369–90.

Bray, A. (1982) *Homosexuality in Renaissance England.* London: Gay Men's Press.

Bhurke, R.A. (1997) *A Matter of Justice.* London: Routledge.

Burke, M. (1993) *Coming Out of the Blue.* London: Cassell.

Chauncey, G. (1994) *Gay New York.* New York: Basic Books.

Chapman, A. and Mason, G. (1999) 'Women, sexual preference and discrimination law: a case study of the NSW jurisdiction', *Sydney Law Review,* 21: 525–66.

Comstock, G.D. (1991) *Violence against Lesbians and Gay Men.* New York: Columbia University Press.

Copley, A. (1989) *Sexual Morality in France 1780–1980.* London: Routledge.

Cover, R.M. (1986) 'Violence and the word', *Yale Law Journal,* 95: 1601–29.

Crane, P. (1982) *Gays and the Law.* London: Pluto.

Crompton, L. (1980) 'The myth of lesbian impunity', *Journal of Homosexuality*, 6 (1–2): 11–32.

Davies, M. (1999) 'Queer property, queer persons: self-ownership and beyond', *Social and Legal Studies*, 8 (3): 327–52.

Derrida, J. (1992) 'Force of law: the mystical foundations of authority', in Drucilla Cornell et al. (eds), *Deconstruction and the Possibility of Justice*. London, Routledge. pp. 68–94.

Devlin, P. (1965) *The Enforcement of Morals*. Oxford: University Press.

Dudgeon (1981) Dudgeon v. UK European Human Rights Reports, 3: 40–62.

Dudgeon (1982) Dudgeon v. UK European Human Rights Reports, 4: 149–187.

Dynes, W.D. (1989) *Homosexuality: A Research Guide*. New York: Garland Press.

Eaton, M. (1994) 'At the intersection of gender and sexual orientation: towards a lesbian jurisprudence', *Southern California Review of Law and Women's Studies*. 183–220.

Eaton, M. (1995) 'Homosexual unmodified: speculations on law's discourse, race and the construction of sexual identity', in D. Herman and C. Stychin (eds), *Legal Inversions*. Philadelphia, PA: Temple University Press. pp. 46–76.

Ellis, H. (1897) *Studies in the Psychology of Sex, Volume 1, Sexual Inversion*. London: The University Press.

Faderman, L. (1981) *Surpassing the Love of Men*. New York: William Morrow.

Faderman, L. (1983) *Scotch Verdict*. New York: William Morrow.

Finnis, J.M. (1970) 'Natural law and unnatural acts', *Heythrop Journal*, 11: 365–87.

Finnis, J.M. (1983) *Natural Law and Natural Rights*. Oxford: Clarendon Press.

Finnis, J.M. (1993) 'Law, morality and "sexual orientation"', *Notre Dame Law Review*, 69: 1049–.

Fitzpatrick (1999) 'Fitzpatrick v. Stirling Housing Association' *All England Law Reports*, 705–50.

Freeman, M.D.A. (1994) *Lloyd's Introduction to Jurisprudence*. London: Stevens and Sons.

Goodich, M. (1979) *The Unmentionable Vice: Homosexuality in the Later Mediaeval Period*. Santa Barbara: Ross-Erikson.

Goodrich, P. (1986) *Reading the Law*. Oxford: Blackwell.

Goodrich, P. (1990) *Languages of Law*. London: Weidenfeld.

Gooding, C. (1992) *The Trouble with the Law? A Legal Handbook for Lesbians and Gay Men*. London: Gay Men's Press.

Grosz, E. (1994) *Volatile Bodies*. Bloomington, IN: Indiana University Press.

Halley, J.E. (1993) 'The construction of heterosexuality', in M. Warner (ed.), *Fear of a Queer Planet: Queer Politics and Social Theory*. Minneapolis: University of Minnesota Press. pp. 82–104.

Halley, J.E. (1994) 'Bowers v. Hardwick in the Renaissance', in J. Goldberg (ed.), *Queering the Renaissance*. Durham, NC: Duke University Press.

Hart, H.L.A. (1963) *Law, Liberty and Morality*. Oxford: Oxford University Press.

Hart, L. (1994) *Fatal Women*. Princeton, NJ: Princeton University Press.

Heinze, E. (1995) *Sexual Orientation: A Human Right*. Dordrecht: Martiinus Nijhoff.

Herek, G.M. and Berrill, K.T. (1992) *Hate Crimes*. London: Sage.

Herman, D. (1994) *Rights of Passage: Struggles for Lesbian and Gay Legal Equality*. Toronto: University of Toronto Press.

Herman, D. and Stychin, C. (eds) (1995) *Legal Inversions*. Philadelphia, PA: Temple University Press.

Hirschfeld, M. (1898) *Paragraph 175 Reichsstrafgesetzbuchs: Die homosexuelle Frage im Urteile der Zeitgenossen*. Leipzig: Spohr.

Humphreys, L. (1970) *The Tearoom Trade*, London, Duckworth.

Hunt, A. (1978) *The Sociological Movement in Law*. London: Macmillan.

Hutchinson, D.L. (1999) 'Ignoring the sexualisation of race: heternormativity, critical race theory and anti-racist politics', *Buffalo Law Review*, 41 (Spring/ Summer): 1–116.

Jacobs and Potter (1998) *Hate Crimes*. Oxford: Oxford University Press.

Jefferson, T.R. (1998) 'Notes towards a black lesbian jurisprudence', *Boston College Third World Law Journal*, 18 (Spring): 263–94.

Jennes, V. and Broad, K. (1997) *Hate Crimes: New Social Movements and the Politics of Violence*. Hawthorne, New York: Aldine deGruyter.

Jennes, V. and Grattet, R. (2001) *Building the Hate Crime Policy Domain: From Social Movement Concept to Law Enforcement Practice*. New York: Russell Sage Foundation.

Kaplan, M. (1997) *Sexual Justice*. New York, Routledge.

Katz, J.N. (1992) *Gay American History: Lesbians and Gay Men in the USA*. New York: Meridian.

Kinsman, G. (1987) *The Regulation of Desire*. Montreal: Black Rose Books.

Kirby, P.J. (2000) 'Developments in gay rights', *New Law Journal*, 14 April: 550–1.

Krafft-Ebing, R. (1947) *Psychopathia Sexualis* (originally published in 1876). Trans. F.J. Rebman. New York: Pioneer Publications.

Krenshaw, K. (1989) 'Demarginalizing the intersection of race and sex. A black feminist critique of antidiscrimination doctrine, feminist theory and antiracist politics', *Chicago Legal Forum*, 139–65.

Krenshaw, K. (1991) 'Mapping the margins: intersectionality, identity, politics and violence against women of color', *Stanford Law Review*, 43: 1241–94.

Kwan, P. (1997) 'Jeffrey Dahmer and the cosynthesis of categories', *Hastings Law Journal*, 48: 1257–92.

Lauritsen, J. and Thorstad, D. (1974) *The Early Homosexual Rights Movement (1864–1935)*. New York: Times Change Press.

Leinen, S. (1993) *Gay Cops*. New Brunswick, Rutgers University Press.

Leventhal, B. and Lundy, S.E. (eds) (1999) *Same-Sex Domestic Violence*. Thousand Oaks, CA: Sage.

Lobel, K. (ed.) (1986) *Naming the Violence: Speaking out about Lesbian Battering*. Boston: Seal Press.

Loizidou, E. (1998) 'Intimate queer celluloid: heavenly creatures and criminal law', in L. Moran, D. Monk and S. Beresford (eds), *Legal Queeries*. London: Cassell. pp. 167–84.

Lombroso, C. and Ferrero, W. (1895) *The Female Offender*. New York: D. Appleton and Co.

MacIntosh, M. (1968) 'The homosexual role', *Social Problems*, 16 (2): 30–49.

Majury, D. (1994) 'Refashioning the unfashionable: claiming lesbian identities in the legal context', *Canadian Journal of Women and the Law*, 7 (2): 286–306.

Mason, G. (1995) '(Out)laws: acts of proscription in the sexual order', in Margaret Thornton (ed.), *Public and Private: Feminist Legal Debates*. Oxford: Oxford University Press.

Mason, G. (1997a) 'Boundaries of sexuality: lesbian experience and feminist discourse on violence against women', *Australasian Gay and Lesbian Law Journal*, 7: 40–56.

Mason, G. (1997b) 'Sexuality, violence: questions of difference' in Chris Cuneen et al. (eds), *Faces of Hate: Hate Crime in Australia*. Sydney. Hawkins Press. pp. 115–36.

Mason, G. (2001) *The Spectacle of Violence*. London: Routledge.

Mason, A. and Palmer, A. (1996) *Queer Bashing: A National Survey of Hate Crimes Against Lesbians and Gay Men*. London, Stonewall.

Mason, G. and Tomsen, S. (eds) (1997) *Homophobic Violence*. Sydney: Hawkins Press.

Modinos (1986) Modinos v Cyprus, *European Human Rights Reports*, 16, 485–504.

Mohr, R.D. (1988) *Gays/Justice: A Study of Ethics, Society and Law*. New York: Columbia University Press.

Moran, L.J. (1996) *The Homosexual(ity) of Law*. London: Routledge.

Moran, L.J. (1997) Special edition of *Social and Legal Studies 'Legal Perversions'*. London: Sage.

Moran, L.J. (ed.) (2001) 'Hate crime: critical reflections', Special Edition *Law and Critique* 12 (3): 201–365.

Moran, L.J., Monk, J. and Beresford, S. (eds) (1998) *Legal Queeries*. London: Cassell.

Morrison, C. and Mackay, A. (2000) *The Experience of Violence and Harassment of Gay Men in the City of Edinburgh*. Edinburgh: Scottish Executive Central Research Unit.

Munt, S. (1994) *Murder by the Book?* London: Routledge.

Norris (1989) Norris v Ireland, *European Human Rights Reports*, 13, 186–203.

Norton, R. (1992) *Mother Clap's Molly House*. London: Gay Mens Press.

Phelan, S. (1995) 'The space of justice: lesbians and democratic politics', in A. Wilson (ed.), *A Simple Matter of Justice*, London: Cassell. pp. 193–220.

Phelan, S. (ed.) (1997) *Playing with Fire: Queer Politics, Queer Theories*. New York, Routledge.

Phillips, O. (1997) 'Zimbabwean law and the production of a white man's disease', *Social and Legal Studies*, 6 (4): 471–93.

Plant, M. et al. (1999) *Experiences and Perceptions of Violence and Intimidation of the Lesbian, Gay, Bisexual and Transgender Community in Edinburgh*. Edinburgh: Edinburgh City Council.

Robson, R. (1992) *Lesbian (Out)law*. Ithaca, New York: Firebrand.

Robson, R. (1998) *Sappho goes to Law School*. New York: Columbia University Press.

Segwick, E.K. (1991) *The Epistemology of the Closet*. Hemel Hempstead: Harvester Wheatsheaf.

Scalettar, L. (2000) 'Resistance, representation, and the subject of violence: reading Hothead Paisan', in J.A. Boone et al., *Queer Frontiers: Millenial Geographies, Genders and Generations*. Madison, WI: University of Wisconsin. pp. 261–78.

Sharpe, A. (1998) 'Institutionalising heterosexuality: the legal exclusion of "Impossible" (trans)sexualities' in L. Moran, J. Monk and S. Beresford (eds), *Legal Queeries*. London: Cassell. pp. 26–43.

Sharpe, A. (1999) 'Transgender performance and the discriminating gaze: a critique of anti-discrimination regulatory regimes', *Social and Legal Studies*, 8 (1): 5–24.

Stanko, B. and Curry, P. (1997) 'Homophobic violence and the self at risk', *Social and Legal Studies*, 6 (4): 513–32.

Stychin, C. (1995) *Laws Desire*. London: Routledge.

Stychin, C. (1998) *Nation by Rights*. Philadelphia: Temple University Press.

Stychin, C. and Herman, D. (2000) *Sexuality in the Legal Arena*. London: Athlone.

Stychin, C. (forthcoming 2001) 'Sexual citizenship in the European Union', *Citizenship*.

Symmonds, J.A. (1928) *Sexual Inversion*. (1984 reprint edition). New York: Bell Publishing.

Tatchell, P. (1992) *Europe in the Pink*. London: Gay Mens Press.

Taylor, J. and Chandler, T. (1995) *Lesbians Talk Violent Relationships*. London: Scarlet Press.

Thomas, K. (1992) 'Beyond the privacy principle', *Columbia Law Review*, 92: 1431–516.

Toonen (1994) Toonen v. Australia, *International Human Rights Reports*, 97.

Valdes, F. (1995) 'Sex and race in queer legal culture', *Review of Law and Women's Studies*, 5: 25–71.

Valdes, F. (1997) 'Queer margins, queer ethics: a call to account for race and ethnicity in the law, theory, and politics of "sexual orientation"', *Hastings Law Journal*, 48: 1293–341.

Valdes, F. (1998) 'Beyond sexual orientation in queer legal theory: majoritarianism, multidimensionality, and responsibility in social justice scholarship', *Denver University Law Review*, 75 (4): 1409–64.

Valdes, F. (1999) 'Theorizing "outcrit" theories: coalitional method and comparative jurisprudential experience. race crits, queer crits, lat crits', *University of Miami Law Review*, 53: 1265–322.

Waaldijk, K. (1993) *Homosexuality: A European Community Issue*. Dordrecht: Nijhoff.

Weeks, J. (1977) *Coming Out*. London: Quartet.

Whittle, S. (1998) 'Gemeinschaftsfremden – or how to be shafted by your friends: sterilization requirements and legal status recognition for the transsexual', in L. Moran, J. Monk and S. Beresford (eds), *Legal Queeries*. London: Cassell. pp. 42–56.

Whittle, S. (2000) *The Transsgender Debate*. London: South Street Press.

Wintermute, R. (1995) *Sexual Orientation and Human Rights: The United States Constitution, the European Convention, and the Canadian Charter*. Oxford: Clarendon Press.

Wittig, M. and Zeig, S. (1979) *Lesbian Peoples: Material for a Dictionary*. New York: Avon.

Wolfenden, J. (1957) *Report of the Departmental Committee on Homosexual Offences and Prostitution Cmnd. 247*. London: HMSO.

Wotherspoon, G. (1991) *City of the Plain: History of a Gay Sub-Culture*. Sydney: Hale and Iremonger.

18

Religious Views of Homosexuality

DAWNE MOON

Religion is a solemn affair, heavy with pretension, and lumpy with love. Listening to a religious debate on sex is like reading an academic thesis on jokes. It misses the point.

(Rabbi Lionel Blue, 'Godly and Gay,' 1995: 123)

This chapter focuses on Western religious views of homosexuality.[1] Current debates about such topics as same-sex marriage involve many complicated and subtle arguments, but these debates are easier to understand if we start by sorting out two main themes: nature and scripture. This chapter begins by looking at scholarly and theological approaches to the traditional assumption that homosexuality is 'unnatural'. It looks at two different, sometimes competing definitions of nature, one a scientific definition and the other a moral definition, and shows how these definitions fit into Western religious worldviews. It then examines different approaches to scripture. Focusing on two different ways people can approach scripture, it shows how different religious thinkers select parts of their scripture and traditions to argue either that homosexuality is sinful or that it is compatible with a righteous life.

The chapter then looks briefly at contemporary debates about same-sex marriage, showing how concerns about tradition and social change are shaped by differing views about nature, scripture, and God. Overall, I show that, from a sociological perspective, religions are inherently neither pro-gay nor anti-gay, and that people can use the same approaches within a religion to argue very different things. I conclude by suggesting questions for future research into religious debates and attitudes about homosexuality.

NATURE, SCIENCE AND MORALITY

For those coming from a Western perspective, nature is a key theme in discussions of religion, morality, and sex. 'Crime against nature' was the traditional English euphemism for sexual transgressions, and many of the religious debates about homosexuality in the West implicitly or explicitly center around the question of whether homosexuality is unnatural. As Dutch scholar Pim Pronk (1993) points out, however, arguments based on a language of nature tend to confound different meanings of the word *natural*. While Pronk focuses on three aspects of nature, I will modify his approach for our purposes here and highlight two. The first formulation of what is natural pertains to science, as in that which may be observed in the natural world. The second formulation of nature is the Ancient Greek one, also used by the Apostle Paul, in which natural means moral. Many of the debates in Christianity and Judaism are confounded, as Pronk shows, when people use competing definitions of nature without acknowledging them. Regardless, it is clear that people may base claims about homosexuality in ideas about nature, whether their intentions are pro-gay or anti-gay.[2]

This section examines various challenges within religious groups to the commonsense assumption that homosexuality is unnatural. It starts by looking at how people participating in these religious debates use cross-cultural evidence and Western historical evidence to challenge the idea that human beings naturally reject homosexuality. It then looks at how pro-gay religious thinkers may challenge the assumption that contemporary, dominant standards of sexual behavior could exist for every society throughout time. I then examine pro-gay attempts to argue that homosexuality is natural by using evidence from science, and show how these uses of nature can help us as scholars to shape questions for study. In the final part of this section, I look at the argument that sex is naturally for reproduction, an argument which uses a moral rather than scientific definition of nature. By looking at this argument and the pro-gay challenge to it, we begin to see how people with different viewpoints can understand the same passage of scripture to mean very different things about the moral status of homosexuality.

Arguments about nature shape contemporary Western debates about homosexuality, as anti-gay religious thinkers assume that homosexuality is unnatural and their pro-gay counterparts must challenge that assumption. Many religious thinkers assume that homosexuality is a sign of humanity's fall, that human beings were created heterosexual and that homosexuality is a part of society's degeneration. Others argue that God did not necessarily create human beings to be heterosexual in the first place. These thinkers refer to secular gay and lesbian scholarship which has shown, for example,

that sexuality differs across different cultures, establishing that humanity is not inherently, or by nature, 'heterosexual'. Anthropologist Gilbert Herdt, for instance, contributed a great deal to Western understandings of sexual variation in his studies of ritual homosexuality in Melanesia, where he observed that oral sex between young initiate boys and older boys was a ritualized phase of life (Herdt, 1981; Herdt and Stoller, 1990). Walter L. Williams (1986), Will Roscoe (1997) and Paula Gunn-Allen (1981, 1986) made similar contributions in their writings about Native American *berdaches*. In a number of Native American nations, a *berdache* was, or is, a person who was thought to have especial spiritual power by embodying both male and female attributes, and most often was someone with a male body but who wore women's clothes and married a man (sometimes as a second wife), or a person with a female body who served the traditionally male role as a hunter or warrior and who sometimes had a wife (see Baum, 1993, for an extensive overview). Such scholarship refutes the claim that human beings all by nature share traditional Western taboos around sex and gender.

A second way scholars have challenged the common sense that homosexuality has been everywhere and always considered 'unnatural' has been to examine Western history itself. Historians of the European tradition have uncovered information about various forms of homosexuality in the so-called Western tradition, such as Bernard Sergent's (1986 [1984]) and David Halperin's (1989, 1993) work on ancient Greece and John Boswell's (1980, 1994) studies of early and pre-modern Christianity in Europe. These scholars have pointed out that not only do different human societies and human religions recognize same-sex sexual practices as legitimate or even sacred, but even early Western philosophers did not share the beliefs about sex that tend to prevail in the West today.

For example, arguing that much historical research tends to be shaped by the researchers' own prejudices against homosexuality,

Boswell uncovers evidence of same-sex relationships between Saints Serge and Bacchus and Saints Perpetua and Felicitas. He argues that these relationships were intimate and were not seriously condemned throughout the first millennium of Christianity. Boswell and others (most notably Horner, 1978) also go so far as to argue that the Bible itself gives evidence of same-sex intimate love, for instance, the love of Jonathan and David, which 'passed the love of women' (II Samuel 1: 26) and even the relationship between John, the beloved disciple, and Jesus, who, upon his death referred to his own mother as John's mother (John 19: 26–7). These thinkers show that homosexuality may not have always been considered unnatural or wrong, even in Western religious traditions.

While some theologians draw from such scholarship to show that homosexuality has not always and everywhere been considered sinful or wrong, others assert that people of faith should not give modern categories of sexuality religious significance, as our contemporary system of sexual categories has not always existed. Many scholars, most famously Michel Foucault (1978), have pointed out that the terms *heterosexuality* and *homosexuality* did not even exist until they were coined by doctors in late nineteenth century Europe, and thus, our conventional ways of attributing different sexual practices to specific *kinds* of people can hardly be considered either universal or 'natural'. In keeping with this historicizing trend, biblical scholars such as Robin Scroggs (1983) and Tom Horner (1978) have pointed out that the way sex has organized people's lives in nineteenth- or twentieth-century Europe and North America was unheard of in biblical times (and vice versa). People making this argument believe that the timeless message of religion is, overall, to help people to treat each other with love and compassion, and that these ethics apply to all people regardless of sexual orientation (see also Olyan, 1997, Scanzoni and Mollenkott, 1994).

Foucault sees as peculiar contemporary Western society's notion that humanity is naturally divided into the two distinct species of heterosexuals and homosexuals. However, many pro-gay religious thinkers (gay and non-gay) believe that our contemporary sexual categories have existed for all time and are, in that sense, natural. They argue that gay men and lesbians are born gay or lesbian. In this view, since gay men and lesbians are made that way by God, homosexuality is part of God's good creation and cannot be considered unnatural or sinful. Episcopal Bishop John Shelby Spong (1988), for instance, argues that sexuality is determined in fetal development and thus, God creates some people to be homosexuals. Other theologians, especially among liberal Jews and Protestants, look with hope to the day that scientists will prove that gay people are naturally and immutably gay (see, for instance, Fuller, 1994, Kahn, 1997 [1989]). In response to popular argument that Christians should 'hate the sin and love the sinner' (Dallas, 1991; Geis and Messer, 1994), some pro-gay church members critique the 'hate the sin' perspective by asserting that gay people are inherently gay. Being constituted as gay, they argue, cannot be separated from doing gay things, including having gay sex.

When people make the 'born gay' argument in religious contexts, they rely on the findings of science to back their moral claims, a task science was not designed to fulfil. More importantly, this perspective overlooks a key feature of many Western religious viewpoints, that people are moral agents who can *choose,* to some extent or other, to do what is moral, what is right, what God calls them to do. As Lewis R. Gordon reflects:

> That theological discussions of homosexuality have focused on homosexuality as sin has locked gays into the world of the unnatural. It is no wonder that a discourse on the naturalness of being gay – that is, not having *chosen* being gay but having been *born* gay – has dominated gay resistance to the charge of violating nature. The defense is, however, a 'Catch 22', for in denying that there is something intrinsically wrong with being gay, one need also assert that one would

choose to be gay if one were to have the choice. It is an existential positioning of a simple ethical challenge: is not part of loving oneself the willingness to choose, eternally, to be oneself? (1998: 175).

When pro-gay people of faith try to make their religious communities support gay people by insisting that gay people have no choice, they deny that gay people may have the ability to act as full participants in religious life. In effect, what eludes many pro-gay liberals, is the possibility that gay people may be *called* to be gay; that God might *demand* that they live with integrity as they challenge their societies' family, gender and sexual norms. They ignore that choosing to live as gay, or lesbian or bisexual or queer might itself be a moral choice to make.

The question, then, for queer scholars, is why so many pro-gay people of faith base their arguments about homosexuality on discourses of science rather than on discourses of morality. Why is it so difficult for many people to imagine the possibility that God would want, demand, and ask people to choose to run against the social conventions of man-woman marriage, including by being lesbian, transgendered, gay or bisexual (or, for that matter, ex-gay)? What happens to religious beliefs if they start from the assumption that sex between (or among) some people of the same sex is *good*, rather than in need of justification?[3] What makes that assumption so difficult to imagine, even for people who believe in an omnipotent and infinite God?

At one level, as we have seen, when Western religious participants in debates about homosexuality invoke the theme of nature, they focus on a question of creation – what is or has been observable in human creation, and whether the acceptance of same-sex sexual orientations or sexual fluidity fits into that. Another view of nature in Western thought characterizes a behavior as unnatural if it is not what God intends for people to do, if it is considered wrong. Many Roman Catholics, Protestants, Jews and Muslims point to God's creating Adam and Eve, and commanding them to 'be fruitful and multiply' as evidence both that human beings are supposed to be have sex only within one-man-one-woman marriage and that homosexuality is therefore wrong, or unnatural. As they say on the talk-shows: 'God created Adam and Eve, not Adam and Steve'. The popular Jewish intellectual and talk-show host Denis Prager elaborates:

> In order to become fully human, male and female must join. In the words of Genesis, 'God created the human ... male and female He created them'. The union of male and female is not merely some lovely ideal; it is the essence of the biblical outlook on becoming human. To deny it is tantamount to denying a primary purpose in life. (1997 [1990]: 65)

For many people, the story of Adam and Eve is the central story of God's creation. For Prager and others, it is a story of heterosexuality as an essential component of being human (see also Novak, 1998).

Detractors criticize this argument in several ways. Some maintain that the statement, 'God created humankind in his image, in the image of God he created them; male and female he created them' (Genesis 1: 27 – including the part that Prager, curiously, chose to leave out) points to the maleness *and* femaleness of God and all persons, which in itself runs contrary to heterosexist thinking (for instance, see Goss, 1993 and Trible, 1987). Others point out that if human beings were all created in God's image, then that includes gay people (see, for instance, Alpert, 1989; Goss, 1993; Nelson, 1978; Sarah, 1995; Shulman, 1995). These commentaries look deeply into human understandings of nature and God and challenge the sexism of much religious thought. However, they tend to assume that gay people are a different *kind* of person, with a different nature. With the exception of Nelson, these commentaries do not confront the central assumption that God does not intend for people to engage in erotic practices with people of their same sex.

Prager's argument that marriage and reproduction are primary purposes in life echoes much of Roman Catholic thought, which is best elaborated in what is known as Natural Law philosophy. This philosophy relies heavily on a view of nature as moral. For instance, John Finnis (1995) argues that male–female marriage is intrinsically good and therefore natural, while non-marital sexuality, including homosexuality, is not good and therefore, not natural. Finnis argues that companionship, not reproduction, is the ultimate and good end product of the marital union of man and woman. However, he claims, 'parenthood and children and family are the intrinsic fulfillment of a communion which, because it is not merely instrumental, can exist and fulfill the spouses even if procreation happens to be impossible for them' (1995: 27). In Finnis's view, sexual activity outside of reproductive marriage – including homosexuality, prostitution, masturbation and 'deliberately contracepted' intercourse (within or outside the institution of marriage) – cannot provide the fulfillment of companionship and is pleasurable only as an individual, physical outlet.

This view is based on circular logic. It says that homosexuality and these other practices are wrong because they are not spiritually fulfilling, and that they are unfulfilling because they are wrong. Many religious thinkers, such as Michael J. Perry (1995), point out such logical flaws, and argue that if companionship and fulfillment are the purposes of intimate relationships, then whether or not a couple can or chooses to reproduce is irrelevant. Taking the critique a step further, and directing it toward those Protestants who argue that sex is primarily for reproduction, Eugene Rogers (1998) argues that the purpose of sex is not to fulfil an instrumental goal of producing children, but to help human beings to experience the love and desire God has for them.

In Rogers's argument, people should see having children as a gift of grace, not as a mandate or near-requirement of being human. In his view, God's amazing gift of love is itself what humanity should focus on. Rogers says:

The shock and wonder of God's self-determining love in creation has a better analogy, according to

biblical metaphor, in the contingency of the love of one human being for another, than in procreation ...

As traditional marriage and childrearing are gifts of grace more than human achievements, and means of sanctification more than satisfaction, so too monogamous, committed gay and lesbian relationships are also gifts of grace, means of sanctification, upbuilding of the community of the people of God.

The chief end of sex is not to make children of human beings, but to make children of God. And Christians best imitate God's relation to them as children not when they bear and beget them, but when they adopt them. (Rogers, 1998: 138–41)

For Rogers, then, the self-giving of committed relationships mirrors God's choice to love and foster humanity. Therefore, in his argument, simply reproducing out of duty has less to do with God's covenant with humanity than do the relationships where someone *chooses* to commit to love another, such as in adoption or in a chosen committed love relationship. Given today's tremendous social pressures to form heterosexual and not same-sex unions, Rogers implies that same-sex relationships have the potential to be more freely chosen and thus *more* like God's covenant with humanity than conventional relationships, although he does not go so far as to make that claim.[4]

The distinction between Finnis and Rogers has to do with a great deal more than the fact that one is Roman Catholic and the other Protestant, as many Protestants also believe that same-sex sexual activity is wrong partly because it cannot lead to reproduction. The difference between these views of sexuality comes not only from different understandings of how God created human nature, but also from different understandings of how God intends for people to use Scripture. For Finnis, Prager, and others like them, the story of Adam and Eve is an allegory about why male and female should be united in reproductive (or reproductive-looking) heterosexuality. For Rogers and others like him, the story of Adam and Eve is a story not about the mandate to reproduce, but about the mandate to love, regardless of gender or sexual orientation.

These examples show how people of faith can use the same scriptures, but arrive at vastly different conclusions about how God created human nature and what God intends for people. The next section looks more closely at different approaches to the parts of scripture that people often invoke in debates about homosexuality.

SCRIPTURE AND HOMOSEXUALITY

Just as nature may be invoked for either pro-gay or anti-gay ends, people also invoke scripture to determine what is moral, but they may come to either pro-gay or anti-gay conclusions.[5] When considering scripture, it is important to keep in mind the comment of Hendrik Hart in his 1993 foreword to Pronk's work, that Christians have an authoritative text, with no authoritative reading of it. When we analyse the ways that people (Christian or otherwise) use religious writings, we should ask such questions as: when do people choose one text over another, or ignore a text completely? In what historical, social, economic conditions are different texts or approaches to texts favored? What possible interpretations are unthinkable to people, and why?

This section begins by defining the terms *modernism* and *fundamentalism*, showing why we must be careful not to categorize people in debates about homosexuality as modernists or fundamentalists. I then distinguish between two ways of reading scripture, literalism and contextualism, and examine literalist readings of the scriptures that are seen as condemning homosexuality, and pro-gay contextual views of those passages. Finally, I look at more literalist readings of scripture as they are used for pro-gay ends.

Many people see debates about homosexuality as battles between fundamentalists and modernists. While this distinction does not help us to understand why some people think homosexuality is sinful and why others do not, this century-old split provides the backdrop for today's debates about homosexuality. Fundamentalism, in Judaism, Christianity and Islam, can be loosely defined for our purposes as a belief that scriptural truths are spelled out in the text as written, and that the written truths of scripture constitute God's clear and unconflicted will for all times. Modernism emerged in the USA and Europe when science began to show that the Bible did not correctly explain everything in the universe. Seeking to reconcile the tensions between science and the scripture, some people began to understand God's truth as constantly being revealed to people, a view which, by extension, saw social change as moving towards God's ideal rather than away from it.[6] In this view, furthermore, scripture began to be seen as the stories told, and eventually written, to help people to understand the world and live well in it; truth could be found in these stories, but a truth which lay in their overarching messages rather than in their specific words and images.

While fundamentalism and modernism do shape today's debates about homosexuality, we must not be too quick to stereotype holders of various viewpoints on homosexuality as modern*ists* or fundamental*ists,* as these monikers obscure more than they explain. While James Davison Hunter (1991) and Robert Wuthnow (1988) both see a radical division in the USA, separating two opposed camps in what Hunter calls a culture war, much sociological evidence suggests that many people are more ambivalent about homosexuality, and many people try to resolve the conflicting arguments and feelings that these debates invoke (Williams, 1997).

Furthermore, many people can seem to adhere to either modernism or to fundamentalism, while holding a view about homosexuality that seems, on the surface, not to go with these other beliefs. For instance, the United Fellowship of Metropolitan Community Churches (MCC) is a Protestant denomination which maintains fairly conservative beliefs about how to understand scripture and the nature of Jesus and salvation, while maintaining that homosexuality conflicts in no way with Christian teaching (Warner, 1995).[7] On the other hand, other people can hold modernist views about women's roles and evolution, while still maintaining that homosexuality is sinful.

Because the split between fundamentalism and modernism is so politically loaded, these terms are not the most clear or useful for characterizing different approaches to scripture. Many people instead see the main divide as falling between literalists, those who take scriptures as word-for-word truth, and contextualists, those who believe that the truth carried by scripture is bigger than human language, and must be understood in the context in which it was read in order for people to begin to discern the greater truths within. Again, characterizing people as literal*ists* or contextual*ists* is not the most useful strategy for understanding these debates, since most people use both more literal-seeming and more context-based readings of scripture.

Very few believers take every word of scripture literally. For instance, even though Jesus is reported to have said 'if your right eye causes you to sin, pluck it out', very few of his contemporary followers would believe that Jesus wants people gouging out their eyes. Likewise, almost all believers take at least some part of scripture literally. For instance, one would be hard-pressed to find any Jews, Muslims or Christians who would say that 'do unto others as you would have them do unto you' is unimportant for today. The question for students of religious belief and behavior is *when* people decide to take a certain part of scripture literally, and *when* people decide to take it as rooted in its own time, as metaphor or as allegory.[8] Our task is to understand contemporary society historically, understand why particular readings make sense, what is at stake for those people who believe homosexuality to fit into their religion and what is at stake for those who believe homosexuality to be sinful.

People can understand the same passage of scripture to mean different things, as we have seen with the story of Adam and Eve.

Those who believe that homosexuality is sinful often turn to the several scriptural passages that appear to condemn it, reading them as clear statements of God's eternal truth. Pro-gay people, on the other hand, tend to view those passages as rooted in historical context, even though they may take other passages much more literally. I will look at different views of several such passages in turn, beginning with those that appear to condemn homosexuality.

Many of those who believe homosexuality is sinful look also to the story of Sodom and Gomorrah (Genesis 19: 1–29), where God spared the family of Lot but rained fire on the rest of his city to wipe it of its extreme and irredeemable sinfulness. For those Christians, Muslims, and Jews who believe that homosexuality is sinful, it seems clear that God's decision to destroy the city was spurred on by the townsmen's demands to have sex with Lot's visitors, two male angels sent by God to see if there were any righteous people in the city. Critics of this interpretation tend to see this story as being about the lack of hospitality the townsmen showed the visitors or about the rampant rape in the story, not about the more loving and egalitarian same-sex intimacy that can exist today (see Countryman, 1988; Mariner, 1995, Scanzoni and Mollenkott, 1994, and Umansky, 1997).

Another key scriptural passage which people see as referring to homosexuality would be that found in the book of Leviticus, with its dietary restrictions, codes of dress and other laws for maintaining order and distinction. These codes include a variety of rules about sexual behavior, including prohibitions on intercourse while a woman is menstruating and sex between men (Leviticus 18: 19, 18: 22 and 20: 13). Many scholars see these rules as having been designed to distinguish the ancient Israelites from practitioners of other ancient religions, whose customs often included things forbidden to the Israelites (see Alpert, 1989; Countryman, 1988; Horner, 1978; Olyan, 1997).

As Leviticus was written down as Jewish law, Jews, Muslims and Christians tend to differ on how they interpret this book. Within Judaism, given millennia of rabbinical teaching and social change, there are widely divergent opinions about the Levitical prohibitions of sex between men. Some see those passages as wholly relevant today, and reflective of a fundamental truth about humanity (see, for instance, the analysis of Jewish anti-gay thought in Alpert, 1989; Olyan, 1997; Olyan and Nussbaum, 1998; Sarah, 1995; Solomon, 1995; Umansky, 1997). Critics, however, point out that Jewish law was written in and for a different time, a time when people assumed that marriage consisted of the absolute submission of a woman to a dominant man, and that sex between men would, in this worldview, render at least one of the men 'submissive' (Horner, 1978; Sarah, 1995; Scroggs, 1983). In this argument, God's way is constantly being revealed to humanity, and society can only progress when people look past their socially ingrained ways of thinking and acting.[9]

Muslims and Christians do not maintain Leviticus as law, and Muslims who believe homosexuality is sinful do not appear to cite this passage as much as they cite the stories of Adam and Eve and of Sodom in denouncing homosexuality. However, many Christians do invoke Leviticus to prove that homosexuality is sinful. Such uses of scripture invite us to inquire into the surrounding social conditions, to ask what makes the particular passages about intercourse between men seem essential for Christians, when the surrounding passages seem, to many people today, irrelevant.

For many Christians, the Apostle Paul's letters to the early Christian church affirm that homosexuality is abominable (Romans 1: 26–27, I Corinthians 6: 9, I Timothy 1: 9–10). For instance, in I Corinthians 6: 9 Paul includes the ancient Greek words *malakoi* and *arsenokoitai* in a list of evildoers, which many translations of the Bible interpret to refer to any homosexuality between men.[10] The inclusion of homosexuality as sin in the New Testament shows many Christians that homosexuality is not like other things prohibited in Levitical law, that this prohibition

holds true for Christians. Detractors suggest a more contextually based reading. Acknowledging that Paul's letters portray homosexuality as a vice, they point out that Paul also says that women should submit to their husbands (Ephesians 5: 22–24, Colossians 3: 18), that women should not speak in church or teach men (I Corinthians 14: 34–36, I Timothy 2:12), and that slaves should obey their masters (Ephesians 6: 5–8, 1 Peter 2: 18–21, Colossians 3: 22). Many people, regardless of their beliefs about homosexuality, give numerous reasons to show that these sentences do not mean today what they appear to us on the surface to mean, that these passages must be understood as rooted in the ancient context in which they were written.

Those who believe homosexuality to be sinful do not see the Apostle Paul's proscriptions against homosexuality as requiring similarly contextual readings, and see such analyses as going to extremes to make the Bible conform to a pro-gay agenda. On the other hand, those who believe homosexuality is not sinful see the relevant passages from Romans, I Corinthians, and I Timothy as requiring contextual understandings of what same-sex sexual practices meant at the time (including man–boy and master–slave relations, as well as temple prostitution), as opposed to the kinds of relationships gay men, bisexuals and lesbians have today.[11] A task for scholars is to understand how people draw the line between what to read more literally and what to interpret given historical context.

Many pro-gay people of these faiths argue that religious truth about homosexuality cannot be found in specific readings of scriptural texts, because societies are so different today from what they were thousands of years ago. For the truth about homosexuality, many argue that the scriptures' overall message is that God often goes against people's expectations and societally entrenched laws, shaking things up. For instance, the prophets in the Hebrew scriptures rejected their families and livelihoods and roamed the countryside; Ruth refused to leave her widowed and childless mother-in-law; the shepherd David grew to become the great King of the Israelites; Jesus healed on the Sabbath, associated with prostitutes and money lenders' and taught people how to love their neighbors by telling a story of a hated Samaritan (see, for instance, Goss, 1993; Heyward, 1984, 1989; Rogers, 1998; Scanzoni and Mollenkott, 1994). Similarly, these thinkers argue gay men, lesbians, transgenderists and bisexuals listen to God when they live and love in non-traditional ways, and hold a godly potential to shake up firmly entrenched human conventions.

These thinkers draw from what they see as the overall message of scripture, the deeper truth. Those who believe that homosexuality is sinful do the same, for instance, when they advocate ministries to help gay people to overcome their homosexuality (becoming 'ex-gay'), with reference to Jesus's overarching message of transformation of the heart. Thus, neither literalism nor contextualism *necessarily* leads to particular views about homosexuality. The major thing that seems to distinguish which side a person fits on seems to be her or his own experience with sexuality and with gay people. Those whose experience forces them to see gay men, transgenderists, bisexuals and lesbians as fully equal to heterosexuals in religiously significant ways, including being loved by God and able (as much as they believe any person can) to understand God's will. Once someone understands sexual or gender orientation as making people simply different, rather than inferior, a more 'traditional' reading of scripture as anti-gay ceases to make sense.

Because a large part of the scholarly theological work on homosexuality has focused on uncovering the context in which apparently anti-gay scripture was written, I have so far given a great deal of attention to pro-gay contextual readings of scripture. I have also looked briefly at anti-gay contextual uses of Scripture, and described the fairly obvious anti-gay literalist readings as well. Pro-gay people can also read scripture more literally for evidence of the acceptability of same-sex relationships to God as well. We have already seen some pro-gay uses of

scriptural literalism. For instance, when scholars point to the intimate relationship between Jonathan and David, and even that between Jesus and John, they hope to show that homosexuality is indeed compatible with religious tradition, teachings and ethics.[12] Likewise, those who refer to the scriptural statements that human beings are created in God's image and commands to love one's neighbor, see these passages as clearly stating an eternal truth.

One final example should serve to show how the framework of scripture can allow not only for sexual repression, but also for sexual liberation. Mary McClintock Fulkerson (1997) uses Paul's letter to the Galatians, where he addressed church members' concerns about whether one must be a Jew before one can be a Christian. He wrote: 'There is no longer Jew or Greek, there is no longer slave or free, there is no longer male and female; for all of you are one in Christ Jesus' (Galatians 3: 28). Many readers, like Fulkerson, see this passage as denying that any worldly identity matters once people are 'one in Christ Jesus'. She concludes that gay men, lesbians, bisexuals and transgendered people might use the passage from Galatians to challenge the church to accept all people as full equals and members in terms of God's infinite love and inclusion. Thus Fulkerson uses a fairly literal reading of scripture to make a radical claim about accepting sexual difference.

TODAY'S DEBATES: SOCIAL ORDER AND SAME-SEX MARRIAGE

Many Protestant denominations and Jewish movements have debated, and continue to debate, whether or not homosexuality is compatible with religious teaching and a life of faith. Some major religious groups have allowed clergy to bless same-sex unions.[13] Even so, because people do not have to agree with every policy of the religious group to which they belong, members of these groups still disagree over the propriety of same-sex marriage or homosexuality in general. Furthermore, debates about homosexuality and same-sex marriage rage on within such groups as Presbyterians, Lutherans, United Methodists, Quakers, American Baptists, Mennonites, Episcopalians, and the Conservative movement in Judaism. This section looks broadly at these debates about same-sex marriage, showing how concerns about tradition and social change fit in with the themes of nature and scripture that we have already explored.

Opponents of religious same-sex marriage generally believe that blessing same-sex unions would take something away from the institution of marriage. For some, like John Finnis and James P. Hanigan (1998), this means that no social recognition should be granted same-sex couples, as any recognition would show children that same-sex relationships were acceptable. Organizations like the Family Research Council, which lobby government leaders from a conservative religious perspective, argue that same-sex marriage would contribute greatly to what they see as civilization's decay and decline, as legitimating homosexuality would reflect a greater acceptance of ways of living that seem contrary to tradition as well as 'nature'.

For others, like ethicist Jean Bethke Elshtain (1997 [1991]), same-sex unions should be granted civil status and protections, but not be equated with marriage, as such unions lack something present in one-man-one-woman marriage. While many in this camp argue that what is lacking is the possibility of procreation, critics suggest that what is 'lacking' is the hierarchy of male over female, which makes same-sex relationships seem to be missing something (see, for instance, Goss, 1993; Shulman, 1995). These critics argue that same-sex marriage does not lack anything significant when compared to traditional marriage, since many same-sex couples do have children, and more importantly, since marriage is supposed to be about love and companionship, not procreation (Rogers, 1998; Solomon, 1995).

Arguments about traditional marriage and same-sex marriage relate to a similar tension that appears in many religions, a tension between tradition and social change. People like Elshtain and Finnis clearly show a concern that if the institution of marriage is consciously altered by the church, that act will dramatically erode not only tradition, but social stability. Finnis makes this most clear when he characterizes homosexuality, along with prostitution, adultery, masturbation, and contraception within marriage as all inherently selfish and animalistic. In a widely cited piece on Judaism and homosexuality, Norman Lamm (1978) also expresses concerns about the social disorder to be hastened by the acceptance of homosexuality, when he argues that same-sex marriage could lead to the widespread acceptance of necrophilia and cannibalism (also cited in Umansky, 1997) and when he accepts an earlier concern that men will leave their wives for the (implicitly more enjoyable) sex with men.

Some pro-gay Christians and Jews accept that the family, and the married couple, are essential building blocks of an orderly society. Rather than seeing this as proof that homosexuality is immoral or unnatural, however, they see this assumption as proving that same-sex marriage should be both legal and religiously sanctioned, to help to curb promiscuity. For example, Episcopal Bishop John Shelby Spong (1988) argues that the church should recognize and bless same-sex relationships, saying:

> A willingness on the part of the church and society to accept, bless, affirm, and encourage long-term faithful relationships among gay and lesbian people would be just and proper. But above all it would indicate to the homosexual minority that there is a recognized alternative to the loneliness of celibacy on the one hand and the irresponsibility of sexual promiscuity on the other. (1988: 202)

Spong does not mean to suggest that gay men and lesbians are all 'promiscuous', as he does consider promiscuity to be rare among both straight and gay people. However, he sees promiscuity among gay men and lesbians to be a result of society's denial of legitimation to same-sex couples. In his view, creating official church rituals to bless and affirm same-sex relationships would help to foster a just social order, one that recognizes that the times have changed and peopling the world is not as important now as it was five thousand years ago.

As we have seen, people who believe homosexuality is sinful or unnatural tend to assume, first, that humanity has always and everywhere despised homosexuality. Furthermore, they assume that people can only revere their religious traditions if they shape social policies to discourage homosexuality and encourage marital heterosexuality. We have seen how many scholars and theologians have discredited the first assumption by showing that sex is organized into people's lives differently in different societies, and that even Western Christian history has not always deplored – and should thus not today discourage – intimate relationships between people of the same sex.

Others challenge the second assumption, by denying that the rejection of homosexuality is intrinsic or necessary to their tradition. Many Jews, Christians and Muslims believe that God's truth is big enough to include social change, including social acceptance of homosexuality. These thinkers believe that the traditional rejection of homosexuality is far less essential to their faith than other parts of their traditions. For instance, Shahid Dossani (1997) argues that Islam has always recognized social change. Dossani draws from the Muslim belief that Judaism was correct in its time and Christianity in its time, but that Islam replaced both. This view recognizes that people can evolve and learn more about God's truth. Dossani thus argues that such evolution did not stop with the founding of Islam, that God understands that society changes and that therefore, God recognizes that humanity has evolved to a stage where it is acceptable for some people, including some Muslims, to be gay.

Others explicitly include same-sex marriage within their accounts of religious traditions of freedom and justice. For instance, Charles Curran (1998) argues that same-sex marriage would not threaten tradition and social order, while it would strengthen the church's traditional valuation of human freedom. Similarly, many Protestant clergy members have deliberately violated their denomination's rules forbidding same-sex marriage, citing other traditions they deem more important. For instance, the Reverends Jimmy Creech and Greg Dell, both United Methodists, have challenged their denomination's doctrinal statement that 'homosexuality is incompatible with Christian teaching' (*Book of Discipline*, para. 65G) and openly blessed same-sex unions. Both have argued that they do so in keeping with the United Methodist tradition of seeking justice for and showing God's love and grace to all persons, including gay persons. Many other pro-gay religious thinkers make similar points (Alexander and Preston, 1996; Comstock, 1993; Heyward, 1984, 1989; Nelson, 1978; Plaskow, 1998; Scanzoni and Mollenkott, 1994; Spong, 1988).

While people certainly find arguments for supporting homosexuality within their tradition, at another level, they may also point out that tradition should not hold society back. While many religious thinkers believe that God prefers that society not change significantly, others see much of tradition as unjust, ignorant, or simply outdated, and believe God's way is revealed through social change.[14] Liberal theologians, informed by understandings of science and history as constantly progressing toward the better, believe that their religions do not conflict with changing family patterns and changing meanings of sexuality. Thus, they believe that traditions or scriptural teachings that originated in a different time do not necessarily apply word-for-word to contemporary situations.[15]

A number of gay theologians see prohibitions on homosexuality or same-sex marriage as rooted in a male-dominated Western tradition of oppressing women and repressing the erotic (Nelson, 1978; Plaskow, 1998). Many of these thinkers draw from Audre Lorde (1984), seeing God as speaking to people and inhering in the erotic, which they define as the passionate connections between people that occur physically, emotionally, and intellectually. In this view, sexual experiences can help people to commune with others and with God (see Goss, 1993; Heyward, 1984, 1989; Nelson, 1978; Plaskow, 1989). Spong argues that the church should develop liturgies for the betrothal of unmarried sex partners and the recognition of marital dissolution, as well as same-sex unions. For these religious thinkers, social change does not move people away from God; the church moves people away from God when it refuses to keep up with social change.

In any debate about social change, including those debates about same-sex marriage, scholars are led to ask what is at stake for participants in their desire to maintain an existing order or to promote change. What do participants in these debates stand to lose or gain in terms of money, power, or legitimacy? Similarly, a strain of religious thought known as liberation theology has long looked at what is at stake in demands for social order, as these demands are often made by people with some kind of power. Episcopal priest Carter Heyward (1984) writes:

> For our sake as well as that of the rest of humanity, we need to realize that it is more often than not the *same* economic interests, the *same* governmental interests, the *same* ecclesiastical interests, and the *same* special interest groups that line up *against* the revolutions in Latin America and Zimbabwe, *against* aid to the cities, *against* welfare and day care and provisions for safe medical abortions, *against* gay/lesbian liberation and women's ordination ... black power, Native American grievances, and 'communism', and *against* most if not all ecclesiastical change .... These are the people who tend to stand firm in their opposition to the relinquishment of any hard-earned privilege – by men, white men, rich white men, rich white private-enterprising men who see themselves as God's special people on the earth. (1984: 113–14)

For Heyward, love and justice are part of her theological tradition, but so are structures of domination and dependence; she believes the role of Christians, and everyone, should be to challenge the system of power that makes connections among oppressions hard to see, to speak about, and to challenge. Unlike those who see religious tradition as wholly good, Heyward and other liberation theologians see religious tradition as a human creation and thus, having both good and bad elements. In her view, religious and social traditions of heterosexism and homophobia are among the many guises of power that people of faith must challenge in the name of God, love and justice. For her, the specific rights of gay people and same-sex couples should not be pursued apart from the essential goals of justice for all people.

DIRECTIONS FOR FUTURE STUDY

When we think about religious debates and attitudes about homosexuality, we can think about some specific questions to help us to analyse their arguments. These include asking what themes people use in a particular religion to make their case. How do they know, for instance, when to use scripture literally or read it in context or as allegory? How do they know how to apply tradition to contemporary life? How do the different themes people use keep them from understanding each other's concerns and addressing them, and how do these failures to address each other weaken their own case?

We can ask a more general level of question as well. What economic, political, cultural, or family patterns or identities contribute to how people view sexuality, marriage, gender roles, and the like? How do people, in their every day interactions, thoughts, and actions create and respond to these conditions? What conditions allow for these political debates to take place, or not take place? What conditions allow people to become exceptions to the rules that prevail in their culture?

As debates about homosexuality within the religious communities I have discussed become more prevalent, the topic of homosexuality becomes a terrain on which people of faith play out various tensions in their beliefs about who and what God is and what God demands of people. These debates force people to articulate the beliefs they have rarely needed to articulate, and thus, they provide an opportunity for participants in and observers of these debates to better understand their deeply-held assumptions about God, humanity, life and love.

NOTES

1 I use the word *Western* in this chapter to refer to Judaism, Christianity, and Islam, even though within that broad category, different religious groups vary to the extent to which they even debate homosexuality at all. I categorize them together because of their shared God and scriptures. For overviews on homosexuality in world religions, see Swidler (1993).

2 I use *pro-gay* here to refer to the wide range of opinions sharing the general premise that homosexuality is not sinful. Similarly, I use *anti-gay* to refer to the view that homosexuality is sinful, which is not to say that people who believe that homosexuality is sinful necessarily or consciously hate gay people.

3 This is a version of the question that queer theory poses to social theory (Warner, 1993), which is why I would call such a formulation about the innate goodness of non-normative sex or gender expression 'queer'. Comstock (1993), Goss (1993), Heyward (1984, 1989), and Rogers (1998) are examples of this kind of thinking in Christianity; Balka and Rose (1989) and Magonet (1995) show the same kind of thinking coming out of a Jewish context, and many of the pieces in Boswell and Henking (1997) do so from a variety of contexts. However, these arguments are not often made outside of gay theological circles.

4 Other Christian thinkers go further than Rogers from the traditional standards of moral relationships. For instance, Marie M. Fortune (1995) develops five standards for loving in a Godly way, in right relationship with others. These standards are that: 1. Intimate partners must be peers, with equal power. 2. Both partners must be free to give authentic consent to the relationship with the information, awareness, and equality necessarily to choose to say no or yes. 3. Both partners must wisely care for each other's and their own bodies and lives and develop trust. 4. Each should be concerned for the pleasure of the other. 5. Each must be faithful to whatever promises and commitments have been made, and commitments must be

changed as people change, hopefully through open and honest communication.

5 I hope that some of the arguments/techniques I present here may be useful to people analysing uses of grounding texts of different religions. For instance, a scholar of Hinduism might ask under what conditions do people accentuate one eternal human goal over another, for instance, the *dharma* (duty) over the *kama* (pleasure)? (Sharma [1993] describes dominant views of homosexuality at different periods in the history of Hinduism.)

For religions where sin is not operative, people may nonetheless use historical and philosophical writings to discern the value of erotic activity between people of the same sex, even though such actions fit under completely different rubrics than in Western religions. (see Swidler, 1993).

6 See Marsden (1980) for a detailed account of this tension in American Protestantism.

7 Also see Comstock (1993) and Gray and Thumma (1997) for more about the MCC and other gay Protestant worship experiences.

8 Different things constitute common sense at different points in history. For instance, for many people well into the nineteenth century in the United States, the Bible seemed unquestionably to support or even mandate slavery, while very few people today believe that God could ever allow slavery. (See Swartley, 1983 for a careful explanation of the historical viewpoints on both sides of the slavery debate and three other Christian debates about scripture.) Some believe that anti-gay beliefs will some day appear just as incompatible with God's true intention as slavery appears today.

9 Spong (1988) and Goss (1993) make similar arguments.

10 These ancient Greek words are translated in many different ways, but generally refer to male temple prostitutes and the men who hired their services, even though different versions of the Bible often lump the two together as 'homosexuals' (an anachronism) or as 'passive homosexuals' and 'active homosexuals' or even 'defilers of themselves with mankind'. There is a great deal of commentary on these words, including Boswell (1980), Countryman (1988), Horner (1978), Scanzoni and Mollenkott (1994), and Scroggs (1983).

11 See Boswell (1980), Comstock (1993), Horner (1978), Scanzoni and Mollenkott (1994), Scroggs (1983). These authors as well as Mariner (1995) make similar arguments about sodomy in the Hebrew Bible.

12 Horner (1978) also argues that Ruth and Naomi may have had a sexual relationship, though such a claim seems slightly shakier.

13 As of July 2000, the Reform and Reconstructionist movements in Judaism allow clergy to officiate over same-sex unions, and the Unitarian Universalist Association recognizes same-sex marriages. Other groups in the United States, such as the United Methodists, the Episcopalians, the Presbyterians and the United Church of Christ

have come close to recognizing same-sex unions in recent years.

14 See Marsden (1980) for a general overview of Protestant modernism, as it first developed in response to nineteenth-century scientific developments. Also see Maitland (1995) for a less historical iteration of a general modernist Protestant theology.

15 See, for instance, Ackelsberg (1989), Goss (1993), Heyward (1984, 1989), Rogers (1998), Scanzoni and Mollenkott (1994), Spong (1988), Umansky (1997).

REFERENCES

Ackelsberg, Martha A. (1989) 'Redefining family: models for the Jewish future', in Christie Balka and Andy Rose (eds), *Twice Blessed: On Being Lesbian or Gay and Jewish*. Boston: Beacon Press. pp. 107–17.

Alexander, Marilyn Bennett and Preston James, (1996) *We Were Baptized Too: Claiming God's Grace for Lesbians and Gays*. Louisville, KY: Westminster John Knox Press.

Allen, Paula Gunn (1981) 'Lesbians in American Indian cultures', *Connections*, 7, 1: 67–86.

Allen, Paula Gunn (1986) *The Sacred Hoop: Recovering the Feminine in American Indian Traditions*. Boston: Beacon Press.

Alpert, Rebecca T. (1989) 'In God's image: coming to terms with Leviticus', in Christie Balka and Andy Rose (eds), *Twice Blessed: On Being Lesbian or Gay and Jewish*. Boston: Beacon Press. pp. 61–70.

Balka, Christie and Rose, Andy (eds) (1989) *Twice Blessed: On Being Lesbian or Gay and Jewish*. Boston: Beacon Press.

Baum, Robert M. (1993) 'Homosexuality and the traditional religions of the Americas and Africa', in Arlene Swidler (ed.), *Homosexuality and World Religions*. Harrisburg, PA: Trinity Press International. pp. 1–46.

Blue, Lionel (1995) 'Godly and gay', in Jonathan Magonet (ed.), *Jewish Explorations of Sexuality*. Providence: Berghahn Books. pp. 117–31.

Book of Discipline of the United Methodist Church (1996) Nashville, TN: The United Methodist Publishing House.

Boswell, John (1980) *Christianity, Social Tolerance and Homosexuality: Gay People in Western Europe from the Beginning of the Christian Era to the Fourteenth Century*. Chicago: University of Chicago Press.

Boswell, John (1994) *Same-Sex Unions in Premodern Europe*. New York: Random House.

Comstock, Gary David (1993) *Gay Theology Without Apology*. Cleveland: Pilgrim Press.

Comstock, Gary David (1996) *Unrepentant, Self-Affirming, Practicing: Lesbian/Bisexual/Gay People within Organized Religion*. New York: Continuum.

Comstock, Gray David and Henking Susan E. (eds) (1997) *Que(e)rying Religion: A Critical Anthology*. New York: Continuum.

Countryman, William (1988) *Dirt, Greed, and Sex: Sexual Ethics in the New Testament and their Implications for Today*. Philadelphia, PA: Fortress Press.

Curran, Charles E. (1998) 'Sexual orientation and human rights in American religious discourse: a Roman Catholic perspective', in Saul M. Olyan and Martha C. Nussbaum (eds), *Sexual Orientation and Human Rights in American Religious Discourse*. New York: Oxford University Press. pp. 85–100.

Dallas, Joe (1991) *Desires in Conflict: Answering the Struggle for Sexual Identity*. Eugene, OR: Harvest House Publishers.

Dossani, Shahid (1997) 'Being Muslim and gay', in Gary David Comstock and Susan E. Henking (eds), *Que(e)rying Religion: A Critical Anthology*. New York: Continuum. pp. 236–7.

Elshtain, Jean Bethke (1997 [1991]) 'Against gay marriage', in Andrew Sullivan (ed.) *Same-Sex Marriage: Pro and Con, A Reader*. New York: Vintage Books. pp. 57–60.

Finnis, John M. (1995) 'Law, morality, and "sexual orientation"', *Notre Dame Journal of Law, Ethics and Public Policy*, 9 (1): 11–40.

Foucault, Michel (1978) *The History of Sexuality, Volume I: An Introduction*. New York: Vintage Books.

Fortune, Marie M. (1995) *Love Does No Harm: Sexual Ethics for the Rest of Us*. New York: Continuum.

Fulkerson, Mary McClintock (1997) 'Gender – being it or doing it? The church, homosexuality, and the politics of identity', in Gary David Comstock and Susan E. Henking (eds), *Que(e)rying Religion: A Critical Anthology*, New York: Continuum. pp. 188–201.

Fuller, Ruth L. (1994) 'What does science teach about human sexuality?', in Sally B. Geis and Donald E. Messer (eds), *Caught in the Crossfire: Helping Christians Debate Homosexuality*. Nashville, TN: Abingdon Press. pp. 78–87.

Geis, Sally B. and Messer, Donald E. (eds) (1994) *Caught in the Crossfire: Helping Christians Debate Homosexuality*. Nashville, TN: Abingdon Press.

Gordon, Lewis R. (1998) 'Introduction: three perspectives on being gay in African-American ecclesiology and religious thought', in Saul M. Olyan and Martha C. Nussbaum (eds), *Sexual Orientation and Human Rights in American Religious Discourse*. New York: Oxford University Press. pp. 171–7.

Goss, Robert (1993) *Jesus Acted Up: A Gay and Lesbian Manifesto*. San Francisco: Harper San Francisco.

Gray, Edward R. and Thumma, Scott L. (1997) 'The gospel hour: liminality, identity, and religion in a gay bar', in Penny Edgell Becker and Nancy L. Eiesland (eds), *Contemporary American Religion: An Ethnographic Reader*. Walnut Creek, CA: Alta Mira Press. pp. 79–98.

Halperin, David M. (1989) 'Sex before sexuality: pederasty, politics, and power in classical Athens', in Martin Duberman, Martha Vicinus and George Chauncey, Jr. (eds), *Hidden From History: Reclaiming the Gay and Lesbian Past.* New York: Meridian. pp. 37–53.

Halperin, David M. (1993) 'Is there a history of sexuality?', in Henry Abelove, Michèle Aina Barale and David M. Halperin. *The Lesbian and Gay Studies Reader.* New York: Routledge. pp. 416–31.

Hanigan, James P. (1998) 'Sexual orientation and human rights: a Roman Catholic View', in Saul M. Olyan and Martha C. Nussbaum (eds), *Sexual Orientation and Human Rights in American Religious Discourse.* New York: Oxford University Press. pp. 63–84.

Herdt, Gilbert H. (1981) *Guardians of the Flutes: Idioms of Masculinity.* New York: McGraw Hill.

Herdt, Gilbert H. and Stoller, Robert J. (1990) *Intimate Communications: Erotics and the Study of Culture.* New York: Columbia University Press.

Heyward, Carter (1984) *Our Passion for Justice: Images of Power, Sexuality, and Liberation.* Cleveland, OH: Pilgrim Press.

Heyward, Carter (1989) *Touching Our Strength: The Erotic as Power and the Love of God.* New York: HarperCollins.

Horner, Tom (1978) *Jonathan Loved David: Homosexuality in Biblical Times.* Philadelphia, PA: Westminster Press.

Hunter, James Davison (1991) *Culture Wars: The Struggle to Define America.* New York: Basic Books.

Kahn, Yoel H. (1997 [1989]) 'The *Kedushah* of homosexual relationships', in Andrew Sullivan (ed.), *Same-Sex Marriage: Pro and Con, A Reader.* New York: Vintage Books. pp. 71–7.

Lamm, Norman (1978 [1974]) 'Judaism and the modern attitude to homosexuality', in Menachem Marc Kellner (ed.), *Contemporary Jewish Ethics.* New York: Hebrew Publishing Company. pp. 375–99.

Lorde, Audre (1984) *Sister/Outsider: Essays and Speeches.* Trumansburg, New York: Crossing Press.

Magonet, Jonathan (ed.) (1995) *Jewish Explorations of Sexuality.* Providence: Berghahn Books.

Maitland, Sara (1995) *A Big-Enough God: A Feminist's Search for a Joyful Theology.* New York: Riverhead Books.

Mariner, Rodney (1995) 'The Jewish homosexual and the *Halakhic* tradition', in Jonathan Magonet (ed.), *Jewish Explorations of Sexuality.* Providence: Berghahn Books. pp. 83–93.

Marsden, George M. (1980) *Fundamentalism and American Culture: The Shaping of Twentieth-Century Evangelicalism, 1870–1925.* New York: Oxford University Press.

Nelson, James B. (1978) *Embodiment: An Approach to Sexuality and Christian Theology.* Minneapolis: Augsburg Publishing House.

Novak, David (1998) 'Religious communities, secular society, and sexuality: one Jewish opinion', in Saul M. Olyan and Martha C. Nussbaum (eds), *Sexual Orientation and Human Rights in American Religious Discourse.* New York: Oxford University Press. pp. 11–28.

Olyan, Saul M. (1997) '"And with a male you shall not lie the lying down of a woman"': on the meaning and significance of Leviticus 18: 22 and 20: 13', in Gary David Comstock and Susan E. Henking (eds), *Que(e)rying Religion: A Critical Anthology.* New York: Continuum. pp. 398–414.

Olyan, Saul M. and Martha C. Nussbaum (eds) (1998) *Sexual Orientation and Human Rights in American Religious Discourse.* New York: Oxford University Press.

Perry, Michael J. (1995) 'The morality of homosexual conduct: a response to John Finnis', *Notre Dame Journal of Law, Ethics and Public Policy,* 9 (1): 41–74.

Plaskow, Judith (1989) 'Towards a new theology of sexuality', in Christie Balka and Andy Rose (eds), *Twice Blessed: On Being Lesbian or Gay and Jewish.* Boston: Beacon Press. pp. 141–51.

Plaskow, Judith (1998) 'Sexual orientation and human rights: a progressive Jewish perspective', in Saul M. Olyan and Martha C. Nussbaum (eds), *Sexual Orientation and Human Rights in American Religious Discourse.* New York: Oxford University Press. pp. 29–45.

Prager, Dennis (1997 [1990]) 'Homosexuality, the Bible, and us – a Jewish perspective', in Andrew Sullivan (ed.), *Same-Sex Marriage: Pro and Con, A Reader.* New York: Vintage Books. pp. 61–6.

Pronk, Pim (1993) *Against Nature? Types of Moral Argumentation Regarding Homosexuality.* Grand Rapids, MI: Eerdmans Publishing Co.

Rogers, Eugene F. (1998) 'Sanctification, homosexuality, and God's triune life', in Saul M. Olyan and Martha C. Nussbaum (eds), *Sexual Orientation and Human Rights in American Religious Discourse.* New York: Oxford University Press. pp. 134–60.

Roscoe, Will (1997) 'We'wha and Klah: the American Indian berdache', in Gary David Comstock and Susan E. Henking (eds), *Que(e)rying Religion: A Critical Anthology.* New York: Continuum. pp. 89–106.

Sarah, Elizabeth (1995) 'Judaism and lesbianism: a tale of life on the margins of the text', in Jonathan Magonet (ed.), *Jewish Explorations of Sexuality,* Providence: Berghahn Books. pp. 95–102.

Scanzoni, Letha and Mollenkott, Virginia Ramsey (1994) *Is the Homosexual My Neighbor? A Positive Christian Response.* San Francisco: Harper.

Scroggs, Robin (1983) *The New Testament and Homosexuality: Contextual Background for Contemporary Debate.* Philadelphia, PA: Fortress Press.

Sergent, Bernard (1986 [1984]) *Homosexuality in Greek Myth.* Transl. by Arthur Goldhammer. Boston: Beacon Press.

Sharma, Arvind (1993) 'Homosexuality and Hinduism', in Arlene Swidler (ed.), *Homosexuality and World Religions*. Harrisburg, PA: Trinity Press International. pp. 47–80.

Shulman, Sheila (1995) 'What is our love?', in Jonathan Magonet (ed.), *Jewish Explorations of Sexuality*. Providence: Berghahn Books. pp. 103–114.

Solomon, Mark (1995) 'A strange conjunction', in Jonathan Magonet (ed.), *Jewish Explorations of Sexuality*. Providence: Berghahn Books. pp. 75–82.

Spong, John Shelby (1988) *Living in Sin? A Bishop Rethinks Human Sexuality*. San Francisco: Harper and Row.

Sullivan, Andrew (ed.) (1997) *Same-Sex Marriage: Pro and Con, A Reader*. New York: Vintage Books.

Swartley, Willard (1983) *Slavery, Sabbath, War and Women: Case Issues in Biblical Interpretation*. Scottsdale, PA: Herald Press.

Swidler, Arlene (ed.) (1993) *Homosexuality and World Religions*. Harrisburg, PA: Trinity Press International.

Trible, Phyllis (1987) *God and the Rhetoric of Sexuality*. Philadelphia, PA: Fortress Press.

Umansky, Ellen M. (1997) 'Jewish attitudes towards homosexuality: a review of comtemporary sources', in Gary David Comstock and Susan E. Henking (eds), *Que(e)rying Religion: A Critical Anthology*. New York: Continuum. pp. 181–7.

Warner, Michael (1993) *Fear of a Queer Planet: Queer Politics and Social Theory*. Minneapolis: University of Minnesota Press.

Warner, R. Stephen (1995) 'The Metropolitan Community churches and the gay agenda: the power of pentacostalism and essentialism', in *Religion and the Social Order. Volume 5*. Greenwood, CT: JAI Press Inc. pp. 81–108.

Williams, Rhys H. (ed.) (1997) *Culture Wars in American Politics: Critical Reviews of a Popular Myth*. New York: Aldine de Gruyter.

Williams, Walter L. (1986) *The Spirit and the Flesh: Sexual Diversity in American Indian Cultures*. Boston: Beacon Press.

Wuthnow, Robert (1988) *The Restructuring of American Religion*. Princeton, NJ: Princeton University Press.

19

Gays and Lesbians as Workers and Consumers in the Economy

MARIEKA M. KLAWITTER

The emergence of sexual orientation as a component of personal identity was closely tied to changes in the organization of economic activity in the past century. Industrialization and urbanization allowed many men and women to separate from farm-based families and from prescribed productive and reproductive roles (D'Emilio, 1983). Urban wage labor markets provided the economic means for men and women to create lives apart from heterosexual marriage and to create sexual and affectional identities (Matthaei, 1997). Throughout the world, the ability to live as gay or lesbian is still greatly affected by the level of economic development and by personal wealth.

Economic relationships have also been an enduring target for advocates for and against gay rights in industrialized countries. In the 1950s and 1960s, gay bars, bathhouses and other businesses were targets for those seeking to wipe out homosexuality (Escoffier, 1997). Patrons of those businesses risked losing their jobs if arrested in a public raid or if otherwise identified as homosexual. Since then, attitudes about homosexuality have changed and gay businesses have greatly expanded in number and variety. Many cities have developed gay neighborhood

business districts and directories of gay businesses. Similarly, some workplaces have been transformed from dangerous places for known homosexuals to gay family-friendly institutions. Some private organizations and governments have created anti-discrimination policies that protect gays and lesbians from employment discrimination based on sexual orientation.

The incredible changes in gay rights and social acceptance, though not uniform, have allowed many gays and lesbians to openly participate in the economy. In this chapter, I will explore how sexual orientation continues to affect economic participation as workers and consumers. The first section analyzes the recent evidence of discrimination in labor markets. It also considers how sexual orientation affects employment through choices in education, location, occupation, and work time. The second section reviews the effects of sexual orientation on consumption behavior and activities.

GAYS AND LESBIANS AS WORKERS

Earnings from employment are the most important source of income for most individuals and families. As such, earnings are an important determinant of economic well-being and work is an important economic activity. The amount written on a paycheck is determined by a complex set of decisions and outcomes negotiated by individual workers, their families, and employers. Differences in average earnings could be a reflection of discrimination (different treatment or opportunities), different choices, or both. Are gays and lesbians different than others in labor market opportunities and choices that affect their paychecks? Here we'll explore the determinants of earnings, the concept of discrimination, evidence of sexual orientation discrimination in labor markets, and the possibility of different employment choices made by gays and lesbians.

IS THERE DISCRIMINATION IN LABOR MARKETS?

Labor market discrimination is differential hiring, firing, promotion, or wages for individuals based on their real or perceived group membership. The past history of employment discrimination based on sexual orientation by government and private employers is well documented in court cases (*Harvard Law Review*, Editors, 1989: 44–74). However, some have questioned whether gays and lesbians are still subject to labor market discrimination (Hewitt, 1995). Widespread discrimination should lower average earnings by closing off job and promotion opportunities and encouraging gays and lesbians to trade off high wages for more supportive working conditions (a 'compensating differential').

The best quantitative evidence in the discrimination debate comes from econometric studies that use national random samples. These studies use multivariate statistics to assess the effects of sexual orientation on average earnings, after disentangling the effects of other factors. Overall, the econometric evidence of sexual orientation

discrimination is mixed. There is stronger evidence of discrimination against gay men than against lesbians.

Badgett (1995) used data from the US General Social Survey from 1989 to 1992 to study annual earnings. She estimated that men who had same-sex sexual experiences earned 11 to 27 per cent less, on average, than did other men, after controlling for age, education, occupation, marital status and region of residence. Average earnings were also lower for women who had same-sex sexual experiences, but the differences were not statistically significant. Two newer studies replicated Badgett's work with additional years of data and alternative definitions of sexual orientation (Blandford, 2000; Black et al., 1999). Both studies found that gay men earned less than heterosexual men and that lesbians earned more than heterosexual women.

My co-author, Victor Flatt and I (1998) used the 1990 US Census data to compare average earnings for members of different-sex couples (married and unmarried) and same-sex couples. After controlling for differences in individual characteristics and labor market conditions, we found that men in same-sex couples earned about 26 per cent less than married men, but about the same as men in unmarried different-sex couples. Women in same-sex couples earned significantly more than women in married couples and women in unmarried different-sex couples. However, the higher earnings for women in same-sex couples were almost completely explained by the greater hours and weeks worked by that group. Beyond the effects of sexual orientation, *per se,* men and women in same-sex couples had higher average levels of education and were more likely to live in urban areas. Both of these factors contribute to higher levels of earnings.

These studies show mixed evidence of earnings discrimination against gays and lesbians. In contrast, there have always been large earnings gaps between people of color and whites and between women and men that were not explained by other characteristics. Is it possible that labor market discrimination might not show up in the average amount of paychecks?

There are two primary explanations for the lack of consistently large differences in average earnings: the ability to pass as straight and differences in work effort based on gender roles. If gays and lesbians are not 'out' at work, then they may face less discrimination and avoid lower wages. As I discuss below, most workers are out to some, but not all co-workers. The second explanation is based on the gender of the worker and his or her partner. The pattern of gay men earning less than married men and lesbians earning more than married women (before accounting for hours of work) is consistent with workers making adjustment to their own work effort based on potential earnings from a partner. Because women still earn significantly less than men on average do, a lesbian can expect significantly less income from a potential partner than can a gay man. She may increase her work effort (e.g., number of hours and weeks of work, investment in job training) to compensate. I'll discuss this possibility more when I consider intrahousehold work decisions below. The effects of gender on work could offset lower earnings due to sexual orientation discrimination for lesbians.

Other evidence of employment discrimination is available from surveys of the general public and of gays and lesbians. Data from national random samples show that Americans have increased general support for equal job opportunities for gays and lesbians from 56 per cent in 1977 to 84 per cent in 1996 (Yang, 1998: 6). However, in 1996 only 55 per cent of Americans thought that 'homosexuals' should be hired as elementary school teachers and only about half thought being lesbian or gay should not disqualify someone from being president of the USA (ibid.: 10–11). Sherrill (1996) found that US public attitudes (on a 'feeling thermometer') toward gays and lesbians were worse than those toward any other group except illegal aliens. These statistics suggest that public support for employment discrimination is decreasing, but still not negligible.

Surveys of gays and lesbians have generally found that 25 to 30 per cent believe that they have experienced sexual orientation discrimination (Badgett, 1997b). In addition, most respondents were 'out' to some but not all co-workers which suggests significant fear of discrimination. Similarly, Woods (1993) describes the incredible efforts by some gays to hide their sexual orientation from co-workers and employers. These studies point to perceptions of discrimination, but are not from random samples and therefore may not be representative of the experience of the general gay and lesbian population.

Some countries and many states, provinces, or cities have laws that prohibit discrimination based on sexual orientation in public or private employment (International Gay and Lesbian Human Rights Commission, 1999). Many European nations adopted antidiscrimination legislation in the late 1990s and South Africa became the first country to include sexual orientation as a protected category in its constitution in 1996.

As of 2000, the USA does not have federal legislation that bans private employers from discriminating as it does for race, sex, religion, national origin, age, and disability. However, this type of legislation has been introduced in the US Congress as the Employment Non-Discrimination Act. There are currently 11 states and many local governments that do have antidiscrimination legislation for private employment (van der Meick, 2000: p4; General Accounting Office, 1997). Local policies have usually been adopted in urban areas with higher than average levels of education and numbers of non-family households (Klawitter and Hammer, 1999; Haeberle, 1996; Wald et al., 1996). These characteristics, not surprisingly, also predict lower levels of antigay feeling and higher levels of average earnings.

Studies of the federal legislation banning discrimination based on race and sex suggest that these laws contributed to labor market gains for blacks and for women (Burstein, 1985; Donohue and Heckman,

1991; Gunderson, 1989). However, we did not find similar gains for members of same-sex couples covered by antidiscrimination policies (Klawitter and Flatt, 1998). Using multivariate analysis, we estimated the earnings effects of living in a state or local area that had sexual orientation in its employment non-discrimination policy. Our results showed that these policies were adopted in places that had higher average wages for people in both same-sex and different-sex couples, but there was no differential effect for same-sex couples. We also did not find that the policies were generally adopted in places with relatively higher wages for people in same-sex couples (after accounting for the effects of education and urban location). These results could reflect the lack of enforcement of non-discrimination policies, an unwillingness of gays and lesbians to initiate legal action, or lack of clearly identifiable employment discrimination.

Employment benefits make up another significant part of compensation for employment and gays and lesbians often do not have the same access to these benefits. Overall, benefits average almost 30 per cent of all compensation for work (Economic Benefits Research Institute, 1999). Many married workers can obtain health insurance for spouses who are self-employed, working in jobs without health benefits, or not in the labor market. Although a growing number of government and private employers offer benefits to domestic partners of unmarried employers, this coverage remains scarce. A 1999 study found that only 12 per cent of workers worked for an employer who offered benefits for same-sex domestic partners (Economic Benefits Research Institute, 2000). Access to health benefits for domestic partners would allow families a wider array of opportunities for combining employment and home work.

Discrimination may also affect other job characteristics such as the ability to socialize with co-workers and to participate in the workplace community. Ellis and Riggle (1995) found that gays and lesbians who were out were more satisfied with their relationships

with co-workers and those working for companies with anti-discrimination policies were more satisfied with their jobs. An early study found that lesbians were more likely to be out in jobs where they worked in small organizations, in female-dominated human services occupations, when they did not work with children, and when their incomes were low (Schneider, 1987). Schneider did not find that being out had a direct effect on the chances of socializing with co-workers outside of the workplace. The choice of strategy for 'managing' sexual orientation at work may dictate the level of social integration. Woods (1993) found that some gay professional men chose to 'play straight' at work or to maintain strict boundaries between their personal and professional lives. These strategies might minimize possible discrimination, but would also exact a toll by limiting social interaction at work.

DO GAYS AND LESBIANS MAKE DIFFERENT CHOICES IN THE LABOR MARKET?

Individuals and families make choices about schooling, work, and home that affect wages and earnings. The effects of gender and sexual orientation on these choices could explain some differences in labor market outcomes for gays and lesbians. Also, real or potential discrimination in the labor market could feed back to affect these choices.

Education

Economists use the term 'human capital' to refer to skills and knowledge that are valuable (and therefore rewarded) in the labor market. Job experience and schooling are the most common forms of human capital.

Several studies have found higher levels of education for gays and lesbians than for others, among both men and women (Blumstein and Schwartz, 1983; Klawitter, 1998; Black et al., 2000). Black et al. (1999) found that the higher level of education for gay men was not likely the result of reporting self-selection because the education levels for fathers of gay men were similar to the levels for fathers of other men. If men from higher socio-economic backgrounds were more likely to identify themselves as members of a same-sex couple, then we would expect to see higher average education levels for their fathers.

Gay men and lesbians might get more education to offset expected earnings effects of discrimination in employment. Alternatively, educational settings may be relatively gay-friendly and encourage longer stays for gays and lesbians. Either way, education is one of the strongest predictors of earnings and higher levels push earnings up for gays and lesbians. This is one of the reasons that econometric studies that account for the effects of education are important in assessing earnings discrimination.

Location

Gays and lesbians are more likely to be located in urban areas than are other people (Badgett, 1995; Black et al., 2000). Indeed, Black et al. (2000: 148) found that 59 per cent of men in same-sex couples were clustered in the twenty cities with the largest gay population (compared to only 26 per cent of the general US population in those cities). Lesbians were somewhat less clustered; 45 per cent were in the top twenty cities (with 25 per cent of the US population).

Gays and lesbians may move to urban areas to find a supportive gay community and to find tolerant labor markets. Because wages (and the cost of living) are generally higher in urban areas than in suburban and rural areas, this pattern should lead to higher earnings for gays and lesbians. Consistent with this, our findings showed that same-sex couples lived in areas with higher average wages (Klawitter and Flatt, 1998). However, we did not find that those labor markets were so much more tolerant that average wages were differentially higher for gays and lesbians after accounting for other characteristics.

Occupation

Popular images of gay men as hairdressers and decorators and lesbians as construction workers convey the notion that sexual orientation affects occupational choice. Occupational choice is a complex process tied up with schooling decisions, lifestyle choices, and work opportunities.

Badgett and King (1997) studied occupational choice by gays and lesbians and how closely it followed the occupational patterns of anti-gay sentiments. They hypothesized that gays and lesbians might choose occupations based on the potential for harassment (anti-gay sentiment), the ability to hide sexual orientation (level of social requirements on the job), and compatibility with family structure (less frequent child-rearing for gays and lesbians). They found that levels of anti-gay sentiments did seem to vary by occupation, but that urban location, education levels, and age explained much of the variation. Although hampered by very small sample size, their results also suggest that gay men may cluster in more tolerant occupations, but that lesbians do not. In my work, I found that women in same-sex couples were more likely than women in different-sex couples to be in managerial or professional jobs and much less likely to be in technical/sales or operator/fabricator jobs (Klawitter, 1998). Blandford (2000) found a similar pattern by sexual orientation for women in technical occupations, but a different pattern for those in service and operator occupations. For men, Blandford found that unmarried gay men were more likely than heterosexual men to be in managerial and technical occupations, and less likely to be in production or operator occupations.

On the whole, grand patterns of occupation choice by sexual orientation have not materialized. However, it does seem that occupational choice may affect the wage gap by sexual orientation. Badgett's (1995) estimates of sexual orientation discrimination were larger for men and smaller for women when she controlled for occupational choice. I found that occupational choice partially accounted for higher wages for women in same-sex couples (Klawitter, 1998). Similarly, when Blandford (2000) used more detailed occupational information he found that less of the difference in average earnings was attributable to sexual orientation for both men and women. Further work on the interrelations of occupational choice and sexual orientation might help sort out the patterns.

Work Time

Earnings are greatly affected by the amount of time spent working. Having a partner or having children can change the incentives to work in the market and the amount of time devoted to work for wages. In traditional husband/wife families, marriage and child-rearing increase work time and earnings for husbands and decrease them for wives.

Black et al. (2000) estimated that about 40 per cent of lesbians and about 20 to 30 per cent of gay men had partners living with them. In contrast, more than half of all adults are married and another 3 per cent cohabit with different-sex partners (Bureau of Census, 1993: Table 16). Black et al. also estimated that there were children living with 22 per cent of lesbian couples, 5 per cent of gay male couples, 36 per cent of unmarried different-sex couples, and 59 per cent of married couples. They estimated higher levels of child-rearing for all gays and lesbians (not just couples): 28 per cent for lesbians and 14 per cent for gay men.

Economists and sociologists have generally assumed that family members jointly make decisions about work. There is a large literature on intrahousehold allocation of home work and labor market work for heterosexual couples and a smaller amount on allocation for homosexual couples. Economists have viewed the allocation within families as reflecting the comparative advantage of partners in home and labor markets (Becker, 1973). This model suggests that the partner with the greatest opportunities in the labor market (highest potential wage) will spend more time on a job and less time doing home work. The other partner will then 'specialize' in home production – using time and market goods to cook, clean, and make a happy home life. The economic approach is very useful in recognizing some incentives for household allocation (for example, wage rates and overall income), but generally ignores the importance of gender roles or other cultural influences.

The effects of gender are at once diminished and amplified in same-sex couples. For same-sex couples, gender roles are less useful as a tool for assigning work tasks within the family. Gender may matter less for an individual's labor market decisions (and a partner's gender may matter more). For example, women with female partners may work more in the market (and thereby take on a less traditionally feminine role) to offset lower expected partner earnings (due to gender). Similarly, men with male partners may work less because they expect male-sized earnings from their partner. However, gender may be amplified by the presence of two people with similar gender socialization and by an effort to maintain gender identification while doing work that is normally reserved for the other gender. For example, Carrington tells how he found that partners seemed to portray their partners' work as gender appropriate by mis-remembering or mis-reporting who had completed household tasks (1999: 51–2).

In my work using US census data (1995), I found that same-sex couples were much less likely to have one member specialize in the labor market than were married couples. (Unmarried different-sex couples were in-between.) Partners in gay male couples were the most likely to work similar numbers of weeks in a year and hours in a week, followed by lesbian couples. Earnings for partners was the most similar for lesbian couples ($r = .42$) then for gay male couples ($r = .29$)

and unmarried different-sex couples ($r = .26$). Married couples had the lowest correlation in earnings for partners ($r = .12$). High correlation shows a lack of labor market specialization, but it may also reflect the matching gender for partners – hence matching gendered labor market opportunities. However, gay and lesbian couples are less closely matched on age, education and race than are married couples (Klawitter, 1995) and this could work to lower the earnings correlations for same-sex couples.

Several studies have found that gender and sexual orientation affect the division of home work (Blumstein and Schwartz, 1983; Kurdek, 1993). Kurdek found that lesbian couples tended to share home work by alternating tasks or doing them together, while gay male couples tended to split up the tasks. In married couples the wife usually did most of the household tasks. Based on an extensive qualitative study of San Francisco area same-sex couples, Carrington (1999) argues that equality in household work in gay and lesbian households is a myth. It seems that gay and lesbian families share market and home work more equally or fairly (not solely on the basis of gender) than do married couples, but the allocation is not simply 50–50.

Specialization may be economically efficient, but it is a risky strategy for those specializing in home production because a break-up would leave them without income (England and Kilbourne, 1990). This is probably one of the reasons that unmarried different-sex do not specialize as much as married couples (Blumstein and Schwartz, 1983; Klawitter, 1995). Similarly, Lundberg and Rose (1999) found that specialization was much less likely in married couples that later divorced. Same-sex couples (like other unmarried couples) lack the legal protections of marriage that might allow home specialists to share assets after separation. For example, Carrington (1999: 180–4) tells the story of a gay man who experienced a huge decrease in income after leaving a high-earning partner. The man did not expect any compensation or a share of the property acquired as a couple despite having done a majority of home work during the relationship.

To summarize, families make decisions about household work and labor market work and those decisions follow patterns based on sexual orientation and legal marriage. The implications for earnings are that we might expect women in same-sex couples to work more in the labor market than other women because of the need for more income, the lesser effect of gender roles in the household, and the lack of legal protections. Similarly, gay men might work less than married men because they have a male partner's earnings and lower gender role expectations in the home, but this might be offset by the lack of legal marriage protections. These influences may partly explain the patterns of earnings by sexual orientation found in the quantitative studies. The remaining influence of gender roles on behavior may mitigate these effects by encouraging gay men to work in the labor market and lesbians to work in the household.

CONSUMPTION ORIENTATION

The other side of the family balance sheet involves expenditures – using income to buy goods and services. In a simple economic model, consumers buy goods and services to increase their 'utility', subject to the constraints of prices and income. But in the world we live in, people shop for entertainment, consume to create identity, and are categorized and targeted by marketers seeking to influence consumption decisions. In this section, I will review research on how sexual orientation affects consumption decisions and experiences. Do gays and lesbians make different consumption choices than others? Do they face discrimination in consumption markets? How are gays and lesbians targeted by marketers and what are the implications for consumers and for the gay community?

Few studies of consumption patterns distinguish between consumers by sexual orientation. Some marketing studies have suggested that, compared to heterosexuals, gays and lesbians are more likely to spend money, spend more on luxury goods (travel, entertainment, expensive clothing), and are more brand-loyal and fashion conscious (Penaloza, 1996: 26). These studies generally reflect the tastes and habits of a non-representative sample of gays and lesbians and are used to bolster claims of a lucrative and under-tapped market.

Other sources of information confirm the idea that gay and lesbian consumers at least partly create their sexual identity through their consumption choices – what they buy and where they shop. Interviews conducted by Freitas et al. (1996) support the notion that some gays and lesbians use clothing and jewelry to help define themselves as part of a queer subculture. Carrington (1999: 154) described how some of the families in his study consciously shopped in gay-owned businesses in spite of paying higher prices – they labelled it the 'gay tax'. Especially in areas with gay-identified neighborhoods, the act of shopping may become part of the performance of sexual orientation.

Do gays and lesbians face discrimination in consumption markets? In a small but carefully scripted study of retail stores, Walters and Curran (1996) found that straight students posing as gay or lesbian couples were treated much differently than were those posing as heterosexual couples. The straight couples received quick, courteous treatment while the gay and lesbian couples were helped more slowly (if at all) and were subjected to pointing, laughing, and rude comments. Similarly, Jones (1996) found that gay couples had less success making hotel reservations than did straight couples.

Much of the hype about the new gay market is based on claims of high income for gays and lesbians based on results of non-representative surveys from marketers (Badgett, 1997a). There is, however, some merit to the idea of gay men as having relatively high household incomes. Using 1990 census data, I found that average incomes were $58,489 for gay male couples, $47,192 for married couples, $45,756 for female same-sex couples, and $37,518 for unmarried different sex couples (Klawitter, 1995). After accounting for location and individual characteristics for partners, male same-sex couples and married couples had similar incomes; female same-sex and unmarried different sex couples had lower incomes. Combining earnings for two men leads to higher average income for gay couples, despite the estimates of lower individual earnings for men in same-sex couples (as I discussed above). Similarly, women in same sex couples earned significantly more than other women (before controlling for other characteristics), but live in households without a male-sized income. These figures do not, however, include people who are not partnered and the best estimates suggest that fewer gay men and lesbians are partnered than are heterosexuals. However, for marketing purposes, family income and family spending habits are likely to be the appropriate metric, unlike comparisons for employment discrimination.

Gays and lesbians may benefit as a 'target market' because it may encourage the development of products and services that affirm queer culture and better serve family consumption needs (for example his and his monogrammed bathrobes, all-women travel packages, or baby bibs with rainbow flags). In addition, having advertisements and products for gays and lesbians serves to legitimize the community as participants in the economy. However, some have worried that marketing hype has provided fodder for anti-gay campaigns that portray gays and lesbians as privileged, frivolous, and not in need of anti-discrimination protection (Gluckman and Reed, 1997). Also, there may be a tension between being a target market and being a social or political movement (Penaloza, 1996; Freitas et al., 1996). Focus on marketing images of consumption by 'beautiful' people may de-emphasize political goals and lead to the alienation and ostracism of people less centrally situated in mainstream culture.

CONCLUSION

My overview of the social science literature suggests that sexual orientation plays a large role in work outcomes, but that there is mixed evidence of discrimination in average earnings for gays and lesbians. The influence of gender on work in both markets and families seems to trump sexual orientation. In consumption markets, gays and lesbians have moved from being targeted by police in gay bars to being targeted by marketers. Of course these changes, like the changes in the labor market, are neither universal nor uniformly seen as progressive. Individuals sometimes face discrimination when buying goods or services in spite of being legitimized as buyers through some marketing campaigns.

The quality and quantity of research on the economics of sexual orientation have grown immensely in the past thirty years. However, many areas remain unexplored or inadequately understood. How do sexual orientation and gender separately and jointly affect family economic decisions? How do the effects of sexual orientation on employment change over the life cycle? How much of our understanding of sexual orientation will be relevant in the changing social, economic, and historical context? How do economic opportunities for gays and lesbians vary by geographic location and social context? How have public policies affected the opportunities and choices for gays and lesbians?

Changes in the social and legal context have enhanced our ability to research issues of sexual orientation. Researchers can publish work on sexual orientation, funding agencies and foundations will support the research, and respondents will answer questions about sexual behavior or identity. Yet, the availability of good quantitative and qualitative data has lagged behind our willingness to analyse the data. I hope that the new century brings new data collection efforts aimed at exploring the economics of sexual orientation.

There have been remarkable changes in how gays and lesbians live and work in the past thirty years. Today many of us participate fully and openly in society and the economy. However, some still face serious discrimination and barriers in employment or consumption. For all, sexual orientation and gender still serve as categories that determine the way families and individuals participate in the economy.

REFERENCES

Badgett, M.V. Lee (1995) 'The wage effects of sexual orientation discrimination' *Industrial and Labor Relations Review*, 48 (4): 726–39.
Badgett, M.V. Lee (1997a) 'Beyond biased samples: challenging the myths on the economic status of lesbians and gay men', in Amy Gluckman and Betsy Reed (eds), *Homo Economics: Capitalism, Community, and Lesbian and Gay Life*. New York: Routledge. pp. 65–71.
Badgett, M.V. Lee (1997b) 'Vulnerability in the workplace: evidence of anti-gay discrimination', *Angles: The Policy Journal of the Institute for Gay and Lesbian Strategic Studies*, 2 (1).
Badgett, M.V. Lee and King, Mary C. (1997) 'Lesbian and gay occupational strategies', in Amy Gluckman and Betsy Reed (eds), *Homo Economics: Capitalism, Community, and Lesbian and Gay Life*. New York: Routledge. pp. 73–85.
Becker, Gary S. (1973) 'A theory of marriage: part I', *Journal of Political Economy*, 81: 813–46.
Black, Dan, Gates, Gary, Sanders, Seth and Taylor, Lowell (2000) 'Demographics of the gay and lesbian population in the United States: evidence from available systematic data sources', *Demography*, 37 (2): 139–54.
Black, Dan A., Makar, Hoda R., Saunders, Seth G. and Taylor, Lowell (1999) 'The effects of sexual orientation on earnings', unpublished manuscript.
Blandford, John M. (2000) 'Evidence of the role of sexual orientation in the determination of earnings outcomes', unpublished manuscript.
Blumstein, Philip and Schwartz, Pepper (1983) *American Couples*. New York: Pocket Books.
Bureau of the Census (1993) '1990 Census of population: Social and economic characteristics', Washington DC: US Government Printing Office.
Burstein, Paul (1985) *Discrimination, Jobs, and Politics: The Struggle for Equal Opportunity in the United States since the New Deal*. Chicago: The University of Chicago Press.
Button, James W., Rienzo, Barbara A. and Wald, Kenneth D. (1997), *Private Lives, Public Conflicts: Battles over Gay Rights in American Communities*. Washington, DC: Congressional Quarterly, Inc.
Carrington, Christopher (1999) *No Place Like Home: Relationships and Family Life among Lesbians and Gay Men*. Chicago: The University of Chicago Press.

D'Emilio, John (1983) *Sexual Politics, Sexual Communities: The Making of a Homosexual Minority in the United States 1940–1970*. Chicago: University of Chicago Press.

Donohue, John J. III and Heckman, James (1991) 'Continuous versus episodic change: the impact of civil rights policy on the economic status of blacks', *Journal of Economic Literature*, 29 (4): 1603–43.

Economic Benefits Research Institute (1999) *Compensation Costs in Private Industry, March 1987 to March 1999*. Facts from EBRI, September 1999. www.ebri.org.

Economic Benefits Research Institute (2000) *Domestic Partner Benefits: Facts and Background*. Facts from EBRI, June 2000. www.ebri.org.

Ellis, Alan L. and Riggle, Ellen D.B. (1995) 'The relation of job satisfaction and degree of openness about one's sexual orientation for lesbians and gay men', *Journal of Homosexuality*, 30 (2): 75–85.

England, Paula and Kilbourne, Barbara Stanek (1990) 'Markets, marriages, and other mates: the problem of power', in Roger Friedland and G.F. Robertson (eds), *Beyond the Market*. New York: Aldine de Gruyter.

Escoffier, Jeffrey (1997) 'The political economy of the closet: notes toward an economic history of gay and lesbian life before Stonewall', in Amy Gluckman and Betsy Reed *Homo Economics: Capitalism, Community, and Lesbian and Gay Life*. New York: Routledge.

Freitas, Anthony, Kaiser, Susan and Hammidi,Tania (1996) 'Communities, commodities, cultural space, and style', *Journal of Homosexuality*, 31 (1/2): 83–107.

General Accounting Office (1997) *Sexual-Orientation-Based Employment Discrimination: States' Experience With Statutory Prohibitions*. Washington, DC. Report number OGC-98–7R.

Gluckman, Amy and Reed, Betsy (1997) 'The gay marketing moment', in Amy Gluckman and Betsy Reed (eds), *Homo Economics: Capitalism, Community, and Lesbian and Gay Life*. New York: Routledge.

Gunderson, Morley (1989) 'Male-female wage differentials and policy responses', *Journal of Economic Literature*, 27 (1): 46–72.

Haeberle, Steven (1996) 'Gay men and lesbians at City Hall', *Social Science Quarterly*, 77 (1): 190–7.

Harvard Law Review (1989) *Sexual Orientation and the Law*. Cambridge, MA: Harvard University Press.

Hewitt, Christopher (1995) 'The socioeconomic position of gay men: a review of the evidence', *American Journal of Economics and Sociology*, 54 (4): 461–79.

International Gay and Lesbian Human Rights Commission (1999) *Antidiscrimination Legislation: April 1999, A Worldwide Summary* http://www.iglhrc.org/.

Jones, David A. (1996) 'Discrimination against same-sex couples in hotel reservation policies', *Journal of Homosexuality*, 31 (1/2): 153–60.

Klawitter Marieka M. (1995) 'Did they find each other or create each other?: Labor market linkages between partners in same-sex and different-sex couples', unpublished manuscript.

Klawitter, Marieka M. (1998) 'The determinants of earnings for women in same-sex and different-sex couples', unpublished manuscript.

Klawitter, Marieka M. and Flatt, Victor (1998) 'The effects of state and local antidiscrimination policies for sexual orientation', *Journal of Policy Analysis and Management*, 17 (4): 658–86.

Klawitter, Marieka M. and Hammer Brian (1999) 'Spatial and temporal diffusion of local antidiscrimination policies for sexual orientation', in Ellen Riggle and Barry Tadlock (eds), *Gays and Lesbians in the Democratic Process*. New York: Columbia University Press.

Kurdek, Lawrence A. (1993) 'The allocation of household labor in gay, lesbian, and heterosexual married couples', *Journal of Social Issues*, 49 (3): 127–39.

Lundberg, Shelly and Rose, Elaina (1999) 'The determinants of specialization within marriage', unpublished manuscript.

Matthaei, Julie (1997) 'The sexual division of labor, sexuality, and lesbian/gay liberation', in Amy Gluckman and Betsy Reed (eds), *Homo Economics: Capitalism, Community, and Lesbian and Gay Life*. New York: Routledge.

Penaloza, Lisa (1996) 'We're here, we're queer, and we're going shopping! A critical perspective on the accommodation of gays and lesbians in the US marketplace', *Journal of Homosexuality*, 31 (1/2): 9–41.

Schneider, Beth E. (1987) 'Coming out at work: bridging the private/public gap', *Work and Occupations*, 13 (4): 463–87.

Sherrill, Kenneth (1996) 'The political power of lesbians, gays, and bisexuals', *PS: Political Science and Politics*, 29: 469–73.

van der Meick, Wagne (2000) 'Legislating equality: A review of laws affecting gay, lesbian, bisexual and transgendered people in the United States', Washington DC: The policy Institute of the National Gay and Lesbian Task Force.

Wald, Kenneth D., Button, James W. and Rienzo, Barbara A. (1996) 'The politics of gay rights in American communities: explaining antidiscrimination ordinances and politics', *American Journal of Political Science*, 40 (4): 1152–78.

Walters, Andrew S. and Curran, Maria-Cristina (1996) 'Excuse me, sir? May I help you and your boyfriend?: salespersons' differential treatment of homosexual and straight customers', *Journal of Homosexuality*, 31 (1/2): 135–52.

Woods, James D. with Jay H. Lucas (1993) *The Corporate Closet: The Professional Lives of Gay Men in America*. New York: The Free Press.

Yang, Alan S. (1998) *From Wrongs to Rights: Public Opinion on Gay and Lesbian Americans Moves Toward Equality*. Washington, DC: National Gay and Lesbian Task Force.

20

Sweating in the Spotlight

Lesbian, Gay and Queer Encounters with Media and Popular Culture

JOSHUA GAMSON

'The big lie about lesbians and gay men,' the late Vito Russo wrote in *The Celluloid Closet*, his 1980s' landmark study of homosexuality in the movies, 'is that we do not exist.'

> America was a dream that had no room for the existence of homosexuals. Laws were made against depicting such things on screen. And when the fact of our existence became unavoidable, we were reflected, on screen and off, as dirty secrets. We have cooperated for a very long time in the maintenance of our own invisibility. And now the party is over. (Russo, 1987: xii)

Indeed. By the start of the twenty-first century, gay and lesbian characters were all over American popular culture and, at least most of the time, neither secret nor particularly dirty. Gays and lesbians now routinely appear in US mainstream newspaper and popular magazine coverage, often sympathetically or matter-of-factly; entertainment and sports stars such as Ellen DeGeneres, Anne Heche, Greg Louganis, Martina Navratilova, Ian McKellen, Rupert Everett, and Melissa Etheridge are out and about in American culture, gracing magazine covers and celebrity gossip news; gay, lesbian, bisexual, and transgendered characters

abound in Hollywood films and independent films too numerous to list, and have appeared as lead and recurring characters on many television programs, from the famous *Ellen* coming-out episode to *Will and Grace, Dawson's Creek, Felicity, NYPD Blue*, and *South Park*, to name just a few; major companies such as Ikea, Budweiser, United Airlines, Subaru, and American Express have targeted gay and lesbian consumers with flattering images of themselves, often published in slick gay and lesbian magazines or on well-trafficked gay and lesbian Internet sites (Chasin, 2000; Walters, 2001). Even Disney World has an annual gay event.

Although the effects of such cultural changes on public opinion – which has become increasingly supportive of lesbian and gay civil equality while remaining morally disapproving (Yang, 1999) – are never direct or obvious, the shifts have been stunning in both breadth and rapidity. As Suzanna Danuta Walters puts it in *All the Rage*, a scant twenty years after Russo, 'the love that dare not speak its name became the love that would not shut up' (Walters, 2001: 29).

The study of the relationship of lesbians and gay men to popular culture and media roughly tracks and responds to this dramatic move into the cultural spotlight, a move that has not only been actively pursued by lesbian and gay social movements but has also exacerbated long-standing divisions within them. Lesbian and gay media and culture studies, like lesbian and gay studies in general, are partly shaped by their close relationship to lesbian and gay social movements (Epstein, 1996; Gamson, 2000), and they have thus reproduced key, interesting tensions in the movement. For those generally assuming stable identity categories, who see gays and lesbians as a minority group subject to unjust discrimination, the concern has tended to be with the fate of 'positive images' of gays and lesbians in media and popular culture; for those who see sexual identities as fluid, multiple and constructed, and aim to question and deconstruct those categories as a means to social change, the concern tends to be with 'queering' popular culture. In an overlapping but not identical tension, those celebrating 'mainstreaming' and assimilation as a means to gay power tend to view cultural visibility, implicitly or explicitly, as political progress; those who want to see the goal of gay politics as the pursuit of major changes in, rather than integration into, the dominant culture, cultural visibility in its more commercialized forms tends to be seen as problematic and sometimes regressive.

Thus, within lesbian and gay media and pop-culture studies – much stronger, notably, than within lesbian and gay communities at large – a profound and growing ambivalence has emerged along with, and about, the increased cultural visibility of lesbians and gay men.[1] This is the story of a field of study that is still catching up with, and struggling to understand, the enormous changes in the cultural terrain: from suppression and stereotyping of gay people's images and voices to their circulation in the spectacles of mass media; from often covert, self-created relationships to heterosexually-oriented popular culture to overt visions, produced or distributed by commercial cultured industries, of unapologetically lesbian and gay people. If the invisibility party is over, new questions are still circulating about the new visibility party that has taken its place: who is invited, and by whom, and at what price, and with what political and social consequences.

INVISIBILITY, STEREOTYPING, AND SENSIBILITIES: THE MINORITY MODEL

Sustained scholarly attention to the relationships between gays and lesbians and popular media began in the late 1970s, and grew out of the burgeoning gay and lesbian movements of that time. Much of the work, in fact, was conducted by scholars explicitly identifying as activists, whose scholarship was as much a political intervention as an intellectual one. For the most part, these early studies operated from a 'minority model', in which a shared, fixed sexual orientation is the basis for a quasi-ethnic minority status for gay people (Epstein, 1987); the question was primarily one of the kinds of images of homosexuals and homosexuality that had been and were being produced, especially in Hollywood. The often explicit goal was to help transform the social and political status of lesbians and gay men: to demonstrate the kinds of distortions and exclusions of gay people produced, and prejudices being encouraged and reproduced, in cultural forms.

Coming primarily out of cinema studies, scholars such as Russo (1987), Parker Tyler (1972), and Richard Dyer (1984), brought home the key point that homosexuals, when not being written out of the culture entirely, were scripted in narrow, stereotyped roles – as comic devices, as sissies and tomboys, as suicidal and self-hating, as targets of violence, or as violent predators. When they were not being treated as laughable, that is, gay people were either killing themselves or killing others. Examining the images of lesbians in film, for instance, Andrea Weiss argued that 'Hollywood cinema, especially, needs to repress lesbianism in order to give free rein to its endless variations on heterosexual romance,' and that the result, when lesbian images managed to surface at all, were ones that 'helped determine the boundaries of possible representation' – the 'lesbian vampire, the sadistic or neurotic repressed woman, the pre-Oedipal "mother/daughter" lesbian relationship, the lesbian as sexual challenge or titillation to men' (Weiss, 1992: 1).

Stereotypes, such scholars have suggested, are the majority culture's ideological means of legitimizing the political oppression of sexual minorities. As Larry Gross summarized it, nicely capturing the merger of scholarship and minority-group politics:

Mostly, [lesbians and gay men] are ignored or denied – symbolically annihilated ... The stereotypic depiction of lesbians and gay men as abnormal, and the suppression of positive or even 'unexceptional' portrayals serves to maintain and police the boundaries of the moral order. It encourages the majority to stay on their gender-defined reservation, and tries to keep the minority quietly hidden out of sight. For the visible presence of healthy, non-stereotypic lesbians and gay men does pose a serious threat: it undermines the unquestioned normalcy of the status quo, and it opens up the possibility of making choices to people who might never otherwise have considered or understood that such choices could be made. (1991: 26, 30)

The stigmatization function of popular culture, from this perspective, serves to keep gay people, as individuals and as a group, mired in self-hatred, to justify their status as, at best, second-class citizens, and to legitimize a moral and political order that is deeply discriminatory.

Such minority-model study of gay and lesbian cultural representation, with its focus on distortions and exclusions, has remained one of the dominant approaches in the field (Fejes and Petrich, 1993; Gross, 1994). Gay and lesbian identity and community, in these studies, are treated as stable; the gay minority is seen as facing straight-majority prejudices that are encoded in popular culture and institutionalized in cultural organizations. In a useful review essay, for instance, Fred Fejes and Kevin Petrich argue that, while media discourse has become less homophobic, it remains deeply heterosexist.

Overall, mainstream network television does not present gays and lesbians in the context of their own identity, desire, community, culture, history or concerns, but rather as woven into the dominant heterosexual metanarrative. ... Aspects of gay and lesbian identity, sexuality and community that are not compatible or that too directly challenge the heterosexual regime are excluded. (1993: 401, 412)

Thus, a gay character may appear on *Melrose Place*, for instance, but seems to have neither a sex life nor any ties to a gay and lesbian community (Walters, 2001); lesbians may become 'chic' advertising icons, while 'the representation of lesbian identity politics' is precluded, since within the ads 'there is no lesbian community' (Clark, 1993: 195–6).

Pointing out the homophobic and heterosexist aspects of popular culture, for both scholars and activists operating within gay-minority politics – who by the 1970s were routinely targeting cultural institutions with 'zaps' and lobbying – has been a means to undermine stigma and challenge a discriminatory moral and political order. Indeed, the anti-defamation work of media advocacy organizations such as the Gay and Lesbian Alliance Against Defamation (GLAAD) has been directly informed by, and has directly informed, research of this kind (Alwood, 1996; Montgomery, 1989). In protests against television shows such as 1980s' *Midnight Caller,* films such as *Cruising* and *Basic Instinct,* and radio hosts such as Rush Limbaugh and Laura Schlesinger, activists have translated into action the basic arguments of minority-based gay media criticism: popular culture routinely discriminates against lesbians and gay men, through stereotypes and invisibility, and that must be challenged.[2] Even strategies by radical activists, who eschew the assimilation-oriented work of more reformist activists, have often emphasized membership in and obligation to the gay minority. When in the early 1990s some advocated 'outing' public figures rumored to be gay, its 'most radical aspect' was in fact 'the argument that all homosexuals are members of a community, whether they admit it or not' (Gross, 1993: 126; Mohr, 1992; Signorile, 1993).

Despite a heavy early emphasis in the scholarship on film and television, it is not only entertainment media that have been subject to scrutiny and analysis. Edward Alwood's (1996) comprehensive historical study of gays, lesbians and the news media, for example, charts the dramatic change from 1950s' news coverage, in which homosexuals were routinely referred to as 'perverts', 'sex deviates', 'fags', and 'child molesters', to 1960s' discussions of 'the sad gay life', to the coverage of Stonewall ('Homo Nest Raided, Queen Bees Are Stinging Mad', read the *New York Daily News* headline) and the 'militant' gay minority and the gay 'lifestyle' in the 1970s, to the increasingly sympathetic coverage of gay civil rights struggles and the renewed victims-and-villains frameworks in 1980s' AIDS coverage.

Like many of his colleagues studying entertainment culture, Alwood's explanatory framework is largely structural. In trying to understand 'how and why the news media perpetuated antigay stereotypes throughout much of this century', Alwood turns not to 'the prejudice and bigotry of individual journalists' or 'slipshod reporting', but to 'a structural bias of the media, one that causes journalists to favor the established power base and defend the status quo while shunning the perspectives of those who are politically powerless' (Alwood, 1996). Objectivity, balance, and fairness, Alwood argues, are 'myths' that 'cannot assure that the news will be accurate, fair, or objective' (ibid.: 7). Journalists 'frequently fall short of their own standards, particularly in covering minorities' – Alwood includes gays and lesbians in the category 'minorities' – and need to be accountable for the resulting double standards, exclusions, and

derogatory stereotypes. When journalists and news organizations grasp that it is 'unfair for them to render gays invisible or paint them as a menace', they will mend their ways, including more minority managers, reflecting all segments of society, and getting rid of stereotypes (ibid.: 327–8). The logic here quite typifies the minority-model study of popular culture: the subject in question is the reality of lesbian and gay experience, which is assumed to be relatively stable and unified; the goal is fair and accurate reporting of that reality; the obstacle is bias and institutionalized homophobia and heterosexism; the solutions are enlightenment and the reform of the practices and institutional arrangements that encourage bias.

The study of the media and popular culture treatments of AIDS has also been quite firmly influenced by this tradition of study, in part because the stakes of misrepresentation were especially clear: if coverage followed the invisibility and stereotyping pattern, policy-makers and the majority of the public were unlikely to see AIDS as a disease in need of resource provision. Indeed, research confirmed that this was, at least early on, pretty much the case. Early media accounts of the disease linked it to homosexuality, and drew on the stereotype of gay promiscuity; gay male identity, which had only recently overcome the stigma of homosexuality-as-disease, was being remedicalized through AIDS; the victim-or-villain dichotomy of earlier years was being reinstated in both fictional and nonfictional accounts, as was the treatment of gay men as spectacular 'others'. Distorting social divisions of race, gender, class and sexuality were reinstated culturally: AIDS was represented as a white gay disease *or* a disease of heterosexual drug users of color; some people with AIDS were 'guilty' while others were 'innocent'. At the root of these sorts of representations, most analysts suggested, was a combination of homophobia and generic institutional dynamics (such as assessments of newsworthiness, or disease-of-the-week TV movie conventions) (Alwood, 1996; Cohen, 1999;

Cook and Colby, 1992; Gross, 1994; Kinsella, 1989; Netzhammer and Shamp, 1994; Watney, 1987). The result was not unidirectional of course – the re-stigmatization of homosexuality and bisexuality (for men, especially) also triggered renewed sympathy for, and mobilization of, gay activism. But many scholars saw in the AIDS crisis a crucial example of how majority prejudice and ignorance played out in popular culture and media, with great costs to a gay minority.

Another key aspect of minority-model gay and lesbian media and culture studies has been the flip side of the invisibility-and-stereotyping arguments: documenting the positive contributions to popular culture, and uses of popular culture, by homosexuals. This scholarship, too, has been deeply informed by the affirmative 1970s' identity politics from which it was born: it shows the creative, complex ways lesbians and gay men have bent the stigmatizing culture to their own positive purposes, creating their own culture and identities from it, and how elements of 'gay sensibilities' have, for all the attempts to write them out, become woven into American culture. Although some simple, romanticized, essentialist versions of 'gay sensibility' – as the inevitable, transcultural, transhistorical result of an innate sexual orientation – have circulated here and there, for the most part such analyses, with nods to the social constructionism that would soon dominate the field, considered gay culture in its historical and cultural context.

These studies are less about charting a minority group's representations than about calling attention to the uses of popular culture in the group's self-construction. In part because gays and lesbians, until recently, were rarely addressed directly as an audience, they have a rich history of turning pieces of heterosexually-oriented popular culture into their own expressions of individual and collective identity, or of generating their own subcultural languages, which are sometimes then picked up by the dominant culture.[3] In *The Homosexualization of America,* Dennis Altman, for instance,

distinguished the 'traditional gay culture', built on the needs for concealment and evasion, with camp as its signature, from post-Stonewall 'contemporary gay [and lesbian] culture,' built on self-affirmation and assertion, with its 'preoccupation with realism ... and with authenticity' (Altman, 1982: 152, 158). These different sorts of self-created subcultures demonstrated, one with subversive wit and the other with assertive sexuality, the creative resistance of gay people to their oppression and the weaving of that creativity into the fabric of popular culture (Bronski, 1984, 1998).

Camp has been one prime example of the gay male (and, to some degree, lesbian as well) poaching of popular culture, and also of gay male cultural contributions. The camp sensibility has been seen as 'a strategy for rewriting and questioning the meanings and values of mainstream representations' (Newton, 1972; Creekmur and Doty, 1995: 2; Cleto, 1999). Writing on camp typically defined it in relation to gayness, as 'those elements in a person, situation, or activity which express, or are created by a gay sensibility', and that sensibility as 'a creative energy reflecting a consciousness that is different from the mainstream ... a perception of the world which is colored, shaped, directed and defined by the fact of one's gayness' (Babuscio, 1984: 40). Many analysts saw in the experience of pre-Stonewall male homosexual life, in particular, the roots of camp's humorous, ironic, subversive, theatrical celebration of 'any highly incongruous contrast between an individual or thing and its context or association' – exaggerated, hyper-feminine drag may be the prototype – especially incongruities of gender (ibid.: 41). 'To gay men,' as Russo put it, 'camp has been both a lifeline and an anchor' (1979: 206).

Gay men's adoration of film stars such as Judy Garland, similarly, and lesbians' admiration of stars such as Greta Garbo, have been seen as a means of expressing and celebrating a marginalized identity (Dyer, 1986; Weiss, 1992). Lesbians, Andrea Weiss has argued, have also 'looked to the cinema ... to create ways of being lesbian, to form and affirm their identity as individuals and as a group' (ibid.: 1). Weiss traced the ways the 'faint traces and coded signs' that result from Hollywood's restricted and restricting treatment of lesbians are 'especially visible to lesbian spectators', who use them for their own identity work (Weiss, 1992: 1; Straayer, 1985). Even the strategy, used by some marketers since the 1980s, of 'gay window advertising' – ads that target gay and lesbian consumers with subcultural codes or subtexts that straight viewers are unlikely to pick up – can be a means for affirming and strengthening the identity it is unwilling to explicitly name. Lesbians and gays can 'read into' such ads 'certain subtextual elements that correspond to experiences with or representations of gay/lesbian subculture,' Danae Clark has argued, finding, if not politics, at least a space for identification, pleasure, and validation (1993: 188, 195–6). For gay people, that is, popular culture has not been simply a site of repression and stigmatization, but a crucial site of self-expression, identification, and individual and collective identity construction.

WHOSE IDENTITY IS IT ANYWAY?:
THE CHALLENGES OF DIFFERENCE
AND THE RISE OF QUEER THEORY

By the 1980s and 1990s, the gay and lesbian 'minority studies' model had come under scrutiny and fire from a variety of directions, shaking the theoretical ground on which many scholars – including students of media and popular culture – were standing. Within gay and lesbian movements in the 1980s, the strong gay-minority emphasis on what people with same-sex inclinations have in common was met with resistance from many of those who did not see themselves included in the 'we' of gay and lesbian culture. Social differences *within* gay and lesbian communities, especially racial, class, and gender differences, erupted. Mainstream gay culture – exactly what was

being traced and celebrated in minority-model studies – was criticized for its exclusion of the 'experiences, interests, values, and unique forms of life' of people of color and working-class people (Seidman, 1996: 10). The gay rights movement was criticized from within, by lesbian feminists in particular, for its male bias; the lesbian-feminist wing was itself then challenged by sex radicals in the feminist 'sex wars', and by working-class women and women of color, for its assumption of a unified lesbian sexual identity based on women's shared characteristics and circumstances (Phelan, 1989). From multiple fronts, then, the 'homosexual' subject at the heart of minority-model studies was criticized for posing unproblematically as 'us', while actually representing the viewpoint and experiences of white, middle-class gay men, and sometimes women; only a select piece of the gay 'minority' was becoming visible enough to even *be* stereotyped.

On one level, these criticisms gave energy to a project of filling in gaps in the field: writings focused on the specific representations of lesbians and lesbianism in film (Holmlund, 1991; Weiss, 1992), television (Moritz, 1994), popular music (Stein, 1994), and advertising (Clark, 1993); on the representation of Asian American men in gay male pornography (Fung, 1991) and black gay men on television (Hemphill, 1990) and music (Thomas, 1995); on images of bisexuals (Garber, 1995) and transgendered people (Bornstein, 1994; Meyerowitz, 1998). The logic of these accounts, however, has never simply been additive, never simply filling in the missing pieces in the puzzle of gay-minority representation. They also posed a challenge to the notions of identity underlying much of the work that preceded them.

As gay men and lesbians of color, for example, asserted and voiced their own specific identities, much of their attention went to the exclusion and distortion of those identities not only by mainstream, white, heterosexual popular culture but also by both straight-dominated black popular culture and white-dominated gay and lesbian popular culture. Marlon Riggs, whose film *Tongues Untied* was a ground-breaking exploration of black gay male identities, wrote of 'the determined, unreasoning, often irrational desire to discredit my claim to blackness and hence to black manhood' in 'the cinematic and television images of and from black America as well as the words of music and dialogue that now abound and *seem* to address my life as a black gay man' (Riggs, 1995: 471). Robert Reid-Pharr pointed to what he called the tendency to 'spectacle-ize Black bodies' that pervades not only American culture in general, but also American lesbian and gay culture; taking the example of the popular documentary *Paris Is Burning*, which took viewers into the world of New York City black and Latino 'houses', he argued that 'the black image is still used by whites, even and especially white gays, to entertain themselves, and more importantly to validate their position as the dominant people of the Americas' (Reid-Pharr, 1993: 65). Film-maker Isaac Julien and film scholar Kobena Mercer wrote of the new images of masculinity in gay life that 'depend on the connotations of power inscribed in symbols of *white* masculinity' (1991: 168).

> As black men, we are implicated in the same landscape of stereotypes in the gay subculture, which is dominated by the needs and demands of white males. Black men fit into this territory by being confined to a narrow repertoire of types – the supersexual stud and the sexual savage on the one hand, the delicate and exotic 'Oriental' on the other. (ibid.: 169)

As Julien and Mercer summed it up, 'White women and men, gay and straight, have more or less colonized cultural debates about sexual representation', exhibiting a 'profound absence of any political awareness of race among white gays' (ibid.: 167).

In the course of these studies, the ideas of a unified minority and a clear homosexual subject (or, for that matter, black or white or female subject), to be represented or distorted in popular culture and media, became much harder to assume. In calling attention to the unexamined assumptions of whiteness in gay culture, and in studies of popular culture, for instance, critics were calling attention to the complexity of gay identities and culture: to the fact of multiple, intersecting, overlapping identities rather than one overarching shared gay identity, to the fact of a diverse, shifting, often divided community in tenuous coalition rather than a fixed, unified 'gay minority'. As Kobena Mercer (1991) put it, 'There is no such thing as a homogeneous and unitary ... community, but only *communities,* in the plural, made of interdependent, and sometimes contradictory, identities.'

These critical voices dovetailed with, and pushed along, those emerging more strictly within the academy, of the assumptions about identity inherent in the minority model – voices that congealed into what became known in the 1990s as 'queer theory'. Queer theory's roots, of course, were in the 'social constructionist' thinking that took hold in the 1970s and 1980s; put simply, constructionists view sex, and especially categories like 'homosexual' and 'heterosexual', as social rather than natural. Heavily influenced by Michel Foucault's history of sexuality – the movement from sodomy as 'a category of forbidden acts' to the homosexual as 'a personage, a past, a case history, a life form' (Foucault, 1990: 43) – social constructionists confronted the dominant, 'essentialist' notion of homosexuality as the outward expression of an innate homosexual nature (Epstein, 1987; Stein, 1992). Constructionists thus documented the different ways 'the homosexual' came into being historically and cross-culturally (Greenberg, 1988).

As queer theory took shape, it both built on and went beyond constructionism, presenting a 'challenge to what has been the dominant foundational concept of both homophobic and affirmative homosexual theory: the assumption of a unified homosexual identity', and putting in its place the assertion that identities are 'always multiple or at best composites', that identity construction is 'arbitrary, unstable, and exclusionary', necessarily entailing 'the silencing and exclusion of some experiences of forms of life' (Seidman, 1996: 11–12). 'I'm permanently troubled by identity categories,' wrote Judith Butler, for instance, 'consider them to be invariable stumbling-blocks, and under stand them, even promote them, as sites of necessary trouble' (1991: 14). Identity is, she argued, a 'necessary error' (Butler, 1993: 21). This was quite a departure from the identity-affirmation politics that informed much of lesbian and gay cultural studies, which saw the error not as identity itself, but as the distortions of that identity by an anti-gay cultural system.

Influenced by post-structuralist social theory, queer theory, as Steven Seidman has described it, shifted the focus from the emergence of the modern homosexual to 'questions of the operation of the hetero/homosexual binary, from an exclusive preoccupation with homosexuality to a focus on heterosexuality as a social and political organizing principle, and from a politics of minority interest to a politics of knowledge and difference' (Seidman, 1996: 9). As Seidman explains,

> Queer theorists view heterosexuality and homosexuality not simply as identities or social statuses but as categories of knowledge, a language that frames what we know as bodies, desires, sexualities, identities. This is a normative language as it shapes moral boundaries and political hierarchies. ... Queer theory is suggesting that the study of homosexuality should not be a study of a minority – the making of the lesbian/gay/bisexual subject – but a study of those knowledges and social practices that organize 'society' as a whole by sexualizing – heterosexualizing or homosexualizing – bodies, desires, acts, identities, social relations, knowledges, culture, and social institutions. (Seidman, 1996: 12–13)

It was thus not so much the lives or identities of gays and lesbians, or the construction of homosexual identities or minority status, that required attention, but the ways the very homo-hetero distinction underpinned all aspects of contemporary life. 'An understanding of virtually any aspect of modern Western culture,' wrote Eve Kosovsky Sedgwick, for example, in *Epistemology of the Closet*, generally considered the founding text of queer theory, 'must be, not merely incomplete, but damaged in its central substance to the degree that it does not incorporate a critical analysis of modern homo/heterosexual definition' (1990: 1). The deconstruction and criticism of 'heteronormativity' in its various forms and guises, of the notion that 'humanity and heterosexuality are synonymous' (Warner, 1993: xxiii) became a key goal and rallying cry of queer studies. As opposed to 'lesbian and gay', Rosemary Hennessy suggested:

> [queer] embraces a proliferation of sexualities (bisexual, transvestite, pre- and post-op transsexual, to name a few) and the compounding of outcast positions along racial, ethnic, and class, as well as sexual lines – none of which is acknowledged by the neat binary division between hetero- and homosexual. 'Queer' not only troubles the gender asymmetry implied by the phrase 'lesbian and gay,' but potentially includes 'deviants' and 'perverts' who may traverse or confuse hetero-homo divisions and exceed or complicate conventional delineations of sexual identity and normative sexual practice. (Hennessy, 1994–95: 34)

Or, as Alexander Doty put it, 'Queerness should challenge and confuse our understanding and uses of sexual and gender categories' (1993: xvii).

As opposed to the criticism of gay people's cultural invisibility or stereotyping, queer theory-influenced studies of popular culture have thus largely involved a project of deconstruction and criticism of the dichotomous sexual and gender categories promoted in pop culture. Indeed, as Michael Warner put it, 'almost everything that could be called queer theory is about ways in which texts – either literature or mass culture or language – shape sexuality' (1992). Queer 'readings' of popular culture often aimed to demonstrate the covert operation of the homosexual-heterosexual 'binary' in cultural texts, and of the ways in which the texts of 'heteronormativity' are never entirely successful at suppressing the complexities of sexual desire and gender identity. 'Connotation,' Doty has argued, 'has been the representational and interpretive closet of mass culture queerness for far too long,' and queer readings of mass culture aim to remove 'mass culture queerness from the shadowy realm of connotation' (1993: xi). Pop-culture subjects such as Michael Jackson (Erni, 1998), Hitchcock films (Berenstein, 1995; Miller, 1990), Paul Lynde (Hainley, 1994), *I Love Lucy* and *Laverne and Shirley,* (Doty, 1993), Madonna (Schwichtenberg, 1993), and Pee-Wee Herman (Balfour, 1993; Bruce, 1995) began to be mined for queer meanings and subtexts, or were themselves 'queered' by the reading of the scholar, who stood in for readers and viewers 'adopting reception positions that can be considered "queer" in some way, regardless of a person's declared sexual and gender allegiances' (Doty, 1993: xi).

John Erni, for instance, found in Michael Jackson a 'queer figure', one whose 'hyperbolic poses of the body and other significatory practices [are] drawn toward the parodic dramatizing, and the political questioning, or normalcy'; looking at the media treatment of the scandal over Michael Jackson's alleged child molestation, he traces 'the meanings of non-normative – and specifically queer – subjectivity in the discursive layers of the scandal', finding in the scandal 'an assemblage of a social discourse about queer eroticism and identity politics out of a history and iconography of "weirdness" attached to a name branded to the problems of secrecy and sexual ambiguity' (Erni, 1998: 159, 164). Sasha Torres, analysing the 1980s' prime-time drama *HeartBeat*, demonstrates how the series' lesbian character, Marilyn, was written as simultaneously similar to and different from the straight characters. The 'often-confused and always-implicit vacillations between universalizing and minoritizing depictions of Marilyn,' she wrote, in an explicit reference to Sedgwick's work, 'themselves demonstrate the productive possibility, as well as the evident limitations, of such liberal representations' (Torres, 1993: 183). Ian Balfour, one of a number of cultural studies scholars to turn their attention to the 'gay subtext, intertext, or just plain text' of

Pee-Wee's Playhouse, argues that 'a principal effect of Pee-wee's histrionics … is to unsettle culturally codified notions of masculine and feminine, indeed to twist them around' (1993: 143, 145–6). In one episode among many in which gender is treated as an ambiguous playhouse, Balfour notes, Pee-wee coaches a character named Cowboy Curtis for a date with the big-haired Miss Yvonne.

> The Cowntess (a cow who occasionally wears a muumuu) ropes Pee-wee into pretending to be Miss Yvonne for Curtis's benefit. Pee-wee protests that he doesn't 'want to be a girl.' But the Cowntess urges him to 'Have some fun with it.' Pee-wee then cheerfully adopts a falsetto voice and revels in his role as a woman …. muses about lipstick, hairspray and the dress he'll wear, while flirting with Cowboy Curtis, and decorum is only restored at the moment when Pee-wee balks at Curtis's attempt to kiss him goodnight. The explicit moral of this episode … is 'Be Yourself.'

The exhortation to be yourself, Balfour concludes, 'includes the possibility of being your twisted self, which is to say a self less twisted according to prefabricated structures of desire' (Balfour, 1993: 145–6). Queer media and culture studies pursue these twisted possibilities with a vengeance: on the one hand, the transgressive, disparate sexual identities and practices present, if suppressed, in popular culture, and, on the other, the myriad ways in which the oppressive, binary categories of sex and gender (gay versus straight, male versus female) are routinely purveyed by popular culture.

MARGINS AND MAINSTREAMS: THE NORMALIZATION OF GAYS AND LESBIANS IN POPULAR CULTURE

'The most effective force of resistance to the hegemonic force of the dominant media,' communications scholar Larry Gross wrote, 'is to speak for oneself,' and 'the ultimate expression of independence for a minority audience struggling to free itself from the dominant culture's hegemony is to become the creators and not merely the consumers of media images' (Gross, 1991: 41). For a time in the earlier parts of the contemporary gay and lesbian movements' history, much energy had been devoted to creating alternative institutions, some of which gave rise to an alternative popular culture by and for gay people: lesbian feminist singers recorded on the Olivia Records label and played at the Michigan Womyn's Music Festival (Taylor and Rupp, 1993); local papers emerged, along with national magazines such as *The Advocate,* to provide news and information that the mainstream press ignored or distorted (Streitmatter, 1995); gay-produced films such as *Word Is Out, The Times of Harvey Milk*, and *Tongues Untied* documented aspects of gay experience, and played at lesbian and gay film festivals.[4]

Until recently, however, the cultural images gays and lesbians produced were known and distributed mostly within lesbian and gay communities, and the images in the popular culture at large were produced by and for heterosexual audiences – although, of course, homosexuals were among their most avid consumers. Over time, in a process that began slowly in the 1970s, picked up over the 1980s, and sped up like crazy in the 1990s, the volume of mainstream popular culture featuring gays and lesbians, and of gay- or lesbian-produced culture 'crossing over' into the culture at large, mushroomed dramatically (Bronski, 1998).

In large part, this newfound visibility was, in fact, the result of the erosion of corporate caution about being associated with gay and lesbian culture, which opened up big new revenue and investment sources for cultural products featuring, or targeting, gays and lesbians. The gay and lesbian 'community' had, largely through the efforts of some of its own (for instance, firms specifically geared towards helping companies market towards gay and lesbian consumers), been transformed into a market niche (Chasin, 2000; Gluckman and Reed, 1997; Lukenbill, 1995; Strub, 1997). Although various studies have challenged the idea that gay men and lesbians earn more than heterosexuals

(Badgett, 1998), and statistics on stigmatized populations are notoriously difficult to collect, the perception that lesbians and gay men are a huge, untapped, brand-loyal group with lots of disposable income began to become conventional business wisdom. Thus major advertisers, such as airlines and music companies and alcohol companies, sought ways to penetrate the gay market. One of those ways was through gay-and-lesbian produced popular culture, especially the glossy magazines such as *Out, 10 Per cent, Genre*, and *Curve*, which emerged in the 1990s, and long-standing magazines such as *The Advocate.* 'The growing visibility of the gay and lesbian community,' as Michael Bronski put it, 'has been largely a direct result of the emergence of the gay market and the commodification of gay life' (1998: 145).

The visibility grew not only in print advertising and magazines. The decreased perception of financial risk on the part of corporations loosened up investment in gay- and lesbian-themed film and television projects, and a series of test cases proved that they could be profitable. The AIDS drama *Philadelphia* demonstrated that audiences might not turn away from Hollywood films with gay central characters; the indie film *Go Fish*, which centered around a group of twenty-something lesbians, became a hit in 1996, demonstrating that films emerging from the budding gay and lesbian independent film world could be highly profitable. The episode in which the title character of *Ellen* came out proved to be a ratings bonanza, demolishing the idea that gay topics were too controversial to retain TV viewers' valuable attention – which had informed earlier advertiser pullouts from episodes of television shows, such as *LA Law* and *Roseanne*, in which same-sex desire was a key storyline, and which had kept networks from supporting programs with gay or lesbian lead characters. Film companies became less cautious about producing and marketing gay-themed films, distributors were on the lookout for independently produced films about lesbian and gay characters that had 'crossover' potential, and advertisers became less skittish about sponsoring television programs with lesbian or gay characters. By the late 1980s, the 'funding, production, and distribution opportunities' for people pursuing lesbian and gay themes in independent media, and the field of lesbian and gay film and video itself, were 'expanding, exploring, exploding' (Gever et al., 1993: xiii); lesbian and gay cultural producers who a few years before would have been ignored found eager commercial sponsors and distributors. Lesbian and gay images have made a fast march towards the center of American popular culture. 'Gay life and identity,' as sociologist Susannah Walters says, 'defined so much by the problems of invisibility, subliminal coding, double entendres and double lives, has now taken on the dubious distinction of public spectacle' (2001: 10).

Very few observers dispute the claim that the recent pop cultural visibility of gays and lesbians has primarily taken the form of emphasizing gay people's similarity to their heterosexual counterparts, that as opposed to their stereotyping as scary, deviant 'others' in the years preceding it, they have become increasingly 'normal' cultural figures. Even their deviance, in fact, has become normalized: gays and lesbians, who had been relegated to occasional talk show appearances in the 1970s and 1980s on which the morality of their practices and identities was the topic, for example, were in the 1990s integrated into the tabloid world of daytime talk shows, as nasty and loud as most everyone else on the shows (Gamson, 1998a).

What scholars and other observers disagree about, however, is whether and how the new visibility is a cause for celebration. For students of media and popular culture, the mainstreaming of lesbian and gay people in the late twentieth and early twenty-first century has generated new questions, and reproduced once again the political tension between those advocating assimilation and normalization as routes to social progress and those pursuing a 'queer' challenge to

norms as a social change strategy. For more conservative critics, the new visibility is progress, a sign that the culture at large is getting over its stereotypes and ignorance and accepting gay people. In *After the Ball: How America Will Conquer Its Fear and Hatred of Gays in the 90s*, for instance, Marshall Kirk and Hunter Madsen described a strategy of 'good propaganda' that seemed to then play out almost as if drawn from their pages. In a reiteration of a conformity-oriented strategy with a long history in gay politics (D'Emilio, 1983), they proposed producing 'favorably sanitized images' and a 'single-minded' focus on 'gay rights issues and nothing more' (Kirk and Madsen, 1989: 170, 180).

> You must help them relate to you and your humanity, to recognize that you and they share many good things in common, and that they can like and accept you *on their own terms* ... Persons featured in the media campaign should be wholesome and admirable by *straight standards*, and completely unexceptional in appearance; in a word, they should be *indistinguishable from the straights* we'd like to reach. In practical terms, this means that cocky mustachioed leathermen, drag queens, and bull dykes would not appear in gay commercial and other public presentations. (ibid.: 174, 183; my emphasis)

This is exactly one of the major objections to others witnessing the movement of gays and lesbians into the mainstream of popular culture. 'Far too often this new visibility and acceptance,' writes Walters, 'is predicated on a comparative model: the straight person (or character in a film or TV show) can only "accept" the gay person once he or she has interpreted that person as "just like me"' (2001: 16). Normalization, some critics have pointed out, comes at a price, the need to 'tone down, clean up, straighten up gay life and gay identity' (ibid.: 285), a neglect of the diversity of gay populations, and a writing out of the sexually transgressive and politically challenging aspects of the lesbian and gay communities and movements.

Most critical analysts point to the distortions provided by the commodification of gay and lesbian life, the driving force behind the new cultural visibility. 'Not only is much recent gay visibility aimed at producing new and potentially lucrative markets, but as in most marketing strategies, money, not liberation, is the bottom line,' writes Rosemary Hennessy. 'The increasing circulation of gay and lesbian images in consumer culture has the effect of consolidating an imaginary, class-specific gay subjectivity for both straight and gay audiences' (Hennessy, 1994–95: 32). The overwhelming majority of advertising material in which gay people appear, Alexandra Chasin has found, for instance, 'depicts that "community" as white, affluent, educated, healthy, youngish adults' (Chasin, 1997: 14–15). 'In the world of the market,' Walters adds, 'all the gays are men, all the men are white, and all the whites are rich' (2000: 313). Recent gay magazines, cultural critic Daniel Harris argues in *The Rise and Fall of Gay Culture*, 'have consolidated their economic base by catering exclusively to the needs of the emerging youth constituency and perpetrating pictorial genocide on men over the age of 40, who have been ethnically cleansed from their pages, leaving behind a racially pure group of young, prosperous beauties' (Harris, 1997: 71). Gay activism, he continues, has been redefined to include 'things like shopping and careering', and images of gay culture 'have been completely desexualized' (ibid.: 77). The new magazines, Harris argues:

> strive to create a sanitized forum that will satisfy even the most conservative businesses … [Editors] drive home to their advertisers the normality of gay people whose Middle American mediocrity is celebrated in article after article … The methods of sterilization involved in creating an ad-friendly marketing vehicle capable of pacifying the fears of large corporations involves the annihilation of gay identity, the eradication of every vestige of difference between ourselves and the heterosexual markets the advertiser is accustomed to addressing. (ibid.: 80–2)

The new visibility, the more radical observers suggest, has brought new distortions. At a minimum, the move of some gay people into the cultural mainstream has heightened the tension between assimilationist and anti-assimilationist wings in gay politics.

It has also called attention to analytical and political difficulties that were not present when the task was simply documenting and opposing images that were blatantly demeaning (Gamson, 1998b). The assumption that a 'positive' image is easily recognizable, is no longer so easy to hold. 'Is it any image that avoids the harshest stereotypes?' asks Jane Schacter.

> Is it a highly assimilated image that makes it impossible to 'tell' if someone is straight or gay? Is it an image that attributes transgressive gender roles to a gay character – an 'effeminate' man or 'masculine' woman – but does so from a 'sympathetic' perspective? It is simply any such 'transgressive' image, available for a potentially empowering appropriation by lesbian and gay viewers, irrespective of the ways in which nongay viewers might react? (Schacter, 1997: 727–8)

These are questions triggered by the move into the spotlight of popular culture, and their answers are primarily normative ones – they depend on where one stands on the *value* of transgression, assimilation, and normalization.

CONCLUSION: LOOKING TO THE FUTURE

These are never bad questions to ask, not least because gay people's ambivalent relationship to media and popular culture – as stigmatizing enemy and destigmatizing savior – is productive. They also force new and difficult issues, about the politics of visibility, into the forefront of the field. It is no longer so easy to assume that visibility, for instance, is always and necessarily a political step forward. The means by which much of the new cultural visibility was achieved – the promotion of an affluent, powerful gay market – has become one of the organizing tools for the anti-gay right, for instance.

Now, as Michael Bronski sums up the results of these 'myths created by means of market research', gay people are seen by some not just as a sexual threat, but 'a sexual threat with economic and social power' (Bronski, 1998: 148–150). 'It is at least possible,' Schacter points out:

> that representations of happy, healthy, well integrated lesbian and gay characters in film or television would create the impression that, in a social, economic, and legal sense, all is well for lesbians and gay men. To the extent that some viewers believe that media images reflect the 'real world,' perhaps these images will induce or confirm their belief that lesbians and gay men are already 'equal' – accepted, integrated, part of the mainstream ... It is at least possible that 'positive' images of gay and lesbian characters, untethered to any representation of the legal status of homosexuality, might prompt in some viewers the rallying cry of 'special rights' that has been so central to the antigay campaigns. (Schacter, 1997: 729)

There is, thus far, no indication that new cultural visibility translates into new political and social rights and fuller, freer citizenship for gay people. Indeed, the impact of popular culture on political opinion, the impact of this new visibility – whether the exposure has generated tolerance or backlash – remains to be seen and studied.

That is a difficult question to transform into research, of course, but its prominence calls attention to one of the largest gaps in the field of lesbian and gay media and pop-culture studies: the dearth of cross-cultural comparison. As this chapter itself reveals, most of the work in the field has focused on North American and British culture, not surprisingly, since those are arguably the sites with the most active and visible gay and lesbian presence in popular culture. Especially as world culture continues to compress, and cultural industries continue to consolidate and globalize, it becomes even more crucial to look beyond the American and British cases alone for clues to the difficult, less-than-obvious relationship between cultural visibility and political freedom.

NOTES

1 While lesbian and gay media studies is primarily shaped by its links to lesbian and gay movements, and by developments within the larger lesbian and gay studies field, it has of course also been influenced by paths in media and popular culture studies. As I tell the story of lesbian and gay studies' attempts to make sense of how and with what consequences popular culture has defined homosexuals and homosexuality, and how and with what consequences lesbians, gay men, bisexuals, and transgendered people have moved onto the pop-culture map, I am also telling the story of the development of media and cultural studies more generally – a growth of interest in spectatorship and reception studies, for instance, and a heavy influence of post-structuralist cultural theory since the 1980s (see Frow and Morris, 2000; Mukerji and Schudson, 1991).

2 These studies, it should be noted, like the political movements from which they emerged, have kept their focus quite firmly not just on images, but on the institutions producing them. Russo charted, for instance, a change from a period in which explicit portrayals of homosexuals – which, though certainly stereotyped, were a regular feature of the early years of film – to the period of the Hollywood Production Code, from the 1930s to 1950s, when such images were erased or went underground, becoming carefully coded subtexts (Russo, 1987). In the early 1990s, Michelangelo Signorile, similarly, exposed the homophobic actions of powerful people, both closeted-gay and openly heterosexual, in entertainment, news media, and politics (Signorile, 1993). The social organization of Hollywood production was part of the analysis of the discursive organization of sexuality – an institutional focus that dropped off quite significantly with the later rise of queer theory.

3 These sorts of studies have also taken cues from the last two decades of media studies more generally, in which a focus on audiences, their meaning-construction activities, and the pleasures and uses they derive from media culture, have come to the forefront (Cruz and Lewis, 1994; Lewis, 1991).

4 While much of the self-produced gay and lesbian culture emerged as part of a minority-building project, not all of it played by the rules of identity politics. 'Queer' theory and politics have also informed gay and lesbian cultural production. As Martha Gever, John Greyson, and Pratibha Parmar, the editors of a 1989 volume on lesbian and gay film and video described their point of view at the time, for example: 'We were bored with tired seventies notions of positive role models, tired of boring seventies preoccupations with classic narrative structures ... We were particularly influenced by the cross-disciplinary critical debates, both in the academy and on the street, that were contesting and deconstructing representations of race and gender (Gever et al., 1993: xiv).

REFERENCES

Altman, Dennis (1982) *The Homosexualization of America.* Boston: Beacon.

Alwood, Edward (1996) *Straight News: Gays, Lesbians, and the News Media.* New York: Columbia University Press.

Babuscio, Jack (1984) 'Camp and the gay sensibility', in R. Dyer (ed.), *Gays and Film.* New York: Zoetrope. pp. 40–57.

Badgett, M.V. Lee (1998) *Income Inflation: The Myth of Affluence Among Gay, Lesbian, and Bisexual Americans.* New York: Policy Institute of the National Gay and Lesbian Task Force and Institute for Gay and Lesbian Strategic Studies.

Balfour, Ian (1993) 'The playhouse of the signifier: reading Pee-Wee Herman', in C. Penley and S. Willis (eds), *Male Trouble.* Minneapolis: University of Minnesota Press. pp. 143–55.

Berenstein, Rhona (1995) '"I'm not the sort of person men marry": monsters, queers, and Hitchcock's *Rebecca*', in C. Creekmur and A. Doty (eds), *Out in Culture.* Durham, NC: Duke University Press. pp. 239–61.

Bornstein, Kate (1994) *Gender Outlaw: On Men, Women, and the Rest of Us.* New York: Vintage Books.

Bronski, Michael (1984) *Culture Clash: The Making of Gay Sensibility.* Boston: South End Press.

Bronski, Michael (1998) *The Pleasure Principle: Sex, Backlash, and the Struggle for Gay Freedom.* New York: St Martin's Press.

Bruce, Bruce La (1995) 'Pee-Wee Herman: the homosexual subtext', in C. Creekmur and A. Doty (eds), *Out in Culture.* Durham, NC: Duke University Press. pp. 382–8.

Butler, Judith (1991) 'Imitation and gender insubordination', in D. Fuss (ed.), *Inside/Out.* New York: Routledge. pp. 13–31.

Butler, Judith (1993) 'Critically queer', *GLQ*, 1: 17–32.

Chasin, Alexandra (1997) 'Selling out', *Sojourner*, 22: 14–15.

Chasin, Alexandra (2000) *Selling Out: The Gay and Lesbian Movement.* Basingstoke: Palgrove.

Clark, Danae (1993) 'Commodity lesbianism', in H. Abelove, M.A. Barale and D. Halperin (eds), *The Lesbian and Gay Studies Reader.* New York: Routledge. pp. 186–201.

Cleto, Fabio (1999) *Camp: Queer Aesthetics and the Performing Subject.* Ann Arbor, MI: University of Michigan Press.

Cohen, Cathy J. (1999) *The Boundaries of Blackness: AIDS and the Breakdown of Black Politics.* Chicago: University of Chicago Press.

Cook, Timothy and Colby, David (1992) 'The mass-mediated epidemic: the politics of AIDS on the nightly network news', in E. Fee and D. Fox (eds), *AIDS: The Making of a Chronic Disease.* Berkeley, CA: University of California Press. pp. 84–122.

Creekmur, Corey K. and Doty, Alexander (1995) 'Introduction', in C.K. Creekmur and A. Doty (eds), *Out in Culture: Gay, Lesbian, and Queer Essays on Popular Culture.* Durham, NC: Duke University Press. pp. 1–11.

Cruz, Jon and Lewis, Justin (1994) *Viewing, Reading, Listening: Audiences and Cultural Reception.* Boulder, CO: Westview Press.

D'Emilio, John (1983) *Sexual Politics, Sexual Communities: The Making of a Homosexual Minority in the United States.* Chicago: University of Chicago Press.

Doty, Alexander (1993) *Making Things Perfectly Queer: Interpreting Mass Culture.* Minneapolis: University of Minnesota Press.

Dyer, Richard (1984) *Gays and Film.* New York: Zoetrope.

Dyer, Richard (1986) 'Judy Garland and gay men', in R. Dyer (ed.), *Heavenly Bodies: Film Stars and Society.* London: Routledge. pp. 141–94.

Epstein, Steven (1987) 'Gay politics, ethnic identity: the limits of social constructionism', *Socialist Review*, 17: 9–54.

Epstein, Steven (1996) 'A queer encounter: sociology and the study of sexuality', in S. Seidman (ed.), *Queer Theory/Sociology.* Cambridge, MA: Blackwell. pp. 145–67.

Erni, John Nguyet (1998) 'Queer figurations in the media: critical reflections on the Michael Jackson sex scandal', *Critical Studies in Mass Communication*, 15: 158–80.

Fejes, Fred and Petrich, Kevin (1993) 'Invisibility, homophobia and heterosexism: lesbians, gays and the media', *Critical Studies in Mass Communication*, Vol. 10, 396–422.

Foucault, Michel (1990) *The History of Sexuality, Volume 1.* New York: Vintage.

Frow, John and Morris, Meaghan (2000) 'Cultural studies', in N.K. Denzin and Y.S. Lincoln (eds), *Handbook of Qualitative Research.* Thousand Oaks, CA: Sage Publications. pp. 315–46.

Fung, Richard (1991) 'Looking for my penis', in B.O. Choices (ed.), *How Do I Look? Queer Film and Video.* Seattle: Bay Press. pp. 145–68.

Gamson, Joshua (1998a) *Freaks Talk Back: Tabloid Talk Shows and Sexual Nonconformity.* Chicago: University of Chicago Press.

Gamson, Joshua (1998b) 'Publicity traps: television talk shows and lesbian, gay, bisexual, and transgender visibility', *Sexualities*, 1: 11–41.

Gamson, Joshua (2000) 'Sexualities, queer theory, and qualitative research', in N.K. Denzin and Y.S. Lincoln (eds), *Handbook of Qualitative Research.* Thousand Oaks, CA: Sage Publications. pp. 347–65.

Garber, Marjorie (1995) *Vice Versa: Bisexuality and the Eroticism of Everyday Life.* New York: Simon and Schuster.

Gever, Martha, Greyson, John and Parmar, Pratibha (1993) *Queer Looks: Perspectives on Lesbian and Gay Film and Video*. New York: Routledge.

Gluckman, Amy and Reed, Betsy (1997) 'The gay marketing moment', in M. Duberman (ed.), *A Queer World*. New York: New York University Press. pp. 519–25.

Greenberg, David (1988) *The Construction of Homosexuality*. Chicago: University of Chicago Press.

Gross, Larry (1991) 'Out of the mainstream: sexual minorities and the mass media', in M. Wolf and A. Kielwasser (eds), *Gay People, Sex, and the Media*. New York: Haworth Press.

Gross, Larry (1993) *Contested Closets: The Politics and Ethics of Outing*. Minneapolis: University of Minnesota Press.

Gross, Larry (1994) 'What is wrong with this picture? Lesbian women and gay men on television', in R.J. Ringer (ed.), *Queer Words, Queer Images: Communication and the Construction of Homosexuality*. New York: New York University Press.

Hainley, Bruce (1994) 'Special guest star, Paul Lynde', *The Yale Journal of Criticism*, 7: 51–84.

Harris, Daniel (1997) *The Rise and Fall of Gay Culture*. New York: Hyperion.

Hemphill, Essex (1990) 'In living color: toms, coons, mammies, faggots and bucks', *Outweek*, December 26: 32–40.

Hennessy, Rosemary (1994–95) 'Queer visibility in commodity culture', *Cultural Critique*, Winter: 31–75.

Holmlund, Christine (1991) 'When is a lesbian not a lesbian? The lesbian continuum and the mainstream femme film', *Camera Obscura*, 145–78.

Julien, Isaac and Mercer, Kobena (1991) 'True confessions: a discourse on images of black male sexuality,' in E. Hemphill (ed.), *Brother to Brother*. Boston: Alyson. pp. 167–73.

Kinsella, James. (1989) *Covering the Plague: AIDS and the American Media*. New Brunswick, NJ: Rutgers University Press.

Kirk, Marshall and Madsen, Hunter (1989) *After the Ball: How America Will Conquer Its Fear and Hatred of Gays in the 90s*. New York: Plume.

Lewis, Justin (1991) *The Ideological Octopus: An Exploration of Television and Its Audience*. New York: Routledge.

Lukenbill, Grant (1995) *Untold Millions: The Gay and Lesbian Market in America*. New York: HarperCollins.

Mercer, Kobena (1991) 'Skin head sex thing: racial difference and the homoerotic Imaginary', in B.O. Choices (ed.), *How Do I Look?* Seattle: Bay Press.

Meyerowitz, Joanne (1998) 'Sex change and the popular press: historical notes on transsexuality in the United States, 1930–1950', *GLQ*, 4: 159–88.

Miller, D.A. (1990) 'Anal rope', *Representations*, 32: 114–33.

Mohr, Richard D. (1992) *Gay Ideas: Outing and Other Controversies*. Boston: Beacon Press.

Montgomery, Kathryn C. (1989) *Target: Prime Time: Advocacy Groups and the Struggle Over Entertainment Television*. New York: Oxford University Press.

Moritz, Marguerite J. (1994) 'Old strategies for new texts: how American television is creating and treating lesbian characters,' in R.J. Ringer (ed.), *Queer Words, Queer Images*. New York: New York University Press. pp. 122–42.

Mukerji, Chandra and Schudson, Michael (1991) 'Introduction: rethinking popular culture', in C. Mukerji and M. Schudson (eds), *Rethinking Popular Culture*. Berkeley, CA: University of California Press. pp. 1–61.

Netzhammer, Emile C. and Shamp Scott A. (1994) 'Guilt by association: homosexuality and AIDS on prime-time television', in R.J. Ringer (ed.), *Queer Words, Queer Images: Communication and the Construction of Homosexuality*. New York: New York University Press.

Newton, Esther (1972) *Mother Camp: Female Impersonators in America*. Chicago: University of Chicago Press.

Phelan, Shane (1989) *Identity Politics: Lesbian Feminism and the Limits of Community*. Philadelphia: Temple University Press.

Reid-Pharr, Robert F. (1993) 'The spectacle of blackness', *Radical America*, 24: 57–65.

Riggs, Marlon (1995) 'Black macho revisited: reflections of a Snap! queen', in C. Creekmur and A. Doty (eds), *Out in Culture: Gay, Lesbian, and Queer Essays on Popular Culture*. Durham, NC: Duke University Press. pp. 470–5.

Russo, Vito (1979) 'Camp', in M.P. Levine (ed.), *Gay Men: The Sociology of Male Homosexuality*. New York: Harper & Row. pp. 205–10.

Russo, Vito (1987) *The Celluloid Closet: Homosexuality in the Movies*. New York: Harper & Row.

Schacter, Jane S. (1997) 'Skepticism, culture and the gay civil rights debate in post-civil-rights era', *Harvard Law Review*, 110: 684–731.

Schwichtenberg, Cathy (1993) 'Madonna's postmodern feminism: bringing the margins to the center.' in C. Schwichtenberg (ed.), *The Madonna Connection*. Boulder, CA: Westview. pp. 129–45.

Sedgwick, Eve Kosovsky (1990) *The Epistemology of the Closet*. Berkeley, CA: University of California Press.

Seidman, Steven (1996) 'Introduction', in S. Seidman (ed.), *Queer Theory/Sociology*. Cambridge, MA: Blackwell. pp. 1–29.

Signorile, Michelangelo (1993) *Queer in America: Sex, the Media, and the Closets of Power*. New York: Anchor Books.

Stein, Arlene (1994) 'Crossover dreams: lesbianism and popular music since the 1970s', in D. Hamer and B. Budge (eds), *The Good, the Bad, and the Gorgeous: Popular Culture's Romance with Lesbianism*. London: Pandora.

Stein, Edward (1992) *Forms of Desire: Sexual Orientation and the Social Constructionist Controversy*. New York: Routledge.

Straayer, Chris (1985) 'Personal best: a lesbian feminist audience analysis', *Jump Cut*, 29: 40–4.

Streitmatter, Rodger (1995) *Unspeakable: The Rise of the Gay and Lesbian Press in America*. Boston: Faber & Faber.

Strub, Sean (1997) 'The growth of the gay and lesbian market', in M. Duberman (ed.), *A Queer World*. New York: New York University Press. pp. 514–18.

Taylor, Verta and Rupp, Leila J. (1993) 'Women's culture and lesbian feminist activism', *Signs*, 19: 32–61.

Thomas, Anthony (1995) 'The house the kids built: the gay black imprint on American dance music', in C. Creekmur and A. Doty (eds), *Out In Culture: Gay, Lesbian, and Queer Essays on Popular Culture*. Durham, NC: Duke University Press. pp. 437–46.

Torres, Sasha (1993) 'Television/feminism: HeartBeat and prime time lesbianism', in H. Abelove, M.A. Barale, and D.M. Halperin (eds), *The Lesbian and Gay Studies Reader*. New York: Routledge. pp. 176–85.

Tyler, Parker (1972) *Screening the Sexes: Homosexuality in the Movies*. New York: Holt, Rinehart and Winston.

Walters, Suzanna Danuta (2001) All the rage: the story of gay visibility in America', unpublished manuscript.

Warner, Michael (1992) 'From queer to eternity', *Voice Literary Supplement*, June, p. 19.

Warner, Michael (1993) *Fear of a Queer Planet*. Minneapolis: University of Minnesota Press.

Watney, Simon (1987) *Policing Desire: Pornography, AIDS, and the Media*. Minneapolis: University of Minnesota Press.

Weiss, Andrea (1992) *Vampires and Violets: Lesbians in Film*. New York: Penguin.

Yang, Alan (1999) *From Wrongs to Rights: Public Opinion on Gay and Lesbian Americans Moves Towards Equality*. New York: The Policy Institute of the National Gay and Lesbian Task Force.

21

Queer Families Quack Back

JUDITH STACEY AND ELIZABETH DAVENPORT

That's what I like…. How we as queers get to choose our families. It's like picking the right color scheme for your house. We don't have to accept what the state has given us. We accessorize. – ('George', in Mann, 1999)

The buzz around this year's Millennium March on Washington doesn't tout glitter or pageantry. It boasts the addition of a 'family area' with activities for the kids; it tells you where to rent a baby stroller. (Hank Stuever, 2000)

'If it looks like a duck, and it walks like a duck, and it quacks like a duck, then it *is* a duck!' Thus ran the verdict pronounced by opponents of the historic legislation by which Vermont became the first state in the USA to grant lesbian and gay couples the right to form civil unions. Debating the bill's provisions in March 2000, hostile lawmakers complained that a civil union was nothing less than marriage by another name, while a flock of little yellow plastic ducks brooded disconsolately on desks throughout the chamber.

Should gay or lesbian couples be allowed by law to marry? Should some form of domestic partnership be recognized as an alternative to marriage, perhaps for heterosexual couples also? Should lesbians and gay men conceive and rear children? Is there really any single way of being 'family' nowadays? Such questions preoccupy citizens and policy-makers alike at the dawn of the new millennium, not only in the United States but in parliaments and public squares around the world. Just a month before the Vermont debate, Canada amended its federal regulations pertaining to spouses to extend to same-sex couples all rights and obligations enjoyed by those of mixed sex. The weekend prior to that, thousands of noisy demonstrators gathered in Paris to protest against the French government's decision to offer unmarried couples, regardless of gender, many benefits and duties that French married couples receive. *'Oui au mariage'* (yes to marriage), they chanted, implying that those who would not, or could not, marry should not be entitled to equality in the eyes of the law.

But if it looks like a duck, and it walks like a duck, is it then a duck … ? Nowhere in the world as yet can same-sex couples actually marry under exactly the same terms and in exactly the same manner as their heterosexual counterparts. Although the conservative owners of the little yellow ducks in Vermont failed to defeat the civil unions bill, they did successfully reserve the word 'marriage' for the union of a man and a woman. Likewise, Canadian law recognizes only married persons as spouses and classifies gay and lesbian partners along with unmarried heterosexual couples of at least twelve months duration as common law mates. And the French government has never proposed extending *mariage* itself to those whom it now legally acknowledges as registered partners.

But that marriage, and such related issues as the legal relationship of a non-biological parent to his or her children, should have become part of the much-vaunted 'homosexual agenda' at all would have appeared ludicrous had anyone prophesied it even a short time ago. Most gay liberationists of the 1960s and 1970s had no interest in imitating or assimilating into heterosexual norms. Those who first broke down the tightly secured door of the closet, deliberately spilling its contents all over the floor, never imagined they might be clearing the way for a new culture of domesticity. The queens of Stonewall so quickly laid to one side by gay and lesbian couples proudly chasing the latest advances in reproductive technology in the quest for their own little princes and princesses – who would have guessed it?

In this chapter we examine the queer political environment in which our putative ducklings – gay and lesbian families in their many plumed varieties – must sink or swim. In the course of what follows, we ask whether lesbian, gay, and other queer genres of kinship represent the brave new families of the twenty-first century, pointing to ways that those in more conventional families might also renegotiate the demands of love and labor. Or conversely, does the gay movement's embrace of family discourse in fact signify capitulation – a retirement from activism to couch potato viewing of *Leave it to Beaver* re-runs?

NO PLACE LIKE HOME: THE POSTMODERN FAMILY CONDITION

Let us begin with a bird's eye view of the context in which queer families of all kinds have hatched. The first thing to notice is how easily these fowl blend into their surrounding terrain. An image of 'Beaver' rather than a duck evokes the 'fabled family of Western nostalgia', signifying the bygone 1950s' era of the modern nuclear family system to which we can no longer return. *Leave it to Beaver*, a popular TV sitcom of that era, idealized a world when proper men were breadwinners and proper women homemakers, when marriage was for life and homosexuality was not a fit topic for family dinner table conversation. However, even before the sitcom could make it into reruns, a global post-industrial world began to supplant the industrial economy that had underwritten the Cleavers' family regime. The 'patriarchal bargain' of the modern family order (Kandiyoti, 1988) – in which women subordinated their individual interests to those of husbands and children in exchange for economic support and social respectability – would soon unravel. Rates of maternal employment, developments in contraception and reproductive technology, and no-fault divorce petitions advanced apace, while feminist and gay liberation movements spurred women and men to question received understandings of gender, sexuality, and family life and to pursue what sociologist Anthony Giddens (1992) terms the modern ideal of a 'pure relationship' of 'confluent love'.

In place of the supposedly 'normal' American family immortalized by 1950s' sitcoms, most people today seek love and intimacy within the denaturalized world of the postmodern family condition. The postmodern family represents no new normal family structure, but instead an irreversible condition of family diversity, choice, flux, and contest. The sequence and packaging of romance, courtship, love, marriage, sex, conception, gestation, parenthood, and death are no longer predictable. Now that there is no consensus on the form a normal family should assume, every kind of family has become an alternative family. Lesbigay or queer families occupy pride of place in this cultural smorgasbord which includes familiar varieties that were historically most prevalent among the poor – such as stepfamilies, unwed motherhood, blended families, bi-national families, divorce-extended kin, cohabiting coupledom, and grandparent-headed families – along with such newer developments as at-home fatherhood, deadbeat dads, and open adoption – as well as innovations made possible by new commerce and technology – surrogacy, sperm banks, ovum exchange, genetic screening, gender selection, frozen embryos, and the no-longer-distant specter of human cloning.

As family innovations proliferate, the mass media energetically broadcast provocative images on a global scale. British journalists gave front-page coverage in late 1999 to the story of a gay male couple who challenged the time-honored passage of citizenship through the mother's line. Returning home to London with infant twins borne by an American surrogate mother, the two men were identified as 'parent one' and 'parent two' on the babies' birth certificates (Gibb, 1999; BBC, 2000). Singer Melissa Etheridge, her former partner Julie Cypher, and David Crosby, their proud celebrity sperm donor, have graced the glossy pages of entertainment monthlies as symbols of new ways to be family. Hollywood gave its first twenty-first century Oscar for best actress to Hilary Swank for her performance as the transgendered 'boyfriend' of Chloe Sevigny in *Boys Don't Cry* (to traditionalists' dismay, the transgendered can truly quack like ducks by legally entering into marriage with a 'same-gendered' partner). And in *The Adventures of Priscilla, Queen of the Desert*, the young son of one of the bus travelers is portrayed enthusiastically applauding the drag show that dad and his mates perform in a little Australian outback town where the boy lives with his mother.

Of course, similar topics now grace the pages of academic journals in numerous disciplines (from sociology, psychology and law, to political science, anthropology, cultural studies, religion, history, and medicine). Whereas appropriate motherhood has long been the focus of scholarly debate, now fathers too have become contested subjects – whether as deadbeat or at-home dads, or as cells in turkey basters. Scholars on the conservative end of the spectrum have begun to claim that not only can children experience too little fathering (as in the case of fathers absent through disappearance or divorce, imprisonment or inertia), but also too much (as in the case of gay men co-parenting).

Perhaps it should not surprise us that the sight of such unfamiliar courses of intimacy gives conservative diners indigestion. Confronted by so much novelty, threatened forces train their rifles at the handiest targets, and campaigns for lesbigay family rights have become difficult to miss. Queer families occupy the vanguard of the postmodern family condition, because they make the denaturalized and contingent character of family and kinship impossible to ignore. How irresistible these sitting ducks must appear to backlash troops mustered for target practice; and their frustration can only be magnified as they begin to suspect the futility of their cause. For by the turn of the millennium, it was already obvious that the historic move toward the legalization of gay marriage had gathered such a head of steam that was it no longer a matter of *if*, but of *when* or *where* it would first secure full legal status. And indeed, in April 2001, the Netherlands led the way and same gendered couples began to be wed. Other nations seem likely to follow suit, including Denmark, Sweden, Canada, and Norway.

Even in the United States, where progress will undoubtedly be slower, popular anti-gay sentiment is steadily declining. Early in 2000, *Newsweek* conducted a poll which showed 83 per cent of all Americans favoring protection from discrimination at work for gay people (up from 56 per cent in 1977), with almost 60 per cent considering gay partners entitled to shared health benefits, and more than one-third supporting the legalization of gay marriage (Leland, 2000). Those viewing homosexuality as a sin were down to 46 per cent (from 54 per cent only two years earlier, in 1998). And indeed, in California, a poll taken in the aftermath of a bitterly fought ballot initiative – designed to restrict marriage to the union of a man and a woman – indicated that the 'debate' itself raised consciousness in this regard: while 42 per cent of Californians said they considered homosexuality morally wrong, no fewer than 54 per cent came out against homophobia (Warren, 2000). Another poll found 41 per cent of all Americans saying yes to civil unions as a means of extending benefits normally associated with marriage (*Los Angeles Times*, 2000). Early French surveys concerning the new civil unions (*pactes civils de solidarité*, or PACS, as the French more colorfully name them) indicated that almost half the population approved of offering them to gay and lesbian couples, and an even greater percentage supported PACS for straight couples. Indeed, startlingly high numbers of heterosexuals have presented themselves to be 'PACS-ed' even though for them marriage remains an option (*New York Times*, 2000).

But although other nations have surged ahead of the United States on the road to making marriage open to all, jurisdictions in the USA lead in providing legal pathways for planned lesbigay parenthood. Here, dramatic legal, popular, and technological gains in the area of lesbian and gay parental rights have preceded the advent of civil unions or marriage. Consistent with this trend, the *Newsweek* poll (Leland, 2000) showed a higher proportion of respondents favoring adoption rights for gay partners (39 per cent) than the percentage approving marriage (34 per cent).

QUEER FAMILY VALUES: A CASE OF CONFORMITY?

Although gay family rights issues now enjoy immense grassroots support among lesbians and gay men in many corners of the world, not all gay theorists or activists find this trend ducky. The same ideological and strategic differences that characterize other contemporary lesbian, gay, and queer discourses undergird the family quarrels: should the ultimate goal be normalization or subversion? Do the politics of accommodation or resistance promise to pave the royal road to 'Home'?

Scholars and activists of diverse ideological leanings continue to debate the consequences of legalizing same-sex marriage. They ask whether it augurs to democratize and degender the institution of marriage, or simply to exacerbate existing inequalities between haves and have-nots, couples and singles, women and men, and among members of different racial and ethnic groups. Would gay marriage increase social acceptance of lesbians and gays, or would it merely promote sexual conservatism and conformist, white picket-fence values? Lesbian and gay studies scholars also cross quills over domestic partnership legislation. Is this best viewed as a desirable and even preferable alternative, a strategic stepping stone, or as a second-class stepsister to full marriage rights? Similarly, what can be said about the current character of gay family relationships? Are they indeed more egalitarian and less violent than their heterosexual counterparts, as enthusiasts frequently claim? Are gay people – gay male people in particular – less inclined to monogamy, and if so, is that cause for regret or applause? Are queer family forms inherently more innovative, more unstable, and/or more considered than mainstream ones?

At the very least it is evident that lesbians and gay men do not share a common set of family values with each other, not to mention with those who occupy less common frequencies on the queer rainbow bandwidth. Indeed, the very notion of 'queer family values' is somewhat oxymoronic, signifying a quixotic wish to fuse subversion with normalization. Even so, for just this reason queer family values may serve as a fitting parodic figure to represent the paradigmatic paradoxes of postmodern intimacy! After examining some of the thickets and thorns of these debates, we will argue for the somewhat frustrating claim that the best answer to most of these questions is 'all of the above'. That is to say, contemporary lesbigay or queer family agendas necessarily house elements of liberation and accommodation, political success and co-option, hand in hand.

RIGHTS AND RITES: THE
DEBATE OVER MARRIAGE

Perhaps nowhere do disagreements over queer family values proceed as visibly or with such volatility as in the debate over legalizing same-sex marriage. While momentum for this goal gathers popular force, gay and lesbian scholars and activists continue to disagree over whether campaigning for the right to marry represents a subversive or normalizing project – or both. Disputes still rage, as anthropologist Ellen Lewin (1998) notes in her engaging book about gay weddings, *Recognizing Ourselves: Ceremonies of Lesbian and Gay Commitment*, 'over whether same-sex marriage constitutes a callow effort to fit into the mainstream or a bold rebellion against the limitations of a rigid gender hierarchy' (ibid.: 35).

In some respects, the major fault lines in the seismic terrain lie between a moderate reformism and a radical oppositional stance, between national gay rights organizations and queer direct action politics, and to some extent along gender and racial lines, with comparatively affluent, socially ambitious, white gay men typically more enthusiastic and prominent in the drive for marriage rights than less privileged, more dissident, lesbian feminists and gay people of color. In fact, lesbian critic Julie Abraham (2000) goes so far – perhaps a bit too far – as to charge that 'the new gay and lesbian constituency being constructed through the marriage debates is a wholly white, conventionally gendered as well as sexually circumspect crowd ...'. However, one of the more attractive (or pernicious, depending on one's standpoint) features of the marriage debate is that scholars do not all line up neatly as pro-marriage conservatives on one side and anti-marriage libertines on the other. Instead, arguments for opening matrimony to all comers, regardless of gender combination can be, and are, readily made from feminist, radical, liberal, and conservative corners alike. Likewise, cogent cases

against the gay marriage crusade rest upon equivalent incommensurate ideological underpinnings – including queer theory, feminism, socialism, anarchism, and libertarianism, along with the more obvious assists from conservative religious doctrines and unadulterated homophobic sentiments.

The intra-community debate over gay marriage was forcefully joined in 1989 in a now classic pair of articles by Tom Stoddard and Paula Ettelbrick, both then attorneys with the Lambda Legal Defense and Education Fund. Responding to Stoddard's (1992) seemingly self-evident equal rights argument that since marriage exists and confers economic and other benefits, it should be open to all, Ettelbrick (1992) took the classic militant position that to affirm marriage ran contrary to the values of gay identity and culture. What of other kinds of relations than monogamous pairings? What of challenging privilege rather than being co-opted into its halls? 'Being queer is more than setting up house, sleeping with a person of the same gender, and seeking state approval for doing so,' she protested.

Criticisms like Ettelbrick's were habitually thrown at those few lesbian and gay couples who dared to venture down the aisle toward even a virtual altar twenty years or more ago. Suzanne Sherman (1992) cites the experience of a lesbian couple who planned a commitment ceremony back then:

> We were a very, very small handful of lesbians who got married. We took a lot of flak from other lesbians, as well as heterosexuals. In 1981, we didn't know any other lesbians, not a single one, who had had a ceremony in Santa Cruz, and a lot of lesbians live in that city. Everybody was on our case about it. They said, What are you doing?; How heterosexual. We really had to sell it. (ibid.: 191).

Now, however, lesbian and gay weddings routinely receive recognition in mainstream newspapers, through 'bridal' registries, and on prime-time TV, while purveyors of classy (or camp!) gay or lesbian wedding commodities mail their catalogs by the thousands. Gay weddings, it seems, are already big business, at least for those who can afford them. Their political meanings are quite complex, however, often lying, as Lewin (1998) shows, in the eye of the beholder: 'Symbols couples intend to invoke resistance may instead suggest complicity with cultural norms, while other symbols explicitly meant to suggest conformity may be understood to subvert and undermine heteronormativity' (1998: 46). Indeed, as Lewin's book ably demonstrates, the line between rituals of resignation and of resistance is traced on shifting sands.

In an influential 1991 article, 'Marriage, law, and gender: a feminist inquiry', feminist legal theorist Nan Hunter suggested that several events of 1989 served to shift the cultural contours of that line and contributed to a 'rapidly developing sense that the legalization of marriage for lesbian and gay Americans [was] politically possible at some unknown but not unreachable point in the future' (ibid.:10). In May 1989, the city of San Francisco became the first major city in the United States to introduce a proposed domestic partnership ordinance, and the California State Bar Association passed a resolution calling upon the state to amend marriage laws to include gay and lesbian couples. In June 1989, Denmark became the first country in the world to open a 'registered partnership' category which conferred upon gay and lesbian couples all of the economic and social benefits of marriage – with the significant exception of rights to parental custody for non-biological parents. Following rapidly in July, the New York State Court of Appeals issued a landmark ruling in favor of a gay partner's claim to protection from eviction, based upon his 'family' relation to the deceased tenant-of-record. And in August, New York City Mayor Ed Koch authorized bereavement leave for the domestic partners of city employees. Within this context, the tide of gay and lesbian resistance to gay marriage began to ebb, reconfiguring and layering the shifting contours of the ideological shoreline.

It's about sex discrimination, pure and simple – not gay rights, not privacy, not freedom of intimate association, but just sex discrimination – gay legal activists argued in the 1993 Hawaiian state court case, an argument which reverberated so widely that the prospect of gay marriage at once became a national electoral issue. It's also about family values, added Lambda Legal Defense and Education Fund attorney Evan Wolfson (1994–95), commenting during the Hawaii case for which he was the plaintiffs' lead attorney: 'Inclusion at the level of marriage is uniquely revolutionary, conservatively subversive, singularly faithful to true American and family values in a way that few, if any, other gay and lesbian victories would be' (ibid.: 580).

Marriage is worth fighting for, posits philosopher Richard Mohr (1994), not just for equal rights or benefits but because it defines and creates social relations. It is a conduit for justice at times of crisis such as illness, death, or financial collapse. And, lest anyone be concerned about its sexual shackles, it is plainly compatible with non-monogamy, he adds: if the ability of many gay men to sustain long-term relationships built on factors other than promises of sexual exclusivity is not witness enough, look to the fact that adultery has been widely decriminalized for heterosexuals in recent decades!

The debate is also about redefining the entire institution of marriage, say those who share Tom Stoddard's (1992) reading that marriage 'may be unattractive and even oppressive as it is currently structured and practiced … [but] enlarging the concept to embrace same-sex couples would necessarily transform it into something new' (ibid.: 13). Indeed, marriage is a state long associated with changing mores, as Nan Hunter (1991) expounds. Even its recent history demonstrates that rigid institutionalizations of gender (or race) have frequently been rapidly discarded as times change: the courts no longer hold to their once key assumption of a husband's authority over his wife, for example, and bans on interracial marriage seem to belong to another era (despite the fact that the last existing such ban, in Alabama, was eliminated only in 1999, more than thirty years after the 1967 *Loving vs. Virginia* Supreme Court decision striking down miscegenation laws). Hunter deduces, therefore, that marriage itself would be enriched and democratized rather than damaged by opening it to same-gendered partners, since this would serve to 'radically denaturalize the social and political construction of male/female difference as authority/dependence relationships that courts have deemed essential to the definition of marriage' (1991: 9). Marriage is simply a social construction without any natural existence outside of particular laws and customs, she asserts, and as cultures change, marriage changes with them.

It is clearly the case that marriage has carried vastly different meanings in different times and places, and does still to this day among different classes and social groups, as lesbian social historian E.J. Graff (1999) documents in her aptly-named volume, *What is Marriage For? The Strange Social History of our Most Intimate Institution.* Time was when the vast civil disobedience of young heterosexuals today, living in pairs in great numbers without benefit of marriage, would have been considered greatly shocking. Today more people are shocked by past generations' assumptions that marriage was primarily about the transfer of estate and other property (including the bride herself) from one family to another. For not until the messy marriage law reforms of the eighteenth century did the day dawn when, in Graff's words, 'marriage for love – long the dubious privilege of the poor, nearly a guarantee of penury, a weird refusal to see that one could love wherever duty lay – started to become its own holy ideal all across the West' (1999: 26).

Perhaps the most significant historical shift with regard to the meaning of marriage at the present time, however, has been the recognition in most quarters that procreation is no longer its necessary complement or goal. Lewin (1998) notes that even those who cannot have sexual relations at all (on account of physical disability, or incarceration, for example) are nowadays encouraged to marry for the 'spiritual' or cultural worth of doing so. And once the time arrives that marriage is sacred even without babies. (Graff, 1999, flags the 1965 Supreme Court ruling in *Griswold vs. Connecticut* on contraception as a private matter between couples, as such a moment), then the exclusion from the married state of those for whom sexual relations can never lead to natural conception becomes more tenuous. Hence, like Hunter (1991), Graff believes that same-sex marriage can deal a feminist *coup de grâce* to male supremacy: 'Same-sex marriage will imply that the *sexes* are deeply and fundamentally equal' (ibid.: 159). However, unlike Hunter, Graff has no objection to the likelihood that 'opening marriage to same-sex couples may well shift our society's sexual dividing line from the current and temporary line between homosexual and heterosexual back to one more historically familiar, a divide between monogamous and promiscuous' (ibid.: 190).

But this is simply shameless capitulation to suburban conformity, scoff many critics from within. Queer theorists and leftists often charge that the recent outbreak of 'mad vow disease', as one witty, scornful critic dubbed the gay marriage campaign (Kate Clinton in Warner, 1999), uncritically embraces bourgeois values, monogamy, and state regulation of intimacy. Emulating heterosexual marriage will strengthen the inequitable and repressive status quo, they complain, for what happily married gay or lesbian couple will turn around to oppose the assignment of benefits they thereby gain? 'In the modern era,' Michael Warner charges, 'marriage has become the central legitimating institution by which the state penetrates the sexuality of its subjects; it is the "zone of privacy" outside which sex is unprotected' (1999: 128). Moreover, expanding the marital tent will do more to reinforce than to eradicate gender prescriptions, many lesbian theorists add, unconvinced by the more optimistic predictions made by Hunter (1991) or Graff (1999). Marriage is an inherently problematic institution, its practice terminally riddled with patriarchy, Nancy Polikoff (1993) maintains. Likewise, Ruthan Robson (1994) posits that to theorize lesbian relations in the context of family law inevitably serves only to domesticate and depoliticize lesbianism (should lesbians allow themselves the unfortunate compliment of being classed as 'good' sexual deviants if they happen to be monogamous and focused on the family?).

Neoconservative gay male intellectuals, such as Andrew Sullivan (1995, 1997), Jonathan Rauch (1994), and Bruce Bawer (1993), unabashedly embrace the goal of opening marriage to gay men and lesbians in precisely these terms, explicitly endorsing the assimilationist project. They do not wish to change anything about the institution of marriage beyond the mixed-gender entry permit to its privileged status, for they champion the very conservative family, sexual, gender, and property values that most queer theorists, lesbians, and feminists oppose. Sullivan goes so far as to suggest that opening social rites such as marriage to gay men and lesbians is the most that a democratic society can tolerate, and that efforts to fight discrimination in other environs cross the line of acceptability. Teasing opponents of gay marriage in terms calculated to raise hackles in both conservative and progressive quarters, he proposes: 'Since persecution is not an option in a civilized society, why not coax gays into traditional values rather than rail incoherently against them?' (1989: 22).

Traditional values, of course, are precisely what more radical critics reject. Echoes of the feminist 'sex wars' and of the queer theory 'sex panic' debate reverberate in the controversy over gay marriage. Radicals do not wish merely to expand access to a one-size-fits-all garment, but rather to redesign and multiply the models for intimacy, sexuality, and kinship available in the family wardrobe. They disagree among themselves, however, over whether marriage should remain one of the selections on the rack. 'The strategic question facing lawyers,' as Warner explains, 'is whether to

extend benefits and recognition even further beyond conventional marriage or to extend the status of marriage and thereby restrict entitlements and recognition to it' (1999: 138). Warner represents a dwindling number of white gay male opponents of same-sex marriage, but many lesbian and feminist theorists, such as Robson (1994), Abraham (2000), and Martha Fineman (1995), still advocate a politics of resistance, aiming to abolish policies that make benefits contingent upon marital status, or indeed to discard the category of 'family' altogether.

But of course such an approach readily attracts the charge of unattainable utopianism, as political theorist Valerie Lehr (1999) notes, in *Queer Family Values: Debunking the Myth of the Nuclear Family*: 'Political theory can provide powerful arguments against seeking inclusion into the institution of marriage, but these arguments may have little persuasive power for lesbian and gay couples trying to confront challenges such as the denial of health care benefits to partners' (ibid.: 30). And as political events unfolded over the 1990s, even former critics like Ettelbrick began to draw closer to the pro-marriage fold. Interviewed in 2000 by a *New York Times* reporter just after Vermont approved civil unions, Ettelbrick acknowledged that she and her partner had 'always told each other in good feminist fashion that they would never marry'; but, she confessed:

> I will admit to being very awed by the developments in Vermont, and just personally, it has made me rethink the opportunity it might provide for me and for my children … The possibility of a border state to New York allowing something like this is very emotional, and part of it is that it signifies a very long road to being included as citizens of this country. (in Goldberg, 2000)

As Warner concedes,

> It is possible, at least in theory, to imagine a politics in which sex-neutral marriage is seen as a step toward the more fundamental goals of sexual justice: not just formal equality before the law, based on a procedural bar to discrimination, but a substantive justice that would target sexual domination, making possible a democratic cultivation of alternative sexualities. (1999: 124)

To do so, however, would require articulating this more liberatory vision in the public discourse of the gay marriage crusade, because, as Warner correctly notes, 'the public sphere in which the discussion takes place is one of the contexts that *define* marriage' (ibid.: 149). Warner charges that the advocates of gay marriage have not made this case.

We disagree somewhat. As we have shown, some feminists like Hunter (1991), Ettelbrick (1992), and Lehr (1999) do indeed advocate marriage as part of a liberatory vision not only of sexuality, but of gender and social justice as well. However, their more critical and visionary perspectives rarely make their way into the circumscribed and polarized discursive constructs through which the mainstream media and the male-dominated national gay press and rights organizations produce and circulate 'the gay marriage debate'. Like these more marginalized voices, we would wish to decouple most individual economic and social entitlements from the already socially privileged domain of coupledom. However, particularly in a society like the United States in which there are scant grounds for presuming that the institution of marriage will soon fade away, and in which grassroots support for same-sex marriage is so keen, it strikes us as both elitist and politically misguided for more critical voices to cede the discursive struggle over marriage to the assimilationist camp.

SEPARATE BUT EQUAL? DOMESTIC PARTNERSHIP AND OTHER ALTERNATIVE MODELS

Paradoxically, while queer and feminist theorists wish to resist the normalizing implications of same-sex marriage, no nation or state has yet dared to present such an option to same-sex couples. Denmark, Norway, Sweden, Iceland, Germany, Finland, France, Vermont … all have chosen the politically 'safer' bargain of domestic partnership as a way of offering such couples most, but not all, of the benefits of marriage. Other states and nations are moving in this direction (at the time of writing, Canada, Australia, South Africa, and Israel and also some US states, including California, have created variations on the 'common-law spouse' theme). But though conservative opponents in Vermont view civil unions as tantamount to marriage (if it quacks like a duck, remember?), gay and lesbian couples who seek the same rights and benefits as other citizens are barely likely to be satisfied with anything that merits the tag 'separate but equal.' Separate has never proven equal before, they rightly aver. That the French PACS are proving highly attractive to young straight couples wanting a pledge of their commitment to one another but not yet ready to plunge fully into marriage, indicates that the two are not the same. And indeed, it is hard to sustain any argument that says domestic partnership is not a second-class status so long as marriage remains an exclusively heterosexual institution.

This does not mean, however, that domestic partnership is inherently an inferior family form. Anyone disliking a one-size-fits-all model is predisposed to consider alternative arrangements for creating family a worthy goal (the sting remaining, of course, that something 'alternative' must indeed be an alternative and not the only choice available). In fact, many queer and feminist theorists prefer domestic partnership over marriage as an option for those who so desire, given the historical ties of marriage to other unwanted baggage. Valerie Lehr (1999) reminds her readers that the gay liberation movement sprang up in the midst of a far broader questioning of a racist, sexist, capitalist economy. Noting that current family narratives (in the West) contain assumptions rooted in the consolidation of industrial capitalism, and tracing the ways in which those of other classes and ethnic backgrounds have rarely been able (or wanted?) to imitate the privatized household of families headed by a middle-class, white, male wage-earner, she urges leaving aside the values of the dominant culture and creating a new ethical framework that allows for traditional ways without excluding other choices.

Feminist legal theorist Martha A. Fineman (1995) proposes a more fundamental rejection of Western definitions of family, arguing that making the sexual pairing of adults the root of family is misguided because it renders women and children economically vulnerable to the vagaries of adult erotic and emotional attachments. Risking the charge of gender 'essentialism', Fineman calls instead for making the mother/child unit the base for state support and, where necessary, intervention. Meanwhile, queer theorists such as Warner (1993, 1999) and Frank Browning (1994) oppose allowing monogamous sexual coupling of any kind to serve as the basis for entitlements or regulation.

Others call for wide-ranging redefinitions of marriage, or of what Fineman calls the sexual family. Neil Miller, for example, quotes a Danish lesbian activist as saying, 'If I am going to marry it will be with one of my oldest friends in order to share pensions and things like that. But I'd never marry a lover. That is the advantage of being married to a close friend. Then, you never have to marry a lover!' (1992: 350). Of course, as Fineman (1995) and others protest, the question left begging is why pensions, health benefits, and so forth should ever have been tied to marital status in the first place. In Scandinavian societies, where this is not the case, all children and adults receive such basic entitlements, and child poverty has been nearly eradicated.

Hunter, fruitfully in our view, advocates offering domestic partnership alongside marriage, multiplying options in the direction of greater family diversity for all. On the one hand, she concludes, domestic partnerships 'go farthest from removing the state from the regulation of intimate relationships' (1991: 24); but, on the other hand, she asks whether this is always a good thing, since non-interference from the state in family matters has historically served chiefly to buttress patriarchy. Moreover,

Hunter adds, domestic partnerships may be more of a burden for those with fewer financial resources since they still lack protections which must then be added by cumbersome and costly legal processes. But simply removing the bar to same-sex marriage would provide nothing by way of alternative, and would limit the ways by which those who so desired could challenge its customs.

That is why the 'all of the above' approach – extending both marriage and domestic partnership to any and all comers – seems the best strategy for addressing the inherent diversity and contradictions of the postmodern family condition. Moreover, any public debate that considers expanding civil rights and protecting sexual (or other) minorities from abuse and discrimination has political value in itself. More at issue, perhaps, are the most effective political strategies for achieving these goals. Impatient with the extravagant drain of labor and finances needed to resist – defensively, and unsuccessfully – the wave of backlash state initiatives designed to pre-empt same-sex marriage, critics such as Eric Rofes (2000) and William Rubenstein (2000) have proposed the more 'up close and personal' strategy of a marital boycott. Until such time as marriage is open to all, they ask sympathetic heterosexuals to refuse to collude with unjust public policy by taking advantage of their heterosexual privilege, and they challenge queer folks to turn down invitations to attend legal weddings with pointed explanations as to their reason for so doing. But to those who continue to insist that even talking about gay marriage is reactionary, Evan Wolfson simply replies, 'The ship has sailed' (1994–95: 660). Marriage is on the gay agenda, like it or not.

HEATHER'S MOMMIES AND OTHER RELATIVES: RESEARCHING QUEER FAMILIES

In a cartoon published not so long ago in the *New Yorker*, a brisk-looking elementary school teacher poses a decidedly postmodern math problem to her young charges. 'If Heather has two mommies,' she asks, 'and each of them has two brothers, and one of those brothers has another man for a "room-mate", how many uncles does Heather have?'[1] The question artfully exposes the way in which the mapping of a family tree, a project rather more commonly assigned by elementary school teachers, is problematic to a child whose family does not match assumed genealogical norms. Must a house-hold reflect some particular cultural pattern (father, mother, and 2.1 children of assorted gender, for example) in order to be consi-dered a family by others?

The notion of 'families we choose' (the discourse-setting title of anthropologist Kath Weston's 1991 study of lesbian and gay families in and around San Francisco) challenges essentialist understandings of kinship. Weston identified the widespread gay experience of rejection by families of origin and the need to construct alternative support structures (a need dramatically heightened by the first ravages of the AIDS epidemic among gay men), as foundational to the creativity with which lesbians and gay men began structuring their own families of choice during the last decades of the twentieth century. Multi-household support networks, the blending of selected biological and chosen kin, early lesbian experiments in planned parenthood via donor insemination were but some of the 'chosen' family forms she investigated.

Families We Choose rightly serves as a portal into the lesbian and gay studies liter-ature on family formation, for it presciently traced the historic shift – at a time when that shift was still young and raw – from the anti-family stance of the early gay liberation movement to the sense of entitlement increasingly voiced by gays and lesbians in their struggle for family recognition and rights as enjoyed by others. Such demands, as Weston noted, are not inherently reac-tionary, reformist, or even progressive. Whether gay family discourse replicates or resists mainstream family 'values' depends upon the particular social and political context. She read the move toward establish-ing families of choice as a sign of a growing sense of political confidence and entitlement among lesbians and gay men. Even Weston might have been surprised, however, to find that within the decade, gay and lesbian parents and their children would become the feted subjects of cover stories in *Newsweek* and other mainstream publications.

AND BABY MAKES THREE (OR TWO, OR FIVE): PARENTING IN QUEER FAMILIES

How many uncles does – or should – Heather acknowledge, indeed? And a few years later, will students find themselves asking in high school biology how Heather herself was conceived ... by artificial insemination from one of the uncles to his sister's female partner, or by sperm donated by an unknown biological 'parent' (or even, nowadays, sperm stored by one of the 'moms' in anticipation of a lesbian coupling, prior to her undergoing male-to-female sex reassignation surgery)? With ovum exchange or fusion? With a pre-birth cus-tody decree attached? Or one of the many other variants rapidly gaining in popularity? Two or more gay men sharing with one, two or more women in the raising of children sharing all their genetic material? And any other co-mothers out there? A former part-ner, perhaps, and her own new partner, all equally, or perhaps competitively, devoted to Heather and to her healthy growth to maturity? Or non-sexual co-parents, defying the modern Western norm that the family be inherently sexual by definition? Or other kinship relations consciously forged in ways that might be emulated by heterosexual parents also?

The 'gayby boom' (or, more accurately, 'lesbaby boom') of the past two decades has been nothing short of spectacular. By the late 1970s, as Weston (1991) documented, lesbians on the west coast and in other urban centers of the United States had begun deciding to bear their own biological children (aided by new assisted reproduction techniques). By the 1990s, gay men were joining the planned parenthood brigade, via adoption, surrogacy, or joint parenting arrangements. Prior to this time, of course, children raised by gay men or lesbians had typically been born in the context of an earlier heterosexual relationship, and few parents who came out of the closet in those days were able to win contests for custody of their children.

Heterosexual procreation and parenthood, after all, represent the ideological lynchpin of Western gender and family conventions. The advent of planned lesbian and gay parenting has spawned a growing mixture of political controversies in the USA and Europe, as well as a new social science industry. Do children need a biological or a social father? A mother? All, or none of the above? Are lesbian and gay parents better, worse, or different from straight parents, and how do their children fare? Queer parenting experiments and the custody rights issues these pose have, interestingly, birthed a natural laboratory for the study of the effects of parental gender and sexual orientation upon child development.

As might be expected, conservative scholars have predicted dire outcomes; and their pejorative views dominated the perspectives of judges and legislators who dealt with the first wave of child custody conflicts and demands. Conservatives claim, for example, that homosexual parents are more sexually promiscuous and more likely to molest their own children; that their children suffer a greater risk of losing a parent to AIDS, substance abuse, or suicide; that the children are more apt to be confused about gender and sexual identities and to become homosexual themselves; that the social stigma and embarrassment of having a homosexual parent unfairly ostracize children and damage their ability to form peer relationships, and that as a consequence of all this, such children suffer higher levels of depression and other emotional difficulties

(e.g. Cameron and Cameron, 1996; Cameron, et al., 1996; Wardle, 1997). Opponents of homosexual parenthood insist also that children of lesbians suffer the supposed ill effects of 'fatherlessness'. 'It is now undeniable,' a Brigham Young professor of family law asserts, 'that, just as a mother's influence is crucial to the secure, healthy, and full development of a child, [a] paternal presence in the life of a child is essential to the child emotionally and physically' (Wardle, 1997: 860).

On the contrary, although the research record has limitations, more than two decades of studies have failed to substantiate such claims. The vast majority of studies to date attempt to compare child outcomes among offspring reared by heterosexual and lesbian mothers. However, since most of these children were born within heterosexual marriages which later dissolved, it has proved very difficult to isolate the effects of parental sexual orientation from such factors as divorce, coming out, step-parenting, or declines and other changes in living standards. But a new literature is growing up as fast as the children themselves, to study the children of self-identified lesbians and gay men consciously choosing to become parents through various means.

This research remains fledgling and constrained by methodological challenges, but thus far researchers almost uniformly report no meaningful differences in the measures of child outcomes they have employed; and this emerging social scientific consensus has helped to shift custody policies and decisions in a more progressive direction. Over time, increasing numbers of state courts and legislatures are extending custody, adoption, and foster care rights to lesbian and gay parents. Not surprisingly, this trend has provoked a backlash assault on the reputed ideological purposes of such research and renewed, sporadically successful, efforts to restrict parenting rights explicitly to heterosexuals.[2]

The available research, however, in our view, suffers more from its defensive response to homophobia than from ideological partisanship. For although few reputable social scientists now subscribe to the view that homosexual parents subject their children to serious risks, too many sympathetic researchers have felt compelled to adopt an implicitly heteronormative defense of gay parenting which accepts heterosexual parenting as the gold standard and therefore sets out to investigate whether or not homosexual parents are indeed inferior. Too often scholars seem to believe that this precludes discovering any differences in child outcomes at all. Thus a characteristically defensive review of research on lesbian-mother families concludes: 'a rapidly growing and highly consistent body of empirical work has failed to identify significant differences between lesbian mothers and their heterosexual counterparts or the children raised by these groups. Researchers have been unable to establish empirically that detriment results to children from being raised by lesbian mothers' (Falk, 1994: 151).

While it is easy to understand and sympathize with the reasoning behind this defensive stance, the impulse to downplay or deny any finding of difference serves to forfeit a unique opportunity for exploring the effects of parental gender and sexual identity, ideology, and behavior on children. This is particularly unfortunate for the domain of gender and sexual theory. Indeed, foreclosing the most interesting questions, researchers report findings that some might find perverse, defensively claiming that children of gay and lesbian parents turn out to be heterosexual in virtually the same proportion as those raised by heterosexual parents. However, while there is no evidence that parental sexual orientation *per se* has a notable impact on children's general psychological, intellectual or social development (nor reason that it should, apart from the social stigma involved), it seems as likely as it should be acceptable that gay parents affirmatively expose their children to a greater range of gender and sexual options. Indeed, there are scattered findings in the published studies that support such a view (see Tasker and Golombok, 1997; Stacey and Biblarz, 2001).

Moreover, should the day in fact come when homosexuality is no longer stigmatized, would it matter anyway how many kids did turn out to be gay? It should seem self-evident to all but the most biased observer that more heterosexual parents, as well as the dominant culture, are likely to attempt to influence their children to follow in their heterosexual footsteps than are gay parents to deliberately 'bring their kids up gay' (to quote Eve Kosofsky Sedgwick's teasingly titled monograph). As Sedgwick (1993: 76) wryly notes, 'advice on how to help your kids turn out gay, not to mention your students, your parishioners, your therapy clients, or your military subordinates, is less ubiquitous that you might think'.

The other minor differences reported in the research on lesbian parenting derive from the special demographic characteristics, values, and quality of relationships such parents currently represent. Given the social and economic requisites involved, lesbians (and especially gay men) who choose to become parents tend to be older and better educated than parents in general, and more often reside in urban settings. And as the means of assisted reproduction and independent adoption are more readily available to those in dominant social groups, such parents are more likely to be white and comparatively affluent. Not surprisingly, the majority of studies to date focus on the group easiest to identify, namely, white lesbian mothers in major cities, and their children. Their tantalizing findings prompt a rash of questions in their turn. Lesbian co-mothers studied, for example, seem to have higher parenting skills than heterosexual stepfathers. But is this related to their sexual orientation, their gender, or other factors? Do gay fathers parent any differently than dads in general, and, if so, why? Would the findings be the same if more racially diverse populations of gay parents were included? And, indeed, are the very categories 'lesbian mother' and 'gay father' ethnocentric, historically transitional and conceptually flawed, as queer theory would imply, since they presume sexual orientation to be fixed and dichotomous rather than fluid, inconsistent, and more multiple? Might we not learn more of interest by studying the gender and number of parents in given families, and their diverse biological and social routes to parenthood, rather than emphasizing effects of their sexual orientation?

Valerie Lehr helpfully summarizes some of the issues researchers might usefully seek to address in this context:

> By highlighting the contradictory roles that queer people create when we enter families, we can perhaps identify some of the challenges that queer families pose for dominant understandings of family: How do we understand lesbian non-biological mothers who live with a child's biological mother? Are lesbian partners mothers or fathers in those relationships? Can a lesbian be a father? Similarly, how do we understand the roles played by two male parents? Are they fathers, mothers, or some of each? ... If a child has three or more parents, how do we identify them? (1999: 103).

Or, as Graff (1999) puts it, bemoaning her own lack of legal status as a potential co-parent, 'if a dead man, or an uncle, or an absent cuckold, or a holy ghost, or a sperm-bank-supplemented husband can be a sociological "father," why can't I?' (ibid.: 105).

LIBERTY, EQUALITY, DIVERSITY?

While some researchers spend their efforts measuring lesbigay families against tacit heteronormative standards, others are more interested in assessing whether queer family relationships are superior – more liberated and liberating – than the *ancien régime* of compulsory heterosexual marriage and gender-divided parenting. Three prominent areas of current concern involve sexual practice and ethics, distributions of labor and power, and racial or ethnic differences in family formation and ideology.

The thorny issue of variance in sexual practice and ethics is not of course one unique to gay people. Values with regard to monogamy, promiscuity, sexual sport, and sex outside of love and relationships are ubiquitous subjects of debate among sexual ethicists and the general public, not to mention the US Congress! Many gay men, however, pursue this dispute with particular energy, passion and creativity. For the gay male 'culture of desire' – which queer theorists like Frank Browning (1994) affirm – creates special challenges for those gay men who question the colonization of sexuality in the name of respectability or of redemption or of 'safe' sex after the devastating terrors of AIDS, but who nonetheless seek the semblance of intimate family bonds. Navigating some of the choppiest channels in the currents of eros and domesticity, such gay men experimentally invent new genres of the 'sexual' family. That is precisely what makes homosexuality so threatening to self-appointed defenders of civilization, Browning claims:

> What is wrong with us homosexual people to straight society is that we are always available (potentially); what threatens them [*sic*] is their anxiety that *all* men harbor a desire to be penetrated and to surrender to the universal impulse toward wildness, an impulse that if allowed to go unchecked would proliferate into a thousand jungles of desire. (1994: 100)

Although data on sexual practice is difficult to gather and decode, most research supports the view that quite a few gay men do indeed seem to walk on the wild side with greater abandon than most of the rest of the population. *Homosexualities*, A.P. Bell and M.S. Weinberg's (1978) classic study on this matter, reports quite formidable levels of gay male sexual activity. Almost half of the white gay men interviewed and one-third of black gay men claimed to have had at least 500 different sex partners in their lives, and more than 90 per cent of the white gay men reported 25 partners or more. Moreover, more than one-quarter of the white gay men reported sexual activity with more than 50 partners during the year of the study, a second quarter indicated between 20 and 50, and more than half of the 29 per cent who considered themselves coupled at the time of their interview depicted their relationships as non-monogamous. Similarly, Gary Dowsett's (1996) *Practicing Desire*, an ethnographic study of gay male sexual practice in Australia, records extensive numbers of sexual partners. The majority of lesbians in the Bell and Weinberg (1978) study, by contrast, claimed to have had fewer than ten partners, with another quarter reporting fewer than five. Almost three-quarters of the women said that they were currently in a stable relationship with another woman which integrated love and sex (despite a culture of jokes about lesbian bed-death), and far more of these than the men believed that sexual infidelity would cause their relationship to fail. And, indeed, despite their greater tolerance for open relationships, Bell and Weinberg record considerable instability in gay male couple relationships.

More recently, voices claim to detect a move away from sexual libertinism, particularly among younger gay men, partly the result of AIDS, and partly a classic historical/ political generational shift. Some critics complain that current family discourse represents a conservative retreat from the defense of sexual liberty and pleasure (paralleling feminist sex wars over pornography). 'Sex Panic' critics, like Browning (1994), Warner (1993, 1999), Douglas Crimp (1988), and Kobena Mercer (1994), castigate prominent mainstream gay authors, including Sullivan (1995, 1997), Bawer (1993), Michelangelo Signorile (1997), and Gabriel Rotello (1997), for fostering such a retreat. And while lesbians certainly divide along similar ideological lines, it is as striking as it is unsurprising that this is a discourse dominated by men.

But who, if anyone, dominates the household when couples cannot resort to default mode gender scripts? Studies of the division of domestic labor and power have become a major area of sociological research ever since feminists focused attention on the politics of housework. Because same-sex couples offer an exceptional social laboratory for gender theory and practice, research on how gay and lesbian couples and co-parents share household duties and expenses is a thriving enterprise, assessing the great gay hope that their relationships are more egalitarian and just than heterosexual ones. The record thus far provides grounds for both self-congratulation and caution. *American Couples*, the 1983 classic study by Philip Blumstein and Pepper Schwartz, which compared married and cohabiting straight couples with their gay male and lesbian counterparts, did find that gender served as a potent determinant across the spectrum of money, work, and sex. Lesbians were most likely to share domestic tasks equally, they reported, and gay men to divide them by interest, but both were more egalitarian and more economically autonomous than married couples. Later studies of lesbian co-parents report similar results. For example, Raymond Chan, Risa Brooks et al. (1998) found that lesbian co-mothers shared childcare tasks more equally than heterosexual parents and that more egalitarian couples were also more satisfied with their relationships. Likewise, Maureen Sullivan (1996) found that lesbian co-parents tended to perform equal childcare duties and enjoy equal status in the home as long as both remained employed. But if one (and not necessarily the birth mother) became a full-time homemaker, her breadwinner partner seemed to assume more of the kind of decision-making power that male breadwinners have traditionally enjoyed. A recent ethnographic study, however, more skeptically asks if such findings owe more to romantic, self-congratulatory ideological investments than to quotidian practice. After closely observing more than fifty families, Christopher Carrington (1999) claims that domestic tasks were, in fact, far from equally shared, but that investment in egalitarianism led lesbians to credit partners who contribute little with more than they in fact do, while dominant gay male partners worked hard to counter any perceived emasculation of the more domesticated partner by stressing that partner's non-domestic activities.

The fond myth that a same-gendered relationship is inherently shielded from patriarchal patterns of dominance and subordination can even make lesbians and gays particularly vulnerable to more threatening conse-quences. For it fosters a tendency to deny what divorce lawyers have known all along, namely that attempts to anchor romantic affairs in the turbulent waters of domesticity are beset by all kinds of dangers, including violence in the home. The emergence of dis-appointing data pointing to the prevalence of partner abuse among gay men and lesbians – which preliminary surveys indicate to be no less rampant than in heterosexual relation-ships – has led to community-based efforts to provide domestic violence intervention and prevention services, at least in urban centers (National Coalition of Anti-Violence Programs, 1997, 1998, 1999). Service pro-viders emphasize the need for concerted efforts to increase the sensitivity of health care and law enforcement agencies to victims of same-gendered domestic violence. For example, a battered lesbian rightly fears that her partner can gain the same access as she to the network of women's shelters, and a gay man might report an assault by his partner as perpetrated by a stranger. Confronting the tendency within lesbian and gay groups to deny the existence of such violence remains a major challenge. Lesbians, in particular, have been reluctant to acknow-ledge that loving women does not in itself grant them immunity from domestic abuse. And feminist theory must confront the com-plex question of whether and why families in all their new varieties might retain as much potential for violence and danger as when gender seemed to explain all.

However long the 'families we choose' literature may be on matters of liberty and equality, it falls significantly behind – like much else in lesbian and gay studies – on matters of racial and ethnic diversity. This is a disproportionately white discourse, both among authors and subjects, reflecting the unwitting ethnocentrism of categories like gay, queer, and choice. After all, communi-ties constructed around sexual identity tend to be white-dominated in Western countries, because the identification of 'gay' with 'white' points to the relatively privileged position of those who can afford to make sexuality the central axis of their identity.[3] As the late Joseph Beam, a black gay poet, observed with some bitterness before he died of AIDS: 'We ain't family. Very clearly, gay male means: white, middle-class, youth-ful, nautilized, and probably butch; there is no room for black gay men within the con-fines of this gay pentagon' (1986: 14). And, of course, the word 'family' itself often signifies differently among communities of color, not to mention among peoples of non-Western nations.

Consequently, the emergent literature on the family formations of lesbigay people of color builds on the premise that most are likely to regard the racial groups to which they belong as a stronger source of solidarity and identity (and marginality) than they do their sexual affinities. Indeed, lesbigay people of color appear to be more apt than whites to remain semi-closeted, embedded within their own racial kin groups and neighborhoods, and to pursue homoerotic interests within racial bonds (see, e.g., Hawkeswood, 1996). Keith Boykin, Execu-tive Director of the National Black Gay and Lesbian Leadership Forum, recounts how he came to such a stance: 'The shared racial identity develops a much stronger family bond than any presumed identity based on sexual orientation. I never polled my family members, but ultimately I decided that some would be more disturbed by my dating a white woman, while others would be more upset by my dating a black man' (1996: 23).

Likewise, gay men and lesbians of color are less likely to participate in the planned gayby boom, partly because of economic barriers which disproportionately affect people of color; partly because they are less likely to live within communities which support and foster this choice; and partly because of the relative paucity of non-white sperm donors. As Boykin notes, 'Homopho-bia and heterosexism are frequently seen not as prejudices but as survival skills for the black race or the black individual' (1996: 167). Black gay and lesbian people – where their existence is even acknowledged – are sometimes viewed by their own families, communities, and churches as lacking commitment to the race on a similar scale to heterosexuals who intermarry. Boykin admits that a 'black man who dates only men raises the specter of the extinction of the family name, potentially causes embarrassment to the family, and often suggests an irresponsible disregard for the need to create strong, black families' (ibid.: 23). A black gay couple caring for their own children are likely not counted a 'strong, black family' in this sense.

For similar reasons, one finds few gay people of color leading the race to the altar. For some, the gay marriage crusade represents a distraction from more urgent racial causes. Indeed, one can readily make the case that in the USA, access to marriage is becoming a major form of class and race privilege, in addition to its status as an exclusively heterosexual club. Paradoxically, however, gay and lesbian family rights activists of all colors frequently cast *themselves* as the inheritors of the struggles for black civil rights. They cite the historic Supreme Court decisions, *Loving vs. Virginia*, 1967, which struck down anti-miscegenation laws, and *Palmore vs. Sidoti*, 1984, which affirmed a divorced white woman's right to retain custody of her children after she married a black man, as precedents for granting similar protections to queer marriage and family goals. And beyond the US borders, journalist Neil Miller (1992) found the prospect of gay marriage capturing the imagination of black people in the townships of South Africa, and inspiring gay people the world over. Moreover, because South Africa's post-apartheid constitution is the first in the world to bar discrimination against people on the basis of any social identity, including sexuality, that nation is actively considering full legalization of same-sex marriage and family rights.

Indeed, one can readily argue that the improvisational diversity of family practices which African-Americans and South Africans forged in response to racial subordination and poverty – such as 'other-mothering' and

multi-household families – foreshadowed many features of the postmodern family condition in the West as a whole. Certainly, the explosive national discourse on black 'matriarchy' in the USA provoked by the 1965 *Moynihan Report* foreshadowed preoccupations of the contemporary politics of 'family values' more generally, as in the Murphy Brown discourse. That is why, in theory, it seems clear that forging a 'rainbow coalition' to support queer family values could benefit both communities of color and gay people of every hue. Translating such theory into practice, however, will require far more awareness and respect than has yet been achieved for the genuine diversity of family definitions, priorities and vulnerabilities that divide racial and ethnic communities here and elsewhere.

SO DUCK OR NO DUCK?

If it looks like a duck, and it walks like a duck, and it quacks like a duck, then is it a duck? We began by asking whether the Vermont experiment in creating civil unions for same-sex couples represents marriage in all but name. So does it? Does the demand of so many lesbian and gay people, in so many parts of the world at once, for equal recognition of their pairings presage an irreversible move toward the embrace of conventional forms of family life? Are lesbigay family forms really just the same as everyone else's, differing only by the gender combination of sexually-bonded adults? Does gay marriage really threaten to undo civilization, as conservatives fear? As Frank Browning observes, 'Worse even than the sexual perversions they practice, gay people's more damning threat to traditionalists is their claim to family parity, their claim to family life as a right' (1994: 142).

Given our claim that queer family developments signal the frontier of global changes in family structure inherent in the postmodern family condition, we could say that in that sense, families created by lesbians and gay men are truly not distinct from other families. They simply heighten the visibility of the fact of irreversible diversity. They bring us face to face with inescapable contests over legitimate relations of gender, sexuality, and family. The decline of the modern (Western) nuclear family system, as we have noted, has left us with no prevailing culturally mandated family pattern – as any third-grader trying to fill in those blanks on a traditional family tree quickly discovers. All forms of intimacy now contend with instability, contradiction, experimentation. Yet family life itself has by no means been discarded. Instead, many are reinventing it with ingenuity and passion. And here gay men and women (and especially those who defy dichotomization as men or women at all) are leading the pack.

The political meanings of family sentiments, practices, and discourse among gay men and lesbians cannot be defined by checking any one box (progressive, reactionary, and so forth), other than the one marked 'all of the above'. Most reforms are two-edged, often contradictory, and can be read as progressive and co-optive, subversive and accommodationist all at once, depending upon social, economic, and political contexts. Extending marriage to same-gendered couples, as we saw, could simultaneously redefine the institution by eroding gender meanings and homophobia, but also exacerbate class inequities and couple privilege, further marginalizing the single, dissidents, sexual radicals, and all who lack economic resources. Choosing to bear children might help to combat homophobia as Heather's mommies take their place as soccer moms, at PTA meetings, and in church and temple, and other children come to see two mommies as yet another norm. But it could also foster more puritanical and conformist values, as critics charge, and sap collective energies from other ongoing political and social battles, as well as ignoring the needs of the elderly gay, or of disenfranchised youth.

The way a society treats its gay families has broad implications for all families. Just as we refuse to protect the family bonds of children because their parent(s) are gay, denying them equal access to health care or to inheritance or to appropriate custody arrangements, so too we punish children for other parental infractions, such as being born to a single mother on welfare or belonging to another group subject to social prejudice. Queer family discourse is not likely to disappear until we come to understand that, as one of us has argued elsewhere, 'all our families are queer'. Gay and lesbian families simply display with added intensity the characteristics of broader family and social realities today, helping to expose the dangerous disjunction between popular 'family values' rhetoric and the complex lived realities of contemporary families. Not the same as other families, nor an alternative to 'the family', lesbigay families expose the social and historical character of every definition of family. Promoting queer family values within a multi-hued rainbow coalition to support all shapes and colors of families could establish family diversity itself as normal in a democracy.

EPILOGUE

Perhaps we might end by suggesting that newly emerging gay and lesbian family forms might better be compared not to plastic ducks but to the ugly duckling of the children's fairy-tale. Hatched as if in prophetic anticipation of the current technological revolution in methods of reproduction as one of a brood of ducklings, one offspring quickly appears different from his nest-mates. Everyone who sees the ugly duckling considers him disturbingly queer. 'Quack, Quack! Get out of town!' they derisively sing. But in time, the queer duckling quacks back, for to his own surprise and theirs he survives their taunts and emerges a magnificent swan, the pride of the pond. Not a duck at all, although the egg from which he came had been laid among their kind. And wouldn't it be dull if the only species our pond could sustain were identical little yellow plastic ducks?

NOTES

1 *The New Yorker*, 8 March, 1999, with reference to Leslea Newman, 1991. *Heather Has Two Mommies*. Boston: Alyson Publications.

2 In Utah, for example, Wardle drafted regulations limiting adoption and foster care placements to households in which all adults were related by blood or marriage (later passed by the state legislature), shortly after publishing his 1997 article impugning the methods, merits, and motives of social science research on lesbian and gay parenting.

3 Note Steven Seidman's assertion that: 'Lesbians and gay men of color have contested the notion of a unitary gay subject and the idea that the meaning and experience of being gay are socially uniform. Indeed, they argue that a discourse that abstracts a notion of gay identity from considerations of race and class is oppressive because it invariably implies a white, middle-class standpoint' (1993: 120). Valerie Lehr (1999) suggests that the fact that racial/ethnic identity is more likely to be central to self-definition for people of color in the USA may result in greater sexual freedom because of the consequently lessened need to embrace a fixed sexual identity. She further wonders, conversely, whether bisexuality is undercounted in white communities.

REFERENCES

Abraham, Julie (2000) 'Public relations: why the rush to same-sex marriage? And who stands to benefit?', *Women's Review of Books*, 17 (8): 12–14.

Bawer, Bruce (1993) *A Place at the Table: The Gay Individual in American Society.* New York: Poseidon.

Beam, Joseph. (1986) 'Leaving the shadows behind', in Joseph Beam (ed.), *In The Life: A Black Gay Anthology.* Boston: Alyson Publications.

Bell, Alan P. and Weinberg Martin S. (1978) *Homosexualities: A Study of Diversity among Men and Women.* London: Mitchell Beazley.

Blumstein, Philip and Schwartz, Pepper (1983) *American Couples.* New York: William Morrow.

Boykin, Keith (1996) *One More River to Cross: Black and Gay in America.* New York: Anchor.

British Broadcasting Corporation (2000) 'Gay couple's babies "denied citizenship"', *BBC News Online* (2 January). www.news.bbc.co.uk/

Browning, Frank (1994) *The Culture of Desire: Paradox and Perversity in Gay Lives Today.* New York: Random House.

Cameron, Paul and Cameron, Kirk (1996) 'Homosexual parents', *Adolescence*, 31: 757–76.

Cameron, Paul, Cameron, Kirk and Landess, Thomas (1996) 'Errors by the American Psychiatric Association, the American Psychological Association, and the National Educational Association in Representing Homosexuality in Amicus Briefs about Amendment 2 to the U.S. Supreme Court', *Psychological Reports*, 79: 383–404.

Carrington, Christopher (1999) *No Place Like Home: Relationships and Family Life among Lesbians and Gay Men.* Chicago: University of Chicago Press.

Chan, Raymond W., Brooks, Risa C. et al. (1998) 'Division of labor among lesbian and heterosexual parents: association with children's adjustment', *Journal of Family Psychology*, 12 (3): 402–19.

Crimp, Douglas (1988) *AIDS: Cultural Analysis/Cultural Activism.* Cambridge: MIT Press.

Dowsett, Gary W. (1996) *Practicing Desire: Homosexual Sex in the Era of AIDS.* Stanford, CA: Stanford University Press.

Ettelbrick, Paula (1992) 'Since when is marriage a path to liberation?', in Suzanne Sherman (ed.), *Lesbian and Gay Marriage: Private Commitments, Public Ceremonies.* Philadelphia: Temple University Press. pp. 20–6.

Falk, Patrick J. (1994) 'The gap between psychosocial assumptions and empirical research in lesbian-mother child custody cases,' in A.E. Gottfried and A.W. Gottfried (eds) *Redefining Families: Implications for Children's Development.* New York: Plenum. pp. 131–56.

Fineman, Martha A. (1995) *The Neutered Mother, The Sexual Family, and Other Twentieth Century Tragedies.* New York: Routledge.

Gibb, Frances (1999) 'Gay couple will be the legal parents of twins', *The Times*, 28 October, p. 5.

Giddens, Anthony (1992) *The Transformation of Intimacy: Sexuality, Love and Eroticism in Modern Societies.* Stanford, CA: Stanford University Press.

Goldberg, Carey (2000) 'Gay couples welcoming idea of civil union', *The New York Times*, 18 March.

Graff, E.J. (1999) *What Is Marriage For? The Strange Social History of Our Most Intimate Institution.* Boston: Beacon Press.

Hawkeswood, William G. (1996) *One of the Children: Gay Black Men in Harlem.* Berkeley, CA: University of California Press.

Hunter, Nan (1991) 'Marriage, law, and gender: a feminist inquiry', *Law and Sexuality*, 1 (1): 9–30.

Kandiyoti, Deniz (1988) 'Bargaining with patriarchy', *Gender and Society*, 2 (3): 274–90.

Lehr, Valerie (1999) *Queer Family Values: Debunking the Myth of the Nuclear Family.* Philadelphia: Temple University Press.

Leland, John (2000) 'Shades of gay', *Newsweek*, 20 March: 46–9.

Lewin, Ellen (1998) *Recognizing Ourselves: Ceremonies of Lesbian and Gay Commitment.* New York: Columbia University Press.

Los Angeles Times (2000) 'Poll finds split on gay rights and marriages', 1 June: A31.

Mann, William J. (1999) 'The family: friends are family in gay life', *Frontiers Newsmagazine*, 18 (6) (23 July): 59–62.

Mercer, Kobena (1994) *Welcome to the Jungle: New Positions in Cultural Studies*. New York: Routledge.

Miller, Neil (1992) *Out in the World: Gay and Lesbian Life from Buenos Aires to Bangkok*. New York: Random House.

Mohr, Richard (1994) *A More Perfect Union*. Boston: Beacon Press.

National Coalition of Anti-Violence Programs (1997) *1997 Report on Lesbian, Gay, Bisexual, Transgender Domestic Violence*. Los Angeles.

National Coalition of Anti-Violence Programs (1998) *Annual Report on Lesbian, Gay, Bisexual, Transgender Domestic Violence*. Los Angeles.

National Coalition of Anti-Violence Programs (1999) *Lesbian, Gay, Transgender and Bisexual Domestic Violence in 1998: A Report of the National Coalition of Anti-Violence Programs*. Los Angeles.

Newman, Leslea (1991) *Heather Has Two Mommies*. Boston: Alyson Publications.

New York Times (2000) 'French couples take plunge that falls short of marriage', 18 April: 1.

Polikoff, Nancy D. (1993) 'We will get what we ask for: why legalizing gay and lesbian marriage will not "dismantle the legal structure of gender in every marriage"'. *Virginia Law Review*, 79 (7): 1535–50.

Rauch, Jonathan (1994) 'A pro-gay, pro-family policy', *The Wall Street Journal*, 29 November.

Robson, Ruthan (1994) 'Repositioning the family: repositioning lesbians in legal theory', *Signs*, 19 (Summer): 975–96.

Rofes, Eric (2000) 'Life after Knight: a call for direct action and civil disobedience', Essay distributed via e-mail (10 March).

Rotello, Gabriel (1997) *Sexual Ecology: AIDS and the Destiny of Gay Men*. New York: Dutton.

Rubenstein, William (2000) 'Why do straight people invite us to their weddings, and why do we go?', Lecture at University of California, Los Angeles.

Sedgwick, Eve Kosofsky (1993) 'How to bring your kids up gay', in Michael Warner (ed.), *Fear of a Queer Planet: Queer Politics and Social Theory*. Minneapolis: University of Minnesota Press. pp. 69–81.

Seidman, Steven (1993) 'Identity and politics in a 'postmodern' gay culture: some historical and conceptual notes', in *Fear of a Queer Planet: Queer Politics and Social Theory*. Minneapolis: University of Minnesota Press. pp. 105–42.

Sherman, Suzanne (1992) *Lesbian and Gay Marriage: Private Commitments, Public Ceremonies*. Philadelphia, PA: Temple University Press.

Signorile, Michelangelo (1997) *Life Outside – The Signorile Report on Gay Men: Sex, Drugs, Muscles, and the Passages of Life*. New York: Harper Collins.

Stacey, Judith (1996) *In The Name of the Family: Rethinking Family Values in the Postmodern Age*. Boston: Beacon.

Stacey, Judith, and Biblarz Timothy (2001) '(How) Does the Sexual Orientation of Parents Matter?' *American, Sociological Review*. 66: 2, pp. 159–183.

Stoddard, Thomas B. (1992) 'Why gay people should seek the right to marry', in Suzanne Sherman (ed.), *Lesbian and Gay Marriage: Private Commitments, Public Ceremonies*. Philadelphia: Temple University Press. pp. 13–19.

Stuever, Hank (2000) 'Is gay mainstream?', *The Washington Post*, 27 April.

Sullivan, Andrew (1989) 'Here comes the groom: a (conservative) case for gay marriage', *The New Republic*, 28 August.

Sullivan, Andrew (1995) *Virtually Normal: An Argument About Homosexuality*. New York: Knopf.

Sullivan, Andrew (1997) *Same-Sex Marriage: Pro and Con, A Reader*. New York: Vintage.

Sullivan, Maureen (1996) 'Rozzie and Harriet? Gender and family patterns of lesbian coparents', *Gender and Society*, 10 (6): 747–67.

Tasker, Fiona L. and Golombok, Susan (1997) *Growing Up in a Lesbian Family*. New York: Guilford.

Wardle, Lynn D. (1997) 'The potential impact of homosexual parenting on children', *University of Illinois Law Review*, 833–919.

Warner, Michael (1993) *Fear of a Queer Planet: Queer Politics and Social Theory*. Minneapolis: University of Minnesota Press.

Warner, Michael (1999) 'Normal and normaller: beyond gay marriage', *Gay and Lesbian Quarterly*, 5 (2): 119–71.

Warren, Jennifer (2000) 'Gays gaining acceptance in state, poll finds', *The Los Angeles Times*, 14 June: A1/27.

Weston, Kath (1991) *Families We Choose: Lesbians, Gays, Kinship*. New York: Columbia University Press.

Wolfson, Evan (1994–95) 'Crossing the threshold: equal marriage rights for lesbians and gay men and the intracommunity critique', *New York Review of Law and Social Change*, XXI (3): 567–615.

Part IV

POLITICS

22

Making a Minority

Understanding the Formation of the Gay and Lesbian Movement in the United States[1]

STEPHEN ENGEL

Referring to the 2000 presidential election cycle for the 31 January 2000 edition of *Time* magazine, columnist Margaret Carlson wrote

> In 1992, not only would no one bring up gaydar, but also the subject of gays in the military was not nearly the preoccupation it is this time ... what this campaign shows is that the country has moved some distance in its acceptance of gays. Two years ago, gay bashing was a staple of the Republican right. Lately, Republicans have largely gone quiet since their pollsters warned them to knock it off. Spreading scare stories about gays just wasn't working. Too many people had come out, and too may blue-haired mothers in the heartland didn't like hearing that their gay son or daughter was worthless or immoral.

Carlson succinctly isolates a shift in the national political culture in the United States. What has happened in recent history that made these 'blue-haired mothers' come out in defense of their gay sons and daughters? Why has the Republican Party, the party of 'traditional family values', refrained from overt bashing of so-called sexual deviance? Why is the slang term 'gaydar' suddenly becoming appropriated

into national discourse? The visibility and acceptance of gay men and lesbians in cultural and political media are higher now than they have ever been as discussions regarding gays in the military are re-opened, as the controversy over the possibility of gay marriage looms and civil unions become a reality, as gay characters are now prominently featured in prime-time television. To be blunt, where did all this gayness come from?

To more fully comprehend the current status of gay and lesbian political and cultural visibility, we must understand the development of the social movement that has both enabled and promoted this visibility. A social movement embodies a sustained collective challenge against political elites and authorities led by people with a common purpose and who lack regular access to existing political institutions (Tarrow, 1994: 2, 4). Often when studying social movements, we develop a theory composed of certain variables which, in turn, represent the questions we ask. Multiple social movement theories exist; some may be compatible, others may not, but usually and most importantly, *no one theory is able to elucidate all aspects of these events*. No one theory is either mutually exclusive or collectively exhaustive. Divergent understandings of social movements derive from the different questions that are asked. The aim, when understanding social movements, is not to develop a totalizing theory that accounts for every potential variable, but to isolate key questions in order to provide a comprehensive understanding of the movement. In general, when investigating the formation of a movement, we seek to discover *why* people participate, *how* they (afford to) participate, and *when* they participate. Each of these questions underlies a specific focus whether it be oriented toward individual motivation, organizational resources, or the external/institutional environment. A theory which can address the interrelated nature of each of these questions without necessarily privileging one above the others will provide the most comprehensive understanding of social movements and the communities that they foster. This chapter identifies three crucial factors necessary for the development of collective insurgency and the formation of a social movement – changing opportunity, pre-existing organizational strength, and cognitive liberation which leads to collective identity formation – each of which correspond to the three questions asked above (McAdam, 1997: 172–92).

Commonly referred to as the political process model, the hypothesized interaction adheres to the following pattern. A change in the opportunity structure creates the possibility for collective organizing by a minority group that usually has little or no access to political power. Yet, the mere opportunity for such mobilization is quite different from and does not guarantee the existence of a movement. Some type of pre-existing organizational network that can enable further member recruitment, select leaders, and facilitate communication must exist to harness this opportunity and convert it into organized and sustainable protest (Tarrow, 1994: 178–82). The disenfranchised minority must experience a cognitive shift characterized

by a relinquishment of a victimized self-perception, an endorsement of a rights-based agenda, and a new sense of efficacy and agential power (ibid.: 183). Thus, all three factors are integrally tied in the evolution of a movement. While these factors are interdependent and necessary for successful collective action, the model presupposes the existence of some type of opportunity in the existing socio-economic and political environment such as an electoral realignment.

A historical analysis of the American gay and lesbian movement utilizing this tri-factor developmental model seeks to answer a variety of questions. What changing opportunity enabled the movement even to be contemplated? What organizations existed to capitalize on this opportunity? When did members of this disenfranchised minority realize their inherent agential power thereby experiencing cognitive liberation? What organizations did the movement spur? What response did the movement elicit from both the government and other citizens? How has the movement changed over the course of its existence? What factors have influenced this change? This chapter addresses these inquiries by studying the evolution of the American gay and lesbian movement throughout the post-World War II period.

WORLD WAR II AND THE 1950s: EMERGING OPPORTUNITY

The emergence of the gay and lesbian movement in the United States is often pinpointed to an exact date and time: 1:20 a.m. on Saturday, 28 June 1969. On this day, police officers raided a well-known gay bar, the Stonewall Inn, on Christopher Street in Greenwich Village. The police raid was not uncommon; however, the reaction of the patrons was extraordinary: they fought back, sparking two days and nights of riotous confrontation between approximately four hundred New York police officers and two thousand gay men and women, especially people of color (Cruickshank, 1992: 69;

D'Emilio, 1983: 232). This event is so crucial because it signifies the emergence of group action among a previously docile, invisible, and seemingly powerless minority. Soon after the riots, various organizations including the Gay Liberation Front (GLF) were created to mobilize gay men and lesbians into a viable political force. As historian John D'Emilio notes, a curious contradiction developed between GLF rhetoric and the reality of the homosexual community. Activists of the early 1970s denounced the invisibility and silence that many felt characterized the homosexual lifestyle. However, leaders of liberation movement organizations demonstrated an uncanny ability to mobilize these supposedly silent and isolated masses: by the middle of the 1970s over one thousand gay and lesbian organizations existed in the United States (1983: 1–2). This apparent inconsistency can be resolved if we take D'Emilio's advice: 'clearly what the movement achieved and how lesbians and gay men responded to it belied the rhetoric of isolation and invisibility. Isolated men and women do not create, almost overnight, a mass movement premised upon a shared group identity' (1983: 2). In other words, the gay and lesbian movement did not suddenly start at a given hour on a certain day following a specific event; rather, it embodies an historical process marked by diverse opportunities, multiple organizational networks, and instances, such as the Stonewall riots, which ushered in a shift in the personal perspectives of gay men and lesbians themselves.

D'Emilio suggests that the first significant opportunity for homosexual identity formation was World War II. The altered social conditions of the war, i.e., a sex-segregated society marked both by soldiers under the strain of warfare and a large influx of women into the domestic labor force, provided a critical opportunity for gay men and lesbians to come into contact with one another. The sex-segregated atmosphere created by militarization immensely disrupted the heterosexual patterns of peace-time life; this phenomenon is no more apparent than in the armed forces. First, by asking recruits if they had ever felt any erotic attraction for members of the same sex, the military was rupturing the silence that shrouded a tabooed behavior, sometimes introducing men to the concept for the first time (D'Emilio, 1983: 24). Second, the war brought previously isolated homosexuals together. Given that the recruits could merely lie about their sexual inclinations and that the draft preferred young and single men, it was likely that the armed forces would contain a disproportionately high percentage of gay men relative to civilian society (ibid.: 25). Third, heterosexual men sometimes engaged in 'situational homosexuality' to attain a level of physical intimacy deprived by the war experience (Vaid, 1995: 48). It was not uncommon for men to dance together at canteens, to share beds at hotels when on leave, or to share train berths while in transit (D'Emilio, 1983: 25–6). The critical point is not that the war experience fostered homoerotic feelings and a rise in homosexuality. Rather, the war's disruption of the social environment provided the *opportunity* for homosexuals to meet, to realize others like themselves existed, and to abandon the isolation that characterized the homosexual lifestyle of the pre-war period. The war created a sexual situation where individuals with homosexual feelings or tendencies could more readily explore them without the absolute fear of exposure.

The return of peace brought the re-establishment of pre-war heterosexual gender norms. Yet, the war had enabled gay men and women to discover one another and to start building networks than could not easily be torn down. The immediate post-war years witnessed early forms of homosexual organizations and the proliferation of novels which featured gay characters and themes. The Veterans Benevolent Association was established by several honorably discharged gay men in New York City in 1945 to function as a social club for gay ex-servicemen hosting parties and dances. In Los Angeles, interracial homosexual couples organized the Knights of the Clock to discuss mutual problems (D'Emilio, 1983: 32). Claire Morgan's *The Price of Salt* (1951) and Jo Sinclair's *The Wasteland* (1946) relayed the stories of strong lesbians and their acceptance of their sexuality while Charlie Jackson's *The Fall of Valor* (1946) discussed the homoerotic social environment experienced by men during the war. While these texts tended to bow to contemporary beliefs on homosexuality, portraying the characters as usually unhappy and fundamentally tragic, their publication signals a small opening of social mores and a shift in the traditional attitude toward homosexuality (D'Emilio, 1983: 32).

Gay subcultural institutions proliferated during the immediate post-war period. Gay bars, while more common in large cities such as New York City or Los Angeles before the war, opened in smaller cities such as Worcester, Massachusetts and Kansas City, Missouri (Berube, 1990: 271–2). The gay bar provided a relatively safe place for gay men to meet each other without having to maintain a façade of heterosexuality (D'Emilio, 1983: 32–3). The bars also shaped a gay identity that went beyond so-called individual 'affliction' toward a sense of community (Berube, 1990: 271). The gay bar therefore functioned as a vehicle by which to promote a primitive notion of collective identity before the 1970s' era of gay liberation. As Urvashi Vaid (1995: 48) notes, the bars helped to establish a 'nascent post-war community of gay men and women [which] was, like its nongay counterparts, ripe for political organizing. As the climate grew more overtly hostile toward gay men and lesbians, a new social movement came into being.'

Despite these advances in gay subcultural and community development, gay men, lesbians, and any other individuals who failed to fit into the heteronormative pattern of post-war life encountered oppression from the religious, legal, and medical fields. Judeo-Christian tradition denounced homosexuality as a sin. At this time, engaging in consensual homosexual sex was a criminal act throughout the United States. The

medical sphere tended to view homosexuals as mentally ill (D'Emilio, 1983: 12). Yet, within this last field, homosexuals tended to make the most advances, even if such advances were indirect. Although widely discredited now, Alfred Kinsey's *Sexual Behavior of the Human Male* and *Sexual Behavior of the Human Female*, published in 1948 and 1953 respectively, provided the most comprehensive study of the sexual behavior of caucasian Americans at the time (D'Emilio, 1983: 34). After interviewing more than 10,000 subjects of both sexes, Kinsey drafted a seven-point scale to detail the fluidity of sexual orientation in which at least 18 per cent of Americans did not consider themselves universally or mostly heterosexual (1948: 636–41, 650). Such results led Kinsey to conclude that 'persons with homosexual histories are to be found in every age group, in every social level, in every conceivable occupation, in cities and on farms, and in the most remote areas of the country' (ibid.: 627). These findings helped to tear away the ideological barriers that hindered equality for gays and lesbians by opening up for discussion the formerly taboo topic of sexuality. In short, the reports enlarged the already existing opportunity structure provided by the war; the political environment was ripening for the formation of a homosexual movement. Yet, the Kinsey reports were also utilized throughout the 1950s as ammunition against the increased visibility of homosexuality in the United States.

The onset of Cold War anti-Communist panic marked the 1950s as a decade rife with political repression. Communists were not the only target; individuals who did not conform to the mainstream heteronormative image reminiscent of the pre-war period were perceived as enemies of the state (Adam, 1995: 61). Amidst growing fears that homosexuals – one such non-conforming group – were infiltrating the highest levels of government and threatening national security, the Senate Investigations Subcommittee of the Committee on Expenditures in the Executive Department began an inquiry in June of 1950 and released its report, 'Employment of Homosexuals and Other Sex Perverts in the U.S. Government', in December of 1950. The report's attack on homosexuals was twofold: it degraded the personal character of gay men and lesbians, and it contended that homosexuals embodied a threat to national security. The report used Kinsey's conclusions regarding the higher prevalence of homosexuality than previously thought to promote a sense of paranoia: these diseased individuals were everywhere and, worse yet, they could not be detected by any physical features. The committee concluded that homosexuals exhibited emotional instability and moral weakness. According to the Senate report, employing homosexuals would not only put fellow workers at risk, but would endanger national integrity (Blasius and Phelan, 1997: 241–51). The report's ultimate conclusion was that homosexuals were fundamentally unsuited for employment in the federal government. Between 1947 and 1950, the dismissal rate of homosexuals from an executive branch office averaged five per month (D'Emilio, 1983: 44; Adam, 1995: 62). Homosexuals were officially banned from the government with the passage of Executive Order 10450 under President Eisenhower in April of 1953 (D'Emilio, 1983: 44). In total, between 1947 and 1950, 1,700 applicants for government positions were turned away because of professed homosexuality, 4,380 individuals were discharged from military service, and 420 gay men and lesbians were dismissed or forced to resign from government posts (Adam, 1995: 62–3).

While the national government endorsed an anti-homosexual stance, gay men and lesbians encountered the more immediate danger of police harassment. Bar raids were prevalent. In the 1950s, approximately one hundred gay men were arrested each month in Philadelphia on misdemeanor charges, and approximately one thousand gay men were arrested each year in Washington, DC. During the 1953 New York City mayoral election, raids on gay bars increased

dramatically (D'Emilio, 1983: 50–1). In 1954, after the murder of a gay man in Miami, one newspaper 'demand[ed] that the homosexuals be punished for tempting "normals" to commit such deeds' (Adam, 1995: 63). In such a seemingly backward environment where the victim was blamed for murder, the American Civil Liberties Union refused to support gay and bisexual individuals in their attempts to attain equality (Blasius and Phelan, 1997: 274–5).

World War II, coupled with the Kinsey studies of the late 1940s created the *opportunity* for men and women unsure of their sexual orientation or already aware of their homosexuality or bisexuality to meet others like themselves. The proliferation of gay bars enabled the community development and identity formation started by the war to continue. However, military and government witch hunts and bar raids continued to demonstrate the enormous challenges that gay men and lesbians encountered daily. The increasing attacks on homosexuals may have promoted community development by making homosexuality a topic for national-level discourse; indeed, sociologists Barry Adam, Jan Willem Duyvendak, and Andre Krouwel (1999: 344), found that 'politicization of a social group seems to be facilitated, rather than hampered, when political repression is evident but not too strong'. D'Emilio (1983: 52) makes a similar point by contending that these attacks 'hastened the articulation of homosexual identity and spread the knowledge that they [gay men and women] existed in large numbers …. Ironically, the effort to root out the homosexuals in American society made it easier for them to find one another.' Even if they could find one another, the widespread condemnation of homosexuality would lead many gays and lesbians to consider homosexuality to be an individual problem indicative not of injustice but disease (ibid.: 53). Nevertheless, the juxtaposition of the opportunity provided by World War II for gay men and lesbians to explore their identity and the subsequent repressive environment of the 1950s fostered a dissonant atmosphere from which the first politically active gay and lesbian organizations emerged.

1960s: COMING TOGETHER AND EARLY ORGANIZING

Founded by Harry Hay in April of 1951 in Los Angeles and modeled after the communist party, the Mattachine Society was the first organization of what would become the homophile movement (Adam, 1995: 67–8). The secret hierarchical and cell-like structure was necessitated, according to the founders, by the oppressive environment fostered by McCarthyism. Yet, Mattachine drew on communism for more than an organizational template; Marxist ideology laid the blueprints to mobilize a mass homosexual constituency for political action. Adapting a Marxist understanding of class politics, Hay and the other founding members theorized that homosexuals constituted an oppressed minority group. Homosexuals, like members of the proletariat, were trapped in a state of false consciousness purported and defended by the heterosexual majority which maintained homosexuality to be a morally reprehensible individual aberration (D'Emilio, 1983: 65–6). Hence, the early Mattachine attempted to promote a measure of cognitive liberation and homosexual collective identity; it advocated the development of a group consciousness similar to that of other ethnic minority groups in the United States. Mattachine, under Hay's direction, whether intentional or not, was capitalizing on a master frame which has had a great deal of cultural resonance in the United States: minority demands for civil rights. By asserting that homosexuals constituted a minority comparable to recognized ethnic groups, Mattachine defined itself rather than being defined by the dominant culture: homosexuality was distinct from and morally equivalent to heterosexuality. Furthermore, the comparison to ethnic minorities provided a model for action: homosexuals should follow the lead of other groups and politically organize for equal civil rights (Vaid, 1995: 52).

By 1953, the Mattachine Society had an estimated 2000 members and one hundred discussion groups stretching from San Diego to Santa Monica, California (Vaid, 1995: 71). Given the rise of McCarthyism, some members became increasingly uncomfortable with the organization's secretive structure and leftist orientation. In order to mitigate growing dissension, the original five members called for a convention in April of 1953 to convert the Mattachine Society into an above-ground organization. The conference exacerbated the division between moderate and militant perspectives. Hay and the other founders were confronted by demands that emphasized assimilation and suggested that homosexual behavior was a minor characteristic that should not create a rift with the heterosexual majority (ibid.: 77). The growing fears about the current leaders' communist backgrounds led to a dramatic shift in leadership. The assimilationist tendency gained control of the organization and steered it towards what D'Emilio (1983) calls a 'retreat to respectability'.

Abandoning its communist-based ideology, the post-convention Mattachine Society no longer sought to promote a homosexual culture or mass movement. Instead, it perceived homosexuality as primarily an individual problem, and it turned to psychology to provide theories on homosexuality. The new leadership proposed and members endorsed the elimination of any mention of 'homosexual culture' from the statement of purpose. *One*, the organization's magazine established in 1953 and devoted to topics relating to homosexuality, remained vibrant, attracting the more radical elements of the Mattachine (D'Emilio, 1983: 85, 87–9).

By the end of 1955, Mattachine Society chapters were set up in San Francisco, New York, and Chicago. On September 21, 1955, another homophile organization, the Daughters of Bilitis (DOB), was established by four lesbian couples in San Francisco, though Del Martin and Phyllis Lyon are credited with maintaining it in early years (D'Emilio, 1983: 89, 102). This organization, similar to the assimilationist Mattachine, emphasized education and self-help activities. The DOB's 'Statement of Purpose' cites as its main goals 'education of the variant, with particular emphasis on the psychological, physiological and sociological aspects, to enable her [the lesbian] to understand herself and make her adjustment to society in all its social, civic, and economic implications' (Blasius and Phelan, 1997: 328). Despite its commitment to legal reform, stated as its final aim in its statement of purpose, the DOB functioned ultimately as a safe meeting space for lesbians and bisexual women who did not feel comfortable in the lesbian bar scene (D'Emilio, 1983: 104). In contrast to the early Mattachine, the DOB had no interest in collectively organizing lesbians for political action; it had no agenda to promote group identity. Its main function, like that of the latter Mattachine, was to integrate the homosexual into heterosexual society by de-emphasizing sexual difference and seeking acceptance from the majority culture.

Relative to gay men, lesbians had to navigate a dual identity that suffered a dual oppression. Lesbians were oppressed because they were lesbians, but also more generally because they were women; consequently, an internal debate erupted in many women about whether to remain active in the homophile movement through DOB or whether to defect to the women's movement through networks such as the National Organization of Women. Personifying this struggle, activist Shirley Willer, in a 1966 address to the National Planning Committee of Homophile Organizations, contended that problems such as police harassment and sodomy law, which seemed to make up the majority of the homophile agenda, did not affect women (Marotta, 1981: 52–3). Willer further claimed that 'there has been little evidence however, that the male homosexual has any intention of making common cause with us [lesbians]. We suspect that should the male homosexual achieve his particular

objective in regard to his homosexuality he might possibly become more of an adamant foe of women's rights that the heterosexual male has been'(Blasius and Phelan, 1997: 344). Such harsh comments were mitigated by Willer's simultaneous desire to maintain the DOB's participation in the homophile movement so as to at least expand the perspective of the male-dominated movement.

The ascension of the moderate perspective did not drown out more radical voices seeking direct action. One such radical was Frank Kameny who started a Washington, DC, branch of the Mattachine Society (MSW) in 1961. In a speech given to the Mattachine Society of New York (MSNY) in 1964, Kameny was angered by the homophile preoccupation with discovering a cause of homosexuality and the deferment to the psychology establishment's labeling of homosexuality as a mental sickness. Homosexuality, in Kameny's view, was not an illness; it was a characteristic of a particular group of people. In his speech he utilized the cultural frame established by the African-American civil rights movement. He contended

> I do not see the NAACP or CORE worrying about which chromosome and gene produces black skin or about the possibility of bleaching the Negro. I do not see any great interest on the part of the B'nai B'rith Anti-Defamation League in the possibility of solving the problems of anti-semitism by converting Jews to Christians ... we are interested in obtaining rights for our respective minorities as Negroes, as Jews, and as homosexuals. Why we are Negroes, Jews, or homosexuals is totally irrelevant, and whether we can be changed to whites, Christians, or heterosexuals is equally irrelevant. (Marrota, 1981: 24)

Beyond a mere scolding of current homophile leaders for guiding the movement down a path that failed to lead to homosexual equality, the above passage reveals a resurgence of the ethnic minority model utilized by Hay and the founders of Mattachine. Yet, by the middle and late 1960s, activists no longer had to rely on Marxist ideology to learn about the development of collective consciousness and social insurgence. Kameny drew on the burgeoning civil rights movements and feminist movements in the United States. Both of these movements, especially the later stages in which black power and radical feminism took hold, exemplified the development of New Left politics. The New Left engendered renewed militancy in the homophile movement and led to a situation ripe for the emergence of a gay rights movement by the end of the 1960s and the beginning of the 1970s.

While various organizations of the homophile movement were mired in an unending moderate versus militant debate, mainstream attitudes toward homosexuality continued to inch toward a more liberal perspective. The Mattachine Society successfully defended its right to publish *The Mattachine Review* to the US Supreme Court in 1958. Throughout the 1960s, gay and lesbian-oriented novels such as Jean Genet's *Our Lady of Flowers*, Herbert Selby's *Last Exit to Brooklyn*, and John Rechy's *City of Night* were published. Bestsellers of the decade including Allen Drury's *Advise and Consent* and James Baldwin's *Another Country* contained gay characters and gay-themed subplots. In October of 1961, the Production Code Administration of Hollywood allowed homosexuality to be portrayed in film. In 1962 and 1963, films such as *The Children's Hour, Walk on the Wild Side*, and *The Best Man* all had gay characters; however, they usually portrayed the gay and lesbian characters as experiencing some kind of tragic end, thereby reinforcing common tropes of loneliness and self-destructive behavior stereotypically linked to homosexuality. In December of 1963, *The New York Times* published a front-page feature detailing the emergence of a gay subculture, and related articles appeared in *Newsweek, Time, Harpers*, and *Life* (D'Emilio, 1983: 134–9). In 1961, Illinois became the first state to adopt the Model Legal Code of the American Law Institute that decriminalized private consensual homosexual sex (Adam, 1995: 75).

Relative to the previous decade, the 1960s embodied a great deal of reform and liberalization of attitudes toward homosexuality. In the legal field, this change was not necessarily represented through an actual alteration or repeal of existing laws, but rather a broadening of support among the heterosexual community for an expansion of civil rights and the attainment of some measures of gay and lesbian equality. For example, only Illinois and Connecticut repealed their anti-sodomy legislation; however, Americans for Democratic Action, the New York Liberal Party, and Wisconsin's Young Democrats accepted the principle of a basic right to private consensual sex. The supreme courts of California, New Jersey, New York, and Pennsylvania all recognized the basic right of gay men and women to congregate thereby providing legal protection to gay bars and recognition of the growing gay subculture. More gay-related legal cases were reaching federal appellate courts. Between 1960 and 1964 only 12 cases were heard, but this number increased 250 per cent between 1965 and 1969. Finally, in 1967, the ACLU accepted the premise that individuals have a fundamental right to privacy, reversed its policy towards homosexuals, and guaranteed them legal support (D'Emilio, 1983: 211–13).

In the medical field, the model of homosexuality as indicative of mental illness came under increasing attack. In 1967, Evelyn Hooker was appointed by the National Institute of Mental Health to study homosexuality; the investigative committee's report, released in 1969, gave credence to the liberal notion that human sexuality covered a wide spectrum of behavior and that homosexuals exhibited no inherent signs of mental illness (D'Emilio, 1983: 215–17). *In short, the political and cultural environment had undergone a liberalizing shift that created the opportunity for the emergence of a mass homosexual movement.* Despite this increasingly liberal environment and consequent ripening of opportunity, and despite a multitude of gay and lesbian organizations throughout the country, a mass gay rights movement failed to materialize at this time for three reasons. First, few examples of the positive effects of gay mobilization existed. Coming out was considered too risky if social change had not yet been proven to be feasible, and the DOB and Mattachine had yet to demonstrate their ability to make any significant political changes. Second, while the political environment was entertaining more debate on homosexuality both in popular culture and medical circles, the vast majority of this debate was led by heterosexuals (D'Emilio, 1983: 124–5, 147). Third, the homophile movement, after the 1953 convention and before the resurgence of militancy, engaged in the paradoxical process of disassembling itself. By advocating that homosexuals should assimilate, and that the only difference between homosexuality and heterosexuality was fundamentally unimportant, it destroyed any possibility of mass mobilization because it devastated the potential for collective identity formation (Marotta, 1981: 68). Not until many more gay men and women were willing to participate, overcome their self-perception as mentally ill or isolated, and recognize homosexuals as an oppressed minority with potential for collective action, would a full movement become possible.

1970s: COMING OUT AND COGNITIVE LIBERATION

What we now perceive as the lesbian, gay, bisexual, and transgender (LGBT) movement at the beginning of the twenty-first century planted its roots in the 1970s; however, the movement that took shape in that decade bears little resemblance to its modern form of various and highly organized state and national-level organizations. To conceive of a gay and lesbian rights movement in the 1970s is to confront a decentralized history of numerous short-lived organizations, clashing personalities, grassroots, local, and state-level activism, the rise of a religiously-based conservative backlash, and the curious denouement of a movement before it seemingly reached

political climax. The struggle for gay and lesbian rights in the 1970s unfolded in New York City, San Francisco, Los Angeles, Washington, DC, Miami, Boston, Minneapolis-St. Paul, Eugene, Oregon, and Wichita, Kansas. The cast of activists is wide and varied: Craig Rodwell, Jim Owles, Jim Fouratt, Marty Robinson, Frank Kameny, Elaine Noble, Harvey Milk, Virginia Apuzzo, Barbara Gittings, Rita Mae Brown, Bruce Voeller, Steve Endean, Kerry Woodward, Jean O'Leary, Midge Costanza, Reverend Troy Perry, Barney Frank, Allan Spear, David Goodstein, Sheldon Andelson, David Mixner, and countless others. For the first time, the gay and lesbian rights movement attracted nationally-known or soon-to-be-known politicians: Senator Edward Kennedy, President Jimmy Carter, President Ronald Reagan, Governor Jerry Brown, Senator Diane Feinstein, and Washington, DC, Mayor, Marion Barry among others.

The movement engendered a powerful countermovement. Spearheaded by Anita Bryant's 'Save Our Children' Campaign to repeal Dade County, Florida's gay rights ordinance, the message of traditional family values, carried forth by Jerry Falwell and Pat Robertson, led to a rash of anti-gay initiatives and/or the repeal of recently-won expanded civil rights protections inclusive of sexual orientation throughout the late 1970s. Yet, as the movement took shape in the 1970s, it suffered also from repeated internal fractures as lesbians fought to distinguish and ultimately separate from a gay male culture seemingly preoccupied with sodomy reform and other laws related to sexual activity. It struggled through each internal rupture managing to establish numerous lobby organizations and political action committees including the Gay Liberation Front, the Gay Activist Alliance, the National Gay Task Force, the Municipal Elections Committee of Los Angeles, and the Gay Rights National Lobby. The decade ended with the unprecedented March on Washington for Lesbian and Gay Rights on 14 October 1979 that attracted anywhere from the Parks Service estimate of 25,000 to marchers' estimate of 250,000 participants (Clendinen and Nagourney, 1999: 408).

By the end of the decade the political side of the gay and lesbian rights movement almost seemed to fizzle faster than any of its predecessors. Spun out of similar concerns that grounded the civil rights and feminist movements, the gay and lesbian rights movement emerged as much of the leftist energy began to wane and as the national culture turned conservative. Having established a vibrant culture and exuberant lifestyle in safe enclaves of San Francisco's Castro or New York City's Greenwich Village, the movement appeared to de-politicize just as it acquired the numbers, public visibility, and cultural confidence to become political. Characterizing the culture of the gay male community as it entered the 1980s, Dudley Clendinen and Adam Nagourney note: 'These men had no inkling of gay liberation ... and, by all appearances, very little notion of oppression, at least now that they had escaped their home-towns for the gay life of San Francisco. Gay liberation had somehow evolved into the right to have a good time – the right to enjoy bars, discos, drugs and frequent impersonal sex' (1999: 445). Afraid to come out of the closet at the end of the 1960s, only ten years later gay men enjoyed an unprecedented hedonism that pushed political activism into an increasingly secondary position relative to embracing the new liberating gay lifestyle.

Gay liberation, in part, evolved from one transcendental moment which symbolized the shift from victim to empowered agent and came in the late evening of Friday, June 27, 1969 at a seedy gay bar, the Stonewall Inn, in Greenwich Village. Patrons of this particular bar ranged in age from late teens to early thirties and included what historian Toby Marotta (1981: 74) has called 'particularly unconventional homosexuals', e.g., street hustlers and drag queens. When officers raided the bar, numerous customers did not flee the scene. As the police arrested some drag queens, the crowd became restless, and, as escapes were attempted, rioting broke out. The July 3, 1969 edition of *The Village Voice* reported that:

Limp wrists were forgotten. Beer cans and bottles were heaved at the windows and a rain of coins descended on the cops. ... Almost by signal the crowd erupted into cobblestone and bottle heaving ... From nowhere came an uprooted parking meter – used as a battering ram on the Stonewall door. I heard several cries of 'let's get some gas,' but the blaze of flame which soon appeared in the window of the Stonewall was still a shock. (D'Emilio, 1983: 232)

Perhaps their unconventionality freed these rioters from more reserved tactics; they could rebel because their personal circumstances enabled them to proclaim their homosexuality without the threat of gravely negative circumstances. Before the end of the evening, approximately two thousand individuals battled nearly four hundred police officers (D'Emilio, 1983: 232).

On Saturday morning a message was haphazardly scrawled on one of the bar's boarded-up windows: 'THEY INVADED OUR RIGHTS ... LEGALIZE GAY BARS, SUPPORT GAY POWER' (Duberman, 1993: 202). Rioting continued Saturday evening; by most accounts, it was less violent than the previous evening. On Sunday morning a new sign was posted on the outside of the bar: WE HOMOSEXUALS PLEAD WITH OUR PEOPLE TO PLEASE HELP MAINTAIN PEACEFUL AND QUIET CONDUCT ON THE STREETS OF THE VILLAGE – MATTACHINE' (ibid.: 207). These two messages encapsulate the growing rift of ideology in the existing homophile movement. The former advocated a militant, adversarial, and radical position while the latter maintained more staid and conformist tactics. The use of words such as 'gay' as opposed to 'homosexual' indicate a radical shift in self-perception. Phrases such as 'gay power' belie how dependent the gay liberation movement was on the precedent-setting cultural frames used by both the black power and radical feminist movements.

The movements that embodied the New Left – the student movement, the anti-war movement, the black power movement, and the feminist movement – began to utilize a new vocabulary to describe their present circumstances. Instead of viewing themselves in terms of discrimination, minority groups spoke of structural oppression inherent in the capitalist system. *Instead of aiming for equality and integration, the goal shifted to liberation and self-determination* (D'Emilio, 1983: 224–5). These movements represented a new blend of politics and culture that moved beyond standard Marxist concentration on economic class to incorporate other areas of oppression that were perhaps now more relevant. Black power perceived oppression as fundamentally racial; feminism introduced the notion of gender as systematically enforced; and gay liberationists contended that underlying sexism was heterosexism (ibid.: 224–8; D'Emilio and Freedman, 1988: 321–1; Echols, 1989: 6–11, 15–18). Gay men and lesbians often participated in both the civil rights and feminist movement, although often without disclosing their sexual orientation. Carl Whitman, who wrote 'A Gay Manifesto' in 1970, was a national president for Students for a Democratic Society (SDS). Robin Morgan, Charlotte Bunch, and Leslie Kagan were lesbians who were all heavily affiliated with the women's movement (Vaid, 1995, 56). Yet, despite the New Left's commitment to equality, the movements that composed it were rampant with sexism and homophobia. Stokely Charmichael, one of the leaders of the Student Non-violent Coordinating Committee, remarked that 'the only position for a woman in the SNCC is prone' (Adam, 1995: 79) and that 'homosexuality is a sickness, just as are baby-rape or wanting to be head of General Motors' (Marotta, 1981: 135).

The gay liberation theory which emerged in the post-Stonewall era was essentially New Leftist in that it was not concerned with the goals of gays and lesbians alone, but with overturning the white male hegemony that characterized modern capitalism. The theory entailed a shift away from the class-based Marxist principles to a struggle over cultural representation. By asserting that all individuals were innately sexually androgynous, gay liberation theory attempted to obliterate the boundaries of the patriarchal gender dynamic that insist on masculine/feminine and homo/hetero division (Seidman, 1993: 109–13). Gay liberationists contended that since they questioned heterosexuality itself, they were necessarily combating notions of sexism. In this sense, they saw themselves as not only integrally tied to the New Left but as the vanguard of New Left political action (Seidman, 1993: 115).

Liberation theory was organizationally embodied in the Gay Liberation Front (GLF). Gay men and women, but especially the former, disgusted with the moderate tactics and assimilationist aims of the New York Mattachine Society, established this new organization in July of 1969 as a militant arm of the New Left. The GLF proclaimed itself to be 'a revolutionary homosexual group of men and women formed with the realization that complete sexual liberation for all people cannot come about unless existing social institutions are abolished' (D'Emilio and Freedman, 1988: 322). The GLF was not preoccupied with discriminatory employment practices, ending police harassment, or repealing of anti-sodomy laws. The GLF made no explicit statement on the attempt to achieve civil rights legislation or work through the existing political system at all. Rather, as its name suggests, the organization sought liberation from constraint inherent in capitalism itself. It intended to work in concert with all oppressed minorities: women, blacks, workers, and the third world for revolutionary social change (Marotta, 1981: 88–91).

In order to end structural oppression, the GLF, following the lead of radical feminists, sponsored consciousness-raising sessions. Consciousness-raising served to bring gay men and women together, to share their experiences, and to discover commonality. Similarity of experience fostered a collective identity. It also encouraged the notion that such similarity could not exist if oppression were not inherent in the system itself (Adam, 1995: 83; Jay and Young, 1992: 193–7).

The liberationist ideology that infused consciousness-raising sessions inspired cognitive liberation; it provided gay men and women with a basis to reject legal, medical, and religious definitions of homosexuality and, for the first time, to define themselves. Such definition is apparent in the name 'Gay Liberation Front'. The term homosexual was imposed upon gay men and women by the medical establishment as a term of illness. The term 'homophile' symbolized the assimilationist tactics of the Mattachine and DOB (Marotta, 1981: 91). Radicals chose the word 'gay' because it was how homosexuals referred to each other; the word symbolized self-definition and, as such, was a recognition of internal power.

Gay liberation also fundamentally restructured the definition of 'coming out' in order to build and strengthen a mass movement. Whereas the phrase had previously referred to an individual acknowledgment of homosexuality to oneself, gay liberationists transformed it into an extremely public and political act. Coming out symbolized a total rejection of the negative definitions that society inflicted on the homosexual and substituted both acceptance and pride in one's gayness. Coming out was the ultimate means to conflate the personal and political. Coming out was no longer perceived as a simple one-time act, but as the adoption of an affirmative identity (D'Emilio and Freedman, 1988: 322–3). Furthermore, by acknowledging one's homosexuality, a person exposed himself or herself to social injustice ranging from verbal discrimination to physical violence. Hence, individuals who did come out had a personal tie to the success of a gay liberation movement (D'Emilio, 1983: 236). Through the process of coming out, the victim status was discarded; homosexuality was transformed from a stigma to be hidden to a source of pride to celebrated. Indeed, by coming out, the homosexual became gay. Coming out was the necessary psychological break necessary to do what the homophile movement could never accomplish – attract a large following.

The ideology of liberation was that critical element that had been missing from the earlier attempts to mobilize gay men, lesbians, and bisexuals. Even if individuals did not actively participate in the political movement, notions of prideful identity trickled into the subculture. Yet, despite their importance in promoting mobilization and insurgency, the GLF, like Mattachine before it, was soon wracked with internal division. The disagreement centered on the extent to which the GLF should foster the aims of other New Left organizations as opposed to focusing on gay oppression as a single issue. Numerous activists – including Arthur Evans, Jim Owles, and Marty Robinson – contended that the GLF was spreading its energy too thin, that its meetings devolved into tedious theoretical discussions that never manifested action, and that its avoidance of hierarchical structure fostered a fundamentally disorganized group (Adam, 1995: 86–7; Marotta, 1981: 140–7). Recognizing the benefits of the liberationist philosophy, i.e., the emphasis on consciousness-raising and coming out, and also understanding that MSNY was too mild and regressive, these activists established an organization in December of 1969 that lay between these two extremes: the Gay Activist Alliance (GAA). The GAA stressed working *within* the system to promote improvement in the every-day concerns of gay men and women by sponsoring candidates, holding rallies, converting its firehouse headquarters into a fund-raising massive gay disco on the weekends, and utilizing chaotic mixes of street theater and politics called zaps to attain media attention. Indeed, its first act, the promotion of a gay rights bill prohibiting employment discrimination against gays and lesbians, could not have more starkly marked the different guiding principles of the GLF and GAA (Clendinen and Nagourney, 1999: 50–6).

As the 1970s progressed and the ideological rift between a single-issue and multi-issue perspective widened, the movement experienced further gender-based schisms. The dual oppression of lesbians strained their allegiance to the women's movement and the gay liberation movement. In the late 1960s, Betty Friedan denounced lesbianism as a 'lavender menace' that threatened the integrity and credibility of feminism. Yet, in 1971, following the Second Congress to Unite Women in New York, NOW reversed its stance declaring that the oppression of lesbians was a legitimate feminist issue. With the women's movement's relative acceptance of lesbians, women began to abandon the gay movement in increasing numbers between 1971 and 1973 (Adam, 1995: 99–103). The GLF and GAA, which were overwhelmingly male from their beginnings, tended to ignore the structural oppression which lesbians faced as women. As activist Marie Robertson claimed, 'Gay liberation, when we get right down to it, is the struggle for gay men to achieve approval for the only thing that separates them from the "Man" – their sexual preference' (Adam, 1995: 99). Gay organizations responded to the female exodus too late and often viewed these lesbians with confusion and/or resentment as they established an autonomous feminist-lesbian subculture throughout the decade.

The 1970s ushered in an entirely new stage of gay and lesbian rights. Whereas the GLF had collapsed by 1973, the cognitive liberation produced by a redefinition of 'coming out' and homosexuality itself profoundly affected gays throughout the nation. While the revolution for which liberationist theorists hoped never occurred, the movement witnessed incredible growth. In 1969, before the Stonewall riot, fifty homophile organizations existed in the United States; by 1973, there were over eight hundred gay and lesbian groups, and by the end of the decade they numbered into the thousands. One such organization, the National Gay Task Force established in 1973 and renamed the National Gay and Lesbian Task Force in 1986, would become one of the leading LGBT rights organizations in the United States. Gay bars continued to proliferate, but now gay-friendly and gay-owned health clinics, book stores, cafés, law offices, travel agencies, and churches and synagogues

(most notably Troy Perry's Metropolitan Community Church) also sprang up. In 1974, the American Psychiatric Association de-listed homosexuality from its register of mental illnesses. In 1975, the ban on gays in the Civil Service was lifted (D'Emilio and Freedman, 1988: 324). The gay press expanded, producing magazines and newspapers such as *The Advocate, Washington Blade, Gay Community News, Philadelphia Gay News*, and the *Windy City Times* (Vaid, 1995: 66). Before the end of the decade, Detroit, Boston, Los Angeles, San Franciso, Houston, and Washington, DC, incorporated sexual preference into their civil rights codes. Openly gay and lesbian officials were elected to office including Elaine Noble to the Massachusetts State Assembly, Karen Clark and Allen Spear to the Minnesota State Assembly, and Harvey Milk to the San Francisco Board of Supervisors. In 1980, the Democratic Party adopted a gay and lesbian rights plank at the national convention and an African-American gay man, Mel Boozer, was nominated to be the Democratic Vice Presidential candidate (D'Emilio and Freedman, 1988, 324; Shilts, 1988: 32). Before the end of the decade, a national gay and lesbian civil rights bill had been introduced in both the House and Senate (Clendinen and Nagourney, 1999: 405, 426). As historian Dennis Altman notes, the 1970s produced a gay male that was 'non-apologetic about his sexuality, self-assertive, highly consumerist and not at all revolutionary, though prepared to demonstrate for gay rights' (1971: 52). Perhaps the most stunning example of the effect that cognitive liberation had on the growth of the moment is that the July 4, 1969 march at Independence Hall in Philadelphia attracted seventy-five participants, whereas the first National March for Lesbian and Gay Rights on 14 October 1979 – a mere decade later – attracted between 100,000 and 200,000 participants (Duberman, 1993: 209; Vaid, 1995: 67).

Despite these strides, by the end of the decade a new political conservatism swept across the nation and the gay and lesbian movement encountered an active New Right counter-movement. Anita Bryant spearheaded 'Save Our Children' and rallied for the repeal of a gay rights ordinance in Dade County, Florida, in 1977. Following Bryant's precedent, recently passed gay rights ordinances were repealed in Wichita, Kansas, Eugene, Oregon, and St. Paul, Minnesota (Clendinen and Nagourney, 1999: 290–330). These defeats fostered a massive initiative to prevent passage of the Proposition 6 (the Briggs Initiative) in California. This bill, which advocated the removal of homosexual teachers from public schools, was defeated 58 to 42 per cent after then-Governor Ronald Reagan came out against it (Clendinen and Nagourney, 1999: 377–390). San Francisco Supervisor Harvey Milk was assassinated on 11 November, 1978 by Dan White, an ex-Supervisor; White was convicted of manslaughter and received a sentence of eight years and seven months. Shock at the lenient sentencing on 21 May 1979 led to riots at San Francisco's City Hall. By the end of the 1970s, opportunity for movement expansion dissipated. Gay liberation as a tenable ideology had died, the movement was weakened by diverse aims among gay men and lesbians, and political conservatism bolstered by a growing radical Christian right began to tear away at the inroads that movement organizations had made earlier in the decade. In short, the 1970s ushered into existence and concretized a highly visible gay male and lesbian culture. By the end of the decade, gay politics appeared to be subsumed by an ever-expanding gay cultural lifestyle; however, the increased visibility and attention given to that subculture by both mainstream media and a backlashing counter-movement testify to the political impact of that cultural visibility. By the early 1980s, gay and lesbian rights were being actively debated at all levels of government despite or because gay cultural institutions were coming out of the closet. Yet, the nature and content of these debates on civil rights and privacy would dramatically shift after the discovery

of a microscopic retrovirus that would come to be known as the Human Immunodeficiency Virus.

1980s: THE DOUBLE-EDGED IMPACT OF AIDS

In 1981, *The New York Times* reported that five gay men had acquired a curious cancer; in the nineteen years since its discovery, over 300,000 Americans have died from that disease now identified as Acquired Immune Deficiency Syndrome (AIDS), approximately 210,000 of whom were gay men (Vaid, 1995: 72, 81). If only measured in terms of its massively destructive impact, AIDS has fundamentally altered the gay and lesbian movement. Yet, to measure the disease's influence only by positioning the death rate within a specific community dramatically and dangerously oversimplifies how AIDS has affected the movement. In numerous ways, the AIDS crisis produced a variety of positive externalities; however, not only did AIDS provide further anti-gay fodder for the New Right, it also spawned a related but distinct movement increasingly in competition with the equal rights agenda of the gay and lesbian movement. The AIDS movement had distinct aims from the gay and lesbian movement, but, perhaps more importantly, it achieved those aims through strategies never conceived as possible by gay rights activists in the 1970s. AIDS, therefore, dramatically shifted the tactics of sexual minority movement organizations throughout the 1980s and 1990s.

The most immediate impact of AIDS was the incredible rapidity with which it spread throughout the 1980s. By the end of 1981, 225 cases were reported nationwide. In the spring of 1983, this increased to 1,400; only two years later, AIDS cases rose by over 900 per cent to 15,000. In 1987, this figure increased to 40,000 cases reported (D'Emilio and Freedman, 1988: 354). The disease's seemingly unstoppable nature coupled with the government and mainstream media's silence and lack of concern regarding both the virus itself and its most prominent class of victims in the United States, i.e., gay men, forced the gay community to mobilize itself. Hundreds of community-based organizations including Shanti, Coming Home Hospice, Project Open Hand of San Francisco, and, most notably, Gay Men's Health Crisis (GMHC), developed to provide services to individuals coping with the virus (Cruikshank, 1992: 182). The sexual minorities community also shaped the early response by supporting more open and frank discussions of sexuality in the media and by spearheading campaigns for 'safer sex' (Adam, 1995: 157–8).

The onset of the AIDS crisis also fostered a dramatic increase in the amount of people who were willing to come out. The lack of an adequate response from the Reagan and Bush administrations forced gay men and women to believe that they were being abandoned by their government. Gay men who would not publicly express their homosexuality in the pre-AIDS era were becoming involved. GMHC itself was started by men who were relatively uninvolved in gay and lesbian politics during the 1970s including Larry Kramer, Nathan Fair, Paul Popham, Paul Rapoport, Larry Mass, and Edmund White. Many of these individuals brought money, contacts, and business experience that pre-AIDS organizations never mustered (D'Emilio and Freedman, 1988: 356; Vaid, 1995: 91; Clendinen and Nagourney, 1999: 460).

As AIDS also forced a variety of celebrities out of the closet, the most notable of whom was Rock Hudson in 1986, it received expanding media coverage. By extension, the visibility of the gay and lesbian community dramatically increased. Books such as *And the Band Played On* by Randy Shilts, published in 1987, and films including *Philadelphia*, released in 1993, demonstrated the greater willingness of heterosexuals to come to terms with both the AIDS epidemic and a politically active gay and lesbian minority (Bersani, 1995: 17–9). Linking gay visibility with AIDS explicitly,

Urvashi Vaid (1995: 81) notes that 'perversely put, we won visibility for gay and lesbian lives because we died in record numbers'. Gay visibility also increased as a result of many pre-AIDS organizations becoming nationally-oriented in order to lobby the government more effectively for support. While gay liberation was predominantly a grassroots and local political movement, the AIDS movement functioned at a national level. The National Gay and Lesbian Task Force (NGLTF) moved its headquarters from New York City to Washington DC, and the ACLU hired a lobbyist specifically to cover AIDS issues for its Washington office (Vaid, 1995: 74). Hence, AIDS enabled gay and lesbian politics to be heard in national public policy debates and electoral politics. Whereas most gay movement interest groups had acted with local and state political institutions, they now began to promote agenda implementation through Congress and the office of the President.

AIDS also re-established and strengthened gay male ties with both the lesbian and straight communities. Lesbians often wavered in their commitment to the gay movement throughout the 1970s, opting to join the feminist movement instead and fostering an independent subculture focusing on women's needs and marked by women-only festivals, bookstores, and cafés. AIDS, or rather the Right's exploitation of and the government's ignorance of AIDS, showed many lesbians and bisexual women that homophobia was still deeply ingrained in American culture (Vaid, 1995: 89). Furthermore, the families of people with AIDS (PWAs) became involved in movement politics, taking part in marches such as the 1987 March on Washington for National Gay and Lesbian Rights. AIDS and straight allies featured prominently in this demonstration, which attracted approximately 650,000 participants. The Names Project AIDS Quilt was displayed on the Washington, DC, Mall on 11 October 1987, and the parents of PWAs were invited to lead a candlelight march that evening (Rofes, 1990, in

Blasius and Phelan, 1997: 654). Whereas the
gay liberation movement of the 1970s
attracted predominantly young countercul-
tural white participants, the AIDS movement
of the 1980s attracted Caucasians, African-
Americans, Asian-Americans, Latinos,
women, men, gays, straights, and bisexuals.

Finally, the intransigence of the Reagan
and Bush administrations as well as the relative lack of visibility in the more mainstream press revitalized direct action protest
tactics reminiscent of the liberationist zaps
of the 1970s. The AIDS Coalition to
Unleash Power (ACT UP) was created in
March 1987 to promote media attention for
the AIDS crisis in hopes of raising universal
awareness and acquiring political leverage.
ACT UP espoused a democratic and participatory culture reminiscent of the GLF; it
often belittled more reform-orientated and
'political insider' organizations such as the
Human Rights Campaign or GMHC for
working too slowly and utilizing behind-
the-scene tactics that were so-called unde-
mocratic and failed to represent anyone
except the middle-class gay white male
(Vaid, 1995: 94–102). ACT UP was bolstered
by the above-mentioned silence of the
Republican-dominated executive branch, its
visibility at the 1987 March on Washington,
increased media coverage, and the inability
of more conservative AIDS groups to compete for participants. On 11 October 1987,
the day following the March, 5,000 individuals staged a National Civil Disobedience
protest on the steps of the Supreme Court.
The demonstration ignited enthusiasm for
such activism. ACT UP's popularity derived
from its ability to acquire media exposure
even if only in the short term. ACT UP's
rallies, speak-outs, placard-painting, and
leaflet-distribution represented a wide range
of participatory opportunities and were all
oriented to attract media coverage.

However, just as AIDS enabled many of
these positive externalities – media visibility, further political organization at the local
and national levels, expanded support from
both the gay and straight communities, a
resurgence of direct action – many of these

same benefits carried with them negative
impacts on the movement. To mention
nothing of the death toll or the vehement
attack orchestrated by the New Right, AIDS
engendered negative visibility for the gay,
lesbian, and bisexual community, fundamentally derailed the movement's original
agenda from equal rights to medical and
social service provision, and produced an
offshoot movement utilizing different
methods and having distinct goals.

The New Right exploited AIDS as a
weapon with which to maintain inequality,
to overturn the achievements of the 1970s,
and to return the nation to an era of more
traditional heteronormative values. After
fighting and winning the de-listing of homosexuality as a mental illness, gays and lesbians now confronted conservatives' use of
AIDS to re-link homosexuality with sickness. Two-time Republican candidate for
President, Pat Buchanan, furthered the myth
that AIDS was a gay disease: 'The poor
homosexuals – they have declared war upon
nature, and now nature is exacting an awful
retribution' (*The Gay Almanac*, 1996: 77).
Conservatives discussed quarantining early-
identified high risk groups, i.e., gay men, IV
drug users, and black and Hispanic men.
The United States military imposed manda-
tory testing. Congress required all immigrants to be tested and forbade entry to
anyone who was HIV-positive. Bathhouses
and bars, staples of the gay subculture, shut
down in record numbers (D'Emilio and
Freedman, 1988: 354; Adam, 1995: 155).
The ultimate legislative achievement of the
New Right was the passage of the Helms
Amendment in 1987 which prohibited the
use of federal funds to 'provide Aids education, information, or prevention materials
and activities that promote or encourage,
directly or indirectly, homosexual sexual
activities'(133 Congressional Record, 14
October 1987, S14216 in Stychin, 1995: 50).

Far more damaging than any attack from
conservatives was the derailing effect
AIDS had on the celebratory concepts of
coming out and gayness introduced by gay
liberation philosophy. The visibility that

AIDS conferred on gay men and women was characterized by prominent queer theorist Leo Bersani (1995: 21) as 'the visibility of imminent death, of promised invisibility. Straight America can rest its gaze on us, let us do our thing over and over in the media, because what our attentive fellow citizens see is the pathos and impotence of a doomed species'. In this analysis, homophobic reactions in the media are declining because AIDS has essentially usurped the role of the homophobe.

In an effort to attain media coverage and government support in combating the virus, many gay and lesbian organizations attempted to 'de-gay' AIDS and de-sexualize homosexuality. Existing institutionalized homophobia meant that AIDS could not be successfully combated if it was continually thought of as a 'gay disease'. In promoting the truthful notion that heterosexuals were also susceptible, the gay and lesbian movement abandoned the overarching and long-term aims of equality and fighting institutionalized homophobia for the immediate need of survival. 'De-gaying' the disease also inhibited people from coming out since people could donate to AIDS organizations without the stigma of being associated with a gay organization (Vaid, 1995: 76–7). 'De-gaying' has also paradoxically led to a measure of invisibility of a minority which accounts for 70 per cent of all AIDS cases in the United States. For example, at the 1987 March on Washington, no mention was given to the gay or lesbian community in the program regarding the Names Project AIDS Quilt nor during the five speeches given during the candlelight vigil (Rofes, 1990 in Blasius and Phelan, 1997: 645–5).

While AIDS did attract wider participation from the gay and straight communities, especially among upper middle-class gay men, such participation further steered the movement away from its traditionally leftist orientation. The influx of this group, while bringing immense resources, also brought political conservatism: 'in place of liberation, the AIDS movement substituted nondiscrimination; instead of building a movement, it built agencies and bureaucracies; instead of placing its political faith in training and organizing gay and lesbian people, and our allies, into an electoral coalition, it placed faith in friends in high places' (Vaid, 1995: 91). This more conservative tendency also led to a de-sexualization of homosexuality itself, disregarding the connection between sexual freedom and gay liberation; since AIDS exposed gay sexuality, gay men and women often responded by de-emphasizing that liberated sexuality and promoting a new image espousing monogamy and safer sex.

While the virus may have caused higher rates of involvement in various AIDS-related organizations, such groups rarely maintained the civil rights oriented agendas of earlier social movement groups. Most AIDS organizations did not directly promote sodomy reform, but were instead primarily social service groups that focused on goals enabling survival rather than the long-term objective of overcoming homophobia (Vaid, 1995: 88). The immense public health crisis which AIDS had created pushed organizations such as the National Gay and Lesbian Task Force to focus on national-level politics and concentrate less on grass-roots activism aiming for legislation at the local and state level. In this sense, the gay and lesbian and the AIDS movements are distinct entities. The latter grew out of the former, but the latter also dramatically impacted and altered the strategies of the former: 'The spread of the AIDS epidemic also drew more and more gays and lesbians to the view that federal intervention on gay-related issues was essential' (Rayside, 1998: 285). Furthermore, the AIDS movement responded to a fundamentally different opportunity – the onset of a public health crisis – and, as such, it more readily attracted non-gay allies, increasingly distanced itself from the gay and lesbian movement, and became a competitor with that movement for legislative and popular support.

Most circumstances engendered by the AIDS crisis carried dual implications. Visibility was gained, but much of it was negative. It acquired national prominence, but

AIDS overshadowed gay and lesbian rights at the national level. The movement expanded, but became increasingly main-streamed into the Washington political power structure at the expense of grassroots participation. Direct action was rejuvenated, but at the expense of both movement soli-darity and heterosexual support. These dra-matic changes brought about by the AIDS crisis established the gay and lesbian move-ment as a major minority constituency in mainstream American politics; yet, as the various circumstances of the 1990s illustrate, this achievement, so vigorously fought for since the early 1950s, is now paradoxically threatening to weaken the movement itself.

THE GAY 90s AND BEYOND: (IN)VISIBILITY AND THE MOVEMENT TODAY

The American gay and lesbian movement, or rather gayness in general, has become increasingly visible in politics and popular culture throughout the 1990s. Enormous volumes of pro- and anti-gay legislation have been debated, passed, and rejected mostly at the state level, but also at the national level, and the movement has con-tinued to fight against an increasingly powerful Christian right. Yet, such visibility, while enormously powerful in promoting the civil rights-based agenda of the move-ment, has revealed the multiple factions that currently exist in the movement – most importantly, the exclusion of people of color – as well as threatened the viability of earlier liberationist aims to end institutionalized heterosexism. While gays and lesbians may have received new prominence in national electoral politics – revealed by the 1992 presidential election and the resurgence of controversy over 'Don't Ask, Don't Tell' and hate crimes legislation in the 2000 elec-tion – the movement also demonstrated its political weakness and lagging mainstream cultural acceptance at the national level by its inability to achieve a full lifting of the

ban on homosexuals in the military, its failure to secure passage of the Employment Non-Discrimination Act (ENDA) in 1996, and its inability to secure national hate crimes legislation.

Throughout the 1970s and the 1980s, the struggle for gay rights has been viewed as a primarily white male movement. The con-cerns of women and people of color were never foremost on the gay agenda. The essential 'whiteness' of the movement became startlingly visible as gay African-Americans, Asians, and Latinos established separate sexual minority rights and AIDS organizations to help members of those particular ethnic minorities cope with both civil rights violations and the illness. The establishment of the Latino/a Lesbian and Gay Organization (LLEGO), the Native American AIDS Task Force, the National Gay Asian and Pacific Islander Network, and the National Black Gay and Lesbian Leader-ship Forum revealed that mainstream gay and AIDS organizations failed to recognize internalized elements of racism and sexism (Vaid, 1995: 90; Rayside, 1998: 286).

Queer Nation attempted to overcome internal division within the movement and set forth a new seemingly post-identity-based agenda in which all elements of the gay, lesbian, bisexual, and transgender com-munity could come together under a single unifying banner. Queer Nation developed in the summer of 1990 and drew upon the direct action tactics of ACT UP. Unlike ACT UP, which sought to attain media visi-bility and subsequent political response for the AIDS crisis, Queer Nation aimed to bring to the forefront the fundamental issues that AIDS had subsumed and sidetracked, namely combating institutionalized homo-phobia and achieving full gay equality (Fraser, 1996: 32–5; Epstein, 1999: 60–4). In doing so, Queer Nation sought to move away from the racial and gender divisions that plagued the movement by asserting a new unitary identity of 'queer':

Being queer means leading a different sort of life. It's not about the mainstream, profit margins, patriotism, patriarchy or being assimilated. It's not about executive director, privilege and elitism. It's about being on the margins, defining ourselves; it's about gender-fuck and secrets, what's beneath the belt and deep inside the heart; it's about the night. Being queer is 'grass roots' because we know that everyone of us, every body, every cunt, every heart and ass and dick is a world of pleasure waiting to be explored. Everyone of us is a world of infinite possibility. (Anonymous in Blasius and Phelan, 1997: 774)

Queer Nation struggled to create a unified group of sexually marginalized individuals. By uniting under the label, 'queer', these activists took a once derogatory term and transformed it into a statement of pride, power, and militancy. Assuming the label of 'queer' was, in this sense, a second form of cognitive liberation that many activists experienced. The Stonewall generation, through coming out and proclaiming their gayness, overcame the self- and societally-inflicted victimization of being homosexual. By asserting their queerness, queer nationals countered the damage incurred by the AIDS crisis and the resurgence of the far Right.

Defining oneself as queer, as the Stonewall generation defined themselves as gay, was as much an expression of individuality as it was one of collective identity. In some sense, being queer was not so much a positive identification as it was identifying as what someone was *not*. Such negative and reflexive identification enabled a disparate group of individuals to come under one banner. By attempting to stand as a representative for all disempowered individuals, Queer Nation affirmed a unity built out of difference. By blaming heterosexual society for constructing this difference, it denied the existence of any essential distinctive identity ultimately suppressing the internal differences which it sought to represent (Seidman, 1993: 133). Hence, instead of working through the gender and racial rifts which have damaged the movement, queer nationalism subsumed and belittled them in order to preserve cohesion. Filmmaker Marlon T. Riggs (1991: 15) found the centrality of white middle-class concerns of Queer Nation profoundly alienating: 'the

New [Queer] Nationalists, on the rare occasion they acknowledged my existence at all, spoke of me with utter contempt, spat and twisted my name like the vilest obscenity'. Queer Nation did not, as its advocates contended, become the ultimate unifier, but rather an expression of the internal factions – age, gender, race, and class – that the movement has confronted since its emergence.

Similar to ACT UP, the prevalence of Queer Nation chapters and other queer groups such as Lesbian Avengers and Women's Action Coalition, as well as the occurrence of direct action tactics have declined steadily throughout the 1990s. Some activists became tired of the protests that were extremely energy-intensive. Some members of the gay and lesbian community could not relate to the 'in-your-face' brand of activism and were disinclined to contribute. Queer Nation was heavily identified as a youth movement to which many in the sexual minorities community could not subscribe. In its attempts to avoid labels and promote an ideology of fluid sexuality, Queer Nation struggled to find an organizational premise, and thus succumbed to a similar problem which afflicted the Gay Liberation Front. Many of the original supporters died of AIDS. Queer Nation may have been a short-lived organizational network, but its long-term legacy lies in cultural transformations ranging from the advent of queer theory to the positive connotation of 'queer' to the fashion craze of body piercing which queer identity popularized. Yet Queer Nation not only succumbed to internal disorganization and disunity, but failed because the in-your-face politics which it espoused no longer appeared as relevant or appropriate given the political climate taking shape by 1992. Both the political and popular cultural environment became increasingly open to gay visibility; in 1993, Andrew Kopkind wrote in *The Nation* that 'Gay invisibility, the social enforcement of the sexual closet, is hardly the problem anymore. Overexposure is becoming the problem.' By then, especially in the presidential election of 1992, it seemed that gay issues were becoming mainstreamed, and suddenly the gay and lesbian community was no longer shunned, but courted ... at least by the Democratic Party.

The 1992 election found the incumbent Republican President Bush battling an economic recession, a gay minority and its straight supporters increasingly disillusioned with the Republican response to AIDS, and an increasingly powerful Christian right which aimed to revive 'traditional' family values. AIDS and the Right's negative response towards the disease brought gay issues to the forefront of the election forcing each Democratic contender to take a stance on gay rights. The position they took contrasted starkly to their Republican opponents. Every major Democratic candidate promised to increase AIDS funding and to lift the ban on gays in the military. Gay rights had been a topic on which the Democratic Party had wavered since the 1972 election, and which party leadership had chosen to downplay in 1988 after Walter Mondale's poor showing against Ronald Reagan in 1984. However, the gay constituency had money and votes. Indeed, Bill Clinton's emergence as the candidate to receive the overall endorsement of the gay community had less to do with his stance on gay rights – a law criminalizing same-sex sodomy was passed while he was attorney general of Arkansas – and more to do with the fact that he actively sought the gay vote, in direct contrast to anti-gay Republican sentiment couched in traditional family values rhetoric (Rayside, 1998: 289–91). Nor did the help of an openly gay political consultant, David Mixner, harm Clinton's campaign. Mixner advised Clinton to tailor his speeches to stress the inclusion of gays and lesbians in his cabinet as well as a sincere desire to use federal resources to stem the AIDS crisis. An estimated 75 per cent of the gay vote helped Clinton secure the presidency (Gallagher and Bull, 1996: 69–79).

The unprecedented visibility of gays and lesbians at the 1992 Democratic Convention and the prevalence of the 'gay issue' in the election, especially in relation to the military ban, brought the movement into the realm of mainstream politics. Gay visibility increased in popular cultural arenas as well, however, such visibility has had both positive and negative consequences. This visibility promotes and reflects greater tolerance of homosexuality; homosexuality is considered a legitimate topic of exploration, as demonstrated by the proliferation of gay and lesbian studies at the university level as well as the increased portrayal of gays on the small and large screen. Popular musicians such as Melissa Ethridge, Ani DiFranco, and k.d. lang, and actors including Ellen DeGeneres, Anne Heche, Rupert Everett, and Nathan Lane are all open about their homosexuality or bisexuality. The musical *Rent*, which discusses AIDS and gay sexuality, won the 1996 Tony Award for best musical. Tony Kushner's gay-themed play *Angels in America* won a Pulitzer Prize. Films such as *Philadelphia* (1993) – nominated for various academy awards and for which Tom Hanks won an academy award for best actor – confronted the impact of AIDS on gay men. Popular films that have reached a mainstream audience and that have explored gay themes or had gay characters include *My Own Private Idaho* (1991), *Threesome* (1994), *Clueless* (1995), *The Birdcage* (1996), *Chasing Amy* (1997), *My Best Friend's Wedding* (1997), *In and Out* (1997), *As Good as it Gets* (1997), *High Art* (1997), *The Object of My Affection* (1998), *Wild Things* (1998), *Go* (1999), *Cruel Intentions* (1999), *Big Daddy* (1999), *Trick* (1999), *American Beauty* (1999) and *The Next Best Thing* (2000). Gay and lesbian characters abound on television. MTV's *The Real World* is always careful to select a gay, lesbian, or bisexual individual as one of its seven housemates on the popular docudrama. Other mainstream prime-time shows that have had recurring gay characters or have had episodes exploring gay themes include: *L.A. Law, Thirtysomething, The Golden Girls, Friends, Mad About You, Frasier, Roseanne, Melrose Place, Beverly Hills 90210, Party of Five, My So-Called Life, Veronica's Closet, South Park, E.R.,*

Chicago Hope, Spin City, NYPD Blue, Ally McBeal, That Seventies Show, Felicity, Buffy the Vampire Slayer, Queer as Folk, Six Feet Under, Sex and the City, and *The West Wing.* A huge amount of media attention was focused on openly lesbian comedian *Ellen* Degeneres; her character, Ellen Morgan, came out of the closet on the sitcom Ellen, aired on April 30, 1997. The show earned the highest ratings the American Broadcasting Company (ABC) had all season, and DeGeneres became the first and only gay leading role in a television show (Stockwell, 1998: 92). In 1998, the National Broadcasting Company (NBC) premiered its now-popular sitcom, *Will and Grace,* which features two gay men – Will Truman and Jack McFarland – as lead characters. In 1999, the Warner Brothers (WB) Network introduced Jack McFee, a gay high school student as a lead character to its immensely popular teen drama, *Dawson's Creek.* While such visibility suggests an immense degree of mainstream cultural acceptance, the inherent danger in this visibility is that it legitimates only particular elements of the movement. The gay image that mainstream culture has appropriated tends to be that of the middle-class white gay male.

Indeed, the graver danger is that movement organizations, viewing that certain representations of the gay subject are acceptable to the heterosexual majority, will privilege that identity at the expense of silencing non-conforming members of its own community. This has been the experience of some gays and lesbians of color who, throughout the 1980s and 1990s, led a backlash against 'mainstream' gay culture. Theorist Barbara Smith (1981: 121) claimed that the creation of a separatist lesbian feminist subculture 'seems much like a narrow kind of politics and ... it seems to be only viably practiced by women who have certain kinds of privilege: white-skinned privilege, class privilege'. Joseph Beam isolated racism in the gay and lesbian movement:

It is possible to read thoroughly two or three consecutive issues of the *Advocate* [a national gay and lesbian news magazine] ... and never encounter, in the words or images, Black gay men .... We ain't family. Very clearly, gay male means: white, middle-class, youthful, Nautilized, and probably butch, there is no room for Black gay men within the confines of this gay pentagon. (Seidman, 1993: 119)

This kind of selective visibility both promotes and reflects greater tolerance of homosexuality, thereby signaling the erosion of heteronormative values and institutions. Yet, it utilizes a narrow but presently widely-accepted and innocuous image of the homosexual to do so.

The movement has attained a high degree of visibility in the political arena in the 1990s through the 'don't ask, don't tell' compromise; ironically, the policy was, in part, intended to maintain gay invisibility within the military. No longer is the homosexual act grounds for discharge, but rather the mere verbal expression of the act. According to theorist Leo Bersani, coercing soldiers to keep their sexual orientation secret illustrates an awareness of the potential threat of queer politics to the maintenance of patriarchal institutions. The enforced silence further bolsters, or at least avoids the destabilization of, heteronormativity (Bersani, 1995: 17–18).

The gay and lesbian movement's inability to press for a successful lifting of the ban also exposes the movement's weakness at the national level. The military ban was not at the forefront of the gay and lesbian agenda when the movement started to organize heavily at a national level; AIDS was. Furthermore, the leftist ideological bias of the post-Stonewall generation included a heavy anti-militarist bent (Vaid, 1995: 157). Despite the creation of the Military Freedom Project (MFP) in 1988, which aimed to repeal the ban, the ban did not receive much media attention until Pete Williams, the Department of Defense's chief spokesperson was outed as gay in the *Advocate,* a national gay and lesbian news magazine. This event forced Dick Cheney, the Secretary of Defense, to assert that the military ban was outdated and that its repeal should be considered. Yet, despite increasing media attention on gays in the military and high-level support for change, the vast majority of activists were concerned that the military ban had replaced AIDS as the prominent gay-themed issue of the election (Vaid, 1995: 159–61).

Once Clinton was elected, national movement organizations such as the National Gay and Lesbian Task Force (NGLTF) and the Human Rights Campaign (HRC) encountered uncharted territory of interacting with the first gay-friendly administration. Instead of coordinating with each other, different organizations lobbied on their respective issues. They organized independent demonstrations and failed to put together a coherent agenda that could be presented to the Clinton administration (Vaid, 1995: 163). Both movement organizations and the Clinton administration underestimated the conservative congressional culture of Washington as well as the increasing power of the religious right. While NGLTF and HRC pushed for an executive order to lift the military ban, i.e., a fundamentally top-down approach, the Christian Coalition was conducting a more successful grassroots campaign to ensure that the ban remained intact. Organizations such as MFP (which now included HRC, NGLTF, ACLU, and NOW), the Ad Hoc Military Group, the Joint Chiefs, the Gay and Lesbian and Bisexual Veterans, the respective staffs of Representative Gerry Studds, Representative Barney Frank, Senator Bob Dole, and Senator Sam Nunn, failed to coordinate their efforts and often engaged in outright conflict, despite working on the same issue (Vaid, 1995: 166–7). Furthermore, despite amassing vast resources relative to both their past history and to any other sexual minorities movement around the world, the American gay and lesbian organizations could not compete with the resources of a growing Christian right counter-movement that fought for the maintenance of the ban (Rayside, 1998: 242–3). In short, the movement ignored signals that the administration was deeply divided on the issue, failed to

muster a grassroots campaign to counter that of the right, and President Clinton, lacking military credibility for being an alleged 'draft-dodger', latched onto Representative Frank's 'don't ask, don't tell' compromise as political cover (Vaid, 1995: 170–1; Gallagher and Bull 1996: 151–60).

The failure to lift the ban and the implementation of a far more homophobic standard – the institutionalization of the closet in the armed forces – demonstrate that the gay and lesbian movement is at a dramatic crossroads at the turn of the new century. First, movement organizations are much more successful at attaining legislation at the state then at the national level. Second, and more importantly, gays, lesbians, bisexuals, and all others who do not conform to the heterosexual norm, have achieved a potentially dangerous kind of pseudo-equality, what Urvashi Vaid terms 'virtual equality'. The movement has secured a large degree of civil rights legislation at the state level. It has achieved positive Supreme Court litigation outcomes such as *Romers v. Evans* (1996).[2] The 1990 Hate Crimes Bill included sexual orientation as a category that signaled a bias crime. The ban on gay immigrants was lifted in 1991. AIDS funding increased significantly under the Clinton administration. Despite its failure in 1996, the Employment Non-Discrimination Act missed passage by only one vote – a remarkable achievement given that most politicians considered the bill untenable only three years prior (Rayside, 1998: 310–11). These successes do not include the gay and lesbian community's unprecedented degree of mainstream cultural visibility attained over the last decade. Yet, such achievements threaten the movement since they inadvertently misrepresent the movement's level of success, providing a false sense of security for the sexual minorities community. The movement is still far from achieving its most fundamental aim: the destruction of institutionalized homophobia or even the passage of national level civil rights legislation inclusive of sexual orientation. The maintenance and, indeed, strengthening of the military ban as well as the power and popular resonance of Christian right anti-gay rhetoric, vividly reflect this failure. In order to counter successfully the mobilization of the far right, the movement must create a dual agenda focusing on civil rights legislation at all government levels, on the one hand, and liberation and cultural reform on the other. It must combine a grassroots with a top-down approach to ensure that its constituents are mobilized and their voices heard.

CONCLUSIONS

In one sense, the modern American gay and lesbian movement *did* commence at 1:20 a.m. on Saturday, June 28, 1969. At that moment, the cognitive liberation necessary to spark a movement took shape. The organizations and the opportunity existed, but until a shift from victim to empowered agent occurred, there was no modern movement. The riots themselves were the symbolic critical moment for gays and lesbians that provided that crucial cognitive liberation without which no cohesive social movement could occur. The riots inspired gay men and lesbians to shed their internalized victim status imposed upon them by heteronormative society. Coming out was transformed into a profoundly political act that helped accomplish what the homophile organizations could not: attract a large number of participants.

Changing opportunity was fostered by World War II, the publication of the Kinsey studies, and the expansion and legitimization of a movement culture throughout the 1960s. Black power and radical feminism especially provided the frame that would inspire gay liberation in the 1970s. Organizations such as the Mattachine Society and Daughters of Bilitis exploited these opportunities and testify that proto-movement developments existed before the Stonewall riots; however, they were unable to establish a mass movement because their assimilationist

tendencies failed to provide the basis for an affirmative and prideful collective identity. Such an identity emerged after the Stonewall riots in the shape of gay liberation. Increasing gay and lesbian political visibility engendered the lifting of the ban on gays in the Civil Service in 1974, the de-listing of homosexuality as a mental illness from the APA register in 1974, and the election of openly gay individuals to political office.

Once the movement started to accomplish its aims within the realm of civil rights legislation at the local and state level, it was challenged by both a powerful religion-based conservative counter-movement, first expressed in Bryant's 'Save Our Children' Campaign, and, far more devastatingly, by AIDS. AIDS was both a crisis and an opportunity; it fostered the development of more and diverse movement organizations, helped to mobilize non-gay allies, provided another policy angle by which to achieve gay visibility and legislation, reoriented the strategies of gays and lesbians toward national-level politics, further broke down the closet door, and vastly increased the number of movement participants. AIDS created an offshoot movement with its own organizations, such as GMHC and ACT UP. The AIDS crisis acts as the changing opportunity that interacts with the pre-existing gay rights organizations and affirmative collective gay identity to produce the AIDS movement with its own interest groups. Queer identity, while not directly linked to an AIDS movement, was inspired by ACT UP and provided another element of cognitive liberation. The inadequate response to the AIDS crisis by the Reagan administration (and to a lesser extent by the Bush government), given legislative shape in the Helms Amendment, also provided an opportunity which helped to foster this new form of queer cognitive liberation.

The fundamental conclusion of this study is that the American gay and lesbian movement exhibits a developmental history emphasizing changing opportunity structures, pre-existing organizations to manipulate this opportunity, and cognitive liberation leading to collective identity formation. Research also suggests that AIDS both promoted and derailed the gay and lesbian rights movement, providing greater political visibility, expanding movement membership, attaining new allies, and forcing national level mobilization while reinvigorating grassroots activism. Yet, it inflicted huge casualties on the community, forced a shift from a long-term human rights agenda to a public health service provision and survival orientation, subjected gays and lesbians to negative visibility, and provided anti-gay fodder for the religious right. Finally, the tail-end of the twentieth century has witnessed an explosive growth of media representation of gays and lesbians in popular television and film, however, the representation is often one-sided and exclusionary, focusing on the members of the gay and lesbian community who do not pose a substantial threat to the prevailing middle-class heteronormative gender dynamic. Gays and lesbians, to make no mention of bisexuals and transgenders, who do not fit the middle-class, white, and usually male paradigm remain beyond the pale of current American media representation.

Future research might carry this investigation of movement formation beyond the boundaries of the United States to explore whether a similar tri-factor pattern can account for movement development in other nations. Preliminary research suggests that this theory holds for the gay and lesbian movement in the United Kingdom, however, the model's robust quality may be strained if the analysis is shifted to a non-Anglican culture, i.e., France, Germany, the Netherlands, Japan, or Brazil. Different national cultures may condition movements to form in diverse manners.

The analysis could also be extended beyond examining movement formation to exploring movement maintenance; such research might evaluate how interest groups interact with political institutions; the investigator might want to select specific examples, such as the Defense of Marriage Act (DOMA), the Employment Non-Discrimination Act

(ENDA), or the recent state Supreme Court decisions regarding gay marriage in Hawaii and Vermont to understand not only why certain bills or court battles succeed or fail, but why certain institutional venues are targeted, and which is the most open in terms of agenda access for the movement. This type of analysis could easily develop into a comparative study that ascertains not only why movements develop differently in distinct national settings, but also the reasons why different movements have achieved distinct levels of politico-cultural freedom. The reasons may lie as much with the movement as with the political institutional environment of a given country. In short, much more investigation and analysis is called for that links social movements to mainstream questions regarding social movement theory. Not only would such research enable a better understanding of movement strategy, but it would continue to evaluate the validity and usefulness of certain theoretical models as well.

NOTES

1 Some of the themes of this essay echo those of my more detailed study, *The Unfinished Revolution: Social Movement Theory and the Gay and Lesbian Movements*, (Cambridge: Cambridge University Press: 2001). This chapter benefited from extensive critique from Steven Seidman and Phil Higgins. Any deficiencies that remain are mine alone.
2 In this case, laws that forbade barring discrimination base on sexual orientation were deemed unconstitutional.

REFERENCES

Abelove, Henry, Barale, Michele Aina and Halperin, David M. (eds) (1993) *The Lesbian and Gay Studies Reader*. New York: Routledge.
Adam, Barry (1995) *The Rise of the Gay and Lesbian Movement*. New York: Twayne Publishers,
Adam, Barry, Duyvendak, Jan Willem, and Krouwel, André (eds) (1999) 'Gay and lesbian movements beyond borders? National imprints of a worldwide movement', in Barry D. Adam, Jan Willem Duyvendak and André Krouwel (eds), *The Global Emergence of Gay*

and Lesbian Politics: National Imprints of a Worldwide Movement, Philadelphia: Temple University Press.

Altman, Dennis (1971) Homosexual Oppression and Liberation. New York: Outerbridge and Drenstfrey.

American Civil Liberties Union (1997) 'Homosexuality and civil liberties: policy statement adopted by the Union's Board of Directors', 7 January 1957, in Mark Blasius and Shane Phelan (eds), We Are Everywhere. New York: Routledge, Inc.

Anonymous (1990) 'Queers read this: I hate straights', in Mark Blasius and Shane Phelan (eds), We Are Everywhere. New York: Routledge.

Bennett, Lisa (1999) Mixed Blessings: Organized Religion and Gay and Lesbian Americans in 1998. Washington, DC: Human Rights Campaign.

Bersani, Leo (1995) Homos. Cambridge MA.: Harvard University Press.

Berube, Allan (1990) Coming Out under Fire: The History of Gay Men and Women in World War Two. New York: The Free Press.

Blasius, Mark (1994) Gay and Lesbian Politics: Sexuality and the Emergence of a New Ethic. Philadelphia: Temple University Press.

Blasius, Mark and Shane Phelan (eds) (1997) We Are Everywhere. New York: Routledge.

Bull, Chris (1997) 'A clean sweep', The Advocate, 22 July: 35–8.

Burns, Ken (1997) 'The homosexual faces a challenge: a speech to the Third Annual Convention of the Mattachine Society', published in Mattachine Review (1956) in Mark Blasius and Shane Phelan (eds), We are Everywhere. New York: Routledge.

Button, James W., Rienzo, Barbara A. and Wald, Kenneth D. (1997) Private Lives, Public Conflicts. Washington, DC: Congressional Quarterly Inc.

Carlson, Margaret (2000) 'McCain and his gaydar', Time, 31 January, 43.

Clendinen, Dudley and Nagourney, Adam (1999) Out for Good: The Struggle to Build a Gay Rights Movement in America. New York: Simon & Schuster.

Cory, Donald Webster [Edward Sagarin] (1997) 'The society we envisage', The Homosexual in America: A Subjective Approach (1951) in Mark Blasius and Shane Phelan (eds), We Are Everywhere. New York: Routledge, Inc.

Cruikshank, Margaret (1992) The Gay and Lesbian Liberation Movement. New York: Routledge.

Daughters of Bilitis (1997) 'Statement of purpose' (1955) in Mark Blasius and Shane Phelan (eds), We Are Everywhere. New York: Routledge, Inc.

D'Emilio, John (1983) Sexual Politics, Sexual Communities: The Making of a Homosexual Minority in the United States, 1940–1970. Chicago: University of Chicago Press.

D'Emilio, John and Freedman, Estelle B. (1988) Intimate Matters: A History of Sexuality in America. New York: Harper and Row Publishers.

Duberman, Martin, Vicinus, Martha and Chauncey Jr. George (eds) (1989) Hidden from History: Reclaiming the Gay and Lesbian Past. New York: Penguin Books USA, Inc.

Duberman, Martin, Vicinus, Martha and Chauncey, George (eds) (1993) Stonewall. New York: Penguin Books USA, Inc.

Echols, Alice (1989) Daring to Be Bad. Minneapolis: University of Minnesota Press.

Epstein, Steven (1999) 'Gay and lesbian movements in the United States: dilemmas of identity, diversity, and political strategy', in Barry D. Adam, Jan Willem Duyvendak, and André Krouwel (eds), The Global Emergence of Gay and Lesbian Politics: National Imprints of a Worldwide Movement. Philadelphia: Temple University Press, pp. 30–90.

Faludi, Susan (1991) Backlash: The Undeclared War Against American Women. New York: Doubleday, Inc.

Foucault, Michel (1978) The History of Sexuality: An Introduction: Volume I. New York: Vintage Books, Random House, Inc.

Fraser, Michael R. (1996) 'Identity and representation as challenges to social movement theory: a case study of Queer Nation', in Michael, Morgan and Susan Leggett (eds), Mainstream(s) and Margins: Cultural Politics in the 90s.Westport, CT: Greenwood Press.

Gallagher, John and Bull, Chris (1996) Perfect Enemies. New York: Crown Publishers Inc.

A Gay Male Group (1992) 'Notes on gay-male consciousness-raising', Out of the Closets: Voices of Gay Liberation. Karla Jay and Allen Young, eds. New York: New York University Press. pp. 293–301.

Hamill, Pete (1995) 'Confessions of a heterosexual', Esquire, August 1990: 55–7.

Harris, Sherry, Haynes, Todd, Hollibaugh, Amber, James, John S., LeVay, Simon, Schulman, Sarah, Shilts, Randy, and Vaid, Urvashi (1993) 'We can get there from here', The Nation, 5 July: 26–31.

Jay, Karla and Allen Young (eds) (1992) Out of the Closets: Views of Gay Liberation. New York: New York University Press.

Jenkins, J. Craig (1995) 'Social movements, political representation, and the state: an agenda and comparative framework', in J. Craig Jenkins, and Bert Klandermans (eds), The Politics of Social Protest: Comparative Perspectives on States and Social Movements. Minneapolis: University of Minnesota Press.

Jenkins, J. Craig and Bert Klandermans (1995) 'The politics of social protest' in J. Craig Jenkins, and Bert Klandermans, (eds), The Politics of Social Protest: Comparative Perspectives on States and Social Movements, Minneapolis: University of Minnesota Press.

Kameny, Franklin (1969) 'Gay is good' in Mark Blasius and Shane Phelan (eds), We Are Everywhere. New York: Routledge, 1997.

Kinsey, Afred C., Pomeroy, Wardell B. and Martin, Clyde E. ([1948] 1988) Sexual Behavior in the Human Male. Bloomington: Indiana University Press (originally published in 1948 by W.B. Saunders Company).

Kitschelt, Herbert, P. (1995) 'Political opportunity structures and political protest: anti-nuclear movements in four democracies', in Theda Skocpol and John L. Campbell (eds), *American Society and Politics*. New York: McGraw-Hill, Inc. pp. 320–44.

Kopkind, Andrew (1994) 'The gay moment', *The Nation*, 3 May 1993: 577, 590–602.

Kriesi, Hanspeter (1995) 'The political opportunity structure of new social movements: its impact on their mobilization', in J. Craig Jenkins, and Bert Klandermans, (eds), *The Politics of Social Protest: Comparative Perspectives on States and Social Movements*. Minneapolis: University of Minnesota Press.

Marotta, Toby (1981) *The Politics of Homosexuality*. Boston: Houghton Mifflin Inc.

McAdam, Doug (1997) 'The political process model', in Steven M. Buechler and F. Kurt Cylke, Jr. (eds), *Social Movements: Perspectives and Issues*. Mountain View, CA: Mayfield Publishing Company. pp. 172–92.

Murphy, Walter F., Flemming, James E. and Barber, Sotirios A. (eds) (1995) 'The right to intimate sexual choice', *American Constitutional Interpretation*. Westbury, New York: The Foundation Press.

National Museum and Archive of Lesbian and Gay History. (1996) A Program of the Lesbian and Gay Community Services Center – New York *The Gay Almanac*. New York: Berkley Books.

O'Conner, John (1997) 'Drawing rave reviews after years out of sight', *New York Times*, 21 April, C14.

Owens, Craig (1987) 'Outlaws: gay men in feminism', in Alice Jardine and Paul Smith, (eds), *Men in Feminism*. New York: Routledge. pp. 219–32.

Patton, Cindy, (1993) 'Tremble, hetero swine.' in Michael Warner, (ed.), *Fear of a Queer Planet*. Minneapolis: University of Minnesota Press. pp. 143–177.

Radicalesbians (1992) 'The woman-identified woman', in Karla Jay and Allen Young (eds), *Out of the Closets: Views of Gay Liberation*. New York: New York University Press, pp. 172–7.

Radicalesbians (New York City) (1992) 'Leaving the gay men behind', Karla Jay and Allen Youngs, (eds), *Out of the Closets: Voices of Gay Liberation*. New York: New York University Press, pp. 290–3.

Rayside, David M. (1998) *On the Fringe: Gays and Lesbians in Politics*. Ithaca, New York: Cornell University Press.

Riggs, Marlon T. (1991) 'Ruminations of a Snap! queen: what time is it?!', *Outlook*, Spring.

Rofes, Eric E. (1997) 'Gay Lib vs. AIDS: averting civil war in the 1990s', *Out/Look* in Mark Blasius and Shane Phelan (eds), *We Are Everywhere*. New York: Routledge.

Rudnick, Paul 'Out in Hollywood', *The Nation*, 5 July 1993, 36–8.

Seidman, Steven (1993) 'Identity politics in a "Postmodern" gay culture: some historical and conceptual notes', in Michael Warner (ed.), *Fear of a Queer Planet*. Minneapolis: University of Minnesota Press. pp. 105–42.

Shea, Lois R. (1998) 'Analysts cautious on gay-rights loss', *The Boston Globe*, 12 February, B1, B17.

Shilts, Randy (1988) *And the Band Played On: Politics, People, and the AIDS Epidemic*. New York: Penguin Books USA.

Skocpol, Theda and Campbell John L. (1995) 'Perspectives on social movements and collective action', in Theda Skocpol and John L. Campbell (eds), *American Society and Politics*. New York: McGraw-Hill, Inc. pp. 284–8.

Smith, Barbara (1981) 'Across the kitchen table: a sister-to-sister dialogue', in Cherrie Moraga and Gloria Anzaldúa (eds), *This Bridge Called My Back*. New York: Kitchen Table: Women of Color Press. pp. 113–27.

Smith, Barbara (1993) 'Where's the revolution?', *The Nation*, 5 July 12–16.

Smith, Ralph R. and Windes Russel R. (1999) 'Identity in political context: lesbian/gay representation in the public sphere', *Journal of Homosexuality*, 37 (2): 25–39.

'Statement of Purpose of the Mattachine Society' ([1951] 1997) in Mark Blasius and Shane Phelan (eds), *We Are Everywhere*. New York: Routledge.

Stockwell, Ann (1998) 'Yep, she Rules', *The Advocate*, 20 January.

Stychin, Carl F. (1995) *Law's Desire: Sexuality and the Limits of Justice*. London: Routledge.

Tarrow, Sidney (1994) *Power in Movement*. New York: Cambridge University Press.

Taylor, Verta and Nancy Whittier (1995) 'Analytical approaches to social movement culture: the culture of the women's movement', in Hanks Johnston and Bert Klandermans (eds), *Social Movements and Culture*. Minneapolis: University of Minnesota Press, pp. 163–87.

Taylor, Verta and Nancy Whittier (1995) 'Collective identity in social movement communities: lesbian feminist mobilization', in Theda Skocpol and John L. Campbell (eds), *American Society and Politics*. New York: McGraw-Hill, Inc. pp. 344–57.

Tourraine, Alain (1985) 'An introduction to the study of social movements', *Social Research*, 52: 749–87.

United States Senate Investigations Subcommittee of the Committee on Expenditures in the Executive Departments (1997) 'Employment of homosexuals and other sex perverts in the U.S. Government', in Mark Blasius and Shane Phelan (eds), *We Are Everywhere*. New York: Routledge, Inc.

Vaid, Urvashi (1995) *Virtual Equality: The Mainstreaming of Gay and Lesbian Liberation*. New York: Anchor Books, Doubleday.

Weber, Max (1958) 'Politics as a vocation', in H.H. Gerth and C. Wright Mills (eds), in *From Max Weber: Essays in Sociology*. New York: Oxford University Press. pp. 77–128.

Willer, Shirley ([1966] 1997) 'What concrete steps can be taken to further the homophile movement?', *The Ladder* (1966) in Mark Blasius and Shane Phelan, (eds), *We Are Everywhere*. New York: Routledge.

23

Anti-Gay and Lesbian Violence and its Discontents

VALERIE JENNESS AND KIMBERLY D. RICHMAN

In 1998 a single homicide in the USA marshaled unprecedented national media attention. In Laramie, Wyoming, Matthew Shepard, a young gay man, was pistol-whipped, tied to a fence, and left to die. Shepard was not discovered until 18 hours later, and he died days later in a Colorado hospital. His assailants, Aaron McKinney and Russell Henderson, were convicted of murder with aggravating circumstances and sentenced to multiple life sentences without the possibility of parole. These convictions came after separate prosecutors argued that the defendants' crime was motivated by homophobia; at the same time, one defense attorney argued that the crime was caused by 'gay panic' (namely, an alleged sexual advance by Shepard toward McKinney caused McKinney to fly into an uncontrollable rage and kill Shepard). Six months after the murder of Matthew Shepard, 39-year-old Billy Jack Gaither, a gay man, was beaten to death with an axe handle, slashed at the throat, and set afire on a pile of tires in Alabama. Again, the assailants were acquaintances of Gaither, outwardly homophobic, and claimed to have acted in response to perceived sexual advances.

Violence targeting gays and lesbians – or people presumed to be gay or lesbian – is not new nor is it anomalous. What is new, however, is that for the first time in history, cases such as those represented by the murder of Shepard and Gaither have inspired journalists, activists, politicians, educators, community representatives, and other members of the morally concerned citizenry to focus national attention on gay-bashing in the USA (Jenness and Grattet, 2001; Perry, 2001). In particular, at the end of the twentieth century and the beginning of the twenty-first century, unprecedented activist, scholarly, and policy-making attention has been devoted to understanding what Rovella (1994: A1), in the *National Law Journal,* called 'the decade of hate – or at least hate crime', including hateful acts of violence directed at gays and lesbians. Violence born of bigotry, manifest as discrimination, and directed towards gays and lesbians is finally forcing a series of related questions. Namely, what are the parameters and epidemiology of anti-gay and lesbian violence? Why does this type of violent conduct occur? And finally, what measures have been taken to curb such violence? This chapter answers those questions. But first we argue that it is important to remember that the conduct is as old as humankind. This sets the stage for understanding how 'gay-bashing' has been constructed as a contemporary social problem in the USA and, to a lesser degree, elsewhere.

A HISTORY OF ANTI-GAY AND LESBIAN VIOLENCE

Violence against homosexuals and people presumed to be homosexual has been documented for as long as the lives of gay men and lesbians have been documented. For example, Boswell (1980) documented violence against gay men and lesbians by Western Europeans from the beginning of the Christian era to the fourteenth century. In the process, he revealed that intolerance toward those with same sex desire increased noticeably in the latter part of the twelfth century. The rise of urbanization and absolutist governments during this time was accompanied by an array of violence, including, most notably for our purposes here, violence directed at homosexuals and perpetrated by government and religious officials. The earliest official government action against gay men, according to Boswell (1980), was a law drafted in Jerusalem by Europeans that punished 'sodomites' with death by fire. Later, in the fourteenth century in France, the legal school of Orleans adopted a law requiring that male homosexual conduct be punished with castration on the first offense, dismemberment on the second offense, and burning on the third offense. In contrast, female homosexuals were punished with dismemberment for the first two offenses.

Moving forward in time, in *Gay American History*, which covers a period of over 400 years, from 1566 to 1966, Jonathan Katz (1976) documented a history of violence directed toward individuals because of their (real or imagined) sexual orientation, identity, or same sex behavior. Historically, such violence included castration, beatings, imprisonment, burning, choking, electrical shocks, and execution. For example, Katz documented many historical moments in which the official government sanction for sodomy or other homosexual acts or behavior was death by hanging, drowning, or some other means. These actions were accepted as legitimate and necessary responses to homosexuality or gender inappropriate behavior, commonly referred to as an 'abomination', 'crime against nature', 'sin', and 'perversion'. Indeed, known or suspected homosexuals were referred to as 'monsters', 'erotopaths', and 'sexual perverts'. Again, these views and acts of violence represented official state policies and were perpetrated by representatives of the state as well as private citizens.

More recently, the National Gay and Lesbian Task Force (1991) has documented literally thousands of incidents of violence against gay men and lesbians in the USA throughout the latter part of the twentieth century. Collecting incidents of reported violence, as well as many acts of violence that have gone unreported, the National Gay and Lesbian Task Force has focused on an array of manifestations of violence against gay men and lesbians, including homicide, AIDS-related incidents, harassment and assault, conspiracy, attacks on gay and lesbian establishments, police abuse and negligence, violence on college campuses, violence by family members, violence in jails and prisons, and most frequently, anti-gay and lesbian defamation. Published reports of this violence include both qualitative and quantitative overviews of the widespread nature of violence against gays and lesbians, despite significant changes in law (Sloan and Gustavsson, 1998) and social attitudes toward homosexuality (*Los Angeles Times*, 2000).

Documented cases of anti-gay and lesbian violence throughout history and across societies provides evidence for a claim made by Virginia Apuzzo, former Executive Director of the National Gay and Lesbian Task Force: 'to be gay or lesbian is to live in the shadow of violence' (cited in Comstock, 1991: 54). Clearly, from a historical and social science point of view, it is difficult to discredit this claim. It is however, useful to ask 'who is doing what to whom, how often, and with what consequences?' After addressing these questions, we turn to another central question 'why does this happen?' More specifically, 'what is the nature of the connection between heterosexism, homophobia, and anti-gay and lesbian violence?'

A CONTEMPORARY EPIDEMIOLOGICAL PORTRAIT OF ANTI-GAY AND LESBIAN VIOLENCE

Despite an undeniable history of violence against gays and lesbians, systematic and reliable information on the causes, manifestations, and consequences of anti-gay and lesbian violence is scant. It is only since the late 1980s that empirical work on the epidemiology of violence against gays and lesbians that is needed to address these questions has been accumulating. As a result, trends in violence against homosexuals is only beginning to be discerned, thus we are only now somewhat situated to provide an empirical portrayal of the epidemiology of anti-gay and lesbian violence. As we discuss below, this empirical portrayal derives from government reports, official state data, and self-report studies undertaken and completed by academics and activists within the gay and lesbian community.

Despite many calls for the government to monitor bias crime in the USA, including violence against gays and lesbians, it was not until the late 1980s that the federal government heeded the call of many civil rights groups and minority constituencies and began to study the nature of bias-motivated violence. In one of the first government-sponsored efforts to assess the scope of violence directed toward minorities in the USA, the US Justice Department commissioned a report on bias-motivated violence in 1987. This report found that 'the most frequent victims of hate violence today are Blacks, Hispanics, Southeast Asians, Jews, and gays and lesbians. Homosexuals are probably the most frequent victims' (cited in Vaid, 1995: 11).

Shortly after the release of this pathbreaking, report, the Federal Bureau of Investigation (FBI) began to collect data on crimes committed because of bias toward homosexuals as part of its larger effort to track bias-crime in the USA. Beginning in the early 1990s, the Uniform Crime Report (UCR) released annual data on the violence against people because of their sexual orientation (see Table 23.1). As 'official data', these are only 'crimes known to the police'; thus, they are necessarily underestimates and they reflect the select nature of data collection by police. Nonetheless, these data reveal three important trends in *reported* violence against homosexuals *because of* their homosexuality. First, from 1991 to 1998 bias-motivated violence directed toward both male and female homosexuals has increased. Second, from 1991 to 1998 violence based on sexual orientation is the second most frequently reported type of hate crime in the USA, with race-based violence being the most frequently reported type of bias-crime in the USA. And third, from 1991 to 1998 officially reported violence directed toward gay men is more common than violence directed toward lesbians.

Official data from state agencies confirm the patterns revealed in national data. For example, reported hate crime in California is increasing and in 1998 the California Department of Justice reported that anti-homosexual crime in California comprised the second largest category of hate crime in the state. Specifically, in 1998 almost 20 per cent of the reported hate crime in the state was based on sexual orientation, compared to 67.2 per cent of the reported hate crime in California being based on race/ethnicity (California Department of Justice, 1999: 7). Moreover, in 1998 15.5 per cent of the reported hate crime in the state was anti-male homosexual, while only 3.1 per cent of the reported hate crime in California was anti-female homosexual crimes (California Department of Justice, 1999: 7).

In addition to government reports, various non-government sponsored studies reveal the contours of crimes against

Table 23.1 *Bias-motivated Offenses Reported by the Uniform Crime Reports, 1991–1998*

Type of Bias-Motivation	1991	1992	1993	1994	1995	1996	1997	1998
Race	2,963	5,050	5,085	4,387	6,170	6,767	5,898	5,360
anti-White	888	1,664	1,600	1,253	1,511	1,384	1,267	989
anti-Black	1,689	2,884	2,985	2,668	3,805	4,469	3,838	3,573
anti-American Indian/Alaskan Native	11	31	36	26	59	69	44	66
anti-Asian/Pacific Islander	287	275	274	267	484	527	437	359
anti-Multi-racial group	88	198	190	173	311	318	312	373
Ethnicity/national origin	450	841	701	745	1,022	1,163	1,083	919
anti-Hispanic	242	498	414	407	680	710	636	595
anti-other ethnicity/national	208	343	287	338	342	453	447	324
Religion	917	1,240	1,245	1,232	1,414	1,500	1,483	1,475
anti-Jewish	792	1,084	1,104	1,080	1,145	1,182	1,159	1,145
anti-Catholic	23	18	31	17	35	37	32	62
anti-Protestant	26	29	25	30	47	80	59	61
anti-Islamic	10	17	13	16	39	33	31	22
anti-other religious group	5	77	58	72	122	139	173	138
anti-multi-religious group	11	14	11	14	25	27	26	45
anti-atheism/agnosticism/etc.	4	1	3	3	1	2	3	2
Sexual Orientation	425	944	938	780	1,266	1,256	1,925	1,439
anti-male homosexual	–	–	665	513	915	927	932	972
anti-female homosexual	–	–	113	119	189	185	220	265
anti-homosexual	421	928	111	77	125	91	410	170
anti-heterosexual	3	13	28	16	19	34	14	13
anti-bisexual	1	3	1	2	18	12	10	19
Disability	–	–	–	–	–	–	12	27
anti-physical	–	–	–	–	–	–	9	14
anti-mental	–	–	–	–	–	–	3	13
Multiple bias	–	–	–	–	23	20	10	15
Total	4,755	8,075	7,969	7,144	9,895	10,706	9,861	9,235
# of participating agencies	2,771	6,181	6,551	7,356	9,584	11,354	11,211	10,461
# of states, including DC	32	42	47	44	46	50	49	46
% of US population represented	n/a	51	58	58	75	84	87	79

Source: US Department of Justice. US Government. Washington, DC.

homosexuals. For example, a recent report on 'Anti-Lesbian, Gay, Bisexual, and Transgender Violence in 1998' was released in 1999 by the National Coalition of Anti-Violence Projects. Summarizing known incidents of violence that occurred throughout 1998 against lesbian, gay, bisexual, or transgender individuals in sixteen distinct cities, states, and/or regions across the USA, this report highlights the following trends: the number of actual or suspected anti-gay murders in the reporting cities, states, and regions increases 136 per cent; serious assaults (one in which the victim(s) sustained major injuries) grew 12 per cent, despite an 11 per cent decline in the number of assaults generally; the number of weapons reported in conjunction with assaults against gay, lesbian, bisexual, and transgendered individuals grew at an unprecedented rate, with the use of firearms increasing 71 per cent, the use of bats, clubs, and blunt objects increasing 46 per cent, the use of vehicles increasing 150 per cent, the use of ropes and restraints increasing 133 per cent, and the use of knives and sharp objects increasing 13 per cent. In addition, the report documented a 242 per cent increase in the number of incidents committed by hate groups; a 103 per cent increase in the number of incidents occurring at or near lesbian, gay, bisexual, or transgendered community public events, such as parades and rallies; and a deterioration in police responses to anti-gay and lesbian violence, indicated by a 155 per cent increase in instances of verbal harassment and abuse of victims by police officers and a 866 per cent increase in reports of physical abuse by police officers (National Coalition of Anti-Violence Projects, 1999). Based on these findings, the National Coalition of Anti-Violence Projects concluded, 'acts of anti-gay violence are neither random nor chaotic. They are the predictable consequence of much more fundamental flaws in the nation's social, cultural, and political fabric.'

Complementing the findings produced by government and activist groups, a growing body of academic studies based on self-report data suggests a number of trends. Namely, the majority of gay men and lesbians have experienced actual violence or the threat of violence because of their sexual orientation (such as having objects thrown at them and being chased, punched, hit, kicked, and/or beaten); gays and lesbians of color are at an increased risk for violent attack because of their sexual orientation and their race/ethnicity; and compared to gay men, lesbians report higher rates of verbal harassment by family members and a greater fear of anti-gay violence as well as a higher rate of victimization in non-gay identified public settings and in their homes and a lower rate of victimization in school and public gay-identified areas (Herek and Berrill, 1992). In addition, a growing body of evidence reveals that violence against gays and lesbians continues to take a variety of forms, from symbolic to fatal assaults; and they implicate a range of perpetrators, from intimates to strangers to institutions such as the state, religion, and medicine. Recent studies suggest that the typical perpetrator of anti-gay and lesbian violence is young, white, and male (Comstock, 1991; Herek and Berrill, 1992). Finally, self-report studies reveal that gays and lesbians often are unwilling to report violence directed at them because of their sexuality. For example, von Schulthess (1992) found that only 15 per cent of lesbians who had been victimized because of their sexuality reported the incident to the police; and many of the respondents reporting that harassment is an inevitable part of life as a lesbian. Comstock's (1991) research suggests that violence against gay men and lesbians frequently goes unreported because of fear of abuse by police, fear of public disclosure, and the perception that law enforcement officials are anti-homosexual.

Finally, moving beyond these specific findings, a growing body of comparative work suggests a number of trends. First, by many accounts, violence motivated by homophobia and heterosexism represents the most frequent, visible, violent, and culturally legitimated type of 'hate crime' in the USA (Comstock, 1991; Herek and Berrill, 1992; National Gay and Lesbian Task Force, 1991). Second, hate-motivated violence perpetuated against gays and lesbians, or people presumed to be gay or lesbian, constitutes one of the most rapidly growing forms of hate crime in the USA (National Gay and Lesbian Task Force, 1991). Third, violence against gays and lesbians continues to take a variety of forms, from verbal harassment to institutional vandalism to murder (National Coalition of Anti-Violence Projects, 1999; National Gay and Lesbian Task Force, 1991). Fourth, documented cases of violence against gays and lesbians across societies illustrate that physical, psychological, and symbolic violence against lesbians crosses racial, ethnic, religious, nationality, and age boundaries (Herek and Berrill, 1992; Katz, 1976; National Coalition of Anti-Violence Projects, 1999; National Gay and Lesbian Task Force, 1991).

To make sense of these many empirical findings and trends requires articulating the nature of the complex connection between homophobia, heteronormativity, heterosexism, and anti-gay and lesbian violence.

Thus, in the next, section we turn our attention to these concepts, as well as the processes and structures they delineate.

EXPLAINING ANTI-GAY AND LESBIAN VIOLENCE: SOURCES OF BIAS

The most common explanation for violence directed at gays and lesbians – as well as bisexual and transgendered people – is routinely offered by scholars, activists, and policy-makers alike who have been devoted to establishing and explaining a causal connection between heterosexism, homophobia and so-called 'gay-bashing'. To greater or lesser degree, the relationship between heterosexism, homophobia, and gay-bashing is implied, but often not rendered specific, in a slew of empirical studies assessing people's beliefs about homosexuality, attitudes towards homosexuals, willingness to participate in/actual participation in discriminatory acts against gay, lesbian, bisexual, and transgendered people, and the larger sociopolitical context in which all are situated. A consideration of this literature requires a view of 'anti-homosexuality' that is multilayered, dynamic, and structured (for an excellent review, see O'Brien, 2001; also, see Perry, 2001).

Scholars generally agree that anti-homosexual bias can be understood to exist on three levels: the individual, which implies individual psychology; the institutional, which is condoned or perpetrated through the law or by other official means; and the structural or cultural, including societal values, moral codes, and the like (Onken, 1998). O'Brien (2001) further delineates between these levels by identifying three corresponding theoretical approaches and terms: homophobia, heteronormativity, and heterosexism. Focusing on these concepts facilitates an understanding of anti-gay and lesbian violence.

The term homophobia is used to apply to the individual – or psychological – level and is primarily conceived as a personality trait that serves specific psychological functions for the individual. According to Herek (1992), the 'experiential function' helps individuals make sense of and reconcile their own previous interactions with gay men or lesbians, or anticipate dealing with future interactions. For example, Herek and Berrill (1992) relates the story of a young man who did not get along with his gay boss. After this experi- ence, the young man felt he could claim with some certainty that all of the negative stereotypes he had heard about gay men were true. The 'social identity function' of anti-gay or lesbian prejudice, on the other hand, allows individuals to affirm their own values, self-concepts, and sense of belonging to a particular group (Herek and Berrill, 1992). For example, one might feel the need to express homophobic sentiments in order to prove him or herself a 'good Christian'. Finally, homophobia may serve an ego-defense function insofar as it provides a venue through which a release for anxiety stemming from unconscious confusion or conflict regarding one's own sexuality can occur. For example, a man who is or has been accused of being particularly effeminate may compensate or act defensively by expressing strong anti-gay prejudice.

O'Brien (2001) refers to the cultural level of anti-gay and lesbian bias as heteronormativity and argues that it can best be analysed in terms of its manifestations in discourse. Most notably, scholars of cultural/literary studies and queer theory emphasize heteronormativity as a discursive practice that pervades literature, fine arts, education, legal language, religion, and other domains of culture (Seidman, 1997). For example, despite a growth in the number of gay and lesbian characters on prime-time television, heterosexuality is routinely presented as the normal way of doing intimate, sexual relationships, with the lives of gays and lesbians representing fodder to dramatic or comedic plotlines. As a dominant discourse in western society, heteronormativity emphasizes the 'correctness' of heterosexuality and traditional family forms, while censuring, punishing, or rendering invisible homosexuality in all of its manifestations (Herek and Berrill, 1992; O'Brien, 2001).

Finally, O'Brien (2001) uses the term heterosexism to describe anti-homosexual bias on the structural or institutional level. Most often studied by anthropologists and sociologists, heterosexism at the level of social structure cements personal anti-homosexual bias(es) and cultural discourses in existing institutions such as law, religion, family, and the economy. Institutional heterosexism both maintains these forms of prejudice and serves as implicit permission – particularly when manifested in official or legal ways – to discriminate, chastise, and perhaps even perpetrate violence against those who deviate from conventional sexualities, identities, or practices. With regard to religion, for example, O'Brien explains:

Most contemporary religions treat homosexuality as problematic. In some cases a distinction is made between homosexual feelings and homosexual acts (e.g., Catholic Catechism, 1989). The experience of homosexual inclinations may be considered an affliction – a 'cross to bear' – but to act on one's homosexual feelings is considered a sin. Many religious leaders advocate celibacy for those 'afflicted' with homosexual tendencies. Some religious organizations sponsor intensive therapy programs intended to help the individual who is 'suffering' from homosexuality recover. Similar to medical institutions, religious institutions take heterosexuality for granted as the normal and desired form of sexual organization and treat homosexuality as deviant, undesirable, dysfunctional and, additionally, sinful. (2001: 3–4)

The legal arena is a particularly salient home for institutional heterosexism:

The extent to which homophobia is an institution is indicated in the decisions of law enforcement officials and judges who consider homosexuality sufficient grounds for justifying acts of prejudice, discrimination and violence. This tacit approval constitutes a form of permissible prejudice. Persons presume their prejudices to be legitimate or permissible when these prejudices are condoned by persons in positions of authority. (ibid.: 5)

Taking this threefold scheme at face value, then, we can begin to ask a complicated question: what is the connection between psychological, cultural, and structural support for anti-gay or lesbian – what O'Brien aptly calls 'permissible prejudice' – and the actual perpetration of violence toward gays, lesbians, and other non-normative sexualities? To be blunt, individual prejudice, having been learned and reinforced at the cultural and social structural levels, can be conceived as a necessary, but *in*sufficient precursor to the perpetration of anti-gay or lesbian violence. Upon consideration of the available data, it would be difficult, if not impossible, to conclude that the existence of homophobia, heterosexism and heteronormativity – no matter how engrained and supported by societal institutions – is, in and of itself, a causal explanation for the occurrence of anti-gay and lesbian violence. That explanation is simply too simple considering public opinion data and behavioral data simultaneously.

A recent nation-wide poll by the *Los Angeles Times* (2000) found that 64 per cent of Americans believe that homosexuality is unacceptable. However, one would be hard-pressed to make the case that nearly two-thirds of the United States' population are gay-bashers. The limited available data on hate crime perpetration do not support such a claim (Comstock, 1991; US Department of Justice, 1998). In fact, a recent statewide poll in California revealed that 42 per cent of respondents said they believed homosexuality is morally wrong; yet even more – 54 per cent – indicated that they felt homophobia (and presumably its violent manifestations) to be morally wrong as well (*Los Angeles Times*, 2000).

The findings on public attitudes toward homosexuality and homophobic acts reveal a complicated relationship between heterosexist beliefs, anti-gay and lesbian attitudes, and violence directed at gays, lesbians, and other non-heterosexuals. On one hand, epidemiological evidence suggests that young, white, males are the modal category of perpetrators of violence against gays and lesbians; at the same time, young males express the most virulent homophobic beliefs (Comstock, 1991; Herek and Berrill, 1992; National Coalition of Anti-Violence Projects, 1999; O'Brien, 2001; Sloan and Gustavsson, 1998). On the other hand, however, the vast majority of young white males do *not* engage in physical violence directed at gays and lesbians. Stated more boldly, most homophobes do *not* assault gays and lesbians. Thus, the relationship between homophobic beliefs and attitudes and physical violence aimed at gays and lesbians cannot be reduced to a simple cause-and-effect statement. It is increasingly obvious and empirically verifiable that many situational, interactional, and structural variables intervene in a larger process that allows individual beliefs and ideas to translate into behavior. In this case, ideas about homosexuals only occasionally – indeed, statistically speaking, rarely – result in actual violence towards homosexuals. Accordingly, the most promising line of research on the topic is undertaken by social scientists, especially psychologists and sociologists, who continue to search for psychological, situational, interactional, and structural variables that inhibit or facilitate violence, including violence against gays and lesbians (see, for example, Herek and Berrill, 1992; Perry, 2001).

THE SOCIAL CONTROL OF ANTI-GAY AND LESBIAN VIOLENCE

Regardless of the social structures and processes that lead to violence against gays and lesbians, it is increasingly defined as an unacceptable expression of contempt for homosexuals and others who represent non-normative identities, lifestyles, and sexual behaviors. Defined by sexism, heterosexism, and at times racism, classism, anti-Semitism, and ageism, anti-gay and lesbian violence has been greeted with an array of legal and extralegal responses designed to bring attention to and curb violence directed at gays and lesbians. In the process, gay-bashing has, for the first time in history, been deemed a national social problem and,

in certain jurisdictions, a bona fide hate crime (Jenness and Broad, 1997; Jenness and Grattet, 2001; Perry, 2001).

As a new century begins, even public officials and religious officials who oppose homosexuality as an identity, behavior, or lifestyle have begun to speak out in defense of homosexuals as undeserving targets of discriminatory violence. As Senator Gordon Smith (R-Oregon) argued on the US Senate floor in June of 2000 in an effort to get his fellow Republicans to favor federal legislation to protect homosexuals from violence,

I think many [religious conservatives] in the Senate are reflexively inclined to vote no. I understand that because I shared those feelings for a long, long, time. You don't have to agree with everything the gay community is asking. I don't, but we ought to agree on protecting them and all Americans. (*Los Angeles Times*, 2000b: A14)

He is not alone in expressing and promoting this sentiment.

Consistent with Senator Gordon's (R-Oregon) pleas, there has been a growth in both extralegal and legal responses to violence motivated by prejudice and directed toward gays and lesbians. With regard to extralegal responses, in the latter part of the twentieth century a plethora of community-based activism defined anti-gay and lesbian violence as a social problem in need of remedy. Most notably, throughout the 1980s and the 1990s gay- and lesbian-sponsored anti-violence projects emerged and proliferated in the USA and abroad. As extensions of the gay and lesbian movement in the USA and abroad, these organizations document and publicize the incidence and prevalence of anti-gay and lesbian violence, establish crisis intervention and victim assistance programs, sponsor public education campaigns, and undertake surveillance efforts in the form of street patrols (Jenness and Broad, 1997). Combined, these activities comprise an 'unprecedented level of organizing against violence' (National Gay and Lesbian Task Force, 1991: 22) that has ensured that anti-gay and lesbian violence has 'finally taken its place among such societal concerns as violence against women, children and ethnic and racial groups' (Comstock, 1991: 1). As Vaid (1995: 207–8), the former Director of the National Gay and Lesbian Task Force, noted in her book on the gay and lesbian movement:

> From 1982 to today, the [gay and lesbian] movement has won near-universal condemnation of gay-bashing from governmental, religious, and civil bodies. We got gay-bashing classified as a crime motivated by prejudice and hate, secured the passage of bias-penalty bills, produced studies into the causes and solutions to homophobic violence, and secured funding for a range of service programs.

To achieve these changes, according to Jenness and Broad (1997), gay- and lesbian-sponsored anti-violence projects have framed anti-gay and lesbian violence similar to the ways in which feminist-sponsored anti-violence against women campaigns in the latter part of the twentieth century framed violence against women. Namely, recent anti-gay and lesbian activism framed the problem of violence against gays and lesbians as a violent crime rather than as a sexual one; moreover, it cast hate-motivated violence directed at gays and lesbians as criminal sexual assault. However, unlike feminist activism dealing with violence against women, which has been anchored in an all-encompassing critique of patriarchy, activism concerning anti-gay and lesbian violence has ignored patriarchy and the gender relations that sustain and reflect it. Gay and lesbian activism has been explicitly preoccupied with homophobia, only implicitly concerned with institutionalized heterosexism, and not at all concerned with patriarchy (Jenness and Broad, 1994).

This critical point of departure ensured that gay and lesbian anti-violence projects in particular and the public more generally have not incorporated a gendered understanding of violence against gay men and lesbian *women* (Jenness and Broad, 1994). At the same time, gay and lesbian sponsored anti-violence projects have affirmed the invisibility of violence directed at lesbians of color because they are lesbians and/or women of color. As a result, the linkage between race-hate, gay-hate, and

misogyny is evident (Sheffield, 1992: 389), but the centrality of race and gender in the gay and lesbian activism dealing with violence is negligible. Sheffield (1992: 395) argued that this is 'not only a profound denial of the most pervasive form of violence in the United States, but an attempt to deny the reality of patriarchal/sexist oppression. [I]t is an attempt to have it both ways: that is, to rage against such hate-violence when the victims are males (and occasionally females) and yet protect male superiority over women.' Distinguishing between violence directed at gay men and violence directed at lesbian women is crucial insofar as a defining characteristic of violence against lesbians is that it exists on a continuum, from exclusively anti-women to exclusively anti-gay conduct (Comstock, 1991; von Schulthess, 1992). Lesbians who experience harassment and violence often have a difficult time distinguishing whether the violence was motivated by 'anti-woman' or 'anti-lesbian' sentiment because a typical incident involves a scenario in which violence begins as anti-woman and then escalates such that it is recognizable as anti-lesbian (Comstock, 1991; von Schulthess, 1992).

Consistent with activism described above, by the end of the twentieth century jurisdictions across the USA had passed laws to enhance the penalty for crimes that manifest evidence of prejudice based on sexual orientation, presumably to deter gay-bashing in the USA (Perry, 2001). For example, in 1982 Washington State passed a law that specified:

> A person is guilty of malicious harassment if he or she maliciously and intentionally commits one of the following acts because of his or her perception of the victim's race, color, religion, ancestry, national origin, gender, sexual orientation, or mental, physical, or sensory handicap. (Rev. Code Wash. 9A.36.080)

Using the language of civil rights – now extended to gays and lesbians – California law specifies that:

> No person, whether or not under color of law, shall by force or threat of force, willfully injure, intimidate, interfere with, oppress, or threaten any

other person in the free exercise or enjoyment of any right or privilege secured to him or her by the Constitution or the laws of the United States because of the other person's race, color, religion, ancestry, national origin, disability, gender, or sexual orientation, or because he or she perceives that the other person has one or more of these characteristics. (Ca Penal Code 422.7)

Consistent with these particular laws, by 1999 21 states had adopted hate crime legislation that includes provisions for 'sexual orientation' as a protected status (Jenness and Grattet, 2001). Moreover, many of the remaining states continue to debate the passage of similar legislation.

Following these states' lead, in the 1990s the Federal Government passed two laws and continues to debate a third bill that recognizes violence against gays and lesbians as an important social problem in need of public resources and legal redress. First, in 1990 President Bush signed into law the Hate Crimes Statistics Act of 1990, which required the Attorney General to collect data on:

[C]rimes that manifest evidence of prejudice based on race, religion, sexual orientation, or ethnicity, including where appropriate the crimes of murder, non-negligent manslaughter; forcible rape; aggravated assault, simple assault, intimidation; arson; and destruction, damage or vandalism of property. (Public Law 101–275)

As a data collection law, the Hate Crimes Statistics Act merely requires the Attorney General to gather and make available to the public data on bias-motivated crime in order to generate the empirical data necessary to develop more effective policy by identifying and counting bias-motivated crimes, measuring trends, fashioning effective responses, designing prevention strategies, and developing sensitivity to the particular needs of victims of hate crimes, including those victimized because they are or are imagined to be homosexual. These data are summarized in Table 23.1.

Second, in 1994, Congress passed the Hate Crimes Sentencing Enhancement Act. This law identifies eight predicate crimes – murder; non-negligent manslaughter; forcible rape; aggravated assault; simple assault;

intimidation; arson; and destruction, damage, or vandalism of property – for which judges are allowed to enhance penalties of 'not less than three offense levels for offenses that finder of fact at trial determines beyond a reasonable doubt are hate crimes' (Public Law 103–322). For the purposes of this law, hate crime is defined as criminal conduct wherein 'the defendant intentionally selected any victim or property as the object of the offense because of the actual or perceived race, color, religion, national origin, ethnicity, gender, disability, or *sexual orientation* of any person' (Public Law 103–322). Although broad in form, this law is somewhat narrow in terms of coverage. It addresses only those hate crimes that take place on federal lands and properties.

Finally, the US Senate recently passed the The Hate Crimes Prevention Act. If signed into law by President Bush, the Hate Crimes Prevention Act, would:

[A]mend the Federal criminal code to set penalties for persons who, whether or not acting under the color of law, willfully cause bodily injury to any person or, through the use of fire, firearm, or explosive device, attempt to cause such injury, because of the actual or perceived: (1) race, color, religion, or national origin of any person; and (2) religion, gender, sexual orientation, or disability of any person, where in connection with the offense, the defendant or the victim travels in interstate or foreign commerce, uses a facility or instrumentality of interstate or foreign commerce, or engages in any activity affecting interstate or foreign commerce, or where the offense is in or affects interstate or foreign commerce (S. 1529).

Despite the fact that these federal legislative efforts are limited – the Hate Crimes Statistics Act does not mandate punishment for offenders of anti-gay and lesbian violence, the Hate Crime Penalty Enhancement Act only covers a limited and minority set of circumstances in which anti-gay and lesbian violence occurs, and the Hate Crimes Prevention Act is not yet law – the inclusion of 'sexual orientation' in each piece of legislation proved controversial. To quote Fernandez (1991: 272), proposals to include a provision for sexual orientation in the Hate

Crimes Statistics Act 'prompted an assault on the bill by conservatives in the House and Senate'. Senator Jesse Helms (R-North Carolina), for example, opposed including sexual orientation in the bill and claimed that Congress was being 'hoodwinked' into passing the 'flagship of the homosexual, lesbian legislative agenda' (*Congressional Record*, 1990: 1076). Helms (R-North Carolina) argued:

> [W]here do you think the idea of legislation to require the collection of statistics on so-called hate crimes originated? If this is such a wonderful crime fighting tool, it sure must have originated with a group known for its tough stance on crime, right? Wrong. This idea was dreamed up by the National Gay and Lesbian Task Force. That is a matter of record. [I]t is clear that the militant homosexuals have been building up the numbers of complaints – not, let me emphasize, of criminal offenses or charges. They have been building up numbers of complaints to bolster their case that this type of legislation is necessary. [T]he evidence is clear, Mr. President. Studying hate crimes against homosexuals is a crucial first step toward achieving homosexual rights and legitimacy in American society. This Senator cannot, and will not, be party to any legislation which fuels the homosexual movement. (*Congressional Record*, 1990: 1076)

However, this type of opposition was ultimately overcome as representatives of the gay and lesbian community successfully framed violence against gays and lesbians as a crime and argued for the appropriateness of including the provision in federal hate crime law (Jenness, 1999; Jenness and Broad, 1997). As Jenness (1999: 566) concluded after examining all of the congressional hearings and debates leading up to the passage of federal hate crime laws,

> Shortly after federal hate crime law was envisioned, proposals were made by outsider claimsmakers, most notably social movement representatives [from the gay and lesbian movement], to further differentiate hate crime victims by adding 'sexual orientation' to the list of provisions in federal hate crime law. Through direct and sustained testimony, [gay and lesbian] SMO representatives were able to bestow empirical credibility upon the violence connected with this provision (i.e., antigay violence). In addition,

they successfully engaged in discursive tactics that rendered the meaning of sexual orientation more similar to than dissimilar from the meanings already attached to race, religion, and ethnicity. By successfully engaging in these linking strategies of persuasion, [gay and lesbian] SMOs proved crucial to the expansion of hate crime law to cover sexual orientation. In other words, the addition of sexual orientation was contingent upon the presence and viability of direct, sustained social movement mobilization coupled with particular discursive moves that prove decisive in social problems talk.

Combined, state and federal laws have, in effect, created a new category of criminal conduct – anti-gay and lesbian violence. In so doing, they reflect and bring newfound attention to the age-old problem of gay-bashing. The consequence of legal reform being brought to bear on the problem of gay-bashing in the USA is perhaps best revealed in a 1988 case involving the beating to death of an Asian-American gay man. In the process of adjudicating this case, a Broward County [Florida] circuit judge jokingly asked the prosecuting attorney, 'That's a crime now, to beat up a homosexual?' The prosecutor answered, 'Yes sir. And it's also a crime to kill them.' The judge replied, 'Times have really changed' (Hentoff, 1990: n.p.).

As the twentieth-first century begins, heterosexism and homophobia were alive and well and gay-bashing continues to occur. But, unlike previous eras, violence against gays and lesbians is increasingly greeted with condemnation. Social movement mobilization, legislative reform, judicial decision-making, and law enforcement practices in the USA have merged to reconstruct gay-bashing as criminal conduct (Jenness and Grattet, 2001).

REFERENCES

Boswell, John (1980) *Christianity, Social Tolerance, and Homosexuality*. Chicago: University of Chicago Press.

California Department of Justice (1999) *Hate Crime in California: 1997*. Sacramento, CA: Division of Criminal Justice Information Services.

Comstock, Gary (1991) *Violence Against Lesbians and Gay Men*. New York: Columbia University Press.

Congressional Record (1990) 8 February: 1067–1092.

Fernandez, Joseph (1991) 'Bringing hate crimes into focus', *Harvard Civil Rights-Civil Liberties Law Review*, 26: 261–92.

Hentoff, Nat (1990) 'The violently attacked community in America', *The Weekly Newspaper of New York*, 25 September.

Herek, Gregory and Berrill, T., Kevin (1992) 'Psychological heterosexism and anti-gay violence: The social psychology of bigotry and bashing', in *Hate Crimes: Reporting Violence against Lesbians and Gay Men*. London: Sage Publications. pp. 149–169.

Herek, Gregory and Berrill, T., Kevin (1992) *Hate Crimes: Confronting Violence Against Gay Lesbian and Gay Men*. Thousand Oaks, CA: Sage Publications.

Jenness, Valerie (1999) 'Managing differences and making legislation: social movements and the racialization, sexualization, and gendering of federal hate crime law in the U.S., 1985–1999', *Social Problems*, 46: 548–71.

Jenness, Valerie and Broad, Kendal (1994) 'Anti-violence activism and the (in)visibility of gender in the gay/lesbian movement and women's movement', *Gender & Society*, 8: 402–23.

Jenness, Valerie and Broad, Kendal (1997) *Hate Crimes: New Social Movements and the Politics of Violence*. Hawthorne, New York: Aldine de Gruyter, Inc.

Jenness, Valerie and Grattet, Ryken (2001) *Building the Hate Crime Policy Domain: From Social Movement Concept of Law Enforcement Practice*. New York: Russell Sage Foundation.

Katz, Jonathan (1976) *Gay American History: Lesbians and Gay Men in the U.S.A.* New York: Thomas Y. Crowell Company.

Los Angeles Times (2000) 'Public more accepting of gays, poll finds': A3.

National Coalition of Anti-Violence Projects (1999) *Anti-Lesbian, Gay, Bisexual and Transgender Violence in 1998*. New York: New York City Gay and Lesbian Anti-Violence Project.

National Gay and Lesbian Task Force (1991) *Anti-Gay/Lesbian Violence, Victimization, and Defamation in 1990*. Washington, DC: National Gay and Lesbian Task Force Policy Institute.

O'Brien, Jodi (2001) 'Homophobia and heterosexism', in *International Encyclopedia of the Social and Behavioral Sciences*. London: Elsevier Science Limited.

Onken, Steven (1998) 'Conceptualizing violence against gay, lesbian, bisexual, intersexual, and transgendered people', in Lacey M. Sloan and Nora S. Gustavsson (eds), *Violence and Social Injustice Against Lesbian Gay and Bisexual People*. New York: The Hawthorne Press, Inc. pp. 5–24.

Perry, Barbara (2001) *In the Name of Hate: Understanding Hate Crimes*. New York: Routledge.

Rovella, David E. (1994) 'Attack on hate crime is enhanced', *National Law Journal*, 29: A1.

Seidman, Steven (1997) *Difference Troubles: Queering Social Theory and Sexual Politics*. New York: Cambridge University Press.

Sheffield, Carole J. (1992) 'Hate violence', in Paula Rothenberg (ed.), *Race, Class, and Gender in the United States*. New York: St. Martin's Press. pp. 388–97.

Schulthess, Beatrice von (1992) 'Violence in the streets: anti-lesbian assault and harassment in San Francisco', in Gregory Herek and Kevin Berrill (eds), *Hate Crimes: Confronting Violence Against Gay Lesbian and Gay Men*. Newbury Park, CA: Sage Publications. pp. 65–75.

Sloan, Lacey M. and Gustavsson, Nora S. (1998) *Violence and Social Injustice Against Lesbian Gay and Bisexual People*. New York: The Hawthorne Press, Inc.

United States Department of Justice (1998) 'Hate crime statistics', in the *Uniform Crime Report*. Washington, DC: Federal Bureau of Investigation.

Vaid, Urvashi (1995) *Virtual Equality: The Mainstreaming of Gay and Lesbian Liberation*. New York: Anchor Books.

STATUTES CITED

Ca Penal code 422.7.
Public Law 101–275
Public Law 103–322
Rev. Code Wash. 9A.36.080.

BILLS CITED

S. 1529 – Hate Crimes Prevention Act

24

Globalization and the International Gay/Lesbian Movement[1]

DENNIS ALTMAN

If by globalization we understand all those processes – social, economic, political and cultural – by which people, goods and ideas move increasingly across borders, then changes in our understandings of and attitudes to sexuality are both affected by and reflect the larger changes of globalization. Moreover, as with globalization itself, the changes are simultaneously leading to greater homogeneity and greater inequality. As all but insignificant pockets of the world's peoples are brought within the scope of global capitalism a consumer culture is developing which cuts across borders and cultures, and is universalized through advertising, mass media and the enormous flows of capital and people in the contemporary world.

While globalization has become central to much work in the social sciences over the past decade, it has hovered on the fringes of gay/lesbian/queer studies. Perhaps this is a reflection of the fact that g/l/q work remains marginalized in the academy, and is almost entirely produced in the centres of the Atlantic world. Thus even a work with as promising a title as *Fear of a Queer*

Planet remains exclusively North American in its content.[2] There are of course exceptions – a few recent anthologies do try to include discussions from outside the First World, but too often the inclusions are so thin that they appear tokenistic, and merely underscore the extent to which the dominant paradigm is based in North America and Northern Europe.[3] This is hardly surprising, though when one examines the specific literature on individual non-western countries there is far more available than is often recognized, as will be discussed later.[4] Perhaps the most egregious example is the renaming of the *Harvard Gay and Lesbian Review* to become *The Gay and Lesbian Review Worldwide*, while remaining almost exclusively American-centric in its focus.

Yet debates on globalization are particularly relevant to what appears to be a rapid spread of gay/lesbian identities, and indeed the emergence of a politicized homosexuality in countries as different as Indonesia, Peru and Zimbabwe may be one of the most potent markers of globalization itself.

HOMOSEXUAL IDENTITIES AND MOVEMENTS

The very idea of a universal homosexual category – reflected in the language of an international gay and lesbian movement – is thus a product of globalization. While homosexual behavior has existed in most societies at most times in history, the creation of a specific identity based upon homosexual behavior is a far more recent and limited phenomenon. The term 'homosexual' was coined in 1869 by the Hungarian doctor Karoly Benkert, but there is some evidence that people defined by a shared sexual attraction to the same gender had already formed loose social groupings in several European cities. More common, however, was a range of understandings of sexuality and gender which saw homosexual behavior as part of an undifferentiated range of possible sexual behaviors, and an equal range of acceptance and condemnation of such behaviors. Such understandings were always heavily gendered, and often ignored the potential for female homosexuality.

There is some debate about just when the 'homosexual', in our understanding of that term, emerged, but the rapid spread of the concept in the nineteenth century was linked to the rapid diffusion of ideas and affluence which grew out of the expansion of capitalism. Moreover, the growing scientific awareness of homosexuality owed a great deal to the growth of European colonialism, and the accompanying interest in other ways of organizing sexuality and gender in non-European societies.[5] By the end of the nineteenth century the idea of the homosexual existed to a sufficient extent that it became possible to imagine the creation of both social and political organizations for those people who identified with the term. The first overtly political organization, the Scientific-Humanitarian Committee, was founded by a German, Magnus Hirschfeld, in 1897, and campaigned for the decriminalization of homosexuality.

Hirschfeld believed that homosexuals constituted a 'third sex', and therefore were inherently different, and no more deserving of condemnation than, say, someone born left-handed. However against the idea of the 'third sex' Freud postulated a universal 'polymorphous perversity', so that childhood experiences determined whether or not one developed a primarily heterosexual or homosexual orientation. While many psychoanalysts developed a strong antipathy to homosexuality, seeing it as a pathology to be cured through therapy, another tradition, which would emerge in the 1960s, used Freud's works to argue against the idea of a heterosexual norm.

After World War I both Europe and the United States saw the development of small homosexual social groups in major cities, most famously Paris and Berlin. Hirschfeld's organization was ended brutally by the Nazis, and it was not until the aftermath of World War II that new organizations emerged – COC (originally the Shakespeare Club) in the Netherlands; Arcadie in France; der Kreis in Switzerland. COC remains by far the longest-lived gay/lesbian organization in the world. In the United States the first groups were established in the 1950s (the Mattachine Society in 1951; Daughters of Bilitis in 1955) but these groups remained largely underground, although some overt political protest began in the early 1960s.[6]

In Europe and North America the dislocations of World War II meant that millions of people came in contact with underground gay and lesbian worlds, and although the post-war organizations remained very small, homosexual communities developed in most major western cities through the 1950s and 1960s.[7] It was the presence of both social and commercial networks which allowed for the rapid emergence of a new sort of gay/lesbian movement in the aftermath of the major social and political upheavals in most liberal democracies from the end of the 1960s.

The contemporary gay/lesbian movement was born out of the political, social and cultural changes of 'the sixties', symbolized by the growing freedom which surrounded discussion of sexuality, the rebirth of feminism and the student movements of 1968. In France and Italy it was the events of May '68 which led to the emergence of a radical gay movement; in the United States the turning point is usually assumed to be the riots which followed a raid on the Stonewall Inn in Greenwich Village, out of which emerged the New York Gay Liberation Front. The gay/lesbian movement of this period saw itself as part of a larger radical assault on hegemonic cultural and political ideas and institutions, and was closely linked to various elements of New Left theory.[8] Small gay liberation groups also appeared in Canada, Britain, Scandinavia, Australasia[9] and some Latin American countries: Argentina in 1969; Mexico in 1971; Puerto Rico in 1974; Brazil in the early 1970s.[10] The first Israeli gay/lesbian organisation was established in 1976.

The post-1968 movement differed from its predecessors in its willingness to assert a new sense of gay/lesbian identity which demanded complete equality, at both an individual and a communal level. Although the original use of the term 'gay' included both women and men, tensions quickly emerged along gender lines, in part because of the strong interconnection between radical lesbianism and feminism, which had no equivalent for gay men.[11] During the 1970s there was increasing divergence between lesbian and gay male organizations, as a growing commercial gay world opened up new ways of living as a homosexual, particularly for men. As one novelist wrote: 'Almost through an act of will, I had made myself embrace this new identity of mine and never look back. I had gay friends. I ate at gay restaurants. I went to gay bars. I had my apartment near DuPont Circle ...'[12]

While 'gay ghettoes' such as that described here only developed in a few cities outside the United States – or, as in the case of Paris's Marais, developed a decade later – the growth of gay and lesbian commercial space has been a feature of almost all western countries from the 1970s on. In many capitalist societies the 'pink dollar' has become seen as an important niche market, and this has made possible a flourishing gay press and an expansion of businesses and professional services aimed at a specifically gay and lesbian market. By the 1990s government authorities in a number of countries were promoting services for lesbian and gay travellers, and Sydney's Gay & Lesbian Mardi Gras was recognized as one of Australia's most successful tourist attractions. The gay/lesbian press, originally an expression of the political movement, has become increasingly preoccupied by 'lifestyle' issues and the need to attract 'mainstream' advertisers.

Meanwhile, women developed a parallel if sometimes overlapping world, and developed a set of social institutions which allowed room for a 'women-centred' politics, sometimes extended to a rejection of anything that could be seen as male-dominated.[13] In some countries links were maintained between women and men through common political organizations such as the National Gay (later Gay and Lesbian) Task Force in the United States. As the radical energies of the early 1970s dissipated so too did organized lesbian and gay politics, though the trajectory of the movements is rather different in different countries. Even in the western world there were significant differences between the English-speaking democracies, where decriminalization of homosexual behavior seemed the top priority; the countries of northern Europe, especially the Netherlands and Denmark, where social acceptance seemed most assured; and those of southern Europe whose laws were less repressive and where a language of universal rights was often used to argue against any sort of identity politics.

The 1970s and 1980s saw a rapid shift in most western countries in attitudes towards homosexuality, with growing recognition of gay men and lesbians as constituting legitimate communities with a certain political influence. Openly lesbian and gay legislators were elected in Norway, Canada and the United States, and almost all western countries abolished remaining laws which decriminalized homosexual activity. The great exception was the United States, where homosexual acts remain illegal in a number of states, in part because of a decision by the Supreme Court in 1986 which upheld Georgia's sodomy laws. The rate of change was particularly rapid in cases such as Spain, which democratized during this period, a shift that would be echoed in Latin America in the late 1980s and some parts of Eastern Europe in the 1990s.[14]

The rapidity of changes in attitudes towards homosexuality meant a corresponding backlash from moral conservatives, most pronounced in the United States. The mobilization of religious conservatives by groups such as the Moral Majority led to bitter attacks on homosexuality, both in the political arena and, not infrequently, in direct violence. While there were examples of similar reactions elsewhere, such as the Thatcher government's prohibitions on 'the promotion of homosexuality', it is probably true that the gains for gay and lesbian rights were rapid and irreversible in most western democracies. Over the past decade these gains have increasingly spread to non-western societies.

GLOBALIZATION AND THE EMERGENCE OF GAY/LESBIAN IDENTITIES

Over the past several decades the processes of globalization have ensured a greater number of people outside the liberal western world have adopted gay/lesbian identities.[15] It is often assumed that homosexuals are defined in most 'traditional' societies as a third sex, but that too is too schematic to be universally useful. As Peter Jackson points out, the same terms in Thailand can be gender *and* sexual categories.[16] This is not as different from western assumptions as is sometimes suggested. Insofar as there is a confusion between sexuality and gender in the 'traditional' view that the 'real' homosexual is the man who behaves like a woman (or, more rarely, vice versa), this is consistent

with the dominant understanding of homosexuality in western countries during the hundred years or so before the birth of the contemporary gay movement. George Chauncey has argued that the very idea of a homosexual/heterosexual divide only became dominant in the United States in the mid-twentieth century:

> The most striking difference between the dominant sexual culture of the early twentieth century and that of our own era is the degree to which the earlier culture permitted men to engage in sexual relations with other men, often on a regular basis, without requiring them to regard themselves – or be regarded by others – as gay … Many men … neither understood nor organised their sexual practices along a hetero-homosexual axis.[17]

If one reads or views contemporary accounts of homosexual life in, say, Central America, Thailand and Côte d'Ivoire,[18] one is immediately struck by the parallels. In many 'traditional' societies there were complex variations across gender and sex lines, with 'trans-gender' people (Indonesian *warias*, Thai *kathoey*, Moroccan *hassas*; Turkish *kocek*; Luban *kitesha* in parts of Congo) characterized by both transvestite and homosexual behavior. These terms are usually – not always – applied to men, but there are other terms sometimes used of women, such as *mati* in Suriname, which also disrupt simplistic assumptions about sex and gender.[19] As Gilbert Herdt wrote: 'Sexual orintation and identity are not the keys to conceptualizing a third sex and gender across time and space.'[20]

Certainly most of the literature about Latin America stresses that a homosexual *identity* (as distinct from homosexual practices) is related to rejection of dominant gender expectations, so that 'a real man' can have sex with other men and not risk his heterosexual identity. As Roger Lancaster put it: 'Whatever else a *cochon* might or might not do, he is tacitly understood as one who assumes the receptive role in anal intercourse. His partner, defined as 'active' in the terms of their engagement, is not stigmatized, nor does he acquire a special identity of any sort.'[21] Thus the *nature* rather than the *object* of the sexual act becomes the key factor. However, there is also evidence that this is changing, and a more western concept of homosexual identity is establishing itself, especially among the middle classes.

Sexuality becomes an important arena for the production of modernity, with 'gay' and 'lesbian' identities acting as markers for modernity.[22] There is an ironic echo of this in the Singapore government's bulldozing of Bugis Street, once the centre of transvestite prostitution in the city – and its replacement by a Disneyland-like simulacrum, where sanitized drag shows are performed.[23] There is an equal irony in seeing the decline of a homosexuality defined by gender nonconformity as 'modern' just when transsexuals and some theorists in western countries are increasingly attracted by concepts of the malleability of gender.[24] From one perspective the fashionable replica of the stylized 'lipstick lesbian' or 'macho' gay man is less 'post-modern' than the *waria* or the Tongan *fakaleiti*.[25]

Speaking openly of homosexuality and transvestism, which is often the consequence of western influence, can unsettle what is accepted but not acknowledged. Indeed, there is some evidence in a number of societies that those who proclaim themselves as 'gay' or 'lesbian', that is seek a public identity based on their sexuality, encounter a hostility that may not have been previously apparent. But there is a great deal of mythology around the 'acceptance' of gender/sexual nonconformity outside the West, a mythology to which for different reasons both westerners and non-westerners contribute. Romanticized views around homoeroticism in many non-western cultures, often based on travel experiences, disguise the reality of persecution, discrimination and violence, sometimes in unfamiliar forms. First-hand accounts make it clear that homosexuality is far from being universally accepted – or even tolerated – in such apparent 'paradises' as Morocco, the Philippines,Thailand or Brazil:

Lurking behind the Brazilians' pride of their flamboyant drag queens, their recent adulation of a transvestite chosen as a model of Brazilian beauty, their acceptance of gays and lesbians as leaders of the country's most widely practised religion and the constitutional protection of homosexuality, lies a different truth. Gay men, lesbians and transvestites face widespread discrimination, oppression and extreme violence.[26]

The emphasis of post-modern theory on pastiche, parody, hybridity, etc. is played out in a real way by women and men who move, often with considerable comfort, from apparent obedience to official norms to their own sense of gay community. Middle-class homosexuals in places like Kuala Lumpur, Mexico City and Istanbul will speak of themselves as part of 'a gay (sometimes 'gay and lesbian') community', but the institutions of such a community will vary considerably depending on both economic resources and political space. Those who take on gay identities often aspire to be part of global culture in all its forms, as suggested by this quote from a Filipino anthology of gay writing: 'I met someone in a bar last Saturday … He's a bank executive. He's mestizo (your type) and … loves Barbara Streisand, Gabriel Garcia Marquez, Dame Margot Fonteyn, Pat Conroy, Isabel Allende, John Williams, Meryl Streep, Armistead Maupin, k.d. lang, Jim Chappell, Margaret Atwood and Luciano Pavorotti.'[27]

Similarly, magazines, like *G & L* in Taiwan – a 'lifestyle' magazine launched in 1996 – mixes local news and features with stories on international, largely American, gay and lesbian icons. As mobility increases, more and more people are travelling abroad and meeting foreigners at home. It is as impossible to prevent new identities and categories travelling as it is to prevent pornography travelling across the Internet. As part of the economic growth of South and East Asia, the possibilities of computer-based communications have been grasped with enormous enthusiasm. They have created a new set of possibilities for the diffusion of information and the creation of (virtual) communities. Whereas the gay movements of the 1970s in the West depended heavily on the creation of a gay/lesbian press, in countries such as Malaysia, Thailand or Japan the Internet offers the same possibilities, with the added attraction of anonymity and instant contact with overseas, thus fostering the links with the diaspora.

It is precisely this constant dissemination of images and ways of being, moving disproportionately from north to south, which leads some commentators to savagely criticize the spread of sexual identities as a new step in neocolonialism: 'The very constitution of a subject entitled to rights involves the violent capture of the disenfranchised by an institutional discourse which inseparably weaves them into the textile of global capitalism.'[28] This position is argued with splendid hyperbole by Pedro Bustos-Aguilar who attacks both 'the gay ethnographer ... [who] kills a native with the charm of his camera' and 'the union of the New World Order and Transnational Feminism' that asserts neocolonialism and western hegemony in the name of supposed universalisms.[29]

Bustos-Aguilar's argument is supported by the universalist rhetoric that surrounded the celebration of the twenty-fifth anniversary of Stonewall, and the pressure to support the rights of 'gay, lesbian, bisexual and transgender people' everywhere, even though this is a particularly American formulation. It finds a troubling echo in the story of an American, Tim Wright, who founded a gay movement in Bolivia, and after four years was found badly beaten and amnesiac: 'And things have gone back to being what they were.'[30] A more measured critique comes from Ann Ferguson, who has warned that the very concept of an international lesbian *culture* is politically problematic, because it would almost certainly be based upon western assumptions, even though she is somewhat more optimistic about the creation of an international *movement*, which would allow for self-determination of local lesbian communities.[31] While western influences were clearly present, it is as true to see the emergence of

groups in much of Latin America, in South-East Asia and among South African blacks as driven primarily by local forces (and successful in South Africa because of links established under apartheid with the African National Congress).

It is certainly true that the assertion of lesbian/gay identity can have neo-colonial implications, but given that many anti-/post-colonial movements and governments deny existing homosexual traditions it becomes difficult to know exactly whose values are being imposed on whom. Both the western outsider and the local custodians of national culture are likely to ignore existing realities in the interest of ideological certainty. Those outside the West tend to be more aware of the difference between traditional homosexualities and contemporary gay identity politics, a distinction sometimes lost by the international lesbian/gay movement in its eagerness to claim universality. New sexual identities mean a loss of certain traditional cultural comforts while offering new possibilities to those who adopt them.

THE IMPACT OF HIV/AIDS

The first reports of what was to be named 'AIDS' (acquired immune deficiency syndrome) accompanied severe illness and death among young homosexual men on both American coasts, and for a short time the new disease was known as 'gay-related immune deficiency syndrome'. Within a few years it became clear that the syndrome was transmitted through sexual and blood contact, and in many parts of the world the bulk of sexual transmission was heterosexual. Nonetheless the epidemiological link to homosexuals in the rich world has a continuing impact on how the epidemic is perceived, and has had a major impact upon gay organization. The first responses to the new disease came from gay communities in major western cities, with the Gay Men's Health Crisis (GMHC) in New York (founded in 1982) becoming a model for groups such as the various Australian state AIDS Councils, the Terrence Higgins Trust in Britain and the Deutsche AIDS Hilfe (Germany).

During the 1980s the need to lobby governments, to provide information and preventive education, and to develop home-care and emotional support for those with HIV/AIDS, dominated gay movements in most western countries, and sometimes involved considerable numbers of lesbians as well. As the epidemic was discovered to be growing very rapidly in Africa and parts of Latin America, AIDS was to be the focus for a new wave of homosexual organizing in a number of 'developing' countries. (Homosexual transmission continues to be significant in many parts of the poor world, even if it is not the major mode of transmission in most countries.) Groups such as Pink Triangle in Malaysia or Triangulo Rosa in Costa Rica came into existence as *de facto* homosexual organizations because of the epidemic.[32] The development of People With AIDS groups built on the earlier gay movement concept of 'coming out'.

Programs around HIV/AIDS have often made use of identities such as 'sex worker' or 'gay/bisexual men'/'men who have sex with men' (MSMs), thus assisting the further globalization of movements based on such identities. (Ironically the term 'men who have sex with men' was coined to reach men who rejected any sense of identity based upon their sexual practices, but fairly quickly became used in ways that just repeated the old confusions between behavior and identity.) Even while recognizing the diversity of sexualities, and the fact that for most people behavior does not necessarily match neat categories, there is a gradual shift towards conceptualizing sexuality as a central basis for identity in most parts of the world in which HIV programs have played a significant role. To quote from one example, a report from Proyecto Girasol, an HIV prevention program in El Salvador:

When the work started in 1994, few people imagined that this kind of organizing would be

accepted or could have an impact. But the space was opened and defended with organization and visibility, and the project built self-esteem within the sex-workers and gay community, 'changing their self-destructive image into a constructive one'. For the first time a positive self-identified gay community was established in El Salvador.[33]

The impact of AIDS on the gay/lesbian movement varied from country to country, but overall it meant a much closer relationship between the state and gay organizations, particularly in countries such as Denmark, Switzerland, Canada and Australia where the epidemic remained largely due to homosexual transmission and national strategies incorporated community responses. At a global level the development of international responses through the Global Program on AIDS and then UNAIDS saw some institutional support for community organizations, including gay ones.

THE DEVELOPMENT OF AN INTERNATIONAL GAY/LESBIAN MOVEMENT

In 1978 the International Gay (later Lesbian and Gay) Association (ILGA) was formed at a conference in Coventry, England. While ILGA has largely been driven by northern Europeans, it now has member groups from over seventy countries and has organized meetings in several southern cities. (Its attempt to win observer status at the United Nations Economic and Social Council was stymied by attacks on some of its members as allegedly sympathetic to pedophilia.) Other networks, often linked to feminist and AIDS organizing, have been created in the past two decades, and emerging lesbian and gay movements are increasingly likely to be in constant contact with groups across the world. Such networks argue for a certain universality of homosexual identity, and their major strategy has involved appeals to universal norms of human rights to oppose persecution and discrimination against homosexuals across the world.

It is striking that while the dominant image of gay and lesbian identity and culture is undoubtedly American, the development of international networks has owed comparatively little to American leadership. On the other hand, the two largest international gay/lesbian 'networks' are probably those based around the Metropolitan Community Church and the Gay Games, both American in origin.

In many cases homosexual identities are asserted without an apparent gay/lesbian movement. The best example of a non-political gay world can probably be found in Thailand where there is a growing middle-class gay world, based neither on prostitution nor on traditional forms of gender nonconformity (as in the person of the *kathoey*) but only a small lesbian group, Anjaree, and no gay male groups at all since the collapse of a couple of attempts to organize around HIV in the late 1980s.[34] In late 1996 controversy erupted in Thailand after the governing body of the country's teacher training colleges decreed that 'sexual deviants' would be barred from entering the colleges. While there was considerable opposition to the ban (subsequently dropped), apart from Anjaree most of this came from non-gay sources. In the ensuing public debate one could see contradictory outside influences at work – both an imported fear of homosexuals and a more modern emphasis on how such a ban infringed human rights. As Peter Jackson concluded: 'A dynamic gay scene has emerged ... in the complete absence of a gay rights movement'.[35]

Indeed, it may be that a political movement is the least likely part of western concepts of homosexual identity to be adopted in many parts of the world, even as some activists enthusiastically embrace the mores and imagery of western queerdom. The particular form of identity politics that allowed for the mobilization of lesbian/gay electoral pressure in countries like the United States, the Netherlands or even France may not be appropriate elsewhere, even if western-style liberal democracy

triumphs. The need for western lesbian/gays to engage in identity politics as a means of enhancing self-esteem may not be felt in other societies. Even so, one should read Jackson's comment about Thailand with some caution. Already when he wrote it there was an embryonic group in Bangkok around an American-owned and run gay bookstore. At the end of 1999 one of the country's gay papers organized a gay festival and twilight parade in the heart of Bangkok, announcing it as: 'the first and biggest gay parade in Asia where Asian gay men have a basic human right to be who they want to be and love who they want to love.'[36] The following year there was speculation in the press of the role of 'the pink vote' in Bangkok's elections. Similarly, accounts of homosexual life in Japan alternate between assuming a high degree of acceptance – and therefore no reason for a political movement – and severe restrictions on the space to assert homosexual identity as against behavior, though the gay group OCCUR has recently gained a certain degree of visibility.

The western lesbian/gay movement emerged in conditions of affluence and liberal democracy, where despite other large social issues it was possible to develop a politics around sexuality that is more difficult in countries where the basic structures of political life are constantly contested. Writing of contemporary South Africa Mark Gevisser notes: 'Race-identification overpowers everything else – class, gender and sexuality.'[37] In the same way basic questions of political economy and democratization will impact on the future development of gay/lesbian movements in much of Asia and Africa. Yet in Latin America and Eastern Europe gay/lesbian movements have grown considerably in the past decade, and there are now signs of their emergence in some parts of Africa, for example, in Botswana and in Zimbabwe where President Mugabe has consistently attacked homosexuality as the product of colonialism.[38] Similar rhetoric has come from the leaders of Kenya,[39] Namibia and

Uganda, whose President Museveni has denounced homosexuality as 'western' – using the rhetoric of the Christian right to do so.[40] (Anglican bishops from Africa – though not South Africa – were crucial in defeating moves to change the Church of England's attitudes towards homosexuality at the 1998 decennial Lambeth Conference.)

While many African officials and clergy maintain that homosexuality is not part of pre-colonial African culture, the evidence for its existence – and the slow acknowledgment of its role in African life – are happening across the continent. One might speculate that the strong hostility from some African political and religious leaders towards homosexuality as a 'western import' is an example of psychoanalytic displacement, whereby anxieties about sexuality are redirected to continuing resentment against colonialism and the subordinate position of Africa within the global economy. Western-derived identities can easily become markers of those aspects of globalization that are feared and opposed. Thus a 1994 Conference for gay/MSMs in Bombay was opposed by the National Federation of Indian Women, an affiliate of the Communist Party of India, as: 'an invasion of India by decadent western cultures and a direct fall-out of our signing the GATT agreement.'[41]

Six years later a number of such conferences had been held in India and there were also signs of growing political hostility, as in the protest directed against Deepa Mehta's film *Fire* for its lesbian content. The twin impact of globalization and the discourses of international human rights are likely to see a strengthening of both gay/lesbian identities and arguments to include homosexuality within the framework of international human rights in the future, but there is also the likelihood of increasing fundamentalist hostility to any form of sexual-based identity politics. The question, as Richard Parker has posed it, is whether: 'We can transform the politics of identity into the politics of solidarity.'[42]

NOTES

1 This chapter draws in part from my book *Global Sex* (Chicago: University of Chicago Press, 2001).

2 Michael Warner (ed.), *Fear of a Queer Planet* (Minneapolis: University of Minnesota Press, 1993).

3 Of the 42 chapters in the influential *Lesbian and Gay Studies Reader* (eds, H. Abelove, M. Barale and D. Halperin, London: Routledge, 1993), three deal with non-western countries – all by professors in American universities. Of the 840-plus pages in Mark Blasius and Shane Phelan's *We Are Everywhere* (New York: Roultledge, 1997), more are devoted to the history of the Mattachine Society and the Daughters of Bilitis than to the entire non-Atlantic world. Ken Plummer's *Modern Homosexualities* (London: Routledge, 1992) devotes two of its nineteen chapters to non-western societies. A significant exception is B. Adam, J.W. Duyvendak and A. Krouwel, *The Global Emergence of Gay and Lesbian Politics* (Philadelphia: Temple University Press, 1999), although even here most of the non-western chapters are written by first world academics.

4 Examples of edited volumes where there has been a genuine attempt to locate both non-western topics and contributors are Peter Aggleton: *Bisexualities and AIDS* (London: Taylor & Francis, 1996) and *Men Who Sell Sex* (London: UCL, 1999); and Peter Drucker, *Different Rainbows* (London: GMP, 2000).

5 See Neville Hoad, 'Arrested development or the queerness of savages', *Postcolonial Studies Journal*, 3 (2): 2000.

6 John d'Emilio, *Sexual Politics, Sexual Communities* (Chicago: University of Chicago Press, 1983).

7 See, e.g., John Loughery, *The Other Side of Silence* (New York: Holt, 1998, Part III); Elizabeth Kennedy and Madeline Davis, *Boots of Leather, Slippers of Gold* (New York: Routledge, 1993); Garry Wotherspoon, *City of the Plain: History of a Gay Sub-Culture*, (Sydney: Hale and Iremonger, 1991); David Higgs (ed.), *Queer Sites: Urban Histories Since 1600* (New York: Routledge, 1999).

8 Dennis Altman, *Homosexual: Oppression and Liberation* (New York: Outerbridge and Dienstfrey, 1971) (new edition, New York University Press, 1996).

9 See Jeffrey Weeks, *Coming Out: Homosexual Politics in Britain from the Nineteenth Century to the Present*, revised edition (London: Quartet, 1990) Gary Kinsman, *The Regulation of Desire: Sexuality in Canada* (Montreal: Black Rose Books, 1987) Karen Lutzen, 'Gay and lesbian politics: assimilation or subversion: a Danish perspective', in J. Lofstrom (ed.), *Scandinavian Homosexualities* (Binghampton: Harrington Park Press, 1998: 233–43) Geoffrey Woolcock and Dennis Altman, 'The largest street party in the world: the gay & lesbian movement in Australia' in B. Adam, J.W. Duyvendak and A. Krouwel, *The Global Emergence of Gay and Lesbian Politics* (Philadelphia: Temple University Press, 1999: 326–43).

10 See the bibliography in Daniel Balderston and Donna Guy, *Sex and Sexuality in Latin America* (New York: New York University Press, 1997: 259–77) Stephen Brown, 'Democracy and sexual difference: the lesbian and gay movement in Argentina', in Adam, et al., *The Global Emergence of Gay and Lesbian Politics* (Philadelphia: Temple University Press: 110–32); James Green, *Beyond Carnival* (Chicago: University of Chicago Press, 1999: 262–77); Richard Parker, *Beneath the Equator* (New York: Routledge, 1999) and the special issue of *Culture, Health and Society* on 'alternative sexualities and changing identities among Latin American men', edited by Richard Parker and Carlos Carceres 1:3 July–September 1999.

11 See, e.g., Lillian Faderman, *Surpassing the Love of Men* (New York: Morrow, 1981).

12 Paul Russell, *Sea of Tranquillity* (New York: Dutton, 1994: 23).

13 See Arlene Stein, *Sex and Sensibility* (Berkeley, CA: University of California Press, 1997).

14 Scott Long, 'Gay and lesbian movements in Eastern Europe', in Adams et al. *The Global Emergence of Gay and Lesbian Politics*, op. cit.: 242–65.

15 This assertion needs to be qualified very carefully, as a number of critics have made clear. See my 'On global queering', *Australian Humanities Review* 2, July 1996 (electronic journal: http/www.lib.latrobe.edu.au) and responses by, among others, Chris Berry, Gary Dowsett, David Halperin, Christopher Lane, Fran Martin and Michael Tan. And compare the cover story in *Asia Week*: 'Sex: how Asia is changing', 23 June, 1995 and 'It's normal to be queer', *The Economist*, 6 January 1996.

16 See Peter Jackson: 'Kathoey><gay><man: the historical emergence of gay male identity in Thailand', in Lenore Manderson and Margaret Jolley, *Sites of Desire/Economies of Pleasure* (Chicago: University of Chicago Press, 1997: 166–90).

17 George Chauncey, *Gay New York* (New York: Basic Books, 1994: 65).

18 For example, Annick Prieur *Mema's House Mexico City* (Chicago: University of Chicago Press, 1998) Jacobo Schifter, *From Toads to Queens* (New York: Haworth, 1999); Peter Jackson and Gerard Sullivan (eds), *Lady Boys, Tom Boys, Rent Boys* (New York: Haworth, 1999); *Woubi Cheri*, directed by Philip Brooks and Laurent Bocahut, Paris Dominant Films, September 1998.

19 Gloria Wekker, 'What's identity got to do with it?: Rethinking identity in light of the Mati work in Suriname', in E. Blackwood and S. Wieringa (eds), *Female Desires: Same-Sex Relations and Transgender Practices Across Cultures*, (New York: Columbia University Press 1999: 119–38). Compare the very complex typologies of 'same-sex' groups in S Murray and W. Roscoe (eds), *Boy-Wives and Female Husbands* (New York: St. Martin's Press, 1998: 279–82), and the chapter by Rudolph Gaudio on 'male lesbians and other queer notions in Hausa' ibid.: 115–28.

20 Gilbert Herdt, *Third Sex, Third Gender* (New York: Zone Books, 1994: 47).

21 Roger Lancaster, '"That we should all turn queer?": Homosexual stigma in the making of manhood and the breaking of revolution in Nicaragua', in Richard Parker and John Gagnon, *Conceiving Sexuality* (New York: Routledge, 1995: 150).

22 See Henning Bech, *When Men Meet: Homosexuality and Modernity* (Chicago: University of Chicago Press, 1997); Ken Plummer, *The Making of the Modern Homosexual* (London: Hutchinson, 1981); Steven Seidman, *Difference Troubles: Queering Social Theory and Sexual Politics* (New York: Cambridge University Press, 1997).

23 See Laurence Wai-teng Leong, 'Singapore', in D. West and R. Green, *Sociolegal Control of Homosexuality* (New York: Plenum, 1997: 134) and the remarkable Singapore film *Bugis Street* (1995, directed by Yon Fan) – remarkable for having been made at all.

24 For example, Sandy Stone, 'The empire strikes back: A posttransexual manifesto', in P. Treichler, L. Cartwright and C. Penley (eds), *The Visible Woman* (New York: New York University Press, 1998: 285–309).

25 See Niko Besnier, 'Sluts and superwomen: the politics of gender liminality in urban Tonga', *Ethnos*, 62: 1–2, 1997: 5–31.

26. Sereine Steakley, 'Brazil can be tough and deadly for gays', *Bay Windows* (Boston) 16 June 1994.

27 Jerry Z. Torres, 'Coming out', in Neil Garcia and Danton Remoto, *Ladlad: An Anthology of Philippine Gay Writing* (Manila: Anvil, 1994: 128).

28 Pheng Cheah, 'Posit(ion)ing human rights in the current global conjuncture', *Public Culture*, 1997: 9: 261.

29 Pedro Bustos-Aguilar, 'Mister don't touch the banana', *Critique of Anthropology*, 15 (2) Fall 1995: 149–70.

30 Pedro Albornoz, 'Landlocked state', *Harvard Gay and Lesbian Review*, Winter, 1999: 17.

31 Ann Ferguson, 'Is there a lesbian culture?' in J. Allen (ed.), *Lesbian Philosophies and Cultures*, (New York: Albany State University of New York Press, 1990: 63–88).

32 Dennis Altman, *Power and Community* (London: Taylor and Francis, 1994).

33 Report from Support Proyecto Girasol, NGO Workshop on HIV/AIDS and Human Rights, Geneva June, 1998. Compare Timothy and Richard Wright, 'Bolivia: developing a gay community', in D. West and R. Green, *Sociolegal Control of Homosexuality* (New York: Plenum, 1997: 97–108).

34 See Andrew Matzner, 'Paradise not', *Harvard Gay and Lesbian Review*, 6:1 Winter, 1999: 42–4.

35 Peter Jackson, 'Beyond bars and boys: life in gay Bangkok', *Outrage* (Melbourne), July 1997: 61–3.

36 Statement from *Male* magazine, quoted in *Brother/Sister*, Melbourne, 16 September 1999: 51.

37 Mark Gevisser, 'Gay life in South Africa', in Peter Drucker (ed.), *Different Rainbows* (London: GMP, 2000).

38 Dean Murphy, 'Zimbabwe's gays go "out" at Great Risk', *Los Angeles Times*, 27 July 1998.

39 For one view of the situation in Kenya see Wanjira Kiama, 'Men who have sex with men in Kenya', in Martin Foreman, *AIDS and Men*, op. cit: 115–26.

40 Chris McGreal, 'Gays are main evil, say African leaders', *Guardian Weekly*, 7–13 October: 4.

41 *Times of India*, November 9 1994, quoted by Sherry Joseph and Pawan Dhall, 'No silence please, we're Indians', in Peter Drucker (ed.), *Different Rainbows* (London: GMP, 2000).

42 Richard Parker, *Beneath the Equator*. (New York: Routledge, 1999: 231).

25

Nationalism Has a Lot to Do with It! Unraveling Questions of Nationalism and Transnationalism in Lesbian/Gay Studies

JYOTI PURI

The title of this chapter has already staked out a position on the question of whether nationalism has anything to do with lesbian and gay politics. But, why consider the connections between nationalisms and lesbian and gay politics? If there indeed exists such a link, then what are its characteristics and ramifications? These are the questions that form the basis of this chapter. Although, I would argue that considering the issues and limitations of nationalisms is crucial for any text on lesbian/gay studies, it is not an issue that is typically included. The most obvious reason, of course, to consider the connections between nationalisms and sexualities is that along with gender, race, and ethnicity, national and sexual identities are crucial markers of our selves.[1] Not only do these aspects of our identities influence whether you or I belong to certain communities – let us suppose (North) 'American' or 'Asian American lesbian' – but these identities also help establish who is socially privileged or marginalized. I would hazard that the failure to address issues of nationalism in mainstream lesbian/gay studies within the USA, with some exceptions, is a reflection of two issues: that scholarly concerns against 'compulsory heterosexuality' and homophobia are expressed in other areas of social life; the complacency that comes with carrying a North American passport.

In contrast, I suggest that it is crucial to examine the links between national and lesbian and gay sexual identities for two reasons. First, as I will argue below, such an exploration will help us understand how nationalism privileges heterosexuality and how it excludes certain sexualities. For example, popular descriptives associated with the US nation – superpower, protector, family values – promote masculinity and heterosexuality at the cost of suppressing what are seen as deviant characteristics, such as homosexuality. In order to understand these links between national and sexual identities, I will attempt to bring together insights from feminist and lesbian/gay scholarship; but, given the relative dearth of scholarship on nationalisms in lesbian/gay studies, I will focus on the links between nationalisms and lesbian and gay sexualities. To that extent, then, this discussion is partly an overview of the issues and insights that have emerged in this area of study. But, beyond mapping the issues, I am also concerned with where discussions of nationalisms are present within mainstream lesbian/gay studies. To this aim, I will draw upon the scholarship in Asian American lesbian/gay/queer studies that addresses questions of nationalisms.[2]

Second, I explore the links between nationalism and lesbian and gay sexualities to indicate the limits of nationalism. If, indeed, nationalism attempts to exclude and marginalize lesbian and gay identities, then we need to consider the possibilities of *including* these identities within nationalism.[3] Could lesbian/gay and marginalized racial identities be seen as so innate a part of French nationalism, for example, so that a lesbian/Algerian/citizen belongs fully and unequivocally? Given the breadth of the question, I will address it from the vantage point of Asian American queers to argue that the nation is a limited political and social construct to mount a movement for inclusion. On the contrary, I will identify the importance of examining emergent sexual identities with a transnational, globalizing cultural framework. Hardly a matter of unrestrained celebration, I will argue that it is necessary to carefully investigate this transnational context that both enables and restricts possibilities of sexual identities. Here, I will also suggest that disciplines such as sociology and anthropology bear particular responsibility to shed light on the social and cultural conditions under which we see the proliferation of sexual identities in disparate social contexts.

NATIONALISMS AND SEXUALITIES

While nationalism seems to connote popular images of parades, flags, celebrations of independence in the ex-colonies, and fights between soccer fans from competing countries, these are but a few of its complex and contradictory manifestations. A rich body of scholarship on nationalisms has demonstrated that the concept of nation may appear to symbolize unity between a group of people who imagine themselves with a shared past and a shared future, but it is, in fact invented, exclusionary and hierarchical. In what has by now become the most well-cited book on nationalism, *Imagined Communities: Reflections on the Origins and Spread of Nationalism*, Benedict Anderson (1983) cautions us that 'official nationalisms' are not unreal; instead, they are invented in the sense that although the concept of nation seems to have emerged in the nineteenth century amidst colonial encounters, it is characterized by claims of a deep historical past and of common cultural traditions. For example, although India as a nation came into existence only in the nineteenth century under British colonialism, nationalists claimed that 'India' had existed since antiquity and there were 'ancient Indian traditions'. Nations have also to be invented in the sense that people have to imagine a shared identity with an extended and otherwise impersonal community, according to Anderson. Consider the contemporary Indian nation of approximately one billion people who are marked by an almost unimaginable range of differences in language, ethnicity, color, region, religion, sexualities, genders, opinions, beliefs, and traditions who would have to, or be forced to, buy into the idea of a shared national identity and a sense of belonging to the community of nation. This shared national identity would have to be invented and constantly reinforced in order to seem natural.

Furthermore, the fact that nations are characterized by sharp inequalities of gender, class, race, sexuality, ethnicity, to name a few, belies the claim that all citizens are equal. Some citizens are more equal than others and others are denied claims to citizenship despite shared experiences (permanent, undocumented workers in various parts of the world). And as Anne McClintock (1995) reminds us, no nation gives women and men equal access to the rights and resources of the nation–state. But, if nations are characterized by a fundamental contradiction between the ideology of (equal) citizenship and the reality of profound inequality along vectors of gender, race, ethnicity, and sexuality, then each nation attempts to contain and manage the contradictions through implicit and explicit violence. Clearly, the institutionalization of racism, sexism, and homophobia in the USA through the legal system simultaneously violates the rights of citizens who are of color, women, and lesbian or gay.

Like other dimensions of identity, the meaning of nationalism is possible only within a framework of difference and opposition. Representations of the aggressive and sometimes loud (North) American are contrasted with those of the proper, restrained Englishman. Which American? Which Englishmen? Hardly innate characteristics, these representations come to have meaning only within a framework in which one national identity can be specified only in opposition to another. National identity can be specified within a framework that both recognizes nations as an indisputable reality and permits the endless elaboration of what makes one nation different from another, particularly since there are no inherent qualities of nations. And, if there are no inherent, objective characteristics that identify one nation from another, then it is necessary to call into question the relations of power that produce these differences. The stereotype of the hard-working German is an arbitrary representation of historical relations of power and can only exist in relation to the characterizations of the more laid-back French or the unabashedly racist representations of the lazy but sunny Jamaican. At the same time, without the endless rehashing of representations, however contradictory, of national identity both from within and outside the nation, the inventiveness of nationalism would, indeed, be laid bare.

More specifically, the question of why it is important to theorize issues of nationalisms, sexualities, and genders was first addressed by feminist scholarship on Third World and settler societies. That contrary to putative understandings, issues of gender and sexuality are inextricable from, not irrelevant to, representations of nationalism, was effectively argued by scholars working at the margins of white, Western mainstream feminisms. However, for political reasons, the early feminist scholarship limited its focus to women.[4] This scholarship demonstrated how women's bodies, sexualities, and gender correlates are the mainstays of national identity or what is constituted as national cultural tradition and necessary to identify one kind of nationalism from another. Typically, women of the so-called respectable classes embodied what characterized a nation (such as ideals of womanhood and sexuality helped constitute what is Britishness, Americanness or Indianness) and other groups of women were excluded, marginalized, or used as a foil for oppositional, desirable representations of nationalism. However, these feminist insights are also limited in that the concept of womanhood is assumed and prescribed within the framework of patriarchy and sexuality is seen as synonymous with heterosexuality.

In contrast, another strand of feminist literature problematized notions of womanhood and did not assume heterosexuality, but without fully exploring issues of lesbian and gay sexualities.[5] Moving beyond a narrow focus on womanhood, this feminist scholarship helped clarify how nationalisms are not simply predicated on the bodies and heterosexualities of women; instead, nationalisms thought of in gendered and sexualized terms. Speaking of the profoundly gendered nature of nationalisms, Cynthia Enloe (1989) instructively argues that only rarely have nationalist movements taken women's experiences as the starting point for understanding the self, but, in fact, nationalism has typically sprung from masculinized memory, masculinized humiliation, and masculinized hope. These assertions of masculinity are also rooted in sexism, forms of racism, and homophobia. For example, according to Enloe, that nationalists have frequently assumed that an assault on ethnic Albanian women by Serbian soldiers was a war crime is not widely disputed. At the same time, the sexual assault can be seen as a crime of war insofar as Serbian soldiers raped Albanian women as a way to violate the honor and integrity of the community, and ethnic Albanians and the wider international community also recognize it as such.

What is undoubtedly useful about the above feminist scholarship is that not only does it identify the ways in which gender and sexual identities of women, in particular, are used to define nationalisms, but it also emphasizes the importance of not separating understandings of nationalism from issues of gender and sexuality. Furthermore, this literature effectively emphasizes the role of women in reproducing and resisting the dominant ideologies of nationalism. This literature has mapped the ways in which women are not simply passive recipients of nationalist ideologies, but active participants in reinforcing and challenging such ideologies. However, if the scholarly contribution of this literature lies in its attention to challenging the seemingly gender-neutral conceptualizations of nationalism and emphasizing the centrality of women and women's sexualities thereof, then this also marks its limitations. This literature elaborates the importance of gender and sexuality through an emphasis on women and their sexuality as a corollary of gender. In effect, in some cases feminist literature explicitly reinforces a heterosexual model by assuming a heterosexual model of womanhood and, in other cases, it fails to take on questions of lesbian and gay sexualities more directly. In either case, heterosexuality is not adequately challenged.

LESBIAN AND GAY POLITICS AND NATIONALISMS

In light of feminist considerations of nationalism, gender, and heterosexuality, the limited amount of scholarship within lesbian/gay studies on matters of nationalism is especially puzzling. Aside from the gaps in scholarship, as Gayatri Gopinath (1997) suggests in her essay on lesbian and gay South Asian sexualities, such omissions simply leave intact dominant constructions of the nation as essentially heterosexual. Calling attention to the work on domestic violence within Indian immigrant communities and the patriarchal immigrant perception of women as repositories of 'Indianness' and 'home', Gopinath argues that within this framework, a non-heterosexual Indian woman is a contradiction in terms; not only is she excluded from home/nation, but she is, quite literally, unimaginable.

This omission in lesbian/gay studies, then also leaves unchallenged the ways in which nationalisms and their 'imagined communities' are less likely to include lesbian and gay sexualities. Making this point in the collection, *Nationalisms and Sexualities*, an early and ground-breaking intervention in this area, Parker et al. (1992) suggest that certain sexual identities and practice are less represented and less representable in nationalism. For example, the exclusion of avowed lesbian, bisexual, and gays from the US military is objectionable for several reasons, the least of which is that these women and men are denied the ability to represent the nation and its 'Americanness'. This attempt to erase certain identities and sexual practices from representations of nationalism is yet again reflected in the words of Dr K. Abhayambika, a professor of medicine and state AIDS programme officer in Kerala, India:

> Even at the end of the twentieth century, the Eastern culture is untinged in its tradition of high morality, monogamous marriage system and safe sex behavior. Our younger generation and youth still practice virginity till their nuptial day. The religious customs and God-fearing living habits are a shield of protection against social evils. It will be difficult for the HIV to penetrate this shield except in certain metropolitan populations.[6]

Therefore, these considerations indicate that the challenge is not to merely add to the few studies on lesbian and gay politics and issues of nationalism; rather, it is also important to confront the ways in which nationalisms may privilege heterosexuality while marginalizing other sexualities. Available studies on lesbian and gay politics and issues of nationalism, attempt to address both of these concerns. Based on these studies, there are four major insights that are detailed below.

Strategies for Equal Rights for Marginalized Sexualities and Genders

One of the important concerns within the literature that deals with nationalisms and lesbian and gay sexualities is the way in which sexual minorities are excluded from full participation in social life and the way in which these exclusions can be challenged. In his article on the issue of exclusion of gays and lesbians from participation in the affairs of the nation and the ways in which social identities can enable the exercise of civil rights, Richard K. Herrell (1996) argues that three areas of social life are crucial to the discourse of 'good citizens'. Herrell identifies religious association, family life, and local politics as the crucial spaces where homosexuality is marginalized. He argues that models of lesbian and gay communities and politics since the 1960s, such as banding together to bring change in the public policy on HIV/AIDS, represent changes in self-representation about being gay and lesbian and about claiming the right to be citizens of the nation.

Yet, where this discourse of individual rights comes into conflict with a discourse of collective or communal rights, a rights-based strategy may only be partly effective. This is especially salient for lesbian and gay politics in non-Western cultural contexts that do not unapologetically promote individual rights. Showing how the more individual rights-based language of lesbian and gay identities can be only partly effective, in her discussion on homosexuality in Zimbabwe, Margrete Aarmo (1999) details the unashamed public expression of homophobia by President Mugabe in 1995. Mugabe expressed common perceptions that homosexuality does not exist in African cultures, that it is deeply offensive to the moral cultural fiber, that it is something imposed by foreign cultures, that it is about the inversion of sex roles, and that no rights could be accorded to people avowing such identities. In effect, Aarmo suggests that organizations such as Gay and Lesbians in Zimbabwe (GALZ) and social practices and activities, such as drag shows, are important in enabling gays and lesbian to counter their exclusion from national life, church, and family. However, this self-representation as gays or lesbians appears to signify individualism, Western modernity, and the dissolution of 'traditional' values in the context of Zimbabwe, thereby creating the backlash against them, according to Aarmo.

Echoing these tensions of modernity, nationalisms and more fully addressing the limitations of a politics that foregrounds the rights of sexual and gender minorities, Tan beng hui (1999) raises concerns about the surveillance of female sexuality, and, in particular, deviant female sexuality, as part of the larger project of nation-building in contemporary Malaysia. Beng hui cites the highly publicized case of a 21-year-old Malay woman impersonating a man in order to marry another women to argue that her impersonation represents an available strategy of resistance against the dominant discourse on deviant female sexuality articulated in the nation. In the absence of a politics of individual rights that is the basis of lesbian and gay identities, beng hui shows how a Malay woman would use strategies that might be more effective under the circumstances. Insofar as Western- or US-centered lesbian/gay studies scholarship and politics promote this rights-based politics across social settings, without being attentive to the attendant tensions and limitations, it can only be arbitrarily effective.

Unraveling Dualities of Homo/Hetero in Representations of Nationalism

In contrast to this rights-based focus and its strengths and limitations in multiple contexts, another strand of scholarship is more closely focused on questions of nationalisms and sexualities that are seen in dual terms – homo/hetero sexualities. This strand of scholarship is more attentive to how a binary model of sexuality is actively produced and, contrary to intuitive wisdom, how the privileging of heterosexuality in nationalism is inextricable from the marginalization of homosexuality. In others words, representations of nationalism can explicitly or implicitly promote heterosexuality only insofar as they acknowledge the possibility of non-heterosexuality – in this case, homosexuality. In the case of the Bahamas, Jacqui Alexander (1997) argues that 'good citizenship' is not only linked to heterosexuality, but it also is predicated on the creation of a subordinate class – of lesbians, gay men, prostitutes, those who are HIV-infected, and an oversexed band of citizens. Alexander specifies the three attendant strategies as making violent heterosexuality appear normal in relation to same-sex desire, the organization of a contradictory quasi-scientific discourse that rationalizes homophobia, and the reconstruction of an idyllic past in which the Bahamas were free from signs of Western decadence and lesbians and gay men.

The collection that perhaps best attempted to unravel how dualities such as homo/hetero and masculine/feminine are actively produced through and, in turn, enable characterizations of nation and national identity in multiple contexts was *Nationalisms and Sexualities* (Parker et al., 1992). Not assuming a heterosexual model, this collection brought feminist concerns with nationalism together with Benedict Anderson's theory on nationalism and Foucault's theorizing on sexuality. What this means is looking at how sexualities and nationalisms are the effects of power relations that rely on the proliferation of categories and identities – sexual and national – in order to regulate and control. For example, this approach raises the concern that the two hierarchical categories of hetero/homosexuality might not only be a way to privilege one

kind of sexuality over another, but it might be also a way to regulate sexuality by specifying what it means to be heterosexual and homosexual while erasing other kinds of sexualities.

Seen in this way, the proliferation of sexual and national identities requires careful and critical analysis instead of a celebration of the proliferation of sexual difference. Rather than being suppressed, issues of homosexualities might be kept under control while bolstering claims that heterosexuality is natural and normal. In her article, 'To Die For', Cindy Patton (1997) examines how, counterintuitively, queerness was incorporated in the national project of redefining citizenship in the post-World War II era that was empathically based and predicated on understanding the notion of minority 'experience'. Through an analysis of the film and book versions of *Gentlemen's Agreement,* Patton argues that this new citizenship was directed at accommodating issues of racism and homophobia without disrupting the boundaries between the privileged self and minoritized other. What is especially compelling about this exploration of citizenship and queerness in the post-World War II era is that it offers a radically different way of constructing a genealogy of sexual minority politics. Indeed, Patton argues that rather than reading the persecutions of homosexuals by the House Committee on Un-American Activities as the marker of their evolving status as a political group, it might be more useful to examine how changing definitions of citizenship aided in limiting sexuality to dual sexual identities.

Such analyses, then, call for both, recognition of the interdependent and hierarchical relation of sexual identities such as homo/heterosexuality, but also counterstrategies that would radically challenge the incessant reproduction of these dualities in configurations of citizenship and nations. Seen in this way, this strand of lesbian/gay studies implicitly calls into question the limitations of a right-based discourse that may be important in bringing about necessary social change, but cannot avoid the pitfalls of assimilation or reproducing the dual categories of hetero/homosexuality. In other words by reinforcing dual categories of sexual identity, rights-based sexual politics may in effect neutralize the challenge posed by this strand of scholarship. As Patton crystallizes the concern, a politics, which is based on identifying as gay or homosexual, could be successful only when there is no longer any need for it.

Radical Nationalisms

If indeed nationalisms help reproduce and regulate categories of sexual difference, then the question is whether it is possible to imagine counterhegemonic nationalisms that, at worst, do not rely on the politics of inclusion and exclusion, or, at best, can imagine nationalisms from a lesbian/gay perspective. Whether there can be an 'imagined community' of citizens that does not privilege homosexuality or reproduce the problems of dual categories of sexual difference is the question. Queer Nation, founded at an ACT UP meeting in New York in 1990, is the clearest example of a counter-hegemonic imagination that seeks to both reveal and destabilize the boundaries of straight and gay politics, but is unable to avoid the pitfalls of inclusions and exclusions. In their definitive article on the nature and politics of Queer Nation, Lauren Berlant and Elizabeth Freeman (1993) describe its premise and the limitations. According to Berlant and Freeman, Queer Nation represents an important counter-strategy that entertains the possibility of nationalism as transgression and resistance by drawing on histories of insurgent nationalisms. In its promotion of a national sexuality, Queer Nation shows how hegemonic nationalism does avow and regulate sexualities through the use of laws, policies, and customs. Anti-assimilationist in its stance, Queer Nation not only emphasizes visibility as a means to safe public existence, but it also seeks to use an 'in-your-face' politics to appropriate national icons of spaces of

quotidian life to make them safe for all persons in an everyday and embodied sense, according to Berlant and Freeman. Using and manipulating the most corporate of spaces – shopping malls and the print and advertising media – Queer Nation seeks to manipulate homosexuality as a 'product' that consumers find both pleasurable and unsettling in order to transform public culture; if sex sells, then, what better way to invoke the capacity of the body to experience transgressive pleasures? But, by marginalizing economic, racial, ethnic, and non-American cultures, they suggest the Queer Nation is unable to leave behind the fantasies of homogeneity that characterize American nationalism. If it's a gay, white male who is at the centre of these insurgent politics, then the idea of Queer Nation is hardly free from the politics of inclusion and exclusion that is the questionable basis of dominant nationalisms to begin with. As long as Queer Nation is imagined from the perspective of the gay, white male, other racial/sexual identities are once again excluded.

Rethinking the Links and Limitations between Nationalisms and Lesbian and Gay Sexualities

Since questions of nationalism, citizenship, and lesbian and gay sexualities cannot be taken for granted because not all queers have the same legal rights to the benefits and responsibilities of citizenship, clearly these links need to be theorized more systematically. For instance, earlier Herrell (1996) specified the three areas where notions of the 'good citizen' are negotiated within American national life without attending to the fact that many lesbian and gay people are not able to participate in these discussions because they are either of color, immigrants, or indigent. Gopinath (1996) makes a similar charge against Berlant and Freeman arguing that, by sidestepping the vexed relation of many queers of color to the regulatory mechanisms of the state and the nation, their analysis supports a nationalism that presupposes white, male, US citizen queers.

Lesbian/gay studies scholarship on nationalisms that privilege gay, white males raises at least two urgent concerns. For queers of color, notions of citizenship and belonging can hardly be taken for granted. This fundamental tension between the promise of nationalism and citizenship and the systematic exclusion of lesbians and gays of color is ignored in mainstream lesbian/gay studies. On the flip side, this also helps explain the complacency in white, Western mainstream scholarship on issues of nationalism and lesbian and gay sexualities. But, as the above discussions suggest, questions of nationalism are not altogether absent. What is striking, but perhaps not unexpected under the circumstances, is that the most careful attention to this issue comes from queers of color. The second related concern has to do with the vantage point from which one explores the links between nationalisms and lesbian and gay sexualities. Since there are no generic lesbian and gay communities, for the purpose of this discussion, I will briefly explore these issues by focusing on Asian American lesbian/gay studies. In so doing, I will try to shed light on what it means to be Asian American, queer, and displaced from the place to which one may have belonged, i.e. to be in diaspora. But to the extent that the displacement means that concepts of 'nation', 'home', and belonging are constantly negotiated, this vantage point also indicates the limitations of nationalism. Where does the second-generation queer Taiwanese American 'belong?' What is 'home?' Which communities can s/he belong to? These are not only difficult questions that must be constantly faced, but they also indicate how confining the idea of the nation–state as 'home' or place of belonging is especially for lesbian and gay Asian Americans.

It is indisputable that intersections of race, ethnicity, nationality, and sexuality make it impossible for Asian Americans to take notions of citizenship or expectations of full participation in public life in the contemporary USA for granted. Indeed, in his article on diaspora, queerness, and Asian

American studies, David Eng (1997) argues that for Asian Americans the claim to citizenship within the US nation–state is dubious at best. Describing this sense of displacement that does not allow any neat alignment between 'nation' and 'home', Eng suggests that Asian Americans feel permanently disenfranchised from 'home' as they remain suspended between departure and arrival. When such ambivalent feelings remain unexamined, they can produce a kind of cultural nationalism that promotes an ideal Asian American citizen – male, heterosexual, working-class, American-born, and English-speaking. In order to claim their place in the US nation–state and counter the feminine and homosexual stereotypes of Asian American men, Asian American cultural nationalists might effectively marginalize those men and women who do not fit this ideal image – particularly queer Asian American. Thus, contrary to inadvertent assumptions underlying (white) queer and gay and lesbian studies, questions of 'nation', 'home', 'belonging', and 'community' are pressing for Asian American queers.

If we can understand nation from a queer perspective, what it means to be queer is also shaped by perceptions of nation and 'home'. In his article, 'Searching of community', Martin F. Manalansan IV (1996) takes on this task of exploring the shaping of 'gay' and 'Filipino' identities and community. While, elsewhere, Manalansan (1994) calls for an examination of the disjunctures between hegemonic representations and practices of gay Filipinos to understand the complex if ongoing nature of the negotiations, agency, and symbolic resistance, in this ethnography Manalansan focuses on the mutual articulations of what it means to be 'gay' and 'Filipino'. Based on his ethnography among fifty gay men, he notes important differences of social class, ethnic/racial affiliations, and varying cultural traditions and practices of homosexuality shaped how they articulated their homosexuality in his study. Filipino men, Manalansan suggests, whether American or Filipino born draw on more than one tradition of being homosexual – the

American (hyper-masculine gay culture) and the *bakla* (socially constructed transvestite and/or effeminized being that occupies an in-between position between men and women). Invoking one and sometimes denigrating the other appears to allow these Filipino men to project differences in what it means to be homosexual. Yet, despite the cleavages that run across this group, there appear to be historical instances – such as the AIDS pandemic, the controversy regarding Miss Saigon, the changing flow of migrants and exiles – that make it necessary to continually reshape the cultural traditions of being 'gay' and 'Filipino', and I would argue, being 'American'.

LIMITATIONS OF NATIONALISM

If this literature on the Asian American studies sheds light on the links between sexualities and nationalisms, then it also foregrounds the problems with limiting the analysis to hegemonic nationalisms. When approached from a critical viewpoint, the links between lesbian and gay sexualities and nationalisms indisputably dispel assumptions that nationalism is equally accessible to all citizens. On the contrary, it is clear that nationalism is thoroughly imbued with the inflections of genders and sexualities, just as representations of genders and sexualities are inflected with the politics of nationalism. More than anything else, the interrelations of sexualities and dominant nationalisms uncover the lines of inclusion and exclusion that are embodied in definitions of citizenship. Who counts as a citizen? What normative expectations of sexuality and gender mark this citizen? Who is excluded? Are some citizens more equal than others? The lines of inclusion and exclusion that are inherent to the liberal notions of citizen make it impossible to argue that dominant nationalisms can ever be completely inclusionary. In their 'Introduction' to *Feminist Genealogies, Colonial Legacies and Democratic Futures*,

the editors, M. Jacqui Alexander and Chandra Talpade Mohanty (1997) suggest that if anything the gender, race, class, and sexually contoured 'universal citizen' of capitalist democracies is supported by a legal system that transforms what are differences between 'citizens' into institutionalized inequality. Not only does the legal apparatus make heterosexuality seem normal and natural, but it also reneges on its promise to protect all citizens against violence, such as homophobia, according to them. Thus, while it is important to understand the links between sexualities and nationalisms, the inherent limitations of nationalism also necessitate analysing concepts of belonging, home, and communities from a different lens.

When viewed from the lens of the Asian American diaspora, the limitations of nationalism as the space in which to articulate rights and the demands to inclusion are especially obvious; in the case of communities that experience mobility, displacement, exile, and resettlement, questions of nationalisms, home, belonging, and inclusion are fraught. When 'belonging' and 'home' are plural and fraught, then the function of the nation, any nation, as a political site is inadequate. This is not to argue that the desire and fantasy of inclusion as an (equal) citizen of the nation is not present or worth fighting for, but 'the nation' does not augur well. There is more than one nation at stake, more than one history, and more than one community to belong to.

Finally, the adequacy of the nation as a political space from and to which lesbian and gay sexualities should articulate demands of full participation is debatable due to the diminishing importance of the nation–state. As Mohanty (1991) notes in her essay, 'Cartographies of struggle: Third World women and the politics of feminism', with the proliferation of transnational economic structures and massive migrations of ex-colonial populations leading to multi-ethnic and multi-racial social contexts, the nation–state is no longer an adequate unit of analysis. However, argues Stuart Hall (1997), insofar as entities of power are more threatening at the moment of decline, the erosion of nation–states, national economies, and national cultural identities under the onslaught of globalization represents a dangerous moment. Thus, it may be argued that the turn into the twenty-first century represents a paradoxical moment. On the one hand, the importance of the nation–state is declining due to socio-economic factors and, on the other hand, nationalisms may be heightened under the onslaught of global, transnational cultural and economic influences.

Although others would insist that despite these changes, global capital nonetheless exerts its demands within the confines of the nation–state (for example, Eng, 1997), these arguments cannot explain how representations of cultural and sexual identities can be both somewhat homogeneous across national boundaries and different in their local manifestations. Sexual identities, such as 'gay' and 'lesbian', across a wide range of national cultural contexts are a case in point. It is crucial to understand the conditions under which sexualities can express themselves as identity across cultural contexts, as well as the differences between what 'gay' and 'lesbian' mean from one context to another. It is indisputable that national identity is materially relevant in contemporary life; indeed, the discussion over the last many pages supports the extant significance of the nation and nationalisms. However, it would be short-sighted to ignore the similarities and differences in sexualities across national boundaries. To that extent, then, it is necessary to understand and contest the significance of nationalisms to lesbian and gay politics, but also to understand the transnational, globalizing framework that shapes the expression of these sexual identities.

SEXUALITIES AND TRANSNATIONALISM

In this section, I wish to briefly explore the importance of juxtaposing a critique of nationalism with a transnational approach to lesbian and gay sexualities.[7] By a transnational approach, I mean a method that is critical of nations as a unit of analysis and is, instead, attentive to the links, similarities, and power differences that exist across cultural settings within and across nation–states (for example, queer 'Indians' from cities like New Delhi and queer South Asians in New York or London). While it is crucial to understand how the 'imagined communities' of nationalism include and exclude lesbian and gay sexualities and to what extent these sexualities are shaped by notions of national cultural identity and the desire for unequivocal inclusion within the national imaginary, it is equally important to understand how and why 'lesbian' and 'gay' identities can proliferate outside of their national units. I use these terms within quotes to suggest that even though these are the political terms avowed by various groups, they may not necessarily connote the same meanings. I emphasize the importance of including a transnational approach to lesbian and gay sexualities for two reasons: to help understand the emergence of lesbian and gay sexualities as *identities* across national contexts; and to consider possibilities for transnational political alliances between such groups marginalized from national cultural life.

In his article, 'Rupture or continuity? The internationalization of gay identities', Dennis Altman (1996) addresses the apparent internationalization of social and cultural identity based on homosexuality, and wonders to what extent a proliferating 'universal gay identity' is the product of economic and cultural forces of globalization that engender a common consciousness and identity based on homosexuality. According to Altman:

> There is great temptation to 'explain' differences in homosexuality in different countries with reference to cultural tradition. What strikes me is that *within* a given country, whether Indonesia or the United States, Thailand or Italy, the *range* of constructions of homosexuality is growing, and that in the past two decades there has emerged a definable group of self-identified homosexuals – to data many more men than women – who see

themselves as part of a global community, whose commonalities override but do not deny those of race and nationality. (1996: 424)

If Altman is correct that increasingly women and men identify with a global community based on their sexualities, then this proliferation of sexual identities raises important concerns: to what extent is this about the dominance of a Western style of identity and politics?; to what extent is this proliferation about the regulation and containment of sexual identities?; to what extent does this enable and limit homoerotic sexual politics?

If the visibility of sexual identities is indeed about the domination of a Western modernity and its humanist, individual model of politics, then this, in turn, raises the anxiety that such a model of sexual politics would marginalize other non-Western forms of lesbian and gay sexualities. Insofar as a Western binary model of sex/gender and sexuality is privileged, it might end up suppressing other possibilities, and not just in the so-called non-Western parts of the world. On the surface, the proliferation of 'lesbian' and 'gay' identity politics into various cultural, national contexts marks the expansion of a Westernized category and politics rooted in categories of identity. Altman (1996, 1997) defines this contemporary form of homosexuality as one that recognizes a difference in sexual and gender identities, and is marked by an emphasis on emotional and sexual relationships and the development of public homosexual worlds, such as a gay press, gay social and political organizations, etc. However much this model may be avowed by groups in various parts of the world – South Africa, Thailand, England, France, India, to name a few – it does not speak to the concern that other instances of the sex-gender system that involve homoeroticism, but cannot be categorized as 'lesbian' or 'gay', may be suppressed or marginalized. Echoing this fear, Manalansan (1995) wonders to what extent the globalization of the language of gay and lesbian oppression is masking hierarchical relations between the first world

and third world, between the urban and suburban. There is particular concern that the dominance of this Western model is more specifically and implicitly privileging an 'Americanization' of sexual politics. Expressing similar unease, John Champagne (1999) cautions that US gay culture has played so dominant a role in this transnational sphere that the Anglo-American subject may have come to stand in for the transnational queer. Put briefly, the seeming proliferation of sexual identities may, in fact, be the predominance of a Western/US hegemonic model of sexual identity politics.

Therefore, ignoring a careful analysis of sexual identities in a transnational context might either obscure other expressions of homoerotic sexualities, or color all lesbian and gay sexualities by a Western/US lens, characterized by dual categories male–female and homo–heterosexuality. Arguing against this sidelining of homoerotic sexualities in non-Western contexts, Rosalind Morris (1994) analyses the category of *kathoey* in contemporary Thailand in order to explode Western ethnocentric assumptions about dual sex-gender systems and dual sexual identities. Not easily translatable into the idiom of English, *kathoey* (transvestite/transsexual/hermaphrodite) possibly represents a naturalized third possibility of sexual identity for biological males.[8] However, Morris cautions, this is a system of sexual and gendered identities, not of hetero–and homosexualities. In contrast to this system of three sexualities, Morris describes a second, co-existent (Westernized?) sex/gender system. Unlike the first system, this system is characterized by dual categories of male–female and hetero–homosexuality, where sexual activity is seen as the product of sexual identity. This second, co-existent system acknowledges four sexualities – homosexual women or men and heterosexual women or men – and *kathoeys* may pass as gay men or as women. Through this instructive approach, Morris demonstrates not only the importance of a careful, contextual analysis of homoeroticism, but also the value of understanding the interactions between 'Western' and 'non-Western' models of homoeroticism.

But there is another concern related to the meaning of the proliferation of sexualities as identities across cultural contexts. The concern is that this dual model of hetero and homosexuality that undergirds 'lesbian' and 'gay' identity may challenge compulsory heterosexuality and homophobia only in a limited way. In fact, even in its Western context, this binary model of sexual identity, which is at the heart of lesbian/gay studies, is an important point of concern. The work of queer theorists such as Eve Sedgwick (1990) compellingly demonstrates that the dual categories of homo/hetero might represent more a strategy of accommodation than a politics of liberation. Speaking to the concerns with identity-based politics, Steven Seidman (1993) notes that if 'heterosexuality' and 'homosexuality' are mutually determining, hierarchical terms, then a politics of identity necessarily reproduces the relationship of what is considered normal and what is excluded. For example, referring back to the discussion on Queer Nation, attempting to include alternative sexualities only ends up privileging certain identities (gay, white, male) and marginalizing others. Seen in this way, it is both crucial to explore the conditions under which there is an apparent proliferation of 'lesbian', 'gay', and, more recently, 'bisexual' identities, their contextual meanings, and the possibilities of an oppositional politics thereof.

Earlier, I mentioned the importance of a transnational approach insofar as it also enables the possibilities of a politics of empowerment and political alliances across national contexts. The transnational proliferation of lesbian and gay identities may raise concerns about the possible hegemony of a specific US/Western gay politics or that such identities may end up limiting rather than liberating. However, what is indisputable is that these identities also enable and empower individuals and groups to challenge homophobia and heterosexuality. Sexual identities, such as 'lesbian' and 'gay'

present a basis for a politics of resistance and social change. For example, in what may be considered a definitive report on the status of homosexuality in India, *Less Than Gay: A Citizen's Report on the Status of Homosexuality in India*, the authors (ABVA, 1991) purposefully claim the term 'gay' as a politicized self-identity that challenges the suppression and control of homosexuality. According to them,

> When we employ the word 'gay' we do not mean to reduce these rich and varied exotic spaces into a medical model of 'heterosexual', 'homosexual' and 'bisexual' behavior. We use it consciously both as a description of people who see themselves as gay and as a sensibility encompassing the entire area of same-sex eroticism. We feel that 'gay' should be used as a politically desirable intervention in a context of state (legal and medical) regulation of homo/sexuality. (1991: 5)

In his comments on the narratives of South Asian queers, Nayan Shah (1993) astutely notes the emphasis on 'coming out', a process that is an essential aspect of gay politics. According to Shah, these narratives explain the process of developing a queer identity and how sexual desire is shaped by a political model.

If these models of sexual identities can be politically strategic and empowering, then they also present the possibilities for fostering transnational alliances. Elsewhere I (Puri, 1999) have analysed the example of *Trikone*, the oldest surviving gay and lesbian South Asian organization. I have argued that this organization presents an example of the importance of establishing alliances between lesbians and gays across national context. The founder of the organization, Arvind Kumar, suggests that this kind of networking is a matter of survival and establishing mutual relationships. What appears to distinguish these transnational alliances is that these alliances are sought on the basis of common histories of marginality of lesbian and gay sexualities, or what Mohanty (1991) has elsewhere called a common context of struggle.

However, even as we explore the possibilities for transnational alliances of sexual identities and the ways in which that might shape their expressions, we need to consider when this transnational framework of gay politics may also be limiting in some ways. In a particularly interesting consideration of the ban on gay teachers by the Ratchabat Institute that provides teacher training in Thailand, Morris (1997) identifies the pitfalls of a transnational framework that enables gay politics. Noting that the state chose to enforce the ban only after a three-year period in which it lay dormant, Morris argues that this was an attempt to eliminate lesbian and gay sexualities in response to transnational discourses on sex and sexuality that paradoxically helped incite national cultural conservatism. The Institute's ban may be seen as a conservative reaction to gay activism by pathologizing lesbian and gay identities. But, in a particularly ironic twist, the Institute's ban on gay teacher trainers also suggests that it acknowledges the concept of 'gayness' as its problem, even as it attempts to displace 'gayness' as foreign or alien.

My point in the foregoing discussion is not to argue both sides of the issue. On the contrary, what I am leading up to is that while we can acknowledge the importance of taking a transnational approach in lesbian/gay studies and entertain both the possibilities and limitations of the proliferation of sexual identities thereof, we have few studies to provide much needed direction. There are few empirical and theoretical studies that attempt to address the politics of the emergence of lesbian and gay sexual identities within a transnational context. Nonetheless, there is emerging consensus on the importance of understanding the significance of the expansion of capital and the proliferation of sexual identities in a transnational context.[9] Indeed, Manalansan (1995) argues that 'gay' is synonymous with capitalist expansion. Without suggesting that sexual identities – 'lesbian' and 'gay' – are necessarily identical across cultural settings, this scholarship indicates that the expansion of capital and attendant social changes may have facilitated the expression of these identities.

What is undeniably necessary is more theoretical work and careful ethnographies of sexual identities in various cultural contexts to answer pressing questions. What are the social, cultural conditions that appear to encourage the proliferation of sexual identities? What explains this 'internationalization'? What kinds of networks of power and resistance effect sexualities as identities? How is sexual desire in diverse contexts shaped and produced through this political model? What kinds of lesbian and gay sexualities are thereby marginalized? What alternative models of sexual liberation may exist? This is where lesbian/gay studies has more work to do and much to contribute. Particularly when coupled with sociological methodology, lesbian/gay studies can shed needed light on the commonalities and differences across social contexts that are witnessing the emergence of 'lesbian' and 'gay' identities. Tracing, rather than assuming, the meaning of categories such as lesbian and gay in their cultural contexts would be especially useful to understand how these sexual identities are shaped by national context and, at the same time, invoke political models of resistance that are not limited to the incentive nature of national culture. In effect, exploring the conditions and meanings of sexual identities would be about not only understanding the possibilities of these politicized identities but also their attendant limitations.

However, I am not simply calling for 'internationalization' of lesbian/gay studies because such a move would reinforce the collusion of a mainstream Western-oriented lesbian/gay studies with the dominance of an US/Western style of sexual politics. On the contrary, I am suggesting that given the productive history of the discipline of lesbian/gay studies, what might be useful is to re-examine the meanings of categories of sexual identity, their meanings and ramifications, and their possibilities and limitations across disparate settings. Such theoretical and ethnographic considerations would not only inform the possible range of meanings of categories such as lesbian and gay, but they would also counter the risk of, to rephrase Champagne's unease, seeing the lesbian or gay subject as Anglo-American. Rather than seeing sexual desire as the result of 'sexual difference' that can be truthfully expressed through 'coming out', it might be more useful to interrogate the cultural conditions that tend to shape a range of experiences of lesbian and gay sexual identities across cultural settings in a transnational, globalizing context. What are the cultural conditions under which the stories of middle-class lesbian and gay youth in Mumbai (formerly known as Bombay), India, seem remarkably similar to those told by their counterparts in Boston, USA – the expectations of 'coming out', of knowing one's difference since an early age, of isolation? What are the differences between the stories? And, finally, if some stories are possible only as others are suppressed, then what kinds of issues, differences, sexualities, and possibilities are not being told?

CONCLUSION

In this chapter, my primary aim was to explore the relevance and meaning of dominant nationalisms from a lesbian and gay perspective. As should have been clear from the above discussion, this task would be difficult without juxtaposing feminist theory on nationalism alongside the literature within lesbian/gay studies. Aside from the fact the useful insights on nationalism and gender and sexuality were first articulated within feminist theory, albeit from a limited perspective, bringing it together with lesbian and gay scholarship on nationalisms is necessary to avoid reproducing the division of labor that has been faulted by many others – that feminist theory primarily attends to issues of gender while lesbian/gay studies mostly takes on issues of lesbian and gay sexualities.

A related aim in this chapter was also to help mainstream questions of nationalism in lesbian/gay studies. Parallel to the feminist scholarship on nationalisms, attention to lesbian and gay sexualities and nationalisms

comes from the more marginalized sectors within lesbian/gay studies. In that sense, critical analysis of the ways in which nationalisms constrain and contain sexual identities and how sexual identities and their politics are shaped within this national cultural unit remains ghettoized within lesbian/gay studies. Perhaps not totally unexpectedly, with the exception of scholars such as Cindy Patton, the most careful and crucial insights come from queers of color. In this chapter, I chose to focus on scholarship within Asian American lesbian/gay studies to map salient issues and debates in the field.

My second, and equally important, aim was to suggest that looking at issues of lesbian and gay sexualities and nationalisms, especially from the perspective of Asian American lesbian/gay studies, indicates the limitations of nationalism as an analytical and political category. In this latter section, I argued the usefulness of a transnational approach that would enable us to recognize the complex meaning of the proliferation of 'lesbian' and 'gay' sexual identities; to explore the possible hegemony of such a model and its political possibilities and limitations. Therefore, in a more concrete and methodological turn, I suggested the importance of unraveling categories of lesbian and gay sexual identities within lesbian/gay studies across disparate, Western and non-Western cultural contexts. I suggested that this move would be necessary to shed light on the meaning, ramifications, possibilities and limitations of categories of 'lesbian' and 'gay' identity. What would be especially useful is to consider the social and cultural conditions under which certain identities appear possible and, ultimately, normal.

In effect, my purpose was to also suggest the useful directions that lesbian/gay studies could take in order to further investigate this propagation of sexual identities without reproducing in lesbian/gay studies the hegemony of the US/Western lesbian and gay style of politics. Because in the last instance, given the history of the discipline of lesbian/gay studies, without a less ethnocentric focus and a willingness to re-examine familiar categories and politics, the discipline would undermine its commitment to an oppositional politics.

NOTES

Many thanks to Hyun Sook Kim for her insightful comments and feedback on this chapter.

1 This is the starting premise of the collection, *Nationalisms and Sexualities* (Parker et al., 1992), which is discussed more fully below.

2 While there are important differences between lesbian and gay and queer studies, in this chapter I use the terms lesbian/gay and queer interchangeably. Also, given the burgeoning, distinct areas of bisexual and transgender studies, I deliberately do not address bisexual and transgender issues in this chapter.

3 By 'we', I refer to those learning and working within the field of lesbian/gay studies.

4 For example, see the collections (Yuval-Davis and Anthias, 1989) *Woman-Nation-State* (Jayawardena, 1986) *Feminism and Nationalism in the Third World*, and (Kandayoti, 1991) *Women, Islam, and the State*.

5 This includes collections such as (Mohanty et al., 1991) *Third World Women and the Politics of Feminism*, (Sangari and Vaid, 1989) *Recasting Women: Essays in Indian Colonial History* (Pierson and Chandhuri, 1998) *Nation, Empire, Colony, Tensions of Empire*, along with books such as *Nation and its Fragments* and (McClintock, 1995) *Imperial Leather*.

6 As quoted in *Less Than Gay: A Citizen's Report on the Status of Homosexuality in India* (ABVA, 1991: 48).

7 For this approach, I draw upon the framework of transnational feminist cultural studies, most prominently developed by scholars such as Inderpal Grewal (1994, 1996) and Caren Kaplan (1994).

8 In a later article, Morris (1997) retracts this reading of *kathoey* as a third gender possibility to suggest that it can be understood within a binary gender system in which *kathoey*, by displacing the instability of masculinity, reinforces the distinctions between masculinity and femininity.

9 See citations by Dennis Altman, John Champagne, Gayatri Gopinath, Martin F. Manalansan IV, and Rosalind Morris.

REFERENCES

Aarmo, Margrete (1999) 'How homosexuality become "un-African": the case of Zimbabwe', in E. Blackwood and S.E. Wieringa (eds), *Female Desires: Same-Sex Relations and Transgender Practices Across Cultures*. New York: Columbia University Press. pp. 255–80.

ABVA (1991) 'Homosexuality in India: culture and heritage', in *Less Than Gay: A Citizen's Report on the Status of Homosexuality in India*. New Delhi: ABVA.

Alexander, M. Jacqui (1997) 'Erotic autonomy as a politics of decolonization: an anatomy of feminist and state practice in the Bahamas tourist economy', M.J. Alexander and C.T. Mohanty (eds), *Feminist Genealogies, Colonial Legacies and Democratic Futures*. New York: Routledge. pp. 63–100.

Alexander, M.J. and Mohanty, C.T. (eds) (1997) *Feminist Genealogies, Colonial Legacies and Democratic Futures*. New York: Routledge.

Altman, D. (1996) 'Rupture or continuity? The internationalization of gay identities', *Social Text*, 48, 14 (3): 77–94.

Altman, D. (1997) 'Global gaze/global gays', *GLQ*, 3: 417–36.

Anderson, Benedict (1983) *Imagined Communities: Reflections on the Origins and Spread of Nationalism*. London: Verso.

beng hui, Tan (1999) 'Women's sexuality and the discourse on Asian values: cross-dressing in Malaysia', in E. Blackwood and S.E. Wieringa (eds), *Female Desires: Same-Sex Relations and Transgender Practices Across Cultures*. New York: Columbia University Press. pp. 281–307.

Berlant, Lauren and Freeman, Elizabeth (1993) 'Queer nationality', in M. Warner (ed.), *Fear of a Queer Planet: Queer Politics and Social Theory*. Minneapolis, London: University of Minnesota Press. pp. 193–229.

Champagne, J. (1999) 'Transnationally queer? A prolegomenon', *Socialist Review*, 27 (1, 2): 143–64.

Chatterjee, Partha (1993) *The Nation and Its Fragment: Colonial and Postcolonial Histories*. Princeton, NJ: Princeton University Press.

Duggan, L. (1994) 'Queering the state', *Social Text*, 39: 1–14.

Eng, D.L. (1997) 'Out here and over there: queerness and diaspora in Asian American studies', *Social Text*, 52/53, 15 (3, 4): 31–52.

Enloe, Cynthia (1989) *Bananas, Beaches, and Bases: Making Feminist Sense of International Politics*. Berkeley, CA: University of California Press.

Gopinath, G. (1996) 'Funny boys and girls: notes on a queer South Asian planet', in R. Leong (ed.), *Asian American Sexualities: Dimensions of the Gay and Lesbian Experience*. New York and London: Routledge. pp. 119–27.

Gopinath, G. (1997) 'Nostalgia, desire, diaspora: South Asian sexualities in motion', *positions*, 5 (2): 467–89.

Grewal, Inderpal (1996) *Home and Harem: Nation, Gender, Empire, and the Cultures of Travel*. Durham, NC, and London: Duke University Press.

Grewal, Inderpal and Kaplan, Caren (1994) 'Introduction: transnational feminist practices and questions of postmodernity', in I. Grewal and C. Kaplan (eds), *Scattered Hegemonies: Postmodernity and Transnational Feminist Practices*. Minneapolis: University of Minnesota Press. pp. 1–33.

Hall, S. (1997) 'The local and the global: globalization and ethnicities', in A.D. King (ed.), *Culture, Globalization, and the World-System: Contemporary Conditions for the Representation of Identity*. Minneapolis: University of Minnesota Press. pp. 19–40.

Herrell, R.K. (1996) 'Sin, sickness, crime: queer desire and the American state', *Identities*, 2 (3): 273–300.

Jayawardena, Kumari (1986) *Feminism and Nationalism in the Third World*. New Delhi: Kali for Women.

Kandayoti, Denise (ed.) (1991) *Women, Islam and the State*. Philadelphia: Temple University Press.

Kaplan, C. and Grewal, I. (1994) 'Transnational feminist cultural studies: beyond marxism/poststructuralism/feminism divides', *positions*, 2 (2): 430–45.

Manalansan, M.F. IV (1994) '(Dis)Orienting the body: locating symbolic resistance among Filipino gay men', *positions*, 2 (1): 73–90.

Manalansan, M.F. IV (1995) 'In the shadows of Stonewall: examining gay transnational politics and the diasporic dilemma', *GLQ*, 2: 425–38.

Manalansan, M.F. IV (1996) 'Searching for community: Filipino gay men in New York City', in R. Leong (ed.), *Asian American Sexualities: Dimensions of the Gay and Lesbian Experience*. New York and London: Routledge. pp. 51–64.

McClintock, Anne (1995) *Imperial Leather: Race, Gender, and Sexuality in the Colonial Contest*. New York: Routledge.

Mohanty, Chandra T. (1991) 'Cartographies of struggle: Third world women and the politics of feminism', in C.T. Mohanty, A. Russo and L. Torres (eds), *Third World Women and the Politics of Feminism*. Bloomington and Indianapolis: Indiana University Press. pp. 1–47.

Morris, R. (1994) 'Three sexes and four sexualities: redressing the discourses on gender and sexuality in contemporary Thailand', *positions*, 2 (1): 15–43.

Morris, R. (1997) 'Educating desire: Thailand, transnationalism, and transgression', *Social Text*, 52/53, 15 (3, 4): 53–79.

Parker, A., Russo, M., Summer, D. and Yaeger, P. (eds) (1992) *Nationalisms and Sexualities*. New York: Routledge.

Patton, Cindy (1997) 'To die for', in E.K. Sedgwick (ed.), *Novel Gazing: Queer Readings in Fiction*. Durham, NC, and London: Duke University Press.

Pierson, R.R. and Chaudhuri, N. (eds) (1998) *Nation, Empire, Colony: Historicizing Gender and Race*. Bloomington and Indianapolis: Indiana University Press.

Puri, Jyoti (1999) *Woman, Body, Desire in Post-colonial India: Narratives of Gender and Sexuality*. New York: Routledge.

Sangari, K. and Vaid, S. (eds) (1989) *Recasting Women: Essays in Colonial History*. New Delhi: Kali for Women.

Sedgwick, Eve K. (1990) *Epistemology of the Closet*. Berkeley, Los Angeles: University of California Press.

Seidman, Steven (1993) 'Identity and Politics in a 'postmodern' gay culture: some historical and conceptual notes', in M. Warner (ed.), *Fear of a Queer Planet: Queer Politics and Social Theory*. Minneapolis, London: University of Minnesota Press. pp. 105–42.

Shah, Nayan (1993) 'Sexuality, identity, and the use of history', in R. Ratti (ed.), *Lotus of Another Color*. Boston: Alyson Publications, Inc. pp. 113–34.

Stoler, Ann (1995) 'Sexual affronts and racial frontiers: European identities and the cultural politics of exclusion in colonial Southeast Asia', in F. Cooper and A. Stoler (eds), *Tensions of Empire: Colonial Cultures in a Bourgeois World*. Berkeley, Los Angeles: University of California Press. pp. 198–237.

Takagi, D.Y. (1996) 'Maiden voyage: excursion into sexuality and identity politics and Asian America', in R. Leong (ed.), *Asian American Sexualities: Dimensions of the Gay and Lesbian Experience*. New York and London: Routledge. pp. 21–35.

Yuval-Davis, N. and Anthias, F. (eds) (1989) *Woman-Nation-State*. New York: St Martin's Press.

26

Sexual Citizenship

Marriage, the Market and the Military

DAVID BELL AND JON BINNIE

The notion of 'sexual citizenship' has become an important way of thinking about contemporary issues in sexual politics. The return of citizenship to political and legal theory in the closing decades of the twentieth century, matched by the increased use of the discourse of citizenship in party politics and policy formulations, in part accounts for the emergence of the sexual citizen as a politically legible figure. At the same time, the move toward rights-based political and legal action by lesbian and gay groups in many liberal democracies has also led to a focus on issues of sexual citizenship (Bell and Binnie, 2000; Stychin, 1998), in line with similar agitations by other groups fighting for 'minority rights', often under the banner of identity politics (Isin and Wood, 1999). However, the emergence of rights-based claims for equality based around the idea of sexual citizenship can be intensely problematic, since they inevitably raise a number of crucial questions – questions that we shall be focusing on in this chapter: is the concept of citizenship the best way to mobilize sexual politics? Who is a sexual citizen? How can we use the notion to begin to interrogate the intersections of law, politics and identity?

The background to the debates on sexual citizenship is critical work on the notion of citizenship itself. Particularly important here are feminist and postmodern revisionings of citizenship, which work to critique the universalizing tendencies of citizenship discourse and rights discourse. The first part of our chapter, therefore, introduces very briefly those elements of critical approaches to citizenship which have resonances for sexual citizenship. We follow that with a short, critical appraisal of two recent attempts to define the terrain of sexual citizenship, by Jeffrey Weeks (1999) and Diane Richardson (1998). In the light of their distinct formulations, we then move on to explore competing readings of attempts to mobilize citizenship discourse in the context of sexual politics.

CITIZENSHIP

The concept of citizenship has both excited and vexed political, social and cultural theorists for some time now. There have been numerous attempts to define the core components of citizenship as it is inscribed in legal, political and civil discourses, as well as critical engagements that have sought to expand existing conceptions in the wake of broad transformations in those terrains. Attempts at definition are always flawed, in that they cannot fully account for the many different ways in which the notion of citizenship is mobilized; this often renders proposed definitions either overly prescriptive or overly vague. The concept is, without a doubt, inherently 'baggy', always subject to particular inflections in particular contexts. But, if we do have to settle on a working definition to guide our analysis, perhaps we should go with one provided in Engin Isin and Patricia Wood's book *Citizenship and Identity*: 'Citizenship can be described as *both* a set of practices (cultural, symbolic and economic) and a bundle of rights and duties (civil, political and social) that define an individual's membership in a polity' (Isin and Wood, 1999: 4, emphasis in original). This is a useful description, in bringing together many different domains in which citizenship is enacted. It might be better to say, however, that those practices, rights and duties which together form the substance of citizenship define an individual's membership in a polity in both positive and negative ways: citizenship is an exclusionary concept just as much as an inclusionary one. The grounds of exclusion are many layered and often shifting in the context of specific articulations of citizenship; the boundaries of the included (citizens) and the excluded (non-citizens) are always on the move, expanding and contracting:

> Citizenship ... has always been a group concept – *but it has never been expanded to all members of any polity*. Still today, in modern democratic states there are many members who are denied the legal status of citizenship on the basis of their place of birth. Moreover, many members of polities are excluded from the scope of citizenship even if they are legally entitled to its benefits. (Isin and Wood, 1999: 20, emphasis in original).

There are, then, as Sarah Benton (1991: 154) writes, two kinds of non-citizen to be considered: 'those who have never been admitted, and those who are exiled'. What this exclusionary logic means, of course, is that battles around citizenship are battles to be recognized and included in the polity. Given the rights-duties coupling that citizenship invokes, fighting for inclusion often means conceding to perform certain duties or responsibilities in a barter for rights. As we shall see, this can usher in compromises that are often intensely problematic, both theoretically and politically. But before we focus on that aspect of the citizenship question, we should say a few short words about formulations of citizenship with different theoretical agendas.

The particular starting point for understandings of the modern condition of citizenship is the work of T.H. Marshall, especially his 1950 essay *Citizenship and Social Class*. Revisions, critiques and extensions of Marshall's theorizing have filled many volumes (see, for example, Turner, 1990, 1993). Subsequently, three broad perspectives have emerged in citizenship theory: civic liberalism, civic republicanism (often seen as manifest in communitarianism), and radical democracy. The civic liberalist tradition in citizenship theory is most closely aligned to Marshall, with its analysis of the state's paternal role in securing the welfare and rights of its citizens, as well as binding citizens together in sociality. Civic republicanism places more stress on obligation often mediated through 'political participation in communal affairs' (Ellison, 1997: 711). The nation–state is placed centre stage in civic republicanist conceptions of citizenship, as is national identity. Pluralist, feminist and post-structuralist takes on citizenship, which we can (perhaps a little untidily, even uneasily) group under the banner of radical democratic citizenship theory, have become increasingly prominent in the academy, chiming as they do with the reinvention of politics under postmodernity (Yeatman, 1994). Most commentators assert that there is something within the notion of citizenship that can further a radical democratic project, despite recuperation by 'New Right' politicians – mobilized in the UK, for example, around the figure of the 'active citizen' and in the drafting of a Citizen's Charter, and in America through neoconservative discourses around welfare and the family (Cooper, 1993b; Roche, 1992). By adding in insights from post-structuralist and feminist theory – such as critiques of the gendered assumptions about citizenship's location in the public sphere and its simultaneous propagation in the private sphere (especially in the family) and work on the 'decentring' of the subject – these approaches seek to complicate (and simultaneously re-energize) the figure of the citizen and its relation to forms of 'identity politics'. As Anne Phillips (1993: 87) writes: '[t]he value of citizenship lies in the way it restates the importance of political activity … [T]his might prove itself as a way of dealing with the politics of an extraordinary time.' Reflecting the post-structuralist perspective, this 'extraordinary time' is described in Paul Clarke's *Deep Citizenship* as one of transformation: 'the world into which we are moving is fractured in multiple ways, … its meta-narratives have collapsed, … its old ideologies have fallen into disrepute and … its old certainties have been transformed into new uncertainties' (1996: 116). That sense of fragmentation, of 'new uncertainties', certainly provides one of the motor mechanisms for restating citizenship in political discourse. It also affords the opportunity to radically rethink what being a citizen is all about; shifting the boundaries, then, of a particular form of political (but not only political) identity. This raises an important question about *how* citizens are engaged in politics – and about what we mean by the *politics of citizenship* itself.

A useful critical summary of the roles available to citizens in the current polity is offered by Holloway Sparks (1997), in an essay on 'dissident citizenship'. Sparks argues that the political role of citizens within current citizenship theory is both limited and limiting, and suggests the need to expand our conception of citizenship to incorporate dissent which, she argues, has 'fallen through the cracks of much mainstream citizenship theory', which has

focused on attempts to secure rights within the public sphere of advanced capitalist market societies (Sparks, 1997: 77). This theorization advances a model of 'participatory democracy', Sparks argues, that sidelines dissent as a political practice. Importantly, Sparks concludes that her revisioning of citizenship is valuable in that it suggests we must acknowledge 'the political agency of dissidents and 'marginals' as the agency of *'citizens'*, as well as broadening our 'understanding of where political participation takes place' (ibid.: 100–1). That these concepts have clear resonances with the kinds of politics mobilized by *sexual dissidents* will become clear later. With this in mind, we shall now turn our attention to attempts to mobilize the concept of citizenship specifically within the context of sexuality, offering a brief but critical reading of some recent contributions to the debate.

SEXUAL CITIZENSHIP

As the notion of citizenship re-emerged in political, academic and popular discourses in the 1980s – spurred on, in the UK, by the Conservative administration's notions of active citizenship, of a Citizen's Charter, and of emphasizing the flipsides of the equation of citizenship (rights *always* come with responsibilities), as well as by a brief flurry of excitement over communitarianism – so it entered the register of sexual politics. With its mobile combinations of the political, the economic, the social, the legal, and the ethical, citizenship seemed to be a neat concept for articulating the field of sexual politics generally. In a period marked by countless transformations – the controversial appearance, negotiations and disputes around queer theory and queer politics; the centralizing of the AIDS crisis in both mobilizing and allying discourses and in homophobic discourses; continuing debate over the form and status of the 'lesbian and gay community'; varieties of 'sex war' recasting notions of a politics rooted in desire; the solidifying of social constructionist notions of sexuality through theories of performativity, plus the contrary re-essentializing of 'gay' identity through biomedical researches; the intensified marketization of sexualities, and so on – the field of sexual politics in its broadest sense seemed likewise to embody many of the debates activated by a focus on citizenship, with its crossing of boundaries between the public and the private, between the collective and the individual, between entitlements and duties.

Diane Richardson (1998) has attempted to survey and summarize existing insights into sexual citizenship, and we would like to here sketch her argument, as well as that made by Jeffrey Weeks (1999). Both writers seek to explore how the notion of sexual citizenship is currently mobilized; Richardson's focus shadows that of feminist critiques of citizenship discourse, by exposing the heterosexualizing of citizenship as an extension of exposing its gendering: 'My starting point is the argument that claims to citizenship status, at least in the West, are closely associated with the institutionalization of heterosexual as well as male privilege' (Richardson, 1998: 88). Following Marshall's delineation of the domains of citizenship – civil, political and social – she charts inequalities faced by two groups of sexual citizens, lesbians and gay men: lack of full equal rights, lack of full political participation and representation, lack of access of welfare entitlements. While she acknowledges that lesbians and gay men are afforded certain rights – usually 'won' as a result of their designation as a 'minority group' – she argues that there is a very high price to pay: sexual citizenship is heavily circumscribed and simultaneously privatized, its limits set by the coupling of tolerance with assimilation: '[l]esbians and gay men are granted the right to be tolerated as long as they stay within the boundaries of that tolerance, whose borders are maintained through a heterosexist public/private divide' – this means that lesbians and gay men can only be citizens if they can be 'good' citizens (ibid.: 89). This cost, in terms of performing 'good'

sexual citizenship, is identified by Carl Stychin (1998) as one of the prime dangers in using citizenship as a model for advancing lesbian and gay rights claims: 'in attempting to achieve legal victories, lesbians and gays seeking rights may embrace an ideal of "respectability", a construction that then perpetuates a division between "good gays" and (disreputable) "bad queers". … The latter are then excluded from the discourse of citizenship (Stychin, 1998: 200).

In addition, Richardson notes that limiting lesbians' and gay men's spaces of citizenship to the private has a contradictory logic to it, in that the private sphere is constructed in a heterosexualized frame, as the space of the family. This helps explain the enduring deployment of reformulations of 'family' in current sexual rights claims – in the notion of 'families we choose' and in arguments for lesbian and gay marriage and parenting: the model of the private into which sexual citizens are projected is one in which only certain articulations are conceivable. Further, as diverse cases including Bowers v. Hardwick and R. v. Brown have shown, the private is a precarious place for sexual citizens, one that is all too easily breached (on these cases, see Halley, 1994; Moran, 1995).

In terms of social citizenship, Richardson defines this in the context of the nation–state, in terms of social membership or belonging. As the growing literature on the relationship between sexuality and the nation shows, despite the imperatives of globalization and transnationalism, citizenship continues to be anchored in the nation, and the nation remains heterosexualized (Stychin, 1998). The arguments over military exclusion of sexual dissidents in the USA and UK can be seen as emblematic of the tensions between sexual and national identity, as we shall see.

Finally, Richardson signals two domains of citizenship not considered by Marshall, but which have come to be seen as central to contemporary citizenship discourses: cultural citizenship and citizenship as consumerism. The first includes struggles over representation and 'symbolic rights' while the second centres on the economic and commercial power of groups to 'buy' themselves rights and recognition. The debates on the so-called 'pink economy' here bring sexual citizens into the broader question of the commodification of citizenship: to what extent do our rights depend on our access to capital? Certainly in the UK, the New Right's make-over of citizenship in the 1980s placed commercial power centrestage; this has been seized upon by some commentators as offering sexual dissidents ways to gain citizenship status that they have previously been denied. As we shall see, economic entryism into citizenship has provoked conflicting responses from commentators.

Jeffrey Weeks' (1999) essay 'The sexual citizen' approaches the subject from a very different angle. Weeks' interest is in the broader social transformations, which have created the preconditions for the figure of the sexual citizen to emerge on the landscape of citizenship.

> The sexual citizen, I want to argue, could be male or female, young or old, black or white, rich or poor, straight or gay: could be anyone, in fact, but for one key characteristic. The sexual citizen exists – or, perhaps better, wants to come into being – because of the new primacy given to sexual subjectivity in the contemporary world … [T]his new personage is a harbinger of a new politics of intimacy and everyday life. (Weeks, 1999: 35)

Set against this backdrop of transformations in identity, intimacy and relationships, this 'new personage', the sexual citizen, is heroized as shifting the very grounds of politics through a version of Giddens' (1991) 'reflexive project of the self':

> The idea of sexual or intimate citizenship is simply an index of the political space that needs to be developed rather than a conclusive answer to it. But in this new world of infinite possibility, but also ever-present uncertainty, we need pioneers, voyagers, experimenters with the self and with relationships. The would-be sexual citizen, I suggest, represents that spirit of searching and of adventure. (Weeks, 1999: 48)

In this sense, the sexual citizen as Weeks conceives him or her, is a marker of transformations in the sphere of personal life, and particularly in its politicization, that have taken place in the West since the 1960s. Weeks identifies the 'moment of citizenship' as a claim for inclusion, arguing that this is often twinned with a 'moment of transgression' in sexual politics: transgressive acts, which Weeks labels 'carnivalesque displays' and 'exotic manifestations of difference', are equated with queer politics (with kiss-ins, mass die-ins, and so on). While such acts make visible that which has otherwise been rendered invisible, Weeks argues that it is the moment of citizenship that allows difference to find 'a proper home' (ibid.: 37). This seems to infer a 'proper' politics, too; one centred on campaigns for welfare, employment and parenting rights, equal protection in law, and domestic partnership or marriage. Here, in an echo of Stychin's (1998) critique of sexual citizenship, transgression can only be a temporary tactic on the path to 'good' citizenship.

Weeks sketches the transformations that have created the possibility of the sexual citizen as threefold: the democratization of relationships, new subjectivities, and new stories. He ends with a list of issues 'likely to be central to post millennial politics':

> achieving a new settlements between men and women;
> elaborating new ways of fulfilling the needs for autonomy and mutual involvement that the family can no longer (if it ever could) fulfil;
> finding ways of dealing with the denaturalization of the sexual: the end of the heterosexual/ homosexual binary divide, the new reproductive technologies, the queering of identities;
> balancing the claims of different communities with constructing new common purposes, recognizing the benefits of individual choice while affirming the importance of collective endeavours;
> learning to live with diversity at the same time as building our common humanity. (Weeks, 1999: 49)

While Weeks is keen to stress that this is neither an agenda nor a map, his utopian projection of twenty-first-century politics clearly (while also rather vaguely) lists new domains of sexual citizenship without offering concrete proposals for the materialization of his wishes. It is almost as if merely living as a sexual citizen will inevitably bring about these further transformations. In fact, in many ways, that kind of logic steers some of the current ways in which the rights claims of sexual citizens are argued: that lesbian and gay marriage, for example, could serve to undermine, even destroy, the whole institution of marriage and all its attendant privileges. We will return to that thread of argument later in the chapter; first, we want to sketch three current 'moments of sexual citizenship', and to interrogate the ways in which each inflects the form of the debate as it stands.

SEXUAL CITIZENSHIP AND THE MARKET

One of the principal ways in which claims to sexual citizenship are currently articulated is via the market. Specifically, the power of the 'pink economy' is seen as offering possibilities for citizenship through consumer muscle (Evans, 1993). Visible consumption spaces (such as gay villages) are therefore recast as *spaces of citizenship*. This obviously raises very real problems of social exclusion; moreover, the notion that citizenship can (or, indeed, must) be 'bought' has to throw into question the kinds of sexual citizenship opportunities that the market can offer.

It has become a common assumption that lesbians, and more notably gay men, are model consumers – miracle workers in the new urban service economy of post-industrial, post-Fordist western society. However, recent analytical work by economists has argued that the pink economy is nothing more than a myth. The discourses of sexual citizenship have become slotted in to this emerging debate on the political economy of sexuality, while also being inflected by the mythologizing of the pink economy – often to contradictory effect. In part, of course, this is as an extension of the broader notion that citizenship is increasingly commodified, as we have already noted. However, the particular problems that this idea raises for the sexual citizen demand further attention.

Among many commentators on 'queer consumption' there is a tendency either to demonize and pathologize gay men as shallow, passive consumers and as both victims and exploiters of capitalism; or to celebrate the creativity, radicality and innovatory nature of gay consumer culture:

> Recently, a new stereotype has crept into the anti-homosexual literature of the right. In addition to being portrayed as immoral, disease-ridden child molesters, gay men and lesbians are now described as superwealthy, highly educated free spenders. The economic arguments that have begun to appear in the past few years are an important part of the same strategy: to split the gay community off from what might have appeared to be its natural allies in a broad, progressive civil-rights movement. (Hardisty and Gluckman, 1997: 218)

Other commentators have argued that lesbian and gay rights can in fact be conceived as commodities to be bought and sold on the open market; thus capitalism can actually secure lesbian and gay liberation. An important arm of this argument is that the visibility that economic muscle provides keeps gay communities in the limelight and makes them better able to resist marginalization: 'The visible existence of gay and lesbian communities is an important bulwark against the tide of reaction; the economic vitality of contemporary lesbian and gay communities erodes the ability of conservatives to reconstruct the closet' (Escoffier, 1997: 131). However, while some commentators champion the growth of the gay market, many gay consumers themselves remain unmoved, even bemused by all the targeting and niche marketing. In addition, the growth of new commercial venues (taken as a barometer of gay economic power – and of its exploitation) is not welcomed with open arms by all. The homogeneity, attitude and high price of some venues are surely nothing new to anyone on the gay scene. People are not duped by the hype surrounding new venues, but instead have a love/hate relationship towards them. People know they are being targeted and exploited, but this does not stop them using the scene just because they know that the rules of the game are rigged. While this sounds somewhat fatalistic – like admitting that citizenship is inevitably and irretrievably commodified, so we just have to live with that as a 'market reality' – an understanding of the economic basis of sexual citizenship is essential as a counter to the reductive arguments thus far advanced either for or against gay consumer citizenship.

We need to move beyond rather simplistic discussions of why gay men (and lesbians) shop. Crucially, we need to trace the evolution of lesbian and gay consumption practices *vis-à-vis* the family orientation of the welfare state. The major reason that the market has provided the stage for the realization of lesbian and gay citizenship has been exclusion from the welfare state. The welfare state was constructed on the basis of a heterosexual assumption, and until very recently the welfare state sought to reproduce heterosexuality and to penalize sexual diversity. A more thorough examination of the heteronormativity of the welfare state is long overdue and must serve as a counter to the rather misleading media and academic commentary on the state of the pink economy. Indeed, as the welfare state itself becomes increasingly marketized, we need to examine the ways in which this impacts on the economics of citizenship in its broadest sense, promoting (and indeed producing) forms of social exclusion that further limit access to citizenship.

LESBIAN AND GAY MARRIAGE

Assimilationist claims to the right to same-sex marriage or registered partnership have been central to current lesbian and gay rights struggles. The arguments made centre on the right to publicly recognize same-sex partnerships in law (and also, related to consumer citizenship, to reap the financial benefits of partnership). At one level, denying the right to marriage limits the citizenship claims of sexual dissidents; on the other hand, marrying into citizenship means sanctioning certain kinds of relationship at the expense of others. While the notion of lesbian and gay marriage has been argued to denaturalize marriage as a heterosexual institution, it naturalizes the stable, monogamous couple-form as the ideal-type of 'families we choose'.

Typical of the pro-registered partnership argument is Morris Kaplan's (1997) work on intimacy and privacy. Kaplan claims that agitation for lesbian and gay marriage asserts 'the positive status of lesbian and gay citizenship' – they represent the 'demands of queer families to enjoy equal social and legal status with their straight counterparts' (Kaplan, 1997: 204). Crucially for Kaplan, lesbian and gay marriage is central to attaining full citizenship and empowerment, since it offers such recognition of the freedom of intimate association, insulated by law. As he concludes: 'Lesbian and gay marriages, domestic partnerships, and the reconceiving of family institutions as modes of intimate association among free and equal citizens all are efforts to appropriate, extend, and transform the available possibilities' (ibid.: 222). It might be instructive to read Kaplan's analysis alongside a number of other considerations of lesbian and gay marriage or registered partnerships. Henning Bech's (1992) modest but insightful 'Report from a rotten state', a commentary on the Danish registered partnership law passed in 1989, for example, distils the terms of the debate by proponents and opponents of the law to show the extent to which political and legal questions get framed in particular, contextualized ways – in this case, both sides argued that their stand on the law was important to say something about *Denmark* (either to protect it from international ridicule, or to position it at the forefront of civilization and human rights). The limits of the Danish law reform – omitting adoption rights and the right to a church wedding – were seen by some activists to have 'cemented the status of homosexuals as second-rate citizens', while also advocating a fixed model of homosexual relationships which 'discouraged an acceptance of homosexuals in their difference and otherness' (Bech, 1992: 136). However, Bech notes that such oppositional critique was relatively marginal to the public debate in Denmark. In a similar vein, Angelia Wilson (1995) sketches a shift in British gay politics, from the Gay Liberation Front's revolutionary calls for the abolition of the family to present agitations based on the rhetorics of rights, justice and equality. In the USA, too, 1970s' gay liberationists critiqued 'the elevation of the family to ideological pre-eminence', arguing that one task of gay liberation must be to support 'issues that broaden the opportunities for living outside traditional heterosexual family units' for gays and straights alike (D'Emilio, 1992: 13). Most forcibly, John D'Emilio, writing at the start of the 1980s, urged that 'solutions should not come in the forms of a radical version of the pro-family position', but rather the building of an 'affectional community' in which 'the family will wane in significance' for all members of society (ibid.: 13–14). The stark contrast between gay liberation's utopian social project (in which gay culture leads), to the 'pro-family' agenda of liberal reformism (where gay culture seeks to replicate heterosexual) is truly striking. By mainstreaming sexual politics, then, the radical edge is blunted, and a 'back-door revolution' advocated, with things like partnership registration held as 'tactical, practical step[s] towards greater justice' (Tucker, 1995: 12). Such moves tread a very fine line – which many of their advocates seem aware of, yet incapable of resolving – as well as revealing tensions within the agendas of different campaigning positions.

Opening up the question of 'lesbian and gay marriage', of course, *can* have far broader impacts, throwing light both on to the constructions of homosexuality and heterosexuality in law, and the limitations of such constructions. Dennis Allen's (1995) discussion of the public debate on same-sex marriage in Hawaii in the light of a suit filed by two lesbian couples and one gay male couple (Baehr v. Lewin) clearly illustrates the destabilizing function of such appeals: as the Hawaii Supreme Court struggled to refine its definiton of 'marriage' (by linking it irrevocably to heterosexuality through the dubious logic of reproductive biologism, while also trying to sidestep sexual discrimination), it revealed 'the logical difficulties, the internal gaps and fissures, not only in the "inevitable" linking of marriage to heterosexuality but within the very idea of heterosexuality itself' (Allen, 1995: 617–18). By having to draw a boundary around marriage defined in relation to reproduction, it excluded involuntarily childless heterosexual couples, and its tortuous attempts to bring them in (by reference to medical technology and the *potential* for reproduction) and threatened to open a door for same-sex couples (who could equally use medical technologies to overcome biological barriers to reproduction). As with legal definitions of sodomy (in Bowers v. Hardwick, for example, where the Georgia law defined sodomy as oral or anal sex without explicitly demarcating the genders of participants), the precariousness of the homo/hetero binary is exposed; in this case, it is heterosexuality that comes to be defined by conduct – using a rather convoluted definition of 'natural' (or at least naturalized), *potential* reproductive conduct. Such problematic defining of sexuality exposes the constructedness of all sexual categories in law.

It is this kind of exposure that advocates of registered partnerships often point towards, and the 'broader agenda' behind such struggles for reform; far from assimilationist, then, same-sex marriage is held as capable of undermining the most solid of social structures ('the family') by infiltrating it and exposing its contradictory logics. The fact that the take-up rate for registered partnerships in Denmark has been very low is thus only of secondary importance when set alongside the bigger picture of both the fact of the *possibility* of partnership registration for those who may want it, and the *threat* to marriage that registered partnerships purportedly pose.

This seems to be the currently dominant political methodology expressed in both academic and activist discourses: the 'quest for justice' within the broad equal rights/citizenship framework, with the suggestion that riding on the back of these claims are more troublesome 'hidden agendas' – of challenging structural homophobia, and thereby questioning the foundational definitions of sexual citizenship. Bowers v. Hardwick, for example, challenged Georgia's sodomy laws through the lens of the right to privacy, while also navigating an uneasy path through the relation of homosexual identity to homosexual conduct (Halley, 1994). The framing of the challenge within rights discourse, which occupies a particular and sensitive place within American law and culture, opened up the terms of the debate in more far-reaching ways, by raising questions about the immutability (or mutability) of homosexual identity (whether or not sexuality is legally analogous to 'race', thus opening up its eligibility for shelter under the Equal Protection Amendment) and about the extent of overlap between 'homosexual conduct' and 'homosexual identity'. The question remains, however, of whether reducing radical activism to claims under law has a positive impact. As Nan D. Hunter (1995b: 120) says, for advocates of legal approaches, 'the process of organising and litigating empowers and emboldens', while for its critics 'the reduction of radical demands into claims of "rights under the law" perpetuates belief systems that teach that other, more transformative modes of change are impossible, unnecessary, or both'.

It is worth examining in more detail the logic of this methodology – and the argument over legal-reformist versus 'radical' action – through the debate on same-sex marriage, since advocates are keen to stress the subversive challenge posed by what can be read as an assimilationist strategy. As Hunter (1995c: 101) points out, the politics of the family have become 'a newly identified zone of social combat', central to agitations for lesbian and gay equality and citizenship. In a sense, marriage is a useful cypher for the whole citizenship debate, since it is seen as a cohesive element of social life, straddling the public and the private, containing a mix of rights and duties, and occupying a central position in political, legal and popular discourses of radically different orientations – from the petitions for the recognition of 'families we choose' to campaigns for a reinstatement of 'family values' as the heart of Christian-democratic political and moral culture. Agitation in the USA for the rights of 'queer families' enable us to witness these competing discourses enacted on the political and legal stage. Like citizenship, then, marriage 'does not exist without the power of the state … to establish, define, regulate and restrict it' (Hunter, 1995b: 110). Hunter suggests that same-sex marriage could potentially 'alter the fundamental concept of the particular institution of marriage', also sending out shockwaves that may shake the foundations of other social institutions that are presently loci of discrimination (ibid.: 112).

Part of Hunter's argument rests with the potential of same-sex marriage to destabilize the *gendered* structure of marriage, fracturing discourses of dependency and authority. It serves, then, to *denaturalize* marriage, to reveal its constructedness, and thereby to 'democratize' it. Paradoxically, however, it seems that such a move could have the function of *reaffirming* marriage as an institution. There are a number of strands to this counterargument. First, by further marginalizing the unmarried, it perpetuates a two-tier system in the recognition of relationship status. It also maintains the (long-term, monogamous) bonds of coupledom as the most legitimate form of lovelife-choice. It 'liberalizes' the institution of marriage, opening it up to those (heterosexual) people who currently oppose its inequalities, as well as comforting those married couples currently uneasy about their privileged status – again reinforcing (and relegitimizing) marriage over and above nonmarried relationships. It puts people currently ineligible to marry under increased moral and legal pressure to wed (such as homosexual couples with children). Meanwhile, it fails to address economic aspects of marriage (whether positive, such as tax breaks, or negative, in terms of welfare and dependency), nor does it address the continuing links between marital status and other forms of legal rights (next of kin status, intestate inheritance, etc.). Perhaps most significantly, it upholds the notions of a particular model of romantic love and commitment, which in many ways are more central to the meaning of marriage than (potentially) procreative coupling, at least outside of legal discourses. A focus exclusively on challenging the legal discourse around marriage, therefore, falls short of considering which aspects of *popular discourse* are contested or reaffirmed by such a move. Since popular discourses then spill over into political and legal process (the recent British moral panic over single mothers, for example), strategies for change need to consider the many meanings of marriage (and nonmarriage) that contribute to its social (as well as legal) status. As Katherine O'Donovan (1993: 87) rightly suggests, marriage retains such an iconic status in society that it is almost inconceivable to think outside its logics: 'there is a kind of uniform monotony to our fates. We are destined to marry or to enter similar relationships.' From this perspective, demanding the right to join that uniform monotony starts to look like a strange political tactic for dissident sexual citizens.

Hunter, meanwhile, reviews calls for same-sex marriage law alongside the alternative strategy of registered partnership legislation, in part examining feminist arguments around both, as well as critiquing work from critical legal studies which has focused on questioning the use of rights discourse in such mobilizations. Registered partnerships offer many practical advantages (and are not hidebound by 'tradition' to construct

contractual obligations along marriage-like lines), but lack the status (in both a legal and cultural sense) of marriage; unless marriage is abolished altogether and replaced by a single system of partnership registration, that distinction will remain, and will carry with it ideological and moral weight.

One aspect of lesbian and gay marriage that is rarely considered in discussions is the so-called mutually beneficial arrangement – the marriage between a lesbian and a gay man for strategic reasons (often immigration status; see Stychin, 2000). While this is often portrayed as a desperate (not to mention dangerous) move, such 'marriages of convenience' could be seen as offering a further, more transgressive strategy. If gay men married lesbians *en masse* as a *political act,* then the status of marriage as the state-licensed public statement of romantic love and life-long commitment would be exposed and undermined. The couple could then have a claim on all the benefits of marriage, without having to bear the responsibilities, while also falling completely outside current discourses of what marriage means (or *is made to mean*).

The strategic claiming of the right of same-sex couples to marry also runs the risk of domesticating sexual practice, lending support to policies which seek to 'clean up' tabooed aspects of gay culture (principally public sex) as well as distancing 'assimilationist' agitation from radical activism – the moment of citizenship versus the moment of transgression. As Eva Pendleton suggests, the assimilationist agenda in American gay politics has a profoundly conservative orientation:

These boys are anxious to recoup the white, middle-class privilege that has previously been denied to openly gay men. Rather than challenge this hegemony, they will do what they can to overcome the political handicap that homosexuality has traditionally represented. The best way to do this, they argue, is to assimilate into Middle America as much as possible. (Pendleton, 1996: 375)

Such a position leads, in Pendleton's words, to 'asexual political activism' (ibid.: 387);

her reading of gay conservative texts such as Bruce Bawer's (1993) *A Place at the Table* uncovers the erotophobia inherent in demands for same-sex marriage. Public sex is especially demonized as a *political* practice (in fact, its politics are erased under the trope of hedonism and irresponsibility). Bawer's take on gay marriage, as outlined by Pendleton, is to suggest that 'the most effective way to preserve the heterosexual nuclear family is to grant homosexuals legal rights' (Pendleton, 1996: 385). The logic of this argument runs thus:

> closeted gay men often marry and have children in order to cover up their true desires. Thus it is actually the stigmatization and secrecy of homosexuality that undermines 'the family'; if gay couples were given equal rights, the sham marriages that eventually destroy families would no longer be necessary. The socially responsible thing for conservatives to do is eliminate the need for homosexuals to use heterosexual marriage as a means of avoiding social stigma – by advocating gay marriage. ... Groups like the Christian Coalition should join with gay conservatives to advance a truly conservative, pro-family agenda for gays and straights alike. (ibid.: 385)

What this exposes is precisely the dangers which assimilationist strategies are prone to: their recuperation by conservative agendas and agenda-setters. Activism based on rights agitation – especially around issues such as partnership/marriage or the right to privacy – can serve to erase aspects of sexual citizenship founded outside the narrow bounds of 'normalcy', reinstating the tension between definitions of the 'good homosexual' and the 'bad homosexual'. Pendleton is at pains to point out, however, that many radical (non-conservative) agitations also valorize monogamy as the 'responsible' mode of sexual citizenship in the time of AIDS. Pervasive sex-negativity can only be further enabled by demands for the right to marry, while arguments based on protecting privacy threaten to further domesticate sexual citizenship by undermining public articulations of sexual identity, such as public sex (Dangerous Bedfellows, 1996). The rush to registered partnerships, held by many as absolutely central to claims for sexual citizenship, is a strategy which must be viewed critically, for we must be aware of the kinds of citizens such a move would produce – and the kinds of non-citizens it would exclude.

GAYS IN THE MILITARY

Equally prominent, and equally problematic, in recent arguments about sexual rights have been the military exclusion policies in the UK and USA. Interrogating the logic of these policies affords a window into crucial aspects of the sexual citizenship debates – the relationship between acts and identities, notions of public and private, the homosocial/homosexual binary. The compromise 'Don't Ask, Don't Tell' stance in the USA shows how these aspects of sexual citizenship are negotiated and contested, giving us an indication of how claims to sexual rights outside the context of the military are likely to fare in law.

The gays in the military debate in the USA can be seen to advocate *passing* as the only possible strategy for homosexuals serving in the forces, since any form of homosexual conduct (including coming out as an 'admitted homosexual' – a definition used in Ben-Shalom v. Marsh) contravenes the Defense Department's policy:

> The identity/conduct distinction that advocates for gay, lesbian and bisexual rights have been so eager to assert is collapsed, in this instance through the mediating category of speech: homosexuality is articulated through speech, and speech has been summarily defined, by the courts, and by the Clinton administration, as conduct. (Currah, 1995: 66)

Even withholding homosexual identity – by passing – can, however, be used as grounds for dismissal. In fact, in Steffan v. Cheney the full force of the US Department of Defense's homophobia apparently centred on *the very act of passing*:

> Steffan was under a positive *duty* as a member of the military to come out because his gay identity was otherwise undetectable but contrary to

regulations. The result of his coming out, though, was his expulsion as unfit for service. Paradoxically, however, in going public he revealed that his sexuality had not rendered him incapable of service. He demonstrated, instead, that absent a public declaration, he remained completely undetectable on the inside of what is, in the end, an institution forged with same-sex bonds. (Stychin, 1995: 94)

Steffan's presence in the navy thus threatened to destabilize (or at least muddy) the distinction between a sanctioned homosociality and an outlawed homosexuality – a distinction actually very precariously enacted in institutions like the military. The navy's fear, put simply, is of *contagion* (backed up by arguments upholding Steffan's expulsion centred on the 'threat' of HIV and AIDS impacting on the 'healthy' military's abilities to defend the nation). Paradoxically, then, as Carl Stychin notes:

Joseph Steffan was defined as an outsider because of his ability to pass – to reveal, through the articulation of a gay identity, that he was an insider all along. However, in assimilating the military with the nation, Steffan is further constructed, not as *being* an insider but as performing the role of the insider – as an espionage agent might perform a role to undermine national security. The underlying concern, then, is not simply that Steffan had successfully performed the role until his own revelation, but that his success had revealed the performativity of the military subject. (1995: 99)

What the gays in the military issue also makes clear, as Hunter points out, is the complex intertwining of privacy, equality and expression central to current forms of sexual citizenship agitation (and to its regulation):

The ban on military service by lesbians, gay men, and bisexuals ... renders identical conduct such as kissing permissible or punishable based on the sexual orientation of the actor. Moreover, the ban restricts self-identifying speech with the justification that homosexual 'conduct' is antithetical to morale, good order and discipline. (1995a: 139)

Further, in order to prohibit the 'public' statement (confession or coming-out) of homosexuality by serving military personnel, the military must itself repeatedly speak the term – generating more of that 'sex-talk'

which Davina Cooper (1993a) identifies as central to the act of making things public so as to render them private; this means constructing a 'homosexual military subject' in order to deny her or his existence. In Judith Butler's (1997: 104) words, '[t]he regulation must conjure one who defines him or herself as a homosexual in order to make plain that no such self-definition is permissible within the military'; the definition of homosexuality must always come from outside (from the state, law, or the military), never from inside. The debate becomes about not gays in the military, but what Butler calls 'gay speech in the military'.

The US military's 'Don't Ask, Don't Tell' ruling, however, offers a strange opt-out clause, or 'rebuttal presumption' – the possibility of renunciation by unchaining identity from conduct (Butler (1997: 116) writes it thus: 'I am a homosexual and I intend not to act on my desire'), or the possibility of writing off an isolated incident of 'homosexual conduct' as a 'mistake' (an exit route also often routinely offered to politicians and other prominent public figures caught in compromising situations).

The debate in the UK has followed the path of that in the USA to a large extent, ushering in the same arguments against homosexual presence in the military: especially the threat to what Derek McGhee (1998: 206) terms the military's 'informal panoptic homosocial habitus'. In addition, the phantom 'general public', always to be relied on as homophobic, is introduced into the debate, on the assumption that homosexual servicemen and women would dent the armed forces' image and reputation in the public's eyes (crucially, in the eyes of parents whose teenage children might be thinking of signing up). The evolving situation in the UK, that of the 'unbanning' of homosexuality in the military, will inevitably have to negotiate these spectres and problems. We await the final outcome of the manoeuvre.

In the meantime, we need to reflect on the relationship between the gays in the military debate and the wider question of sexual citizenship. At its simplest, of course, the argument is that denying homosexuals the right to fight for their country denies them full citizenship, given the continuing durability of the relationship between the citizen and the nation–state. This obviously sidesteps the crucial question of the legitimacy of such a strategy in the context of rights agitation. In the same manner as the debate on lesbian and gay marriage, the gays in the military debate is upheld by some as having a destabilizing, radical function: opening up one of the most heteronormative state institutions to homosexuals begins the task of undermining heteronormativity itself. While there is something appealing about this line of argument, it also needs to be treated with some scepticism, as Carl Stychin notes:

> I remain convinced that the struggle for the inclusion of 'out' gays and lesbians in the United States military, and the fight for same-sex marriage, *could* be discursively deployed to reimagine these central national institutions, and by extension, the ways in which the nation state has been gendered and sexualized. Although I am very sceptical as to whether activism is interested in such a project, these struggles may contain within them the *potential* to destabilize the construction of the nation. (1998: 198)

The framing of Stychin's comment is important, and leads us into our concluding discussion, which concerns theory and politics.

CONCLUSION

As part of his discussion of the UK ban on gays in the armed forces, Derek McGhee takes Carl Stychin to task. In McGhee's eyes, Stychin's 'deconstructive' reading of the US military exclusion policy overstresses 'epistemic panic' and discursive destabilizing at the expense of a recognition of the 'materiality of practice': 'One could say, "so what?" the heterosexualised, homosocial space [of the armed forces] has been denaturalized in a Queer Legal Theorist's article. But will this really change

anything?' (McGhee, 1998: 235). McGhee's disquiet is symptomatic of a broader concern with the abstractions of 'theory' and the mismatch between 'theory' and 'politics'. This tension runs through all the modalities of sexual citizenship we have discussed in this chapter. We share McGhee's disquiet, in that theoretical readings might seem a million miles away from the concrete realities of the experience of sexual citizens and non-citizens. Individuals losing legal cases make 'interesting' studies for theorists to interrogate the inner workings of the law machine, but this cannot always be more broadly productive. In the same way, the destabilizing potential offered by same-sex marriage and gays in the military might never amount to more than *potential* – both areas of rights agitation could equally easily shore up the institutions they are supposed to corrode.

What this suggests, we think, is not that theory cannot play its part in sexual citizenship, but that we need ways to negotiate the void between theory and the 'materiality of practice'. The marketization of sexual citizenship is something we need to attend to with a critical insight, for sure, but one which does not write off the ambiguities inherent in the notions of the pink economy and the lesbian and gay community (and the relations between the two). Same-sex marriage must also be handled with care, and we must stop to think about the consequences of such rights claims rather than accepting them as self-evident. And any reading of the gays in the military debate must tread a similarly careful path between the seductions of textual deconstruction and the material and social outcomes that policies can and do have (Bell and Binnie, 2000). Obviously we need theory to aid us in these interrogations, but we must not lose sight of the lives and experiences of those we theorize about. The debate on sexual citizenship in the twenty-first century is likely to return to this dilemma repeatedly – whether that debate occurs in the academy, in the mass media, in the law courts, or on the streets.

ACKNOWLEDGEMENTS

An earlier version of this chapter appears as 'Sexual citizenship: law, theory and politics', in Janice Richardson and Ralph Sandland (eds), *Feminist Perspectives on Law and Theory* (London: Cavendish, 2000). Thanks to the publishers and editors for permission to reprint it here in revised form – especially to Ruth Massey at Cavendish and Sally Sheldon, series editor. Thanks also to Diane Richardson for asking us to contribute to the *Handbook*.

REFERENCES

Allen, Dennis (1995) 'Homosexuality and narrative', *Modern Fiction Studies,* 41: 609–34.

Bawer, Bruce (1993) *A Place at the Table: The Gay Individual in American Society.* New York: Touchstone Books.

Bech, Henning (1992) 'Report from a rotten state: "marriage" and "homosexuality" in "Denmark"', in Ken Plummer (ed.), *Modern Homosexualities: Fragments of Lesbian and Gay Experience.* London: Routledge. pp. 134–47.

Bell, David and Binnie, Jon (2000) *The Sexual Citizen: Queer Politics and Beyond.* Cambridge: Polity Press.

Benton, Sarah (1991) 'Gender, sexuality and citizenship', in Geoff Andrews (ed.), *Citizenship.* London: Lawrence and Wishart. pp. 151–63.

Butler, Judith (1997) *Excitable Speech: A Politics of the Performative.* New York: Routledge.

Clarke, Paul (1996) *Deep Citizenship.* London: Pluto Press.

Cooper, Davina (1993a) 'An engaged state: sexuality, governance, and the potential for change', *Journal of Law and Society,* 20: 257–75.

Cooper, Davina (1993b) 'The Citizen's Charter and radical democracy: empowerment and exclusion within citizenship discourse', *Social and Legal Studies,* 2: 149–71.

Currah, Paisley (1995) 'Searching for immutability: homosexuality, race and rights discourse', in Angelia Wilson (ed.), *A Simple Matter of Justice?: Theorizing Lesbian and Gay Politics.* London: Cassell. pp. 91–109.

Dangerous Bedfellows (eds) (1996) *Policing Public Sex: Queer Politics and the Future of AIDS Activism.* Boston: South End Press.

D'Emilio, Jon (1992) *Making Trouble: Essays on Gay History, Politics, and the University.* New York: Routledge.

Ellison, Nick (1997) 'Towards a new social politics: citizenship and reflexivity in late modernity', *Sociology,* 31: 697–717.

Escoffier, Jeffery (1997) 'The political economy of the closet: notes towards an economic history of gay and lesbian life before Stonewall', in Amy Gluckman and Betsy Reed (eds), *Homo Economics: Capitalism, Community, and Lesbian and Gay Life.* London: Routledge. pp. 123–34.

Evans, David (1993) *Sexual Citizenship: The Material Construction of Sexualities.* London: Routledge.

Giddens, Anthony (1991) *Modernity and Self-Identity: Self and Society in the Late Modern Age.* Cambridge: Polity Press.

Halley, Janet (1994) 'Sexual orientation and the politics of biology: a critique of the argument from immutability', *Stanford Law Journal,* 36: 301–66.

Hardisty, Jean and Gluckman, Amy (1997) 'The hoax of "special rights": the right wing's attack on gay men and lesbians', in Amy Gluckman and Betsy Reed (eds), *Homo Economics: Capitalism, Community, and Lesbian and Gay Life.* London: Routledge. pp. 209–22.

Hunter, Nan D. (1995a) 'Identity, speech and equality', in Lisa Duggan and Nan D. Hunter, *Sex Wars: Sexual Dissent and Political Culture.* New York: Routledge. pp. 123–41.

Hunter, Nan D. (1995b) 'Marriage, law and gender: a feminist inquiry', in Lisa Duggan and Nan D. Hunter, *Sex Wars: Sexual Dissent and Political Culture.* New York: Routledge. pp. 107–22.

Hunter, Nan D. (1995c) 'Sexual dissent and the family: the Sharon Kowalski case', in Lisa Duggan and Nan D. Hunter, *Sex Wars: Sexual Dissent and Political Culture.* New York: Routledge. pp. 101–6.

Isin, Engin and Wood, Patricia (1999) *Citizenship and Identity.* London: Sage.

Kaplan, Morris (1997) 'Intimacy and equality: the question of lesbian and gay marriage', in Shane Phelan (ed.), *Playing with Fire: Queer Politics, Queer Theories.* New York: Routledge. pp. 201–30.

McGhee, Derek (1998) 'Looking and acting the part: gays in the armed forces – a case of passing masculinity', *Feminist Legal Studies,* 4: 205–44.

Marshall, T.H. (1950) *Citizenship and Social Class.* Cambridge: Cambridge University Press (reprinted 1973).

Moran, Leslie (1995) 'Violence and the law: the case of sado-masochism', *Social and Legal Studies,* 4: 225–51.

O'Donovan, Katherine (1993) 'Marriage: a sacred or profane love machine?', *Feminist Legal Studies,* 1: 75–90.

Pendleton, Eva (1996) 'Domesticating partnerships', in Dangerous Bedfellows (eds), *Policing Public Sex: Queer Politics and the Future of AIDS Activism.* Boston: South End Press. pp. 373–93.

Phillips, Anne (1993) *Democracy and Difference.* Cambridge: Polity Press.

Richardson, Diane (1998) 'Sexuality and citizenship', *Sociology*, 32: 83–100.

Roche, Maurice (1992) *Rethinking Citizenship: Welfare, Ideology and Change in Modern Society*. Cambridge: Polity.

Sparks, Holloway (1997) 'Dissident citizenship: democratic theory, political courage, and activist women', *Hypatia*, 12: 74–110.

Stychin, Carl (1995) *Law's Desire: Sexuality and the Limits of Justice*. London: Routledge.

Stychin, Carl (1998) *A Nation by Rights: National Cultures, Sexual Identity Politics and the Discourse of Rights*. Philadelphia: Temple University Press.

Stychin, Carl (2000) ''A stranger to its laws': sovereign bodies, global sexualities, and transnational citizens', *Journal of Law and Society*, 27: 601–25.

Tucker, Scott (1995) *Fighting Words: An Open Letter to Queer and Radicals*. London: Cassell.

Turner, Bryan (1990) 'Outline of a theory of citizenship', *Sociology*, 24: 187–214.

Turner, Bryan (ed.) (1993) *Citizenship and Social Theory*. London: Sage.

Weeks, Jeffrey (1999) 'The sexual citizen', in Mike Featherstone (ed.), *Love and Eroticism*. London: Sage. pp. 35–52.

Wilson, Angelia (1995) 'Introduction', in Angelia Wilson (ed.), *A Simple Matter of Justice?: Theorizing Lesbian and Gay Politics*. London: Cassell. pp. 1–9.

Yeatman, Anna (1994) *Postmodern Revisionings of the Political*. New York: Routledge.

Index

binaries
   bisexuality 216–17, 225–6
   gender 220, 245
   heterosexual/homosexual 27–44, 242–3
   natural 208
   operation of 346
   public/private 154–5
   science 56
   transgender 243–4
   urban-rural 191
   see also dualisms
Binnie, Jon 443–55
biological
   determinism 58–9, 67–8
   essentialism 6, 18, 20, 56–7
   explanations 61–2, 65–8, 73–4, 222
   signs of queer desire 261–2
   see also genes; health; medicine; science
biomedicine *see* medicine
Birke, Lynda 55–72
bisexuality 109, 193, 199–214, 215–27
black
   family formations 370–1
   gay men 345, 370
   identities 345
   labor market 331–2
   matriarchy 371
   modernity responses 184
   older people 178, 179
   popular culture 344–5
   women scholars 302
   see also African Americans; color
Blumstein, Philip 369
bodies 145–60, 175–6, 253–70
born gay 315–16
Bornstein, Kate 116–17
Boswell, John 314–15, 404
boundaries 130–1, 238, 240
Bourdieu, Pierre 206
Boykin, Keith 370, 371
Brah, Avtar 185, 189–90, 193
brains 58, 60–3, 261–2
breast cancer 259
Briggs Initiative 390
Broad, Kendal 411
Bronski, Michael 348, 351
Brown, M. 151, 152, 156–7
Brown, Wendy 235
Browning, Frank 368, 369, 371
Bryant, Anita 385, 390, 399
Bullen, Elizabeth 279
bulletin board services (BBS) 119, 120–2, 126, 129
Bullough, Vern 86
Bunch, Charlotte 74–5
Burchell, G. 234
Burton, Richard 86, 87
Bustos-Aguilar, Pedros 420
Butler, Judith 18, 124, 154, 272, 346, 454

Butler, R.N. 163
Byne, William 262, 263

camp sensibility 343–4
capitalism 246, 387
Caribbean nation building 239
Carlson, Margaret 377
Carmichael, Stokely 387
Carrington, Christopher 369
Cartesian rationality 285
Castells, Manuel 28, 32
Castro District, San Francisco 99–114, 146–7, 190
chain migration 103
Champagne, John 437, 440
change 209–12, 235–6, 266
Chauncey, George 102, 103, 104, 418
children 80, 276–81, 365–7
choice 223, 316
Christian Right 22, 51, 223, 396, 398
   see also New Right
chromosome block 262–3
Churchill, Wainwright 86
cinema *see* film
citizens
   good 431, 432
   universal 435
citizenship
   cultural 446–7
   see also sexual citizenship
civic liberalism 444
civic republicanism 444
civil rights, demands for 382
civil unions 355, 357–8, 371, 400
   see also registered partnerships; same-sex marriage
Clarke, Paul 445
class 101, 102, 105, 178, 277, 344
Clendinen, Dudley 386
Clifford, James 184, 189, 193
Clinton, Bill 234–5, 275, 396, 397–8
closet
   coming out 10, 32, 155–7, 170–4,
      385–90, 438
   epistemology of the 30, 346
codes, online 124–5
cognitive dissonance 201–2
cognitive liberation 382, 385–90, 395, 399–400
cohort effects 165–6, 178
collective consciousness 383–4
collective rights 431
color
   queers of 108, 344–5, 394, 397, 434, 440
   women of 103, 108, 272, 344, 411
   see also African Americans; black
coming out 10, 32, 155–7, 170–4, 385–90, 438
commercialization 17, 50–1
commodification 194, 349–50, 447
Common Law 299
commonality presumption 193, 216